1,001

LOW-FAT

desserts

SUE SPITLER

Surrey Books
CHICAGO

1,001 LOW-FAT DESSERTS is published by Surrey Books, Inc.,
230 E. Ohio St., Suite 120, Chicago, IL 60611.

First edition: 1 2 3 4 5

This book is manufactured in the United States of America.

Library of Congress Cataloging-in-Publication data:
Spitler, Sue
    1,001 low-fat desserts / by Sue Spitler — 1st. ed.
      688 p.   cm.
    Includes index.
    ISBN 1-57284-028-5 (pbk.)
    1. Desserts.   2. Low-fat diet—Recipes.   I. Title.   II. Title: One
thousand and one low-fat desserts.
TX773.S77   1999   98-53328
641.8'6—DC21   CIP

Editorial and production: *Bookcrafters, Inc., Chicago*
Art direction and book design: *Joan Sommers Design, Chicago*
Nutritional analyses: *Linda R. Yoakam, M.S., R.D.*
Cover illustration: *Vicky Rabinowicz*

For prices on quantity purchases or for free book catalog,
contact Surrey Books at the above address.

This title is distributed to the trade by Publishers Group West.

CONTENTS

ACKNOWLEDGMENTS

A heartfelt thank you, Chef Pat Molden, for your invaluable contributions to this cookbook—your culinary expertise, computer and editing skills, and friendship are immensely appreciated. A four-toque salute to chefs Carol Roessler and Peggy Ferguson and many thanks to Barbara Krueger and Cindy Roth for their superb talents in recipe testing. I'm also grateful to Linda Yoakam, who provided nutritional information for each recipe, to Gene DeRoin for his expert editing, and to publisher Susan Schwartz and her staff for their encouragement and support.

To my many "delicious" friends, because they
love eating desserts with me!

INTRODUCTION

Let them eat cake, decadent and richly flavored! And tender-crusted pies, luscious cheesecakes, custard-filled crisp cream puffs and eclairs, silky custards, delicate soufflés, moist cookie bars, and frosty ice cream delights. Utterly delicious! No one will suspect that every dessert in *1,001 Low-Fat Desserts* is low in fat and calories--unless you tell them!

1,001 Low-Fat Desserts offers an encyclopedic variety of scrumptious low-fat dessert recipes that will appease any sweet tooth and gladden any occasion. You'll find well-loved favorite cakes and pies, such as Black Forest Torte, Boston Cream Cake, Carrot Cake with Cream Cheese Frosting, Flourless Chocolate Cake, German Chocolate Cake, Hot Fudge Pudding Cake, Pineapple Upside Down Cake, Red Velvet Cake, Baked Key Lime Pie, Best Cherry Pie, Black Bottom Pie, Caramel Pecan Pumpkin Pie, Double-Coconut Cream Meringue Pie, Double-Crust Blueberry Pie, Eggnog Pie, Ginger Peachy Pie, Grandma's Lemon Meringue Pie, Mile-High Apple Pie, Rhubarb Pie, Shoofly Pie, Spiced Sweet Potato Pie, and Tarte Tatin.

Cappuccino Cheesecake, Chocolate Caramel Cheesecake, and New York-Style Cheesecake are but a few of the creamy cheesecake recipes, and Chocolate Chip Cookies, Chocolate Indulgence Brownies, Cry Babies, Florentines, Frosted Sugar Cookies, Gingersnappers, Hazelnut Macaroons, Jam Buttons, Kringla, Mississippi Mud Bars, Putting on the Ritz Bars, Raisin Oatmeal Cookies, and Sugared Lemon Squares are the best baker's dozen you'll ever taste!

You'll find special occasion festive desserts and family favorites in other chapters too. Almond Paris Brest, Baklava, Classic Cream Puffs, Fillo Napoleons, Peach Melba Meringues, Berry Lemon Trifle, Caramel Flan, Creamy Rice Pudding, Tiramisu, Baked Alaska, Chocolate Cherry Ice Cream Pie, French Vanilla Ice Cream, Lemon Ice, Apple Crumb Cobbler, Blueberry Clafouti, Autumn Fruit Crisp, Bananas Foster, and Pears Melba in Meringue Shells are tempting finales.

Understanding the demands of busy lifestyles, "Quick Desserts: Cakes, Cookies, and More" is a chapter offering desserts that can be prepared in a flash. Many of these recipes use convenience foods and mixes to streamline preparation. Apricot Sour Cream Cake, Blender

Cheese Pie, Blueberry Bread Cobbler, Campus Bars, Candied Apple Gold Cake, Caramel Bananas Foster, Chocolate Cake Tart, Food Processor Cake, and Zany Brownie Bars are among the varied selection in this helpful chapter.

FREE AND EQUAL® DESSERTS

Many people choose to regulate or eliminate refined sugar in their diets, often to reduce calories for weight control, or to regulate diabetes. The chapter, "Free and Equal® Desserts," has over 90 fabulous dessert recipes that have been made without the addition of refined sugar or natural sweeteners such as honey, corn syrup, or fructose. Equal® for Recipes and Equal® sweetener in packets were used as a sugar substitute in testing these recipes. Equal® sweetens like sugar, but its properties in baking, like bulk, tenderness, and browning, are very different. Recipes therefore have to be specially created—it's not as simple as just substituting Equal® sweetener for sugar!

Recipes in "Free and Equal® Desserts" were tested only with Equal® brand sweetener; if you use another brand of artificial sweetener and want to use these recipes, you may need to experiment.

Recipes using Equal® sweetener were carefully developed with the same low-fat guidelines used throughout the cookbook. The percentage of calories from fat noted in the Nutritional Analysis for these recipes is skewed, however, appearing higher than if the recipes were made with sugar; sugar contains 770 calories per cup and thus effects the mathematical calculation for determining fat percentage. For example, Dark Flourless Chocolate Cake (see p. 573), if made with 1 cup sugar instead of $7^1/_4$ teaspoons Equal® for Recipes, would calculate to be 35 percent calories from fat, rather than 47 percent. Even with the skewed higher figures for fat percentage, two-thirds of the recipes in this chapter meet our criterion of 35 percent calories or less from fat.

LOW-FAT BAKING

How were all of these healthful, tempting desserts created? We substituted the many excellent reduced-fat and fat-free ingredients such as fat-free milk, and low-fat and fat-free yogurt, sour cream, and cream cheese for their full-fat counterparts. We also incorporated other low-fat food alternatives, such as cocoa for baking chocolate, egg whites or egg substitutes for whole eggs or yolks, and fresh fruit and purees for fat and oil. You will find a recipe for Prune Puree (see p. 42), but there is an excellent prune puree for baking available in the baking section of supermarkets which can be substituted.

NUTRITIONAL ANALYSES

The American Heart Association, National Academy of Sciences, National Cancer Institute, and American Diabetes Association all recommend that one's daily intake consist of no more than 30 percent of calories from fat. Although the majority of our dessert recipes are 30 percent calories from fat or less, we've set a top limit of 35 percent, with the consideration that one's daily food intake will include other low-fat or fat-free foods such as lean meats, fruits, vegetables, pasta, grains, breads, and cereals, thus keeping a day's average at or below the 30 percent guideline. Also, desserts might not be eaten with every meal. Some desserts in the "Free and Equal® Desserts" chapter exceed 35 percent calories from fat; this variance is explained above. The top limit set for calories per serving is 375, though most recipes fall well below that figure.

Specific nutritional data are provided for recipes (not including variations) in this book, but nutritional data are not always infallible. The nutritional analyses are derived by using computer software highly regarded by nutritionists and dietitians, but they are meant to be used only as guidelines. Figures are based on actual laboratory values of ingredients, so results may vary slightly, depending upon the manufacturer or brand of an ingredient used.

Other factors that can effect the accuracy of nutritional data include variability in sizes, weights, and measures of fruits, vegetables, and other foods. There is also a possible 20 percent error factor in the nutritional labeling of prepared foods.

If you have any health problems that impose strict dietary requirements, it is important to consult a physician, dietitian, or nutritionist before using recipes in this or any other cookbook. Also, if you are a diabetic or require a diet that restricts calories, fat, or sodium, remember that the nutritional data may be accurate for the recipe as written and tested but not for the food you cooked due to the variables explained above.

Ingredients noted as "optional," "to taste," or "as garnish" are not included in the nutritional analyses. When alternate choices or amounts of ingredients are given, the ingredient or amount listed first has been used for analysis. Similarly, data is based on the first, or lower, number of servings shown, where a range is given.

ONE

Cakes
AND
Frostings

DOUBLE-CHOCOLATE SNACK CAKE

Great for a coffee klatch, or a pot-luck gathering.

9 servings

³/₄ cup Prune Puree (see p. 42)
²/₃ cup packed light brown sugar
¹/₃ cup strong coffee
3 tablespoons margarine, softened
2 tablespoons unsweetened cocoa
1 egg white
2 teaspoons vanilla
2 cups all-purpose flour
1 teaspoon baking soda
¹/₄ teaspoon salt
1 cup reduced-fat semisweet chocolate morsels
Powdered sugar, as garnish

Per Serving
Calories: 372
% Calories from fat: 23
Fat (gm): 10.3
Saturated fat (gm): 7
Cholesterol (mg): 0.1
Sodium (mg): 270
Protein (gm): 4.9
Carbohydrate (gm): 72.1
Exchanges
Milk: 0.0
Vegetable: 0.0
Fruit: 0.0
Bread: 4.5
Meat: 0.0
Fat: 1.0

1. Beat Prune Puree, brown sugar, coffee, margarine, and cocoa in large mixing bowl until smooth; mix in egg white and vanilla. Add combined flour, baking soda, and salt, stirring just until combined. Stir in chocolate morsels.

2. Spoon batter into greased 8- or 9-inch square baking pan. Bake at 350 degrees until toothpick inserted in center of cake comes out clean, 25 to 30 minutes. Cool in pan on wire rack. Sprinkle with powdered sugar.

COFFEE-FROSTED COCOA CAKE

A perfect cake to carry for shared dinners and picnics.

16 servings

1¹/₂ cups sugar
¹/₂ cup margarine, softened
2 eggs
1 teaspoon vanilla
2 cups all-purpose flour
³/₄ cup unsweetened cocoa
2 teaspoons baking soda
1 teaspoon salt
1 cup skim milk
Coffee Frosting (recipe follows)

Per Serving
Calories: 240
% Calories from fat: 27
Fat (gm): 7.6
Sat. fat (gm): 1.6
Cholesterol (mg): 26.9
Sodium (mg): 385
Protein (gm): 3.9
Carbohydrate (gm): 41.6
Exchanges
Milk: 0.0
Vegetable: 0.0
Fruit: 0.0
Bread: 2.5
Meat: 0.0
Fat: 1.5

1. Combine sugar and margarine in large bowl; beat until light and fluffy. Add eggs one at a time, beating well after each addition. Stir in vanilla.

2. Combine flour, cocoa, baking soda, and salt in medium bowl. Mix dry ingredients into egg mixture alternately with milk, blending well. Spread batter in greased and floured 13 x 9-inch cake pan.

3. Bake cake at 350 degrees 25 to 35 minutes or until toothpick inserted in center comes out clean and cake begins to pull away from sides of pan. Cool completely on wire rack. Frost with Coffee Frosting.

Coffee Frosting

makes about ¹/₂ cup

1 tablespoon instant coffee granules
1 tablespoon hot water
1 tablespoon margarine, softened
1 cup powdered sugar
2-3 tablespoons skim milk

1. Dissolve coffee in hot water in medium bowl. Beat in margarine, powdered sugar, and enough milk for spreading consistency.

MINTED CHOCOLATE CAKE SQUARES

A moist, dark chocolate cake with an easy frosting—perfect for picnics!

12 servings

- 1/3 cup Prune Puree (see p. 42)
- 1/2 cup water
- 3 eggs
- 1/2 teaspoon mint extract
- 3 cups powdered sugar
- 1 cup Dutch process cocoa
- 2 ounces semisweet chocolate, melted
- 1 1/2 cups all-purpose flour
- 1 1/2 teaspoons baking soda
- 1/2 teaspoon salt
- 3/4 cup boiling water
  Easy Cocoa-Mint Frosting (recipe follows)

Per Serving
Calories: 345
% Calories from fat: 13
Fat (gm): 5.3
Saturated fat (gm): 3.2
Cholesterol (mg): 53.4
Sodium (mg): 281
Protein (gm): 6.1
Carbohydrate (gm): 69.6
Exchanges
Milk: 0.0
Vegetable: 0.0
Fruit: 0.0
Bread: 4.5
Meat: 0.0
Fat: 0.5

1. Mix Prune Puree, 1/2 cup water, eggs, and mint extract in large bowl until smooth; mix in powdered sugar, cocoa, and melted chocolate. Mix in combined flour, baking soda, and salt. Mix in boiling water.

2. Pour batter into greased 13 x 9-inch baking pan. Bake at 350 degrees until cake springs back when touched lightly in the center, about 35 minutes. Cool on wire rack.

3. Frost cake with Easy Cocoa-Mint Frosting; refrigerate until frosting is set.

Easy Cocoa-Mint Frosting

makes about 2 cups

- 1/4 cup cocoa
- 1/4 cup powdered sugar
- 1/4 cup Prune Puree
- 1/2 teaspoon mint extract
- 2 cups light whipped topping

1. Combine cocoa and powdered sugar in small bowl; mix in Prune Puree and mint extract until smooth. Fold in whipped topping until well blended.

DARK CHOCOLATE CAKE SQUARES

The addition of oats and whole wheat flour makes this cake a little bit different and lends a slightly chewy brownie-type texture. A perfect cake to carry for shared dinner occasions.

12 servings

$^1/_2$ cup quick-cooking oats
$1^1/_2$ cups sugar
1 cup all-purpose flour
$^1/_4$ cup whole wheat *or* all-purpose flour
$^3/_4$ cup unsweetened cocoa
$1^1/_2$ teaspoons baking powder
$1^1/_2$ teaspoons baking soda
$^1/_2$ teaspoon salt
1 cup fat-free milk
$^1/_3$ cup vegetable oil
2 teaspoons vanilla
3 egg whites
1 cup boiling water
1 ounce semisweet chocolate, melted
Cocoa Frosting (recipe follows)

Per Serving
Calories: 353
% Calories from fat: 21
Fat (gm): 8.2
Saturated fat (gm): 1.5
Cholesterol (mg): 0.7
Sodium (mg): 365
Protein (gm): 4.5
Carbohydrate (gm): 66.8
Exchanges
Milk: 0.0
Vegetable: 0.0
Fruit: 0.0
Bread: 4.5
Meat: 0.0
Fat: 1.0

1. Process oats in blender until finely chopped, but not ground. Combine oats, sugar, flours, cocoa, baking powder, baking soda, and salt in large bowl. Mix milk, oil, vanilla, and egg whites; add to flour mixture and beat 2 minutes at medium speed. Mix in boiling water and melted chocolate.

2. Pour batter into 13 x 9-inch baking pan; bake at 350 degrees until cake springs back when touched lightly, about 35 minutes. Cool on wire rack. Frost with Cocoa Frosting.

Cocoa Frosting

makes about 1¹/₄ cups

$2^1/_2$ cups powdered sugar
$^1/_4$ cup unsweetened cocoa
1-2 tablespoons margarine, softened
1 teaspoon vanilla
2-3 tablespoons fat-free milk

1. Mix powdered sugar, cocoa, margarine, vanilla, and enough milk to make spreading consistency.

CHOCOLATE ZUCCHINI CAKE

Bake the cake in two 8- or 9-inch round cake pans if you like; the frosting will need to be doubled to frost layers.

15 servings

1/2 cup margarine
1/2 cup Prune Puree (see p. 42)
1 3/4 cups sugar
2 eggs
1/2 cup reduced-fat buttermilk
1 teaspoon vanilla
2 1/2 cups all-purpose flour
1/4 cup unsweetened cocoa
1 teaspoon baking soda
1/2 teaspoon baking powder
1/2 teaspoon ground cinnamon
1/2 teaspoon ground cloves
2 cups finely chopped or shredded zucchini
1/4-1/2 cup reduced-fat semisweet chocolate morsels
Cocoa Frosting (see p. 5)

Per Serving
Calories: 369
% Calories from fat: 21
Fat (gm): 8.8
Saturated fat (gm): 2.6
Cholesterol (mg): 28.7
Sodium (mg): 207
Protein (gm): 4.2
Carbohydrate (gm): 70.5
Exchanges
Milk: 0.0
Vegetable: 0.0
Fruit: 0.0
Bread: 4.5
Meat: 0.0
Fat: 1.0

1. Beat margarine, Prune Puree, and sugar in large bowl until smooth. Mix in eggs, buttermilk, and vanilla. Mix in combined flour, cocoa, baking soda, baking powder, and spices; mix in the zucchini.

2. Pour batter into greased 13 x 9-inch baking pan; sprinkle with chocolate morsels. Bake at 350 degrees until toothpick inserted in center comes out clean, about 45 minutes. Cool on wire rack. Spread with Cocoa Frosting.

GREEN TOMATO CAKE

Who would guess the secret ingredient in this cake is green tomatoes!

16 servings

1/3 cup margarine, softened

1/3 cup Prune Puree (see p. 42) *or* applesauce

2 cups sugar

3 eggs

2 cups finely chopped green tomatoes

1 tablespoon grated orange rind

2 teaspoons vanilla

2¹/2 cups all-purpose flour

1/2 cup unsweetened cocoa

2¹/2 teaspoons baking powder

2 teaspoons baking soda

1/2 teaspoon salt

1 teaspoon ground cinnamon

1/2 cup fat-free milk

1/2 cup chopped walnuts *or* pecans
Orange Glaze *or* Chocolate Glaze
(see pp. 47, 76)

Per Serving
Calories: 284
% Calories from fat: 22
Fat (gm): 7.2
Saturated fat (gm): 1.2
Cholesterol (mg): 40
Sodium (mg): 376
Protein (gm): 5.1
Carbohydrate (gm): 51.2
Exchanges
Milk: 0.0
Vegetable: 0.0
Fruit: 0.0
Bread: 3.5
Meat: 0.0
Fat: 1.0

1. Beat margarine, Prune Puree, and sugar until blended in large bowl; beat in eggs 1 at a time. Mix in tomatoes, orange rind, and vanilla. Mix in combined flour, cocoa, baking powder, baking soda, salt, and cinnamon alternately with milk, beginning and ending with dry ingredients. Mix in walnuts.

2. Pour batter into greased and floured 12-cup fluted tube pan. Bake at 350 degrees until toothpick inserted in center comes out clean, 55 to 60 minutes. Cool on wire rack 10 minutes; remove from pan and cool. Drizzle with Orange Glaze.

Variation: **Spiced Chocolate Beet Cake**—Make cake as above, substituting shredded cooked or canned beets for the green to-matoes and 1 cup packed brown sugar for 1 cup of the granulated sugar; decrease cocoa to 1/4 cup and stir 2 ounces melted semisweet chocolate into cake batter. Drizzle cake with Chocolate Glaze.

CHOCOLATE CARROT CAKE

Part of the margarine in this moist, chocolatey cake has been replaced with applesauce or Prune Puree.

16 servings

2¹/2 cups all-purpose flour
1 cup granulated sugar
1 cup packed light brown sugar
¹/4 cup unsweetened cocoa
1 teaspoon baking powder
1 teaspoon ground cinnamon
¹/4 teaspoon ground nutmeg
¹/2 cup margarine, softened
¹/2 cup applesauce *or* Prune Puree (see p. 42)
3 eggs
2 teaspoons vanilla
3 cups shredded carrots
¹/2 cup chopped walnuts
¹/2 cup reduced-fat semisweet chocolate morsels
Powdered Sugar Frosting *or* Chocolate Glaze (see pp. 34, 76)

Per Serving
Calories: 349
% Calories from fat: 31
Fat (gm): 12.2
Saturated fat (gm): 3.6
Cholesterol (mg): 39.8
Sodium (mg): 142
Protein (gm): 4.9
Carbohydrate (gm): 57.6
Exchanges
Milk: 0.0
Vegetable: 0.0
Fruit: 0.0
Bread: 4.0
Meat: 0.0
Fat: 1.5

1. Combine flour, sugars, cocoa, baking powder, spices, margarine, applesauce, eggs, and vanilla in large bowl; beat on low speed until ingredients are blended. Beat on high speed 3 minutes. Mix in carrots, walnuts, and chocolate morsels.

2. Pour batter into greased and floured 12-cup fluted tube pan. Bake at 350 degrees until toothpick inserted in center comes out clean, 50 to 60 minutes. Cool in pan on wire rack 10 minutes; remove from pan and cool. Frost top of cake with Powdered Sugar Frosting.

AUNT RUBY'S CHOCOLATE SAUERKRAUT CAKE

Aunt Ruby will never reveal the secret ingredient in this chocolatey, moist cake—is it the sauerkraut or the beer?

15 servings

1^1/$_2$ cups sugar
 ^{1}/$_2$ cup vegetable shortening
  2 eggs
1^1/$_4$ teaspoons vanilla
 ^{1}/$_2$ cup unsweetened cocoa
2^1/$_4$ cups all-purpose flour
  1 teaspoon baking powder
  1 teaspoon baking soda
 ^{1}/$_2$ teaspoon salt
  1 cup beer *or* water
 ^{2}/$_3$ cup well-drained, rinsed sauerkraut, chopped
      Chocolate Cream Cheese Frosting
      (recipe follows)

Per Serving
Calories: 308
% Calories from fat: 27
Fat (gm): 9.2
Saturated fat (gm): 2.8
Cholesterol (mg): 32
Sodium (mg): 324
Protein (gm): 4
Carbohydrate (gm): 51
Exchanges
Milk: 0.0
Vegetable: 0.0
Fruit: 0.0
Bread: 3.0
Meat: 0.0
Fat: 2.0

1. Beat sugar and shortening in large bowl until blended; beat in eggs, vanilla, and cocoa. Mix in combined flour, baking powder, baking soda, and salt alternately with beer, beginning and ending with dry ingredients. Mix in sauerkraut.

2. Spread batter in greased 13 x 9-inch baking pan. Bake at 350 degrees until toothpick inserted in center comes out clean, 40 to 45 minutes. Cool in pan on wire rack; spread with Chocolate Cream Cheese Frosting.

Chocolate Cream Cheese Frosting

makes about 1^1/$_2$ cups

 ^{1}/$_2$ package (8-ounce size) reduced-fat cream cheese, softened
  1 tablespoon margarine, softened
1^3/$_4$-2 cups powdered sugar
  3 tablespoons unsweetened cocoa

1. Beat cream cheese and margarine in medium bowl until smooth; beat in powdered sugar and cocoa.

MAPLE SYRUP COCOA CAKE

This cake contains no eggs or dairy products. Maple syrup adds wonderful flavor and moisture, and whole wheat flour a toothsome texture.

12 servings

1³/₄ cups maple syrup *or* honey
   1 cup water
   5 tablespoons oil
   1 tablespoon vinegar
   1 teaspoon vanilla
1³/₄ cups unbleached all-purpose flour
 ¹/₂ cup whole wheat *or* all-purpose flour
 ¹/₄ cup unsweetened cocoa
 ³/₄ teaspoon baking powder
 ³/₄ teaspoon baking soda
 ¹/₂ teaspoon salt
      Chocolate Glaze (see p. 76)

Per Serving
Calories: 291
% Calories from fat: 18
Fat (gm): 5.9
Saturated fat (gm): 0.8
Cholesterol (mg): 0.1
Sodium (mg): 217
Protein (gm): 2.9
Carbohydrate (gm): 57.5
Exchanges
Milk: 0.0
Vegetable: 0.0
Fruit: 0.0
Bread: 3.5
Meat: 0.0
Fat: 1.0

1. Mix maple syrup, water, oil, vinegar, and vanilla in large bowl until blended. Mix in combined flours, cocoa, baking powder, baking soda, and salt.

2. Pour batter into 2 greased and floured 8-inch round cake pans. Bake at 350 degrees until toothpick inserted in center of cake comes out clean, 30 to 35 minutes. Cool in pans on wire rack 10 minutes; remove from pans and cool completely.

3. Place cake layers on 2 plates. Make Chocolate Glaze, substituting water for the milk; drizzle over cake layers.

TEXAS COWBOY CAKE

Our low-fat version of an old-time favorite.

18 servings

2 cups sugar
1 cup Prune Puree (see p. 42)
1/2 cup unsweetened cocoa
1/2 cup strong coffee
6 tablespoons vegetable oil
2 ounces semisweet chocolate, melted
2 eggs
2 teaspoons vanilla
2²/3 cups all-purpose flour
2 teaspoons baking soda
1/2 teaspoon salt
1/2 cup fat-free sour cream
Texas Frosting (recipe follows)
1/3-1/2 cup chopped walnuts

Per Serving
Calories: 374
% Calories from fat: 19
Fat (gm): 8.2
Saturated fat (gm): 1.9
Cholesterol (mg): 25.5
Sodium (mg): 262
Protein (gm): 4.9
Carbohydrate (gm): 72.2
Exchanges
Milk: 0.0
Vegetable: 0.0
Fruit: 0.0
Bread: 4.5
Meat: 0.0
Fat: 1.0

1. Combine sugar, Prune Puree, cocoa, coffee, oil, and melted chocolate in large bowl; mix well. Mix in eggs and vanilla. Mix in half the combined flour, baking soda, and salt; mix in sour cream, then remaining flour mixture.

2. Spread mixture in greased and floured jelly roll pan, 15 x 10 inches. Bake at 350 degrees until toothpick inserted in cake comes out clean, 25 to 30 minutes. Cool in pan on wire rack.

3. Frost cake with Texas Frosting; sprinkle with walnuts.

Texas Frosting

makes about 2 cups

3 cups powdered sugar
1/4 cup unsweetened cocoa
1/4-1/3 cup fat-free milk
1/4 teaspoon baking soda
2 ounces reduced-fat cream cheese, softened

1. Mix powdered sugar, cocoa, milk, and baking soda in medium saucepan; heat over medium-low heat until steaming. Remove from heat and cool.

2. Add cream cheese to sugar mixture, beating until frosting is spreadable consistency.

MIRACLE WHIP CAKE

Another oldie but goodie, transformed into low-fat goodness. Mayonnaise can be substituted for the salad dressing, if you prefer.

10 servings

2 cups all-purpose flour
1 cup sugar
1/4 cup unsweetened cocoa
2 teaspoons baking soda
1 teaspoon baking powder
1/4 teaspoon salt
1/2 cup salad dressing (Miracle Whip)
1/2 cup applesauce
1 cup warm water
1 teaspoon vanilla
Chocolate Glaze (see p. 76)

Per Serving
Calories: 283
% Calories from fat: 18
Fat (gm): 5.8
Saturated fat (gm): 0.9
Cholesterol (mg): 4.2
Sodium (mg): 434
Protein (gm): 3
Carbohydrate (gm): 55.1
Exchanges
Milk: 0.0
Vegetable: 0.0
Fruit: 0.0
Bread: 3.5
Meat: 0.0
Fat: 1.0

1. Combine flour, sugar, cocoa, baking soda, baking powder, and salt in large bowl. Add salad dressing, applesauce, water, and vanilla; mix at low speed until blended, then mix at medium speed 1 minute longer (batter will be thin).

2. Pour batter into greased and floured 6-cup fluted tube pan or 9-inch square baking pan. Bake at 350 degrees until toothpick inserted in center of cake comes out clean, 40 to 45 minutes. Cool in pan on wire rack 10 minutes; remove from pan and cool. Drizzle with Chocolate Glaze.

GERMAN CHOCOLATE CAKE

One of America's classic cakes, in delicious low-fat, low-calorie style.

16 servings

1 cup granulated sugar
3/4 cup packed light brown sugar
1/2 cup Prune Puree (see p. 42)
1 1/2 cups 1% low-fat milk
1 tablespoon lemon juice
4 ounces German sweet chocolate, melted
1 teaspoon vanilla
2 eggs
2 egg whites
2 cups all-purpose flour
1 teaspoon baking soda
1/2 teaspoon salt
  Coconut Frosting (recipe follows)

Per Serving
Calories: 368
% Calories from fat: 23
Fat (gm): 9.8
Saturated fat (gm): 3.3
Cholesterol (mg): 28.1
Sodium (mg): 265
Protein (gm): 6.2
Carbohydrate (gm): 66.5
Exchanges
Milk: 0.0
Vegetable: 0.0
Fruit: 0.0
Bread: 4.0
Meat: 0.0
Fat: 2.0

1. Mix sugars and Prune Puree, milk, lemon juice, melted chocolate, and vanilla in large bowl. Beat in eggs and egg whites; mix in combined flour, baking soda, and salt.

2. Pour batter into 2 greased and floured 9-inch round cake pans. Bake at 350 degrees until cakes spring back when touched, about 25 minutes. Cool in pans on wire rack 10 minutes; remove from pans and cool completely.

3. Place 1 cake layer on serving plate; spread with 3/4 cup Coconut Frosting; top with second cake layer. Frost top and side of cake.

Coconut Frosting

makes about 2 1/2 cups

3/4 cup sugar
2 tablespoons plus 1 1/2 teaspoons cornstarch
5 tablespoons margarine
1/3 cup light corn syrup
1 1/4 cups evaporated fat-free milk
2 teaspoons vanilla
1/2 cup shredded coconut
1/2-3/4 cup chopped toasted pecans

1. Combine all ingredients, except coconut and pecans, in medium saucepan. Heat to boiling; stir in coconut and pecans. Cool until thick enough to spread, stirring occasionally.

CHOCOLATE BUTTERMILK CAKE WITH MOCHA FROSTING

A chocolate dream come true, this cake is 3 layers high and generously covered with creamy mocha frosting!

16 servings

6 tablespoons vegetable shortening
1 cup granulated sugar
1/2 cup packed light brown sugar
2 eggs
2 egg whites
1 teaspoon vanilla
2 cups cake flour
1/2 cup unsweetened cocoa
2 teaspoons baking powder
1/2 teaspoon baking soda
1/2 teaspoon salt
1 cup reduced-fat buttermilk
Mocha Frosting (recipe follows)

Per Serving
Calories: 351
% Calories from fat: 17
Fat (gm): 6.9
Saturated fat (gm): 1.8
Cholesterol (mg): 27.3
Sodium (mg): 195
Protein (gm): 4.1
Carbohydrate (gm): 71.5
Exchanges
Milk: 0.0
Vegetable: 0.0
Fruit: 0.0
Bread: 4.5
Meat: 0.0
Fat: 1.0

1. Grease and flour three 8-inch round cake pans. Line bottoms of pans with waxed paper.

2. Beat shortening, sugars, eggs, egg whites, and vanilla in large bowl until smooth. Mix in combined flour, cocoa, baking powder, baking soda, and salt alternately with buttermilk, beginning and ending with dry ingredients.

3. Pour batter into prepared pans. Bake at 350 degrees until toothpicks inserted in centers of cakes come out clean, 25 to 30 minutes. Cool in pans on wire racks 10 minutes; invert onto wire racks. Peel off waxed paper and cool cake layers completely.

4. Place 1 cake layer on serving plate; frost with about 1/2 cup frosting. Repeat with second cake layer and frosting. Top with third cake layer; frost top and side of cake.

Mocha Frosting

makes about 2¹/₂ cups

    5 cups powdered sugar
  ¹/₂ cup unsweetened cocoa
  2-3 teaspoons instant coffee granules
  1-2 tablespoons margarine, softened
    1 teaspoon vanilla
  4-5 tablespoons skim milk

1. Combine powdered sugar, cocoa, coffee granules, and margarine in large bowl; beat in vanilla and enough milk for spreading consistency.

SOUR CREAM CHOCOLATE LAYER CAKE

One of our favorite chocolate cakes, rich and moist with sour cream.

16 servings

    1 cup hot water
  ²/₃ cup unsweetened cocoa
 1³/₄ cups sugar
    5 tablespoons margarine, softened
    2 teaspoons vanilla
    3 egg whites
  ¹/₂ cup fat-free sour cream
 1³/₄ cups cake flour
    1 teaspoon baking powder
  ¹/₂ teaspoon baking soda
  ¹/₂ teaspoon salt
      Mocha Frosting (see above)

Per Serving
Calories: 337
% Calories from fat: 12
Fat (gm): 4.4
Saturated fat (gm): 0.9
Cholesterol (mg): 0.3
Sodium (mg): 223
Protein (gm): 2.9
Carbohydrate (gm): 72.3
Exchanges
Milk: 0.0
Vegetable: 0.0
Fruit: 0.0
Bread: 4.5
Meat: 0.0
Fat: 0.5

1. Mix hot water and cocoa, stirring to dissolve cocoa. Cool to room temperature.

2. Mix sugar, margarine, and vanilla in large bowl until blended; beat in egg whites, 1 at a time. Mix in sour cream; beat at high speed 1 minute. Mix in half the combined flour, baking powder, baking soda, and salt; mix in half the cocoa mixture. Mix in remaining flour mixture; mix in remaining cocoa mixture.

3. Pour batter into 2 greased and floured 9-inch round cake pans. Bake at 350 degrees until toothpick inserted in center comes out clean, 25 to 30 minutes. Cool in pans on wire rack 10 minutes; remove from pans and cool completely.

4. Place 1 cake layer on serving plate; frost with generous $^1/_2$ cup Mocha Frosting. Top with second layer; frost top and side of cake.

MOCHA MALLOW CAKE

The flavors of chocolate and coffee are blended in both the cake and the fluffy frosting.

12 servings

1³/₄ cups cake flour
2 cups packed light brown sugar
³/₄ cup unsweetened cocoa
2 teaspoons baking soda
1 teaspoon baking powder
1 teaspoon salt
1 cup hot water
1¹/₂ teaspoons instant espresso powder *or* 1 tablespoon instant coffee granules
1 cup reduced-fat buttermilk
2 eggs
¹/₂ cup vegetable oil
1 teaspoon vanilla
Mocha Mallow Frosting (recipe follows)

Per Serving
Calories: 375
% Calories from fat: 24
Fat (gm): 10.3
Saturated fat (gm): 1.6
Cholesterol (mg): 36.4
Sodium (mg): 541
Protein (gm): 4.6
Carbohydrate (gm): 68.2
Exchanges
Milk: 0.0
Vegetable: 0.0
Fruit: 0.0
Bread: 4.5
Meat: 0.0
Fat: 1.5

1. Combine flour, brown sugar, cocoa, baking soda, baking powder, and salt in large bowl. Combine water and espresso, stirring to dissolve; mix with buttermilk, eggs, oil, and vanilla in small bowl. Beat buttermilk mixture into flour mixture, mixing until well blended.

2. Pour batter into 2 greased and floured 9-inch round cake pans. Bake at 350 degrees until toothpick inserted in center of cake comes out clean, about 50 minutes. Cool cakes in pans on wire rack 10 minutes; remove from pans and cool completely.

3. Place 1 cake layer on serving plate; frost with about ³/₄ cup Mocha Mallow Frosting. Top with second cake layer; frost top and side of cake.

Mocha Mallow Frosting

makes about 4 cups

- 1 cup sugar
- 1/3 cup water
- 3 egg whites
- 1/4 teaspoon cream of tartar
- 1/8 teaspoon salt
- 1/4 cup unsweetened cocoa
- 1 tablespoon instant espresso powder *or* 2 tablespoons instant coffee granules

1. Combine all ingredients, except cocoa and espresso, in top of double boiler. Place over simmering water and beat at high speed until stiff peaks form, 5 to 8 minutes. Remove from heat; beat in cocoa and espresso granules.

MARSHMALLOW FUDGE CAKE

An easy to make one-step cake!

16 servings

- 1³/4 cups all-purpose flour
- 1¹/4 cups fat-free milk
- 1¹/4 cups sugar
- 1/2 cup unsweetened cocoa
- 1/2 cup vegetable shortening
- 1 teaspoon baking powder
- 1 teaspoon baking soda
- 2 teaspoons vanilla extract
- 1/4 teaspoon salt
- 3 large eggs
- Marshmallow Frosting (recipe follows)

Per Serving
Calories: 242
% Calories from fat: 26
Fat (gm): 7.1
Saturated fat (gm): 1.8
Cholesterol (mg): 40.2
Sodium (mg): 179
Protein (gm): 3.9
Carbohydrate (gm): 40.6
Exchanges
Milk: 0.0
Vegetable: 0.0
Fruit: 0.0
Bread: 3.0
Meat: 0.0
Fat: 1.0

1. Measure all ingredients, except Marshmallow Frosting, into large bowl. Mix at low speed until ingredients are just combined; beat at medium speed 2 minutes.

2. Pour batter into 2 greased and floured 9-inch round cake pans. Bake at 350 degrees until cake springs back when touched in the center, about 30 minutes. Cool on wire racks 10 minutes; remove from pans and cool completely.

3. Place 1 cake layer on serving plate and spread with generous $1/2$ cup Marshmallow Frosting; top with second layer and frost top and side of cake.

Marshmallow Frosting

makes about 4 cups

    1   cup sugar
    $1/3$ cup water
    2   egg whites
    $1/4$ teaspoon cream of tartar
        Dash salt

1. Combine all ingredients in top of double boiler. Place over simmering water and beat at high speed until stiff peaks form, 5 to 8 minutes.

CHOCOLATE STRAWBERRY TORTE

Use any berries or combination of berries to decorate this festive dessert offering.

10 servings

    1   cup sugar, divided
    1   cup all-purpose flour
    $1/2$ teaspoon baking powder
    $1/2$ teaspoon baking soda
    $1/4$ teaspoon salt
    1   cup 2% reduced-fat milk
    $1/2$ cup unsweetened cocoa
    2   ounces semisweet chocolate, coarsely
        chopped
    1   teaspoon vanilla
    4   egg whites
    $1/4$ teaspoon cream of tartar
    3   cups plain, *or* chocolate, light whipped
        topping
  1-1$1/2$ pints small strawberries
        Mint sprigs, as garnish

Per Serving
Calories: 233
% Calories from fat: 19
Fat (gm): 4.9
Saturated fat (gm): 3.7
Cholesterol (mg): 2
Sodium (mg): 188
Protein (gm): 4.5
Carbohydrate (gm): 42.5
Exchanges
Milk: 0.0
Vegetable: 0.0
Fruit: 0.0
Bread: 3.0
Meat: 0.0
Fat: 0.5

1. Combine 3/4 cup sugar, flour, baking powder, baking soda, and salt in large bowl. Mix milk and cocoa; heat over medium heat, whisking constantly, until mixture thickens, about 5 minutes. Remove from heat; add chocolate and vanilla, whisking until chocolate is melted. Add milk mixture to dry ingredients, mixing just until blended.

2. With clean bowl and beaters, beat egg whites and cream of tartar in large bowl to stiff peaks; beat to stiff peaks, adding remaining 1/4 cup sugar gradually. Fold about 1/3 of the whites into cake batter; fold batter into remaining egg whites.

3. Pour batter into 2 greased and floured 9-inch round cake pans. Bake at 350 degrees until toothpick inserted in center of cake comes out clean, about 40 minutes. Cool in pans on wire rack 10 minutes; remove from pans and cool completely.

4. Place 1 cake layer on serving plate; frost with 1 cup whipped topping. Top with second cake layer; spread top with remaining whipped topping. Arrange strawberries, pointed ends up, on top of cake. Garnish with mint sprigs.

FLOURLESS CHOCOLATE CAKE

It's hard to believe that a cake so sinfully rich and so wonderful can actually be low in fat! Although regular cocoa can be used, the Dutch process cocoa lends a special flavor.

8 servings

- 1/2 cup Dutch process cocoa
- 3/4 cup packed light brown sugar
- 3 tablespoons flour
- 2 teaspoons instant espresso powder
- 1/8 teaspoon salt
  Pinch pepper
- 3/4 cup fat-free milk
- 1 teaspoon vanilla
- 2 ounces unsweetened, *or* bittersweet, chocolate, chopped
- 2 ounces semisweet chocolate, chopped
- 1 egg

Per Serving
Calories: 350
% Calories from fat: 21
Fat (gm): 8.7
Saturated fat (gm): 4.5
Cholesterol (mg): 27
Sodium (mg): 109
Protein (gm): 6.6
Carbohydrate (gm): 65.8
Exchanges
Milk: 0.0
Vegetable: 0.0
Fruit: 0.0
Bread: 4.0
Meat: 0.0
Fat: 1.5

3 egg whites
1/8 teaspoon cream of tartar
1/3 cup granulated sugar
Rich Chocolate Frosting (recipe
follows)

1. Combine cocoa, brown sugar, flour, coffee granules, salt, and pepper in medium saucepan; gradually stir in milk and vanilla to make smooth mixture. Heat over medium heat, stirring frequently, until mixture is hot and sugar dissolved (do not boil).

2. Remove saucepan from heat; add chocolate, stirring until melted. Whisk about 1/2 cup chocolate mixture into egg; whisk egg mixture back into saucepan. Cool to room temperature.

3. Beat egg whites until foamy in medium bowl; add cream of tartar and beat to soft peaks. Continue beating, adding sugar gradually, until stiff, but not dry, peaks form. Stir about 1/4 of the egg whites into cooled chocolate mixture; fold chocolate mixture into remaining egg whites.

4. Lightly grease bottom and side of 9-inch round cake pan; line bottom of pan with parchment paper. Pour batter into pan. Place pan in large roasting pan on center oven rack; add 1 inch hot water.

5. Bake cake at 350 degrees until just firm when lightly touched, 25 to 30 minutes (do not test with toothpick as cake will still be soft in the center). Cool completely on wire rack; refrigerate, covered, 8 hours or overnight.

6. Loosen side of cake from pan with sharp knife. Remove from pan and peel off parchment. Place on serving plate. Frost with Rich Chocolate Frosting.

Rich Chocolate Frosting

makes about 3/4 cup

1-2 tablespoons margarine, softened
1 1/2 cups powdered sugar
1/4 cup Dutch process cocoa
1/2 teaspoon vanilla
3-4 tablespoons fat-free milk

1. Mix margarine, powdered sugar, cocoa, and vanilla with enough milk to make spreadable consistency.

BLACK FOREST TORTE

A delicious low-fat version of this classic chocolate and cherry combination.

12 servings

3 egg yolks
1³/4 cups sugar, divided
1/2 cup Dutch process cocoa
1/2 cup hot water
1 teaspoon vanilla
1¹/3 cups cake flour
1 teaspoon baking powder
1/4 teaspoon salt
4 egg whites, room temperature
2 cans (16 ounces each) pitted tart cherries in water
1 ounce unsweetened chocolate, coarsely chopped
2 tablespoons cherry-flavored liqueur *or* 1/2 teaspoon cherry extract
Meringue Frosting (see p. 107)
Candied cherries, as garnish
Chocolate curls, as garnish

Per Serving
Calories: 302
% Calories from fat: 9
Fat (gm): 3
Saturated fat (gm): 1.4
Cholesterol (mg): 53.3
Sodium (mg): 135
Protein (gm): 5.4
Carbohydrate (gm): 64.6
Exchanges
Milk: 0.0
Vegetable: 0.0
Fruit: 0.0
Bread: 4.0
Meat: 0.0
Fat: 0.0

1. Beat egg yolks with 1 cup sugar in large bowl until thick and lemon colored, about 5 minutes. Mix cocoa, hot water, and vanilla until smooth; gradually beat into yolk mixture. Continue beating on high speed until mixture is very foamy and increased in volume, 5 to 10 minutes. Fold in combined flour, baking powder, and salt.

2. In a clean bowl with clean beaters, beat egg whites to soft peaks; beat to stiff peaks, gradually adding 1/4 cup sugar. Fold 1/3 of the whites into yolk mixture; fold yolk mixture into remaining whites.

3. Pour batter into ungreased, parchment-lined 9-inch springform pan. Bake at 350 degrees until cake springs back when lightly touched, 35 to 40 minutes. Cool in pan on wire rack until completely cool. Remove cake from pan and peel off parchment. Slice cake horizontally into 3 equal layers.

4. Drain cherries, reserving juice. Heat cherry juice and remaining $^{1}/_{2}$ cup sugar to boiling in medium saucepan; boil until mixture is reduced to $^{3}/_{4}$ cup. Remove from heat; add chocolate, stirring until melted. Stir in liqueur.

5. Place 1 cake layer on serving plate; spread $^{1}/_{3}$ of the chocolate mixture on cake. Spoon $^{1}/_{2}$ of the cherries on top. Top with second cake layer, pressing onto cherries. Spread with $^{1}/_{3}$ chocolate mixture and remaining cherries. Spread cut side of third cake layer with remaining chocolate mixture and place, cut side down, on cake. Frost cake with Meringue Frosting; garnish with candied cherries and chocolate curls.

CHOCOLATE MOUSSE TORTE

This cake is more complex to make, but the soufflé-like flourless cake layers, filled and frosted with rich chocolate mousse, will make any occasion special.

12 servings

5	egg yolks
$^{2}/_{3}$	cup sugar, divided
1	teaspoon almond extract
5	egg whites
$^{1}/_{4}$	teaspoon cream of tartar
$^{1}/_{4}$	cup Dutch process cocoa
	Chocolate Mousse (recipe follows)
$^{1}/_{4}$	cup sliced almonds, toasted

Per Serving
Calories: 247
% Calories from fat: 29
Fat (gm): 8.3
Saturated fat (gm): 3.2
Cholesterol (mg): 125.3
Sodium (mg): 54
Protein (gm): 7.1
Carbohydrate (gm): 39.2
Exchanges
Milk: 0.0
Vegetable: 0.0
Fruit: 0.0
Bread: 2.5
Meat: 0.0
Fat: 1.5

1. Grease bottoms of three 8- or 9-inch round cake pans and line with parchment paper; grease and flour lightly.

2. Beat egg yolks and $^{1}/_{3}$ cup sugar in large bowl until thick and lemon colored, about 5 minutes; mix in almond extract.

3. With clean beaters and bowl, beat egg whites and cream of tartar to soft peaks; beat to stiff peaks, adding remaining $^{1}/_{3}$ cup sugar gradually. Mix $^{1}/_{4}$ of the egg whites into the egg yolk mixture; fold egg yolk mixture into egg whites. Fold in cocoa.

4. Spread batter in cake pans; bake at 350 degrees until toothpick inserted in center comes out clean, 15 to 18 minutes. Cool cakes in pans on wire racks; remove from pans.

5. Place 1 cake layer, parchment side up, in bottom of 9-inch springform pan; discard parchment. Spread cake with 1/3 of the Chocolate Mousse; repeat with remaining cake layers and Chocolate Mousse. Sprinkle top of cake with almonds. Refrigerate 8 hours or overnight.

6. Loosen cake from side of pan with sharp knife; remove side of pan and place cake on serving plate.

Chocolate Mousse

makes about 4 cups

>   1 envelope (1/4 ounce) unflavored gelatin
> 1/4 cup cold water
>   1 cup sugar, divided
> 1/2 cup Dutch process cocoa
> 1 1/4 cups 1% low-fat milk
>   2 egg yolks
>   4 ounces semisweet chocolate, finely chopped
>   2 egg whites
> 1/8 teaspoon cream of tartar

1. Sprinkle gelatin over cold water in small saucepan; let stand 3 to 4 minutes. Heat over low heat until gelatin is dissolved, stirring constantly.

2. Mix 1/2 cup sugar and cocoa in small saucepan; whisk in milk. Heat to boiling over medium-high heat; reduce heat and simmer briskly, whisking constantly, until thickened, 3 to 4 minutes. Whisk about 1/2 the milk mixture into egg yolks; whisk yolk mixture into milk mixture in saucepan. Cook over low heat 1 to 2 minutes, whisking constantly. Remove from heat; add gelatin mixture and chocolate, whisking until chocolate is melted. Refrigerate until cool, but not set, about 20 minutes.

3. Beat egg whites, remaining 1/2 cup sugar, and cream of tartar until foamy in medium bowl; place bowl over pan of simmering water and beat at medium speed until egg whites reach 160 degrees on candy thermometer. Remove from heat and beat at high speed until very thick and cool, about 5 minutes. Mix 1/4 of the egg whites into chocolate mixture; fold chocolate mixture into remaining egg whites.

CHOCOLATE SOUFFLÉ CAKE ROLL

A chocolate soufflé made into a cake roll, generously filled with whipped topping and dusted with cocoa!

8 servings

4 egg yolks
2/3 cup granulated sugar, divided
6 egg whites
1/4 teaspoon cream of tartar
1/8 teaspoon salt
1 teaspoon vanilla
1/2 cup unsweetened cocoa
3-4 cups chocolate whipped topping
Unsweetened cocoa, as garnish
Powdered sugar, as garnish
1 cup raspberries
2 cups Raspberry Sauce (see p. 658)

Per Serving
Calories: 293
% Calories from fat: 28
Fat (gm): 9
Saturated fat (gm): 6.8
Cholesterol (mg): 106.7
Sodium (mg): 106
Protein (gm): 5.2
Carbohydrate (gm): 46.3
Exchanges
Milk: 0.0
Vegetable: 0.0
Fruit: 0.0
Bread: 3.0
Meat: 0.0
Fat: 1.5

1. Grease jelly roll pan, 15 x 10 x 1 inch; line with parchment paper; grease and flour lightly.

2. Beat egg yolks in medium bowl 3 minutes. Beat in 1/3 cup sugar gradually, beating until yolk mixture is thick and lemon colored, about 5 minutes.

3. With clean beaters, beat egg whites, cream of tartar, and salt in large bowl to soft peaks. Beat in remaining 1/3 cup sugar gradually, beating to stiff peaks; beat in vanilla. Fold in 1/2 cup cocoa; mix 1/4 of the egg whites into beaten yolk mixture. Fold yolk mixture into remaining egg whites.

4. Spread batter evenly in prepared pan. Bake at 375 degrees until cake springs back when touched lightly, about 15 minutes. Loosen sides of cake with sharp knife; immediately invert cake onto clean dish towel dusted with cocoa; peel off parchment paper. Cool cake 2 to 3 minutes; roll up in towel, beginning with short edge. Let cool on wire rack.

5. Carefully unroll cake; spread with whipped topping and roll up. Place cake on serving plate. Sprinkle generously with cocoa; sprinkle lightly with powdered sugar. Cut into slices; sprinkle with raspberries and serve with Raspberry Sauce.

CHOCOLATE BUTTERCREAM CAKE ROLL

A luscious buttercream-filled and frosted cake roll, with an apricot accent tucked inside.

14 servings

3 eggs
1 cup sugar
1/3 cup water
1 teaspoon vanilla
3/4 cup all-purpose flour
1/4 cup unsweetened cocoa
1 teaspoon baking powder
1/4 teaspoon salt
3/4 cup apricot spreadable fruit
Chocolate Buttercream (see p. 74)
Chocolate leaves or curls, as garnish

Per Serving
Calories: 345
% Calories from fat: 9
Fat (gm): 3.6
Saturated fat (gm): 0.8
Cholesterol (mg): 45.7
Sodium (mg): 147
Protein (gm): 2.7
Carbohydrate (gm): 76.6
Exchanges
Milk: 0.0
Vegetable: 0.0
Fruit: 0.0
Bread: 5.0
Meat: 0.0
Fat: 0.0

1. Grease jelly roll pan, 15 x 10 x 1 inch; line with parchment paper; grease and flour lightly.

2. Beat eggs at high speed in large bowl until thick and lemon colored, about 5 minutes; gradually beat in sugar. Mix in water and vanilla. Mix in combined flour, cocoa, baking powder, and salt gradually, mixing just until smooth.

3. Pour batter into prepared pan, spreading evenly. Bake at 375 degrees until toothpick inserted in center comes out clean, 12 to 14 minutes. Loosen cake from edges of pan and invert onto clean towel sprinkled generously with cocoa; peel off parchment paper. Roll cake in towel, beginning at short end. Cool on wire rack.

4. Unroll cake; spread with spreadable fruit. Spread with 1 to 1 1/2 cups Chocolate Buttercream and roll up. Place cake roll on serving plate; spread with remaining Chocolate Buttercream. Garnish with chocolate leaves.

Variation: **Yule Log**—Make cake but do not fill or frost with Chocolate Buttercream. Make **Ricotta Cream Filling** as follows: Process 1 cup light ricotta cheese, 1 cup powdered sugar, 1/2 cup fat-free milk, 2 tablespoons softened margarine, and 2 teaspoons vanilla in blender until smooth. After unrolling cooled cake, spread with apricot spreadable fruit and Ricotta Cream Filling and roll up. Frost with 1/2 recipe Chocolate Buttercream. Using fork, make curved lines in frosting to resemble tree bark. Decorate with chopped filberts and chocolate leaves.

COCONUT MERINGUE CAKE ROLL

For variation, or if short on time, the meringue for this recipe can be omitted. Instead, sprinkle the cake roll generously with powdered sugar, or frost with Marshmallow Frosting (see p. 18).

10 servings

$^3/_4$ cup sugar, divided
3 egg yolks
6 egg whites, divided
2 tablespoons melted margarine
1 teaspoon vanilla
1 cup cake flour
1 tablespoon cornstarch
$^1/_4$ teaspoon salt
$^1/_4$ teaspoon cream of tartar
Coconut Cream Filling (recipe follows)
Meringue (recipe follows)
3-4 tablespoons flaked coconut

Per Serving
Calories: 254
% Calories from fat: 22
Fat (gm): 6.2
Saturated fat (gm): 2.5
Cholesterol (mg): 87.8
Sodium (mg): 168
Protein (gm): 7.2
Carbohydrate (gm): 42.3
Exchanges
Milk: 0.0
Vegetable: 0.0
Fruit: 0.0
Bread: 3.0
Meat: 0.0
Fat: 1.0

1. Grease jelly roll pan, 15 x 10 x 1 inch. Line pan with parchment; grease lightly.

2. Mix $^1/_2$ cup sugar, egg yolks, 3 egg whites, and margarine in large bowl; beat at high speed until thick and lemon colored, about 5 minutes. Stir in vanilla. Mix in combined flour, cornstarch, and salt until blended.

3. Beat remaining 3 egg whites and cream of tartar to soft peaks in large bowl; beat to stiff peaks, adding remaining $^1/_4$ cup sugar gradually. Mix $^1/_4$ of egg whites into cake batter; fold cake batter into remaining egg whites.

4. Spread batter evenly in prepared pan. Bake at 450 degrees until cake is browned and springs back when touched, about 6 minutes. Loosen sides of cake with sharp knife and immediately invert onto clean dish towel sprinkled generously with powdered sugar; peel off parchment paper. Let cool 2 to 3 minutes; roll cake up in towel, starting at long end. Cool on wire rack.

5. Unroll cake; spread with chilled Coconut Cream Filling and roll up. Place cake on ovenproof serving platter; spread with Meringue and sprinkle with coconut. Bake at 500 degrees until meringue is browned, 3 to 5 minutes.

Coconut Cream Filling

makes about 2 cups

$^1/_3$ cup sugar
2 tablespoons cornstarch
1$^1/_2$ cups 2% reduced-fat milk
1 egg, slightly beaten
$^1/_4$ cup flaked coconut
1 teaspoon vanilla

1. Mix sugar and cornstarch in small saucepan; whisk in milk. Cook over medium-high heat, whisking constantly, until mixture boils and thickens.

2. Whisk about $^1/_2$ cup of mixture into egg; whisk egg mixture back into milk mixture. Cook over low heat, whisking constantly, until thickened. Stir in coconut and vanilla. Cool to room temperature; refrigerate until chilled.

Meringue

4 egg whites
$^1/_4$ teaspoon cream of tartar
$^1/_2$ cup powdered sugar

1. Beat egg whites and cream of tartar to soft peaks; beat to stiff peaks, adding sugar gradually.

PUMPKIN JELLY ROLL CAKE

This cake can also be filled with Coconut Cream Filling (see above), or 3 to 4 cups of light whipped topping.

8 servings

3 egg yolks
$^1/_2$ cup granulated sugar, divided
$^1/_2$ cup canned pumpkin
$^1/_2$ cup all-purpose flour
$^1/_2$ teaspoon baking powder
1$^1/_2$ teaspoons pumpkin pie spice
$^1/_4$ teaspoon salt
3 egg whites
$^1/_4$ teaspoon cream of tartar
Mock Mascarpone (see p. 161)
1 cup powdered sugar, divided
Powdered sugar, as garnish

Per Serving
Calories: 206
% Calories from fat: 11
Fat (gm): 2.5
Saturated fat (gm): 0.9
Cholesterol (mg): 82.2
Sodium (mg): 289
Protein (gm): 7.9
Carbohydrate (gm): 38.1
Exchanges
Milk: 0.0
Vegetable: 0.0
Fruit: 0.0
Bread: 2.5
Meat: 0.0
Fat: 0.5

1. Grease jelly roll pan, 15 x 10 x 1 inch; line with parchment paper and grease and flour lightly.

2. Beat egg yolks and ¹/₄ cup granulated sugar in medium bowl until thick and lemon colored, 3 to 5 minutes; mix in pumpkin. Mix in combined flour, baking powder, pie spice, and salt.

3. With clean beaters and bowl, beat egg whites and cream of tartar to soft peaks; beat to stiff peaks, adding remaining ¹/₄ cup granulated sugar gradually. Mix ¹/₄ of the egg whites into cake batter; fold cake batter into remaining egg whites.

4. Spread batter evenly in prepared pan. Bake at 375 degrees until cake is browned and springs back when touched, about 12 minutes. Loosen sides of cake with sharp knife and immediately invert onto clean dish towel sprinkled generously with powdered sugar; peel off parchment paper. Let cool 2 to 3 minutes; roll cake up in towel, starting at short end. Cool on wire rack.

5. Make Mock Mascarpone, substituting reduced-fat cream cheese for the fat-free cream cheese; beat in 1 cup of powdered sugar.

6. Unroll cake; spread with Mock Mascarpone and roll up. Place cake on serving plate; sprinkle generously with powdered sugar.

CHOCOLATE-CHERRY PUDDING CAKE

Served warm, this fudgey favorite will bring smiles to kids of all ages.

14 servings

1³/₄ cups all-purpose flour
1¹/₄ cups granulated sugar
¹/₃ cup unsweetened cocoa
3 tablespoons baking powder
³/₄ cup skim milk
¹/₂ cup unsweetened applesauce
1 cup fresh, *or* frozen, sweet cherries, thawed and pitted
¹/₄ cup chopped pecans
1¹/₄ cups packed dark brown sugar
3 cups hot water
¹/₄ cup unsweetened cocoa

Per Serving
Calories: 242
% Calories from fat: 7
Fat (gm): 1.9
Saturated fat (gm): 0.2
Cholesterol (mg): 0
Sodium (mg): 264
Protein (gm): 3.0
Carbohydrate (gm): 55.1
Exchanges
Milk: 0.0
Vegetable: 0.0
Fruit: 1.5
Bread: 2.0
Meat: 0.0
Fat: 0.0

1. Combine flour, granulated sugar, ¹/₃ cup cocoa, and baking powder in large bowl; stir in milk and applesauce just until dry ingredients are moistened. Fold in cherries and pecans. Spoon batter into greased and floured 13 x 9-inch baking pan.

2. Combine brown sugar, hot water, and ¹/₄ cup cocoa in medium bowl, stirring until smooth. Pour brown sugar mixture over batter.

3. Bake at 350 degrees 35 to 40 minutes or until set (cake will have a pudding-like texture). Serve warm or at room temperature.

HOT FUDGE PUDDING CAKE

For the ultimate treat, serve warm, topped with scoops of low-fat ice cream or frozen yogurt.

6 servings

1 cup all-purpose flour
¹/₂ cup packed light brown sugar
6 tablespoons Dutch process cocoa, divided
1¹/₂ teaspoons baking powder
¹/₄ teaspoon salt
¹/₂ cup fat-free milk
2 tablespoons vegetable oil
1 teaspoon vanilla
¹/₃ cup granulated sugar
1¹/₂ cups boiling water

Per Serving
Calories: 259
% Calories from fat: 18
Fat (gm): 5.2
Saturated fat (gm): 0.9
Cholesterol (mg): 0.4
Sodium (mg): 240
Protein (gm): 4.1
Carbohydrate (gm): 49.1
Exchanges
Milk: 0.0
Vegetable: 0.0
Fruit: 0.0
Bread: 3.0
Meat: 0.0
Fat: 1.0

1. Combine flour, brown sugar, 3 tablespoons cocoa, baking powder, and salt in medium bowl. Add combined milk, oil, and vanilla to flour mixture, mixing well. Spoon batter into greased 8- or 9-inch square baking pan.

2. Mix remaining cocoa and granulated sugar; sprinkle over cake batter. Pour boiling water over batter; do not stir.

3. Bake at 350 degrees until cake springs back when touched, about 30 minutes. Cool on wire rack 5 to 10 minutes; serve warm.

Variation: **Mocha Latte Pudding Cake**—Make cake as above, substituting granulated sugar for the brown sugar and adding 1 tablespoon instant espresso and ¹/₂ teaspoon ground cinnamon to flour mixture. Serve warm pudding cake with a scoop of fat-free vanilla or chocolate ice cream and light whipped topping.

LEMON PUDDING CAKE

A luscious combination of moist cake and creamy pudding—for best flavor, use fresh lemon juice.

8 servings

1¹/₄ cups sugar, divided
¹/₂ cup all-purpose flour
¹/₈ teaspoon salt
1 cup 2% reduced-fat milk
¹/₃ cup lemon juice
2 tablespoons margarine, melted
1 egg
1 tablespoon grated lemon rind
3 egg whites
¹/₈ teaspoon cream of tartar

Per Serving
Calories: 208
% Calories from fat: 17
Fat (gm): 4.1
Saturated fat (gm): 1.1
Cholesterol (mg): 28.8
Sodium (mg): 114
Protein (gm): 4
Carbohydrate (gm): 39.9
Exchanges
Milk: 0.0
Vegetable: 0.0
Fruit: 0.0
Bread: 2.5
Meat: 0.0
Fat: 0.5

1. Combine 1 cup sugar, flour, and salt in large bowl. Combine milk, lemon juice, margarine, egg, and lemon rind; mix into dry ingredients.

2. Beat egg whites and cream of tartar to soft peaks in large bowl; beat to stiff peaks, adding remaining ¹/₄ cup sugar gradually. Fold egg whites into cake batter (batter will be slightly lumpy and thin).

3. Pour batter into greased 1¹/₂-quart casserole or soufflé dish. Place casserole in roasting pan on oven rack; add 1 to 2 inches boiling water. Bake at 350 degrees until cake is golden and springs back when touched, about 40 minutes. Cool on wire rack 15 minutes; serve warm.

CHEESECAKE CUPCAKES

No need to frost, as these chocolate cupcakes are baked with a topping of cream cheese.

20 servings (1 cupcake each)

Per Serving
Calories: 136
% Calories from fat: 29
Fat (gm): 4.6
Saturated fat (gm): 2.3
Cholesterol (mg): 22.5
Sodium (mg): 186
Protein (gm): 3.4
Carbohydrate (gm): 21.7
Exchanges
Milk: 0.0
Vegetable: 0.0
Fruit: 0.0
Bread: 1.5
Meat: 0.0
Fat: 0.5

- $3/4$ cup all-purpose flour
- $3/4$ cup sugar
- $1/3$ cup unsweetened cocoa
- $3/4$ teaspoon baking soda
- $1/2$ teaspoon salt
- $3/4$ cup reduced-fat buttermilk
- $1/4$ cup shortening
- 1 egg
- 1 teaspoon vanilla
- Cheesecake Topping (recipe follows)
- $1/2$ cup reduced-fat semisweet chocolate morsels

1. Combine all ingredients, except Cheesecake Topping and chocolate morsels, in large bowl. Beat at low speed until blended; beat at high speed 3 minutes, scraping side of bowl occasionally.

2. Pour batter into paper-lined muffin cups, filling each about $1/2$ full. Spread about 1 tablespoon Cheesecake Topping over batter in each, covering completely. Sprinkle each with about 1 teaspoon chocolate morsels.

3. Bake at 350 degrees until golden, about 30 minutes. Cool in pans on wire rack.

Cheesecake Topping

- 1 package (8 ounces) fat-free cream cheese, room temperature
- $1/2$ cup sugar
- 1 egg

1. Mix all ingredients until smooth.

MACAROON CUPCAKES

Not quite a cake, not quite a meringue, but delicious!

24 servings (1 each)

1¼ cups sugar, divided
¾ cup all-purpose flour
½ teaspoon baking powder
½ teaspoon salt
6 egg whites
½ teaspoon cream of tartar
½ teaspoon vanilla
1¼ cups flaked coconut
Sliced almonds, as garnish

Per Serving
Calories: 77
% Calories from fat: 15
Fat (gm): 1.3
Saturated fat (gm): 1.1
Cholesterol (mg): 0
Sodium (mg): 73
Protein (gm): 1.4
Carbohydrate (gm): 15.2
Exchanges
Milk: 0.0
Vegetable: 0.0
Fruit: 0.0
Bread: 1.0
Meat: 0.0
Fat: 0.0

1. Combine 1 cup sugar, flour, baking powder, and salt; reserve. Beat egg whites and cream of tartar to soft peaks in large bowl; beat to stiff peaks, adding remaining ¼ cup sugar gradually. Beat in vanilla; fold in reserved sugar mixture and coconut.

2. Spoon batter into paper-lined muffin cups; top each with 2 or 3 almond slices. Bake at 300 degrees until just beginning to brown, about 30 minutes. Cool on wire rack.

PEANUT BUTTER CUPCAKES

Frosted with creamy Chocolate Buttercream frosting for the ultimate flavor treat!

24 servings (1 each)

½ cup reduced-fat chunky peanut butter
5 tablespoons margarine, softened
1¼ cups packed light brown sugar
2 eggs
1 teaspoon vanilla
2 cups all-purpose flour
1 tablespoon baking powder
½ teaspoon salt
1¼ cups fat-free milk
Chocolate Buttercream (see p. 74)

Per Serving
Calories: 279
% Calories from fat: 20
Fat (gm): 6.4
Saturated fat (gm): 1.3
Cholesterol (mg): 18
Sodium (mg): 209
Protein (gm): 3.9
Carbohydrate (gm): 52.6
Exchanges
Milk: 0.0
Vegetable: 0.0
Fruit: 0.0
Bread: 3.5
Meat: 0.0
Fat: 1.0

1. Beat peanut butter and margarine until smooth in large bowl; beat in brown sugar. Beat in eggs and vanilla; mix in combined flour, baking powder, and salt alternately with milk, beginning and ending with dry ingredients.

2. Spoon batter into 24 paper-lined muffin cups. Bake at 350 degrees until toothpick inserted in center of cupcake comes out clean, 18 to 22 minutes. Cool on wire rack. Frost cupcakes with Chocolate Buttercream.

GRANNY CAKE

So named because every grandma has a version of this yummy cake—best eaten when still slightly warm.

12 servings

2 cups all-purpose flour
1¹/₃ cups granulated sugar
1 teaspoon baking soda
¹/₂ teaspoon salt
2 eggs
1 can (20 ounces) crushed pineapple *or* fruit cocktail, undrained
¹/₂ cup packed light brown sugar
¹/₄-¹/₂ cup chopped nuts
Granny Frosting (recipe follows)

Per Serving
Calories: 369
% Calories from fat: 24
Fat (gm): 10.1
Saturated fat (gm): 1.9
Cholesterol (mg): 35.7
Sodium (mg): 318
Protein (gm): 4.9
Carbohydrate (gm): 66.1
Exchanges
Milk: 0.0
Vegetable: 0.0
Fruit: 0.0
Bread: 4.0
Meat: 0.0
Fat: 1.5

1. Combine flour, granulated sugar, baking soda, and salt in large bowl; add eggs and pineapple with juice, mixing until well blended.

2. Pour batter into greased 13 x 9-inch baking pan. Sprinkle batter with brown sugar and nuts. Bake at 350 degrees until toothpick inserted in center of cake comes out clean, 40 to 45 minutes. Pour Granny Frosting over hot cake; cool on wire rack (frosting will thicken as it cools).

Granny Frosting

¹/₂ cup margarine
1 cup powdered sugar
¹/₂ cup fat-free evaporated milk
1 teaspoon vanilla

1. Melt margarine in saucepan; stir in powdered sugar, evaporated milk, and vanilla. Heat to boiling; boil, stirring constantly, until thick.

BANANA CINNAMON CAKE

Bananas add flavor and moistness to this picnic-perfect cake.

10 servings

1½ cups all-purpose flour
½ cup packed light brown sugar
2 teaspoons baking powder
1 teaspoon baking soda
1 teaspoon ground cinnamon
¼ teaspoon salt
1 package (6 ounces) reduced-fat custard-style banana yogurt
1 cup mashed ripe banana (1 medium banana)
2 tablespoons margarine, softened
2 egg whites
1 teaspoon vanilla
Powdered Sugar Frosting (recipe follows)

Per Serving
Calories: 233
% Calories from fat: 19
Fat (gm): 5.1
Saturated fat (gm): 1.2
Cholesterol (mg): 1.6
Sodium (mg): 362
Protein (gm): 3.7
Carbohydrate (gm): 43.6
Exchanges
Milk: 0.0
Vegetable: 0.0
Fruit: 0.0
Bread: 2.5
Meat: 0.0
Fat: 1.0

1. Combine flour, sugar, baking powder, baking soda, cinnamon, and salt in large bowl. Mix yogurt, banana, margarine, egg whites, and vanilla; stir into flour mixture and mix well. Pour batter into greased and floured 9-inch square baking pan.

2. Bake at 375 degrees 25 to 30 minutes or until cake springs back when lightly touched in center. Cool in pan on wire rack 10 minutes; invert onto wire rack and cool completely. Spread with Powdered Sugar Frosting.

Powdered Sugar Frosting

makes about ½ cup

1 cup powdered sugar
2 tablespoons margarine, melted
2 tablespoons skim milk

1. Combine powdered sugar, margarine, and milk in small bowl; beat until smooth. Spread frosting over cooled cake.

OATMEAL CAKE

With a Broiled Pecan Frosting, this cake is a comfort food to remember.

15 servings

1 cup quick-cooking oats

1¼ cups boiling water

6 tablespoons margarine

1 cup granulated sugar

1 cup packed light brown sugar

2 eggs

1⅓ cups cake flour

1 teaspoon baking soda

½ teaspoon salt

1 teaspoon ground cinnamon

¼ teaspoon ground nutmeg

Generous pinch ground cloves

Broiled Pecan Frosting (double recipe) (see p. 41)

Per Serving
Calories: 327
% Calories from fat: 28
Fat (gm): 10.6
Saturated fat (gm): 2
Cholesterol (mg): 28.6
Sodium (mg): 273
Protein (gm): 3.3
Carbohydrate (gm): 56.4
Exchanges
Milk: 0.0
Vegetable: 0.0
Fruit: 0.0
Bread: 4.0
Meat: 0.0
Fat: 1.5

1. Mix oats, boiling water, and margarine in large bowl, stirring until margarine is melted; let stand 15 to 20 minutes. Mix in sugars and eggs. Mix in combined remaining ingredients, except Broiled Pecan Frosting.

2. Pour batter into greased 13 x 9-inch baking pan. Bake at 350 degrees until toothpick inserted in center comes out clean, about 35 minutes. Cool on wire rack 10 to 15 minutes.

3. Make double the recipe for Broiled Pecan Frosting, except do not double pecans; spread evenly on cake. Broil 4 inches from heat source until mixture is bubbly and pecans browned, about 1 minute.

NEW ENGLAND CAKE

A true comfort food, from the recipe collection of my great grandmother Rickard.

16 servings

2 cups packed light brown sugar
1/2 cup vegetable shortening
1/2 cup applesauce
2 eggs
3 cups all-purpose flour
1 teaspoon baking powder
1/2 teaspoon salt
1 cup coffee
2 teaspoons unsweetened cocoa
1 teaspoon baking soda
1 cup raisins
1/3 cup chopped nuts
Brown Sugar Frosting (see p. 79)

Per Serving
Calories: 360
% Calories from fat: 20
Fat (gm): 8.4
Saturated fat (gm): 1.8
Cholesterol (mg): 26.5
Sodium (mg): 204
Protein (gm): 4.3
Carbohydrate (gm): 68.2
Exchanges
Milk: 0.0
Vegetable: 0.0
Fruit: 0.0
Bread: 4.5
Meat: 0.0
Fat: 1.0

1. Beat brown sugar, shortening, and applesauce in large bowl until blended; beat in eggs. Mix in combined flour, baking powder, and salt alternately with combined coffee, cocoa, and baking soda. Mix in raisins and nuts.

2. Spread batter in greased 13 x 9-inch baking pan. Bake at 350 degrees until toothpick inserted in center comes out clean, about 40 minutes. Cool on wire rack. Spread with Brown Sugar Frosting.

BANANA STRAWBERRY JAM CAKE

This cake can double as a brunch treat—serve warm with additional strawberry preserves instead of frosting.

12 servings

6 tablespoons margarine, room temperature

1 cup sugar

1 cup strawberry jam

1 large ripe banana, mashed

2 eggs

1 3/4 cups all-purpose flour

1 teaspoon baking powder

1/2 teaspoon baking soda

1 teaspoon ground cinnamon

1/4 teaspoon ground allspice

Generous pinch ground nutmeg

1/2 cup fat-free sour cream

1/2 recipe Raspberry Cream Frosting (see p. 543)

Per Serving
Calories: 314
% Calories from fat: 22
Fat (gm): 7.6
Saturated fat (gm): 2.3
Cholesterol (mg): 35.3
Sodium (mg): 190
Protein (gm): 4
Carbohydrate (gm): 58.5
Exchanges
Milk: 0.0
Vegetable: 0.0
Fruit: 0.0
Bread: 4.0
Meat: 0.0
Fat: 1.0

1. Beat margarine and sugar until blended; add strawberry jam and banana, mixing well. Beat in eggs. Mix in combined flour, baking powder, baking soda, and spices alternately with sour cream, beginning and ending with dry ingredients.

2. Spread batter in greased 13 x 9-inch baking pan. Bake at 350 degrees until toothpick inserted in center of cake comes out clean, about 40 minutes. Cool on wire rack.

3. Make Raspberry Cream Frosting, substituting strawberry jam for the raspberry preserves. Spread on cooled cake; refrigerate.

Variation: **Fourth of July Cake**—Make cake as above, using no jam in the frosting. Frost cake, and make a flag or other design using about 1/2 cup blueberries and 1 1/2 to 2 pints halved strawberries.

PRUNE AND BRANDY CAKE

A cake with spirit! We particularly enjoy this cake during the winter holidays.

8 servings

1 cup coarsely chopped pitted prunes

³/₄ cup brandy *or* ³/₄ cup water and ¹/₂ teaspoon brandy extract

¹/₂ cup packed light brown sugar

3 tablespoons vegetable oil

2 eggs

¹/₄ cup fat-free sour cream

1 teaspoon vanilla

¹/₄ cup yellow cornmeal

¹/₂ cup all-purpose flour

1 teaspoon baking powder

¹/₄ teaspoon salt

Warm Rum Sauce (see p. 54)

2 tablespoons brandy *or* ¹/₂ teaspoon brandy extract

Per Serving
Calories: 353
% Calories from fat: 24
Fat (gm): 9.6
Saturated fat (gm): 1.7
Cholesterol (mg): 53.7
Sodium (mg): 217
Protein (gm): 5.1
Carbohydrate (gm): 46
Exchanges
Milk: 0.0
Vegetable: 0.0
Fruit: 0.0
Bread: 3.0
Meat: 0.0
Fat: 3.0

1. Combine prunes and brandy in small bowl; let stand 30 minutes. Drain, reserving brandy.

2. Mix sugar, oil, and eggs in medium bowl; mix in sour cream and vanilla. Mix in combined cornmeal, flour, baking powder, and salt; mix in prunes.

3. Grease 8-inch round or square cake pan and line with parchment paper; grease and flour parchment. Spread batter in pan and bake at 350 degrees until cake is browned and toothpick inserted in center comes out clean, 20 to 25 minutes. Cool cake in pan on wire rack 10 minutes. Remove from pan and discard parchment. Brush top of cake with reserved brandy.

4. Make Warm Rum Sauce, substituting 2 tablespoons brandy for the rum. Serve sauce over warm cake.

SEMOLINA CAKE

This sugar-syrup-soaked cake, common in Mediterranean countries, is particularly excellent served with fruit.

15 servings

8 egg yolks
1 cup sugar, divided
1¹/₂ cups semolina
¹/₂ cup all-purpose flour
¹/₂ cup water
6 tablespoons margarine, melted
8 egg whites
¹/₂ teaspoon cream of tartar
1 tablespoon grated lemon rind
   Sugar Syrup (recipe follows)
   Light whipped topping, as garnish
   Chopped toasted pine nuts, as garnish

Per Serving
Calories: 312
% Calories from fat: 21
Fat (gm): 7.5
Saturated fat (gm): 1.8
Cholesterol (mg): 113.6
Sodium (mg): 87
Protein (gm): 6
Carbohydrate (gm): 56
Exchanges
Milk: 0.0
Vegetable: 0.0
Fruit: 0.0
Bread: 3.5
Meat: 0.0
Fat: 1.5

1. Beat egg yolks on high speed in large bowl until thick and lemon colored, about 5 minutes; gradually beat in ¹/₂ cup sugar. Fold in semolina and flour; mix in water and margarine.

2. Beat egg whites and cream of tartar to soft peaks in large bowl; beat to stiff peaks, adding remaining ¹/₂ cup sugar gradually. Fold ¹/₄ of the egg whites into yolk mixture; fold yolk mixture and lemon rind into remaining egg whites.

3. Pour batter into greased 13 x 9-inch baking pan. Bake at 350 degrees until edges are browned and toothpick inserted in center comes out clean, about 40 minutes. Cool cake on wire rack 10 minutes; pour warm Sugar Syrup over cake and cool completely. Garnish pieces with whipped topping and pine nuts.

Sugar Syrup

makes about 2 cups

2 cups sugar
2 cups water
1 tablespoon lemon juice

1. Heat all ingredients to boiling in medium saucepan; reduce heat and simmer, uncovered, 10 minutes.

CITRUS DATE CAKE

Cardamom and dates lend Mediterranean flair to this flavorful cake.

6 to 8 servings

1/2 cup sugar
1/3 cup vegetable oil
  1 egg
  1 egg white
  1 teaspoon vanilla
  1 cup all-purpose flour
  1 teaspoon ground cardamom
  1 teaspoon baking powder
1/4 teaspoon baking soda
1/4 teaspoon salt
1/3 cup fat-free sour cream
1/2 cup chopped dates
  1 tablespoon grated lemon rind
  1 tablespoon grated orange rind
     Orange Glaze (see p. 47)

Per Serving
Calories: 364
% Calories from fat: 32
Fat (gm): 13.2
Saturated fat (gm): 1.9
Cholesterol (mg): 35.3
Sodium (mg): 263
Protein (gm): 5.1
Carbohydrate (gm): 57.5
Exchanges
Milk: 0.0
Vegetable: 0.0
Fruit: 0.0
Bread: 3.5
Meat: 0.0
Fat: 2.5

1. Beat sugar and oil until well blended in large bowl, about 2 minutes. Beat in egg, egg white, and vanilla. Mix in combined flour, cardamom, baking powder, baking soda, and salt; mix in sour cream. Mix in dates and citrus rinds.

2. Pour batter into greased and floured 8- or 9-inch round cake pan. Bake at 350 degrees until cake springs back when touched, about 30 minutes. Cool in pan on wire rack 10 minutes.

3. Place cake on serving plate; drizzle with Orange Glaze.

SUGARED PECAN AND DATE CAKE

A cake moist and sweet with dates, topped with a warm, crunchy pecan glaze. Best served warm!

8 to 10 servings

1 cup sugar
1/4 cup margarine, softened
1 teaspoon vanilla
1 egg yolk
1 cup all-purpose flour
1/2 teaspoon baking soda
1/8 teaspoon salt
1/2 cup reduced-fat buttermilk
1/3 cup chopped dates
3 egg whites, beaten to stiff peaks
Broiled Pecan Frosting (recipe follows)

Per Serving
Calories: 378
% Calories from fat: 33
Fat (gm): 13.9
Saturated fat (gm): 2.6
Cholesterol (mg): 27.2
Sodium (mg): 277
Protein (gm): 4.8
Carbohydrate (gm): 60.2
Exchanges
Milk: 0.0
Vegetable: 0.0
Fruit: 0.0
Bread: 4.0
Meat: 0.0
Fat: 2.0

1. Mix sugar, margarine, and vanilla in large bowl; beat in egg yolk. Mix in combined flour, baking soda, and salt alternately with buttermilk, beginning and ending with dry ingredients. Stir in dates; fold in egg whites.

2. Pour batter into greased and floured 9-inch round or square cake pan. Bake at 350 degrees until toothpick inserted in center comes out clean, 20 to 25 minutes. Cool cake in pan on wire rack 10 minutes; remove from pan and cool 10 to 15 minutes.

3. Place cake on ovenproof serving plate or cookie sheet. Spread Broiled Pecan Frosting evenly on cake. Broil 4 inches from heat source until mixture is bubbly and pecans browned, about 1 minute. Serve warm.

Broiled Pecan Frosting

1/2 cup packed light brown sugar
3 tablespoons flour
1/2 teaspoon ground cinnamon
3 tablespoons margarine
2 tablespoons fat-free milk
1/3 cup coarsely chopped pecans

1. Heat all ingredients, except pecans, to boiling in small saucepan, stirring frequently; cook over medium heat 2 minutes, stirring constantly. Remove from heat; stir in pecans.

RUM-SPIKED CARDAMOM CAKE

A flavor combination to surprise and delight! Prepared prune-based fat substitute for baking is available in supermarkets and can be substituted for the homemade Prune Puree.

10 servings

- ²/₃ cup Prune Puree (recipe follows)
- ²/₃ cup packed light brown sugar
- 4 tablespoons margarine, softened
- ¹/₂ teaspoon rum, *or* brandy, extract
- 2 eggs
- 1³/₄ cups all-purpose flour
- 2 teaspoons baking powder
- ¹/₂ teaspoon ground cardamom
- ¹/₄ teaspoon salt
- ¹/₃ cup fat-free milk
  Rum Glaze (recipe follows)

Per Serving
Calories: 269
% Calories from fat: 19
Fat (gm): 5.8
Saturated fat (gm): 1.3
Cholesterol (mg): 42.6
Sodium (mg): 237
Protein (gm): 4.3
Carbohydrate (gm): 51.1
Exchanges
Milk: 0.0
Vegetable: 0.0
Fruit: 0.5
Bread: 3.0
Meat: 0.0
Fat: 0.5

1. Beat Prune Puree, brown sugar, and margarine until fluffy in medium bowl. Mix in rum extract and eggs. Mix in combined flour, baking powder, cardamom, and salt alternately with milk, beginning and ending with flour mixture.

2. Pour batter into 8¹/₂ x 4¹/₂-inch greased and floured loaf pan. Bake until a toothpick inserted in center comes out clean, 50 to 55 minutes. Cool in pan on wire rack 10 minutes; remove from pan and cool completely. Drizzle with Rum Glaze.

Prune Puree

makes about 2 cups

- 1 package (12 ounces) pitted prunes
- ¹/₃ cup light corn syrup
- 1 tablespoon sugar
- ²/₃ cup water, divided

1. Process prunes, corn syrup, sugar, and ¹/₃ cup water in food processor until smooth. Add remaining ¹/₃ cup water and process until smooth. Refrigerate up to 4 weeks or freeze.

Rum Glaze

makes about ¹/₄ cup

- ¹/₂ cup powdered sugar
- ¹/₂ teaspoon rum extract
- 1-2 teaspoons fat-free milk

1. Mix powdered sugar, rum extract, and enough milk to make a glaze consistency.

HATTIE'S HOT MILK CAKE

Our neighbor, Hattie, has baked this cake for years—a family favorite that will become yours too! The secret to success is beating the eggs very well. The recipe can be doubled and baked in a 13 x 9-inch pan.

8 to 9 servings

- 2 eggs
- 1 cup sugar
- 1 teaspoon vanilla
- 1 cup all-purpose flour
- 1 teaspoon baking powder
- ¹/₄ teaspoon salt
- ¹/₂ cup 2% reduced-fat milk
- 1 tablespoon margarine
  Broiled Coconut Frosting (recipe follows)

Per Serving
Calories: 369
% Calories from fat: 35
Fat (gm): 14.7
Saturated fat (gm): 5.3
Cholesterol (mg): 54.3
Sodium (mg): 285
Protein (gm): 4.4
Carbohydrate (gm): 56
Exchanges
Milk: 0.0
Vegetable: 0.0
Fruit: 0.0
Bread: 3.5
Meat: 0.0
Fat: 2.5

1. Beat eggs in medium bowl until light and lemon colored, about 5 minutes. Add sugar to eggs gradually, beating on high speed 4 to 5 minutes longer. Mix in vanilla; mix in combined flour, baking powder, and salt just until blended. Heat milk and margarine in small saucepan until margarine is melted, stirring frequently. Add milk mixture to batter, mixing well.

2. Pour batter into greased 8-inch square baking pan. Bake at 350 degrees until toothpick inserted in center comes out clean, 20 to 25 minutes. Cool on wire rack.

3. Spread Broiled Coconut Frosting over cake; broil 4 to 5 inches from heat source until bubbly and brown, about 3 minutes.

Broiled Coconut Frosting

    1 cup flaked coconut
    $^1/_2$ cup packed light brown sugar
    6 tablespoons margarine melted
    $^1/_4$ cup 2% reduced-fat milk
    $^1/_2$ teaspoon vanilla

1. Mix all ingredients.

YUM YUM CAKE

Mixed right in the pan, this cake can be in the oven in 5 minutes flat!

8 servings

    $1^1/_2$ cups all-purpose flour
    1 cup sugar
    $^1/_4$ cup unsweetened cocoa
    1 teaspoon baking soda
    $^1/_2$ teaspoon salt
    $^1/_4$ cup vegetable oil
    1 tablespoon cider vinegar
    1 teaspoon vanilla
    1 cup fat-free milk
    Chocolate Glaze (see p. 76)

Per Serving
Calories: 320
% Calories from fat: 20
Fat (gm): 7.1
Saturated fat (gm): 1
Cholesterol (mg): 0.8
Sodium (mg): 327
Protein (gm): 3.9
Carbohydrate (gm): 60.6
Exchanges
Milk: 0.0
Vegetable: 0.0
Fruit: 0.0
Bread: 4.0
Meat: 0.0
Fat: 1.0

1. Mix flour, sugar, cocoa, baking soda, and salt in greased 8- or 9-inch square baking pan. Make 2 holes in the dry ingredients; pour oil into one, the vinegar and vanilla into the other. Pour the milk over all and mix until well blended and smooth.

2. Bake at 350 degrees until toothpick inserted in center comes out clean, about 30 minutes. Cool in pan on wire rack. Spread with Chocolate Glaze.

PINEAPPLE RIGHT-SIDE-UP CAKE

This fruit-topped sheet cake is perfect for picnics or potluck occasions. Vary the fruit as you like.

18 servings

2 cups all-purpose flour

1¹/₂ cups granulated sugar

2 teaspoons baking powder

¹/₂ teaspoon salt

¹/₈ teaspoon ground nutmeg

¹/₂ cup margarine, softened

3 eggs

1 teaspoon vanilla

1 can (16 ounces) sliced pineapple in juice, drained

1 can (16 ounces) apricot halves in juice, drained

¹/₂ cup packed light brown sugar

¹/₄-¹/₂ cup sliced almonds

Butter Glaze (see p. 87)

Per Serving
Calories: 281
% Calories from fat: 21
Fat (gm): 7
Saturated fat (gm): 1.4
Cholesterol (mg): 35.4
Sodium (mg): 196
Protein (gm): 3.3
Carbohydrate (gm): 52.7
Exchanges
Milk: 0.0
Vegetable: 0.0
Fruit: 0.0
Bread: 3.5
Meat: 0.0
Fat: 1.0

1. Combine flour, granulated sugar, baking powder, salt, and nutmeg in large bowl; add margarine, eggs, and vanilla and mix on low speed until blended. Beat on medium speed 2 minutes (batter will be stiff).

2. Spread batter in greased jelly roll pan, 15 x 10 x 1 inch. Cut pineapple and apricot halves into halves; arrange on cake batter. Sprinkle with brown sugar and almonds.

3. Bake at 350 degrees until toothpick inserted in center comes out clean, about 45 minutes. Cool on wire rack. Drizzle with Butter Glaze.

MOM'S RHUBARB STREUSEL CAKE

With Mom's approval, we've added a streusel, rich and crispy, and a light orange glaze to this wonderfully moist cake.

12 servings

1/2 cup margarine, softened
1 1/3 cups sugar
1 egg, beaten
1 teaspoon vanilla
2 cups all-purpose flour
1 teaspoon baking soda
1 teaspoon ground cinnamon
1/2 teaspoon ground nutmeg
1/2 teaspoon salt
1 cup reduced-fat buttermilk
2 cups sliced fresh, *or* frozen and thawed, rhubarb (scant 1-inch pieces)
1/3 cup raisins
2 teaspoons grated orange rind
Crisp Streusel (recipe follows)
Orange Glaze (recipe follow)

Per Serving
Calories: 342
% Calories from fat: 27
Fat (gm): 10.4
Saturated fat (gm): 2.2
Cholesterol (mg): 18.4
Sodium (mg): 345
Protein (gm): 4.1
Carbohydrate (gm): 59.3
Exchanges
Milk: 0.0
Vegetable: 0.0
Fruit: 0.0
Bread: 4.0
Meat: 0.0
Fat: 1.5

1. Beat margarine and sugar until smooth; beat in egg and vanilla. Mix in combined flour, baking soda, cinnamon, nutmeg, and salt alternately with buttermilk, beginning and ending with dry ingredients. Mix in rhubarb, raisins, and orange rind.

2. Pour batter into greased and floured 13 x 9-inch baking pan. Sprinkle Crisp Streusel over cake. Bake at 350 degrees until toothpick inserted in center comes out clean, 35 to 40 minutes. Cool on wire rack 15 minutes; drizzle with Orange Glaze.

Crisp Streusel

1/2 cup packed light brown sugar
2 tablespoons quick-cooking oats
2 tablespoons flour
2 tablespoons cold margarine, cut into pieces

1. Combine brown sugar, oats, and flour in small bowl; cut in margarine with pastry blender to form crumbly mixture.

Orange Glaze

makes about ¹/₄ cup

¹/₂ cup powdered sugar
1 teaspoon grated orange rind
2-4 teaspoons orange juice

1. Mix powdered sugar and orange rind with enough orange juice to make glaze consistency.

RHUBARB CAKE WITH RHUBARB JAM

The ultimate cake for rhubarb lovers! Enjoy all year, as either fresh or frozen rhubarb can be used.

15 servings

Mom's Rhubarb Streusel Cake (see p. 46)
1 teaspoon grated orange rind
Rhubarb Jam (recipe follows)

Per Serving
Calories: 329
% Calories from fat: 22
Fat (gm): 8.4
Saturated fat (gm): 1.8
Cholesterol (mg): 14.7
Sodium (mg): 278
Protein (gm): 3.8
Carbohydrate (gm): 61
Exchanges
Milk: 0.0
Vegetable: 0.0
Fruit: 0.0
Bread: 4.0
Meat: 0.0
Fat: 1.0

1. Make Mom's Rhubarb Streusel Cake, omitting raisins and adding 1 additional teaspoon orange rind. Serve with warm Rhubarb Jam.

Rhubarb Jam

12 servings (about ¹/₄ cup each)

³/₄ cup sugar
³/₄ cup orange juice
6 cups sliced fresh, *or* frozen, rhubarb
¹/₂ teaspoon ground cinnamon

1. Heat sugar and orange juice to boiling in small saucepan. Add rhubarb and cinnamon and simmer, uncovered, 10 minutes or until rhubarb is tender and desired sauce consistency, stirring occasionally.

RHUBARB BRUNCH CAKE WITH BOURBON SAUCE

Spiked with bourbon for a spirited dessert! Flavored extract can be substituted if preferred.

15 servings

10	tablespoons margarine, softened, divided
1¹/₂	cups packed light brown sugar, divided
¹/₂	cup granulated sugar
2	egg whites *or* ¹/₄ cup no-cholesterol real egg product
3	tablespoons bourbon *or* brandy *or* 1 teaspoon brandy extract
2	cups all-purpose flour
1	teaspoon baking soda
3	teaspoons ground cinnamon, divided
¹/₄	teaspoon salt
³/₄	cup reduced-fat buttermilk
3	cups coarsely chopped rhubarb
	Bourbon Sauce (recipe follows)

Per Serving
Calories: 327
% Calories from fat: **23**
Fat (gm): **8.6**
Saturated fat (gm): **1.7**
Cholesterol (mg): **0.4**
Sodium (mg): **256**
Protein (gm): **2.9**
Carbohydrate (gm): **58.1**
Exchanges
Milk: 0.0
Vegetable: 0.0
Fruit: 0.0
Bread: 3.5
Meat: 0.0
Fat: 1.5

1. Beat 8 tablespoons margarine, 1 cup brown sugar, and granulated sugar in medium bowl until fluffy. Beat in egg whites and bourbon; mix in combined flour, baking soda, 1 teaspoon cinnamon, and salt alternately with buttermilk, beginning and ending with flour mixture. Mix in rhubarb.

2. Spread batter evenly in greased and floured 13 x 9-inch baking pan. Combine remaining 2 tablespoons margarine, ¹/₂ cup brown sugar, and 2 teaspoons cinnamon; crumble mixture over cake batter.

3. Bake cake at 350 degrees until toothpick inserted in center comes out clean, about 40 minutes. Cool in pan on wire rack. Serve slightly warm with Bourbon Sauce.

Bourbon Sauce

makes about 2 cups

- 1 cup packed light brown sugar
- 2 tablespoons cornstarch
- 1¹/₂ cups water
- 2 tablespoons bourbon or brandy *or* ¹/₂-1 teaspoon brandy extract
- 1 tablespoon margarine

1. Mix brown sugar and cornstarch in small saucepan; mix in water and heat to boiling. Boil, stirring constantly, until thickened, about 1 minute. Remove from heat; stir in bourbon and margarine.

GLAZED BLUEBERRY CAKE

Head for the blueberry patch for this cake! Frozen berries are fine for off-season baking.

8 servings

- ¹/₂ cup margarine, softened
- 1 cup sugar
- 2 eggs
- ¹/₂ cup fat-free milk
- 1 teaspoon vanilla
- 2 cups all-purpose flour
- 2 teaspoons baking powder
- Generous pinch ground nutmeg
- ¹/₂ teaspoon salt
- ³/₄-1 cup fresh, *or* frozen, blueberries
- Grated rind of 1 lemon
- Lemon Glaze (see p. 62)

Per Serving
Calories: 375
% Calories from fat: 31
Fat (gm): 12.9
Saturated fat (gm): 2.7
Cholesterol (mg): 53.3
Sodium (mg): 426
Protein (gm): 5.6
Carbohydrate (gm): 60.2
Exchanges
Milk: 0.0
Vegetable: 0.0
Fruit: 0.0
Bread: 4.0
Meat: 0.0
Fat: 2.0

1. Beat margarine and sugar until blended in large bowl; beat in eggs, milk, and vanilla. Mix in combined flour, baking powder, nutmeg, and salt; fold in blueberries and lemon rind.

2. Pour batter into greased 8- or 9-inch square baking pan. Bake at 350 degrees until toothpick inserted in center comes out clean, 30 to 35 minutes. Cool on wire rack. Drizzle with Lemon Glaze.

AUTUMN APPLE CAKE

Peeling the apples is the most difficult part of making this easy sweetly spiced cake! The recipe can be doubled and baked in a 13 x 9-inch baking pan.

9 servings

2 cups chopped, peeled tart baking apples
2/3 cup sugar
1 1/2 cups all-purpose flour
1 teaspoon baking powder
1/2 teaspoon baking soda
1/4 teaspoon salt
3/4 teaspoon ground cinnamon
1/4 teaspoon ground nutmeg
1/8 teaspoon ground mace
1/4 cup vegetable oil
1 egg
1 teaspoon vanilla
Brown Sugar Glaze (recipe follows)

Per Serving
Calories: 261
% Calories from fat: 26
Fat (gm): 7.6
Saturated fat (gm): 1.1
Cholesterol (mg): 23.6
Sodium (mg): 205
Protein (gm): 3
Carbohydrate (gm): 46.1
Exchanges
Milk: 0.0
Vegetable: 0.0
Fruit: 0.0
Bread: 3.0
Meat: 0.0
Fat: 1.0

1. Toss apples and sugar; let stand 15 minutes.

2. Combine flour, baking powder, baking soda, salt, and spices in medium bowl; add combined oil, egg, and vanilla, mixing well. Mix in apples.

3. Spoon batter into greased and floured 8- or 9-inch square baking pan. Bake at 350 degrees until toothpick inserted in center comes out clean, 35 to 40 minutes. Cool in pan on wire rack. Drizzle with Brown Sugar Glaze.

Brown Sugar Glaze

makes about 1/4 cup

1 1/2 teaspoons margarine
1 tablespoon packed light brown sugar
1/2 cup powdered sugar
2 teaspoons hot water

1. Heat margarine and brown sugar in small saucepan until margarine is melted. Remove from heat and stir in powdered sugar and hot water; stir over medium-low heat until mixture is smooth, stirring constantly. Add a few drops more hot water if necessary to make glaze consistency.

APPLESAUCE STREUSEL CAKE

Oatmeal in both the cake and streusel add to the homey goodness of this dessert. Serve warm with reduced-fat ice cream or frozen yogurt.

9 servings

- 1/2 cup margarine, softened
- 3/4 cup packed light brown sugar
- 1 egg
- 3/4 cup applesauce
- 1 teaspoon vanilla
- 1 cup all-purpose flour
- 1/2 cup whole wheat flour
- 1/2 cup quick-cooking oats
- 2 teaspoons baking powder
- 1/2 teaspoon salt
- 1/2 teaspoon ground cinnamon
- 1/4 teaspoon baking soda
- 1/4 teaspoon ground cloves
- Crisp Streusel (see p. 46)

Per Serving
Calories: 348
% Calories from fat: 35
Fat (gm): 13.8
Saturated fat (gm): 2.8
Cholesterol (mg): 23.6
Sodium (mg): 441
Protein (gm): 4.3
Carbohydrate (gm): 53.3
Exchanges
Milk: 0.0
Vegetable: 0.0
Fruit: 0.0
Bread: 3.5
Meat: 0.0
Fat: 2.0

1. Beat margarine and sugar in large bowl until blended; beat in egg, applesauce, and vanilla. Mix in combined remaining ingredients, except Crisp Streusel, stirring until well blended.

2. Pour batter into greased 8- or 9-inch square baking pan. Sprinkle with Crisp Streusel. Bake at 350 degrees until toothpick inserted in center of cake comes out clean, 35 to 40 minutes. Cool on wire rack.

ORANGE-GLAZED GINGERBREAD CAKE

Lightly spiced and orange-glazed, cake pieces may be served with scoops of lemon frozen yogurt or sherbet.

6 servings

- $^1/_3$ cup packed light brown sugar
- $^1/_2$ cup fat-free milk
- $^1/_4$ cup light molasses
- $^1/_3$ cup melted margarine
- 2 tablespoons honey
- 1 egg white
- 1 cup all-purpose flour
- $^3/_4$ teaspoon baking powder
- 1 teaspoon ground ginger
- $^3/_4$ teaspoon ground cinnamon
- $^1/_2$ teaspoon ground nutmeg
- $^1/_4$ teaspoon ground cloves
- $^1/_4$ teaspoon salt
- 2 dashes black pepper
  Orange Glaze (see p. 47)

Per Serving
Calories: 324
% Calories from fat: 28
Fat (gm): 10.4
Saturated fat (gm): 2.1
Cholesterol (mg): 0.4
Sodium (mg): 307
Protein (gm): 3.7
Carbohydrate (gm): 55.2
Exchanges
Milk: 0.0
Vegetable: 0.0
Fruit: 0.0
Bread: 3.5
Meat: 0.0
Fat: 1.5

1. Combine brown sugar, milk, molasses, margarine, honey, and egg white in large bowl; mix well. Add combined flour, baking powder, spices, salt, and pepper, mixing well.

2. Pour batter into 8-inch square baking pan. Bake at 350 degrees until toothpick inserted in center of cake comes out clean, about 25 minutes. Cool on wire rack. Drizzle with Orange Glaze.

MOLASSES CREAM CAKE

The cake can also be baked in 9-inch round cake pans; spread Molasses Cream between the cooled layers.

12 servings

2¹/₂ cups all-purpose flour
¹/₄ cup sugar
1 teaspoon baking soda
1 teaspoon ground ginger
1 teaspoon ground cinnamon
¹/₂ teaspoon salt
1 cup dark molasses
³/₄ cup hot water
¹/₂ cup margarine, softened
1 egg
Molasses Cream (see p. 66)

Per Serving
Calories: 281
% Calories from fat: 29
Fat (gm): 9.2
Saturated fat (gm): 2.7
Cholesterol (mg): 17.7
Sodium (mg): 312
Protein (gm): 3.3
Carbohydrate (gm): 45.8
Exchanges
Milk: 0.0
Vegetable: 0.0
Fruit: 0.0
Bread: 3.0
Meat: 0.0
Fat: 1.5

1. Combine all ingredients, except Molasses Cream, in large bowl. Beat on low speed until blended; beat on high speed 2 minutes.

2. Pour batter into greased 13 x 9-inch baking pan. Bake at 350 degrees until toothpick inserted in center comes out clean, about 35 minutes. Cool on wire rack. Spread Molasses Cream over cooled cake; refrigerate.

PUMPKIN GINGER CAKE WITH WARM RUM SAUCE

Moist with pumpkin and savory with spices, a perfect choice for fall and winter holidays.

8 servings

- $^1/_2$ cup canned pumpkin
- $^1/_2$ cup packed light brown sugar
- $^1/_4$ cup margarine, softened
- $^1/_4$ cup light molasses
- 1 egg
- $1^1/_2$ cups all-purpose flour
- $^1/_2$ teaspoon baking powder
- $^1/_2$ teaspoon baking soda
- $^1/_2$ teaspoon ground allspice
- $^1/_2$ teaspoon ground cloves
- $^1/_2$ teaspoon ground ginger
- Warm Rum Sauce (recipe follows)

Per Serving
Calories: 306
% Calories from fat: 28
Fat (gm): 9.5
Saturated fat (gm): 2
Cholesterol (mg): 27.2
Sodium (mg): 248
Protein (gm): 4.8
Carbohydrate (gm): 49
Exchanges
Milk: 0.0
Vegetable: 0.0
Fruit: 0.0
Bread: 3.0
Meat: 0.0
Fat: 2.0

1. Combine pumpkin, brown sugar, margarine, molasses, and egg in large mixer bowl; beat at medium speed until light and fluffy.

2. Combine flour, baking powder, baking soda, allspice, cloves, and ginger in medium bowl; add to pumpkin mixture. Blend at low speed until moistened. Pour batter into greased and floured 8-inch square baking pan.

3. Bake cake at 350 degrees until toothpick inserted in center comes out clean, 30 to 40 minutes. Cool in pan on wire rack 10 minutes; remove from pan. Cool completely on wire rack. Serve with Warm Rum Sauce

Warm Rum Sauce

makes $1^1/_2$ cups

- $^1/_4$ cup sugar
- 1 tablespoon cornstarch
- $1^1/_4$ cups fat-free milk
- 2 tablespoons rum *or* $^1/_2$ teaspoon rum extract

2 tablespoons margarine
1/2 teaspoon vanilla
1/8 teaspoon ground nutmeg

1. Mix sugar and cornstarch in small saucepan; stir in milk and rum. Cook over medium heat until mixture boils and thickens, stirring constantly.
2. Remove from heat; stir in margarine, vanilla, and nutmeg. Serve warm.

MOIST GINGERBREAD WITH LEMON SAUCE

Pungently spiced and unbelievably moist, the gingerbread can be served with Tart Lemon Sauce or dusted generously with powdered sugar.

12 servings

1/2 cup margarine, softened
1/2 cup packed light brown sugar
1 egg
1 cup light molasses
1 cup boiling water
2 teaspoons baking soda
2 1/2 cups all-purpose flour
1/4 cup chopped crystallized ginger
1 tablespoon ground ginger
1 teaspoon ground cinnamon
1/2 teaspoon salt
Tart Lemon Sauce (see p. 650)

Per Serving
Calories: 359
% Calories from fat: 26
Fat (gm): 10.6
Saturated fat (gm): 2.2
Cholesterol (mg): 35.3
Sodium (mg): 445
Protein (gm): 4
Carbohydrate (gm): 63.7
Exchanges
Milk: 0.0
Vegetable: 0.0
Fruit: 0.0
Bread: 4.0
Meat: 0.0
Fat: 1.5

1. Beat margarine and brown sugar until fluffy in large bowl; beat in egg. Mix molasses, boiling water, and baking soda; mix into margarine mixture. Mix in combined flour, crystallized ginger, spices, and salt.
2. Pour batter into greased and floured 13 x 9-inch baking pan. Bake at 350 degrees until toothpick inserted in center comes out clean, 25 to 30 minutes. Cool in pan 20 minutes; remove from pan and cool 10 to 15 minutes. Serve warm with warm or chilled Tart Lemon Sauce.

GINGERBREAD CAKE WITH CIDER FRUIT SAUCE

A delicious combination of flavors that welcome autumn holidays.

16 servings

3 eggs
2 egg whites
³/4 cup light molasses
1²/3 cups packed light brown sugar
Grated rind of 1 large lemon
2 tablespoons ground ginger
Generous pinch ground cinnamon
Generous pinch ground allspice
Generous pinch ground cloves
Generous pinch ground nutmeg
Generous pinch ground pepper
2 cups all-purpose flour
¹/4 cup vegetable oil
³/4 cup reduced-fat buttermilk
1 teaspoon baking soda
Cider Fruit Sauce (recipe follows)

Per Serving
Calories: 347
% Calories from fat: 12
Fat (gm): 4.8
Saturated fat (gm): 0.9
Cholesterol (mg): 40.1
Sodium (mg): 129
Protein (gm): 4.5
Carbohydrate (gm): 75.3
Exchanges
Milk: 0.0
Vegetable: 0.0
Fruit: 2.0
Bread: 3.0
Meat: 0.0
Fat: 0.5

1. Beat eggs and egg whites in large bowl at high speed until thick and lemon colored, about 5 minutes. Mix in molasses. Mix in combined brown sugar, lemon rind, and spices. Mix in flour and oil alternately, beginning and ending with oil. Mix buttermilk and baking soda; mix into batter.

2. Pour batter into greased and floured 10-cup fluted tube pan. Bake at 350 degrees until toothpick inserted in center of cake comes out clean, 50 to 60 minutes. Cool cake in pan on wire rack 10 minutes; remove cake from pan and cool 10 to 15 minutes. Serve warm with Cider Fruit Sauce.

Cider Fruit Sauce

makes about 4 cups

3 cups mixed dried fruit
3 cups apple cider
¹/4 cup packed light brown sugar

1. Heat dried fruit and 3 cups cider to boiling in medium saucepan; reduce heat and simmer until fruit is softened and mixture is desired sauce consistency, about 20 minutes. Add sugar, stirring until dissolved.

Variation: **Fruited Gingerbread Cake with Penuche Frosting—** Make cake as above, spreading batter in 2 greased and floured 9-inch round cake pans. Bake at 350 degrees until toothpick inserted in center of cake comes out clean, about 30 minutes. Cool cake in pans on wire rack 10 minutes. Remove from pans and cool completely.

Make Cider Fruit Sauce as above, using 1 cup dried fruit, 1 cup cider, and 1 to 2 tablespoons brown sugar; cook to a thick filling consistency and cool. Spread filling between cake layers; frost with Penuche Frosting (see p. 69).

GINGERED PEAR CAKE

We serve this cake simply topped with sweetened sour cream and ginger; a drizzle of Citrus Glaze (see p. 63) is also delicious.

12 servings

1 cup packed light brown sugar
1/4 cup margarine, softened
3 egg whites
1 1/2 cups all-purpose flour
1 1/2 teaspoons baking soda
1/4 teaspoon salt
1 teaspoon ground ginger
1/4 teaspoon ground cloves
2 tablespoons chopped crystallized ginger
2 small pears, unpeeled, cored, shredded
Gingered Sour Cream Topping (recipe follows)

Per Serving
Calories: 228
% Calories from fat: 22
Fat (gm): 5.7
Saturated fat (gm): 2.11
Cholesterol (mg): 6.7
Sodium (mg): 287
Protein (gm): 4
Carbohydrate (gm): 40.7
Exchanges
Milk: 0.0
Vegetable: 0.0
Fruit: 0.0
Bread: 2.5
Meat: 0.0
Fat: 1.0

1. Beat brown sugar, margarine, and egg whites in large bowl until thoroughly mixed. Mix in combined flour, baking soda, salt, ground ginger, cloves, and crystallized ginger. Gently mix in pears.

2. Pour batter into greased and floured 6-cup fluted tube pan. Bake at 350 degrees until toothpick inserted in center comes out clean, 50 to 60 minutes. Cool cake in pan on wire rack 10 minutes; remove from pan and cool completely.

3. Serve cake slices with Gingered Sour Cream Topping.

Gingered Sour Cream Topping

makes 1 to 1¹/₂ cups

1-1¹/₂ cups reduced-fat sour cream
  2-3 tablespoons sugar
  2-4 tablespoons coarsely chopped crystallized
       ginger

1. Mix all ingredients.

SWEET CHERRY CAKE

Enjoy this cake warm with a generous scoop of reduced-fat frozen yogurt or ice cream. Two cans (16 ounces each) of pitted dark sweet cherries, well drained, can be substituted for the fresh cherries.

10 servings

  2 cups all-purpose flour
  1 tablespoon baking powder
¹/₄ teaspoon salt
¹/₂ cup margarine, softened
  1 cup plus 3 tablespoons sugar, divided
  2 eggs
¹/₄ cup fat-free milk
³/₄ teaspoon vanilla
  2 cups pitted dark sweet cherries
 10 tablespoons light whipped topping

Per Serving
Calories: 320
% Calories from fat: 30
Fat (gm): 10.8
Saturated fat (gm): 2.6
Cholesterol (mg): 42.5
Sodium (mg): 329
Protein (gm): 4.6
Carbohydrate (gm): 51.6
Exchanges
Milk: 0.0
Vegetable: 0.0
Fruit: 0.0
Bread: 3.5
Meat: 0.0
Fat: 1.5

1. Combine flour, baking powder, salt, margarine, 1 cup sugar, eggs, milk, and vanilla in large bowl. Beat at low speed until blended; beat at medium speed 3 minutes.

2. Spread batter in greased and floured 9-inch springform pan. Sprinkle cherries over top of batter; sprinkle with remaining sugar. Bake at 350 degrees until toothpick inserted in center comes out clean, 55 to 60 minutes. Cool on wire rack 10 minutes; remove side of pan and cool. Serve with whipped topping.

WALT'S BLACKBERRY CAKE

This cake is a tribute to Walt, who braved poison ivy in the blackberry patch a number of times! Frozen blackberries can be used, and raspberries or strawberries can be substituted.

10 to 12 servings

6 tablespoons margarine, softened
1 cup sugar
1 egg
1³/₄ cups all-purpose flour
¹/₂ teaspoon baking powder
¹/₂ teaspoon baking soda
¹/₄ teaspoon salt
1 teaspoon ground cinnamon
¹/₂ teaspoon ground ginger
¹/₂ teaspoon ground allspice
Pinch ground nutmeg
1¹/₂ cups pureed fresh, *or* frozen, thawed, blackberries
Sugar Glaze (see p. 349)

Per Serving
Calories: 289
% Calories from fat: 23
Fat (gm): 7.6
Saturated fat (gm): 1.5
Cholesterol (mg): 21.3
Sodium (mg): 234
Protein (gm): 3.3
Carbohydrate (gm): 52.9
Exchanges
Milk: 0.0
Vegetable: 0.0
Fruit: 0.0
Bread: 3.5
Meat: 0.0
Fat: 1.0

1. Beat margarine and sugar in large bowl until well blended. Beat in egg. Mix in combined flour, baking powder, baking soda, salt, and spices alternately with blackberries, beginning and ending with dry ingredients.

2. Pour batter into greased and floured 6-cup fluted tube pan. Bake at 350 degrees until toothpick comes out clean, about 45 minutes. Cool cake in pan on wire rack 10 minutes; remove from pan and cool completely. Drizzle with Brown Sugar Glaze.

MAPLE-GLAZED SWEET POTATO CAKE

Sweet potatoes contribute moistness and flavor in this good-for-you dessert. Fresh cooked or canned and drained sweet potatoes can be used.

16 servings

- 1 cup packed light brown sugar
- 1 cup granulated sugar
- 6 tablespoons margarine, softened
- 6 egg whites *or* ³/₄ cup no-cholesterol real egg product
- 2¹/₂ cups mashed cooked sweet potatoes
- 3 cups all-purpose flour
- 1 teaspoon ground cinnamon
- 1 teaspoon baking powder
- 1 teaspoon baking soda
- ¹/₂ teaspoon ground nutmeg
- ¹/₄ teaspoon ground cloves
- ¹/₂ teaspoon salt
- 1 teaspoon maple extract
  Maple Glaze (recipe follows)
- ¹/₄ cup coarsely chopped toasted pecans *or* walnuts

Per Serving
Calories: 328
% Calories from fat: 16
Fat (gm): 5.9
Saturated fat (gm): 1
Cholesterol (mg): 0
Sodium (mg): 266
Protein (gm): 4.9
Carbohydrate (gm): 64.5
Exchanges
Milk: 0.0
Vegetable: 0.0
Fruit: 0.0
Bread: 4.0
Meat: 0.0
Fat: 1.0

1. Beat sugars and margarine in large bowl until well blended. Add egg whites, beating well; mix in sweet potatoes. Mix in combined remaining ingredients, except Maple Glaze and pecans (batter will be stiff).

2. Pour batter into greased and floured 12-cup fluted tube pan. Bake at 350 degrees until toothpick inserted in center comes out clean, about 1¹/₂ hours. Cool in pan on wire rack 10 minutes; remove from pan and cool completely.

3. Arrange cake on serving plate; drizzle with Maple Glaze and sprinkle with pecans.

Maple Glaze

makes about ¹/₂ cup

- 1 cup powdered sugar
- 1 teaspoon maple extract
- 1-2 tablespoons fat-free milk

1. Mix powdered sugar, maple extract, and enough milk to make glaze consistency.

LEMON POPPY SEED CAKE

Lemon-scented and flecked with poppy seeds—serve this cake with Tart Lemon Sauce (see p. 650), if you wish.

12 servings

1¹/₄ cups granulated sugar, divided
¹/₂ cup fat-free milk
¹/₃ cup vegetable oil
¹/₃ cup fat-free sour cream
¹/₃ cup unsweetened applesauce
 2 egg yolks
¹/₂ teaspoon lemon extract
 2 cups cake flour
 1 teaspoon baking powder
¹/₄ teaspoon baking soda
¹/₂ teaspoon salt
 2 egg whites
¹/₈ teaspoon cream of tartar
 3 tablespoons plus 1 teaspoon poppy
   seeds, divided
 1 tablespoon grated lemon rind
   Lemon Glaze (recipe follows)

Per Serving
Calories: 260
% Calories from fat: 28
Fat (gm): 8.1
Saturated fat (gm): 1.2
Cholesterol (mg): 35.7
Sodium (mg): 186
Protein (gm): 3.8
Carbohydrate (gm): 43.7
Exchanges
Milk: 0.0
Vegetable: 0.0
Fruit: 0.0
Bread: 3.0
Meat: 0.0
Fat: 1.0

1. Mix 1 cup granulated sugar, milk, oil, sour cream, applesauce, egg yolks, and lemon extract in large bowl; mix in combined flour, baking powder, baking soda, and salt.

2. Beat egg whites and cream of tartar to soft peaks in medium bowl; beat to stiff peaks, adding remaining ¹/₄ cup sugar gradually. Fold egg whites, 3 tablespoons poppy seeds, and lemon rind into cake batter.

3. Pour batter into greased and floured 12-cup plain or fluted tube pan. Bake at 350 degrees until toothpick inserted in center comes out clean, about 45 minutes. Cool in pan on wire rack 10 minutes; remove from pan and cool completely.

4. Place cake on serving plate; drizzle with Lemon Glaze and sprinkle with remaining 1 teaspoon poppy seeds.

Lemon Glaze

makes about 1/4 cup

- 1/2 cup powdered sugar
- 1-2 teaspoons finely grated lemon rind
- 3-4 teaspoons lemon juice

1. Mix powdered sugar, lemon rind, and enough lemon juice to make glaze consistency.

Variations: **Lemon-Blueberry Cake**—Make cake as above, substituting reduced-fat custard-style lemon yogurt for the sour cream and deleting poppy seeds; fold 1 to 1 1/2 cups fresh or frozen blueberries into cake batter. Bake and glaze as above.

Cranberry-Orange Cake—Coarsely chop 1 cup cranberries; mix with 1/4 cup of the sugar and let stand 10 minutes. Make cake as above, using 3/4 cup sugar, substituting reduced-fat custard-style orange yogurt for the sour cream, orange rind for the lemon rind, and omitting poppy seeds. Fold cranberry mixture into cake batter. Bake as above and glaze with Orange Glaze (see p. 47).

ORANGE POPPY SEED CAKE

This citrus-fresh cake is a perfect ending to any meal.

12 servings

- 1/2 cup sugar
- 6 tablespoons margarine, softened
- 2 egg whites
- 1 egg
- 3/4 cup reduced-fat sour cream
- 2 tablespoons frozen orange juice concentrate, thawed
- 2 cups cake flour
- 2 tablespoons poppy seeds
- 1 teaspoon baking powder
- 1/2 teaspoon baking soda
- 1/4 teaspoon salt
  Citrus Glaze (recipe follows)

Per Serving
Calories: 231
% Calories from fat: 32
Fat (gm): 8.1
Saturated fat (gm): 2.3
Cholesterol (mg): 22.7
Sodium (mg): 233
Protein (gm): 4
Carbohydrate (gm): 35.6
Exchanges
Milk: 0.0
Vegetable: 0.0
Fruit: 0.0
Bread: 2.0
Meat: 0.0
Fat: 2.0

1. In large bowl, beat sugar and margarine until smooth and fluffy. Beat in egg whites, egg, sour cream, and orange juice until smooth.

2. Combine cake flour, poppy seeds, baking powder, baking soda, and salt in medium bowl; add to sour cream batter. Beat on medium-high speed until smooth, about 1 to 2 minutes. Pour batter into greased and floured 6-cup fluted tube pan.

3. Bake cake at 350 degrees 40 to 55 minutes or until toothpick inserted in center comes out clean. Cool in pan on wire rack 25 to 30 minutes; invert onto wire rack and cool. Spoon Orange Glaze over cake.

Citrus Glaze

makes about ¹/₂ cup

    1 cup powdered sugar
    Orange juice

1. Combine sugar and enough orange juice to make glaze consistency.

BANANA PECAN CAKE

This cake keeps beautifully, tasting even better the second or third day!

12 servings

    1³/₄ cups mashed ripe bananas (about 3 large)
    ²/₃ cup packed light brown sugar
    ¹/₄ cup honey
    ¹/₄ cup margarine, melted
    2 cups all-purpose flour
    1 teaspoon baking powder
    1 teaspoon baking soda
    ¹/₂ teaspoon salt
    Generous pinch ground nutmeg
    ¹/₃ cup chopped pecans
    Banana Glaze (recipe follows)

Per Serving
Calories: 250
% Calories from fat: 22
Fat (gm): 6.3
Saturated fat (gm): 1
Cholesterol (mg): 0
Sodium (mg): 293
Protein (gm): 3
Carbohydrate (gm): 47.2
Exchanges
Milk: 0.0
Vegetable: 0.0
Fruit: 0.0
Bread: 3.0
Meat: 0.0
Fat: 1.0

1. Beat bananas, brown sugar, honey, and margarine in large bowl until well blended. Mix in combined flour, baking powder, baking soda, salt, and nutmeg; mix in pecans.

2. Spoon batter into greased 6-cup fluted tube pan. Bake at 350 degrees 50 to 55 minutes or until toothpick inserted in center comes out clean. Cool in pan on wire rack 10 minutes; remove from pan and cool completely. Drizzle with Banana Glaze.

Banana Glaze

makes about 1/4 cup

1/2 cup powdered sugar
1/4 teaspoon banana extract
3-4 teaspoons fat-free milk

1. Mix powdered sugar, banana extract, and enough milk to make glaze consistency.

CARROT-WALNUT CAKE

An old favorite, chock-full of crunchy walnuts.

16 servings

1 cup granulated sugar
3/4 cup packed light brown sugar
1 cup Prune Puree (see p. 42)
1/3 cup vegetable oil
3 eggs
1 teaspoon vanilla
4 cups shredded carrots
3 cups all-purpose flour
1 tablespoon baking powder
1/2 teaspoon salt
1/2-3/4 cup chopped walnuts, divided
Caramel Glaze (recipe follows)

Per Serving
Calories: 369
% Calories from fat: 19
Fat (gm): 8.1
Saturated fat (gm): 1.1
Cholesterol (mg): 40
Sodium (mg): 245
Protein (gm): 5.5
Carbohydrate (gm): 71.3
Exchanges
Milk: 0.0
Vegetable: 0.0
Fruit: 0.0
Bread: 4.5
Meat: 0.0
Fat: 1.0

1. Combine sugars, Prune Puree, oil, eggs, and vanilla in large bowl, mixing well; mix in carrots. Mix in combined flour, baking powder, and salt. Reserve 3 tablespoons walnuts; stir remaining walnuts into batter.

2. Pour batter into greased and floured 12-cup fluted tube pan. Bake at 350 degrees until toothpick inserted in center comes out clean, 1 to 1 1/4 hours. Cool cake in pan on wire rack 10 minutes; remove from pan and place on rack on cookie sheet. Pierce top of cake with long-tined fork. Spoon warm Caramel Glaze over warm cake; sprinkle with reserved 3 tablespoons walnuts.

Caramel Glaze

makes about 1/2 cup

  1 cup sugar
  1/2 cup 1% low-fat buttermilk
  2 tablespoons light corn syrup
  1/2 teaspoon baking soda

1. Mix all ingredients in small saucepan. Cook over medium-low heat until glaze turns a golden color and foaming begins to subside, 10 to 12 minutes, stirring constantly (watch carefully, as mixture can burn easily).

PENNSYLVANIA DUTCH CARROT CAKE

The mixing method for this cake is a bit different, yielding a cake that is dense and moist. The flavor is reminiscent of spiced gingerbread, perfectly accented with Molasses Cream topping.

12 servings

  1 cup granulated sugar
  1/3 cup packed light brown sugar
  1 1/3 cups cold water
  3/4 cup raisins
  1/4 cup margarine
  1 cup shredded carrots
  1/2 cup chopped nuts
  2 cups all-purpose flour
  1 teaspoon baking soda
  1/2 teaspoon salt
  1 teaspoon ground cinnamon
  3/4 teaspoon ground allspice
  1/4 teaspoon ground nutmeg
  1/8 teaspoon ground cloves
      Molasses Cream (recipe follows)

Per Serving
Calories: 293
% Calories from fat: 24
Fat (gm): 8
Saturated fat (gm): 2
Cholesterol (mg): 0
Sodium (mg): 254
Protein (gm): 3.9
Carbohydrate (gm): 52.7
Exchanges
Milk: 0.0
Vegetable: 0.0
Fruit: 0.0
Bread: 3.5
Meat: 0.0
Fat: 1.0

1. Heat sugars, water, raisins, margarine, and carrots to boiling in large saucepan; reduce heat and simmer, uncovered, 5 minutes. Cool. Stir in combined remaining ingredients, except Molasses Cream.

2. Pour batter into greased 13 x 9-inch baking pan. Bake at 350 degrees until cake pulls from side of pan and springs back when touched, 55 to 60 minutes. Cool on wire rack. Serve each piece with a generous dollop of Molasses Cream.

Molasses Cream

makes about 1¹/₂ cups

> 1¹/₂ cups light whipped topping
> ¹/₄ cup powdered sugar
> 2 teaspoons molasses
> Generous pinch ground nutmeg

1. Mix all ingredients; refrigerate.

CARROT CAKE WITH CREAM CHEESE FROSTING

Moist and sweetly spiced, you'll make this cake over and over again.

16 servings

> 3 cups shredded carrots
> ¹/₂ cup raisins for baking
> 1 cup packed light brown sugar
> ¹/₃ cup vegetable oil
> 3 eggs
> 2 cups all-purpose flour
> 1 teaspoon baking powder
> 1 teaspoon baking soda
> 1 teaspoon ground cinnamon
> ¹/₄ teaspoon ground allspice
> ¹/₄ teaspoon ground nutmeg
> ¹/₄ teaspoon salt
> Cream Cheese Frosting (recipe follows)

Per Serving
Calories: 319
% Calories from fat: 23
Fat (gm): 8.1
Saturated fat (gm): 2.2
Cholesterol (mg): 44.7
Sodium (mg): 229
Protein (gm): 4.2
Carbohydrate (gm): 58.1
Exchanges
Milk: 0.0
Vegetable: 0.0
Fruit: 0.0
Bread: 3.5
Meat: 0.0
Fat: 1.5

1. Mix carrots, raisins, brown sugar, oil, and eggs in large bowl. Mix in combined remaining ingredients, except Cream Cheese Frosting.

2. Pour batter into 2 greased and floured 8-inch round cake pans. Bake at 350 degrees until toothpick inserted in cake comes out clean, 25 to 30 minutes. Cool in pans on wire rack 10 minutes; remove from pans and cool.

3. Place 1 cake layer on serving plate and frost. Top with remaining cake layer; frost top and side of cake.

Cream Cheese Frosting

makes about 2¹/₂ cups

- ³/₄ package (8-ounce size) reduced-fat cream cheese, softened
- 1 tablespoon margarine, softened
- 3¹/₂-4 cups powdered sugar
- 1 teaspoon vanilla

1. Beat cream cheese and margarine in medium bowl until smooth; beat in powdered sugar and vanilla.

Variation: **Blueberry-Carrot Cake**—Make cake as above, deleting raisins; stir ³/₄ to 1 cup fresh or frozen blueberries into cake batter. Bake in greased and floured 12-cup fluted cake pan until toothpick inserted in center comes out clean, 50 to 60 minutes. Cool on wire rack 10 minutes; remove from pan and cool. Drizzle cake with Cream Cheese Glaze (see p. 498).

PRUNE AND RAISIN SPICE CAKE

Delicious warm, with reduced-fat rum raisin ice cream!

14 servings

- ¹/₂ cup margarine, softened
- 1 cup granulated sugar
- ¹/₂ cup packed light brown sugar
- 3 eggs
- 2 teaspoons vanilla
- 2¹/₂ cups all-purpose flour
- 1 teaspoon baking powder
- 1 teaspoon baking soda
- 1 teaspoon salt
- 1 teaspoon ground cinnamon
- ¹/₂ teaspoon ground allspice
- 1 cup reduced-fat buttermilk
- 1 cup fat-free sour cream
- ¹/₂ cup chopped pecans
- ²/₃ cup golden raisins
- ²/₃ cup chopped pitted prunes
  Rum Glaze (see p. 43)

Per Serving
Calories: 356
% Calories from fat: 27
Fat (gm): 10.8
Saturated fat (gm): 2
Cholesterol (mg): 46
Sodium (mg): 418
Protein (gm): 6.4
Carbohydrate (gm): 59.8
Exchanges
Milk: 0.0
Vegetable: 0.0
Fruit: 0.0
Bread: 4.0
Meat: 0.0
Fat: 1.5

1. Beat margarine and sugars until blended in large bowl. Beat in eggs and vanilla. Mix in combined flour, baking powder, baking soda, salt, and spices alternately with combined buttermilk and sour cream, beginning and ending with dry ingredients. Mix in pecans, raisins, and prunes.

2. Pour batter into greased and floured 12-cup fluted tube pan. Bake at 350 degrees until toothpick inserted in center comes out clean, about 1¹/₄ hours. Cool cake in pan on wire rack 10 minutes; remove from pan and cool. Drizzle with Rum Glaze.

MOIST RAISIN CAKE

Thank you, Mrs. Rosencran's, for sharing your dairy-free recipe! The cake is also excellent without the spices—try Orange Glaze (see p. 47) too.

12 servings

1	cup raisins
2	cups water
¹/₂	cup margarine, room temperature
1³/₄	cup all-purpose flour
1	cup granulated sugar
1	teaspoon baking soda
1	teaspoon salt
¹/₂	teaspoon ground cinnamon
¹/₂	teaspoon ground nutmeg
	Powdered sugar, as garnish

Per Serving
Calories: 235
% Calories from fat: 29
Fat (gm): 7.8
Saturated fat (gm): 1.6
Cholesterol (mg): 0
Sodium (mg): 389
Protein (gm): 2.4
Carbohydrate (gm): 40.3
Exchanges
Milk: 0.0
Vegetable: 0.0
Fruit: 0.0
Bread: 2.5
Meat: 0.0
Fat: 1.5

1. Heat raisins and water to boiling in medium saucepan; reduce heat and simmer, uncovered, 10 minutes. Add margarine, stirring until melted. Cool.

2. Add combined remaining ingredients, except powdered sugar, mixing well. Pour batter into greased 13 x 9-inch baking pan. Bake at 350 degrees until cake springs back when touched, about 35 minutes. Cool on wire rack; sprinkle with powdered sugar.

SPICE CAKE WITH PENUCHE FROSTING

The flavor combination of sweet cake spices and creamy caramel fudge (penuche) frosting is too good to be true!

10 servings

4 tablespoons margarine, softened
3/4 cup sugar
1 egg
1/2 teaspoon vanilla
1 1/3 cups all-purpose flour
2 teaspoons baking powder
3/4 teaspoon ground cinnamon
1/4 teaspoon ground nutmeg
1/4 teaspoon ground ginger
1/4 teaspoon salt
2/3 cup skim milk
Penuche Frosting (recipe follows)

Per Serving
Calories: 342
% Calories from fat: 23
Fat (gm): 8.7
Saturated fat (gm): 1.8
Cholesterol (mg): 21.6
Sodium (mg): 233
Protein (gm): 3.1
Carbohydrate (gm): 63.6
Exchanges
Milk: 0.0
Vegetable: 0.0
Fruit: 0.0
Bread: 4.0
Meat: 0.0
Fat: 1.5

1. Beat margarine, sugar, egg, and vanilla in large bowl until smooth. Mix in combined flour, baking powder, spices, and salt alternately with milk, beginning and ending with dry ingredients. Pour batter into greased and floured 8- or 9-inch round cake pan.

2. Bake at 350 degrees until cake is browned and springs back when touched, about 40 minutes. Cool in pan on wire rack 10 minutes; remove from pan and cool to room temperature.

3. Place cake on serving plate; spread top and side with Penuche Frosting.

Penuche Frosting

makes about 1 1/2 cups

3 tablespoons margarine
1/2 cup packed light brown sugar
2-2 1/2 cups powdered sugar
1/2 teaspoon vanilla
2-4 tablespoons skim milk

1. Melt margarine in medium saucepan; stir in brown sugar and cook over medium heat until bubbly. Stir in powdered sugar, vanilla, and enough milk to make spreading consistency.

Tip: Use the frosting immediately as it tends to thicken quickly. If frosting becomes too thick, thin with a few drops of hot water.

HONEY SPICE CAKE

Whole wheat flour gives the cake a pleasant toothsome texture; all-purpose flour can be substituted.

12 servings

1/2 cup margarine, softened
1 cup honey
1 1/2 cups all-purpose flour
1/2 cup whole wheat flour
1 teaspoon baking powder
1/2 teaspoon baking soda
1 teaspoon ground cinnamon
3/4 teaspoon ground nutmeg
1/2 teaspoon ground cloves
1/2 teaspoon ground ginger
1/2 teaspoon salt
2 eggs, lightly beaten
1/2 cup flaked coconut
   Molasses Cream (see p. 66)
1 tablespoon honey

Per Serving
Calories: 290
% Calories from fat: 32
Fat (gm): 10.7
Saturated fat (gm): 3.7
Cholesterol (mg): 35.3
Sodium (mg): 292
Protein (gm): 3.7
Carbohydrate (gm): 46.4
Exchanges
Milk: 0.0
Vegetable: 0.0
Fruit: 0.0
Bread: 3.0
Meat: 0.0
Fat: 1.5

1. Beat margarine and honey in large bowl until blended. Mix in combined flours, baking powder, baking soda, spices, and salt alternately with eggs, beginning and ending with dry ingredients. Mix in coconut.

2. Pour batter into greased 13 x 9-inch baking pan. Bake at 350 degrees until toothpick inserted in center comes out clean, 30 to 35 minutes. Cool on wire rack.

3. Make Molasses Cream, substituting 1 tablespoon honey for the molasses; spoon over cake pieces.

HONEY GRAHAM CAKE

A firm-textured cake, with a lovely honey accent. Serve with fruit and light whipped topping.

24 servings

1/2 cup vegetable oil
1 cup packed light brown sugar
4 eggs
1 cup honey
3 tablespoons lemon juice
3 1/2 cups all-purpose flour
1 1/2 teaspoons baking powder
1 1/2 teaspoons baking soda
1/2 teaspoon salt
2 teaspoons ground cinnamon
3/4 cup fat-free milk
1/2 cup graham cracker crumbs
1/2 cup finely ground pecans
Lemon Soaking Syrup (recipe follows)

Per Serving
Calories: 260
% Calories from fat: 25
Fat (gm): 7.7
Saturated fat (gm): 1.1
Cholesterol (mg): 35.4
Sodium (mg): 187
Protein (gm): 3.7
Carbohydrate (gm): 45.8
Exchanges
Milk: 0.0
Vegetable: 0.0
Fruit: 0.0
Bread: 3.0
Meat: 0.0
Fat: 1.0

1. Beat oil, sugar, eggs, honey, and lemon juice in large bowl until blended. Mix in combined flour, baking powder, baking soda, salt, and cinnamon alternately with milk, beginning and ending with dry ingredients; beat on high speed 2 minutes. Mix in graham cracker crumbs and pecans.

2. Pour batter into greased and floured 12-cup fluted tube pan. Bake at 350 degrees until toothpick inserted in center comes out clean, 50 to 60 minutes. Cool in pan on wire rack 10 minutes; remove from pan and cool 10 minutes. Spoon warm Lemon Soaking Syrup over warm cake; cool completely.

Lemon Soaking Syrup

1 cup sugar
1/3 cup lemon juice

1. Heat sugar and lemon juice to boiling in small saucepan, stirring to dissolve sugar; cool 5 minutes.

GRAHAM CAKE

Swirled with a cloud of whipped topping and ribboned with Caramel Topping, this cake is a thing of beauty as well as a taste treat.

12 servings

6 egg yolks
1 1/2 cups granulated sugar, divided
1 teaspoon baking powder
2 teaspoons vanilla
6 egg whites
1/2 teaspoon cream of tartar
1/2 teaspoon salt
2 cups graham cracker crumbs
1/2 cup finely chopped walnuts
2 cups light whipped topping
1/4 cup powdered sugar
Caramel Topping (recipe follows)

Per Serving
Calories: 359
% Calories from fat: 32
Fat (gm): 13
Saturated fat (gm): 3.7
Cholesterol (mg): 124.2
Sodium (mg): 281
Protein (gm): 6.4
Carbohydrate (gm): 54.6
Exchanges
Milk: 0.0
Vegetable: 0.0
Fruit: 0.0
Bread: 3.5
Meat: 0.0
Fat: 2.0

1. Beat egg yolks at high speed in medium bowl until thick and lemon colored, about 5 minutes. Beat in 1 cup granulated sugar gradually; beat in baking powder and vanilla.

2. With clean bowl and beaters, beat egg whites, cream of tartar, and salt to soft peaks in large bowl. Beat to stiff peaks, adding remaining 1/2 cup granulated sugar gradually. Fold 1/4 of the egg whites into egg yolks; fold egg yolk mixture, graham crumbs, and walnuts into remaining egg whites.

3. Pour batter into 2 greased and floured 9-inch round cake pans. Bake at 325 degrees until wooden pick inserted in center comes out clean, about 25 minutes. Cool cakes in pans on wire rack 10 minutes; remove from pans and cool.

4. Combine whipped topping and powdered sugar. Place 1 cake layer on serving plate; spread with 1/2 the whipped topping. Add second cake layer and spread remaining whipped topping. Drizzle cake with Caramel Topping.

Caramel Topping

makes about ¹/₂ cup

  1 egg, lightly beaten
¹/₂ cup packed light brown sugar
  2 teaspoons flour
  2 tablespoons margarine
  2 tablespoons fat-free milk
  1 teaspoon vanilla

1. Mix all ingredients until smooth in small saucepan; cook over medium-low heat until thick and smooth, about 5 minutes. Cool to room temperature.

WHITE CAKE WITH MARSHMALLOW FROSTING

The perennial favorite white cake with fluffy Marshmallow Frosting. Be sure to try the Maraschino Party Cake variation that follows.

12 servings

2¹/₄ cups cake flour
  1 tablespoon baking powder
¹/₂ teaspoon salt
¹/₂ cup vegetable shortening
1¹/₃ cups sugar
³/₄ cup 2% reduced-fat milk
  4 egg whites
      Marshmallow Frosting (see p. 18)

Per Serving
Calories: 315
% Calories from fat: 24
Fat (gm): 8.5
Saturated fat (gm): 2.2
Cholesterol (mg): 1.1
Sodium (mg): 255
Protein (gm): 3.9
Carbohydrate (gm): 56.1
Exchanges
Milk: 0.0
Vegetable: 0.0
Fruit: 0.0
Bread: 3.5
Meat: 0.0
Fat: 1.5

1. Combine all ingredients, except egg whites and Marshmallow Frosting, in large bowl; beat on medium speed 2 minutes. Add egg whites; beat 2 minutes longer.

2. Pour batter into 2 greased and floured 8- or 9-inch round cake pans. Bake at 350 degrees until toothpick inserted in center comes out clean, 30 to 35 minutes. Cool cakes in pans on wire rack; remove from pans and cool completely. Place 1 cake layer on serving plate; spread with ¹/₂ cup Marshmallow Frosting. Top with remaining cake layer and frost.

Variation: **Maraschino Party Cake**—Make cake as above, adding ¹/₃ cup finely chopped pecans, ¹/₃ cup finely chopped maraschino cherries, and substituting ¹/₄ cup maraschino cherry juice for ¹/₄ cup of the milk. Garnish top of cake with drained maraschino cherries.

CHOCOLATE BUTTERCREAM GOLD CAKE

Slathered in Chocolate Buttercream, this flavorful cake will be one you make often. Great with Marshmallow Frosting (see p. 18) too!

16 servings

2 cups all-purpose flour
1 1/3 cups sugar
1 tablespoon baking powder
1/2 teaspoon salt
1/3 cup vegetable shortening
1/2 teaspoon lemon extract
1 teaspoon vanilla
1 cup 2% reduced-fat milk, divided
2 eggs
Chocolate Buttercream (recipe follows)

Per Serving
Calories: 377
% Calories from fat: 17
Fat (gm): 7.2
Saturated fat (gm): 1.8
Cholesterol (mg): 27.9
Sodium (mg): 213
Protein (gm): 3.3
Carbohydrate (gm): 75.4
Exchanges
Milk: 0.0
Vegetable: 0.0
Fruit: 0.0
Bread: 5.0
Meat: 0.0
Fat: 0.5

1. Combine all ingredients, except 1/3 cup milk, eggs, and Chocolate Buttercream, in large bowl; mix at medium speed 2 minutes. Add remaining 1/3 cup milk and eggs; beat 2 minutes longer.

2. Pour batter into 2 greased and floured 8- or 9-inch round cake pans. Bake at 350 degrees until toothpick inserted in center of cake comes out clean, 25 to 30 minutes. Cool cakes in pans on wire rack 10 minutes; remove from pans and cool completely. Place 1 cake layer on serving plate; spread with 1/2 cup Chocolate Buttercream. Top with remaining cake layer and frost cake.

Chocolate Buttercream

makes about 3 cups

6 cups powdered sugar
1/2 cup unsweetened cocoa
3 tablespoons margarine, softened
1 teaspoon vanilla
5-6 tablespoons fat-free milk

1. Mix powdered sugar, cocoa, margarine, vanilla, and enough milk to make desired spreading consistency.

BOSTON CREAM CAKE

A family favorite, with chocolatey glaze and a luxurious cream filling.

12 servings

8 tablespoons margarine, softened
1 1/4 cups sugar
2 eggs
1 teaspoon vanilla
2 2/3 cups all-purpose flour
1 tablespoon baking powder
1/2 teaspoon salt
1 2/3 cups fat-free milk
Vanilla Cream Filling (recipe follows)
Chocolate Glaze (recipe follows)

Per Serving
Calories: 338
% Calories from fat: 24
Fat (gm): 9.1
Saturated fat (gm): 2
Cholesterol (mg): 54
Sodium (mg): 354
Protein (gm): 5.6
Carbohydrate (gm): 58.8
Exchanges
Milk: 0.0
Vegetable: 0.0
Fruit: 0.0
Bread: 4.0
Meat: 0.0
Fat: 1.0

1. Beat margarine, sugar, eggs, and vanilla until smooth in medium bowl. Mix in combined flour, baking powder, and salt alternately with milk, beginning and ending with dry ingredients.

2. Pour batter into 2 greased and floured 8- or 9-inch round cake pans. Bake at 350 degrees until cakes spring back when touched, about 40 minutes. Cool in pans on wire rack 10 minutes; remove from pans and cool to room temperature.

3. Place 1 cake layer on serving plate; spread with Vanilla Cream Filling. Top with second cake layer and spoon Chocolate Glaze over.

Vanilla Cream Filling

makes about 1 1/4 cups

1/4 cup sugar
2 tablespoons cornstarch
1 cup fat-free milk
1 egg, beaten
1/2 teaspoon vanilla

1. Mix sugar and cornstarch in saucepan; stir in milk. Heat over medium-high heat, stirring constantly, until mixture comes to a boil; boil, stirring constantly, until thickened.

2. Whisk about 1/2 of milk mixture into beaten egg in small bowl; whisk egg mixture back into saucepan. Cook over very low heat, whisking constantly, 30 to 60 seconds. Remove from heat; stir in vanilla and cool.

Chocolate Glaze

    1   cup powdered sugar
    2   tablespoons unsweetened cocoa
    1/2 teaspoon vanilla
    1-2 tablespoons fat-free milk

1. Combine powdered sugar and cocoa in small bowl; stir in vanilla and enough milk to make glaze consistency.

RED VELVET CAKE

Also known as Waldorf Astoria Cake, this colorful red dessert is reputed to trace its origins to the famed hotel. The cake can also be frosted with Cream Cheese Frosting (see p. 67).

16 servings

    1 1/2 cups sugar
    6   tablespoons vegetable shortening
    2   eggs
    1   teaspoon vanilla
    2   bottles (1 ounce each) red food coloring
    1/4   cup unsweetened cocoa
    2 1/4 cups all-purpose flour
    1   teaspoon baking soda
    1/2   teaspoon salt
    1   cup reduced-fat buttermilk
    1   tablespoon white distilled vinegar
          Buttercream Frosting (see p. 542)

Per Serving
Calories: 361
% Calories from fat: 17
Fat (gm): 6.9
Saturated fat (gm): 1.7
Cholesterol (mg): 27.1
Sodium (mg): 207
Protein (gm): 3.4
Carbohydrate (gm): 71.8
Exchanges
Milk: 0.0
Vegetable: 0.0
Fruit: 0.0
Bread: 5.0
Meat: 0.0
Fat: 0.0

1. Beat sugar and shortening until well blended in large bowl. Add eggs and vanilla, blending well; beat in food coloring and cocoa until well blended. Mix in combined flour, baking soda, and salt alternately with combined buttermilk and vinegar.

2. Pour batter into 2 greased and floured 9-inch round cake pans. Bake at 350 degrees until toothpick inserted in center of cake comes out clean, 25 to 30 minutes. Cool in pans on wire rack 10 minutes; remove cakes from pans and cool completely.

3. Place 1 cake layer on serving plate; spread with generous 1/2 cup Buttercream Frosting. Top with remaining layer; frost cake.

SPICED STRAWBERRY CAKE

Gently spiced and dotted with strawberries, this cake is perfect to serve with summer's ripe berries or other fresh fruit.

12 servings

1²/₃ cups plus ¹/₄ cup sugar, divided
6 tablespoons margarine, softened
3 eggs
2¹/₃ cups all-purpose flour
³/₄ teaspoon baking powder
³/₄ teaspoon baking soda
¹/₂ teaspoon salt
¹/₄ teaspoon ground allspice
Generous pinch ground nutmeg
Generous pinch ground pepper
³/₄ cup reduced-fat buttermilk
5 cups sliced strawberries, divided
¹/₄ cup finely chopped toasted almonds, optional
2 teaspoons grated lemon rind
Marshmallow Frosting (see p. 18)

Per Serving
Calories: 374
% Calories from fat: 18
Fat (gm): 7.5
Saturated fat (gm): 1.6
Cholesterol (mg): 53.6
Sodium (mg): 315
Protein (gm): 5.6
Carbohydrate (gm): 72.7
Exchanges
Milk: 0.0
Vegetable: 0.0
Fruit: 0.0
Bread: 4.5
Meat: 0.0
Fat: 1.0

1. Beat 1²/₃ cups sugar and margarine until well blended in large bowl. Mix in eggs one at a time, blending well after each addition. Mix in combined flour, baking powder, baking soda, salt, allspice, nutmeg, and pepper alternately with buttermilk, beginning and ending with dry ingredients.

2. Mash 1 cup strawberries; mix into cake batter with almonds, if using, and lemon rind. Pour batter into 2 greased and floured 9-inch round cake pans. Bake at 350 degrees until toothpick inserted in center comes out clean, about 30 minutes. Cool cakes in pans on wire rack 10 minutes; remove from pans and cool completely.

3. Place 1 cake layer on serving plate; spread with about ¹/₂ cup Marshmallow Frosting. Top with second cake layer; frost top and side of cake. Mix remaining 4 cups strawberries and remaining ¹/₄ cup sugar; serve over cake slices.

Variation: **Strawberry Cake with Strawberry Rhubarb Filling—** Make cake and frosting as above, but do not assemble cake. To make **Strawberry Rhubarb Filling,** mix ¹/₄ cup sugar and 2 teaspoons cornstarch in small saucepan; add 1 cup fresh or frozen sliced rhubarb. Heat over medium-high heat to boiling; reduce heat and simmer until rhubarb is tender and mixture thickened, 3 to 4 minutes, stirring frequently. Coarsely mash 1 cup strawberries with 2 tablespoons sugar; stir into rhubarb mixture and cook 1 minute. Cool. Spread mixture between cake layers and frost cake with Marshmallow Frosting.

MOM'S APPLE DAPPLE CAKE

The absolute all-time favorite dessert of my "little brother," Gary!

16 to 24 servings

⅓ cup vegetable oil
⅔ cup applesauce
2 cups sugar
3 eggs
2 teaspoons vanilla
3 cups all-purpose flour
1 teaspoon baking soda
½ teaspoon salt
3 cups peeled chopped apples
½ cup chopped walnuts
    Brown Sugar Syrup (recipe follows)

Per Serving
Calories: 358
% Calories from fat: 27
Fat (gm): 10.8
Saturated fat (gm): 1.6
Cholesterol (mg): 39.8
Sodium (mg): 205
Protein (gm): 4.8
Carbohydrate (gm): 61.9
Exchanges
Milk: 0.0
Vegetable: 0.0
Fruit: 0.0
Bread: 4.0
Meat: 0.0
Fat: 1.5

1. Mix oil, applesauce, sugar, eggs, and vanilla until well blended in large bowl; mix in combined flour, baking soda, and salt. Mix in apples and walnuts.

2. Pour batter into greased and floured 12-cup fluted tube pan. Bake at 350 degrees until toothpick inserted in center comes out clean, about 60 minutes. Remove from oven and cool on wire rack 5 minutes. Pierce cake with long-tined fork and pour hot Brown Sugar Syrup over cake. Let cake cool in pan 2 hours. Invert onto serving plate.

Brown Sugar Syrup

makes about 1 cup

1 cup packed light brown sugar
¼ cup fat-free milk
¼ cup margarine

1. Heat all ingredients to boiling, stirring to melt margarine; boil 3 minutes.

EDDIE'S BANANA CAKE

One of the best banana cakes you'll ever eat! Eddie bakes the cake in layers, although it can be baked in a single 13 x 9-inch pan.

16 servings

2¹/₂ cups cake flour

1²/₃ cups sugar

1¹/₄ teaspoons baking powder

1¹/₄ teaspoons baking soda

Pinch salt

¹/₂ cup vegetable shortening

²/₃ cup reduced-fat buttermilk, divided

1¹/₄ cups mashed ripe banana (1 large)

2 eggs

¹/₂ cup chopped nuts

Brown Sugar Frosting (recipe follows)

Per Serving
Calories: 361
% Calories from fat: 26
Fat (gm): 10.6
Saturated fat (gm): 2.2
Cholesterol (mg): 26.9
Sodium (mg): 180
Protein (gm): 3.8
Carbohydrate (gm): 64.3
Exchanges
Milk: 0.0
Vegetable: 0.0
Fruit: 0.0
Bread: 4.0
Meat: 0.0
Fat: 1.5

1. Combine flour, sugar, baking powder, baking soda, and salt in large bowl. Add vegetable shortening, ¹/₃ cup buttermilk, and the banana; beat at medium speed 2 minutes. Add remaining buttermilk and eggs; beat at medium speed 2 minutes. Mix in nuts.

2. Pour batter into 2 greased and floured 9-inch round cake pans. Bake at 350 degrees until toothpick inserted in center comes out clean, about 35 minutes. Cool in pans on wire rack 10 minutes; remove from pans and cool.

3. Place 1 cake layer on serving plate; spread with ¹/₂ the Brown Sugar Frosting; top with second layer and spread top with remaining Brown Sugar Frosting.

Brown Sugar Frosting

makes about 1¹/₂ cups

1 cup packed light brown sugar

¹/₄ cup fat-free milk

2 tablespoons margarine

1¹/₂ cups powdered sugar

Fat-free milk, optional

1. Heat brown sugar, milk, and margarine in medium saucepan until mixture is smooth; remove from heat. Mix in powdered sugar and milk, if necessary, to make spreading consistency.

ORANGE MARMALADE CINNAMON CAKE

Topped with fluffy Marshmallow Frosting, this cake is party perfect.

14 servings

2 cups all-purpose flour
1¹/2 cups sugar
1 tablespoon baking powder
¹/2 teaspoon salt
2 teaspoons ground cinnamon
¹/2 teaspoon ground ginger
¹/2 cup vegetable shortening
1 cup fat-free milk, divided
4 egg whites *or* ¹/2 cup no-cholesterol real egg product, divided
Orange Marmalade Filling (recipe follows)
Marshmallow Frosting (see p. 18)

Per Serving
Calories: 341
% Calories from fat: 21
Fat (gm): 8.2
Saturated fat (gm): 2.1
Cholesterol (mg): 15.7
Sodium (mg): 258
Protein (gm): 4.5
Carbohydrate (gm): 63.4
Exchanges
Milk: 0.0
Vegetable: 0.0
Fruit: 0.0
Bread: 4.0
Meat: 0.0
Fat: 1.0

1. Combine flour, sugar, baking powder, salt, and spices in large bowl; add shortening, ¹/2 of the milk, and egg whites. Mix on low speed until blended; beat at high speed 2 minutes. Add remaining milk and egg whites; beat at high speed 2 minutes, scraping bowl occasionally.

2. Pour batter into 2 greased and floured 8- or 9-inch round cake pans. Bake at 350 degrees until toothpick inserted in center comes out clean, 25 to 30 minutes. Cool in pans on wire racks 10 minutes; remove from pans and cool.

3. Place 1 cake layer on serving plate; spread with Orange Marmalade Filling. Top with second cake layer and frost with Marshmallow Frosting.

Orange Marmalade Filling

makes about 1¹/4 cups

¹/4 cup sugar
1 tablespoon cornstarch
¹/8 teaspoon salt
¹/2 cup fat-free milk
1 egg yolk
¹/2 cup orange marmalade
1 tablespoon margarine

1. Mix sugar, cornstarch, and salt in medium saucepan; mix in milk. Heat to boiling, whisking constantly, until thickened.

2. Whisk about ¹/₂ the mixture into egg yolk; whisk yolk mixture back into saucepan. Cook over low heat 1 to 2 minutes, whisking constantly.

3. Remove pan from heat; stir in orange marmalade and margarine. Cool.

BERRY CREAM CHEESE CAKE

Whipped Cream Cheese Topping makes a baked-on "frosting" for this unique cake.

12 servings

- ¹/₂ cup margarine, melted
- ¹/₂ cup sugar
- ¹/₂ cup sour cream
- 2 eggs
- 1 teaspoon vanilla
- 1¹/₃ cups all-purpose flour
- ¹/₂ teaspoon baking soda
- ¹/₂ teaspoon baking powder
- ¹/₄ teaspoon salt
- Whipped Cream Cheese Topping (recipe follows)
- ¹/₂ cup blueberries
- Glazed Strawberry Sauce (see p. 116)

Per Serving
Calories: 344
% Calories from fat: 29
Fat (gm): 11.2
Saturated fat (gm): 3.5
Cholesterol (mg): 40.4
Sodium (mg): 336
Protein (gm): 6.5
Carbohydrate (gm): 51.8
Exchanges
Milk: 0.0
Vegetable: 0.0
Fruit: 0.0
Bread: 3.5
Meat: 0.0
Fat: 2.0

1. Beat margarine, sugar, sour cream, eggs, and vanilla until smooth in medium bowl. Mix in combined flour, baking soda, baking powder, and salt.

2. Pour batter into greased and floured 9-inch round cake pan with removable bottom. Bake at 350 degrees 15 minutes. Spread Whipped Cream Cheese Topping on top of partially baked cake; bake until cake pulls from side of pan and toothpick inserted comes out clean, 10 to 15 minutes. Cool on wire rack 10 minutes; remove from pan and cool completely.

3. Mix blueberries into Glazed Strawberry Sauce; serve with cake.

Whipped Cream Cheese Topping

makes about 1¹/₄ cups

1 package (8 ounces) fat-free cream cheese, softened
¹/₄ cup sugar
¹/₄ cup fat-free sour cream

1. Beat all ingredients until smooth.

PEACH MERINGUE CAKE

Meringues, light as clouds, are layered with cake and peach cream filling.

12 servings

8 tablespoons margarine, softened
¹/₂ cup sugar
4 egg yolks
1 teaspoon vanilla
1 cup all-purpose flour
2 teaspoons baking powder
¹/₄ teaspoon salt
¹/₃ cup fat-free milk
Peach Cream Filling (recipe follows)
Meringue Layers (recipe follows)

Per Serving
Calories: 263
% Calories from fat: 36
Fat (gm): 10.4
Saturated fat (gm): 3
Cholesterol (mg): 71.1
Sodium (mg): 243
Protein (gm): 3.5
Carbohydrate (gm): 38.8
Exchanges
Milk: 0.0
Vegetable: 0.0
Fruit: 0.0
Bread: 2.5
Meat: 0.0
Fat: 2.0

1. Beat margarine and sugar in large bowl until fluffy; beat in egg yolks and vanilla. Mix in combined flour, baking powder, and salt alternately with milk, beginning and ending with dry ingredients.

2. Spread batter in 2 greased and floured 9-inch round cake pans; bake at 350 degrees until toothpick inserted in center comes out clean, 35 to 40 minutes. Cool cakes in pans on wire rack 10 minutes; remove from pans and cool completely.

3. Place 1 cake layer on serving plate; spread with ¹/₂ cup Peach Cream Filling, top with 1 Meringue Layer, and spread with another ¹/₂ cup Peach Cream Filling. Top with remaining cake layer, Peach Cream Filling, and Meringue Layer.

Peach Cream Filling

makes about 1¹/₂ cups

 1¹/₂ cups light whipped topping
 2 tablespoons peach preserves
 1 tablespoon powdered sugar

1. Mix all ingredients.

Meringue Layers

makes 2

 4 egg whites
 ¹/₈ teaspoon cream of tartar
 1 cup sugar

1. Beat egg whites and cream of tartar to soft peaks in large bowl; beat to stiff peaks, adding sugar gradually.

2. Spread mixture onto greased and floured bottoms of 2 inverted 9-inch round cake pans, spreading to edges of pans. Bake at 350 degrees until meringues are golden and crisp, about 40 minutes. Carefully remove meringues from pan bottoms with metal spatula; cool on wire rack.

MIXED BERRY TORTE

Use the season's freshest berries, or substitute another fruit of your choice.

10 servings

 2 eggs
 1 cup sugar
 1 cup all-purpose flour
 1 teaspoon baking powder
 ¹/₂ teaspoon salt
 1 teaspoon vanilla
 ¹/₂ cup fat-free milk
 1 tablespoon margarine
 Orange Marmalade Filling (see p. 80)
 3-4 cups mixed berries (blueberries, raspberries, blackberries, strawberries)
 Powdered sugar, as garnish

Per Serving
Calories: 259
% Calories from fat: 14
Fat (gm): 4.1
Saturated fat (gm): 1
Cholesterol (mg): 64.1
Sodium (mg): 250
Protein (gm): 4.1
Carbohydrate (gm): 53.3
Exchanges
Milk: 0.0
Vegetable: 0.0
Fruit: 0.0
Bread: 3.5
Meat: 0.0
Fat: 0.0

1. Beat eggs in medium bowl at high speed until thick and lemon colored, 3 to 5 minutes; beat in sugar gradually. Mix in combined flour, baking powder, and salt; mix in vanilla. Heat milk and margarine in small saucepan just until hot; mix into batter, blending well.

2. Pour batter into greased and floured 9-inch springform pan. Bake at 350 degrees until toothpick inserted in center comes out clean, 20 to 25 minutes. Cool in pan on wire rack 10 minutes; remove side of pan and cool.

3. At serving time, spread top of cake with Orange Marmalade Filling and arrange berries on top. Sprinkle top of berries with powdered sugar.

DATE-WALNUT CAKE

One of our favorite cakes! Three layers of richly flavored cake, topped off with the creamiest of cream cheese frostings.

16 servings

1³/₄ cups sugar
¹/₂ cup margarine, softened
1¹/₂ teaspoons butter extract
2 egg yolks
2 cups all-purpose flour
1 teaspoon baking soda
¹/₄ teaspoon salt
1 cup reduced-fat buttermilk
¹/₃-¹/₂ cup chopped walnuts
¹/₃ cup chopped dates
6 egg whites, beaten to stiff peaks
Cream Cheese Frosting (see p. 67)

Per Serving
Calories: 371
% Calories from fat: 25
Fat (gm): 10.5
Saturated fat (gm): 2.8
Cholesterol (mg): 32.1
Sodium (mg): 278
Protein (gm): 5.6
Carbohydrate (gm): 64.6
Exchanges
Milk: 0.0
Vegetable: 0.0
Fruit: 0.0
Bread: 4.5
Meat: 0.0
Fat: 1.5

1. Mix sugar, margarine, and butter extract in large bowl; beat in egg yolks, one at a time. Mix in combined flour, baking soda, and salt alternately with buttermilk, beginning and ending with dry ingredients. Stir in walnuts and dates; fold in egg whites.

2. Pour batter into 3 greased and floured 8- or 9-inch round cake pans. Bake at 350 degrees until toothpick inserted in center comes out clean, 20 to 25 minutes. Cool cakes in pans on wire racks 10 minutes; remove from pans and cool completely.

3. Place 1 cake layer on serving plate and frost with ¹/₂ cup Cream Cheese Frosting; repeat with second layer. Top cake with remaining layer; frost top and side of cake.

RASPBERRY JAM CAKE

Although raspberry jam is our choice, any jam or preserve will be delicious in this cake.

10 servings

1/2 cup 2% reduced-fat milk
1 teaspoon vanilla
2 tablespoons margarine
2 egg whites
1/2 cup sugar
2 egg yolks
1 cup cake flour
1 teaspoon baking powder
1/8 teaspoon salt
3/4 cup seedless raspberry jam
Marshmallow Frosting (see p. 18)

Per Serving
Calories: 260
% Calories from fat: 12
Fat (gm): 3.7
Saturated fat (gm): 0.9
Cholesterol (mg): 43.6
Sodium (mg): 144
Protein (gm): 3.5
Carbohydrate (gm): 55.1
Exchanges
Milk: 0.0
Vegetable: 0.0
Fruit: 0.0
Bread: 3.5
Meat: 0.0
Fat: 0.5

1. Heat milk, vanilla, and margarine over medium-high heat just to simmering, stirring occasionally to melt margarine; cool.

2. Beat egg whites in medium bowl to soft peaks; beat to stiff peaks, adding sugar gradually. Beat in egg yolks. Mix in combined flour, baking powder, and salt alternately with milk mixture, beginning and ending with flour mixture.

3. Pour batter into greased and floured 8-inch round cake pan. Bake at 350 degrees until toothpick inserted in center of cake comes out clean, 25 to 30 minutes. Cool in pan on wire rack 10 minutes; remove from pan and cool completely.

4. Using serrated knife, cut cake into 2 layers. Place bottom layer on serving plate; spread with half the jam. Top with second cake layer and spread with jam. Frost top and side of cake with Marshmallow Frosting.

BUTTER-GLAZED POUND CAKE

Moistened with Buttery Soaking Syrup and glazed, this cake is delicious alone or served with fresh fruit. See the tropical coconut variation below. Serve with a medley of tropical fruit—mango or papaya, pineapple, and kiwi.

24 servings

2³/₄	cups sugar
10	tablespoons margarine, softened
10	egg whites *or* 1¹/₄ cups no-cholesterol real egg product
1	teaspoon butter extract
4¹/₄	cups cake flour
1	teaspoon baking soda
¹/₄	teaspoon salt
1¹/₂	cups reduced-fat sour cream
	Buttery Soaking Syrup (recipe follows)
	Buttery Glaze (recipe follows)

Per Serving
Calories: 284
% Calories from fat: 19
Fat (gm): 6.2
Saturated fat (gm): 2
Cholesterol (mg): 5
Sodium (mg): 167
Protein (gm): 4.2
Carbohydrate (gm): 53.4
Exchanges
Milk: 0.0
Vegetable: 0.0
Fruit: 0.0
Bread: 3.5
Meat: 0.0
Fat: 1.0

1. Beat sugar and margarine until blended in large bowl. Gradually add egg whites and butter extract, beating well. Mix in combined flour, baking soda, and salt alternately with sour cream, beginning and ending with dry ingredients.

2. Spread batter into greased and floured 12-cup fluted tube pan. Bake at 325 degrees until toothpick inserted in center of cake comes out clean, 1¹/₄ to 1¹/₂ hours. Cool in pan on wire rack 10 minutes; remove from pan and cool completely.

3. Pierce cake with long-tined fork and drizzle with warm Buttery Soaking Syrup; spoon Buttery Glaze over.

Buttery Soaking Syrup

makes about 1 cup

²/₃	cup water
¹/₂	cup sugar
¹/₂	teaspoon butter extract

1. Heat water, sugar, and butter extract to boiling in small saucepan, stirring to dissolve sugar. Cool slightly.

Buttery Glaze

makes about ³/₄ cup

>   2 cups powdered sugar
>   ¹/₂ teaspoon butter extract
>   3-4 tablespoons fat-free milk

1. Mix powdered sugar, butter extract, and enough milk to make thick glaze consistency.

Variation: **Tropical Coconut Pound Cake**—Make cake as above, substituting coconut extract for the butter extract. Substitute light coconut milk for the water in the Buttery Soaking Syrup and for the milk in the Buttery Glaze; substitute coconut extract for the butter extract in both the syrup and glaze. Sprinkle top of glazed cake with toasted coconut.

MARBLE POUND CAKE

A cake you'll make often because of its versatility. Serve plain, or top with sliced fruit or Brandied Cherry Sauce (see p. 655).

12 servings

>   1 cup reduced-fat buttermilk
>   1 teaspoon vanilla
>   ¹/₂ teaspoon baking soda
>   8 tablespoons margarine, softened
>   1¹/₃ cups sugar
>   3 egg whites
>   2 cups cake flour
>   ¹/₈ teaspoon salt
>   1¹/₂ ounces semisweet chocolate, melted
>   Chocolate Glaze (see p. 76)

Per Serving
Calories: 291
% Calories from fat: 27
Fat (gm): 9.1
Saturated fat (gm): 2.3
Cholesterol (mg): 0.8
Sodium (mg): 203
Protein (gm): 3.5
Carbohydrate (gm): 50
Exchanges
Milk: 0.0
Vegetable: 0.0
Fruit: 0.0
Bread: 3.0
Meat: 0.0
Fat: 1.5

1. Mix buttermilk, vanilla, and baking soda; let stand 2 to 3 minutes. Beat margarine and sugar until fluffy in large bowl. Beat in egg whites one at a time, beating well after each addition. Mix in combined flour and salt alternately with buttermilk mixture, beginning and ending with flour mixture.

2. Reserve 2 cups batter; stir melted chocolate into remaining batter. Spoon batters alternately into greased and floured 9 x 5-inch loaf pan; swirl gently with knife.

3. Bake at 350 degrees until wooden pick inserted in center comes out clean, 60 to 70 minutes. Cool in pan on wire rack 10 minutes; remove from pan and cool completely.

4. Place cake on serving plate; drizzle with Chocolate Glaze.

Variation: **Orange-Glazed Pound Cake**—Make cake, omitting chocolate and vanilla and adding 1 teaspoon orange extract; bake as above. Heat $3/4$ cup powdered sugar and $1/2$ cup orange juice to boiling in small saucepan, stirring until sugar is dissolved. Cool slightly. Pierce top of cake at 1-inch intervals with long-tined fork; spoon warm syrup over cake. Cool, remove from pan, then drizzle with Orange Glaze (see p. 47).

CHOCOLATE COFFEE POUND CAKE

All the flavor of the richest pound cake, with half of the fat! Serve with espresso for an elegant ending to a fine meal.

12 servings

6 tablespoons margarine, softened

$1^1/_3$ cups sugar

2 large eggs

1 cup all-purpose flour

$1/_3$ cup Dutch process cocoa

$1/_2$ teaspoon baking soda

$1/_4$ teaspoon baking powder

$1/_4$ teaspoon salt

2 tablespoons instant espresso *or* instant coffee granules

2 tablespoons hot water

1 teaspoon vanilla

6 tablespoons fat-free sour cream

Coffee Glaze (recipe follows)

Per Serving
Calories: 246
% Calories from fat: 28
Fat (gm): 7.8
Saturated fat (gm): 1.8
Cholesterol (mg): 35.3
Sodium (mg): 207
Protein (gm): 3.3
Carbohydrate (gm): 41
Exchanges
Milk: 0.0
Vegetable: 0.0
Fruit: 0.0
Bread: 2.5
Meat: 0.0
Fat: 1.5

1. Beat margarine and sugar in large bowl until light and fluffy. Add eggs one at a time, beating well after each addition. Combine flour, cocoa, baking soda, baking powder, and salt. Dissolve espresso powder in hot water; add vanilla and stir into sour cream. Add dry ingredients to margarine mixture alternately with sour cream mixture, beginning and ending with dry ingredients.

2. Pour batter into greased and floured 6-cup fluted tube pan. Bake at 350 degrees until toothpick inserted in center of cake comes out clean, 35 to 40 minutes. Cool cake in pan on rack 10 minutes; remove from pan and cool completely. Drizzle Coffee Glaze over cake.

Coffee Glaze

makes about ¹/₃ cup

>   ³/₄ cup powdered sugar
>   1 tablespoon margarine, melted
> 2-3 tablespoons strong coffee

1. Mix powdered sugar, margarine, and enough coffee to make glaze consistency.

RICH LEMON POUND CAKE

Savor the richness of this cake—serve with Tart Lemon Sauce (p. 650), if desired.

12 servings

> ³/₄ cup sugar
> ¹/₃ cup margarine, softened
>   1 cup reduced-fat sour cream
>   3 egg whites
>   2 teaspoons lemon juice
>   1 tablespoon grated lemon rind
> 2¹/₂ cups cake flour
>   1 teaspoon baking soda
> ¹/₄ teaspoon salt
>   Lemon Syrup (recipe follows)
>   Powdered sugar, as garnish

Per Serving
Calories: 234
% Calories from fat: 27
Fat (gm): 6.9
Saturated fat (gm): 2.4
Cholesterol (mg): 6.7
Sodium (mg): 240
Protein (gm): 4.2
Carbohydrate (gm): 39
Exchanges
Milk: 0.0
Vegetable: 0.0
Fruit: 0.0
Bread: 2.5
Meat: 0.0
Fat: 1.0

1. Beat sugar and margarine in large bowl until light and fluffy. Beat in sour cream, egg whites, lemon juice, and lemon rind until smooth. Mix in combined flour, baking soda, and salt, beating until smooth, about 1 minute. Spoon batter into greased and floured 6-cup fluted tube pan.

2. Bake cake 40 to 50 minutes or until toothpick inserted in center comes out clean. Cool in pan on wire rack 20 minutes; invert onto wire rack.

3. With a skewer or tines of fork, pierce cake top at 1-inch intervals. Spoon warm Lemon Syrup over cake; sprinkle with powdered sugar.

Lemon Syrup

makes about 2/3 cup

> 2/3 cup powdered sugar
> 1/4 cup lemon juice
> 3 tablespoons water

1. Combine sugar, lemon juice, and water in small saucepan. Heat to boiling, stirring constantly until sugar is dissolved. Cool slightly.

CRANBERRY JEWEL CAKE

A rich-tasting cake with pound cake texture, covered with a sparkling cranberry glaze.

12 servings

> 1 1/2 cups packed light brown sugar
> 3/4 cup fat-free milk
> 3 tablespoons vegetable oil
> 2 teaspoons grated orange rind
> 1/2 teaspoon orange extract
> 2 1/4 cups cake flour
> 1/2 cup fat-free dry milk powder
> 2 teaspoons baking powder
> 1/2 teaspoon salt
> 1 cup fresh, *or* frozen, cranberries, halved or coarsely chopped
> 4 large egg whites
> Cranberry Glaze (recipe follows)

Per Serving
Calories: 308
% Calories from fat: 10
Fat (gm): 3.7
Saturated fat (gm): 0.5
Cholesterol (mg): 0.8
Sodium (mg): 232
Protein (gm): 4.5
Carbohydrate (gm): 65.6
Exchanges
Milk: 0.0
Vegetable: 0.0
Fruit: 0.0
Bread: 4.0
Meat: 0.0
Fat: 0.5

1. Beat brown sugar, milk, oil, orange rind, and extract in large bowl until smooth. Add combined flour, milk powder, baking powder, and salt, stirring just until combined; mix in cranberries.

2. With clean beaters and bowl, beat egg whites to stiff peaks in large bowl. Fold half the whites into batter; fold remaining egg whites into batter.

3. Pour batter into greased 9-inch springform pan. Bake at 350 degrees until cake springs back when touched, 45 to 50 minutes. Cool on wire rack 10 minutes; remove side of pan and cool completely.

4. Place cake on serving plate. Pour warm Cranberry Glaze over top of cake, spreading evenly. Let stand at least 1 hour before serving.

Cranberry Glaze

  1 cup granulated sugar
  1/4 cup water
  2 cups fresh, *or* frozen, cranberries

1. Heat sugar and water to boiling in medium saucepan, stirring until sugar is dissolved. Boil without stirring until sugar is a deep caramel color, about 10 minutes (watch carefully as caramel can burn easily).
2. Add cranberries to caramel, cooking until berries "pop" and stirring until caramel is smooth, 1 to 2 minutes.

PEACH OATMEAL UPSIDE-DOWN CAKE

The oats lend a chewy texture to this sweet peach dessert.

8 servings

  8 tablespoons margarine, softened, divided
  2 tablespoons light corn syrup
  3-4 tablespoons coarsely chopped pecans
  1 cup packed light brown sugar, divided
  1 can (16 ounces) sliced peaches, drained
  1 egg
  1 teaspoon vanilla
  1 1/4 cups all-purpose flour
  1/3 cup quick-cooking oats
  3/4 teaspoon baking powder
  1/2 teaspoon baking soda
  1/4 teaspoon salt
  1 1/2 teaspoons ground cinnamon
      Generous pinch ground mace
  1/2 cup reduced-fat buttermilk

Per Serving
Calories: 363
% Calories from fat: 34
Fat (gm): 14.2
Saturated fat (gm): 2.8
Cholesterol (mg): 27
Sodium (mg): 374
Protein (gm): 4.6
Carbohydrate (gm): 56.3
Exchanges
Milk: 0.0
Vegetable: 0.0
Fruit: 0.0
Bread: 4.0
Meat: 0.0
Fat: 2.0

1. Heat 2 tablespoons margarine, corn syrup, pecans, and 1/2 cup brown sugar in small saucepan until margarine is melted and mixture is bubbly; pour into 9-inch round cake pan. Slice peaches thinly and arrange over topping in pan.
2. Beat remaining 6 tablespoons margarine and remaining 1/2 cup brown sugar in large bowl until light and fluffy. Beat in egg and vanilla; mix in combined flour, oats, baking powder, baking soda, salt, cinnamon, and mace alternately with buttermilk, beginning and ending with dry ingredients.

3. Pour batter over peaches in pan. Bake at 350 degrees 35 to 40 minutes or until toothpick inserted in center of cake comes out clean. Immediately invert cake onto serving plate.

BING CHERRY UPSIDE-DOWN CAKE

Dark cherries in a rich caramel topping with almonds—you'll never believe it's low in fat. Any canned cherries can be used; use pie cherries if you like a tart flavor.

8 servings

8 tablespoons margarine, softened, divided

2 tablespoons light corn syrup

3-4 tablespoons sliced almonds, toasted

1/2 cup packed light brown sugar

1 can (16 ounces) Bing cherries, drained

2/3 cup granulated sugar

1 egg

1/2 teaspoon almond extract

1 cup all-purpose flour

3/4 teaspoon baking soda

1/4 teaspoon salt

1/2 cup fat-free sour cream

Per Serving
Calories: 372
% Calories from fat: 32
Fat (gm): 13.8
Saturated fat (gm): 2.6
Cholesterol (mg): 27
Sodium (mg): 358
Protein (gm): 4.5
Carbohydrate (gm): 59.5
Exchanges
Milk: 0.0
Vegetable: 0.0
Fruit: 0.0
Bread: 4.0
Meat: 0.0
Fat: 2.0

1. Heat 2 tablespoons margarine, corn syrup, almonds, and brown sugar in small saucepan until margarine is melted and mixture is bubbly. Pour into 9-inch round cake pan. Arrange cherries over topping in pan.

2. Beat remaining 6 tablespoons margarine and granulated sugar in large bowl until light and fluffy. Beat in egg and almond extract; mix in combined flour, baking soda, and salt alternately with sour cream, beginning and ending with dry ingredients.

3. Pour batter over cherries in pan. Bake at 350 degrees 35 to 40 minutes or until toothpick inserted in center of cake comes out clean. Immediately invert cake onto serving plate.

Variation: **Tropical Upside-Down Cake**—Make topping as above in Step 1, substituting 1 cup sliced mango and 1/2 cup pineapple tidbits for the Bing cherries, and sweetened flaked coconut for the almonds. Make and bake cake as above, substituting coconut or rum extract for the almond extract.

ORANGE-PLUM UPSIDE-DOWN CAKE

Great when plums are in season—use your favorite variety, or combine different colors for a "rainbow" effect.

8 servings

8 tablespoons margarine, softened, divided
2 tablespoons light corn syrup
1/2 cup packed light brown sugar
1 1/2 cups thinly sliced pitted plums
2/3 cup granulated sugar
1 egg
1 tablespoon grated orange rind
1/2 teaspoon orange extract
1 cup all-purpose flour
3/4 teaspoon baking soda
1/4 teaspoon salt
1/2 cup reduced-fat buttermilk

Per Serving
Calories: 336
% Calories from fat: 33
Fat (gm): 12.6
Saturated fat (gm): 2.6
Cholesterol (mg): 27
Sodium (mg): 360
Protein (gm): 3.5
Carbohydrate (gm): 54
Exchanges
Milk: 0.0
Vegetable: 0.0
Fruit: 0.0
Bread: 3.5
Meat: 0.0
Fat: 2.0

1. Heat 2 tablespoons margarine, corn syrup, and brown sugar in small saucepan until margarine is melted and mixture is bubbly. Pour into 9-inch round cake pan. Arrange plums over topping in pan.

2. Beat remaining 6 tablespoons margarine and granulated sugar until light and fluffy in large bowl; beat in egg, orange rind, and orange extract. Mix in combined flour, baking soda, and salt alternately with buttermilk, beginning and ending with dry ingredients.

3. Pour batter over plums in pan. Bake at 350 degrees 35 to 40 minutes or until toothpick inserted in center of cake comes out clean. Immediately invert cake onto serving plate.

Variation: **Nectarine-Blueberry Upside-Down Cake**—Make topping as above in Step 1, substituting 1 cup sliced, pitted nectarines and 1/2 cup blueberries for the plums. Make and bake cake as above, substituting reduced-fat custard-style lemon yogurt for the buttermilk, and lemon rind and extract for the orange rind and extract.

BLUEBERRY CORNMEAL UPSIDE-DOWN CAKE

You'll love the taste of cornmeal in this beautiful upside-down cake.

8 servings

8 tablespoons margarine, softened, divided

2 tablespoons light corn syrup

1/2 cup packed light brown sugar

2 cups fresh, *or* frozen, thawed blueberries

2/3 cup granulated sugar

1 egg

1 tablespoon grated lemon rind

1 teaspoon vanilla extract

3/4 cup all-purpose flour

1/2 cup yellow cornmeal

1 teaspoon baking powder

1/2 teaspoon baking soda

1/4 teaspoon salt

1/2 cup reduced-fat buttermilk

Per Serving
Calories: 340
% Calories from fat: 33
Fat (gm): 12.6
Saturated fat (gm): 2.6
Cholesterol (mg): 27
Sodium (mg): 386
Protein (gm): 3.5
Carbohydrate (gm): 55.1
Exchanges
Milk: 0.0
Vegetable: 0.0
Fruit: 0.0
Bread: 3.5
Meat: 0.0
Fat: 2.0

1. Heat 2 tablespoons margarine, corn syrup, and brown sugar in small saucepan until margarine is melted and mixture is bubbly. Pour into 9-inch round cake pan. Arrange blueberries over topping in pan.

2. Beat remaining 6 tablespoons margarine and granulated sugar until light and fluffy in large bowl; beat in egg, lemon rind, and vanilla. Mix in combined flour, cornmeal, baking powder, baking soda, and salt alternately with buttermilk, beginning and ending with dry ingredients.

3. Pour batter over blueberries in pan. Bake at 350 degrees 35 to 40 minutes or until toothpick inserted in center of cake comes out clean. Immediately invert cake onto serving plate.

Variation: **Two-Berry Upside-Down Cake**—Make cake as above, substituting 1 cup each blackberries and raspberries for the blueberries, substituting white cornmeal for the yellow cornmeal, and adding 1/4 cup finely ground toasted hazelnuts and 1/8 teaspoon ground nutmeg to the flour mixture. Bake as above.

APPLE CRANBERRY UPSIDE-DOWN CAKE

Fall apples and glistening cranberries top a moist cake. The cake is leavened only with beaten eggs.

9 servings

2 tablespoons honey

4 tablespoons melted margarine, divided

1/2 cup packed light brown sugar

2 large tart baking apples, peeled, cored, sliced

2/3 cup coarsely chopped cranberries

3 eggs

2 egg whites

1/2 cup granulated sugar

1 teaspoon vanilla

3/4 cup all-purpose flour

1/2 cup graham cracker crumbs

1/4 teaspoon salt

Per Serving
Calories: 267
% Calories from fat: 27
Fat (gm): 8.2
Saturated fat (gm): 1.8
Cholesterol (mg): 70.7
Sodium (mg): 189
Protein (gm): 4.5
Carbohydrate (gm): 45
Exchanges
Milk: 0.0
Vegetable: 0.0
Fruit: 0.0
Bread: 3.0
Meat: 0.0
Fat: 1.0

1. Combine honey and 2 tablespoons melted margarine in 11 x 7-inch baking pan; sprinkle with brown sugar. Arrange apples over topping in pan in rows; sprinkle cranberries between rows of apples.

2. Beat eggs and egg whites in large bowl until foamy; beat in sugar gradually, beating until thick and lemon colored, about 5 minutes. Mix in vanilla; mix in combined flour, graham cracker crumbs, salt, and remaining 2 tablespoons melted margarine.

3. Pour batter over fruit in pan, spreading evenly over fruit. Bake at 350 degrees until cake is golden and springs back when touched, about 30 minutes. Immediately invert cake onto serving plate.

APPLE-DATE UPSIDE-DOWN CAKE

An apple-topped cake fragrant with spices and studded with dates and walnuts.

9 servings

8 tablespoons margarine, softened, divided

2 tablespoons light corn syrup

1/2 cup plus 2/3 cup packed light brown sugar, divided

2 cups thinly sliced, peeled tart apples

1/4 cup light molasses

1 egg

1 1/4 cups all-purpose flour

1 teaspoon ground ginger

1 teaspoon ground cinnamon

1/2 teaspoon ground allspice

1/4 teaspoon ground nutmeg

3/4 teaspoon baking soda

1/4 teaspoon salt

1/2 cup reduced-fat buttermilk

1/3 cup chopped pitted dates

3-4 tablespoons chopped walnuts

Per Serving
Calories: 361
% Calories from fat: 30
Fat (gm): 12.6
Saturated fat (gm): 2.4
Cholesterol (mg): 24
Sodium (mg): 330
Protein (gm): 3.9
Carbohydrate (gm): 60.7
Exchanges
Milk: 0.0
Vegetable: 0.0
Fruit: 0.0
Bread: 2.0
Meat: 0.0
Fat: 1.5

1. Heat 2 tablespoons margarine, corn syrup, and 1/2 cup brown sugar in small saucepan until margarine is melted and mixture is bubbly; pour into 9-inch round cake pan. Arrange apple slices over topping in pan.

2. Beat remaining 6 tablespoons margarine and 2/3 cup brown sugar in large bowl until light and fluffy; beat in molasses and egg. Mix in combined flour, spices, baking soda, and salt alternately with buttermilk, beginning and ending with dry ingredients. Stir in dates and walnuts.

3. Pour batter over apples in pan. Bake at 350 degrees for 35 to 40 minutes or until a toothpick inserted in center of cake comes out clean. Immediately invert cake onto serving plate.

PINEAPPLE UPSIDE-DOWN CAKE

Invert the cake immediately after baking so all the warm caramel topping releases from the pan.

8 to 10 servings

3 tablespoons light corn syrup

5 tablespoons margarine, softened, divided

2/3 cup packed light brown sugar

2-3 tablespoons chopped pecans

1 can (8 ounces) sliced pineapple in its own juice, drained, slices cut in halves

4 maraschino cherries, cut in halves

2/3 cup granulated sugar

1 egg

1/2 teaspoon pineapple extract *or* vanilla

1 1/3 cups all-purpose flour

2 teaspoons baking powder

1/4 teaspoon salt

2/3 cup skim milk

Light whipped topping, as garnish

Per Serving
Calories: 347
% Calories from fat: 23
Fat (gm): 9.1
Saturated fat (gm): 1.7
Cholesterol (mg): 27
Sodium (mg): 264
Protein (gm): 4
Carbohydrate (gm): 63.8
Exchanges
Milk: 0.0
Vegetable: 0.0
Fruit: 0.5
Bread: 3.5
Meat: 0.0
Fat: 1.5

1. Heat corn syrup and 1 tablespoon margarine until melted in small skillet. Stir in brown sugar and pecans and cook over medium heat until mixture is bubbly, 2 to 3 minutes. Pour topping mixture into ungreased 9-inch round cake pan; arrange pineapple slices and cherries on top.

2. Beat remaining 4 tablespoons margarine, granulated sugar, egg, and pineapple extract in medium bowl until smooth. Mix in combined flour, baking powder, and salt alternately with milk, beginning and ending with dry ingredients. Pour batter over topping in pan.

3. Bake at 350 degrees until cake springs back when touched, about 40 minutes. Loosen side of cake with sharp knife and immediately invert onto serving plate. Serve warm with light whipped topping.

PINEAPPLE AND DOUBLE CHEESE UPSIDE-DOWN CAKE

Loaded with taste, you'll love the fruit and cheese flavors in this cake.

10 servings

- 1 can (20 ounces) pineapple slices, undrained, divided
- 1¼ cups packed light brown sugar, divided
- 2-3 tablespoons honey
- ½ package (8-ounce size) fat-free cream cheese, softened
- 2 tablespoons margarine, softened
- 2 eggs
- ¾ cup all-purpose flour
- 1 teaspoon baking powder
- ¼ teaspoon salt
- ½ cup (2 ounces) shredded reduced-fat Colby cheese

Per Serving
Calories: 243
% Calories from fat: 17
Fat (gm): 4.7
Saturated fat (gm): 1.6
Cholesterol (mg): 46.9
Sodium (mg): 217
Protein (gm): 4.9
Carbohydrate (gm): 47
Exchanges
Milk: 0.0
Vegetable: 0.0
Fruit: 0.0
Bread: 3.0
Meat: 0.0
Fat: 0.5

1. Drain pineapple, reserving ¼ cup juice. Process 4 pineapple slices and reserved juice in food processor until smooth.

2. Heat ½ cup brown sugar, honey, and ½ of the pureed pineapple in small saucepan until bubbly; spread in bottom of greased 9-inch round cake pan. Arrange remaining pineapple slices over topping in pan.

3. Beat cream cheese, margarine, and remaining ¾ cup sugar until blended in large bowl; beat in eggs. Mix in combined flour, baking powder, and salt; mix in Colby cheese and remaining pureed pineapple.

4. Pour batter over pineapple in pan. Bake at 350 degrees until toothpick inserted in center comes out clean, about 45 minutes. Immediately invert onto serving plate.

GLAZED ORANGE CHIFFON CAKE

Sometimes called Sunshine Cake, this cake has a perfect, tender texture and a delicate orange flavor.

12 servings

2¹/4 cups cake flour
1²/3 cups granulated sugar
   1 tablespoon baking powder
¹/4 teaspoon salt
³/4 cup orange juice *or* water
¹/3 cup vegetable oil
   5 egg yolks
   1 teaspoon vanilla
   2 teaspoons grated orange rind
   7 egg whites
¹/2 teaspoon cream of tartar
   2 cups powdered sugar
2-3 tablespoons orange juice
     Ground nutmeg, as garnish

Per Serving
Calories: 358
% Calories from fat: 21
Fat (gm): 8.4
Saturated fat (gm): 1.5
Cholesterol (mg): 88.8
Sodium (mg): 163
Protein (gm): 5
Carbohydrate (gm): 66.3
Exchanges
Milk: 0.0
Vegetable: 0.0
Fruit: 0.0
Bread: 4.0
Meat: 0.0
Fat: 1.5

1. Combine flour, granulated sugar, baking powder, and salt in large mixing bowl. Mix orange juice, oil, egg yolks, vanilla, and orange rind in bowl; add to flour mixture and beat at medium speed until smooth.

2. With clean beaters and in separate large bowl, beat egg whites until foamy. Add cream of tartar and beat to very stiff but not dry peaks. Stir about ¹/4 of egg whites into cake batter; fold batter into remaining egg whites. Pour batter into ungreased 12-cup tube pan.

3. Bake at 325 degrees until cake is golden and springs back when touched (cracks in top of cake will appear dry), 55 to 60 minutes. Invert cake pan on a funnel or bottle until cake is completely cool. Loosen side of cake and invert onto serving plate.

4. Mix powdered sugar with enough orange juice to make glaze consistency. Spoon glaze over top of cool cake; sprinkle with nutmeg.

CLASSIC SPONGE CAKE

This luscious, very low-fat cake can be adapted to make many desserts—use your imagination and combine different fillings and frostings to create your own masterpiece! Simply sprinkle with powdered sugar and serve with a medley of berries, or frost with Mocha Mallow Frosting (see p. 17), or drizzle with Rum Soaking Syrup and spread with Chocolate Glaze (see pp. 107, 76).

12 servings

3 egg yolks
1 cup sugar, divided
2 teaspoons vanilla
1/4 cup water
1 cup cake flour
1 teaspoon baking powder
1/4 teaspoon salt
5 egg whites
1/4 teaspoon cream of tartar

Per Serving
Calories: 122
% Calories from fat: 10
Fat (gm): 1.4
Saturated fat (gm): 0.4
Cholesterol (mg): 53.2
Sodium (mg): 114
Protein (gm): 2.9
Carbohydrate (gm): 24.3
Exchanges
Milk: 0.0
Vegetable: 0.0
Fruit: 0.0
Bread: 1.5
Meat: 0.0
Fat: 0.0

1. Beat egg yolks in large mixing bowl, gradually adding 3/4 cup sugar; beat at high speed until yolks are thick and lemon colored, about 5 minutes. Mix in vanilla and water; add combined flour, baking powder, and salt, beating on low speed just until blended.

2. With clean beaters and in separate large bowl, beat egg whites and cream of tartar to soft peaks. Beat to stiff peaks, gradually adding remaining 1/4 cup sugar. Stir 1/4 of the egg whites into batter; fold batter into remaining whites.

3. Pour batter into ungreased 12-cup tube pan. Bake at 350 degrees 35 minutes or until cake springs back when touched lightly. Invert pan onto funnel and cool to room temperature. Loosen side of cake with small metal spatula and remove from pan.

Tip: Cake can be baked in an ungreased 10-inch springform pan. Invert on wire rack or balance on 4 cans or custard cups to cool.

ORANGE CARAMEL FROSTED SPONGE CAKE

A special occasion cake with a unique combination of flavors!

12 servings

Classic Sponge Cake (see p. 100)
1/4 cup orange juice
Orange Caramel Syrup (recipe follows)
Orange Caramel Frosting (recipe follows)

Per Serving
Calories: 363
% Calories from fat: 18
Fat (gm): 7.3
Saturated fat (gm): 4.6
Cholesterol (mg): 71
Sodium (mg): 296
Protein (gm): 6.6
Carbohydrate (gm): 67.2
Exchanges
Milk: 0.0
Vegetable: 0.0
Fruit: 0.0
Bread: 4.5
Meat: 0.0
Fat: 1.0

1. Make Classic Sponge Cake as directed, substituting 1/4 cup orange juice for water in recipe. Bake in ungreased 10-inch springform pan and cool.

2. Slice cake horizontally into 2 layers; brush or spoon Orange Caramel Syrup onto cut sides of cake. Place bottom layer on serving plate; spread with 1/2 cup Orange Caramel Frosting. Top with second layer and frost cake.

Orange Caramel Syrup

makes about 1 1/2 cups

1 1/4 cups sugar
1/2 cup water
2 tablespoons light corn syrup
3/4 cup orange juice
1 tablespoon grated orange rind

1. Heat sugar, water, and corn syrup to boiling in large saucepan, stirring to dissolve sugar; boil without stirring until mixture turns a medium caramel color (watch carefully as mixture can burn easily).

2. Remove from heat and stir in orange juice and rind (mixture will splatter and bubble). Stir over medium heat until caramel dissolves. Pour 1/2 cup syrup into small bowl and reserve for frosting; cool.

Orange Caramel Frosting

makes about 2¹/₂ cups

2 packages (8 ounces each) reduced-fat
  cream cheese, softened
¹/₂ cup reserved Orange Caramel Syrup
1-1¹/₂ cups powdered sugar

1. Beat cream cheese until fluffy in large bowl; gradually beat in reserved Orange Caramel Syrup. Beat in enough powdered sugar for desired spreading consistency.

CITRUS CLOUD CAKE

Tender sponge cake, filled with creamy custard and frosted with fluffy Meringue Frosting.

12 servings

Classic Sponge Cake (see p. 100)
1 tablespoon finely grated orange rind
  Orange Custard Filling (recipe follows)
  Meringue Frosting (see p. 107)

Per Serving
Calories: 297
% Calories from fat: 17
Fat (gm): 5.7
Saturated fat (gm): 2.9
Cholesterol (mg): 116
Sodium (mg): 226
Protein (gm): 6.7
Carbohydrate (gm): 55
Exchanges
Milk: 0.0
Vegetable: 0.0
Fruit: 0.0
Bread: 3.5
Meat: 0.0
Fat: 1.0

1. Make Classic Sponge Cake, adding orange rind with dry ingredients. Bake in ungreased 10-inch springform pan and cool.

2. Slice cake horizontally into 3 layers. Place 1 cake layer on serving plate; spread with half the Orange Custard Filling. Repeat with second layer; place remaining cake layer on top. Frost cake with Meringue Frosting.

Orange Custard Filling

- ¹/₂ cup sugar
- 3 tablespoons cornstarch
- 3 egg yolks
- 1 tablespoon grated orange rind
- 1¹/₂ cups orange juice
- ¹/₄ cup fat-free milk
- 1 package (8 ounces) reduced-fat cream cheese, softened

1. Combine sugar and cornstarch in medium saucepan; mix in egg yolks and orange rind. Whisk in orange juice and milk gradually, blending well. Cook over medium heat, whisking constantly, until mixture boils and thickens.

2. Pour custard into bowl; cover with plastic wrap, pressing onto surface of custard. Refrigerate until cold. Beat cream cheese until smooth and fluffy; gradually beat in cold custard.

LEMON CUSTARD SPONGE CAKE

A beautiful cake that will make any special occasion one to remember.

12 servings

- 3 egg yolks
- ³/₄ cup sugar, divided
- 1 teaspoon vanilla
- 3 egg whites
- ¹/₈ teaspoon cream of tartar
- ¹/₃ cup all-purpose flour
- ¹/₃ cup cornstarch
- ¹/₈ teaspoon salt
- Lemon Custard (recipe follows)
- 2¹/₂ cups light whipped topping, divided
- ¹/₂ cup raspberries
- Lemon rind twists, as garnish
- Mint sprigs, as garnish

Per Serving
Calories: 196
% Calories from fat: 25
Fat (gm): 5.4
Saturated fat (gm): 2.6
Cholesterol (mg): 71.5
Sodium (mg): 126
Protein (gm): 3.2
Carbohydrate (gm): 33
Exchanges
Milk: 0.0
Vegetable: 0.0
Fruit: 0.0
Bread: 2.0
Meat: 0.0
Fat: 1.0

1. Grease 9-inch round cake pan; line with parchment paper and grease and flour.

2. Beat egg yolks and $^1/_2$ cup sugar in small bowl until thick and lemon colored, 3 to 5 minutes; mix in vanilla.

3. With clean, medium bowl and beaters, beat egg whites and cream of tartar to soft peaks; beat to stiff peaks, adding remaining $^1/_4$ cup sugar gradually. Fold egg yolk mixture into egg whites. Gently fold in combined flour, cornstarch, and salt.

4. Spread batter in prepared pan. Bake at 350 degrees until toothpick inserted in center of cake comes out clean, about 30 minutes. Cool cake in pan 10 minutes; remove from pan and cool completely. Remove parchment.

5. Cut cake horizontally in half. Place bottom of cake on serving plate. Spread 1 cup Lemon Custard on cake and top with second layer. Spread remaining 1 cup Lemon Custard on top of cake. Spread 2 cups whipped topping on side of cake. Place remaining $^1/_2$ cup whipped topping in pastry bag with star tip and pipe rosettes around top edge of cake. Garnish rosettes with raspberries, lemon rind twists, and mint sprigs. Refrigerate until serving time.

Lemon Custard

makes about 2 cups

   $^1/_3$ cup sugar
   $^1/_4$ cup cornstarch
   $^1/_4$ teaspoon salt
   $1^1/_3$ cups fat-free milk
     1 egg yolk
     2 tablespoons margarine
     2 teaspoons grated lemon rind
   $^1/_3$ cup lemon juice

1. Combine sugar, cornstarch, and salt in medium saucepan; whisk in milk. Heat to boiling over medium-high heat, whisking constantly; boil, whisking constantly, until thickened, about 1 minute.

2. Whisk about $^1/_2$ cup milk mixture into egg yolk; whisk yolk mixture back into milk mixture. Cook over low heat, whisking constantly, 1 to 2 minutes. Remove from heat; stir in margarine, lemon rind, and lemon juice. Cool; refrigerate until chilled.

Variation: **Sponge Cake with Rosemary Syrup and Blueberries—** Make cake as above; do not make Lemon Custard. Cool uncut cake on wire rack 20 minutes; remove from pan and place on serving plate. To make **Rosemary Syrup,** heat ³/₄ cup sugar, ³/₄ cup water, 2 tablespoons crushed dried rosemary leaves, and 1 tablespoon lemon juice to boiling in small saucepan. Reduce heat and simmer, uncovered, 10 minutes. Pierce top of cake with tines of fork; drizzle ¹/₂ cup warm syrup over warm cake. Mix remaining syrup with 1¹/₂ quarts blueberries; serve over cake slices.

FRESH ORANGE SPONGE CAKE

A fresh orange is finely chopped and incorporated into the cake batter.

16 servings

1 medium orange, unpeeled, cut into wedges and seeded
2 cups sugar, divided
1 cup reduced-fat buttermilk
2 egg yolks
¹/₄ cup vegetable oil
1 teaspoon vanilla
2³/₄ cups cake flour
1 teaspoon baking powder
¹/₂ teaspoon baking soda
¹/₂ teaspoon salt
4 egg whites
¹/₄ teaspoon cream of tartar
Honey Orange Glaze (recipe follows)
Orange slices, as garnish

Per Serving
Calories: 271
% Calories from fat: 14
Fat (gm): 4.4
Saturated fat (gm): 0.7
Cholesterol (mg): 27
Sodium (mg): 175
Protein (gm): 3.5
Carbohydrate (gm): 56
Exchanges
Milk: 0.0
Vegetable: 0.0
Fruit: 0.0
Bread: 3.5
Meat: 0.0
Fat: 0.5

1. Process orange and rind in food processor until finely chopped; add 1¹/₂ cups sugar, buttermilk, egg yolks, oil, and vanilla and process until smooth. Transfer mixture to large bowl; fold in half the combined flour, baking powder, baking soda, and salt. Fold in remaining flour mixture.

2. Beat egg whites and cream of tartar to soft peaks in large bowl; beat to stiff peaks, adding remaining ¹/₂ cup sugar gradually. Stir ¹/₄ of the egg whites into cake batter; fold cake batter into remaining egg whites.

3. Pour batter into greased and floured 12-cup tube pan. Bake at 350 degrees until toothpick inserted in center comes out clean, about 60 minutes. Cool cake in pan on wire rack 10 minutes; remove from pan and cool completely. Pierce top of cake with long-tined fork and drizzle with Honey Orange Glaze. Garnish each slice with an orange slice.

Honey Orange Glaze

makes about 1 1/2 cups

3/4 cup honey
3/4 cup orange juice

1. Heat honey and orange juice in small saucepan until hot; cool slightly.

BLACK WALNUT SPONGE CAKE

You'll savor the distinctive flavor of black walnuts in this light sponge cake. English walnuts, or any other nut, may be substituted, if desired.

10 servings

1/2 cup black walnuts
1 cup cake flour
1 teaspoon baking powder
1/8 teaspoon ground nutmeg
1/8 teaspoon salt
2 large eggs
2/3 cup sugar, divided
1 teaspoon vanilla
2 egg whites
1/8 teaspoon cream of tartar
Rum Soaking Syrup (recipe follows)
Meringue Frosting (recipe follows)

Per Serving
Calories: 285
% Calories from fat: 14
Fat (gm): 4.6
Saturated fat (gm): 0.6
Cholesterol (mg): 42
Sodium (mg): 124
Protein (gm): 5.4
Carbohydrate (gm): 56.3
Exchanges
Milk: 0.0
Vegetable: 0.0
Fruit: 0.0
Bread: 3.5
Meat: 0.0
Fat: 0.5

1. Combine walnuts, flour, baking powder, nutmeg, and salt in food processor; process until the nuts are finely ground.

2. Beat eggs in large mixing bowl, gradually adding 1/3 cup sugar, and beating until thick and lemon colored, about 5 minutes; add vanilla. In a clean, medium bowl with clean beaters, beat egg whites and cream of tartar to soft peaks; beat to stiff peaks, gradually adding remaining 1/3 cup sugar.

3. Whisk 1/4 of the egg whites into the egg mixture. Fold in half the flour mixture, then the remaining whites, followed by the remaining flour mixture.

4. Gently spoon batter into greased and floured 9-inch springform pan. Bake at 375 degrees until cake springs back when lightly touched, 40 to 45 minutes. Cool in pan on wire rack for 10 minutes; remove side of pan and cool completely.

5. Cut cake horizontally in half. Place bottom half on serving plate; brush with half the Rum Soaking Syrup and spread with ³/₄ cup Meringue Frosting. Top with remaining cake layer; brush with remaining Rum Soaking Syrup. Frost top and side of cake with remaining Meringue Frosting.

Rum Soaking Syrup

makes about 1 cup

> ¹/₂ cup water
> ³/₄ cup sugar
> 1 tablespoon dark rum *or* ¹/₂ teaspoon rum
>   extract

1. Heat water and sugar to boiling in medium saucepan; boil, stirring constantly, until sugar is dissolved. Add rum.

Meringue Frosting

makes about 4 cups

> ³/₄ cup sugar
> ¹/₄ cup water
> 2 tablespoons light corn syrup
> 3 egg whites
> ¹/₂ teaspoon cream of tartar

1. Heat sugar, water, and corn syrup to boiling in small saucepan, stirring to dissolve syrup. Boil, covered, 2 minutes. Uncover and boil until syrup reaches 240 degrees on a candy thermometer. Remove pan from heat.

2. While sugar is boiling, beat egg whites and cream of tartar to soft peaks in large bowl. When syrup reaches 240 degrees, immediately pour it, in steady stream, into egg whites, beating constantly at high speed. Continue beating until mixture is cooled to room temperature, about 5 minutes.

Variation: **Mascarpone Walnut Torte**—Make cake as above, substituting English walnuts for the black walnuts; omit Rum Soaking Syrup and Meringue Frosting. Make Mock Mascarpone (see p. 161), beating in 3 to 4 tablespoons sugar to taste. Split cake as above; spread half the Mock Mascarpone on each layer. Stack layers on serving plate; sprinkle with ¹/₃ cup chopped toasted walnuts.

CARAMEL APPLE BLACK WALNUT SPONGE CAKE

Use a favorite tart baking apple to team with the rich caramel and black walnut flavors.

12 servings

²/₃ cup sugar
3 tablespoons water
4 cups thinly sliced peeled apples
Black Walnut Sponge Cake (see p. 106)

Per Serving
Calories: 302
% Calories from fat: 12
Fat (gm): 4.0
Saturated fat (gm): 0.5
Cholesterol (mg): 35.3
Sodium (mg): 103
Protein (gm): 4.6
Carbohydrate (gm): 63.7
Exchanges
Milk: 0.0
Vegetable: 0.0
Fruit: 0.0
Bread: 4.0
Meat: 0.0
Fat: 0.5

1. Wrap bottom of 9-inch springform pan with aluminum foil so that it will not leak. Grease and flour pan.

2. Heat sugar and water to boiling in small saucepan, stirring to dissolve sugar; boil without stirring until mixture is a medium caramel color. Pour into prepared pan. Arrange apples over caramel.

3. Pour cake batter into pan; bake at 375 degrees 40 to 45 minutes or until cake springs back when touched. Loosen side of cake from pan and invert immediately onto serving plate.

MANGO BABA CAKE

Soaked with a sugar syrup like baba au rhum, this luscious cake is topped with mangoes and whipped topping. If fresh mangoes are not available, the jarred can be used.

10 to 12 servings

Classic Sponge Cake (see p. 100)
Sherry Sugar Syrup (recipe follows)
Mango Filling (recipe follows)
3/4 cup light whipped topping
2-4 tablespoons sliced toasted almonds

Per Serving
Calories: 276
% Calories from fat: 11
Fat (gm): 3.4
Saturated fat (gm): 1.2
Cholesterol (mg): 64
Sodium (mg): 139
Protein (gm): 4.3
Carbohydrate (gm): 57
Exchanges
Milk: 0.0
Vegetable: 0.0
Fruit: 1.0
Bread: 3.0
Meat: 0.0
Fat: 0.0

1. Make Classic Sponge Cake, baking in a 9-inch springform pan; cool. Slice cake horizontally into 2 layers.

2. Brush or drizzle warm Sherry Sugar Syrup over cut sides of each layer. Place 1 cake layer, cut side up, on serving plate; spoon half of Mango Filling evenly over cake. Top with second cake layer, cut side up, and spoon remaining Mango Filling over. Spoon dollops of whipped topping on cake and sprinkle with almonds.

Sherry Sugar Syrup

makes about 1 cup

2/3 cup water
1/3 cup sugar
1/4 cup dry sherry *or* 1/4 cup water and 1/2
teaspoon sherry extract

1. Heat water, sugar, and dry sherry to boiling in small saucepan, stirring to dissolve sugar. Cool slightly.

Mango Filling

makes about 3 cups

    3 cups cubed mangoes (4-5 large)
1/4-1/3 cup sugar
  1-2 tablespoons fresh lime juice
  1/2 teaspoon almond extract, optional

1. Mash mangoes coarsely with fork. Mix 1/4 cup sugar into fruit and let stand 30 minutes.

2. Heat mangoes to boiling in small saucepan; reduce heat and simmer until mixture is thick, about 5 minutes, stirring often. Stir in lime juice, almond extract, and remaining sugar, if needed for sweetness. Cool.

COCONUT PECAN CAKE WITH SEAFOAM FROSTING

A spectacular 3-layer sponge cake that will make any occasion all the more special.

16 servings

    2 cups sugar, divided
  1/2 cup margarine, softened
    2 teaspoons butter and nut extract
    3 egg yolks
    2 cups all-purpose flour
    1 teaspoon baking soda
  1/4 teaspoon salt
    1 cup reduced-fat buttermilk
  1/3 cup plus 2 tablespoons chopped pecans
  1/3 cup plus 2 tablespoons toasted coconut
    6 egg whites
  1/2 teaspoon cream of tartar
      Seafoam Frosting (recipe follows)

Per Serving
Calories: 362
% Calories from fat: 24
Fat (gm): 9.9
Saturated fat (gm): 2.3
Cholesterol (mg): 40.5
Sodium (mg): 280
Protein (gm): 4.9
Carbohydrate (gm): 64.9
Exchanges
Milk: 0.0
Vegetable: 0.0
Fruit: 0.0
Bread: 4.0
Meat: 0.0
Fat: 2.0

1. Grease bottoms of three 9-inch cake pans; line with parchment and grease lightly.

2. Beat 1³/₄ cups sugar, margarine, and butter and nut extract until well blended in large bowl. Beat in egg yolks 1 at a time, beating well after each addition. Mix in combined flour, baking soda, and salt alternately with buttermilk, beginning and ending with dry ingredients. Mix in ¹/₃ cup each pecans and coconut.

3. With clean beaters in large, clean bowl, beat egg whites and cream of tartar to soft peaks; beat to stiff peaks, beating in remaining ¹/₄ cup sugar gradually. Stir ¹/₄ of the egg whites into cake batter; fold cake batter into remaining egg whites.

4. Spread batter into prepared cake pans. Bake at 350 degrees until cakes spring back when touched, 20 to 25 minutes. Cool cakes in pans on wire rack 10 minutes; loosen cakes with metal spatula and remove from pans. Remove parchment from cakes; cool completely.

5. Place 1 cake layer on serving plate; frost with ¹/₂ cup Seafoam Frosting; repeat with remaining 2 layers and frost cake. Sprinkle top of cake with remaining 2 tablespoons coconut and pecans.

Seafoam Frosting

makes about 3¹/₂ cups

> 1¹/₂ cups packed light brown sugar
> ¹/₃ cup light corn syrup
> 2 egg whites
> ¹/₄ teaspoon cream of tartar
> ¹/₄ teaspoon salt
> ¹/₄ cup water
> 2 teaspoons vanilla

1. Combine all ingredients except vanilla in top of double boiler. Beat over simmering water until mixture stands in stiff peaks, about 5 minutes. Remove from heat; add vanilla, beating until mixture is very thick, about 5 minutes. Use immediately.

BASIC ANGEL FOOD CAKE

A versatile cake with virtually no fat that can be served quite elegantly alone or topped with fresh fruit, frozen yogurt, or a sauce such as Sweet Lemon Sauce (see p. 651).

12 to 16 servings

12 egg whites
³/4 teaspoon cream of tartar
1 teaspoon lemon juice
1 teaspoon vanilla
1¹/2 cups sugar, divided
1 cup cake flour
¹/2 teaspoon salt
    Vanilla Glaze (see p. 350)

Per Serving
Calories: 189
% Calories from fat: 0
Fat (gm): 0.1
Saturated fat (gm): 0
Cholesterol (mg): 0
Sodium (mg): 153
Protein (gm): 4.3
Carbohydrate (gm): 42.8
Exchanges
Milk: 0.0
Vegetable: 0.0
Fruit: 0.0
Bread: 2.5
Meat: 0.0
Fat: 0.0

1. Beat egg whites and cream of tartar to soft peaks in large bowl. Beat in lemon juice and vanilla; beat just to stiff peaks, adding ¹/2 cup sugar gradually (do not overbeat). Sprinkle ¹/2 cup sugar over egg whites and fold in. Combine remaining ¹/2 cup sugar, flour, and salt; sift half the flour mixture over egg whites and fold in. Repeat with remaining flour mixture.

2. Pour batter into ungreased 12-cup tube pan. Bake until cake is golden and cracks look dry, about 40 minutes. Invert pan on funnel and cool completely. Loosen side of cake from pan with metal spatula and invert onto serving plate. Drizzle with Vanilla Glaze.

Variations: **Peppermint Angel Food Cake**—Make cake as above, folding in ¹/3 cup crushed peppermint candy with last addition of flour. Frost with Marshmallow Frosting (see p. 18), adding ¹/2 teaspoon peppermint extract to the icing and tinting with a few drops red food color. Sprinkle top and side of cake with ¹/2 cup crushed peppermint candy.

Spiced Angel Food Cake—Make cake as above, folding in 1¹/2 teaspoons ground cinnamon, ¹/2 teaspoon ground allspice, and ¹/4 teaspoon ground nutmeg. Frost with Seafoam Frosting (see p. 111) and serve with sliced peaches.

CITRUS POPPY SEED ANGEL FOOD CAKE

My all-time favorite angel food cake—tall, tender, and bursting with sweet citrus flavor!

16 servings

13 egg whites, room temperature
1 teaspoon cream of tartar
2 teaspoons lemon juice
1¹/₂ cups sugar, divided
1 cup cake flour
¹/₂ teaspoon salt
2 tablespoons finely grated orange rind
1 tablespoon finely grated lemon rind
2 tablespoons poppy seeds
Citrus Glaze (see p. 63)

Per Serving
Calories: 149
% Calories from fat: 3
Fat (gm): 0.5
Saturated fat (gm): 0.1
Cholesterol (mg): 0
Sodium (mg): 118
Protein (gm): 3.6
Carbohydrate (gm): 32.8
Exchanges
Milk: 0.0
Vegetable: 0.0
Fruit: 0.0
Bread: 2.0
Meat: 0.0
Fat: 0.0

1. Beat egg whites and cream of tartar to soft peaks in large bowl. Beat in lemon juice; beat just to stiff peaks, adding ¹/₂ cup sugar gradually (do not overbeat). Sprinkle ¹/₂ cup sugar over egg whites and fold in. Combine remaining ¹/₂ cup sugar, flour, and salt; sift half the flour mixture over egg whites and fold in. Repeat with remaining flour mixture. Fold in citrus rinds and poppy seeds.

2. Pour batter into ungreased 12-cup tube pan. Bake until cake is golden and cracks look dry, about 40 minutes. Invert pan on funnel and cool completely. Loosen side of cake from pan with metal spatula and invert onto serving plate. Drizzle with Citrus Glaze.

CHOCOLATE ANGEL FOOD CAKE

Enjoy the extra chocolatey flavor and moist texture of this exceptional cake that contains no fat.

10 servings

8 egg whites
$^1/_2$ teaspoon cream of tartar
1 teaspoon vanilla
$1^1/_4$ cups sugar, divided
$^1/_3$ cup unsweetened cocoa
$^1/_4$ cup cake flour
$^1/_4$ teaspoon salt
Chocolate Glaze (see p. 76)

Per Serving
Calories: 175
% Calories from fat: 0
Fat (gm): 0
Saturated fat (gm): 0
Cholesterol (mg): 0.2
Sodium (mg): 110
Protein (gm): 3.5
Carbohydrate (gm): 40.6
Exchanges
Milk: 0.0
Vegetable: 0.0
Fruit: 0.0
Bread: 2.5
Meat: 0.0
Fat: 0.0

1. Beat egg whites and cream of tartar until foamy in large bowl; beat to soft peaks. Beat in vanilla; beat just to stiff peaks, gradually beating in $^1/_4$ cup sugar (do not overbeat). Sprinkle $^1/_2$ cup sugar over egg whites and fold in. Combine remaining $^1/_2$ cup sugar, cocoa, flour, and salt; sift half the flour mixture over egg whites and fold in. Repeat with remaining flour mixture.

2. Spread mixture in ungreased 12-cup tube pan. Bake at 350 degrees until cake is golden and cracks are dry, 25 to 30 minutes. Invert pan on funnel and cool completely. Loosen side of cake from pan with metal spatula and invert onto serving plate. Drizzle with Chocolate Glaze.

Variation: **Mocha Angel Food Cake**—Make cake as above, adding 1 ounce grated bittersweet chocolate and 1 to 2 tablespoons instant espresso powder to the last addition of flour. Frost with Mocha Mallow Frosting; garnish with chocolate-covered coffee beans, chocolate shavings, or miniature chocolate morsels.

ALMOND ANGEL FOOD CAKE

Delicate in flavor and texture, and drizzled with a light almond glaze.

10 servings

8 egg whites
1/2 teaspoon cream of tartar
1/4 teaspoon almond extract
1 1/4 cups sugar, divided
1 cup cake flour
1/4 teaspoon salt
1/3 cup finely chopped toasted almonds
Almond Glaze (recipe follows)
2-3 tablespoons sliced toasted almonds

Per Serving
Calories: 235
% Calories from fat: 13
Fat (gm): 3.4
Saturated fat (gm): 0.3
Cholesterol (mg): 0.1
Sodium (mg): 105
Protein (gm): 5
Carbohydrate (gm): 47.2
Exchanges
Milk: 0.0
Vegetable: 0.0
Fruit: 0.0
Bread: 3.0
Meat: 0.0
Fat: 0.5

1. Beat egg whites and cream of tartar until foamy in large bowl; beat to soft peaks. Beat in almond extract; beat just to stiff peaks, gradually beating in 1/4 cup sugar (do not overbeat). Sprinkle 1/2 cup sugar over egg whites and fold in. Combine remaining 1/2 cup sugar, flour, and salt; sift half the flour mixture over egg whites and fold in. Repeat with remaining flour mixture. Fold in chopped almonds.

2. Spread mixture in ungreased 12-cup tube pan. Bake at 350 degrees until cake is golden and cracks are dry, 25 to 30 minutes. Invert pan on funnel and cool completely. Loosen side of cake from pan with metal spatula and invert onto serving plate. Drizzle with Almond Glaze; sprinkle with sliced almonds.

Almond Glaze

makes about 1/2 cup

1 cup powdered sugar
1/4-1/2 teaspoon almond extract
2-3 tablespoons fat-free milk

1. Mix powdered sugar, almond extract, and enough milk to make glaze consistency.

STRAWBERRY MERINGUE ANGEL FOOD CAKE

A new guise for baked Alaska—ice cream fills the cake in this meringue-glossed masterpiece. Cake removed from center can be use to make trifle, or can be toasted and processed in a food processor to make crumbs for an ice cream topping.

14 servings

Basic Angel Food Cake (see p. 112)
1-1¹/₂ quarts reduced-fat strawberry ice cream
   or frozen yogurt, slightly softened
4 egg whites
¹/₄ teaspoon cream of tartar
¹/₂ cup sugar
¹/₂ teaspoon vanilla
   Whole strawberries, as garnish
   Glazed Strawberry Sauce (recipe
   follows)

Per Serving
Calories: 354
% Calories from fat: 5
Fat (gm): 1.9
Saturated fat (gm): 1
Cholesterol (mg): 5.8
Sodium (mg): 173
Protein (gm): 6.9
Carbohydrate (gm): 76.3
Exchanges
Milk: 0.0
Vegetable: 0.0
Fruit: 0.0
Bread: 5.0
Meat: 0.0
Fat: 0.0

1. Place cake upside down on plate. Make a "tunnel" in the center of the cake, cutting with a serrated knife and leaving 1 inch of cake on the inner and outer edges; do not cut through base of cake. Pull center of cake out, using fingers and small knife, leaving about 2 inches of cake at the base. Fill cake with ice cream; wrap and freeze until firm, 8 hours or overnight.

2. Beat egg whites and cream of tartar to soft peaks in large bowl; beat to stiff peaks, adding sugar gradually. Beat in vanilla.

3. Invert cake onto ovenproof plate; spread top and side of cake with meringue, sealing to plate. Bake at 450 degrees until meringue is golden, 3 to 4 minutes. Garnish with strawberries. Serve immediately with Glazed Strawberry Sauce.

Glazed Strawberry Sauce

makes about 3¹/₂ cups

3 cups sliced strawberries
¹/₃ cup currant jelly, melted
¹/₃ cup strawberry, *or* orange, liqueur

1. Mix all ingredients.

BEST HOLIDAY FRUITCAKE

Chock-full of dried and candied fruits and nuts, this cake is steeped in brandy for extra goodness.

24 servings

2 cups all-purpose flour
1 teaspoon baking powder
$^1/_2$ teaspoon salt
1 teaspoon ground cinnamon
1 teaspoon ground allspice
$^1/_2$ teaspoon ground mace
$^1/_2$ teaspoon ground nutmeg
$^1/_2$ cup margarine, softened
$^3/_4$ cup packed light brown sugar
$^1/_2$ cup brandy *or* apricot nectar
$^1/_4$ cup honey
$^1/_4$ cup apricot nectar *or* orange juice
3 eggs
$1^3/_4$ cups golden raisins
$^3/_4$ cup chopped apricots
$^3/_4$ cup chopped pitted dates
1 cup glacéed orange peel
$^1/_2$ cup halved glacéed cherries
$^1/_2$ cup glacéed pineapple chunks
$^3/_4$ cup walnut pieces

Per Serving
Calories: 258
% Calories from fat: 23
Fat (gm): 6.9
Saturated fat (gm): 1.2
Cholesterol (mg): 26.5
Sodium (mg): 131
Protein (gm): 3.6
Carbohydrate (gm): 45.4
Exchanges
Milk: 0.0
Vegetable: 0.0
Fruit: 0.0
Bread: 3.0
Meat: 0.0
Fat: 1.0

1. Combine all ingredients, except fruit and walnuts, in large bowl; mix on low speed until blended. Beat on high speed 3 minutes. Mix in fruits and nuts.

2. Spread batter evenly in greased 12-cup tube pan with removable bottom. Bake at 275 degrees until toothpick inserted in center comes out clean, $2^1/_2$ to 3 hours. Cover top of cake with aluminum foil during last hour of baking, if necessary to prevent overbrowning. Cool in pan on wire rack 10 minutes; remove from pan and cool.

3. Wrap cake in cheesecloth dampened with brandy; wrap in plastic bag or aluminum foil. Refrigerate at least 1 month and up to 1 year, dampening cheesecloth with brandy occasionally.

TROPICAL FRUITCAKE

Make the fruitcake several months in advance, as flavors mellow in aging.

14 servings

3/4 cup raisins

3/4 cup glacéed pineapple

1/2 cup chopped dates

1/2 cup coarsely chopped candied mango *or* papaya

2/3 cup light rum, divided

2/3 cup all-purpose flour

1/2 cup packed light brown sugar

1/2 teaspoon baking powder

1/2 teaspoon ground cinnamon

1/2 teaspoon ground mace

1/2 teaspoon ground ginger

1/2 teaspoon ground allspice

1/4 teaspoon salt

1/4 cup margarine, softened

2 eggs

1/2 cup flaked coconut

1/2 cup chopped macadamia nuts

Per Serving
Calories: 248
% Calories from fat: 30
Fat (gm): 8.5
Saturated fat (gm): 2.2
Cholesterol (mg): 30.2
Sodium (mg): 119
Protein (gm): 2.5
Carbohydrate (gm): 36.7
Exchanges
Milk: 0.0
Vegetable: 0.0
Fruit: 0.0
Bread: 2.5
Meat: 0.0
Fat: 1.5

1. Combine fruit and 1/3 cup rum in large bowl; let stand 15 minutes.

2. Combine remaining rum and ingredients, except coconut and macadamia nuts, in large bowl and mix at low speed until blended. Beat at high speed 3 minutes; mix in fruit mixture, coconut, and macadamia nuts.

3. Spread batter in greased and floured 9 x 5-inch loaf pan. Bake at 275 degrees until toothpick inserted in center comes out clean, 2 to 2 1/2 hours. Cover cake during last hour of baking if becoming too brown. Cool on wire rack.

4. Wrap cake in cheesecloth dampened with rum; wrap in plastic bag or aluminum foil. Refrigerate at least 1 month and up to 1 year, dampening cheesecloth with rum occasionally.

PETITE FRUITCAKES

Bake these bite-sized morsels up to 2 weeks in advance.

36 servings (2 each)

    3 cups halved red and green glacéed
      cherries
    3 cups halved red and green glacéed
      pineapple wedges
1 1/2 cups glacéed citron, *or* orange peel
    2 cups chopped pecans
  3/4 cup dry sherry
    1 cup margarine, softened
    1 cup packed light brown sugar
    5 eggs
    2 cups all-purpose flour
    1 teaspoon baking powder
  1/2 teaspoon salt

Per Serving
Calories: 282
% Calories from fat: 32
Fat (gm): 10.2
Saturated fat (gm): 1.6
Cholesterol (mg): 29.4
Sodium (mg): 148
Protein (gm): 2.3
Carbohydrate (gm): 45.6
Exchanges
Milk: 0.0
Vegetable: 0.0
Fruit: 0.0
Bread: 3.0
Meat: 0.0
Fat: 1.5

1. Combine glacéed fruit, pecans, and sherry in bowl; let stand 15 minutes.

2. Combine remaining ingredients in large bowl; beat on low speed until blended. Beat at high speed 2 minutes. Stir in fruit mixture.

3. Spoon mixture into greased miniature muffin tins. Bake at 275 degrees until wooden pick inserted in center comes out clean, about 45 minutes. Cool on wire rack.

4. Line airtight container with cheesecloth soaked in dry sherry; arrange fruitcakes in container and cover with cheesecloth. Refrigerate up to 2 months.

BRANDIED CHOCOLATE FRUITCAKE

Chocolate- or coffee-flavored liqueur can be substituted for the brandy.

24 servings

1 1/2 cups chopped dried apricots
1 1/2 cups chopped dates
1 cup glacéed orange peel
1/2 cup raisins
1 cup chopped walnuts
1/2 cup brandy
1 cup margarine, softened
1 cup packed light brown sugar
1/2 cup molasses
6 eggs
1/2 cup orange marmalade
1/2 cup orange juice
2 ounces semisweet chocolate, melted
2 1/2 cups all-purpose flour
1 1/2 teaspoons baking powder
1/4 teaspoon baking soda
1/4 teaspoon salt
1 1/2 teaspoons ground cinnamon
1/2 teaspoon ground nutmeg

Per Serving
Calories: 355
% Calories from fat: 31
Fat (gm): 12.8
Saturated fat (gm): 2.6
Cholesterol (mg): 53
Sodium (mg): 186
Protein (gm): 5.2
Carbohydrate (gm): 56
Exchanges
Milk: 0.0
Vegetable: 0.0
Fruit: 0.0
Bread: 3.5
Meat: 0.0
Fat: 2.0

1. Combine fruit, walnuts, and brandy in large bowl; let stand 15 minutes.

2. Combine remaining ingredients in large bowl; beat on low speed until blended. Beat at high speed 3 minutes. Stir in fruit mixture.

3. Spread batter in greased and floured 12-cup fluted tube pan. Bake at 275 until toothpick inserted in center comes out clean, 2 1/2 to 3 hours. Cover with aluminum foil during last hour of baking if becoming too brown. Cool on wire rack.

4. Wrap cake in cheesecloth dampened with brandy; wrap in plastic bag or aluminum foil and refrigerate at least 1 month and up to 1 year, dampening cheesecloth with brandy occasionally.

CHRISTMAS CAKE

A cake so full of flavors that you won't be able to wait for Christmas to sample it!

16 servings

1 cup dark raisins
1 cup golden raisins
1 cup currants
$1/2$ cup glacéed orange, *or* lemon, peel
$1/2$ cup chopped glacéed cherries
$1/4$ cup apple cider
$1/4$ brandy *or* apple cider
$1/2$ cup margarine, softened
$1/2$ cup Prune Puree (see p. 42)
$1/4$ cup honey
1 cup packed light brown sugar
4 eggs
$1^1/2$ cups all-purpose flour
$1/2$ teaspoon baking powder
$1/2$ teaspoon ground cinnamon
$1/2$ teaspoon ground cloves
$1/2$ teaspoon ground nutmeg
$1/3$ cup apricot jam, warm
Glacéed cherries, halved, as garnish

Per Serving
Calories: 344
% Calories from fat: 18
Fat (gm): 7.2
Saturated fat (gm): 1.6
Cholesterol (mg): 53
Sodium (mg): 115
Protein (gm): 4.1
Carbohydrate (gm): 67.7
Exchanges
Milk: 0.0
Vegetable: 0.0
Fruit: 0.0
Bread: 4.5
Meat: 0.0
Fat: 0.5

1. Combine fruit, cider, and brandy in bowl; let stand 15 minutes.

2. Beat margarine, Prune Puree, honey, and brown sugar until blended in large bowl. Beat in eggs, 1 at a time, beating well after each addition. Mix in flour, baking powder, and spices; mix in fruit mixture.

3. Pour batter into greased 9-inch springform pan. Bake at 300 degrees until toothpick inserted in center comes out clean, about $2^1/4$ hours. Cool on wire rack 10 minutes; remove side of pan and cool completely.

4. Wrap cake in cheesecloth dampened with brandy; wrap in plastic bag or aluminum foil and refrigerate up to 1 month, dampening cheesecloth with brandy occasionally.

5. Place cake on serving plate; brush with warm apricot jam and garnish with glacéed cherries.

DUNDEE CAKE

Studded with raisins, glacéed orange peel, and almonds, this cake welcomes the holiday season. Glaze with Orange Glaze (see p. 47), if desired.

12 servings

1/2	cup margarine, softened
1	cup sugar
2	cups all-purpose flour
1	teaspoon baking powder
3/4	teaspoon ground cinnamon
1/4	teaspoon ground nutmeg
1/4	teaspoon salt
4	eggs, divided
1	cup currants *or* dark raisins
1	cup golden raisins
1/2	cup glacéed orange peel
1/3	cup chopped almonds
	Blanched whole almonds, as garnish

Per Serving
Calories: 353
% Calories from fat: 28
Fat (gm): 11.4
Saturated fat (gm): 2.3
Cholesterol (mg): 70.7
Sodium (mg): 202
Protein (gm): 6
Carbohydrate (gm): 59.3
Exchanges
Milk: 0.0
Vegetable: 0.0
Fruit: 0.0
Bread: 4.0
Meat: 0.0
Fat: 1.5

1. Beat margarine and sugar in large bowl until blended. Mix in 1/4 of the combined flour, baking powder, spices, and salt, and 1 egg; mix in remaining flour mixture and eggs. Mix in fruit and chopped almonds.

2. Pour batter into greased and floured 8- or 9-inch springform pan. Arrange whole almonds in circles on top of cake. Bake at 350 degrees until toothpick inserted in center comes out clean, about 1 1/2 hours. Cool on wire rack 10 minutes; remove side of pan and cool completely.

HOLIDAY CAKE

Perfect for the holidays, with bright glacéed fruit. For other times of the year, substitute raisins or nuts for the fruit.

12 servings

2 cups all-purpose flour

$1/2$ cup granulated sugar

$1/2$ cup packed light brown sugar

1 tablespoon baking powder

$1/2$ teaspoon salt

$1/2$ teaspoon ground cardamom *or* allspice

$2/3$ cup fat-free milk

1 tablespoon bourbon *or* $1/2$ teaspoon brandy extract

6 tablespoons margarine, softened

2 eggs

$1/4$ cup chopped glacéed orange peel

$1/4$ cup chopped glacéed red and green cherries

Orange Glaze (see p. 47)

Glacéed orange peel and cherries, as garnish

Per Serving
Calories: 244
% Calories from fat: 25
Fat (gm): 6.7
Saturated fat (gm): 1.4
Cholesterol (mg): 35.6
Sodium (mg): 309
Protein (gm): 3.8
Carbohydrate (gm): 41.9
Exchanges
Milk: 0.0
Vegetable: 0.0
Fruit: 0.0
Bread: 2.5
Meat: 0.0
Fat: 1.0

1. Combine all ingredients except glacéed fruit and Orange Glaze in large bowl. Mix at low speed until ingredients are blended; beat at high speed 3 minutes. Mix in chopped glacéed fruit.

2. Pour batter into greased and floured 9 x 5-inch loaf pan. Bake at 350 degrees until toothpick inserted in center comes out clean, 60 to 65 minutes. Cool cake in pan on wire rack 10 minutes; remove from pan and cool completely. Drizzle with Orange Glaze; decorate with glacéed fruit.

DRIED FRUIT FRUITCAKE

With a bounty of dried fruit, this light fruitcake will appeal to people who are not fond of traditional fruitcakes with glacéed fruit.

24 servings

Per Serving
Calories: 241
% Calories from fat: 10
Fat (gm): 2.6
Saturated fat (gm): 1.3
Cholesterol (mg): 39.8
Sodium (mg): 219
Protein (gm): 4.8
Carbohydrate (gm): 50
Exchanges
Milk: 0.0
Vegetable: 0.0
Fruit: 0.0
Bread: 3.5
Meat: 0.0
Fat: 0.0

1	cup granulated sugar
3/4	cup packed light brown sugar
1	package (8 ounces) reduced-fat, *or* fat-free, cream cheese, softened
1	tablespoon grated lemon rind
1	tablespoon grated orange rind
2	teaspoons vanilla
4	eggs
3	cups all-purpose flour
1/2	cup cornstarch
1	teaspoon baking soda
1	teaspoon salt
1	cup fat-free sour cream
1	cup coarsely chopped mixed dried fruit
1/2	cup dried cranberries
1/2	cup dried cherries
1/2	cup dried blueberries
	Citrus Glaze (see p. 63)

1. Beat sugars, cream cheese, citrus rinds, and vanilla until smooth in large bowl; beat in eggs. Mix in combined flour, cornstarch, baking soda, and salt alternately with sour cream. Mix in fruit.

2. Pour batter into greased 12-cup fluted tube pan. Bake at 350 degrees until wooden pick inserted in center comes out clean, about 60 minutes. Cool in pan on rack 10 minutes; remove from pan and cool. Drizzle with Citrus Glaze.

TWO

Pies
AND
Tarts

BASIC PIE CRUST (ALL-PURPOSE FLOUR)

This pastry contains a minimum of margarine yet is not difficult to handle or roll. Use cold margarine and ice water, as the recipe directs.

8 servings (one 8- or 9-inch crust)

1¼ cups all-purpose flour
2 tablespoons sugar
¼ teaspoon salt
4-5 tablespoons cold margarine *or* vegetable shortening
3-5 tablespoons ice water

Per Serving
Calories: 134
% Calories from fat: 39*
Fat (gm): 5.8
Saturated fat (gm): 1.1
Cholesterol (mg): 0
Sodium (mg): 140
Protein (gm): 2.1
Carbohydrate (gm): 18
Exchanges
Milk: 0.0
Vegetable: 0.0
Fruit: 0.0
Bread: 1.0
Meat: 0.0
Fat: 1.0

1. Combine flour, sugar, and salt in medium bowl. With pastry blender or 2 knives, cut in margarine until mixture resembles coarse crumbs. Sprinkle with water, 1 tablespoon at a time, mixing lightly with a fork after each addition until pastry just holds together.

2. Roll dough on lightly floured surface into circle 2 inches larger in diameter than pie pan. Wrap pastry around rolling pin and unroll into 8- or 9-inch pie or tart pan, easing it into bottom and side of pan. Trim edges, fold under, and flute. Bake as pie recipe directs.

Tip: To bake pie crust before filling, line bottom of pastry with aluminum foil and fill with a single layer of pie weights or dried beans. Bake at 425 degrees until browned, about 15 minutes, removing weights and foil 5 minutes before end of baking time. If not using weights or dried beans, piercing the bottom of the pastry with the tines of a fork will help crust remain flat.

*Percentage of calories from fat will decrease in servings of actual pie.

BASIC PIE CRUST (CAKE FLOUR)

This pastry also contains a minimum of margarine but uses cake flour, which is lower in calories than all-purpose flour.

8 servings (one 8- or 9-inch crust)

1¼ cups cake flour

1 tablespoon sugar

¼ teaspoon salt

4-5 tablespoons cold margarine

3-5 tablespoons ice water

Per Serving
Calories: 119
% Calories from fat: 44*
Fat (gm): 5.8
Saturated fat (gm): 1.1
Cholesterol (mg): 0
Sodium (mg): 140
Protein (gm): 1.5
Carbohydrate (gm): 14.9
Exchanges
Milk: 0.0
Vegetable: 0.0
Fruit: 0.0
Bread: 1.0
Meat: 0.0
Fat: 1.0

1. Combine cake flour, sugar, and salt in medium bowl. With pastry blender or 2 knives, cut in margarine until mixture resembles coarse crumbs. Sprinkle in water, 1 tablespoon at a time, mixing lightly with a fork after each addition until pastry just holds together.

2. Roll dough on lightly floured surface into a circle 2 inches larger in diameter than pie pan. Wrap pastry around rolling pin and unroll into 8- or 9-inch pie or tart pan, easing it into bottom and side of pan. Trim edges, fold under, and flute. Bake as pie recipe directs.

Tip: To bake pie crust before filling, line bottom of pastry with aluminum foil and fill with a single layer of pie weights or dried beans. Bake at 425 degrees until browned, about 15 minutes, removing weights and foil 5 minutes before end of baking time. If not using weights or dried beans, piercing the bottom of the pastry with the tines of a fork will help crust remain flat.

*Percentage of calories from fat will decrease in servings of actual pie.

DOUBLE PIE CRUST

Use this crust for traditional fruit pies such as Mile-High Apple Pie (see p.136) or your favorite heirloom recipe.

8 servings (one 8- or 9-inch double crust)

1³/4 cups all-purpose flour

3 tablespoons sugar

¹/2 teaspoon salt

5-6 tablespoons cold margarine, cut into pieces

5-7 tablespoons ice water

Per Serving
Calories: 181
% Calories from fat: 36*
Fat (gm): 7.3
Saturated fat (gm): 1.4
Cholesterol (mg): 0
Sodium (mg): 229
Protein (gm): 2.9
Carbohydrate (gm): 25.6
Exchanges
Milk: 0.0
Vegetable: 0.0
Fruit: 0.0
Bread: 1.5
Meat: 0.0
Fat: 1.5

1. Combine flour, sugar, and salt in medium bowl; cut in margarine with pastry blender until mixture resembles coarse crumbs. Add water, a tablespoon at a time, mixing with fork until dough forms.

2. Roll and bake as recipe directs.

*Percentage of calories from fat will decrease in servings of actual pie.

CORNMEAL DOUBLE PIE CRUST

This unusual Italian-style crust is particularly good with fruit pies.

8 servings (one 8- or 9-inch double crust)

2 cups all-purpose flour

¹/3 cup yellow cornmeal

1 teaspoon baking powder

¹/2 teaspoon salt

5 tablespoons cold margarine, cut into pieces

¹/4 package (8-ounce size) cold fat-free cream cheese, cut into pieces

Per Serving
Calories: 209
% Calories from fat: 33*
Fat (gm): 7.6
Saturated fat (gm): 1.5
Cholesterol (mg): 0.6
Sodium (mg): 351
Protein (gm): 6.1
Carbohydrate (gm): 28.4
Exchanges
Milk: 0.0
Vegetable: 0.0
Fruit: 0.0
Bread: 2.0
Meat: 0.0
Fat: 1.5

3 egg whites *or* ¹/₃ cup no-cholesterol real
egg product

1. Combine flour, cornmeal, baking powder, and salt in bowl; cut in margarine and cream cheese until mixture resembles coarse crumbs. Add egg whites, mixing until dough is moist and crumbly.

2. Roll and bake as pie recipe directs.

*Percentage of calories from fat will decrease in servings of actual pie.

HAZELNUT PASTRY CRUST

Almonds, pecans, or other nuts can be substituted for the hazelnuts.

8 servings (one 8- or 9-inch crust)

¹/₄ cup chopped hazelnuts, toasted
1 cup all-purpose flour
3 tablespoons sugar
¹/₂ teaspoon salt
3 tablespoons cold margarine, cut into pieces
4-5 tablespoons cold water

Per Serving
Calories: 143
% Calories from fat: 46*
Fat (gm): 7.4
Saturated fat (gm): 1
Cholesterol (mg): 0
Sodium (mg): 196
Protein (gm): 2.1
Carbohydrate (gm): 17.4
Exchanges
Milk: 0.0
Vegetable: 0.0
Fruit: 0.0
Bread: 1.0
Meat: 0.0
Fat: 1.5

1. Process nuts, flour, sugar, and salt in food processor until nuts are finely ground. Add margarine and process, using pulse technique, until the mixture resembles coarse crumbs. Sprinkle 4 tablespoons water over and process just until combined, adding additional water if needed.

2. Form dough into a ball and wrap in plastic wrap, flattening into a disk. Chill 1 hour or longer before using.

3. Roll and bake as recipe directs.

*Percentage of calories from fat will decrease in servings of actual pie.

SHORTBREAD CRUST

A tender, sweet crust that is almost like a cookie.

12 servings (one 10- or 12-inch crust)

1¹/₃ cups all-purpose flour
¹/₂ cup powdered sugar
  Pinch salt
5 tablespoons cold margarine, cut into pieces
1 egg, lightly beaten
1 teaspoon vanilla

Per Serving
Calories: 120
% Calories from fat: 40*
Fat (gm): 5.3
Saturated fat (gm): 1
Cholesterol (mg): 17.7
Sodium (mg): 61
Protein (gm): 2
Carbohydrate (gm): 15.7
Exchanges
Milk: 0.0
Vegetable: 0.0
Fruit: 0.0
Bread: 1.0
Meat: 0.0
Fat: 1.0

1. Combine flour, sugar, and salt in medium bowl. Cut in margarine until mixture resembles coarse crumbs. Mix in combined egg and vanilla with fork, stirring just until mixture forms a dough.

2. Form dough into a ball; flatten slightly and wrap in plastic wrap. Chill 1 hour or longer before using.

3. Roll and bake as recipe directs.

*Percentage of calories from fat will decrease in servings of actual pie.

CREAM CHEESE TART CRUST

A rich crust that can be used for many double-crust pies.

12 servings (1 large free-form crust, or 2, 9-inch crusts)

8 tablespoons margarine

1/4 package (8-ounce size) cream cheese

1/2 cup sugar

1 egg

1 teaspoon vanilla

2 1/4 cups all-purpose flour

1/4 teaspoon salt

Per Serving
Calories: 209
% Calories from fat: 42*
Fat (gm): 9.8
Saturated fat (gm): 2.7
Cholesterol (mg): 22.9
Sodium (mg): 157
Protein (gm): 3.4
Carbohydrate (gm): 26.6
Exchanges
Milk: 0.0
Vegetable: 0.0
Fruit: 0.0
Bread: 1.5
Meat: 0.0
Fat: 2.0

1. Beat margarine and cream cheese until smooth in large mixing bowl; add sugar, beating well. Add egg and vanilla and beat at high speed for 1 minute or until very smooth. Add combined flour and salt and mix just until blended.

2. Form dough into a ball; flatten slightly and wrap in plastic wrap. Refrigerate 2 hours or longer before using.

3. Roll and bake as recipe directs.

*Percentage of calories from fat will decrease in servings of actual pie.

MERINGUE PIE CRUST

Light, airy, delicious, and versatile. Fill this crust with scoops of low-fat frozen yogurt or ice cream, and top with a light drizzle of Warm Rum or Bittersweet Chocolate Sauce (see pp. 54, 641).

8 servings (one 8- or 9-inch crust)

  4 egg whites
  1/2 teaspoon cream of tartar
  1 cup sugar

Per Serving
Calories: 106
% Calories from fat: 0
Fat (gm): 0
Saturated fat (gm): 0
Cholesterol (mg): 0
Sodium (mg): 28
Protein (gm): 1.8
Carbohydrate (gm): 25.2
Exchanges
Milk: 0.0
Vegetable: 0.0
Fruit: 0.0
Bread: 1.5
Meat: 0.0
Fat: 0.0

1. Beat egg whites and cream of tartar in medium bowl to soft peaks. Gradually beat in sugar, beating to stiff peaks. Spoon mixture into ungreased 8- or 9-inch glass pie pan, spreading on bottom and up side to form a large bowl shape.

2. Bake at 350 degrees 40 minutes or until crust is firm to touch and very lightly browned. Cool on wire rack.

GRAHAM CRACKER CRUMB CRUST

Mix crumb crusts right in the pan—it's quick and easy!

8 servings (one 8- or 9-inch crust)

  1 1/4 cups graham cracker crumbs
  2 tablespoons sugar
  3 tablespoons margarine, melted
  1-2 tablespoons honey

Per Serving
Calories: 144
% Calories from fat: 47*
Fat (gm): 7.8
Saturated fat (gm): 1.6
Cholesterol (mg): 0
Sodium (mg): 125
Protein (gm): 1.3
Carbohydrate (gm): 18
Exchanges
Milk: 0.0
Vegetable: 0.0
Fruit: 0.0
Bread: 1.0
Meat: 0.0
Fat: 1.5

1. Combine graham crumbs, sugar, and margarine in 8- or 9-inch pie pan; add enough honey for mixture to stick together. Pat mixture evenly on bottom and side of pan.

2. Bake at 350 degrees 8 to 10 minutes or until edge of crust is lightly browned. Cool on wire rack.

*Percentage of calories from fat will decrease in servings of actual pie.

VANILLA CRUMB CRUST

A perfect recipe when a delicately flavored crust is desired.

8 servings (one 8- or 9-inch crust)

1¼ cups vanilla wafer cookie crumbs
2-3 tablespoons margarine, melted
2-3 tablespoons honey

Per Serving
Calories: 117
% Calories from fat: 49*
Fat (gm): 6.4
Saturated fat (gm): 1.6
Cholesterol (mg): 0
Sodium (mg): 94
Protein (gm): 0.6
Carbohydrate (gm): 14.4
Exchanges
Milk: 0.0
Vegetable: 0.0
Fruit: 0.0
Bread: 1.0
Meat: 0.0
Fat: 1.0

1. Combine vanilla crumbs and margarine in 8- or 9-inch pie pan; add enough honey for mixture to stick together. Pat mixture evenly on bottom and side of pan.

2. Bake 8 to 10 minutes or until edge of crust is lightly browned. Cool on wire rack.

*Percentage of calories from fat will decrease in servings of actual pie.

CHOCOLATE COOKIE CRUMB CRUST

You can choose chocolate wafer crumbs, or chocolate sandwich cookie crumbs.

8 servings (one 8- or 9-inch crust)

1¼ cups chocolate cookie crumbs
2 tablespoons sugar
3 tablespoons margarine, melted
1-2 tablespoons honey

Per Serving
Calories: 158
% Calories from fat: 44*
Fat (gm): 8
Saturated fat (gm): 1.5
Cholesterol (mg): 0
Sodium (mg): 225
Protein (gm): 1.3
Carbohydrate (gm): 21.6
Exchanges
Milk: 0.0
Vegetable: 0.0
Fruit: 0.0
Bread: 1.5
Meat: 0.0
Fat: 1.0

1. Mix cookie crumbs, sugar, and margarine in bottom of 8- or 9-inch pie pan; add enough honey for mixture to stick together. Press evenly on bottom and side of 8- or 9-inch pie pan.

2. Bake at 350 degrees 6 to 8 minutes. Cool on wire rack.

Variation: **Chocolate Pecan Crumb Crust**—Make crust as above, decreasing margarine to 1 tablespoon, increasing honey to 3 tablespoons, and adding ¼ cup ground pecans.

*Percentage of calories from fat will decrease in servings of actual pie.

GINGERSNAP CRUMB CRUST

Gingersnaps provide a zesty flavor accent in this crust.

8 servings (one 8- or 9-inch crust)

$1/2$ cup graham cracker crumbs
$1/2$ cup gingersnap cookie crumbs
2-3 tablespoons margarine
2 tablespoons honey

Per Serving
Calories: 102
% Calories from fat: 42*
Fat (gm): 4.9
Saturated fat (gm): 0.9
Cholesterol (mg): 0
Sodium (mg): 104
Protein (gm): 0.9
Carbohydrate (gm): 14.2
Exchanges
Milk: 0.0
Vegetable: 0.0
Fruit: 0.0
Bread: 1.0
Meat: 0.0
Fat: 0.5

1. Combine graham crumbs, gingersnap crumbs, and margarine in 8- or 9-inch pie pan; add enough honey for mixture to stick together. Pat mixture evenly on bottom and side of pan.

2. Bake at 350 degrees 8 to 10 minutes or until edge of crust is lightly browned. Cool on wire rack.

Variation: **Ginger-Raisin Crumb Crust**—Process 3 tablespoons raisins, 2 teaspoons grated orange peel, and cracker crumbs in food processor until raisins are finely chopped, using pulse technique. Combine with remaining ingredients and proceed as above.

*Percentage of calories from fat will decrease in servings of actual pie.

LEMON COOKIE CRUMB CRUST

We enjoy using the lemon cookies that are coated with powdered sugar;
process to fine crumbs in a food processor or with a rolling pin.

8 servings (one 8- or 9-inch crust)

1½ cups lemon cookie crumbs (cookies
    with powdered sugar)
2 tablespoons sugar
2-3 tablespoons margarine, melted
2 tablespoons honey

Per Serving
Calories: 128
% Calories from fat: 43*
Fat (gm): 6.2
Saturated fat (gm): 1.4
Cholesterol (mg): 0.3
Sodium (mg): 46
Protein (gm): 0.1
Carbohydrate (gm): 18.4
Exchanges
Milk: 0.0
Vegetable: 0.0
Fruit: 0.0
Bread: 1.0
Meat: 0.0
Fat: 1.0

1. Mix cookie crumbs, sugar, and margarine in bottom of 8- or
9-inch pie pan; mix in enough honey for mixture to stick together. Press evenly on bottom and side of pan.

2. Bake at 350 degrees 6 to 8 minutes. Cool on wire rack.

*Percentage of calories from fat will decrease in servings of actual
pie.

MILE-HIGH APPLE PIE

Nothing is more American than real homemade apple pie. Enjoy this one
warm with a generous scoop of fat-free frozen yogurt or a slice of reduced-
fat Cheddar cheese.

10 servings

Double Pie Crust (see p. 128)
6 cups peeled, cored, sliced tart baking
    apples
1 cup sugar
4-5 tablespoons all-purpose flour
¾ teaspoon ground cinnamon

Per Serving
Calories: 309
% Calories from fat: 24
Fat (gm): 8.5
Saturated fat (gm): 1.7
Cholesterol (mg): 0
Sodium (mg): 240
Protein (gm): 3
Carbohydrate (gm): 57

1/4 teaspoon ground nutmeg

1/8 teaspoon ground cloves

1/8 teaspoon salt

2 tablespoons margarine, cut into pieces

Exchanges
Milk: 0.0
Vegetable: 0.0
Fruit: 0.0
Bread: 3.4
Meat: 0.0
Fat: 1.0

1. Roll 2/3 of the Double Pie Crust on floured surface to form circle 2 inches larger than inverted 9-inch pie pan; ease pastry into pan.

2. Toss apples with combined sugar, flour, spices, and salt in large bowl; arrange apples in pastry and dot with margarine.

3. Roll remaining 1/3 Double Pie Crust to fit top of pie and place over apples. Trim edges of pastry to within 1/2 inch of pan; fold top pastry over bottom pastry and flute. Cut vents in top crust.

4. Bake pie at 425 degrees until apples are fork-tender and pastry browned, 40 to 50 minutes. Cover pastry with aluminum foil if it is becoming too brown. Cool on wire rack 15 to 20 minutes before cutting.

Variations: **Mile-High Caramel Apple Pie**—Fill pie crust as above, increasing flour to 1/3 cup and omitting margarine. Heat 2/3 package (14-ounce size) caramels and 1/4 cup water in small saucepan until caramels are melted, stirring frequently. Pour caramel mixture over apples; place top crust on pie and bake as above.

Apple 'n Apricot Pie—Prepare pie as above, adding 1/2 cup apricot jam and 1/4 cup chopped pecans to the apple mixture. Cover with top crust and bake as above.

Cherry-Apple Pie—Complete Step 1 above. Reduce sugar to 1/2 cup and combine with flour, spices, and salt, adding 2 teaspoons grated orange peel; sprinkle 3 tablespoons mixture over bottom crust. Combine remaining sugar mixture, 4 cups sliced apples, and 1 can (21 ounces) cherry pie filling. Pour into pie shell. Omit margarine. Cover fruit with top crust and bake as above.

UPSIDE-DOWN APPLE PIE

Topped with a caramel coating, this recipe turns traditional apple pie up-side-down.

10 servings

2 tablespoons margarine
2 tablespoons corn syrup
2/3 cup packed light brown sugar
1/3 cup chopped pecans
   Double Pie Crust (see p. 128)
6 cups peeled, cored, sliced tart baking apples
3/4 cup granulated sugar
3 tablespoons flour
1 tablespoon lemon juice
1 teaspoon ground cinnamon
   Pinch salt

Per Serving
Calories: 369
% Calories from fat: 26
Fat (gm): 11.1
Saturated fat (gm): 1.9
Cholesterol (mg): 0
Sodium (mg): 222
Protein (gm): 3.2
Carbohydrate (gm): 67
Exchanges
Milk: 0.0
Vegetable: 0.0
Fruit: 2.0
Bread: 2.5
Meat: 0.0
Fat: 1.5

1. Heat margarine, corn syrup, brown sugar, and pecans in small saucepan until sugar is melted; cool. Pour into bottom of deep-dish 9-inch pie pan.

2. Roll 2/3 of the Double Pie Crust on floured surface to form circle 2 inches larger than pan; ease pastry into pan, covering sugar mixture.

3. Toss apples with combined granulated sugar, flour, lemon juice, cinnamon, and salt in large bowl; arrange apples in pastry.

4. Roll remaining 1/3 Double Pie Crust to fit top of pie and place over apples. Trim edges of pastry to within 1/2 inch of pan; fold top pastry over bottom pastry and flute. Cut vents in top crust.

5. Bake pie at 425 degrees until apples are fork-tender and pastry browned, 40 to 50 minutes. Cover pastry with aluminum foil if becoming too brown. Cool on wire rack 5 minutes. Invert pie onto serving plate; cool.

STREUSEL APPLE PIE

The crisp, spicy topping provides a wonderful counterpoint to juicy fall apples.

8 servings

Basic Pie Crust (All-Purpose Flour) (see p. 126)
6 cups peeled, cored, sliced tart baking apples
1 tablespoon lemon juice
$^1/_3$-$^1/_2$ cup sugar
3 tablespoons flour
Spiced Streusel Topping (recipe follows)

Per Serving
Calories: 370
% Calories from fat: 26
Fat (gm): 11
Saturated fat (gm): 2.2
Cholesterol (mg): 0
Sodium (mg): 197
Protein (gm): 4.4
Carbohydrate (gm): 65.6
Exchanges
Milk: 0.0
Vegetable: 0.0
Fruit: 2.0
Bread: 2.0
Meat: 0.0
Fat: 2.0

1. Make Basic Pie Crust, using 9-inch pie pan.

2. Toss apples with lemon juice; add combined sugar and flour and toss well. Arrange apples in pastry. Sprinkle with Spiced Streusel Topping.

3. Bake at 350 degrees until apples are fork-tender and topping browned, 55 to 60 minutes. Cover pie with aluminum foil if becoming too brown. Cool on wire rack.

Spiced Streusel Topping

makes about 1$^1/_2$ cups

$^2/_3$ cup quick-cooking oats
$^1/_2$ cup packed light brown sugar
$^1/_3$ cup all-purpose flour
1$^1/_2$ teaspoons ground cinnamon
$^1/_2$ teaspoon ground allspice
$^1/_4$ teaspoon ground ginger
$^1/_4$ teaspoon ground nutmeg
3-4 tablespoons margarine

1. Combine oats, brown sugar, flour, and spices in medium bowl; cut in margarine until mixture resembles coarse crumbs.

Variations: **Apple-Blueberry Streusel Pie**—Make pie as above, using 5 cups coarsely chopped apples and 1 cup dried blueberries. Substitute 2 tablespoons orange juice for the lemon juice, and add 2 teaspoons grated orange rind to fruit before tossing with sugar and flour.

Apple-Rhubarb Streusel Pie—Make pie as above, using 4 cups sliced apples and 2 cups sliced rhubarb. Increase sugar to ³/₄ to 1 cup, and increase flour to ¹/₄ cup.

TARTE TATIN

Caramelized sugar contributes special flavor to this French-style upside-down apple tart.

8 servings

5 cups Granny Smith apples (about 2¹/₂ pounds), peeled, cored, and cut into scant ¹/₂-inch slices
³/₄ cup sugar, divided
¹/₄ teaspoon ground nutmeg
1 tablespoon lemon juice
2 tablespoons margarine
Tatin Crust (recipe follows)

Per Serving
Calories: 245
% Calories from fat: 27
Fat (gm): 7.6
Saturated fat (gm): 1.5
Cholesterol (mg): 0
Sodium (mg): 84
Protein (gm): 1.4
Carbohydrate (gm): 44.8
Exchanges
Milk: 0.0
Vegetable: 0.0
Fruit: 2.0
Bread: 1.0
Meat: 0.0
Fat: 1.0

1. Toss apples with ¹/₂ cup sugar and nutmeg; sprinkle with lemon juice. Set aside.

2. Place remaining ¹/₄ cup sugar in 10-inch skillet with oven-proof handle. Cook over medium heat until sugar melts and is golden brown, about 5 minutes, stirring occasionally (watch carefully as the sugar can burn easily). Add apple mixture and margarine; cook 5 minutes or until apples are just tender, stirring occasionally. Remove from heat.

3. Arrange apples in skillet so they are slightly mounded in the center.

4. On lightly floured surface, roll Tatin Crust into 11-inch circle and place on top of apples; tuck in edges. Cut vents in pastry to allow steam to escape.

5. Bake in skillet at 425 degrees 20 to 25 minutes or until lightly browned. Invert onto serving platter. Serve warm or at room temperature.

Tatin Crust

    1 cup cake flour
    2 tablespoons sugar
    3 tablespoons cold margarine
  2-3 tablespoons ice water

1. Combine cake flour and sugar in medium bowl. Cut in margarine until mixture resembles coarse crumbs. Sprinkle in water, 1 tablespoon at a time, mixing lightly with a fork until dough just holds together. Cover and refrigerate 15 minutes.

Variations: **Caramelized Pear and Almond Tarte Tatin**—Substitute pears for the apples, tossing with combined 1/2 cup sugar, 1/3 cup sliced almonds, 1 tablespoon flour, 1 teaspoon grated lemon rind, 1/2 teaspoon ground cinnamon, and 1/4 teaspoon ground nutmeg. Complete recipe as above, beginning with Step 2.

Apple-Cheddar Tarte Tatin—Make recipe as above, adding 1/3 cup raisins to apples in Step 1. Prepare Tatin Crust, substituting vegetable shortening for the margarine, and adding 1/3 cup shredded reduced-fat or fat-free Cheddar cheese before sprinkling with water; add additional water if necessary.

SOUFFLÉ APPLE PIE

A vanilla soufflé tops apple filling in this unusual pie.

8 servings

    Basic Pie Crust (All-Purpose Flour)
    (see p. 126)
    2 large tart apples, peeled, cored, sliced
  1/4 cup golden raisins
    3 tablespoons margarine, softened
  3/4 cup sugar
    2 egg yolks
  1/4 cup all-purpose flour
  1/4 teaspoon salt
  1/2 cup fat-free milk, hot
    1 teaspoon vanilla
    3 egg whites, stiffly beaten

Per Serving
Calories: 321
% Calories from fat: 32
Fat (gm): 11.5
Saturated fat (gm): 2.4
Cholesterol (mg): 53.5
Sodium (mg): 293
Protein (gm): 5.3
Carbohydrate (gm): 49.8
Exchanges
Milk: 0.0
Vegetable: 0.0
Fruit: 1.0
Bread: 2.5
Meat: 0.0
Fat: 2.0

1. Bake Basic Pie Crust according to recipe, using 9-inch pie pan. Cool on wire rack.

2. Arrange apples and raisins in pastry. Beat margarine, sugar, and egg yolks until light and fluffy in medium bowl; mix in flour and salt. Mix in milk and vanilla gradually; fold in egg whites. Spoon mixture over fruit.

3. Bake at 325 degrees until top is set and browned, about 1 hour. Cool on wire rack.

SOUR CREAM APPLE PIE

Sweet, spicy, and creamy all in one pie!

8 servings

Gingersnap Crumb Crust (see p. 135)
- 1/2 cup graham cracker crumbs
- 1 tablespoon melted margarine
- 1 tablespoon honey
- 1 cup fat-free sour cream
- 1 egg
- 2/3 cup sugar
- 2 tablespoons flour
- 1/2 teaspoon ground cinnamon
- 1/4 teaspoon ground nutmeg
- 2 1/2 pounds tart baking apples, peeled, cored, sliced

Per Serving
Calories: 370
% Calories from fat: 21
Fat (gm): 9.1
Saturated fat (gm): 1.9
Cholesterol (mg): 27
Sodium (mg): 186
Protein (gm): 4.9
Carbohydrate (gm): 70.6
Exchanges
Milk: 0.0
Vegetable: 0.0
Fruit: 2.0
Bread: 2.5
Meat: 0.0
Fat: 1.5

1. Make Gingersnap Crumb Crust, adding 1/2 cup graham cracker crumbs and 1 tablespoon each melted margarine and honey to mixture. Reserve 1/2 cup crumb mixture. Pat remaining mixture evenly on bottom and side of 9-inch pie pan, and bake as directed in recipe.

2. Combine in large bowl sour cream, egg, sugar, flour, and spices; stir in apples and pour into Gingersnap Crumb Crust. Bake at 350 degrees until apples are tender, about 1 hour, sprinkling top with reserved crumbs during last 10 minutes of baking time. Cool on wire rack.

APPLE SPIRAL TART

A European pastry shop presentation with the traditional apple pie flavor!

10 servings

4-5 cups chopped, peeled, cored tart baking apples

$^1/_2$ cup golden raisins

$^1/_4$ cup chopped walnuts

2 tablespoons brandy *or* $^1/_2$ teaspoon brandy extract

$^2/_3$ cup packed light brown sugar

$^1/_3$ cup all-purpose flour

1 teaspoon ground cinnamon

$^1/_4$ teaspoon ground nutmeg

$^1/_8$ teaspoon ground cloves

Double Pie Crust (see p. 128)

$^1/_4$ cup apricot spreadable fruit, warm

Per Serving
Calories: 319
% Calories from fat: 22
Fat (gm): 8
Saturated fat (gm): 1.3
Cholesterol (mg): 0
Sodium (mg): 192
Protein (gm): 4
Carbohydrate (gm): 58.3
Exchanges
Milk: 0.0
Vegetable: 0.0
Fruit: 1.0
Bread: 2.5
Meat: 0.0
Fat: 1.5

1. Combine apples, raisins, nuts, and brandy in large bowl; add combined sugar, flour, and spices and toss. Let stand while rolling Double Pie Crust.

2. Divide Double Pie Crust into 2 equal pieces; roll 1 piece on floured surface into circle 1 inch larger than 9-inch tart pan. Ease pastry into pan and trim. Roll remaining piece into rectangle $^1/_8$ inch thick; cut into long strips $1^1/_2$ inches wide with fluted pastry wheel or knife. Stand pastry strips upright in tart pan, beginning in center and forming a spiral design; spoon apple mixture between strips.

3. Bake at 375 degrees until apple mixture is tender and pastry is browned, about 60 minutes. Cool on wire rack; brush with apricot spreadable fruit.

Variation: **Fruited Spiral Tart**—Make Double Pie Crust as above, adding 1 tablespoon grated orange rind to flour, and substituting orange juice for the water in the recipe. Substitute $^1/_4$ cup each dried cherries, dried blueberries, and chopped dried apricots for the raisins and walnuts in the recipe. Replace the brandy with orange juice. Proceed with recipe as above.

CRANBERRY-APPLE TART

The perfect fall combination, with the crunch of cornmeal crust.

8 servings

- 1 cup sugar
- 2 tablespoons flour
- 1/3 cup water
- 2 teaspoons grated orange rind
- 1/8 teaspoon ground nutmeg
- 4 cups peeled, sliced apples
- 1¹/2 cups fresh, *or* frozen, cranberries
- Cornmeal Double Pie Crust (see p.128)
- Powdered sugar, as garnish

Per Serving
Calories: 360
% Calories from fat: 20
Fat (gm): 8
Saturated fat (gm): 1.6
Cholesterol (mg): 0.6
Sodium (mg): 352
Protein (gm): 6.6
Carbohydrate (gm): 67.1
Exchanges
Milk: 0.0
Vegetable: 0.0
Fruit: 0.0
Bread: 4.5
Meat: 0.0
Fat: 1.0

1. Mix sugar and flour in large saucepan; add water, orange rind, and nutmeg. Heat to boiling, stirring to dissolve sugar; add apples and cranberries. Simmer 10 minutes or until cranberries pop, stirring occasionally. Cool to room temperature.

2. Make Cornmeal Double Pie Crust; scatter ²/3 of the dough in 9-inch pie or tart pan. Pat dough evenly on bottom and side of pan. Roll remaining dough between sheets of waxed paper to ¹/8 inch thickness. Cut into ¹/2-inch strips.

3. Spoon fruit mixture into crust, spreading evenly. Top with pastry strips, weaving strips to form lattice pattern.

4. Bake at 350 degrees until golden, 45 to 50 minutes. Cool on wire rack. Sprinkle with powdered sugar.

PEACH-ALMOND STREUSEL PIE

The taste of the Deep South, with brown sugar, peaches, and the crunch of almonds.

10 servings

Basic Pie Crust (All-Purpose Flour) (see p. 126)

5 cups sliced, peeled peaches

3/4 cup granulated sugar

3/4 cup packed dark brown sugar

1/4 cup all-purpose flour

1 teaspoon ground cinnamon

1/2 teaspoon ground nutmeg

1/4 teaspoon salt

2 tablespoons lemon juice

1 tablespoon grated orange rind

1 teaspoon almond extract

Almond Streusel (recipe follows)

Per Serving
Calories: 357
% Calories from fat: 21
Fat (gm): 8.2
Saturated fat (gm): 1.5
Cholesterol (mg): 0
Sodium (mg): 438
Protein (gm): 3.7
Carbohydrate (gm): 67.4
Exchanges
Milk: 0.0
Vegetable: 0.0
Fruit: 1.0
Bread: 3.0
Meat: 0.0
Fat: 1.5

1. Make Basic Pie Crust, using 9-inch pan.

2. Toss peaches with combined remaining ingredients, except Almond Streusel. Arrange fruit in pastry. Sprinkle with Almond Streusel.

3. Bake on baking sheet at 400 degrees 40 to 50 minutes until fruit is tender and bubbly and streusel browned. Cool on wire rack.

Almond Streusel

makes about 1 cup

- 1/4 cup all-purpose flour
- 1/4 cup packed dark brown sugar
- 1/4 cup quick-cooking oats
- 2 tablespoons cold margarine, cut into pieces
- 1/2 teaspoon almond extract
- 3 tablespoons sliced almonds

1. Combine flour, brown sugar, and oats. Cut in margarine until mixture resembles coarse crumbs; stir in almond extract and almonds.

FRESH PEACH TART

Delicious when peaches are in season, this tart can also be made with frozen peaches.

8 servings

- Shortbread Crust (see p. 130)
- 1/2 cup apricot preserves, divided
- 3 tablespoons flour
- 8 medium peaches, peeled, pitted, sliced
- 1 teaspoon hot water

Per Serving
Calories: 282
% Calories from fat: 25
Fat (gm): 8
Saturated fat (gm): 1.6
Cholesterol (mg): 27
Sodium (mg): 94
Protein (gm): 4
Carbohydrate (gm): 49.5
Exchanges
Milk: 0.0
Vegetable: 0.0
Fruit: 1.0
Bread: 2.5
Meat: 0.0
Fat: 1.0

1. Roll Shortbread Crust between sheets of waxed paper to 12-inch circle. Ease pastry into 10-inch tart pan and trim.

2. Mix 1/4 cup apricot preserves and flour and spread on bottom of prepared pastry. Arrange peaches in spiral pattern on apricot mixture. Thin 2 tablespoons apricot preserves with 1 teaspoon hot water; brush on peaches.

3. Bake tart at 375 degrees until peaches are tender and pastry is brown, 30 to 40 minutes. Melt remaining preserves and brush over baked tart. Cool on wire rack.

PEACH-BERRY PEASANT PIE

Tender, sweet pastry is gently folded over summer's sweet fruit in this country-style pie.

8 servings

Shortbread Crust (see p. 130)
5 cups sliced, peeled peaches
1/2 cup blueberries
1/2 cup blackberries
1/2 cup raspberries
3/4 cup sugar, divided
1/4 cup cornstarch

Per Serving
Calories: 327
% Calories from fat: 22
Fat (gm): 8.1
Saturated fat (gm): 1.6
Cholesterol (mg): 27
Sodium (mg): 93
Protein (gm): 4
Carbohydrate (gm): 61.1
Exchanges
Milk: 0.0
Vegetable: 0.0
Fruit: 2.0
Bread: 2.5
Meat: 0.0
Fat: 1.0

1. Roll Shortbread Crust between sheets of waxed paper to 14-inch circle. Ease pastry into 9-inch pie pan.

2. Toss fruit with 2/3 cup sugar and cornstarch; arrange in pastry. Gently gather and fold outer edge of pastry over fruits, leaving center of pie open. Brush edge of pastry with water and sprinkle remaining sugar over top of pie.

3. Bake at 425 degrees 40 to 50 minutes or until crust is lightly browned and fruit is bubbling and tender. Cool.

PEACH AND STRAWBERRY FLAN

A light cheese filling accents the flavors of sweet fruit.

8 servings

Shortbread Crust (see p. 130)
1¹/4 teaspoons ground cinnamon, divided
1 can (16 ounces) sliced peaches in juice, drained, reserving juice
3 tablespoons sugar, divided
2 teaspoons cornstarch
1 teaspoon lemon juice
1/2 package (8-ounce size) fat-free cream cheese, softened

Per Serving
Calories: 247
% Calories from fat: 30
Fat (gm): 8.1
Saturated fat (gm): 1.8
Cholesterol (mg): 28
Sodium (mg): 172
Protein (gm): 5.6
Carbohydrate (gm): 38.1
Exchanges
Milk: 0.0
Vegetable: 0.0
Fruit: 1.0
Bread: 1.5
Meat: 0.0
Fat: 1.5

2 teaspoons fat-free milk
1/2 teaspoon vanilla
1 cup sliced strawberries

1. Make Shortbread Crust, adding 1 teaspoon cinnamon. Roll pastry between 2 sheets of waxed paper to circle 12 inches in diameter. Ease pastry into 10-inch tart pan; trim. Pierce bottom and side of pastry with fork. Bake at 425 degrees until crisp and golden brown, 10 to 15 minutes. Cool on wire rack.

2. Add enough water to reserved peach juice to make 1 cup; stir in 2 tablespoons sugar, cornstarch, lemon juice, and remaining 1/4 teaspoon cinnamon. Heat to boiling and boil until clear; cool slightly.

3. Beat cream cheese, milk, remaining 1 tablespoon sugar, and vanilla until smooth. Spread over crust. Arrange strawberries and peaches on cheese mixture; spoon glaze over fruit. Chill 2 to 3 hours before serving.

PEACH CHIFFON PIE

This easy version is made with canned peaches; substitute fresh if you like.

8 servings

Gingersnap Crumb Crust (see p. 135)
1 can (8 ounces) sliced peaches, drained
1 carton (8 ounces) fat-free peach yogurt
1 tablespoon honey
1 teaspoon lemon juice
1 envelope unflavored gelatin
1 tablespoon orange juice
4 teaspoons meringue powder
1/4 cup water
2 tablespoons sugar
Ground nutmeg, as garnish

Per Serving
Calories: 154
% Calories from fat: 27
Fat (gm): 4.9
Saturated fat (gm): 1
Cholesterol (mg): 0
Sodium (mg): 138
Protein (gm): 3
Carbohydrate (gm): 25.7
Exchanges
Milk: 0.0
Vegetable: 0.0
Fruit: 0.0
Bread: 1.5
Meat: 0.0
Fat: 1.0

1. Make Gingersnap Crumb Crust, using 8-inch pie pan.

2. Reserve 3 peach slices to use as garnish. Process remaining peaches, yogurt, honey, and lemon juice in blender or food processor until smooth.

3. Sprinkle gelatin over orange juice in small saucepan; let stand until gelatin is softened. Cook over low heat, stirring, until gelatin is dissolved; add to peach mixture with blender running.

4. Beat meringue powder with water until foamy; continue beating, gradually adding sugar, until stiff peaks form. Fold fruit mixture into meringue.

5. Pour filling into crust. Chill 2 to 3 hours before serving. Sprinkle with nutmeg.

PEAR TART WITH CRÈME ANGLAISE

Select pears that are just ripe, but not soft, for this elegant and delicate tart.

8 servings

Basic Pie Crust (Cake Flour) (see p. 127)

2 pounds pears (4 large), peeled, cored, and sliced 1/4-inch thick

1/4 cup all-purpose flour

3 tablespoons sugar

1/2 teaspoon ground cinnamon

1/4 teaspoon ground nutmeg

Crème Anglaise (see p. 640)

Per Serving
Calories: 246
% Calories from fat: 26
Fat (gm): 7.4
Saturated fat (gm): 1.4
Cholesterol (mg): 27.1
Sodium (mg): 156
Protein (gm): 4
Carbohydrate (gm): 43.1
Exchanges
Milk: 0.0
Vegetable: 0.0
Fruit: 0.0
Bread: 3.0
Meat: 0.0
Fat: 0.5

1. Bake Basic Pie Crust according to recipe, using 9-inch tart pan. Cool on wire rack.

2. Toss pears with combined flour, sugar, cinnamon, and nutmeg. Arrange pears in overlapping circles in crust.

3. Bake at 375 degrees 20 to 25 minutes or until pears are tender. Serve warm with Crème Anglaise.

Variation: **Spiced Pear Tart**—Make tart through Step 1 above. Add 2 teaspoons lemon juice, 1/4 teaspoon ground ginger, 1/8 teaspoon ground black pepper, and 1/8 teaspoon ground allspice to spices in Step 2. Complete as above, glazing tart after baking with 1/3 cup heated, strained raspberry jam.

POACHED PEAR TARTE TATIN

Firm ripe pears are gently poached in sweetened red wine, then baked under a flavorful crust.

8 servings

7 pears, peeled, halved, cored
1/2 cup sugar
1/2 teaspoon ground cinnamon
2 1/2 cups dry red wine
Hazelnut Pastry Crust (see p. 129)

Per Serving
Calories: 330
% Calories from fat: 21
Fat (gm): 8
Saturated fat (gm): 1.1
Cholesterol (mg): 0
Sodium (mg): 196
Protein (gm): 2.8
Carbohydrate (gm): 53.3
Exchanges
Milk: 0.0
Vegetable: 0.0
Fruit: 1.0
Bread: 2.0
Meat: 0.0
Fat: 1.5

1. Arrange pears, cut sides up, in 12-inch stainless steel or non-stick skillet; sprinkle with combined sugar and cinnamon. Pour wine over pears. Heat to boiling; reduce heat and simmer, covered, just until pears are tender, 10 to 20 minutes, depending on ripeness of pears. Remove pears with slotted spoon; boil wine mixture until reduced to 1/2 cup.

2. Slice pears and arrange in 10-inch glass pie plate; pour wine mixture over.

3. Roll Hazelnut Pastry Crust between 2 sheets of waxed paper to 12 inch diameter. Place pastry over pears, folding in excess pastry and tucking in edges. Cut several vents in pastry.

4. Bake at 375 degrees until pastry is golden and crisp, about 40 minutes. Cool 5 minutes; invert onto serving plate.

Variation: **Custard Pear Tart**—Roll Hazelnut Pastry Crust as above, easing it into 10-inch tart pan. Line pastry with aluminum foil and fill with a single layer of pie weights or dried beans. Bake at 425 degrees until browned, about 15 minutes, removing weights and foil 5 minutes before end of baking time. Cool. Poach pears as above. Boil wine mixture until reduced to 1/3 cup. Fill pastry with Pastry Cream (see p. 268); arrange sliced pears on top. Brush with reduced wine mixture to glaze. Sprinkle with 3 tablespoons toasted sliced almonds as garnish.

FRESH APRICOT TART

Fresh and colorful as a summer sunset!

8 servings

1/2 recipe Cornmeal Double Pie Crust
(see p. 128)
1 pound apricots, pitted, sliced
3/4 cup raspberries
1/2 cup sugar, divided
3 tablespoons flour
Powdered sugar, as garnish

Per Serving
Calories: 196
% Calories from fat: 18
Fat (gm): 4.1
Saturated fat (gm): 0.8
Cholesterol (mg): 0.3
Sodium (mg): 176
Protein (gm): 4.2
Carbohydrate (gm): 36.6
Exchanges
Milk: 0.0
Vegetable: 0.0
Fruit: 1.0
Bread: 1.5
Meat: 0.0
Fat: 1.0

1. Make 1/2 recipe Cornmeal Double Pie Crust; press dough evenly on bottom and side of 9-inch tart pan. Bake at 400 degrees until lightly browned, about 15 minutes. If dough has puffed, press with spatula to flatten.

2. Toss fruit with 1/4 cup sugar. Combine remaining sugar and flour and sprinkle on bottom of crust. Arrange fruit in crust.

3. Bake at 350 degrees until apricots are tender and juices have thickened, about 40 to 50 minutes. Cool on wire rack. Sprinkle with powdered sugar.

CANNED APRICOT PIE

Peaches, plums, or other canned fruit can be substituted for the apricots, but apricot pie is a special treat.

8 servings

1 cup sugar
1/4 cup all-purpose flour
1/2 teaspoon ground cinnamon
2 cans (16 ounces each) apricot halves, drained (reserve 1/2 cup juice)
2 teaspoons margarine
Double Pie Crust (see p. 128)

Per Serving
Calories: 355
% Calories from fat: 21
Fat (gm): 8.3
Saturated fat (gm): 1.6
Cholesterol (mg): 0
Sodium (mg): 245
Protein (gm): 4
Carbohydrate (gm): 67.6
Exchanges
Milk: 0.0
Vegetable: 0.0
Fruit: 1.0
Bread: 3.5
Meat: 0.0
Fat: 1.0

1. Mix sugar, flour, cinnamon, and 1/2 cup reserved apricot juice in medium saucepan. Heat to boiling; boil, stirring constantly, until thickened. Stir in apricots and margarine; cool.

2. Roll 2/3 of the Double Pie Crust on lightly floured surface to form circle 1 1/2 inches larger than inverted 8-inch pie pan. Ease pastry into pan. Pour fruit into pan.

3. Roll remaining pastry into circle to fit top of pie and place over apricots; trim edges of pastry to within 1/2 inch of pan; fold top pastry over bottom pastry and flute. Cut vents in top pastry.

4. Bake at 425 degrees 10 minutes; reduce heat to 375 degrees and bake until juices are bubbly and crust is golden, about 40 minutes, covering edge of pie with aluminum foil if necessary to prevent excessive browning. Cool on wire rack.

BEST CHERRY PIE

The perfect pie for Washington's birthday!

8 servings

Double Pie Crust (see p. 128)
2 packages (16 ounces each) frozen unsweetened cherries, thawed, drained (about 4 cups)
1/2 teaspoon almond extract
3/4 cup plus 2 teaspoons sugar, divided
1/3 cup all-purpose flour
2 tablespoons cornstarch
1 teaspoon fat-free milk

Per Serving
Calories: 338
% Calories from fat: 21
Fat (gm): 7.9
Saturated fat (gm): 1.6
Cholesterol (mg): 0
Sodium (mg): 231
Protein (gm): 4.5
Carbohydrate (gm): 63.8
Exchanges
Milk: 0.0
Vegetable: 0.0
Fruit: 0.0
Bread: 1.0
Meat: 0.0
Fat: 3.5

1. Roll 2/3 of the Double Pie Crust on lightly floured surface to form circle 1 1/2 inches larger than inverted 8-inch pie pan. Ease pastry into pan.

2. Combine cherries and almond extract; toss with combined 3/4 cup sugar, flour, and cornstarch. Spoon fruit into pastry.

3. Roll remaining pastry into circle to fit top of pie and place over cherries; trim edges of pastry to within 1/2 inch of pan; fold top pastry over bottom pastry and flute. Cut vents in top pastry; brush with milk and sprinkle with remaining 2 teaspoons sugar.

4. Bake at 425 degrees 10 minutes; reduce heat to 375 degrees and bake until juices are bubbly and crust is golden, 45 to 50 minutes, covering edge of pie with aluminum foil if necessary to prevent excessive browning. Cool on wire rack.

Variation: **Coconut Streusel Cherry Pie**—Make Basic Pie Crust (Cake Flour) (see p.127) in 8-inch pie pan. Prepare cherries as in Step 2 above. To make **Coconut Streusel**, combine 1/2 cup all-purpose flour, 1/2 cup packed light brown sugar, 1/3 cup quick-cooking oats, and 1/3 cup coconut. Cut in 3 tablespoons margarine until mixture resembles coarse crumbs. Sprinkle over cherries. Bake pie as in Step 4 above.

CANNED CHERRY PIE

This filling is easy to make, and lemon juice gives it a fresh cherry flavor.

8 servings

3/4 cup sugar

1 1/2 tablespoons cornstarch

1/2 teaspoon salt

2 cans (16 ounces each) pitted red tart cherries, drained (reserve 1/2 cup juice)

2-3 drops red food coloring

1 teaspoon margarine

2-3 teaspoons lemon juice

Double Pie Crust (see p. 128)

Per Serving
Calories: 305
% Calories from fat: 23
Fat (gm): 8
Saturated fat (gm): 1.6
Cholesterol (mg): 0
Sodium (mg): 388
Protein (gm): 3.8
Carbohydrate (gm): 55.9
Exchanges
Milk: 0.0
Vegetable: 0.0
Fruit: 1.0
Bread: 2.5
Meat: 0.0
Fat: 1.5

1. Mix sugar, cornstarch, salt, and cherries in medium saucepan. Add 1/2 cup reserved cherry juice, food coloring, and margarine. Boil, stirring constantly, until thickened. Stir in lemon juice; cool.

2. Roll 2/3 of the Double Pie Crust on lightly floured surface to form circle 1 1/2 inches larger than inverted 8-inch pie pan. Ease pastry into pan. Pour filling into pastry.

3. Roll remaining pastry into circle to fit top of pie and place over cherries; trim edges of pastry to within 1/2 inch of pan; fold top pastry over bottom pastry and flute. Cut vents in top pastry.

4. Bake at 425 degrees 10 minutes; reduce heat to 375 degrees and bake until juices are bubbly and crust is golden, about 40 minutes, covering edge of pie with aluminum foil if necessary to prevent excessive browning. Cool on wire rack.

BLUEBERRY-CHERRY TART

Blueberries team with dried cherries for a sweet-tart accent.

8 servings

Hazelnut Pastry Crust (see p. 129)
1 egg white
1/4 teaspoon salt
1/3 cup sugar
2 tablespoons chopped toasted blanched hazelnuts *or* almonds
1 tablespoon cornstarch
1/2 cup dried cherries
2 cups fresh blueberries
Orange Glaze (see p. 47)

Per Serving
Calories: 279
% Calories from fat: 29
Fat (gm): 9.2
Saturated fat (gm): 1.2
Cholesterol (mg): 0
Sodium (mg): 280
Protein (gm): 3.7
Carbohydrate (gm): 47.9
Exchanges
Milk: 0.0
Vegetable: 0.0
Fruit: 1.0
Bread: 2.0
Meat: 0.0
Fat: 1.5

1. Roll Hazelnut Tart Crust between sheets of lightly floured waxed paper into a 12-inch round. Ease pastry onto greased pizza pan or baking sheet.

2. Beat egg white and salt in small bowl to soft peaks; beat to stiff peaks, adding sugar gradually. Fold in combined nuts and cornstarch. Spread over dough, leaving a 1 1/2-inch border. Sprinkle with cherries. Mound blueberries on top. Gently fold edge of crust over filling (fruit will not be completely enclosed).

3. Bake at 400 degrees 25 to 30 minutes or until crust is browned and blueberries are puffed; cool on wire rack. Drizzle with Orange Glaze.

Variation: **Grape Tart**—Make recipe as above, substituting walnuts for the hazelnuts in the dough and filling, golden raisins for the dried cherries, and halved red or green seedless grapes for the blueberries. Omit glaze; sprinkle cooled tart with powdered sugar.

RASPBERRY-GLAZED BLUEBERRY TART

Imagine this tart, abundant with just-picked, perfectly ripe berries! Top helpings with a small scoop of frozen low-fat vanilla or lemon yogurt.

8 servings

Basic Pie Crust (All-Purpose Flour) (see p. 126)

- 1 tablespoon sugar
- 4 cups fresh blueberries
- 3/4 cup raspberry spreadable fruit
- 1 tablespoon raspberry-flavor liqueur, optional
- 2 teaspoons cornstarch
- 1/4 teaspoon ground cinnamon
- 1/4 teaspoon ground nutmeg

Per Serving
Calories: 214
% Calories from fat: 25
Fat (gm): 6.1
Saturated fat (gm): 1.2
Cholesterol (mg): 0
Sodium (mg): 174
Protein (gm): 2.6
Carbohydrate (gm): 38
Exchanges
Milk: 0.0
Vegetable: 0.0
Fruit: 0.0
Bread: 2.5
Meat: 0.0
Fat: 1.0

1. Make Basic Pie Crust according to recipe, adding 1 tablespoon sugar and using 9-inch tart pan; bake according to recipe. Cool on wire rack.

2. Arrange blueberries in cooled crust. Combine spreadable fruit, liqueur, cornstarch, cinnamon, and nutmeg in small saucepan. Heat to boiling, stirring constantly. Remove from heat and spoon over blueberries. Refrigerate until glaze is slightly firm, about 30 minutes.

LEMON SOUFFLÉ BLUEBERRY PIE

Plump blueberries are topped with lemon soufflé in a luscious pie.

8 servings

    Basic Pie Crust (All-Purpose Flour)
    (see p. 126)
4 cups fresh, *or* frozen, blueberries
1 cup sugar, divided
2 tablespoons water
4 egg yolks
1 1/2 tablespoons flour
1/3 cup lemon juice
4 egg whites
1/8 teaspoon salt
1 tablespoon grated lemon rind

Per Serving
Calories: 318
% Calories from fat: 24
Fat (gm): 8.7
Saturated fat (gm): 2
Cholesterol (mg): 107
Sodium (mg): 212
Protein (gm): 6
Carbohydrate (gm): 56
Exchanges
Milk: 0.0
Vegetable: 0.0
Fruit: 2.0
Bread: 1.5
Meat: 0.0
Fat: 1.5

1. Bake Basic Pie Crust according to recipe, using 9-inch pie pan. Cool on wire rack.

2. Heat blueberries, 1/2 cup sugar, and water to boiling in medium saucepan, stirring to dissolve sugar. Drain; reserve juice.

3. Beat egg yolks in small bowl until thick and lemon colored, 3 to 4 minutes, gradually adding combined 1/4 cup sugar and flour; beat in lemon juice. Transfer to saucepan; cook over medium-high heat, whisking constantly, until mixture boils and thickens, 2 to 3 minutes. Cool to room temperature.

4. Beat egg whites and salt to soft peaks; beat to stiff peaks, adding remaining 1/4 cup sugar gradually. Add 1/4 of the egg whites to the yolk mixture, mixing until smooth; fold yolk mixture into remaining egg whites. Fold in lemon rind.

5. Spoon blueberry mixture into pie crust; drizzle with 3 tablespoons reserved juice. Spread soufflé mixture over pie, sealing to edge of crust.

6. Bake at 400 degrees until golden, 12 to 15 minutes. Cool on wire rack. Refrigerate.

Variation: **Orange Soufflé Pie**—Omit blueberries, 1/2 cup of the sugar, and water. Make pie as above, substituting orange juice and rind for the lemon juice and rind. Combine 1/3 cup orange marmalade and 1 can (11 ounces) drained Mandarin oranges; fill pie and bake as above.

BLUEBERRY CROSTATA

The pastry crust for this pie is made with cornmeal; the filling is like a rich blueberry jam.

8 servings

3 cups fresh, *or* frozen, blueberries
1 cup granulated sugar
1 tablespoon grated lemon rind
$1/8$ teaspoon ground nutmeg
Cornmeal Double Pie Crust (see p. 128)
Powdered sugar, as garnish

Per Serving
Calories: 337
% Calories from fat: 20
Fat (gm): 7.9
Saturated fat (gm): 1.6
Cholesterol (mg): 0.6
Sodium (mg): 355
Protein (gm): 6.5
Carbohydrate (gm): 61.2
Exchanges
Milk: 0.0
Vegetable: 0.0
Fruit: 0.0
Bread: 4.0
Meat: 0.0
Fat: 1.0

1. Combine blueberries, granulated sugar, and lemon rind in medium saucepan; cook, covered, to simmering. Simmer, uncovered, until mixture is reduced to $1^1/2$ cups; stir in nutmeg. Cool to room temperature.

2. Make Cornmeal Double Pie Crust; scatter $2/3$ of the dough in 9-inch tart pan. Pat dough evenly on bottom and side of pan. Roll remaining dough between waxed paper to $1/8$ inch thickness. Cut into $1/2$-inch strips.

3. Spoon blueberry mixture into crust, spreading evenly. Top with pastry strips, weaving strips to form lattice pattern.

4. Bake at 350 degrees until golden, 45 to 50 minutes. Cool on wire rack. Sprinkle with powdered sugar.

DOUBLE-CRUST BLUEBERRY PIE

Nothing's better at the height of summer than fresh blueberry pie, but frozen blueberries can be substituted to give that taste of summer whenever you wish!

8 servings

Double Pie Crust (see p. 128)
4 cups blueberries
1 cup sugar
1/3 cup all-purpose flour
2 teaspoons grated lemon rind
1 teaspoon cinnamon
1/2 teaspoon salt
2 teaspoons margarine

Per Serving
Calories: 347
% Calories from fat: 21
Fat (gm): 8.6
Saturated fat (gm): 1.7
Cholesterol (mg): 0
Sodium (mg): 390
Protein (gm): 4
Carbohydrate (gm): 65
Exchanges
Milk: 0.0
Vegetable: 0.0
Fruit: 1.0
Bread: 3.5
Meat: 0.0
Fat: 1.0

1. Roll 2/3 of the Double Pie Crust on lightly floured surface to form circle 1 1/2 inches larger than inverted 9-inch pie pan. Ease pastry into pan.

2. Combine blueberries, sugar, flour, lemon rind, cinnamon, and salt. Spoon fruit into pastry; dot with margarine.

3. Roll remaining pastry into circle to fit top of pie and place over blueberries. Trim edges of pastry to within 1/2 inch of pan; fold top pastry over bottom pastry and flute. Cut vents in top pastry.

4. Bake at 425 degrees 10 minutes; reduce heat to 375 degrees and bake until juices are bubbly and crust is golden, 40 to 50 minutes, covering edge of pie with aluminum foil if necessary to prevent excessive browning. Cool on wire rack.

Variations: **Black Grape Pie**—Substitute 5 cups seedless black or red grapes for blueberries. Decrease sugar to 2/3 cup, and substitute 3 tablespoons quick-cooking tapioca for the flour. Prepare fruit and bake pie as directed above.

Rhubarb Pie—Make pie as above, substituting 4 cups sliced rhubarb for blueberries. Increase sugar to 1 1/2 cups, and substitute orange rind for the lemon rind. Top with a lattice crust and bake as directed above.

Pineapple Rhubarb Pie—Make pie as above, substituting 3 cups sliced rhubarb and 1 cup crushed canned pineapple, drained, for the blueberries. Increase sugar to 1 1/3 cups and substitute orange rind for the lemon rind; omit cinnamon.

FRENCH BLUEBERRY TART

Fresh blueberries nestled in a tender shortbread crust.

10 servings

Shortbread Crust (see p. 130)
1¹/₄ cups sugar
2 tablespoons cornstarch
¹/₈ teaspoon ground mace
3-4 cups blueberries, divided
1 tablespoon lemon juice
1 teaspoon grated lemon rind
10 tablespoons light whipped topping

Per Serving
Calories: 281
% Calories from fat: 22
Fat (gm): 7
Saturated fat (gm): 1.8
Cholesterol (mg): 21.2
Sodium (mg): 76.2
Protein (gm): 2.7
Carbohydrate (gm): 52.6
Exchanges
Milk: 0.0
Vegetable: 0.0
Fruit: 1.0
Bread: 2.5
Meat: 0.0
Fat: 1.0

1. Roll Shortbread Crust between lightly floured sheets of waxed paper into 12-inch circle. Ease pastry into 10-inch tart pan. Trim excess pastry and pierce bottom with fork. Bake at 350 degrees until golden brown, about 15 minutes. Cool on wire rack.

2. Combine sugar, cornstarch, mace, 1 cup blueberries, lemon juice, and rind in medium saucepan. Cook over medium heat, stirring constantly, until boiling and thickened; cool slightly. Stir in remaining blueberries. Pour into cooled crust. Chill 2 to 3 hours.

3. Cut into wedges and serve with light whipped topping.

Variations: **Raspberry Glacé Pie**—Prepare pie as above, substituting raspberries for the blueberries. Omit mace. Beat ¹/₄ package (8-ounce size) reduced-fat cream cheese, 1 tablespoon sugar, and 1 tablespoon fat-free milk until smooth; spread on bottom of crust. Pour fruit filling over cheese. Chill.

Blueberry Lemon Cheese Pie—Bake Basic Pie Crust (All-Purpose Flour) (see p. 126), using 9-inch pie pan; cool. Beat 1 package (8 ounces) reduced-fat cream cheese until smooth; add 1 can (14 ounces) sweetened condensed milk and ¹/₂ cup lemon juice. Fold in 1 cup blueberries; spoon filling into prepared crust. Chill 1 to 2 hours. Cook sugar, cornstarch, mace, 1 cup blueberries, lemon juice, and rind following Step 2 above; cool and stir in remaining 1 cup berries. Spoon berries over pie; chill before serving.

MIXED BERRY TART

Select as many kinds of berries as you can for beautiful color and texture contrast.

8 servings

Shortbread Crust (see p. 130)
Mock Mascarpone (recipe follows)
3-4 cups mixed berries (raspberries, black-berries, strawberries, blueberries, gooseberries, currants, etc.)
1/4 cup currant, *or* apple, jelly, melted
Powdered sugar, as garnish

Per Serving
Calories: 264
% Calories from fat: 31
Fat (gm): 9
Saturated fat (gm): 2.3
Cholesterol (mg): 30.9
Sodium (mg): 255
Protein (gm): 8
Carbohydrate (gm): 37.9
Exchanges
Milk: 0.0
Vegetable: 0.0
Fruit: 0.5
Bread: 2.0
Meat: 0.0
Fat: 2.0

1. Roll Shortbread Crust between 2 sheets of waxed paper into 12-inch circle. Ease into 10-inch tart pan and trim. Pierce bottom with fork. Bake at 425 degrees until crisp and golden brown, 10 to 15 minutes. Cool on wire rack.

2. Spread Mock Mascarpone evenly on cooled crust; top with berries and drizzle with jam. Dust serving plates with powdered sugar; top with tart slices.

Mock Mascarpone

makes about 1 1/4 cups

1 package (8 ounces) fat-free cream cheese, softened
3 tablespoons reduced-fat sour cream
2-3 tablespoons 2% reduced-fat milk

1. Beat cream cheese until fluffy; mix in sour cream and milk. Refrigerate several hours, or up to several days.

STRAWBERRY-RHUBARB PIE

The classic spring pie, now with a crisp streusel top.

10 servings

1¹/2 cups sugar
3 tablespoons flour
3 tablespoons cornstarch
¹/4 teaspoon ground nutmeg
1 tablespoon lemon juice
3 cups sliced rhubarb
1 cup sliced strawberries
Basic Pie Crust (Cake Flour) (see p. 127)
Spiced Streusel Topping (see p. 139)

Per Serving
Calories: 351
% Calories from fat: 21
Fat (gm): 8.7
Saturated fat (gm): 1.7
Cholesterol (mg): 0
Sodium (mg): 158
Protein (gm): 3.2
Carbohydrate (gm): 66.7
Exchanges
Milk: 0.0
Vegetable: 0.0
Fruit: 1.0
Bread: 3.5
Meat: 0.0
Fat: 1.0

1. Combine sugar, flour, cornstarch, nutmeg, and lemon juice in large saucepan; stir in rhubarb. Heat to boiling; reduce heat and simmer, uncovered, stirring frequently, until mixture is thickened and rhubarb is almost tender, about 3 minutes. Stir in strawberries.

2. Roll Basic Pie Crust on lightly floured surface to form a circle 1¹/2 inches larger than inverted 9-inch pie pan. Ease pastry into pan; trim and flute. Spoon fruit into pan; top with Spiced Streusel Topping.

3. Bake at 350 degrees until juices are bubbly, about 40 minutes, covering pie with aluminum foil if necessary to prevent excessive browning. Cool on wire rack.

PLUM-NECTARINE POUCH PIE

Fresh summer fruit in a delicious free-form crust.

10 servings

Cream Cheese Tart Crust (see p. 131)
2 cups sliced pitted plums
2 cups sliced pitted nectarines
3 tablespoons flour
1/2 cup sugar, divided
1 teaspoon fat-free milk
1/4 cup red currant jelly, melted

Per Serving
Calories: 371
% Calories from fat: 29
Fat (gm): 12.3
Saturated fat (gm): 3.3
Cholesterol (mg): 27.4
Sodium (mg): 191
Protein (gm): 5.2
Carbohydrate (gm): 61.4
Exchanges
Milk: 0.0
Vegetable: 0.0
Fruit: 2.0
Bread: 2.0
Meat: 0.0
Fat: 2.0

1. Roll Cream Cheese Tart Crust between two sheets waxed paper into 14-inch circle (edges do not have to be even). Remove 1 sheet of waxed paper and invert crust onto large greased cookie sheet; remove remaining paper.

2. Toss fruit with combined flour and 1/3 cup sugar. Arrange fruit in center of pastry, leaving a 2- to 3-inch border around outer edge. Gently gather and fold outer edge of pastry over fruit, leaving center uncovered. Brush edge of pastry with milk and sprinkle remaining sugar over fruit and crust.

3. Bake at 400 degrees 20 to 25 minutes or until crust is lightly browned and fruit is tender. Brush fruit with jelly. Cut into wedges and serve warm.

Variation: **Rhubarb-Peach Pouch Pie**—Make pie as above, increasing sugar to 1 cup and substituting 2 cups sliced rhubarb and 2 cups sliced peaches for the plums and nectarines.

RUSTIC COUNTRY FRUIT TART

Perfect for a lazy-day summer picnic—a tumble of garden fruits, lightly glazed and encased in a free-form pastry.

8 servings

Basic Pie Crust (All-Purpose Flour) (see p. 126)

1/2 cup all-purpose flour, divided

2 tablespoons cold margarine

1 pint raspberries

1 pint strawberries, sliced

1 cup seedless grapes

3 medium apricots, cut in halves, pitted

3 medium peaches *or* nectarines, cut in halves, peeled, pitted

1/3 cup sugar

1/2 teaspoon ground cinnamon

1/4 cup apricot spreadable fruit

2 tablespoons water

Per Serving
Calories: 284
% Calories from fat: 28
Fat (gm): 9.2
Saturated fat (gm): 1.8
Cholesterol (mg): 0
Sodium (mg): 184
Protein (gm): 4
Carbohydrate (gm): 48.1
Exchanges
Milk: 0.0
Vegetable: 0.0
Fruit: 1.0
Bread: 2.0
Meat: 0.0
Fat: 2.0

1. Make Basic Pie Crust, adding 1/4 cup flour and 2 tablespoons margarine. Roll pastry on lightly floured surface into a 12-inch circle (edges do not need to be even). Transfer pastry to a 12-inch pizza pan.

2. Toss fruits with combined remaining 1/4 cup flour, sugar, and cinnamon. Arrange fruits in center of pastry, leaving a 2- to 3-inch border around outer edge. Gently gather and fold outer edge of pastry over fruits, leaving center uncovered.

3. Bake at 425 degrees 20 to 25 minutes or until crust is lightly browned and fruit is tender. Heat spreadable fruit and water in small saucepan until warm; brush over fruit. Cut into wedges and serve warm.

Variation: **Apricot-Almond Tart**—Make tart as above, substituting 12 large pitted apricots for the other fruit, and pumpkin pie spice for the cinnamon. Combine 1/4 cup ground almonds and remaining 1/4 cup flour and sprinkle over rolled pastry. Arrange apricots over center of pastry, leaving 2-inch border. Combine sugar and pumpkin pie spice and sprinkle over fruit. Fold in the edges as above and top with 2 tablespoons sliced almonds; bake and glaze as in Step 3.

FRUITS OF THE HARVEST PIE

From your own bounty, or the frozen food section of the supermarket!

8 servings

Double Pie Crust (see p. 128)
2 cups chopped, peeled, cored apple
1 cup sliced fresh, *or* frozen, thawed rhubarb
1 cup fresh, *or* frozen, thawed blueberries
1 cup fresh, *or* frozen, thawed raspberries
1 cup sugar
1/2 cup all-purpose flour
1/2 teaspoon salt
1 tablespoon orange juice
2 teaspoons grated orange rind
2 teaspoons margarine

Per Serving
Calories: 356
% Calories from fat: 21
Fat (gm): 8.7
Saturated fat (gm): 1.7
Cholesterol (mg): 0
Sodium (mg): 388
Protein (gm): 4.3
Carbohydrate (gm): 66.7
Exchanges
Milk: 0.0
Vegetable: 0.0
Fruit: 1.0
Bread: 3.5
Meat: 0.0
Fat: 1.0

1. Roll 2/3 of the Double Pie Crust on lightly floured surface to form circle 1 1/2 inches larger than inverted 9-inch pie pan. Ease pastry into pan.

2. Toss fruit with combined sugar, flour, and salt. Spoon fruit into pastry; sprinkle with orange juice and orange rind, and dot with margarine.

3. Roll remaining pastry into circle to fit top of pie and place over fruit; trim edges of pastry to within 1/2 inch of pan; fold top pastry over bottom pastry and flute. Cut vents in top pastry.

4. Bake at 425 degrees 10 minutes; reduce heat to 375 degrees and bake until juices are bubbly and crust is golden, 30 to 40 minutes, covering edge of pie with aluminum foil if necessary to prevent excessive browning. Cool on wire rack.

GLAZED FRUIT PIE

Choose your favorite fresh fruit and follow this basic recipe—fresh tasting and easy!

8 servings

Basic Pie Crust (All-Purpose Flour)
(see p. 126)
6 cups fresh fruit (peaches, nectarines, pears, strawberries, raspberries, blueberries, etc.)
1 cup sugar
3 tablespoons cornstarch
1/2 cup orange, *or* apple, juice
2 tablespoons lemon juice

Per Serving
Calories: 305
% Calories from fat: 17
Fat (gm): 6
Saturated fat (gm): 1.2
Cholesterol (mg): 0
Sodium (mg): 140
Protein (gm): 3.1
Carbohydrate (gm): 62
Exchanges
Milk: 0.0
Vegetable: 0.0
Fruit: 1.0
Bread: 3.0
Meat: 0.0
Fat: 0.5

1. Bake Basic Pie Crust according to recipe, using 9-inch pie pan. Cool on wire rack.

2. Mash enough fruit to measure 1 cup. Combine sugar and cornstarch in saucepan; stir in orange juice and mashed fruit. Cook over medium heat, stirring constantly until mixture boils and thickens, about 5 minutes; stir in lemon juice. Cool slightly.

3. Pour 1/2 the fruit mixture into baked crust; spread over bottom and up side, completely covering crust. Fill with remaining fruit. Pour remaining glaze over top, covering fruit. Refrigerate 3 hours or longer.

Tip: Peach, nectarines, and pears should be peeled and sliced before using. Berries can be used whole.

Variation: **Strawberry Melon Pie**—Bake crust, following Step 1. Mash 1 cup strawberries and cook with sugar, cornstarch, and juices as above. Beat 1/2 package (8-ounce size) reduced-fat cream cheese with 1 tablespoon fat-free milk until smooth. Spread over bottom of crust. Top with 3 cups cantaloupe and/or honeydew balls or cubes. Pour strawberry mixture over. Chill.

GREEN TOMATO PIE

And you thought this fruit was only good fried and eaten as a vegetable? Try this old-fashioned favorite and see how delicious dessert can be. To peel tomatoes easily, dip in boiling water 30 to 60 seconds.

8 servings

    Cornmeal Double Pie Crust (see p. 128)
- 5 cups thinly sliced, peeled green tomatoes
- 1 cup granulated sugar
- 3 tablespoons flour
- 1/4 teaspoon salt
- 1/4 teaspoon ground cinnamon
- 1/4 teaspoon ground nutmeg
- 1/8 teaspoon ground cloves
- 1 tablespoon grated lemon rind
- 1/4 cup lemon juice
- 1 1/2 tablespoons margarine

Per Serving
Calories: 372
% Calories from fat: 24
Fat (gm): 10
Saturated fat (gm): 2
Cholesterol (mg): 0.6
Sodium (mg): 468
Protein (gm): 8.2
Carbohydrate (gm): 64
Exchanges
Milk: 0.0
Vegetable: 2.0
Fruit: 0.0
Bread: 3.5
Meat: 0.0
Fat: 1.5

1. Roll 2/3 of the Cornmeal Double Pie Crust between sheets of lightly floured waxed paper to form circle 1 1/2 inches larger than inverted 9-inch pie pan. Ease pastry into pan.

2. Toss tomatoes with combined sugar, flour, salt, spices, and lemon rind. Arrange tomatoes in pan; sprinkle with lemon juice. Dot with margarine. Roll remaining pastry between sheets of waxed paper to 1/4 inch thickness. Cut into 1/2-inch wide strips; arrange on top of pie in lattice pattern. Flute edge of crust.

3. Bake at 425 degrees 10 minutes; reduce heat to 375 degrees and bake until juices are bubbly and crust is golden, 40 to 50 minutes, covering edge of pie with aluminum foil if necessary to prevent excessive browning. Cool on wire rack.

Variation: **Green Tomato Apple Pie**—Make pie as above, using 2 cups green tomatoes and 3 cups sliced, peeled apples. Substitute 2/3 cup packed light brown sugar and 1/3 cup granulated sugar for the sugar in recipe. Complete recipe as above.

GRANDMA'S LEMON MERINGUE PIE

A perfect flavor combination of sweet and tart, topped with a mile-high meringue! Be sure to spread the meringue while filling is hot, and seal it to the edge of the crust to prevent weeping.

10 servings

Basic Pie Crust (All-Purpose Flour)
(see p. 126)
2 cups sugar, divided
1/2 cup cornstarch
1 1/2 cups water
1/2 cup lemon juice
1 egg
2 tablespoons margarine
4 egg whites
1/4 teaspoon cream of tartar

Per Serving
Calories: 324
% Calories from fat: 20
Fat (gm): 7.4
Saturated fat (gm): 1.5
Cholesterol (mg): 21.2
Sodium (mg): 168
Protein (gm): 3.8
Carbohydrate (gm): 61.6
Exchanges
Milk: 0.0
Vegetable: 0.0
Fruit: 0.0
Bread: 4.0
Meat: 0.0
Fat: 1.0

1. Bake Basic Pie Crust according to recipe, using 9-inch pie pan. Cool on wire rack.

2. Combine 1 1/2 cups sugar and cornstarch in medium saucepan; stir in water and lemon juice. Heat to boiling; boil, whisking constantly, until thickened, about 1 minute.

3. Beat egg in small bowl; whisk about 1 cup of lemon mixture into egg mixture. Whisk egg mixture back into saucepan; cook over very low heat, whisking constantly, 30 to 60 seconds. Remove from heat; add margarine, stirring until melted. Pour into pie crust.

4. Using clean beaters and large bowl, beat egg whites until foamy; add cream of tartar and beat to soft peaks. Beat to stiff peaks, adding remaining 1/2 cup sugar gradually. Spread meringue over hot filling, sealing well to edge of pie crust.

5. Bake at 400 degrees until meringue is browned, about 5 minutes. Cool to room temperature before cutting. Refrigerate leftover pie.

LEMON SOUR CREAM PIE

A creamy variation of Lemon Meringue Pie.

8 servings

Basic Pie Crust (All-Purpose Flour)
(see p. 126)
1¹/₃ cups sugar, divided
3 tablespoons cornstarch
Dash salt
1 cup fat-free milk
3 egg yolks, beaten
1-2 tablespoons margarine
1 teaspoon grated lemon rind
¹/₄ cup lemon juice
1 cup fat-free sour cream
3 egg whites
¹/₄ teaspoon cream of tartar

Per Serving
Calories: 364
% Calories from fat: 23
Fat (gm): 9.2
Saturated fat (gm): 2
Cholesterol (mg): 80
Sodium (mg): 221
Protein (gm): 7.6
Carbohydrate (gm): 62.6
Exchanges
Milk: 0.0
Vegetable: 0.0
Fruit: 0.0
Bread: 4.0
Meat: 0.0
Fat: 1.5

1. Bake Basic Pie Crust according to recipe, using 9-inch pie pan. Cool on wire rack.

2. Combine 1 cup sugar, cornstarch, and salt in medium saucepan; stir in milk. Heat to boiling; boil, whisking constantly until thickened, about 1 minute. Whisk about ¹/₂ cup of hot mixture into egg yolks; whisk egg mixture into saucepan. Cook over very low heat, whisking constantly, 1 to 2 minutes. Stir in margarine, lemon rind, and juice; cool 10 minutes. Stir in sour cream. Pour into pastry.

3. Using clean beaters and large bowl, beat egg whites until foamy; add cream of tartar and beat to soft peaks. Beat to stiff peaks, adding remaining ¹/₃ cup sugar gradually. Spread meringue over hot filling, sealing to edge of pastry. Bake at 400 degrees until meringue is browned, about 5 minutes. Cool on wire rack.

ELEGANT LEMON TART

This tart proves once again that the simplest things are the best!

10 servings

Cream Cheese Tart Crust (see p. 131)
3 eggs
1 cup sugar
2 tablespoons flour
1/2 cup lemon juice
Powdered sugar, as garnish

Per Serving
Calories: 359
% Calories from fat: 33
Fat (gm): 13.2
Saturated fat (gm): 3.7
Cholesterol (mg): 91
Sodium (mg): 208
Protein (gm): 6.2
Carbohydrate (gm): 54.2
Exchanges
Milk: 0.0
Vegetable: 0.0
Fruit: 0.0
Bread: 2.5
Meat: 0.0
Fat: 2.5

1. Make Cream Cheese Tart Crust, using 9-inch tart pan. Pierce bottom and side with fork; bake at 350 degrees until golden brown, about 15 minutes.

2. Beat remaining ingredients, except powdered sugar, until smooth. Pour into crust; bake until filling is set, about 15 minutes. Sprinkle warm tart with powdered sugar. Cool on wire rack.

Variation: **Melon-Lime Tart**—Make tart as above, substituting lime juice for the lemon juice. Delete powdered sugar. When tart is completely cool, arrange 3 to 4 cups thinly sliced ripe cantaloupe and honeydew melon in overlapping layers over lime filling. Garnish with mint leaves or fresh berries.

SWEET STRIP LEMON PIE

A sweet lemony filling is topped with brown sugar pastry strips to make this unusual pie.

12 servings

Cornmeal Double Pie Crust (see p. 128)

- 1/3 cup packed light brown sugar
- 1 cup granulated sugar
- 1 cup dark corn syrup
- 1 cup cold water
- 2 eggs, lightly beaten
- 3 tablespoons flour
- 2 tablespoons lemon juice
- 2 teaspoons grated lemon rind

Per Serving
Calories: 327
% Calories from fat: 16
Fat (gm): 6
Saturated fat (gm): 1.3
Cholesterol (mg): 36
Sodium (mg): 266
Protein (gm): 5.3
Carbohydrate (gm): 64
Exchanges
Milk: 0.0
Vegetable: 0.0
Fruit: 0.0
Bread: 4.0
Meat: 0.0
Fat: 1.0

1. Make Cornmeal Double Pie Crust, adding 1/3 cup brown sugar. Roll 1/2 the pastry between 2 sheets of lightly floured waxed paper to 11-inch circle. Ease pastry into 9-inch pie pan.

2. Combine remaining ingredients in medium saucepan, whisking until smooth. Heat to boiling, whisking constantly, and cook until thickened, 1 to 2 minutes. Cool slightly; pour into pastry.

3. Roll remaining pastry between sheets of lightly floured waxed paper to 1/4 inch thickness. Cut dough into 1-inch-wide strips. Twist pastry strips and layer over filling in parallel lines; seal strips to edge of pastry and trim.

4. Bake at 350 degrees until golden brown, about 35 minutes. Cool; refrigerate 1 to 2 hours.

LEMON CHESS PIE

Unadulterated lemon for TRUE lemon lovers—but this pie would also be delicious with lime.

10 servings

Basic Pie Crust (All-Purpose Flour)
(see p. 126)

2 tablespoons grated lemon rind, divided
2 cups sugar
1¹/₂ tablespoons flour
¹/₄ cup lemon juice
¹/₄ cup fat-free milk
4 eggs
Light whipped topping, as garnish

Per Serving
Calories: 300
% Calories from fat: 20
Fat (gm): 6.7
Saturated fat (gm): 1.5
Cholesterol (mg): 85
Sodium (mg): 141
Protein (gm): 4.5
Carbohydrate (gm): 56.6
Exchanges
Milk: 0.0
Vegetable: 0.0
Fruit: 0.0
Bread: 3.5
Meat: 0.0
Fat: 1.0

1. Make Basic Pie Crust according to recipe, adding 1 tablespoon lemon rind and using 9-inch pie pan.

2. Beat remaining ingredients, except whipped topping, until smooth. Pour into pastry.

3. Bake at 375 degrees until set, about 45 minutes. Cool on wire rack; refrigerate 2 to 3 hours. Serve with whipped topping.

LEMON PUDDING PIE

As this lemony pie filling bakes, it forms a cake-like layer over sweet lemon pudding.

10 servings

Basic Pie Crust (All-Purpose Flour)
(see p. 126)
2 tablespoons grated lemon rind, divided
1¹/₂ cups sugar
¹/₃ cup all-purpose flour
Pinch salt
¹/₃ cup lemon juice
2 egg yolks
1 tablespoon margarine, melted
1¹/₄ cups fat-free milk
3 egg whites

Per Serving
Calories: 279
% Calories from fat: 22
Fat (gm): 6.9
Saturated fat (gm): 1.5
Cholesterol (mg): 43.1
Sodium (mg): 159
Protein (gm): 4.8
Carbohydrate (gm): 50.1
Exchanges
Milk: 0.0
Vegetable: 0.0
Fruit: 0.0
Bread: 3.5
Meat: 0.0
Fat: 1.0

1. Make Basic Pie Crust according to recipe, adding 1 table-spoon lemon rind and using 9-inch pie pan.

2. Combine sugar, flour, and salt; beat in lemon juice, remaining 1 tablespoon lemon rind, egg yolks, margarine, and milk. Beat egg whites until stiff peaks form; fold into lemon mixture. Pour filling into pastry.

3. Bake at 375 degrees about 50 minutes until filling is set and richly browned. Cool on wire rack.

LEMON CLOUD PIE

Other flavors of this wonderful dessert are easy. Just substitute another low-fat fruit yogurt for the lemon. Strawberry, raspberry, or cherry are possible choices.

8 servings

Meringue Pie Crust (see p. 132)
1½ cups light whipped topping
1½ cups low-fat custard-style lemon yogurt
2 tablespoons lemon rind, grated
Lemon slices, as garnish

Per Serving
Calories: 176
% Calories from fat: 11
Fat (gm): 2.1
Saturated fat (gm): 1.9
Cholesterol (mg): 2.8
Sodium (mg): 58
Protein (gm): 3.7
Carbohydrate (gm): 35.3
Exchanges
Milk: 0.0
Vegetable: 0.0
Fruit: 0.0
Bread: 2.0
Meat: 0.0
Fat: 0.5

1. Make Meringue Pie Crust, using 9-inch pie pan.

2. Combine whipped topping, yogurt, and lemon rind in small bowl. Spoon into center of meringue shell. Garnish with lemon slices. Refrigerate.

Variation: **Summer Cloud Pie**—Prepare pie as above, substituting raspberry or peach custard-style yogurt for the lemon. Add 2 tablespoons orange rind in place of lemon rind. Fill meringue shell as above, and top pie with 2-3 cups combined fresh whole raspberries, blueberries, and sliced strawberries.

BERRY LEMON CREAM PIE

Double lemon, and "berry" sweet. Substitute any fresh berries you like.

8 servings

Lemon Cookie Crumb Crust (see p. 136)
Pastry Cream (see p. 268)
2 tablespoons lemon juice
2 teaspoons grated lemon rind
1 cup light whipped topping
3 cups fresh blackberries
1/3 cup seedless raspberry jam, melted

Per Serving
Calories: 295
% Calories from fat: 28
Fat (gm): 9.3
Saturated fat (gm): 3.2
Cholesterol (mg): 55.9
Sodium (mg): 68
Protein (gm): 2.5
Carbohydrate (gm): 52
Exchanges
Milk: 0.0
Vegetable: 0.0
Fruit: 1.0
Bread: 2.5
Meat: 0.0
Fat: 1.5

1. Make Lemon Cookie Crumb Crust, using 9-inch pie pan.

2. Make Pastry Cream, deleting vanilla, and adding lemon juice and rind; chill. Fold in whipped topping and spoon into crust.

3. Arrange berries on top of filling and brush with jam. Refrigerate at least 1 hour.

Variation: **Ginger Peachy Pie**—Substitute Gingersnap Crumb Crust (see p. 135) for the Lemon Cookie Crumb Crust. Make pie as above, substituting 2 tablespoons chopped crystallized ginger for the lemon juice and rind, and adding 1/2 teaspoon ground ginger to the Pastry Cream. Top with 3 cups sliced, pitted, peeled peaches, and glaze with heated, strained apricot jam.

CITRUS CREAM TART

A delicious light ending to a rich meal, this pie has a wonderful creamy texture in a crispy lemon crust.

10 servings

Lemon Cookie Crumb Crust (see p. 136)
1 can (14 ounces) low-fat sweetened condensed milk
1/3 cup orange juice
3 tablespoons lemon juice
3 eggs
1 tablespoon grated orange rind
1 tablespoon grated lemon rind
1 1/4 cups light whipped topping

Per Serving
Calories: 272
% Calories from fat: 33
Fat (gm): 10.3
Saturated fat (gm): 3
Cholesterol (mg): 74.8
Sodium (mg): 106
Protein (gm): 5.1
Carbohydrate (gm): 40
Exchanges
Milk: 0.0
Vegetable: 0.0
Fruit: 0.0
Bread: 2.5
Meat: 0.0
Fat: 2.0

1. Make Lemon Cookie Crumb Crust, using 9-inch tart pan.

2. Beat remaining ingredients, except whipped topping, until smooth; pour into crust.

3. Bake at 325 degrees until set, about 30 minutes. Cool on wire rack. Serve with whipped topping.

BAKED KEY LIME PIE

The traditional key lime pie, but baked with mile-high meringue.

8 servings

Graham Cracker Crust (see p. 132)
1 can (14 ounces) fat-free sweetened condensed milk
1/2 cup Key lime, *or* Persian lime, juice
1/3 cup water
3 egg yolks, lightly beaten
1 tablespoon finely grated lime rind
4 egg whites
1/4 teaspoon cream of tartar
1/2 cup sugar

Per Serving
Calories: 371
% Calories from fat: 23
Fat (gm): 9.8
Saturated fat (gm): 2.2
Cholesterol (mg): 80
Sodium (mg): 207
Protein (gm): 8.1
Carbohydrate (gm): 63.5
Exchanges
Milk: 0.5
Vegetable: 0.0
Fruit: 0.0
Bread: 3.5
Meat: 0.0
Fat: 2.0

1. Make Graham Cracker Crust, using 9-inch pie pan.

2. Mix sweetened condensed milk, lime juice, water, egg yolks, and lime rind until smooth in large bowl; pour into crust. Bake at 350 degrees 30 minutes; remove to wire rack.

3. During last 5 minutes of baking time, using large, clean bowl and beaters, beat egg whites and cream of tartar to soft peaks. Beat to stiff peaks, adding sugar gradually. Spread meringue over hot filling, sealing to edge of crust.

4. Increase oven temperature to 400 degrees. Bake pie until meringue is browned, about 5 minutes. Cool on wire rack; refrigerate at least 1 hour.

KEY LIME CREAM CHEESE PIE

Named after the Florida Keys, key limes are small in size and yellow in color.

8 servings

Basic Pie Crust (Cake Flour) (see p. 127)

- 3/4 cup sugar
- 1 envelope unflavored gelatin
- 1 1/4 cups fat-free milk
- 6 ounces reduced-fat cream cheese, softened
- 1/3-1/2 cup Key lime, *or* Persian lime, juice
  Lime slices, as garnish
  Fresh mint, as garnish

Per Serving
Calories: 244
% Calories from fat: 29
Fat (gm): 7.8
Saturated fat (gm): 3.2
Cholesterol (mg): 10.7
Sodium (mg): 245
Protein (gm): 4.9
Carbohydrate (gm): 38.6
Exchanges
Milk: 0.0
Vegetable: 0.0
Fruit: 0.0
Bread: 2.5
Meat: 0.0
Fat: 1.5

1. Bake Basic Pie Crust according to recipe, using 9-inch pie pan. Cool on wire rack.

2. Mix sugar and gelatin in small saucepan; stir in milk. Cook over low heat until sugar and gelatin are dissolved, stirring constantly; remove from heat.

3. Beat cream cheese in medium bowl until fluffy; beat in lime juice until smooth. Gradually add milk mixture, mixing until smooth. Pour mixture into cooled pie crust. Refrigerate until set, 2 to 4 hours. Garnish with lime slices and mint.

FROZEN MARGARITA PIE

A key lime pie, touched with tequila and frozen! The pie can be refrigerated instead of frozen, if desired.

8 servings

Vanilla Crumb Crust (see p. 133)
1 can (14 ounces) fat-free sweetened condensed milk
1/2 cup Key lime, *or* Persian lime, juice
1 tablespoon finely grated lime rind
3 tablespoons tequila
1 1/2-2 cups light whipped topping
Lime slices, as garnish

Per Serving
Calories: 306
% Calories from fat: 24
Fat (gm): 7.9
Saturated fat (gm): 3
Cholesterol (mg): 0
Sodium (mg): 146
Protein (gm): 4.5
Carbohydrate (gm): 50.1
Exchanges
Milk: 0.0
Vegetable: 0.0
Fruit: 0.0
Bread: 3.5
Meat: 0.0
Fat: 1.5

1. Make Vanilla Crumb Crust, using 9-inch pie pan.

2. Mix sweetened condensed milk, lime juice, lime rind, and tequila; fold in whipped topping. Spoon mixture into crust; freeze until firm, 6 hours or overnight.

3. Let pie stand at room temperature 15 to 30 minutes before cutting; garnish with lime slices.

KIWI TART

Add other sliced spring or summer fruit to this tart if you wish.

8 servings

Basic Pie Crust (Cake Flour) (see p. 127)
1/4 cup sugar
2 tablespoons cornstarch
1 1/4 cups 2% reduced-fat milk
1 tablespoon lemon juice
1 egg, slightly beaten
5 medium kiwi fruit, peeled and sliced

Per Serving
Calories: 208
% Calories from fat: 31
Fat (gm): 7.4
Saturated fat (gm): 1.8
Cholesterol (mg): 29.3
Sodium (mg): 169
Protein (gm): 4
Carbohydrate (gm): 32.1
Exchanges
Milk: 0.0
Vegetable: 0.0
Fruit: 0.0
Bread: 2.0
Meat: 0.0
Fat: 1.5

1. Bake Basic Pie Crust according to recipe, using 9-inch tart pan. Cool on wire rack.

2. Mix sugar and cornstarch in small saucepan; stir in milk and lemon juice. Cook over medium heat until mixture boils and thickens; boil 1 minute, stirring constantly. Stir about ¹/₂ cup milk mixture into egg; stir egg mixture back into saucepan. Cook over low heat, stirring constantly, until thickened, about 1 minute.

3. Spoon hot custard into cooled pie crust, spreading evenly; cool to room temperature. Lightly cover custard with plastic wrap; refrigerate 2 to 4 hours or until set. Just before serving, arrange kiwi slices in overlapping circles on custard.

ISLAND DREAM PIE

A taste of the Caribbean in this tropical chiffon pie!

8 servings

Vanilla Crumb Crust (see p. 133)
1 medium banana, cut up
1 medium mango, peeled, cut up
¹/₂ cup light rum *or* orange juice
1 tablespoon lemon juice
6 tablespoons sugar, divided
1 envelope unflavored gelatin
2 egg yolks
2 tablespoons banana liqueur *or*
    ¹/₂ teaspoon banana extract
4 teaspoons meringue powder
¹/₄ cup water
2 cups light whipped topping
    Chopped macadamia nuts, as garnish

Per Serving
Calories: 290
% Calories from fat: 30
Fat (gm): 9.8
Saturated fat (gm): 4
Cholesterol (mg): 53.3
Sodium (mg): 111
Protein (gm): 2.4
Carbohydrate (gm): 38.1
Exchanges
Milk: 0.0
Vegetable: 0.0
Fruit: 0.5
Bread: 2.0
Meat: 0.0
Fat: 2.5

1. Make Vanilla Crumb Crust, using 9-inch pie pan.

2. Process fruit, rum, and lemon juice in blender or food processor until smooth. Mix ¹/₄ cup sugar and gelatin in small saucepan. Beat in egg yolks and ¹/₂ cup of the fruit mixture. Cook over medium heat, stirring constantly, until thickened. Remove from heat; stir in remaining fruit mixture and liqueur. Chill until mixture mounds when dropped from a spoon.

3. Beat meringue powder with water until foamy in medium bowl; continue beating, adding remaining 2 tablespoons sugar, until stiff peaks form. Fold fruit mixture into meringue; fold in whipped topping.

4. Pour filling into crust. Chill 2 to 3 hours before serving. Sprinkle with nuts.

Tip: Meringue powder can be purchased in the baking section of many stores. Raw egg whites, which were formerly used in chiffon pies, are considered unsafe.

BANANA-STRAWBERRY CREAM PIE

Strawberries add a new twist to this old favorite. Refrigerate until the cream filling is set and well chilled before slicing.

8 servings

Graham Cracker Crumb Crust (see p. 132)

- 1/4 cup graham cracker crumbs
- 1 tablespoon margarine
- 1/3 cup sugar
- 1/4 cup cornstarch
- 2 tablespoons flour
- 1/3 teaspoon salt
- 2 1/2 cups skim milk
- 3 egg yolks
- 1 teaspoon vanilla
- 1/4 teaspoon ground cinnamon
- 1/4 teaspoon ground nutmeg
- 1 cup sliced strawberries
- 2 medium bananas

Per Serving
Calories: 312
% Calories from fat: 35
Fat (gm): 12
Saturated fat (gm): 2.8
Cholesterol (mg): 81.2
Sodium (mg): 296
Protein (gm): 5.8
Carbohydrate (gm): 46.1
Exchanges
Milk: 0.0
Vegetable: 0.0
Fruit: 0.0
Bread: 3.0
Meat: 0.0
Fat: 2.0

1. Make Graham Cracker Crumb Crust, adding 1/4 cup graham crumbs and 1 tablespoon margarine to recipe and using 9-inch pie pan.

2. Mix sugar, cornstarch, flour, and salt in medium saucepan; stir in milk. Cook over medium heat until mixture boils and thickens; boil 1 minute, stirring constantly.

3. Stir about 1/2 cup of mixture into egg yolks; stir egg mixture back into saucepan. Cook over low heat, stirring constantly, until thickened. Remove from heat; stir in vanilla, cinnamon, and nutmeg. Cool to room temperature, stirring frequently. Refrigerate until chilled, 1 to 2 hours.

4. Set aside 4 to 6 strawberry slices. Slice 11/2 bananas and arrange in crust with remaining strawberries. Spoon custard into crust; refrigerate until set, 4 to 6 hours. Slice remaining banana, and garnish pie with banana and strawberry slices.

BANANA PECAN TART BRULÉE

A custard-topped pie, with a surprise nut layer—delicious served warm from the oven.

12 servings

Shortbread Crust (see p. 130)
1/3 cup ground pecans
1/3 cup sugar
2 egg whites *or* 1/4 cup no-cholesterol real egg product
2 tablespoons margarine, melted
2 bananas, thinly sliced
Pastry Cream (see p. 268)
1/2 teaspoon rum extract
1/4 cup packed light brown sugar

Per Serving
Calories: 274
% Calories from fat: 35
Fat (gm): 10.7
Saturated fat (gm): 2.1
Cholesterol (mg): 54.7
Sodium (mg): 106
Protein (gm): 4.4
Carbohydrate (gm): 41.1
Exchanges
Milk: 0.0
Vegetable: 0.0
Fruit: 1.0
Bread: 2.0
Meat: 0.0
Fat: 1.5

1. Roll Shortbread Crust between sheets of waxed paper into 13-inch circle. Ease pastry into 12-inch tart pan with removable bottom; trim pastry and pierce bottom with a fork. Bake at 350 degrees 15 to 17 minutes, until golden brown.

2. Combine pecans, sugar, egg whites, and margarine. Pour into crust, spreading into an even layer. Bake at 350 degrees until set, about 10 minutes. Cool on wire rack.

3. Arrange bananas on top of nut layer. Mix Pastry Cream and rum extract; spread over bananas in even layer. Sprinkle with brown sugar. Broil 3 minutes or until sugar is melted and bubbly, covering edges of pastry with foil to prevent browning.

Variations: **Caramelized Pineapple Tart**—Prepare the basic recipe through Step 2 as above. Drain 2 cans (16 ounces each) pineapple tidbits, reserving 2 tablespoons of juice. Place juice in large skillet with $^{1}/_{2}$ cup packed light brown sugar, and stir over medium heat until sugar is dissolved. Add pineapple and cook over high heat until syrup is very thick, 8 to 10 minutes, stirring often. Pour pineapple and brown sugar mixture over nut layer. Sprinkle with $^{1}/_{4}$ cup packed light brown sugar, and broil as above.

Bananas Foster Tart—Prepare recipe through Step 2 as above. Combine 2 tablespoons margarine, 1 tablespoon dark rum, and $^{1}/_{2}$ cup packed light brown sugar in large skillet. Stir over medium heat until sugar is dissolved. Cook over high heat until syrup is thick. Add 4 sliced bananas and stir to coat bananas; pour over nut layer. Sprinkle with $^{1}/_{4}$ cup packed light brown sugar and broil as above. Serve with fat-free vanilla ice cream.

Almond-Grape Tart—Prepare recipe through Step 2 as above, substituting almonds for the pecans. Arrange 2 cups halved red and green seedless grapes over nut layer. Glaze with 3 to 4 tablespoons warm strained apricot preserves. Garnish with sliced almonds, if desired.

TOASTED COCONUT CREAM TART

Tucked in a tart pan for a new look, you'll enjoy this updated version of an old favorite.

8 servings

Basic Pie Crust (Cake Flour) (see p. 127)

- $^{1}/_{3}$ cup sugar
- 2 tablespoons cornstarch
- $1^{1}/_{2}$ cups 1% low-fat milk
- 1 egg, slightly beaten
- $^{1}/_{4}$ cup toasted, unsweetened, flaked coconut, divided

Per Serving
Calories: 197
% Calories from fat: 35
Fat (gm): 7.7
Saturated fat (gm): 2.3
Cholesterol (mg): 28.3
Sodium (mg): 171
Protein (gm): 3.8
Carbohydrate (gm): 28.3
Exchanges
Milk: 0.0
Vegetable: 0.0
Fruit: 0.0
Bread: 2.0
Meat: 0.0
Fat: 1.0

1. Bake Basic Pie Crust according to recipe, using 9-inch pie pan. Cool on wire rack.

2. Mix sugar and cornstarch in small saucepan; stir in milk. Cook over medium heat until mixture boils and thickens; boil 1 minute, stirring constantly.

3. Stir about 1/2 cup of the mixture into egg; stir egg mixture back into saucepan. Cook over low heat, stirring constantly, until thickened. Stir in 3 tablespoons of coconut.

4. Pour custard into cooled pie crust, spreading evenly. Sprinkle with remaining 1 tablespoon coconut. Cool to room temperature. Refrigerate until set, 2 to 4 hours.

Variation: **Strawberry Cream Pie**—Make custard as in Steps 2 and 3, deleting coconut and stirring in 1/2 cup reduced-fat or fat-free sour cream, and 1 teaspoon vanilla after removing from heat. Pour into pastry crust; chill. Mash 1 cup strawberries in medium saucepan with 1/2 cup sugar, 2 tablespoons cornstarch, and 1 tablespoon lemon juice. Heat to boiling, stirring until thickened. Remove from heat and stir in 3 cups halved or quartered strawberries. Spread strawberries over custard. Chill at least 2 hours.

DOUBLE COCONUT CREAM MERINGUE PIE

Reduced-fat coconut milk, available in most large groceries, lends a subtle coconut flavor to the pie filling.

8 servings

Basic Pie Crust (All-Purpose Flour) (see p. 126)

1/3 cup plus 1/4 cup sugar, divided

1/3 cup cornstarch

1/8 teaspoon salt

2 cups fat-free milk

1/2 can (14-ounce size) light coconut milk

2 egg yolks

1 teaspoon vanilla

Per Serving
Calories: 298
% Calories from fat: 33
Fat (gm): 11
Saturated fat (gm): 2.9
Cholesterol (mg): 54.3
Sodium (mg): 248
Protein (gm): 6.5
Carbohydrate (gm): 43.2
Exchanges
Milk: 0.0
Vegetable: 0.0
Fruit: 0.0
Bread: 3.0
Meat: 0.0
Fat: 2.0

    1 tablespoon margarine

1/4-1/2 cup plus 2 tablespoons flaked coconut,
       divided

    3 egg whites

  1/4 teaspoon cream of tartar

1. Bake Basic Pie Crust according to recipe, using 9-inch pie pan. Cool on wire rack.

2. Combine 1/3 cup sugar, cornstarch, and salt in medium saucepan; whisk in milk and coconut milk. Heat to boiling over medium-high heat, whisking constantly until thickened, 1 to 2 minutes. Whisk about 1/2 the milk mixture into egg yolks; whisk yolk mixture back into saucepan. Cook over medium-low heat, whisking constantly, 1 minute. Remove from heat; stir in vanilla, margarine, and 1/4 cup coconut. Pour into crust.

3. Beat egg whites and cream of tartar to soft peaks in medium bowl; beat to stiff peaks, adding 1/4 cup sugar gradually. Spread meringue over hot filling, sealing to edge of crust; sprinkle with 2 tablespoons coconut.

4. Bake at 400 degrees until meringue is browned, about 5 minutes. Cool on wire rack. Refrigerate until chilled, 3 to 4 hours.

Variation: **Coconut-Banana Island Pie**—Slice 1 small banana and arrange in cooled pie crust. Make pie as above, substituting 1 cup fat-free milk for the coconut milk and adding 1/2 teaspoon coconut extract. Substitute chopped macadamia nuts for the coconut in the filling and on the meringue.

BUTTERSCOTCH WALNUT PIE

A delicious butterscotch filling, topped with toasted walnuts.

10 servings

Graham Cracker Crumb Crust
(see p. 132)

3 cups fat-free milk

1 cup plus 1 tablespoon packed light brown sugar, divided

1/4 cup cornstarch

1/2 teaspoon salt

3 egg yolks, lightly beaten

1 teaspoon vanilla

1 tablespoon margarine, melted

1/3-1/2 cup chopped walnuts

Per Serving
Calories: 296
% Calories from fat: 34
Fat (gm): 11.4
Saturated fat (gm): 2.2
Cholesterol (mg): 65.2
Sodium (mg): 279
Protein (gm): 5.4
Carbohydrate (gm): 44.3
Exchanges
Milk: 0.0
Vegetable: 0.0
Fruit: 0.0
Bread: 3.0
Meat: 0.0
Fat: 2.0

1. Make Graham Cracker Crumb Crust, using 9-inch pie pan.

2. Combine milk, 1 cup brown sugar, cornstarch, and salt in medium saucepan. Heat to boiling; boil, stirring constantly, 1 minute. Whisk half the milk mixture into egg yolks; whisk egg mixture back into saucepan. Cook over medium heat, stirring until thickened. Stir in vanilla. Pour into crust. Refrigerate 4 hours.

3. Toss margarine and walnuts in small baking pan; bake at 400 degrees until brown, 5 to 8 minutes. Stir in remaining 1 tablespoon brown sugar; sprinkle on top of pie.

SPICED SWEET POTATO PIE

A change from traditional pumpkin, this pie will brighten any winter holiday table.

8 servings

Basic Pie Crust (All-Purpose Flour)
(see p. 126)

1¹/2 cups mashed sweet potatoes, peeled, cooked

³/4 cup packed light brown sugar

1 egg

2 egg whites

1¹/2 cups fat-free milk

1 teaspoon ground cinnamon

1 teaspoon ground ginger

¹/2 teaspoon ground mace

¹/4 teaspoon salt

Light whipped topping, as garnish

Per Serving
Calories: 276
% Calories from fat: 21
Fat (gm): 6.6
Saturated fat (gm): 1.4
Cholesterol (mg): 27.3
Sodium (mg): 268
Protein (gm): 5.9
Carbohydrate (gm): 48.6
Exchanges
Milk: 0.0
Vegetable: 0.0
Fruit: 0.0
Bread: 3.0
Meat: 0.0
Fat: 1.0

1. Bake Basic Pie Crust according to recipe, using 9-inch pie pan. Cool on wire rack.

2. Beat sweet potatoes, brown sugar, egg, and egg whites in medium bowl until smooth. Mix in milk, spices, and salt. Pour into pie crust.

3. Bake at 350 degrees about 45 minutes or until sharp knife inserted near center comes out clean. Serve warm or at room temperature with whipped topping.

Variations: **Sweet Potato Brulée Tart**—Bake Basic Pie Crust in 10-inch tart pan. Complete recipe as above. Cool pie and chill 3 to 4 hours. Press ¹/3 cup brown sugar through a strainer forming an even layer on surface of cold pie. Cover edge of pie with strips of aluminum foil. Broil until sugar is melted and bubbly, 1 to 2 minutes.

Orange Sweet Potato Pie—Make pie as above, substituting fat-free evaporated milk for the milk, and adding 1 tablespoon grated orange rind and 2 tablespoons orange liqueur *or* orange juice to filling. Mix whipped topping with 1 tablespoon orange liqueur, *or* ¹/2 teaspoon orange extract, and 1 teaspoon grated orange rind.

Honey-Walnut Pumpkin Pie—Substitute 1 can (16 ounces) mashed pumpkin for the sweet potato. Substitute 1 cup honey for the brown sugar. Mix pie and bake as above. Cool pie and chill 3 to 4 hours. Sprinkle top of pie with 1/3 cup chopped walnuts and 1/3 cup brown sugar. Cover edge of pie with strips of aluminum foil. Broil 4 to 6 inches from heat until sugar melts and bubbles, 1 to 2 minutes.

SQUASH AND HONEY PIE

A perfect pie for autumn, with cornmeal crust accenting the flavor of fresh winter squash.

8 servings

1 large butternut *or* other winter, squash (about 3 pounds)
1/2 cup honey
1/4 cup packed dark brown sugar
1 teaspoon ground cinnamon
1/2 teaspoon ground ginger
1/4 teaspoon ground allspice
3 eggs
1/2 cup fat-free milk
1/2 recipe Cornmeal Double Pie Crust (see p. 128)

Per Serving
Calories: 297
% Calories from fat: 17
Fat (gm): 5.9
Saturated fat (gm): 1.4
Cholesterol (mg): 80.1
Sodium (mg): 218
Protein (gm): 7.5
Carbohydrate (gm): 57.4
Exchanges
Milk: 0.0
Vegetable: 0.0
Fruit: 0.0
Bread: 3.5
Meat: 0.0
Fat: 1.0

1. Cut squash in half lengthwise; remove seeds. Steam or cook in microwave at high power, covered, until tender, about 20 minutes. Cool. Scrape enough cooked squash from shell to measure 2 cups; process in food processor until smooth. Add remaining ingredients, except Double Cornmeal Crust, and blend until smooth.

2. Make 1/2 recipe Cornmeal Double Pie Crust and press onto bottom and side of 9-inch pie pan; crimp edge of pastry. Pour squash filling into pastry.

3. Bake at 425 degrees 10 minutes; reduce temperature to 350 degrees and bake until set, 25 to 30 minutes. Cool on wire rack.

CARAMEL PECAN PUMPKIN PIE

The caramelized sugar in the filling gives a special flavor to this pie.

10 servings

Basic Pie Crust (All-Purpose Flour)
(see p. 126)

1/2 cup sugar

1 cup light corn syrup

2 tablespoons dark rum *or* 1 teaspoon
   rum extract

1-2 tablespoons margarine

3 large eggs

3/4 cup canned pumpkin

1 teaspoon ground ginger

1/2 cup pecan halves, coarsely chopped

Per Serving
Calories: 320
% Calories from fat: 31
Fat (gm): 11.4
Saturated fat (gm): 1.9
Cholesterol (mg): 63.6
Sodium (mg): 184
Protein (gm): 4.4
Carbohydrate (gm): 51.5
Exchanges
Milk: 0.0
Vegetable: 0.0
Fruit: 0.0
Bread: 3.0
Meat: 0.0
Fat: 2.0

1. Make Basic Pie Crust, using 8-inch pie pan.

2. Cook sugar in heavy saucepan over low heat until melted and a deep caramel color, swirling pan or stirring occasionally with metal fork. Immediately stir in corn syrup, and stir until caramel dissolves. Add rum and margarine. Cool slightly.

3. Beat eggs, adding warm sugar mixture gradually. Mix in pumpkin, ginger, and pecans. Pour into pastry. Bake at 350 degrees until set, about 45 minutes. Cool on wire rack.

PUMPKIN CHIFFON PIE

A light textured alternative to conventional pumpkin pie.

8 servings

Basic Pie Crust (Cake Flour)
(see p. 127)
- 1/2 cup packed light brown sugar
- 1 envelope unflavored gelatin
- 1/4 teaspoon salt
- 1/4 teaspoon ground cinnamon
- 1/4 teaspoon ground nutmeg
- 1 teaspoon finely chopped crystallized ginger
- 3/4 cup canned pumpkin
- 2 egg yolks
- 1/3 cup fat-free milk
- 4 teaspoons meringue powder
- 1/4 cup water
- 1/4 cup granulated sugar

Per Serving
Calories: 230
% Calories from fat: 28
Fat (gm): 7.2
Saturated fat (gm): 1.6
Cholesterol (mg): 53.4
Sodium (mg): 241
Protein (gm): 3.7
Carbohydrate (gm): 38.3
Exchanges
Milk: 0.0
Vegetable: 0.0
Fruit: 0.0
Bread: 2.5
Meat: 0.0
Fat: 1.5

1. Bake Basic Pie Crust, using 8-inch pie pan; cool on wire rack.

2. Combine brown sugar, gelatin, salt, and spices in small saucepan; mix in pumpkin, egg yolks, and milk.

3. Cook over medium heat, stirring constantly, until mixture boils. Refrigerate, stirring occasionally, until mixture mounds slightly when dropped from spoon.

4. Beat meringue powder with water in medium bowl until foamy; beat to stiff peaks, gradually adding granulated sugar. Fold pumpkin mixture into meringue; pour filling into crust. Chill 2 to 3 hours before serving.

RAISIN PIE

This traditional Pennsylvania Dutch pie was often called "Funeral Pie" because raisins were a fruit available year-round when needed for a funeral meal.

12 servings

Double Pie Crust (see p. 128)
3 cups water
4 cups raisins
1 cup sugar
2 tablespoons cornstarch
1 teaspoon grated lemon rind
3 tablespoons lemon juice
1/2 teaspoon salt
1 tablespoon margarine

Per Serving
Calories: 345
% Calories from fat: 15
Fat (gm): 6
Saturated fat (gm): 1.2
Cholesterol (mg): 0
Sodium (mg): 267
Protein (gm): 3.5
Carbohydrate (gm): 73.6
Exchanges
Milk: 0.0
Vegetable: 0.0
Fruit: 3.0
Bread: 1.5
Meat: 0.0
Fat: 1.0

1. Roll 2/3 of the Double Pie Crust on floured surface to form circle 2 inches larger than 9-inch pie pan; ease pastry into pan.

2. Heat water to boiling; stir in raisins. Cook until tender, about 5 minutes. Stir in combined sugar and cornstarch; heat to boiling, stirring constantly for 1 minute. Stir in remaining ingredients and pour into pastry.

3. Roll remaining 1/3 Double Pie Crust to fit top of pie and place over filling. Trim edges of pastry to within 1/2 inch of pan; fold top pastry over bottom pastry and flute. Cut vents in top crust.

4. Bake at 400 degrees until light brown, 35 to 40 minutes. Cool on wire rack.

GRANDMA BYE'S SOUR CREAM RAISIN PIE

A cherished family recipe from the plains of South Dakota.

10 servings

Double Pie Crust (see p. 128)
1 cup reduced-fat sour cream
1 cup sugar
2 eggs, lightly beaten
1 tablespoon ground cinnamon
1/2 teaspoon ground cloves
1/4 teaspoon ground allspice
1 cup raisins

Per Serving
Calories: 311
% Calories from fat: 20
Fat (gm): 7
Saturated fat (gm): 1.5
Cholesterol (mg): 42.4
Sodium (mg): 218
Protein (gm): 5.7
Carbohydrate (gm): 57.5
Exchanges
Milk: 0.0
Vegetable: 0.0
Fruit: 0.0
Bread: 0.0
Meat: 0.0
Fat: 0.0

1. Roll 2/3 of the Double Pie Crust on floured surface to form circle 2 inches larger than 9-inch pie pan; ease pastry into pan.

2. Mix sour cream, sugar, eggs, and spices until smooth. Stir in raisins and pour into pastry.

3. Roll remaining 1/3 Double Pie Crust to fit top of pie and place over filling. Trim edges of pastry to within 1/2 inch of pan; fold top pastry over bottom pastry and flute. Cut vents in top crust.

4. Bake at 400 degrees 15 minutes. Reduce heat to 375 degrees and bake until crust is light brown and sharp knife inserted near center comes out clean, 40 to 45 minutes. Cool on wire rack.

DRIED FRUIT TART

Good at any time of the year, especially in winter months when fresh fruit is limited in availability.

10 servings

Basic Pie Crust (All-Purpose Flour) (see p. 126)
1½ cups coarsely chopped mixed dried fruit
½ cup chopped dates
½ cup apricot nectar *or* orange juice
¼ cup packed light brown sugar
Cinnamon Streusel (see p. 582)
1 tablespoon cold margarine
⅓ cup chopped walnuts

Per Serving
Calories: 326
% Calories from fat: 28
Fat (gm): 10.7
Saturated fat (gm): 1.8
Cholesterol (mg): 0
Sodium (mg): 160
Protein (gm): 4
Carbohydrate (gm): 57.1
Exchanges
Milk: 0.0
Vegetable: 0.0
Fruit: 0.0
Bread: 3.5
Meat: 0.0
Fat: 2.0

1. Bake Basic Pie Crust according to recipe, using 9-inch tart pan. Cool on wire rack.

2. Heat mixed dried fruit, dates, apricot nectar, and brown sugar to boiling in medium saucepan; reduce heat and simmer, uncovered, 1 minute. Process in food processor until smooth. Cool completely; spread in bottom of crust.

3. Make Cinnamon Streusel, adding 1 tablespoon margarine and the walnuts. Sprinkle over the fruit.

4. Bake at 400 degrees until tart is bubbly and streusel browned, 20 to 25 minutes.

OLD-FASHIONED MINCEMEAT PIE

Try this quick version of a traditional holiday treat.

10 servings

4 ounces extra-lean ground beef
2 packages (9 ounces each) condensed mincemeat, crumbled
1 cup chopped peeled apple
¹/₄ cup sugar
2¹/₂ cups water
Double Pie Crust (see p. 128)

Per Serving
Calories: 371
% Calories from fat: 21
Fat (gm): 8.9
Saturated fat (gm): 1.7
Cholesterol (mg): 7
Sodium (mg): 441
Protein (gm): 5.3
Carbohydrate (gm): 67.8
Exchanges
Milk: 0.0
Vegetable: 0.0
Fruit: 0.0
Bread: 4.5
Meat: 0.0
Fat: 1.5

1. Brown ground beef in large saucepan; drain. Add mincemeat, apple, sugar, and water. Heat to boiling; boil 3 minutes, stirring frequently. Cool.

2. Roll ²/₃ of the Double Pie Crust on floured surface to form circle 2 inches larger than 9-inch pie pan; ease pastry into pan.

3. Pour filling into pastry. Roll remaining ¹/₃ Double Pie Crust to fit top of pie and place over filling. Trim edges of pastry to within ¹/₂ inch of pan; fold top pastry over bottom pastry and flute. Cut vents in top crust.

4. Bake at 425 degrees until crust is light brown, 35 to 45 minutes, covering edge of pie with aluminum foil if necessary to prevent excessive browning. Cool on wire rack.

CHEESECAKE-MINCE PIE

The cream cheese and sour cream provide a tangy contrast to the sweet mincemeat filling.

12 servings

Ginger-Raisin Crumb Crust (see p. 135)
2 cups prepared mincemeat
1/3 cup chopped walnuts
1 1/2 packages (8-ounce size) fat-free cream cheese
2 eggs
1/2 cup sugar plus 2 tablespoons, divided
1 tablespoon grated orange rind
1 tablespoon orange juice
1 cup fat-free sour cream
1/2 teaspoon orange extract

Per Serving
Calories: 321
% Calories from fat: 22
Fat (gm): 8.1
Saturated fat (gm): 2.3
Cholesterol (mg): 37.6
Sodium (mg): 392
Protein (gm): 8.3
Carbohydrate (gm): 56.8
Exchanges
Milk: 0.0
Vegetable: 0.0
Fruit: 0.0
Bread: 3.5
Meat: 0.0
Fat: 1.5

1. Make Ginger-Raisin Crumb Crust, using 9-inch pie pan.

2. Mix mincemeat and walnuts; pour into crust. Beat cream cheese, eggs, 1/2 cup sugar, orange rind, and juice until smooth. Pour over mincemeat.

3. Bake at 375 degrees 20 minutes or until set. Combine sour cream, remaining 2 tablespoons sugar, and orange extract; spread evenly over baked pie. Bake 10 minutes longer. Cool on wire rack; refrigerate at least 6 hours or overnight.

PEACHY PECAN PIE

Pecan pie with a luscious fruit twist.

10 servings

Basic Pie Crust (All-Purpose Flour) (see p. 126)

- 2 eggs
- 2/3 cup sugar
- 2/3 cup corn syrup
- 1 teaspoon vanilla
- 1/2 teaspoon salt
- 1 package (10 ounces) frozen sliced peaches, thawed, well-drained, cut up
- 1/2 cup coarsely chopped pecans
- 10 tablespoons light whipped topping

Per Serving
Calories: 313
% Calories from fat: 28
Fat (gm): 10.2
Saturated fat (gm): 2
Cholesterol (mg): 42.4
Sodium (mg): 257
Protein (gm): 3.7
Carbohydrate (gm): 53.1
Exchanges
Milk: 0.0
Vegetable: 0.0
Fruit: 0.0
Bread: 3.0
Meat: 0.0
Fat: 2.0

1. Make Basic Pie Crust, using 9-inch pie pan.

2. Beat eggs, sugar, corn syrup, vanilla, and salt until well blended. Stir in peaches and pecans; pour into pastry.

3. Bake at 375 degrees until filling is set, 35 to 40 minutes. Cool on wire rack. Top each slice with 1 tablespoon of whipped topping.

PECAN CRUNCH TART

We've slashed the calories and created a rich-tasting pecan pie.

8 servings

Basic Pie Crust (All-Purpose Flour)
(see p. 126)

2 eggs

1 cup pure maple syrup *or* pancake syrup

1 tablespoon vanilla

1/8 teaspoon salt

2/3 cup reduced-fat granola

1/3 cup barley-wheat cereal (Grape-nuts)

2/3 cup coarsely chopped pecans

Per Serving
Calories: 367
% Calories from fat: 34
Fat (gm): 14.3
Saturated fat (gm): 2.1
Cholesterol (mg): 53
Sodium (mg): 245
Protein (gm): 6.1
Carbohydrate (gm): 55.5
Exchanges
Milk: 0.0
Vegetable: 0.0
Fruit: 0.0
Bread: 3.5
Meat: 0.0
Fat: 2.5

1. Make Basic Pie Crust, using 10-inch tart pan.

2. Beat eggs, syrup, vanilla, and salt until smooth. Stir in remaining ingredients; pour into pastry. Bake at 350 degrees until set, about 35 minutes.

BRANDIED BROWN SUGAR PIE

Pretty sweet—awfully good!

10 servings

Basic Pie Crust (All-Purpose Flour)
(see p. 126)

2 cups packed light brown sugar

6 tablespoons margarine, melted

3 eggs, lightly beaten

1/4 cup fat-free milk

1 tablespoon brandy *or* 1 teaspoon
brandy extract

1/2 teaspoon salt
Light whipped topping, as garnish

Per Serving
Calories: 361
% Calories from fat: 32
Fat (gm): 13
Saturated fat (gm): 2.7
Cholesterol (mg): 63.7
Sodium (mg): 347
Protein (gm): 3.8
Carbohydrate (gm): 57.8
Exchanges
Milk: 0.0
Vegetable: 0.0
Fruit: 0.0
Bread: 3.5
Meat: 0.0
Fat: 2.5

1. Make Basic Pie Crust, using 9-inch pie pan.

2. Beat remaining ingredients, except whipped topping, in medium bowl until well blended; pour into pastry.

3. Bake at 325 degrees until mixture is set and puffs slightly. Cool. Serve with whipped topping.

OLD-FASHIONED BUTTERMILK PIE

Carry on Grandma's best tradition with this pie!

8 servings

Gingersnap Crumb Crust (see p. 135)
3/4 cup sugar
2 tablespoons margarine, softened
1 egg
2 egg whites
3 tablespoons flour
1/4 teaspoon salt
1 cup reduced-fat buttermilk
Ground nutmeg, as garnish

Per Serving
Calories: 236
% Calories from fat: 32
Fat (gm): 8.6
Saturated fat (gm): 1.9
Cholesterol (mg): 27.6
Sodium (mg): 264
Protein (gm): 3.9
Carbohydrate (gm): 36.7
Exchanges
Milk: 0.0
Vegetable: 0.0
Fruit: 0.0
Bread: 2.5
Meat: 0.0
Fat: 1.0

1. Make Gingersnap Crumb Crust, deleting 1 tablespoon margarine and using 8-inch pie pan. Do not bake.

2. Mix sugar and margarine in medium bowl until blended; beat in egg and egg whites. Stir in flour, salt, and buttermilk until well blended.

3. Pour filling into crust; bake at 350 degrees 40 minutes or until sharp knife inserted near center comes out clean. Sprinkle with nutmeg and serve warm or chilled.

Variation: **Raisin-Pecan Buttermilk Pie**—Make pie as above, substituting brown sugar for granulated, and adding 1/2 cup chopped raisins and 1/3 cup chopped pecans to the filling.

CIDER VINEGAR PIE

An old-time recipe to satisfy modern tastes—try it with raspberry vinegar for a change of pace.

8 servings

Basic Pie Crust (Cake Flour)
(see p. 127)
1¼ cups sugar, divided
⅓ cup cornstarch
Dash salt
1¼ cups water
2 egg yolks
⅓ cup apple cider vinegar
2 egg whites
¼ teaspoon cream of tartar

Per Serving
Calories: 280
% Calories from fat: 23
Fat (gm): 7.1
Saturated fat (gm): 1.5
Cholesterol (mg): 53.2
Sodium (mg): 156
Protein (gm): 3
Carbohydrate (gm): 51.8
Exchanges
Milk: 0.0
Vegetable: 0.0
Fruit: 0.0
Bread: 3.5
Meat: 0.0
Fat: 1.0

1. Bake Basic Pie Crust according to recipe, using 8-inch pie pan.

2. Combine 1 cup sugar, cornstarch, and salt in medium saucepan; stir in water. Heat to boiling, stirring constantly; boil 1 minute, stirring, until thick. Whisk ½ cup hot mixture into egg yolks; whisk yolk mixture back into saucepan. Cook over medium heat, stirring constantly, 1 minute. Stir in vinegar. Pour into crust.

3. Beat egg whites and cream of tartar to soft peaks; beat to stiff peaks, adding remaining ¼ cup sugar gradually. Spread meringue over hot filling, sealing well to edge of crust.

4. Bake at 375 degrees until lightly browned, about 10 minutes.

Variation: **Spiced Raisin Vinegar Pie**—Make pie as above, adding 1 teaspoon ground cinnamon, ¼ teaspoon each ground cloves and nutmeg when making custard. Add ½ cup fat-free sour cream and ½ cup raisins after adding vinegar. Complete recipe as above.

CHOCOLATE RUM PIE

Dutch or European process cocoa gives a special rich chocolate flavor to the filling in this delicious pie.

8 servings

Vanilla Crumb Crust (see p. 133)
1 envelope unflavored gelatin
1 cup 2% reduced-fat milk, divided
1/2 cup sugar
2 tablespoons dark rum
1/2 cup Dutch process cocoa
1 teaspoon rum extract
1 envelope (1.3 ounces) whipped topping mix

Per Serving
Calories: 244
% Calories from fat: 32
Fat (gm): 8.4
Saturated fat (gm): 3.2
Cholesterol (mg): 2.2
Sodium (mg): 114
Protein (gm): 2.9
Carbohydrate (gm): 36.1
Exchanges
Milk: 0.0
Vegetable: 0.0
Fruit: 0.0
Bread: 2.5
Meat: 0.0
Fat: 1.5

1. Make Vanilla Crumb Crust, using 8-inch pie pan.

2. Sprinkle gelatin over 1/2 cup milk in small saucepan; let stand 2 to 3 minutes. Stir in sugar and rum. Cook over low heat, stirring constantly, until gelatin and sugar are dissolved. Remove from heat; stir in cocoa and rum extract.

3. When gelatin mixture is partially set (consistency of unbeaten egg whites), blend whipped topping and remaining 1/2 cup milk in deep bowl; beat at high speed until topping forms soft peaks, about 4 minutes. Fold topping into gelatin mixture. Spoon mixture into cooled crust; refrigerate until set, 2 to 4 hours.

CHOCOLATE FUNNY CAKE PIE

Is it a cake—or is it a pie? A little of both, with a moist chocolate filling.

10 servings

Basic Pie Crust (Cake Flour) (see p. 127)

1½ cups sugar, divided
¼ cup unsweetened cocoa
6 tablespoons water
1 teaspoon vanilla, divided
1 cup all-purpose flour
1 teaspoon baking powder
4 tablespoons cold margarine
1 egg, beaten
½ cup fat-free milk

Per Serving
Calories: 313
% Calories from fat: 28
Fat (gm): 9.8
Saturated fat (gm): 2
Cholesterol (mg): 21.5
Sodium (mg): 230
Protein (gm): 3.8
Carbohydrate (gm): 53
Exchanges
Milk: 0.0
Vegetable: 0.0
Fruit: 0.0
Bread: 3.5
Meat: 0.0
Fat: 1.5

1. Make Basic Pie Crust, using 9-inch pie pan.

2. Mix ½ cup sugar, cocoa, water, and ½ teaspoon vanilla; pour into pastry.

3. Combine flour, remaining 1 cup sugar, and baking powder in medium bowl; cut in margarine until mixture resembles coarse crumbs. Stir in combined egg, milk, and remaining ½ teaspoon vanilla. Spread batter over cocoa mixture.

4. Bake at 350 degrees until toothpick inserted in center comes out clean, about 40 minutes.

BLACK BOTTOM PIE

Triple-layered Southern classic, in a chocolate crust!

10 servings

Chocolate Cookie Crumb Crust
(see p. 134)
2 cups Pastry Cream (double recipe)
(see p. 268)
1 ounce unsweetened chocolate, melted
2 tablespoons unsweetened cocoa
4 teaspoons vanilla, divided
1 envelope unflavored gelatin
$^1/_4$ cup water
2 teaspoons meringue powder
2 tablespoons water
$^1/_4$ cup sugar
2 cups light whipped topping
Grated semisweet chocolate, as garnish

Per Serving
Calories: 341
% Calories from fat: 33
Fat (gm): 12.6
Saturated fat (gm): 4.9
Cholesterol (mg): 88.9
Sodium (mg): 217
Protein (gm): 4.9
Carbohydrate (gm): 52.6
Exchanges
Milk: 0.0
Vegetable: 0.0
Fruit: 0.0
Bread: 3.5
Meat: 0.0
Fat: 2.0

1. Make Chocolate Cookie Crumb Crust, using 9-inch pie pan.

2. Make Pastry Cream, doubling recipe. Mix 1 cup warm Pastry Cream with melted chocolate, cocoa, and 2 teaspoons vanilla in small bowl. Spread evenly over crust. Refrigerate.

3. Sprinkle gelatin over water in small saucepan; let stand 3 to 4 minutes to soften. Cook over low heat, stirring, until dissolved; add to remaining Pastry Cream. Refrigerate, stirring occasionally, until mixture mounds slightly when dropped from spoon.

4. Beat meringue powder with water until foamy; beat to stiff peaks, gradually adding sugar. Beat in remaining 2 teaspoons vanilla. Fold gelatin mixture into meringue. Pour over chocolate layer in crust. Refrigerate 2 to 3 hours. Top with whipped topping; sprinkle with grated chocolate.

Variation: **Banana Black Bottom Pie**—Make pie through Step 2. Slice 3 bananas over chocolate layer. Stir 1 tablespoon banana liqueur, *or* $^1/_2$ teaspoon banana extract, into remaining Pastry Cream. Complete pie as above; sprinkle with chopped pecans and shaved chocolate.

RED BOTTOM PIE

A rum-flavored custard tops a cranberry filling, creating a combination of light and tangy flavors.

8 servings

Lemon Cookie Crumb Crust (see p. 136)

1 package (10 ounces) frozen cranberry relish, thawed

1/4 cup orange juice

1 tablespoon cornstarch

2 egg yolks

1/3 cup sugar

1 envelope unflavored gelatin

1/4 teaspoon salt

1 cup fat-free milk

2 tablespoons dark rum *or* 2 teaspoons rum extract

2 teaspoons meringue powder

2 tablespoons water

1 cup light whipped topping

Per Serving
Calories: 272
% Calories from fat: 28
Fat (gm): 8.6
Saturated fat (gm): 2.8
Cholesterol (mg): 54.1
Sodium (mg): 145
Protein (gm): 2.5
Carbohydrate (gm): 44.7
Exchanges
Milk: 0.0
Vegetable: 0.0
Fruit: 1.0
Bread: 2.0
Meat: 0.0
Fat: 1.5

1. Make Lemon Cookie Crumb Crust, using 9-inch pie pan.

2. Combine cranberry relish, orange juice, and cornstarch in small saucepan; heat to boiling over medium heat, stirring until thickened. Spread on bottom of crust; refrigerate.

3. Mix egg yolks, sugar, gelatin, salt, and milk in small saucepan; heat to boiling over medium heat, stirring constantly. Remove from heat and stir in rum; refrigerate, stirring occasionally, until mixture mounds when dropped from spoon.

4. Beat meringue powder with water until foamy; continue beating until stiff peaks form. Fold gelatin mixture into meringue; fold in whipped topping. Spoon mixture on top of cranberry filling. Chill 3 hours.

Variation: **Eggnog Pie**—Substitute Vanilla Crumb Crust (see p. 133) for the Lemon Cookie Crumb Crust; skip Step 2. Make custard in Step 3, doubling ingredients and stirring in 2 tablespoons each rum and brandy *or* 1 teaspoon each rum and brandy extract. Complete pie as in Step 4, doubling ingredients.

SHOOFLY PIE

Try this molasses-flavored pie, perhaps the most famous pie of the Penn-sylvania Dutch.

8 servings

Basic Pie Crust (Cake Flour) (see p. 127)
- 3/4 cup all-purpose flour
- 1/2 cup packed light brown sugar
- 1/2 teaspoon salt
- 1/2 teaspoon ground cinnamon
- 1/8 teaspoon ground cloves
- 1/8 teaspoon ground ginger
- 1/8 teaspoon ground nutmeg
- 2 tablespoons vegetable shortening *or* margarine
- 3/4 cup water
- 1/2 cup molasses
- 1 egg yolk, beaten
- 1 1/2 teaspoons baking soda

Per Serving
Calories: 296
% Calories from fat: 29
Fat (gm): 9.6
Saturated fat (gm): 2.1
Cholesterol (mg): 26.6
Sodium (mg): 538
Protein (gm): 3
Carbohydrate (gm): 49.6
Exchanges
Milk: 0.0
Vegetable: 0.0
Fruit: 0.0
Bread: 3.0
Meat: 0.0
Fat: 1.5

1. Make Basic Pie Crust, using 9-inch pie pan.

2. Combine flour, brown sugar, salt, and spices in mixing bowl. Cut in shortening until mixture resembles coarse crumbs.

3. Combine remaining ingredients; pour into pastry. Sprinkle crumb mixture over filling. Bake at 400 degrees 10 minutes; reduce temperature to 325 degrees and bake until knife inserted in center comes out clean, about 30 minutes.

MONTGOMERY PIE

Molasses and lemon are a delicious combination in this Pennsylvania Dutch pie.

10 servings

Basic Pie Crust (Cake Flour) (see p. 127)

- 1/2 cup water
- 1 1/4 cups sugar, divided
- 1/4 cup molasses
- 3 tablespoons lemon juice
- 2 eggs, divided
- 1 cup plus 1 teaspoon flour, divided
- 1 teaspoon baking powder
- 4 tablespoons cold margarine
- 1/2 cup fat-free milk
- 1 teaspoon grated lemon rind

Per Serving
Calories: 317
% Calories from fat: 29
Fat (gm): 10.3
Saturated fat (gm): 2.1
Cholesterol (mg): 42.6
Sodium (mg): 241
Protein (gm): 4.2
Carbohydrate (gm): 52.4
Exchanges
Milk: 0.0
Vegetable: 0.0
Fruit: 0.0
Bread: 3.0
Meat: 0.0
Fat: 2.0

1. Make Basic Pie Crust, using 9-inch pie pan.

2. Mix water, 1/4 cup sugar, molasses, lemon juice, 1 egg, and 1 teaspoon flour; pour into pastry.

3. Combine remaining 1 cup flour, 1 cup sugar, and baking powder in medium bowl; cut in margarine until mixture resembles coarse crumbs. Mix in combined remaining egg, milk, and lemon rind. Pour batter over molasses mixture.

4. Bake at 350 degrees until toothpick inserted in center comes out clean, about 45 minutes.

THREE

Cheesecakes

NEW YORK-STYLE CHEESECAKE

There are only accolades for this cheesecake—and no one will believe this is a low-fat version!

12 servings

Graham Cracker Crumb Crust
(see p. 132)
3 packages (8 ounces each) fat-free cream
  cheese, softened
3/4 cup sugar
2 eggs
2 tablespoons cornstarch
1 teaspoon vanilla
1 cup reduced-fat sour cream

Per Serving
Calories: 244
% Calories from fat: 31
Fat (gm): 8.5
Saturated fat (gm): 3.1
Cholesterol (mg): 46.5
Sodium (mg): 417
Protein (gm): 11.4
Carbohydrate (gm): 30.6
Exchanges
Milk: 0.0
Vegetable: 0.0
Fruit: 0.0
Bread: 2.0
Meat: 1.0
Fat: 1.5

1. Make Graham Cracker Crumb Crust, pressing mixture evenly on bottom and 1/2 inch up side of 9-inch springform pan.

2. Beat cream cheese and sugar in large bowl until light and fluffy; beat in eggs, cornstarch, and vanilla. Add sour cream, mixing well.

3. Pour mixture into crust. Bake at 325 degrees until cheesecake is set but still slightly soft in the center, 45 to 50 minutes. Turn oven off; cool cheesecake in oven with door ajar 3 hours. Refrigerate 8 hours or overnight.

Variation: **Latte Cheesecake**—Make cheesecake as above, adding 1/3 cup espresso or double-strength coffee, 2 egg yolks, and 1/8 teaspoon ground nutmeg. Spread top of chilled cheesecake with 2 cups light whipped topping; sprinkle lightly with cinnamon and chocolate shavings.

COLOSSAL CHEESECAKE

A sumptuous dense filling and rich pastry crust are accented with citrus peel and vanilla bean seeds—a truly special cheesecake.

16 servings

Rich Citrus Pastry Crust (recipe follows)

3 packages (8 ounces each) fat-free cream cheese, softened

2 packages (8 ounces each) reduced-fat cream cheese, softened

1³/4 cups sugar

3 tablespoons flour

· 1 tablespoon finely grated lemon peel

1 tablespoon finely grated orange peel

1 vanilla bean, split and seeds scraped out
   or 2 teaspoons vanilla

3 eggs

2 egg whites

¹/2 cup fat-free sour cream

Per Serving
Calories: 314
% Calories from fat: 34
Fat (gm): 11.7
Saturated fat (gm): 5
Cholesterol (mg): 56.4
Sodium (mg): 464
Protein (gm): 12.4
Carbohydrate (gm): 38.5
Exchanges
Milk: 0.0
Vegetable: 0.0
Fruit: 0.0
Bread: 2.5
Meat: 1.0
Fat: 1.5

1. Roll Rich Citrus Pastry Crust on floured surface to ¹/8 inch thickness; cut into 11-inch circle. Reserve and refrigerate scraps. Ease pastry into 10-inch springform pan; press onto bottom and ¹/2 inch up side of pan. Pierce bottom of pastry with fork. Refrigerate 30 minutes. Bake at 400 degrees until browned, about 20 minutes; cool on wire rack.

2. Beat cream cheese until fluffy in large bowl; beat in sugar, flour, citrus peel, and vanilla bean seeds until smooth. Beat in eggs and egg whites 1 at a time, beating well after each addition. Beat in sour cream.

3. Roll pastry scraps on floured surface to ¹/8 inch thickness; cut into 2-inch-wide strips. Press strips to inside of pan, covering side and sealing to bottom crust.

4. Pour filling into crust. Bake at 450 degrees 15 minutes; reduce oven temperature to 200 degrees and bake until center of cheesecake is just set, 50 to 60 minutes. Turn oven off; cool cheesecake in oven with door ajar 1 hour. Cool on wire rack; refrigerate 8 hours or overnight.

Rich Citrus Pastry Crust

     1 cup all-purpose flour
   1/4 cup sugar
     1 teaspoon grated lemon peel
     1 teaspoon grated orange peel
   1/2 small vanilla bean, split and seeds
        scraped out *or* 1/2 teaspoon vanilla
     8 tablespoons cold margarine, cut into
        pieces
     2 egg whites

1. Combine flour, sugar, citrus peel, and vanilla bean seeds in bowl; cut in margarine until mixture resembles coarse crumbs. Mix in egg whites, forming dough. Roll into ball and wrap in plastic wrap, flattening into a disk. Refrigerate at least 1 hour.

RICOTTA CHEESECAKE

A basic ricotta cheesecake with citrus accents that can't be beat for flavor! Top with fresh fruit, or a sauce from the Sauce chapter.

12 servings

        Lemon Cookie Crumb Crust (see
        p. 136)
   3 1/2 cups reduced-fat ricotta cheese
    1/4 cup all-purpose flour
    1/2 teaspoon salt
      1 cup sugar
      2 eggs
      2 egg whites
      1 tablespoon grated orange rind
      1 tablespoon grated lemon rind
      2 teaspoons vanilla
        Ground nutmeg, as garnish

Per Serving
Calories: 253
% Calories from fat: 25
Fat (gm): 7.2
Saturated fat (gm): 2.5
Cholesterol (mg): 48.2
Sodium (mg): 261
Protein (gm): 12.7
Carbohydrate (gm): 34.7
Exchanges
Milk: 0.0
Vegetable: 0.0
Fruit: 0.0
Bread: 2.0
Meat: 1.0
Fat: 1.0

1. Make Lemon Cookie Crumb Crust, pressing mixture evenly on bottom and 1/2 inch up side of 10-inch springform pan.

2. Beat ricotta cheese, flour, and salt in large bowl until well blended. Beat in sugar, eggs, and egg whites; mix in orange rind, lemon rind, and vanilla.

3. Pour filling into crust. Bake at 350 degrees until filling is set, 1 to 1¼ hours. Cool on wire rack; refrigerate 8 hours or overnight. Sprinkle lightly with nutmeg before serving.

WHITE CHOCOLATE CHEESECAKE

Rich, creamy, and delicious. Serve with a combination of Raspberry Sauce and Bittersweet Chocolate Sauce (see pp. 658, 642).

12 servings

Nut Crunch Crust (recipe follows)
2 packages (8 ounces each) fat-free cream cheese, softened
1¼ cups sugar
1 cup fat-free sour cream
3 eggs
¼ cup lemon juice
1 tablespoon grated lemon rind
2 teaspoons vanilla extract
¼ teaspoon ground nutmeg
Pinch salt
6 ounces white baking chocolate, melted

Per Serving
Calories: 266
% Calories from fat: 23
Fat (gm): 6.7
Saturated fat (gm): 3.8
Cholesterol (mg): 58.6
Sodium (mg): 266
Protein (gm): 9.8
Carbohydrate (gm): 40.7
Exchanges
Milk: 0.0
Vegetable: 0.0
Fruit: 0.0
Bread: 3.0
Meat: 0.0
Fat: 1.0

1. Make Nut Crunch Crust; sprinkle over bottom of greased 9-inch springform pan.

2. Beat cream cheese in large bowl until fluffy; beat in sugar, sour cream, eggs, lemon juice, lemon rind, vanilla, nutmeg, and salt. Mix in chocolate.

3. Pour batter into crust; bake at 325 degrees until cheesecake is almost set in the center, 1 to 1¼ hours. Cool on wire rack. Refrigerate 8 hours or overnight.

Nut Crunch Crust

makes one 9-inch crust

1/4 cup wheat-barley cereal (Grape-nuts)
2 tablespoons sugar
1 tablespoon chopped almonds

1. Combine all ingredients in food processor or blender; process until finely ground.

CAPPUCCINO CHEESECAKE

Creamy and rich, with a subtle coffee flavor.

12 servings

Mocha Crumb Crust (recipe follows)
2 cups 1% low-fat cottage cheese
2 eggs
2 egg whites
2 packages (8 ounces each) fat-free cream cheese, softened
1 1/3 cups reduced-fat sour cream
1 1/4 cups sugar
1/3 cup all-purpose flour
1/2 teaspoon ground cinnamon
1/4 teaspoon ground nutmeg
1/4 teaspoon salt
3 tablespoons instant espresso powder
3 tablespoons warm water
Light whipped topping, as garnish
Chocolate-covered coffee beans, as garnish

Per Serving
Calories: 310
% Calories from fat: 27
Fat (gm): 9.3
Saturated fat (gm): 3.7
Cholesterol (mg): 48.9
Sodium (mg): 531
Protein (gm): 15
Carbohydrate (gm): 41.7
Exchanges
Milk: 0.0
Vegetable: 0.0
Fruit: 0.0
Bread: 3.0
Meat: 0.0
Fat: 2.0

1. Make Mocha Crumb Crust, pressing mixture on bottom and 1 inch up side of 9-inch springform pan. Bake at 350 degrees until set, about 8 minutes.

2. Process cottage cheese, eggs, and egg whites in food processor or blender until smooth. Beat cream cheese in large bowl until fluffy; beat in cottage cheese mixture, sour cream, sugar, flour, spices, and salt. Dissolve espresso powder in warm water; add to cheese mixture.

3. Pour batter into crust. Bake at 300 degrees until cheesecake is almost set in the center, 60 to 70 minutes. Turn oven off; cool cheesecake in oven with door ajar, 1 hour. Cool on wire rack. Refrigerate 8 hours or overnight.

4. Garnish cheesecake with whipped topping and coffee beans.

Mocha Crumb Crust

makes one 9- or 10-inch crust

- 1$1/4$ cups graham cracker crumbs
- 2 tablespoons sugar
- 2 tablespoons unsweetened cocoa
- 2 teaspoons instant espresso powder
- $1/2$ teaspoon ground nutmeg
- 3 tablespoons margarine, melted
- 1-2 tablespoons honey

1. Combine all ingredients.

MOCHA RUM CHEESECAKE

A no-bake cheesecake that's ready to eat in 2 hours!

12 servings

Chocolate Pecan Crumb Crust
(see p. 134)
1 envelope unflavored gelatin
1 tablespoon instant coffee granules
1/2 cup water
1 package (8 ounces) fat-free cream cheese, softened
1/3 cup sugar
1/4 cup Dutch process cocoa
2 tablespoons light rum *or* 1 teaspoon rum extract
2 cups light whipped topping
Chocolate curls, as garnish

Per Serving
Calories: 196
% Calories from fat: 31
Fat (gm): 7
Saturated fat (gm): 2.3
Cholesterol (mg): 1.5
Sodium (mg): 234
Protein (gm): 4.3
Carbohydrate (gm): 28.3
Exchanges
Milk: 0.0
Vegetable: 0.0
Fruit: 0.0
Bread: 2.0
Meat: 0.0
Fat: 1.0

1. Make Chocolate Pecan Crumb Crust, pressing onto bottom and 1/2 inch up side of 9-inch springform pan.

2. Mix gelatin, instant coffee, and water in small saucepan; cook over low heat, stirring constantly, until dissolved. Cool. Beat cream cheese in medium bowl until fluffy; beat in sugar, cocoa, and rum. Beat in gelatin mixture; fold in whipped topping.

3. Pour filling into crust, spreading evenly. Sprinkle with chocolate curls. Refrigerate until set, about 2 hours.

CHOCOLATE CHIP CHEESECAKE

A cheesecake with all the flavors of your favorite cookie.

16 servings

Shortbread Crust (see p. 130)
2 cups 1% low-fat cottage cheese
2 eggs
1/4 cup fat-free milk
2 packages (8 ounces each) fat-free cream cheese, softened
1 cup granulated sugar
3/4 cup packed dark brown sugar
1 teaspoon vanilla extract
1/4 teaspoon salt
1 cup reduced-fat semisweet chocolate morsels
2 tablespoons chopped walnuts
3/4 cup chocolate-flavored syrup

Per Serving
Calories: 340
% Calories from fat: 24
Fat (gm): 9.4
Saturated fat (gm): 5.1
Cholesterol (mg): 43.3
Sodium (mg): 373
Protein (gm): 11
Carbohydrate (gm): 56.1
Exchanges
Milk: 0.0
Vegetable: 0.0
Fruit: 0.0
Bread: 3.5
Meat: 0.0
Fat: 2.0

1. Roll Shortbread Crust between two sheets of waxed paper to 1/8 inch thickness; cut into 11-inch circle. Reserve and refrigerate scraps. Ease pastry into 10-inch springform pan; press onto bottom and 1/2 inch up side of pan; pierce bottom of pastry with fork. Bake at 400 degrees until lightly browned, 8 to 10 minutes; cool on wire rack.

2. Process cottage cheese, eggs, and milk in food processor or blender until smooth. Beat cream cheese in large bowl until fluffy; beat in cottage cheese mixture, sugars, vanilla, and salt. Mix in chocolate morsels.

3. Roll pastry scraps on floured surface to 1/8 inch thickness; cut into 2-inch-wide strips. Press strips to inside of pan, covering side and sealing to bottom crust.

4. Pour batter into crust; sprinkle with walnuts. Bake at 350 degrees until cheesecake is almost set in the center, 50 to 60 minutes. Cool on wire rack. Refrigerate 8 hours or overnight. Serve with chocolate-flavored syrup.

MARBLE MINT CHEESECAKE

The flavor is like a chocolate mint candy!

12 servings

Chocolate Cookie Crumb Crust
(see p. 134)

1 teaspoon mint extract

1 package (8 ounces) fat-free cream cheese, softened

1/2 cup sugar

2 eggs

1 tablespoon green crème de menthe *or* 1 teaspoon mint extract

1 cup fat-free sour cream

1 cup reduced-fat semisweet chocolate morsels

1/2 cup chocolate-flavored syrup

2-3 drops green food color

6 chocolate-covered thin mints, halved

Per Serving
Calories: 331
% Calories from fat: 29
Fat (gm): 11.2
Saturated fat (gm): 6.2
Cholesterol (mg): 37
Sodium (mg): 307
Protein (gm): 7.1
Carbohydrate (gm): 54
Exchanges
Milk: 0.0
Vegetable: 0.0
Fruit: 0.0
Bread: 3.5
Meat: 0.0
Fat: 2.0

1. Make Chocolate Cookie Crumb Crust, adding mint extract, and pressing evenly onto bottom and side of 9-inch pie pan. Bake as directed.

2. Beat cream cheese in large bowl until fluffy; beat in sugar, eggs, crème de menthe, and sour cream.

3. Melt chocolate morsels and chocolate syrup in small saucepan over medium heat, stirring constantly until smooth. Remove from heat and stir in 3/4 cup cheese mixture. Add green food color to remaining cheese mixture.

4. Alternately spoon chocolate and mint mixtures into crust; swirl with knife. Bake at 350 degrees until center is almost set, about 30 minutes. Cool on wire rack. Refrigerate 4 hours or overnight. Top with chocolate-covered thin mints.

CHOCOLATE SWIRL CHEESECAKE

If a darker chocolate swirl is desired, mix 1 ounce melted semisweet chocolate into the chocolate cheesecake mixture.

12 servings

Chocolate Cookie Crumb Crust
(see p. 134)

1 carton (16 ounces) 1% low-fat cottage cheese

2 packages (8 ounces each) fat-free cream cheese, softened

1 package (8 ounces) reduced-fat cream cheese, softened

1¹/4 cups sugar, divided

2 eggs

1 teaspoon vanilla

¹/4 cup unsweetened cocoa

4 egg whites

¹/4 teaspoon cream of tartar

Light whipped topping, as garnish

Chocolate curls, as garnish

Per Serving
Calories: 313
% Calories from fat: 29
Fat (gm): 10
Saturated fat (gm): 3.9
Cholesterol (mg): 49
Sodium (mg): 630
Protein (gm): 15.1
Carbohydrate (gm): 40.4
Exchanges
Milk: 0.0
Vegetable: 0.0
Fruit: 0.0
Bread: 2.5
Meat: 1.0
Fat: 1.5

1. Make Chocolate Cookie Crumb Crust, pressing mixture evenly onto bottom and ¹/2 inch up side of 9-inch springform pan.

2. Process cottage cheese in food processor or blender until smooth. Beat cream cheese in large bowl until smooth; beat in cottage cheese, 1 cup sugar, eggs, and vanilla, blending well. Pour ¹/2 of the mixture into medium bowl; stir in cocoa.

3. Using large clean bowl and beaters, beat egg whites and cream of tartar to soft peaks; beat to stiff peaks, adding remaining ¹/4 cup sugar gradually. Mix ¹/4 of the egg whites into cocoa mixture; fold remaining egg whites into plain cheese mixture.

4. Pour plain cheese mixture into crust; spoon large dollops of chocolate mixture over and swirl together with a knife. Bake at 325 degrees until almost set in the center, 40 to 50 minutes. Cool on wire rack; refrigerate 8 hours or overnight.

5. Garnish slices with whipped topping and chocolate curls.

TURTLE CHEESECAKE

*A combination of brownie crust, caramel cheesecake, and pecans smoth-
ered with caramel sauce—who can resist such an incredible offering!*

12 servings

Brownie Crust (recipe follows)

³/₄ package (14-ounce size) caramels
(about 35)

¹/₄ cup fat-free milk

2 packages (8 ounces each) fat-free cream
cheese, softened

¹/₂ cup sugar

2 eggs

¹/₄ cup fat-free sour cream

Caramel Glaze (recipe follows)

¹/₄-¹/₂ cup pecan halves

Per Serving
Calories: 356
% Calories from fat: 22
Fat (gm): 9
Saturated fat (gm): 3.3
Cholesterol (mg): 56.2
Sodium (mg): 279
Protein (gm): 9.6
Carbohydrate (gm): 63.1

Exchanges
Milk: 0.0
Vegetable: 0.0
Fruit: 0.0
Bread: 4.0
Meat: 0.0
Fat: 1.5

1. Make Brownie Crust.

2. Heat caramels and milk in small saucepan over medium-low
heat until melted, stirring occasionally. Pour caramel over
Brownie Crust, spreading evenly. Refrigerate until caramel is
cold, about 20 minutes.

3. Beat cream cheese and sugar in medium bowl until well
blended. Beat in eggs, 1 at a time, beating well after each addition; mix in sour cream.

4. Pour batter over caramel. Place pan on cookie sheet and bake
at 350 degrees 45 minutes or until center is almost set. Run
sharp knife around side of pan to loosen cheesecake; cool on
wire rack. Refrigerate 8 hours or overnight.

5. Remove side of pan; place cheesecake on serving plate. Pour
Caramel Glaze over top of cheesecake; top with pecan halves.

Brownie Crust

makes one 9-inch crust

- 1/2 cup all-purpose flour
- 1/3 cup packed light brown sugar
- 1/3 cup reduced-fat semisweet chocolate morsels, melted
- 3 tablespoons margarine, melted
- 1 egg

1. Mix all ingredients in medium bowl until blended; spread evenly in bottom of greased 9-inch springform pan.

2. Bake at 350 degrees until firm to touch, 13 to 15 minutes; cool on wire rack.

Caramel Glaze

makes about 1 cup

- 1/2 package (14-ounce size) caramels (about 25 caramels)
- 1/3 cup fat-free milk

1. Heat caramels and milk in small saucepan over medium-low heat until melted, stirring occasionally. Let stand, stirring occasionally, until thickened enough to spread, 5 to 10 minutes.

Variations: **Triple-Chocolate Brownie Cheesecake**—Make cheesecake as above, omitting the caramels, milk, and Caramel Glaze and adding 1/4 cup unsweetened cocoa and 1/3 cup reduced-fat semisweet chocolate morsels to the filling. Bake as above.

Peanut Butter Cup Cheesecake—Make cheesecake as above, omitting caramels and milk, substituting brown sugar for the granulated sugar, and adding 3/4 cup reduced-fat peanut butter. Bake and chill as above. Omit Caramel Glaze; drizzle top of cheesecake with 1 ounce melted semisweet chocolate; garnish with halved peanut butter cup candies. Serve with Bittersweet Chocolate Sauce (see p. 642).

BROWNIE SWIRL CHEESECAKE

Our idea of chocolate heaven!

12 servings

1 package (15 ounces) reduced-fat brownie mix

2/3 cup applesauce

2 packages (8 ounces each) fat-free cream cheese

2/3 cup sugar

2 tablespoons cornstarch

1/4 cup fat-free milk

1 egg

1 teaspoon vanilla

2 ounces semisweet chocolate, melted
Chocolate Sauce (see p. 642)

Per Serving
Calories: 314
% Calories from fat: 16
Fat (gm): 5.7
Saturated fat (gm): 2.1
Cholesterol (mg): 21.6
Sodium (mg): 352
Protein (gm): 9
Carbohydrate (gm): 58.5
Exchanges
Milk: 0.0
Vegetable: 0.0
Fruit: 0.0
Bread: 4.0
Meat: 0.0
Fat: 1.0

1. Mix brownie mix and applesauce in bowl; press onto bottom and 1 inch up side of 9-inch springform pan, using spoon if necessary (batter will be stiff).

2. Beat cream cheese until fluffy in large bowl; beat in sugar, cornstarch, milk, egg, and vanilla. Transfer half of the mixture to small bowl and stir in chocolate.

3. Spoon the 2 fillings alternately into crust; swirl with knife. Bake at 350 degrees until almost set in the center, 30 to 35 minutes. Cool on wire rack; refrigerate 8 hours or overnight. Serve with Chocolate Sauce.

CHOCOLATE CARAMEL CHEESECAKE

For an attractive garnish, drizzle 1 ounce melted semisweet chocolate over top of baked cheesecake.

12 servings

Vanilla Crumb Crust (see p. 133)

1 package (14 ounces) chocolate, *or* regular, caramels (about 50 caramels)

1 can (5 ounces) evaporated skim milk

1/2 cup chopped walnuts

2 packages (8 ounces each) fat-free cream cheese, softened

1/2 cup sugar

2 eggs

2 ounces semisweet baking chocolate, melted

1/4 cup unsweetened cocoa

1 teaspoon vanilla

Per Serving
Calories: 347
% Calories from fat: 28
Fat (gm): 11
Saturated fat (gm): 3
Cholesterol (mg): 39.3
Sodium (mg): 307
Protein (gm): 10.1
Carbohydrate (gm): 54.6
Exchanges
Milk: 0.0
Vegetable: 0.0
Fruit: 0.0
Bread: 3.5
Meat: 0.0
Fat: 2.0

1. Make Vanilla Crumb Crust, pressing mixture evenly onto bottom and 1/2 inch up side of 9-inch springform pan.

2. Heat caramels and milk in small saucepan over medium-low heat until melted, stirring occasionally. Pour mixture into crust; sprinkle with walnuts. Refrigerate until caramel is cold, about 20 minutes.

3. Beat cream cheese and sugar in medium bowl until well blended. Beat in eggs, 1 at a time. Mix in chocolate, cocoa, and vanilla.

4. Pour mixture over walnuts in crust. Place pan on cookie sheet and bake at 350 degrees 45 minutes or until center is almost set. Run sharp knife around side of pan to loosen cheesecake; cool on wire rack. Refrigerate 8 hours or overnight.

CHOCOLATE CHEESE PIE

Chocolate all the way!

10 servings

Chocolate Cookie Crumb Crust
(see p. 134)
2 packages (8 ounces each) fat-free cream
cheese, softened
3/4 cup sugar
2 eggs
1 teaspoon vanilla
1 ounce bittersweet chocolate, melted
1/4 cup Dutch process cocoa
2-3 cups light whipped topping
Chocolate curls, as garnish

Per Serving
Calories: 299
% Calories from fat: 32
Fat (gm): 10.8
Saturated fat (gm): 4.2
Cholesterol (mg): 46
Sodium (mg): 441
Protein (gm): 9.5
Carbohydrate (gm): 41.1
Exchanges
Milk: 0.0
Vegetable: 0.0
Fruit: 0.0
Bread: 2.5
Meat: 1.0
Fat: 1.5

1. Make Chocolate Cookie Crumb Crust, using 9-inch pie pan.

2. Beat cream cheese until fluffy in large bowl; beat in sugar, eggs, and vanilla. Mix in melted chocolate and cocoa.

3. Pour filling in crust. Bake at 375 degrees until almost set in the center, 25 to 30 minutes. Cool on wire rack; refrigerate 8 hours or overnight.

4. Spread whipped topping over cheesecake and garnish with chocolate curls.

Variation: **Black Forest Cheesecake**—Press crust mixture evenly onto bottom and 1/2 inch up side of 9-inch springform pan. Make filling as above, increasing chocolate to 2 ounces and substituting 2 tablespoons brandy *or* 1 teaspoon brandy extract for the vanilla. Spoon Brandied Cherry Sauce (see p. 655) over slices.

CHOCOLATE FILLO CHEESECAKE

12 servings

Vegetable cooking spray
2 tablespoons graham cracker crumbs
1 egg white, beaten
2 tablespoons vegetable oil
8 sheets frozen fillo pastry, thawed
3 packages (8 ounces each) fat-free cream cheese, softened
1 cup reduced-fat sour cream
2/3 cup sugar
1/3 cup Dutch process cocoa
2 eggs
3 tablespoons flour
1/2 teaspoon ground cinnamon

Per Serving
Calories: 218
% Calories from fat: 28
Fat (gm): 6.8
Saturated fat (gm): 2.7
Cholesterol (mg): 46.6
Sodium (mg): 405
Protein (gm): 12.6
Carbohydrate (gm): 26.2
Exchanges
Milk: 0.0
Vegetable: 0.0
Fruit: 0.0
Bread: 1.5
Meat: 1.0
Fat: 1.0

1. Lightly spray 9-inch springform pan with cooking spray; sprinkle with graham cracker crumbs.

2. Mix egg white and oil until well blended in small bowl. Lay 1 sheet fillo on clean, dry surface; brush lightly with oil mixture. Top with second sheet fillo, arranging it crosswise over the first; brush with oil mixture. Repeat with remaining fillo and oil mixture, arranging fillo so corners are staggered. Lift fillo and place in pan, fitting against the bottom and side. Bake at 375 degrees 6 to 8 minutes or until lightly browned. Cool on wire rack.

3. Beat cream cheese until fluffy in large bowl; mix in sour cream, sugar, and cocoa. Beat in eggs; mix in flour and cinnamon.

4. Pour mixture into fillo crust; gently fold edges of fillo inward so that edges of fillo do not extend outside of pan. Bake at 350 degrees 50 minutes or until center of cheesecake is almost set. Cover edges of fillo crust with aluminum foil during last 15 or 20 minutes of baking time if beginning to get too brown. Cool on wire rack 10 minutes. Carefully remove side of pan and cool completely; refrigerate 8 hours or overnight.

Variation: **Chocolate Sin Cheesecake**—Omit graham cracker crumbs, egg white, oil, and fillo; skip Steps 1 and 2. Make Chocolate Cookie Crumb Crust (see p. 134); press evenly onto bottom and ¹/₂ inch up side of 9-inch springform pan. Make filling as in Step 3; stir in 2 to 3 ounces melted bittersweet chocolate. Bake and refrigerate as above. Garnish top of cheesecake with light whipped topping and chocolate curls.

CARAMEL FUDGE CHEESECAKE

A marvelous combination of rich chocolate and caramel flavors.

14 servings

Chocolate Cookie Crumb Crust
(see p. 134)
¹/₂ cup reduced-fat semisweet chocolate morsels
¹/₂ cup fat-free caramel sauce
2 packages (8 ounces each) fat-free cream cheese, softened
2 packages (8 ounces each) reduced-fat cream cheese, softened
1 cup packed light brown sugar
¹/₃ cup Dutch process cocoa
1 cup fat-free sour cream
4 egg whites
1 tablespoon vanilla extract
¹/₄ teaspoon salt

Per Serving
Calories: 356
% Calories from fat: 31
Fat (gm): 12.3
Saturated fat (gm): 6.8
Cholesterol (mg): 17.8
Sodium (mg): 561
Protein (gm): 11.9
Carbohydrate (gm): 50.1
Exchanges
Milk: 0.0
Vegetable: 0.0
Fruit: 0.0
Bread: 3.5
Meat: 0.0
Fat: 2.5

1. Make Chocolate Cookie Crumb Crust in 10-inch springform pan, pressing evenly onto bottom and ¹/₂ inch up side of pan. Bake as directed.

2. Heat chocolate morsels and caramel sauce in small saucepan over medium to medium-low heat, stirring constantly until chocolate is melted; cool.

3. Beat cream cheese in large bowl until fluffy; beat in chocolate mixture and remaining ingredients until smooth.

4. Pour filling into crust. Bake at 350 degrees until center is almost set, about 50 minutes. Cool on wire rack; refrigerate 8 hours or overnight.

ALMOND PRALINE CHEESECAKE

If not in the mood to make praline, purchased English toffee bits can be substituted.

12 servings

Vanilla Crumb Crust (see p. 133)
2 cups 1% low-fat cottage cheese
2 packages (8 ounces each) fat-free cream cheese, softened
1/2 cup packed light brown sugar
2 eggs
3 tablespoons almond liqueur *or* 1 teaspoon almond extract
3 egg whites
1/8 teaspoon cream of tartar
2 tablespoons granulated sugar
Almond Praline (recipe follows)

Per Serving
Calories: 284
% Calories from fat: 27
Fat (gm): 8.2
Saturated fat (gm): 2.1
Cholesterol (mg): 40
Sodium (mg): 450
Protein (gm): 13.3
Carbohydrate (gm): 34.6
Exchanges
Milk: 0.0
Vegetable: 0.0
Fruit: 0.0
Bread: 2.5
Meat: 1.0
Fat: 1.0

1. Make Vanilla Crumb Crust, using 10-inch springform pan.

2. Process cottage cheese in food processor or blender until smooth. Beat cream cheese in large bowl until smooth; beat in brown sugar, cottage cheese, eggs, and almond liqueur.

3. Using large, clean bowl and beaters, beat egg whites and cream of tartar to soft peaks; beat to stiff peaks, adding granulated sugar gradually. Mix about 1/4 of the egg whites into cream cheese mixture; fold cream cheese mixture into remaining egg whites. Fold in 1/2 of the Almond Praline.

4. Pour filling into crust. Bake at 325 degrees until almost set in the center, 35 to 40 minutes. Sprinkle top of cheesecake with remaining Almond Praline. Cool on wire rack; refrigerate 8 hours or overnight.

Almond Praline

makes about 3/4 cup

- 1/2 cup sugar
- 1/4 cup water
- 1/2 cup slivered blanched almonds

1. Heat sugar and water to boiling over medium-high heat in small skillet, stirring until sugar is dissolved. Boil without stirring until sugar turns a golden color; stir in almonds and remove from heat.

2. Immediately pour praline into greased jelly roll pan, spreading to a thin layer. Cool.

3. Break praline into small pieces; process in food processor until finely ground.

TOFFEE CHEESECAKE

A satin-smooth cheesecake, flavored with brown sugar and sprinkled with crunchy toffee bits.

16 servings

Graham Cracker Crumb Crust
(see p. 132)

1 1/4 cups packed light brown sugar, divided

3 packages (8 ounces each) fat-free cream cheese, softened

1 cup fat-free sour cream

2-3 teaspoons butter extract

2 eggs

4 egg whites

1/2 teaspoon cream of tartar

Brown Sugar Sour Cream Topping
(recipe follows)

4 ounces English toffee bits

Per Serving
Calories: 283
% Calories from fat: 24
Fat (gm): 7.5
Saturated fat (gm): 2.8
Cholesterol (mg): 37.3
Sodium (mg): 369
Protein (gm): 11
Carbohydrate (gm): 42.5
Exchanges
Milk: 0.0
Vegetable: 0.0
Fruit: 0.0
Bread: 3.0
Meat: 0.0
Fat: 1.5

1. Make Graham Cracker Crumb Crust, substituting 1/4 cup brown sugar for the granulated sugar, and using 10-inch spring-form pan.

2. Beat cream cheese until fluffy in large bowl; beat in remaining 1 cup brown sugar, sour cream, butter extract, and whole eggs.

3. Using large, clean bowl and beaters, beat egg whites and cream of tartar to stiff peaks. Mix about ¹/₄ of the egg whites into cheese mixture; fold cheese mixture into remaining egg whites.

4. Pour filling into crust. Bake at 350 degrees until just set in the center, 45 to 55 minutes. Spread Brown Sugar Sour Cream Topping over cheesecake and sprinkle with English toffee bits; bake just until topping is set, about 5 minutes. Cool on wire rack; refrigerate 8 hours or overnight.

Brown Sugar Sour Cream Topping

makes about 1¹/₂ cups

- 1¹/₂ cups fat-free sour cream
- ¹/₄ cup packed light brown sugar
- 1 teaspoon butter extract *or* vanilla

1. Mix all ingredients.

MAPLE PECAN CHEESECAKE

Superb served with fresh peaches or berries.

12 servings

Graham Cracker Crumb Crust (see p. 132)
- ¹/₄ cup plus 1-2 tablespoons maple syrup *or* pancake syrup
- 3 cups 1% low-fat cottage cheese
- 2 packages (8 ounces each) fat-free cream cheese, softened
- ³/₄ cup packed light brown sugar
- 2 eggs
- 4 egg whites
- ¹/₄ teaspoon cream of tartar
- ¹/₄ cup granulated sugar
- 3-4 tablespoons chopped toasted pecans

Per Serving
Calories: 291
% Calories from fat: 26
Fat (gm): 8.4
Saturated fat (gm): 2.1
Cholesterol (mg): 40.8
Sodium (mg): 554
Protein (gm): 15.7
Carbohydrate (gm): 39
Exchanges
Milk: 0.0
Vegetable: 0.0
Fruit: 0.0
Bread: 2.5
Meat: 1.0
Fat: 1.0

1. Make Graham Cracker Crumb Crust, substituting 1 to 2 tablespoons maple syrup for the honey, and using 10-inch springform pan.

2. Process cottage cheese in food processor or blender until smooth. Beat cream cheese in large bowl until smooth; beat in cottage cheese, brown sugar, remaining 1/4 cup maple syrup, and whole eggs until well blended.

3. With clean bowl and beaters, beat egg whites and cream of tartar until foamy; beat to stiff peaks, adding granulated sugar gradually. Mix about 1/4 of the egg whites into cream cheese mixture; fold cream cheese mixture into remaining egg whites.

4. Pour filling into crust; sprinkle with pecans. Bake at 325 degrees until set, 40 to 45 minutes. Cool on wire rack; refrigerate 8 hours or overnight.

BAKLAVA CHEESECAKE

A spectacular cheesecake, baked in fillo, topped with nuts, and soaked with honey syrup.

16 servings

Vegetable cooking spray
2 tablespoons graham cracker crumbs
3 egg whites, room temperature, divided
2-3 tablespoons melted margarine
8 sheets frozen fillo pastry, thawed
5 packages (8 ounces each) fat-free cream cheese, softened
1 1/2 cups packed light brown sugar
3 tablespoons flour
3 eggs
1/2 cup honey
1 tablespoon finely grated lemon rind
2 teaspoons vanilla
Baklava Crust (recipe follows)
Honey Syrup (recipe follows)

Per Serving
Calories: 365
% Calories from fat: 25
Fat (gm): 10.4
Saturated fat (gm): 2
Cholesterol (mg): 45.4
Sodium (mg): 538
Protein (gm): 15.7
Carbohydrate (gm): 53.9
Exchanges
Milk: 0.0
Vegetable: 0.0
Fruit: 0.0
Bread: 3.5
Meat: 1.0
Fat: 1.5

1. Lightly spray 10-inch springform pan with cooking spray; sprinkle with graham cracker crumbs.

2. Beat 1 egg white and margarine until well blended in small bowl. Lay 1 sheet fillo on clean, dry surface with long edge parallel to surface. Brush left half of fillo lightly with egg white mixture, fold right half over, and brush it lightly with egg white mixture. Place fillo in pan so that 5 inches fillo hangs over edge of pan. Repeat with remaining fillo and egg white mixture, overlapping fillo in pan and covering entire pan.

3. Beat cream cheese until fluffy in large bowl; beat in brown sugar and flour. Beat in eggs and remaining egg whites one at a time, beating well after each addition. Beat in remaining ingredients, except Baklava Crust and Honey Syrup.

4. Pour filling into fillo crust. Fold fillo pastry over filling. Bake at 350 degrees until cheesecake is just set in the center and firm to touch, 60 to 70 minutes. Carefully remove side of pan and place cheesecake on wire rack; make about 12 holes in top of cheesecake with wooden skewer so that steam can escape. Cool completely; refrigerate 8 hours or overnight.

5. Flatten fillo on top of cheesecake if necessary, using pancake turner. Place Baklava Crust on top of cheesecake. Fasten side of pan around cheesecake and place on jelly roll pan; pour hot Honey Syrup over. Cool 1 hour; refrigerate overnight. Let cheesecake stand at room temperature 30 minutes before cutting.

Baklava Crust

    8 sheets frozen fillo pastry, thawed
    1 cup walnut pieces
    2 tablespoons granulated sugar
    1 teaspoon ground cinnamon
    1 egg white, lightly beaten
  2-3 tablespoons melted margarine

1. Stack sheets of fillo; place rim of 10-inch springform pan on fillo and cut through fillo with sharp knife, cutting along inside of pan. Set pan rim on greased cookie sheet.

2. Process walnuts, granulated sugar, and cinnamon in food processor until finely ground. Mix egg white and margarine until well blended in small bowl. Place 1 fillo circle inside pan rim and brush lightly with egg white mixture; place second circle on top and brush with egg white mixture. Repeat with 2 more circles of fillo; sprinkle walnut mixture evenly over fillo. Repeat layers, using remaining fillo and egg white mixture. Score pastry into 16 wedges with sharp knife.

3. Bake at 350 degrees until fillo is browned and crisp, about 30 minutes.

Honey Syrup

- ¹/₄ cup granulated sugar
- ¹/₄ cup honey
- ¹/₄ cup water
- 1 tablespoon lemon juice

1. Heat all ingredients to boiling in small saucepan; boil over medium-high heat until mixture is syrupy, 4 to 5 minutes.

MACADAMIA NUT CHEESECAKE

The taste of the islands—this cheesecake is delicious with Pineapple-Rum Sauce (see p. 654), too.

12 servings

- Nutty Crumb Crust (recipe follows)
- 2 packages (8 ounces each) fat-free cream cheese, softened
- ³/₄ cup packed light brown sugar
- ¹/₃ cup light corn syrup
- 2 eggs
- 2 tablespoons apple juice
- 1 teaspoon almond extract
- 1 teaspoon rum extract
- ¹/₂ teaspoon ground cinnamon
- ¹/₂ cup finely chopped toasted macadamia nuts

Per Serving
Calories: 257
% Calories from fat: 28
Fat (gm): 8.1
Saturated fat (gm): 1.7
Cholesterol (mg): 39
Sodium (mg): 337
Protein (gm): 8.8
Carbohydrate (gm): 38.9
Exchanges
Milk: 0.0
Vegetable: 0.0
Fruit: 0.0
Bread: 2.5
Meat: 0.0
Fat: 1.5

1. Make Nutty Crumb Crust, pressing mixture evenly onto bottom and 1/2 inch up side of 10-inch springform pan. Bake at 350 degrees 5 minutes or until lightly browned. Cool on wire rack.

2. Beat cream cheese in large bowl until fluffy; beat in brown sugar, corn syrup, eggs, apple juice, extracts, and cinnamon. Stir in macadamia nuts.

3. Pour filling into crust; bake at 350 degrees until cheesecake is almost set in the center, 45 to 50 minutes. Cool on wire rack. Refrigerate 8 hours or overnight.

Nutty Crumb Crust

makes one 10-inch crust

- 1 1/2 cups dry plain breadcrumbs
- 2 tablespoons chopped toasted macadamia nuts
- 1/4 cup honey
- 1 tablespoon margarine, melted

1. Combine all ingredients.

Variation: **Coconut Almond Cheesecake**—Substitute Coconut Crust (see p. 261) for the Nutty Crumb Crust. Make filling, adding 1/3 cup toasted coconut; substitute toasted slivered almonds for the macadamia nuts and coconut extract for the rum extract. Bake as above. Serve with Bittersweet Chocolate Sauce (see p. 641), if desired.

CREAMY CHEESECAKE WITH PINEAPPLE-RUM SAUCE

A no-bake cheesecake, quick and easy to make.

12 servings

Gingersnap Crumb Crust (see p. 135)
3/4 cup sugar, divided
2 tablespoons cornstarch
1 envelope unflavored gelatin
1 cup fat-free milk
1 egg, beaten
2 packages (8 ounces each) fat-free cream cheese, softened
1/2 cup fat-free sour cream
1/2 teaspoon rum extract
Pineapple-Rum Sauce (see p. 654)

Per Serving
Calories: 226
% Calories from fat: 17
Fat (gm): 4.3
Saturated fat (gm): 1.2
Cholesterol (mg): 21.1
Sodium (mg): 302
Protein (gm): 8.2
Carbohydrate (gm): 38.4
Exchanges
Milk: 0.0
Vegetable: 0.0
Fruit: 0.0
Bread: 2.5
Meat: 0.0
Fat: 1.0

1. Make Gingersnap Crumb Crust; reserve 2 tablespoons crumbs. Pat remaining crumb mixture on bottom and 1/2 inch up side of 9-inch springform pan and bake according to recipe.

2. Combine 1/4 cup sugar, cornstarch, and gelatin in small saucepan; whisk in milk. Heat to boiling, whisking constantly; boil, whisking, until thickened, about 1 minute. Whisk about 1/2 of the mixture into egg; whisk egg mixture into saucepan. Cook over low heat, whisking constantly, 1 minute. Cool to room temperature.

3. Beat cream cheese and remaining 1/2 cup sugar until fluffy in medium bowl; beat in sour cream and rum extract. Mix in milk mixture. Pour mixture into crust; sprinkle with reserved 2 tablespoons crumbs. Refrigerate until set, 4 to 6 hours.

4. Loosen side of pan and place cheesecake on serving plate. Serve with Pineapple-Rum Sauce.

Variations: **Vanilla Cheesecake with Drunken Berries**—Make cheesecake as above, substituting 2 teaspoons vanilla for the rum extract and deleting Pineapple-Rum Sauce. To make **Drunken Berries**, combine 3 cups blueberries, 1/4 cup sugar, and 2 tablespoons vodka in bowl; let stand 20 minutes, stirring occasionally. Serve over cheesecake slices.

Apple Cider Cheesecake—Heat 2 cups apple cider to boiling in small saucepan; boil until reduced to 1 cup. Cool. Make cheesecake as above, substituting cider for the milk, adding 1/2 teaspoon ground cinnamon and 2 pinches ground nutmeg, and substituting vanilla for the rum extract. Bake as above. Glaze cheesecake with Caramel Glaze (see p. 65); delete Pineapple-Rum Sauce.

PINEAPPLE CHEESECAKE

A generously sized cheesecake, perfect for large gatherings.

12 servings

Graham Cracker Crumb Crust
(see p. 132)

2 packages (8 ounces each) 1% low-fat creamed cottage cheese

3 eggs

3 packages (8 ounces each) fat-free cream cheese, softened

1 cup sugar

2 tablespoons flour

1-1 1/4 teaspoons rum extract

1/4 teaspoon salt

1 can (16 ounces) crushed pineapple, drained

Sugared Sour Cream Topping
(recipe follows)

Per Serving
Calories: 350
% Calories from fat: 20
Fat (gm): 7.7
Saturated fat (gm): 2.2
Cholesterol (mg): 59
Sodium (mg): 644
Protein (gm): 18.2
Carbohydrate (gm): 51.4
Exchanges
Milk: 0.0
Vegetable: 0.0
Fruit: 1.0
Bread: 2.5
Meat: 1.0
Fat: 1.0

1. Make Graham Cracker Crumb Crust, pressing mixture onto bottom and 1/2 inch up side of 10-inch springform pan.

2. Process cottage cheese and eggs in food processor or blender until smooth. Beat cream cheese in large bowl until fluffy; beat in cottage cheese, sugar, flour, rum extract, and salt. Mix in pineapple.

3. Pour batter into crust. Bake at 300 degrees until cheesecake is almost set in the center, 60 to 70 minutes. Turn oven off; cool cheesecake in oven with door ajar 1 hour.

4. Spread top of cake with Sugared Sour Cream Topping; bake at 350 degrees 10 minutes. Cool on wire rack; refrigerate 8 hours or overnight.

Sugared Sour Cream Topping

   2 cups fat-free sour cream
   3 tablespoons sugar
   1 teaspoon vanilla

1. Mix all ingredients.

Variation: **Tropical Cheesecake**—Make cheesecake as above, adding ¹/₂ cup chopped macadamia nuts to the filling and omitting Sugared Sour Cream Topping. Arrange sliced kiwi, mango, and pineapple on top of chilled cheesecake; drizzle or brush with warm honey or melted apple jelly.

RIPE BANANA CHEESECAKE

Ripe bananas flavor this cheesecake on a fruit crust. Try this with Warm Rum Sauce (see p. 54).

12 servings

   Banana Fruit Crust (recipe follows)
   1 package (8 ounces) fat-free cream cheese, softened
   1 package (8 ounces) reduced-fat cream cheese, softened
   1 cup fat-free sour cream
   1 cup mashed ripe banana (1 large)
   ¹/₂ cup packed light brown sugar
   1 egg
   1 tablespoon lemon juice
   1 teaspoon vanilla extract
   ¹/₂ teaspoon rum extract
   ¹/₂ teaspoon ground cinnamon
   1 cup light whipped topping

Per Serving
Calories: 194
% Calories from fat: 21
Fat (gm): 4.5
Saturated fat (gm): 3.1
Cholesterol (mg): 28
Sodium (mg): 218
Protein (gm): 7
Carbohydrate (gm): 31
Exchanges
Milk: 0.0
Vegetable: 0.0
Fruit: 1.0
Bread: 1.0
Meat: 0.0
Fat: 1.0

1. Make Banana Fruit Crust, spreading mixture evenly over bottom of 9-inch springform pan.

2. Beat cream cheese in large bowl until fluffy; beat in remaining ingredients, except whipped topping.

3. Pour filling into crust; bake at 350 degrees until cheesecake is almost set in the center, 30 to 40 minutes. Cool on wire rack; refrigerate 8 hours or overnight. Serve with whipped topping.

Banana Fruit Crust

makes one 10-inch crust

- 1/3 cup chopped dried tropical fruit
- 1/4 cup hot water
- 4 ripe bananas

1. Soak dried fruit in hot water until softened, about 10 minutes. Coarsely mash bananas in medium bowl; add fruit mixture, blending well.

APPLE-CRANBERRY UPSIDE-DOWN CHEESECAKE

This upside-down cheesecake has no crust, but when inverted, has a tempting fruit topping.

12 servings

- 5 cups sliced peeled Granny Smith, *or* Rome, apples
- 1-2 tablespoons margarine
- 1/2 cup dried cranberries
- 1/4 cup packed light brown sugar
- 2 teaspoons grated lemon rind
- 3/4 teaspoon ground cinnamon
- 1/4 teaspoon ground nutmeg
- 2 packages (8 ounces each) reduced-fat cream cheese, softened
- 2/3 cup granulated sugar
- 4 eggs
- 3 tablespoons lemon juice
- 2 cups plain fat-free yogurt

Per Serving
Calories: 247
% Calories from fat: 32
Fat (gm): 8.8
Saturated fat (gm): 4.9
Cholesterol (mg): 89.1
Sodium (mg): 241
Protein (gm): 8
Carbohydrate (gm): 33.7
Exchanges
Milk: 0.0
Vegetable: 0.0
Fruit: 0.5
Bread: 2.0
Meat: 0.0
Fat: 1.5

1. Lightly grease 10-inch springform pan and line with parchment paper.

2. Saute apples in margarine in large skillet 5 minutes. Add cranberries, brown sugar, lemon rind, and spices; cook 2 to 3 minutes or until liquid evaporates, stirring frequently. Cool slightly; arrange apple mixture in bottom of pan, pressing with wooden spoon.

3. Beat cream cheese until fluffy in large bowl; beat in granulated sugar, eggs, and lemon juice. Add yogurt, mixing until well blended.

4. Pour filling over apple mixture in pan. Bake at 350 degrees until just set in the center, about 50 minutes. Cool on wire rack; refrigerate 8 hours or overnight.

5. Remove side of pan; invert cheesecake onto serving plate and remove parchment. Rearrange fruit if necessary.

APRICOT WALNUT CHEESECAKE

This apricot-flavored ricotta cheesecake boasts a walnut crust and apricot glaze. Serve with fresh sliced apricots in season.

10 servings

Walnut Crust (recipe follows)
1 1/2 pounds reduced-fat ricotta cheese
1 package (8 ounces) fat-free cream cheese
3/4 cup sugar
1/4 cup all-purpose flour
8 egg whites *or* 1 cup no-cholesterol real egg product
3/4 cup apricot nectar
1/4 cup lemon juice
3/4 cup apricot preserves, divided
2 teaspoons grated lemon rind
1-2 tablespoons finely chopped walnuts

Per Serving
Calories: 349
% Calories from fat: 19
Fat (gm): 7.6
Saturated fat (gm): 2.5
Cholesterol (mg): 18.3
Sodium (mg): 377
Protein (gm): 13.8
Carbohydrate (gm): 57.4
Exchanges
Milk: 0.0
Vegetable: 0.0
Fruit: 0.0
Bread: 3.5
Meat: 1.0
Fat: 1.0

1. Make Walnut Crust, pressing onto bottom and 1/2 inch up side of 10-inch springform pan.

2. Beat ricotta and cream cheese until fluffy in large bowl; beat in sugar and flour. Beat in egg whites, apricot nectar, lemon juice, 1/4 cup apricot preserves, and lemon rind.

3. Pour filling into crust. Bake at 300 degrees until just set in the center, 1 1/4 to 1 1/2 hours. Turn oven off; cool cheesecake in oven 2 hours. Refrigerate 8 hours or overnight.

4. Remove side of pan and place cheesecake on serving plate. Melt remaining 1/2 cup preserves in small saucepan; brush over top of cheesecake. Sprinkle with walnuts.

Walnut Crust

1 cup finely crushed corn flake cereal
$^1/_4$ cup packed light brown sugar
$^1/_4$ cup finely ground walnuts
$^1/_2$ teaspoon ground cinnamon
$^1/_8$ teaspoon ground nutmeg
2 tablespoons melted margarine
1-2 tablespoons honey

1. Combine all ingredients, adding enough honey for mixture to stick together.

GINGERED PEACH AND ALMOND CHEESECAKE SQUARES

Perfect for picnics or shared dinner occasions.

16 servings

2 Gingersnap Crumb Crusts (see p. 135)
2 packages (8 ounces each) fat-free cream cheese, softened
$^1/_2$ cup granulated sugar
2 eggs
$^1/_2$ teaspoon almond extract
6-8 medium peaches, peeled, thinly sliced
$^1/_3$ cup packed light brown sugar
$^1/_4$ cup chopped toasted blanched almonds

Per Serving
Calories: 209
% Calories from fat: 29
Fat (gm): 6.8
Saturated fat (gm): 1.5
Cholesterol (mg): 29
Sodium (mg): 269
Protein (gm): 6.3
Carbohydrate (gm): 30.7
Exchanges
Milk: 0.0
Vegetable: 0.0
Fruit: 0.0
Bread: 2.0
Meat: 0.0
Fat: 1.0

1. Make Gingersnap Crumb Crusts, pressing mixture evenly onto bottom of jelly roll pan, 15 x 10 inches. Bake at 350 degrees until lightly browned, 6 to 8 minutes. Cool on wire rack.

2. Beat cream cheese and granulated sugar in large bowl until fluffy; beat in eggs and almond extract. Spread mixture evenly on crust. Arrange peaches in rows on top; sprinkle with combined brown sugar and almonds.

3. Bake at 350 degrees until set, about 30 minutes. Cool on wire rack; refrigerate until chilled, 4 to 6 hours.

Variation: **Plum Streusel Cheesecake Squares**—Make recipe as above, substituting 2 Vanilla Crumb Crusts (see p. 133) for the Gingersnap Crumb Crusts, vanilla for the almond extract, and 8 to 10 plums for the peaches; delete brown sugar and almonds. Assemble recipe as above; sprinkle Brown Sugar Granola Streusel (see p. 480) over the plums and bake as above.

PEAR PECAN CHEESECAKE

Ripe pears flavor this rich-tasting cheesecake in a pecan crust.

10 servings

Sweet Pecan Dough (recipe follows)
- 1 package (8 ounces) fat-free cream cheese, softened
- 1/2 cup sugar
- 2 tablespoons flour
- 1/4 teaspoon salt
- 1 cup fat-free sour cream
- 2 egg whites
- 1 teaspoon vanilla extract
- 2 cups thinly sliced, peeled, cored ripe pears

Per Serving
Calories: 229
% Calories from fat: 22
Fat (gm): 5.5
Saturated fat (gm): 1
Cholesterol (mg): 1.8
Sodium (mg): 253
Protein (gm): 7.5
Carbohydrate (gm): 37.5
Exchanges
Milk: 0.0
Vegetable: 0.0
Fruit: 1.0
Bread: 1.5
Meat: 0.0
Fat: 1.0

1. Press Sweet Pecan Dough evenly onto bottom and 1 inch up side of 9-inch springform pan. Chill 30 to 60 minutes.

2. Beat cream cheese, sugar, flour, and salt in large mixing bowl until smooth; beat in sour cream, egg whites, and vanilla.

3. Arrange pears on crust; pour filling over pears. Bake at 350 degrees until set and lightly browned, 45 to 55 minutes. Refrigerate 8 hours or overnight.

Sweet Pecan Dough

makes one 9-inch crust

- 1 cup all-purpose flour
- 1/4 cup powdered sugar
- 3 tablespoons finely chopped toasted pecans
- 3 tablespoons margarine
- 2-3 tablespoons water

1. Combine flour, sugar, and pecans in large mixing bowl; cut in margarine until mixture resembles coarse crumbs. Sprinkle with enough water to form a dough.

GOAT CHEESE CHEESECAKE WITH MIXED BERRIES

Goat cheese imparts a subtle yet distinctive flavor to this unusual cheesecake. Serve at room temperature or chill, if you like.

8 servings

Butter-flavored vegetable cooking spray
- 2 tablespoons graham cracker crumbs
- 1 package (8 ounces) fat-free cream cheese, softened
- 4 ounces reduced-fat goat cheese, softened
- 3/4 cup granulated sugar, divided
- 2 teaspoons lemon juice
- 2 teaspoons finely grated lemon rind
- 1 teaspoon vanilla
- 4 egg yolks
- 3 tablespoons flour
- 4 egg whites
- 1/8 teaspoon cream of tartar
- 2 cups mixed berries (raspberries, blueberries, etc.)
  Powdered sugar, as garnish
- 2 cups Raspberry Sauce (double recipe) (see p. 658)

Per Serving
Calories: 285
% Calories from fat: 19
Fat (gm): 6.3
Saturated fat (gm): 2.9
Cholesterol (mg): 121.4
Sodium (mg): 241
Protein (gm): 10.1
Carbohydrate (gm): 48.8
Exchanges
Milk: 0.0
Vegetable: 0.0
Fruit: 1.0
Bread: 2.5
Meat: 0.0
Fat: 1.0

1. Spray 9-inch cake pan with removable bottom with cooking spray and coat with graham cracker crumbs.

2. Beat cream cheese, goat cheese, and $^1/_2$ cup sugar in large bowl until smooth; beat in lemon juice, lemon rind, vanilla, egg yolks, and flour, blending well.

3. Using large, clean bowl and beaters, beat egg whites and cream of tartar to soft peaks; beat to stiff peaks, adding remaining $^1/_4$ cup sugar gradually. Stir about $^1/_4$ of the egg whites into cream cheese mixture; fold cream cheese mixture into remaining egg whites.

4. Pour batter into prepared pan. Bake at 350 degrees until toothpick inserted in center comes out clean, about 40 minutes. Cool on wire rack.

5. Invert cake onto serving plate; arrange berries on top and sprinkle with powdered sugar.

6. Make Raspberry Sauce, doubling recipe. Drizzle about 1 tablespoon Raspberry Sauce on each serving plate. Arrange cheesecake slices on plates and serve with remaining sauce.

SPRING BERRY CHEESECAKE

You won't believe this cheesecake until you taste it—delectable!

10 servings

$^1/_2$ cup vanilla wafer cookie crumbs

2 tablespoons melted margarine

1 cup 2% reduced-fat cottage cheese

1 package (8 ounces) fat-free cream cheese, softened

1 cup fat-free sour cream

$^1/_3$ plus $^1/_4$ cup sugar, divided

3 eggs

$^1/_2$ cup fat-free milk

2 tablespoons lemon juice

3 tablespoons finely grated lemon rind

3 tablespoons flour

1 teaspoon vanilla

$^1/_8$ teaspoon salt

1 quart strawberries, sliced

Per Serving
Calories: 216
% Calories from fat: 24
Fat (gm): 5.9
Saturated fat (gm): 1.8
Cholesterol (mg): 67.5
Sodium (mg): 337
Protein (gm): 11.1
Carbohydrate (gm): 29.3
Exchanges
Milk: 0.0
Vegetable: 0.0
Fruit: 0.0
Bread: 2.0
Meat: 1.0
Fat: 0.5

1. Combine vanilla wafer crumbs and margarine in bottom of 9-inch springform pan; press evenly onto bottom of pan.

2. Process cottage cheese in food processor or blender until smooth. Transfer cottage cheese to large bowl; add cream cheese, sour cream, and $1/3$ cup sugar and beat until light and fluffy. Add eggs one at a time, beating well after each addition. Add milk, lemon juice, lemon rind, flour, vanilla, and salt, mixing well.

3. Pour mixture into crust. Bake at 325 degrees 50 minutes or until center is set. Cool on wire rack. Refrigerate 8 hours or overnight.

4. Remove side of pan; place cheesecake on serving plate. Combine berries and remaining $1/4$ cup sugar in medium bowl; spoon strawberries over cheesecake slices.

STRAWBERRY SPECTACULAR CHEESECAKE

A large cheesecake with the creamiest texture ever. Perfect with strawberries, but raspberries or blueberries can be used as well.

14 servings

Graham Cracker Crumb Crust (see p. 132)

2 packages (8 ounces each) reduced-fat cream cheese, softened
2 packages (8 ounces each) fat-free cream cheese, softened
1 cup sugar, divided
2 tablespoons flour
$1/2$ teaspoon salt
2 egg yolks
1 tablespoon lemon juice
5 egg whites
$1/2$ teaspoon cream of tartar
2 pints small strawberries
$1/2$ cup currant jelly, melted

Per Serving
Calories: 301
% Calories from fat: 32
Fat (gm): 11
Saturated fat (gm): 5
Cholesterol (mg): 48.2
Sodium (mg): 508
Protein (gm): 10.5
Carbohydrate (gm): 40.3
Exchanges
Milk: 0.0
Vegetable: 0.0
Fruit: 0.5
Bread: 2.5
Meat: 0.0
Fat: 2.0

1. Make Graham Cracker Crumb Crust, using 10-inch spring-form pan.

2. Beat cream cheese until fluffy in large bowl; beat in $3/4$ cup sugar, flour, and salt. Add egg yolks and lemon juice, beating well.

3. Using large, clean bowl and beaters, beat egg whites and cream of tartar to soft peaks; beat to stiff peaks, adding remaining $1/4$ cup sugar gradually. Mix $1/4$ of the egg whites into cheese mixture; fold cheese mixture into remaining egg whites.

4. Pour filling into crust. Bake at 300 degrees until center of cheesecake is almost set, 50 to 60 minutes. Turn oven off; cool cheesecake in oven 2 hours, with door ajar. Refrigerate 8 hours or overnight.

5. Remove side of pan; place cheesecake on serving plate. Arrange strawberries on cheesecake, pointed ends up. Melt jelly; brush or drizzle over strawberries.

Variation: **Glazed Plum Cheesecake**—Make cheesecake as above, omitting strawberries, currant jelly, and Step 5. Heat $3/4$ cup orange juice, $1/2$ cup apple jelly, and $1/4$ cup packed light brown sugar to boiling in large skillet, stirring to dissolve sugar and jelly. Cut 6 to 8 plums into $1/2$-inch slices and add to skillet. Reduce heat and simmer, covered, until plums are tender, 3 to 4 minutes. Remove plums and cool. Boil sugar mixture until thickened to a syrup consistency, 5 to 7 minutes. Arrange plums on cheesecake and drizzle with syrup.

RASPBERRY CHEESECAKE

The fruit is in the cheesecake, rather than on top—serve it with Raspberry Sauce (see p. 658) on the side for even more flavor!

14 servings

Lemon Cookie Crumb Crust (see p. 136)

2 cups fresh, *or* frozen, unsweetened raspberries

2 tablespoons sugar

2 packages (8 ounces each) fat-free cream cheese, softened

1 package (8 ounces) reduced-fat cream cheese, softened

1 can (14 ounces) low-fat sweetened condensed milk

3 eggs

1 teaspoon vanilla

Per Serving
Calories: 235
% Calories from fat: 27
Fat (gm): 7.3
Saturated fat (gm): 1.8
Cholesterol (mg): 57
Sodium (mg): 318
Protein (gm): 10.4
Carbohydrate (gm): 32.3
Exchanges
Milk: 0.0
Vegetable: 0.0
Fruit: 0.0
Bread: 2.0
Meat: 1.0
Fat: 1.0

1. Make Lemon Cookie Crumb Crust in 10-inch springform pan, pressing evenly onto bottom and 1/2 inch up side of pan. Bake as directed.

2. Combine raspberries and sugar in small bowl. Set aside. Beat cream cheese in large bowl until fluffy; beat in remaining ingredients until smooth. Gently fold in raspberry mixture.

3. Pour mixture into crust; bake at 350 degrees until center is almost set, about 45 minutes. Cool. Refrigerate 8 hours or overnight.

Variations: **Blueberry Cheesecake**—Make cheesecake as above, substituting blueberries for the raspberries, brown sugar for the granulated sugar, and orange extract for the vanilla. Add 1 tablespoon grated orange rind to the mixture.

Raspberry Chocolate Cheesecake—Substitute Chocolate Cookie Crumb Crust (see p. 134) for the crust in Step 1. Reduce amount of raspberries in Step 2 to 1 cup. Set aside. Divide cheese mixture into two bowls. Fold 4 ounces melted semisweet chocolate into one bowl. Pour into prepared crust. Fold raspberries into remaining cheese mixture; spoon over chocolate layer. Bake and cool as in Step 3. Serve with Chocolate Sauce or Raspberry Sauce (see pp. 642, 658).

RASPBERRY SWIRL CHEESECAKE

For an added touch, spoon Raspberry Sauce (see p. 658) over each slice.

12 servings

Vanilla Crumb Crust (see p. 133)
3 packages (8 ounces each) fat-free cream cheese, softened
3/4 cup sugar
2 eggs
2 tablespoons cornstarch
1 tablespoon lemon juice
1 cup reduced-fat sour cream
2 cups fresh, *or* frozen, thawed, unsweetened raspberries, divided
Light whipped topping, as garnish
Mint sprigs, as garnish

Per Serving
Calories: 235
% Calories from fat: 29
Fat (gm): 7.6
Saturated fat (gm): 3.1
Cholesterol (mg): 46.5
Sodium (mg): 396
Protein (gm): 11.1
Carbohydrate (gm): 30.5
Exchanges
Milk: 0.0
Vegetable: 0.0
Fruit: 0.0
Bread: 2.0
Meat: 1.0
Fat: 1.0

1. Make Vanilla Crumb Crust, pressing mixture evenly onto bottom and 1/2 inch up side of 9-inch springform pan.

2. Beat cream cheese until fluffy in large bowl. Beat in sugar, eggs, cornstarch, lemon juice, and sour cream. Pour into crust.

3. Process 1 cup raspberries in food processor; strain and discard seeds. Dollop raspberries on top of cheesecake and swirl into cheesecake with a knife.

4. Bake at 350 degrees until almost set in the center, about 60 minutes. Turn oven off; cool cheesecake in oven with door ajar 2 hours. Refrigerate 8 hours or overnight.

5. Remove side of pan and place cheesecake on serving plate. Garnish with whipped topping, remaining 1 cup raspberries, and mint.

RASPBERRY-HAZELNUT CHEESECAKE

A stunning cheesecake for special occasions. For variation, other preserves and nuts can be substituted for the raspberry preserves and hazelnuts.

12 servings

Hazelnut Pastry Crust (see p. 129)
1/4 cup sugar
2 envelopes unflavored gelatin
1/4 teaspoon salt
1 cup fat-free milk
2 eggs
2 packages (8 ounces each) fat-free cream cheese
2 cartons (8 ounces each) reduced-fat custard-style raspberry yogurt
1 teaspoon vanilla
1 1/2 cups light whipped topping
1 cup raspberry preserves, divided
Fresh raspberries, as garnish
Mint leaves, as garnish

Per Serving
Calories: 297
% Calories from fat: 23
Fat (gm): 7.8
Saturated fat (gm): 2.6
Cholesterol (mg): 41.2
Sodium (mg): 445
Protein (gm): 10.4
Carbohydrate (gm): 46.9
Exchanges
Milk: 0.0
Vegetable: 0.0
Fruit: 0.0
Bread: 3.0
Meat: 0.0
Fat: 1.5

1. Roll Hazelnut Pastry Crust between 2 sheets of waxed paper into circle 1 1/2 inches larger than 9-inch springform pan. Ease pastry into pan, pressing against bottom and 1/2 inch up side. Pierce bottom of pastry with fork. Bake at 400 degrees until lightly browned, 10 to 15 minutes. Cool on wire rack.

2. Combine sugar, gelatin, and salt in small saucepan; whisk in milk and eggs until smooth. Whisk constantly over medium-low heat until mixture thickens slightly, about 8 minutes. Remove from heat.

3. Beat cream cheese until fluffy in large bowl; beat in gelatin mixture, yogurt, and vanilla. Fold in whipped topping.

4. Spread 1/2 cup preserves in bottom of crust; pour filling into crust. Refrigerate until cheesecake is set, 3 to 4 hours.

5. Remove side of pan and place cheesecake on serving plate. Spread top of cheesecake with remaining 1/2 cup preserves. Garnish with raspberries and mint.

BLACKBERRY-TOPPED CHEESE PIE

Any berries—boysenberries, raspberries, strawberries, blueberries—can be substituted for the blackberries.

8 servings

Per Serving
Calories: 326
% Calories from fat: 22
Fat (gm): 8.1
Saturated fat (gm): 2.1
Cholesterol (mg): 56.2
Sodium (mg): 299
Protein (gm): 9.8
Carbohydrate (gm): 54.1
Exchanges
Milk: 0.0
Vegetable: 0.0
Fruit: 0.5
Bread: 3.0
Meat: 0.0
Fat: 1.5

Lemon Cookie Crumb Crust (see p. 136)

- 1 package (8 ounces) fat-free cream cheese, softened
- $1/2$ cup 1% low-fat cottage cheese
- 2 eggs
- $1/2$ cup plus 2 tablespoons sugar, divided
- 3 tablespoons lemon juice
- 1 tablespoon finely grated lemon rind
- 1 cup fat-free sour cream
  Blackberry Topping (recipe follows)

1. Make Lemon Cookie Crumb Crust, using 9-inch pie pan.

2. Beat cream cheese in large bowl until smooth; beat in cottage cheese, eggs, $1/2$ cup sugar, lemon juice, and rind.

3. Pour cheese filling into crust. Bake at 350 until just set in the center, 20 to 25 minutes. Reduce oven temperature to 325 degrees. Mix sour cream and remaining 2 tablespoons sugar; spread over top of cheesecake and bake 5 minutes longer. Cool on wire rack. Spoon Blackberry Topping over cheesecake; refrigerate until chilled, 8 hours or overnight.

Blackberry Topping

makes about 1$1/2$ cups

- $1/3$ cup sugar
- 1$1/2$ tablespoons cornstarch
- 2 cups fresh, *or* frozen, unsweetened blackberries, divided
- 2 generous pinches ground nutmeg

1. Mix sugar and cornstarch in small saucepan; add 1 cup blackberries. Heat to boiling over medium-high heat, stirring until thickened. Remove from heat; stir in remaining 1 cup blackberries and nutmeg. Cool.

Variation: **Tart Lemon Cheese Pie**—Make recipe as above, increasing lemon juice to $1/4$ cup and lemon rind to 2 tablespoons; delete sour cream mixture and Blackberry Topping. Bake and refrigerate as above. Serve with chilled Tart Lemon Sauce (see p. 650).

BLUEBERRY CHEESECAKE TART

Baked in a pastry crust and topped simply with blueberries; substitute raspberries if you like.

8 servings

Basic Pie Crust (All-Purpose Flour) (see p. 126)
1 package (8 ounces) fat-free cream cheese, softened
$1/2$ cup sugar
1 tablespoon flour
1 egg
1 tablespoon lemon juice
2-3 cups fresh, *or* frozen, thawed, blueberries
$1/3$-$1/2$ cup currant jelly, melted
Ground nutmeg, as garnish

Per Serving
Calories: 277
% Calories from fat: 22
Fat (gm): 7
Saturated fat (gm): 1.6
Cholesterol (mg): 28.8
Sodium (mg): 309
Protein (gm): 7.4
Carbohydrate (gm): 47.3
Exchanges
Milk: 0.0
Vegetable: 0.0
Fruit: 0.5
Bread: 2.5
Meat: 0.0
Fat: 1.5

1. Bake Basic Pie Crust, using 10-inch tart pan; cool on wire rack.

2. Beat cream cheese in medium bowl until fluffy; beat in sugar and flour until smooth. Mix in egg and lemon juice.

3. Pour filling into crust. Bake at 350 degrees until set, about 20 minutes. Cool on wire rack.

4. Place cheesecake on serving plate. Arrange blueberries on top and brush or drizzle with currant jelly; sprinkle lightly with nutmeg. Refrigerate until chilled, 2 to 3 hours.

LEMON-BLUEBERRY CHEESECAKE

A light textured cheesecake, with a no-bake filling, is glazed with fragrant blueberries.

10 servings

Egg Pastry Crust (recipe follows)
3 tablespoons lemon juice
1 tablespoon water
1 envelope unflavored gelatin
2 packages (8 ounces each) reduced-fat cream cheese, softened
1 cup sugar
1 teaspoon vanilla
1 cup light whipped topping
Blueberry Glaze (recipe follows)
Light whipped topping, as garnish

Per Serving
Calories: 361
% Calories from fat: 33
Fat (gm): 13.1
Saturated fat (gm): 6.8
Cholesterol (mg): 42.4
Sodium (mg): 305
Protein (gm): 6.2
Carbohydrate (gm): 53.5
Exchanges
Milk: 0.0
Vegetable: 0.0
Fruit: 0.0
Bread: 3.5
Meat: 0.0
Fat: 2.5

1. Press Egg Pastry Crust onto bottom and $1/2$ inch up side of 9-inch springform pan; pierce with fork. Bake at 350 degrees until light brown, about 20 minutes. Cool on wire rack.

2. Mix lemon juice, water, and gelatin in small saucepan; stir over low heat until gelatin is dissolved, about 3 minutes.

3. Beat cream cheese until fluffy in large bowl; beat in gelatin mixture, sugar, and vanilla. Fold in whipped topping. Pour filling into crust; refrigerate until set, 2 to 3 hours. Spoon Blueberry Glaze evenly over top. Garnish with whipped topping.

Egg Pastry Crust

$3/4$ cup all-purpose flour
$1/4$ cup sugar
$1/8$ teaspoon salt
4-5 tablespoons cold margarine, cut into pieces
1 egg, beaten
1 tablespoon cold water, if needed

1. Combine flour, sugar, and salt in bowl; cut in margarine until mixture resembles coarse crumbs. Mix in egg; add water, if necessary to form dough. Form into ball and wrap in plastic wrap, flattening into disk; refrigerate at least 1 hour.

Blueberry Glaze

$^1/_2$ cup sugar
2 tablespoons cornstarch
$^1/_2$ cup water
1 tablespoon lemon juice
1 pint fresh, *or* frozen, blueberries, divided
Pinch ground nutmeg

1. Combine sugar and cornstarch in medium saucepan; stir in water and lemon juice. Cook over medium heat, stirring, until sugar is dissolved. Add $^1/_2$ cup blueberries and heat to boiling, stirring until thickened, about 1 minute. Cool.

2. Stir remaining blueberries and nutmeg into glaze mixture.

Variations: **Blueberries 'n Cream Cheesecake**—Omit Egg Pastry Crust. Fill bottom of 9-inch springform pan with single layer of blueberries (about 2 cups). Make Blueberry Glaze, cooking all the blueberries in Step 1; cool. Make cream cheese filling and pour over berries. Spoon dollops of Blueberry Glaze over filling and swirl with knife. Refrigerate as above.

Sherry Trifle Cheesecake—Omit Egg Pastry Crust. Line bottom and side of springform pan with ladyfingers. Brush with $^1/_2$ cup melted raspberry jam. Substitute $^1/_4$ cup cream sherry for the lemon juice and water in the recipe. Prepare filling as in Steps 2 and 3 (p. 246). After chilling, top cheesecake with 2 cups mixed fresh fruit. Delete Blueberry Glaze; serve with light whipped topping and Raspberry Sauce (see p. 658).

LEMON MERINGUE CHEESECAKE

Never has a cheesecake filling been quite as smooth and delicate as this.
The filling is slightly soft, so chill very well before cutting.

12 servings

Basic Pie Crust (All-Purpose Flour)
(see p. 126)
3 packages (8 ounces each) fat-free
cream cheese, softened
2/3 cup lemon juice
2 tablespoons flour
1 cup granulated sugar
1/3 cup cornstarch
2/3 cup water
2 teaspoons grated lemon rind
4 egg yolks
4 egg whites
1/4 teaspoon cream of tartar
1/3 cup powdered sugar

Per Serving
Calories: 269
% Calories from fat: 21
Fat (gm): 6.4
Saturated fat (gm): 1.8
Cholesterol (mg): 75.6
Sodium (mg): 424
Protein (gm): 11.9
Carbohydrate (gm): 41
Exchanges
Milk: 0.0
Vegetable: 0.0
Fruit: 0.0
Bread: 3.0
Meat: 0.0
Fat: 1.0

1. Bake Basic Pie Crust according to recipe, using 9-inch pie pan.

2. Beat cream cheese in medium bowl until smooth; beat in lemon juice and flour.

3. Mix granulated sugar and cornstarch in medium saucepan; stir in water and lemon rind. Cook over medium heat, stirring constantly until mixture thickens and boils; boil 1 minute, whisking constantly. Whisk mixture into egg yolks; return to saucepan and cook over low heat 1 minute, whisking constantly. Gradually beat into cream cheese mixture, mixing well; pour into crust.

4. Using clean bowl and beaters, beat egg whites and cream of tartar to soft peaks in large bowl. Gradually beat in powdered sugar, beating to stiff but not dry peaks. Spread meringue over hot filling, sealing to edge of crust.

5. Bake at 425 degrees until meringue is golden, about 5 minutes. Cool on wire rack; refrigerate at least 4 hours before serving.

Variation: **Lime Blueberry Cheesecake**—Omit Basic Pie Crust. Make Vanilla Crumb Crust (see p. 133), pressing mixture evenly on bottom and 1 inch up side of 9-inch springform pan. Make cream cheese filling as above in Steps 2 and 3, substituting lime juice for the lemon juice. Gently stir 1 cup blueberries into filling and pour into crust. Skip Steps 4 and 5. Cool and refrigerate as above.

SUMMER LEMON CHEESECAKE

A cheesecake that's lemon all the way, including the crust—and topped with fresh ripe berries!

12 servings

Lemon Cookie Crumb Crust (see p. 136)

2 packages (8 ounces each) fat-free cream cheese, softened

$^1/_2$ cup sugar

$1^1/_2$ cups custard-style reduced-fat lemon yogurt, divided

2 eggs

2 tablespoons lemon juice

2 tablespoons finely grated lemon rind, divided

Sugared Crushed Berries (recipe follows)

Per Serving
Calories: 231
% Calories from fat: 23
Fat (gm): 6
Saturated fat (gm): 1.8
Cholesterol (mg): 40.4
Sodium (mg): 269
Protein (gm): 8.1
Carbohydrate (gm): 37.1
Exchanges
Milk: 0.0
Vegetable: 0.0
Fruit: 1.0
Bread: 1.5
Meat: 0.0
Fat: 1.0

1. Make Lemon Cookie Crumb Crust, pressing mixture evenly onto bottom and $^1/_2$ inch up side of 9-inch springform pan.

2. Beat cream cheese in large bowl until fluffy; beat in sugar, $^1/_2$ cup yogurt, eggs, lemon juice, and 1 tablespoon lemon rind.

3. Pour filling into crust. Bake at 350 degrees until almost set in the center, 20 to 30 minutes. Cool on wire rack.

4. Remove side of pan and place cheesecake on serving plate. Spread remaining 1 cup yogurt over top and sprinkle with remaining 1 tablespoon lemon rind. Serve with Sugared Crushed Berries.

Sugared Crushed Berries

makes about 3 cups

2 cups strawberries, divided

2 cups blueberries, divided

$^1/_4$ cup sugar

1. Mash 1 cup strawberries and 1 cup blueberries with sugar; let stand 15 minutes. Stir in remaining berries.

LIGHT LEMON CHEESECAKE WITH CRANBERRY COULIS

An exquisite lemon cheesecake with a cranberry sauce that can be served year round.

8 servings

Butter Crumb Pastry (recipe follows)
1 package (8 ounces) 1% low-fat cottage cheese
1/2 package (8-ounce size) fat-free cream cheese, softened
1/2 cup sugar
2 eggs
2 egg whites
1 tablespoon lemon juice
1 tablespoon finely grated lemon rind
Cranberry Coulis (recipe follows)

Per Serving
Calories: 299
% Calories from fat: 21
Fat (gm): 6.9
Saturated fat (gm): 1.8
Cholesterol (mg): 81.9
Sodium (mg): 312
Protein (gm): 11.2
Carbohydrate (gm): 48.4
Exchanges
Milk: 0.0
Vegetable: 0.0
Fruit: 0.0
Bread: 3.5
Meat: 0.0
Fat: 1.0

1. Press Butter Crumb Pastry on bottom and 1 inch up side of 9-inch-round cake pan with removable bottom.

2. Process cottage cheese in food processor or blender until smooth. Add cream cheese, sugar, eggs, egg whites, lemon juice, and rind to food processor; process until smooth.

3. Pour filling into pastry. Bake at 350 degrees until filling is set, 35 to 40 minutes. Cool on wire rack. Refrigerate 8 hours or overnight. Serve with Cranberry Coulis.

Butter Crumb Pastry

1 1/4 cups all-purpose flour
1 tablespoon sugar
1/2 teaspoon baking powder
3-4 tablespoons cold margarine, cut into pieces
1 egg
1 teaspoon butter extract

1. Combine flour, sugar, and baking powder in bowl; cut in margarine until mixture resembles coarse crumbs. Mix in egg and butter extract to form crumbly dough.

Cranberry Coulis

makes about 1¹/₂ cups

1¹/₂ cups fresh, or frozen, cranberries
1 cup orange juice
3-4 tablespoons sugar
3-4 tablespoons honey

1. Heat cranberries and orange juice to boiling in small saucepan; reduce heat and simmer, covered, until cranberries are tender, 5 to 8 minutes. Add sugar and honey and process mixture in food processor or blender until almost smooth. Serve warm or chilled.

LUSCIOUS LEMON CHEESECAKE

Luscious indeed, and nestled in a cinnamon-spiced sesame crust.

12 servings

Lemon Custard (recipe follows)
Sesame Crumb Crust (recipe follows)
2 packages (8 ounces each) fat-free cream cheese, softened
1 package (8 ounces) reduced-fat cream cheese, softened
¹/₂ cup sugar
¹/₂ cup fat-free sour cream
¹/₄ teaspoon salt
1 tablespoon grated lemon rind
Sesame seeds, as garnish

Per Serving
Calories: 272
% Calories from fat: 30
Fat (gm): 9
Saturated fat (gm): 3.4
Cholesterol (mg): 47.2
Sodium (mg): 498
Protein (gm): 11
Carbohydrate (gm): 36.2
Exchanges
Milk: 0.0
Vegetable: 0.0
Fruit: 0.0
Bread: 3.0
Meat: 0.0
Fat: 1.5

1. Make Lemon Custard and chill.

2. Make Sesame Crumb Crust, pressing mixture evenly on bottom and ¹/₂ inch up side of 10-inch springform pan. Bake at 350 degrees until browned, about 8 minutes.

3. Beat cream cheese until fluffy in large bowl; beat in sugar, sour cream, and salt. Beat in chilled Lemon Custard.

4. Spoon filling into crust, spreading evenly. Sprinkle with lemon rind and sesame seeds. Refrigerate until set, about 4 hours.

Lemon Custard

   $^1/_2$ cup sugar
   2 tablespoons cornstarch
   $^1/_3$ cup lemon juice
   2 eggs
   1 tablespoon grated lemon rind

1. Mix sugar and cornstarch in small saucepan; whisk in lemon juice. Whisk over medium heat until mixture boils and thickens, about 1 minute.

2. Whisk about $^1/_2$ the lemon mixture into eggs; whisk egg mixture into lemon mixture. Whisk in lemon rind. Cook over low heat, whisking constantly, 1 to 2 minutes. Cool; refrigerate until chilled, 1 to 2 hours.

Sesame Crumb Crust

   $1^1/_4$ cups dry bread crumbs *or* vanilla wafer
           crumbs
   3-4 tablespoons toasted sesame seeds
   2 tablespoons sugar
   $^1/_4$ teaspoon ground cinnamon
   3-4 tablespoons margarine, melted
   1-2 tablespoons honey *or* light corn syrup

1. Combine all ingredients, adding enough honey for ingredients to stick together.

Variation: **Daiquiri Cheesecake**—Make cheesecake as above, substituting Vanilla Crumb Crust (see p. 133) for the Sesame Crumb Crust. Substitute lime rind and lime juice for the lemon rind and lemon juice in the filling and custard. Add 2 tablespoons light rum *or* 1 teaspoon rum extract to the custard before combining with eggs. Omit sesame seeds. Serve cheesecake with light whipped topping and garnish with lime slices.

LEMON GINGER CHEESECAKE

The combination of lemon and ginger flavors is surprisingly subtle, and very refreshing. Delicious with Fresh Ginger Sauce (see p. 649).

12 servings

Gingersnap Crumb Crust (see pg. 135)
2 packages (8 ounces each) fat-free cream cheese, softened
1¼ cups fat-free sour cream
3 eggs
1 cup sugar
1 tablespoon vanilla
¼ cup chopped crystallized ginger
1-2 teaspoons ground ginger
3 tablespoons grated lemon rind
Mint sprigs, as garnish
Lemon slices, as garnish

Per Serving
Calories: 237
% Calories from fat: 19
Fat (gm): 5
Saturated fat (gm): 1.4
Cholesterol (mg): 56
Sodium (mg): 315
Protein (gm): 9.3
Carbohydrate (gm): 38.3
Exchanges
Milk: 0.0
Vegetable: 0.0
Fruit: 0.0
Bread: 2.5
Meat: 0.0
Fat: 1.0

1. Make Gingersnap Crumb Crust, pressing mixture evenly on bottom and ½ inch up side of 9-inch springform pan. Wrap pan with aluminum foil to prevent leaking.

2. Beat cream cheese until smooth in large bowl; add sour cream, mixing until smooth. Beat in eggs, sugar, and vanilla; mix until smooth. Mix in ginger and lemon rind, mixing just until blended.

3. Pour mixture into crust. Place springform pan in roasting pan on center oven rack; pour 2 inches hot water into roasting pan. Bake at 350 degrees until cheesecake is set in the center, 45 to 50 minutes. Remove cheesecake from roasting pan. Turn oven off; cool cheesecake in oven with door ajar 2 hours. Refrigerate 8 hours or overnight.

4. Remove side of pan and place cheesecake on serving plate; garnish with mint and lemon slices.

CREAMY CITRUS CHEESECAKE

Orange and lemon combine in this light, flavorful cake.

8 servings

Lemon Cookie Crumb Crust
(see p. 136)

2 cups 1% low-fat cottage cheese

1/2 package (8-ounce size) fat-free cream
cheese, softened

2 egg whites

1/2 cup sugar

3 tablespoons frozen orange juice
concentrate

1 tablespoon grated orange rind

2 teaspoons grated lemon rind

1/2 teaspoon lemon extract

Per Serving
Calories: 248
% Calories from fat: 25
Fat (gm): 7
Saturated fat (gm): 1.9
Cholesterol (mg): 3.9
Sodium (mg): 367
Protein (gm): 10.2
Carbohydrate (gm): 36.3
Exchanges
Milk: 0.0
Vegetable: 0.0
Fruit: 0.0
Bread: 2.5
Meat: 1.0
Fat: 0.5

1. Make Lemon Cookie Crumb Crust, patting mixture evenly on bottom and side of 9-inch pie pan.

2. Process cottage cheese in food processor or blender until smooth. Beat cream cheese in large bowl until fluffy; beat in cottage cheese and remaining ingredients.

3. Pour filling into crust; bake at 350 degrees until cheesecake is almost set in the center, about 30 minutes. Cool on wire rack. Refrigerate 8 hours or overnight.

SUNSHINE CHEESECAKE

Delicately flavored with orange and finished with rich Orange Topping.

12 servings

Graham Cracker Crumb Crust (see p. 132)

1 package (8 ounces) reduced-fat cream cheese, softened

1 package (8 ounces) fat-free cream cheese, softened

2/3 cup sugar

2 tablespoons flour

1/4 cup frozen orange juice concentrate

1/2 teaspoon orange extract

2 eggs

Orange Topping (recipe follows)

Per Serving
Calories: 254
% Calories from fat: 34
Fat (gm): 9.8
Saturated fat (gm): 3.7
Cholesterol (mg): 63.4
Sodium (mg): 287
Protein (gm): 7
Carbohydrate (gm): 34.8
Exchanges
Milk: 0.0
Vegetable: 0.0
Fruit: 0.0
Bread: 2.0
Meat: 0.0
Fat: 2.0

1. Make Graham Cracker Crumb Crust, pressing mixture on bottom and 1/2 inch up side of 9-inch springform pan.

2. Mix cream cheese until fluffy in large bowl; beat in sugar and flour; beat in orange juice concentrate, orange extract, and eggs.

3. Pour mixture into crust. Bake at 350 degrees until filling is just set in the center, 30 to 40 minutes. Cool on wire rack; spoon Orange Topping evenly over top of cheesecake. Refrigerate 8 hours or overnight.

Orange Topping

makes about 3/4 cup

1/4 cup sugar

1 tablespoon cornstarch

1/2 cup orange juice

1 tablespoon lemon juice

1 egg yolk, beaten

1. Combine sugar and cornstarch in small saucepan; whisk in orange and lemon juice. Whisk over medium-high heat until boiling and thickened, 2 to 3 minutes.

2. Whisk 1/2 of the orange juice mixture into egg yolk; whisk yolk mixture into saucepan. Whisk over low heat 1 minute.

Variation: **Macaroon Cheesecake**—Substitute Coconut Crust (see p. 261). Make filling, substituting fat-free milk for the orange juice concentrate, and vanilla for the orange extract; delete Orange Topping. Bake cheesecake at 350 degrees 20 minutes. Beat 1 egg white and 1/2 teaspoon vanilla until soft peaks form; gradually add 1/3 cup sugar, beating to stiff peaks. Fold in 1/2 cup toasted coconut. Spoon evenly over top of cheesecake and bake until browned, 15 to 20 minutes.

MINCEMEAT CHEESECAKE

A holiday pie sure to please—a cream cheese pastry with layers of moist mincemeat and creamy cheesecake.

14 servings

Cream Cheese Tart Crust (see p. 131)
2 packages (8 ounces each) fat-free cream cheese, softened
1/2 cup plus 2 tablespoons sugar, divided
2 eggs
1 tablespoon grated orange rind
1/2 teaspoon orange extract
1 can (16 ounces) mincemeat
1/2 cup chopped walnuts
1 cup fat-free sour cream
Orange segments, as garnish

Per Serving
Calories: 365
% Calories from fat: 31
Fat (gm): 13
Saturated fat (gm): 3.5
Cholesterol (mg): 52.5
Sodium (mg): 406
Protein (gm): 10.9
Carbohydrate (gm): 52.4
Exchanges
Milk: 0.0
Vegetable: 0.0
Fruit: 0.0
Bread: 3.5
Meat: 0.0
Fat: 2.5

1. Roll Cream Cheese Tart Crust between 2 sheets of waxed paper to a circle 1 inch larger than inverted 10-inch pie pan. Ease pastry into pan; trim and flute edge. Pierce bottom of pastry with fork and bake at 350 degrees until lightly browned, about 15 minutes. Cool on wire rack.

2. Beat cream cheese until fluffy in large bowl; beat in 1/2 cup sugar, eggs, orange rind, and orange extract.

3. Mix mincemeat and walnuts; spoon 1 1/2 cups mixture into crust; pour cream cheese mixture over top. Bake until cheesecake is set in the center, 20 to 30 minutes.

4. Mix sour cream and remaining 2 tablespoons sugar; spread over top of cheesecake. Bake 10 minutes longer. Cool on wire rack; refrigerate 8 hours or overnight. Garnish pie with remaining mincemeat and orange segments.

GLACÉED ORANGE CHEESECAKE

Glacéed orange rind accents a traditional dense and creamy cheesecake.

12 servings

Graham Cracker Crumb Crust
(see p. 132)

3 packages (8 ounces each) fat-free cream cheese, softened

1 cup sugar

1 package (8 ounces) fat-free sour cream

2 eggs

3 egg whites

2 tablespoons orange juice concentrate

3/4-1 cup glacéed orange rind

Light whipped topping, as garnish

Glacéed orange rind, as garnish

Per Serving
Calories: 290
% Calories from fat: 21
Fat (gm): 6.9
Saturated fat (gm): 1.9
Cholesterol (mg): 39.9
Sodium (mg): 432
Protein (gm): 12.3
Carbohydrate (gm): 45.4
Exchanges
Milk: 0.0
Vegetable: 0.0
Fruit: 0.0
Bread: 3.0
Meat: 0.0
Fat: 1.5

1. Make Graham Cracker Crumb Crust, pressing mixture evenly in bottom and 1/2 inch up side of 10-inch springform pan.

2. Beat cream cheese in large bowl until fluffy. Beat in sugar, sour cream, eggs, egg whites, and orange juice concentrate. Stir in glacéed orange rind.

3. Pour mixture into crust. Bake at 375 degrees until just set in the center, 40 to 50 minutes. Cool on wire rack; refrigerate 8 hours or overnight.

4. Garnish cheesecake slices with whipped topping and glacéed orange rind.

Variation: **Jewel Cheesecake**—Substitute coarsely chopped glacéed pineapple and cherries for the orange rind; mix with 1/4 cup rum and let stand 30 minutes. Make cheesecake as above, omitting orange concentrate and stirring in glacéed fruit mixture. Bake as above; spread with 1 cup fat-free sour cream mixed with 2 tablespoons sugar and bake 5 minutes longer. Cool as above. Decorate top of cheesecake with glacéed pineapple and cherries before serving.

ORANGE PUMPKIN CHEESECAKE

Flavors of pumpkin and orange marmalade combine in a splendid dessert for the holidays

16 servings

Graham Cracker Crumb Crust
(see p. 132)

- 1/3 cup ground pecans
- 2 teaspoons pumpkin pie spice, divided
- 1 package (16 ounces) 1% low-fat creamed cottage cheese
- 2 packages (8 ounces each) fat-free cream cheese, softened
- 1 package (8 ounces) reduced-fat cream cheese, softened
- 3/4 cup packed light brown sugar
- 2 tablespoons flour
- 1 can (16 ounces) pumpkin
- 2 eggs
- 2 teaspoons finely grated orange rind
- 1/4 teaspoon salt
- 4 egg whites
- 1/2 teaspoon cream of tartar
- 1/4 cup granulated sugar

Marmalade Sour Cream Topping (recipe follows)

- 1 medium orange, thinly sliced
- 1/4 cup orange marmalade, melted

Per Serving
Calories: 318
% Calories from fat: 28
Fat (gm): 10.1
Saturated fat (gm): 3.2
Cholesterol (mg): 36.7
Sodium (mg): 481
Protein (gm): 14.1
Carbohydrate (gm): 43.4
Exchanges
Milk: 0.0
Vegetable: 0.0
Fruit: 0.0
Bread: 3.0
Meat: 0.5
Fat: 1.5

1. Make Graham Cracker Crumb Crust, substituting 1/3 cup pecans for 1/3 cup of the crumbs, and adding 1/2 teaspoon pumpkin pie spice; press evenly on bottom and 1/2 inch up side of 10-inch springform pan.

2. Process cottage cheese in food processor or blender until smooth. Beat cream cheese until fluffy in large bowl; beat in cottage cheese, brown sugar, flour, pumpkin, eggs, orange rind, remaining 1¹/₂ teaspoons pumpkin pie spice, and salt.

3. Using clean bowl and beaters, beat egg whites and cream of tartar to soft peaks in large bowl. Beat to stiff peaks, adding granulated sugar gradually. Mix about ¹/₄ of the egg whites into cream cheese mixture; fold cream cheese mixture into remaining egg whites.

4. Pour filling into crust. Bake at 300 degrees until almost set in the center, 1 to 1¹/₄ hours. Turn oven off; cool cheesecake in oven 1 hour with door ajar.

5. Spread Marmalade Sour Cream Topping over top of cheesecake; bake at 350 degrees 10 minutes. Cool on wire rack; refrigerate 8 hours or overnight.

6. Remove side of pan and place cheesecake on serving plate. Arrange orange slices on top of cheesecake and brush with orange marmalade.

Marmalade Sour Cream Topping

    2 cups fat-free sour cream
¹/₃ cup orange marmalade
    2 generous pinches nutmeg

1. Combine all ingredients.

BRANDIED GINGER CHEESECAKE

Triple-spiced for ginger lovers, this creamy cheese cake has both ground and candied ginger and a wonderful gingersnap crust.

12 servings

Gingersnap Crumb Crust (see p. 135)
1 package (15 ounces) low-fat ricotta cheese
1 package (8 ounces) fat-free cream cheese, softened
1 package (8 ounces) reduced-fat cream cheese, softened
1 cup sugar, divided
2 tablespoons brandy *or* 1 to 2 teaspoons brandy extract
2 eggs
4 egg whites
1/4 teaspoon cream of tartar
3-4 tablespoons sliced crystallized ginger

Per Serving
Calories: 264
% Calories from fat: 28
Fat (gm): 8.4
Saturated fat (gm): 3.8
Cholesterol (mg): 52
Sodium (mg): 348
Protein (gm): 12.6
Carbohydrate (gm): 33.3
Exchanges
Milk: 0.0
Vegetable: 0.0
Fruit: 0.0
Bread: 2.0
Meat: 1.0
Fat: 1.0

1. Make Gingersnap Crumb Crust, pressing mixture evenly on bottom and 1/2 inch up side of 9- or 10-inch springform pan.

2. Beat cheeses in large bowl until smooth; beat in 3/4 cup sugar, brandy, and eggs.

3. With clean beaters and bowl, beat egg whites and cream of tartar to soft peaks; beat to stiff peaks, adding remaining 1/4 cup sugar gradually. Stir 1/4 of the egg whites into cheesecake mixture; fold cheesecake mixture into remaining egg whites.

4. Pour batter into crust. Bake at 325 degrees until almost set in the center, about 50 minutes. Cool on wire rack; refrigerate 8 hours or overnight.

5. Top slices with crystallized ginger.

FROZEN ITALIAN CHEESECAKE

Make this frozen dessert several days in advance so flavors can blend, or make it 2 to 3 weeks in advance for convenience.

8 servings

Coconut Crust (recipe follows)
1 package (7.2 ounces) fluffy white frosting mix
1 package (8 ounces) fat-free cream cheese, softened
1/2 cup fat-free sour cream
2 tablespoons dry sherry *or* 1/2 teaspoon sherry extract
1/4 teaspoon almond extract
1/4 cup chopped toasted almonds

Per Serving
Calories: 279
% Calories from fat: 26
Fat (gm): 8
Saturated fat (gm): 3.6
Cholesterol (mg): 2.3
Sodium (mg): 324
Protein (gm): 7.1
Carbohydrate (gm): 42.9
Exchanges
Milk: 0.0
Vegetable: 0.0
Fruit: 0.0
Bread: 2.5
Meat: 0.0
Fat: 2.0

1. Make Coconut Crust, pressing mixture evenly on bottom of 11 x 7-inch baking dish. Refrigerate until set, about 45 minutes.

2. Make frosting mix according to package directions. Beat cream cheese in large bowl until fluffy; beat in frosting, sour cream, sherry, and almond extract.

3. Pour filling over crust, spreading evenly; sprinkle with almonds. Freeze until firm, 6 hours or overnight.

Coconut Crust

1 1/2 cups finely ground corn flake cereal
1 cup flaked coconut, toasted
2 tablespoons margarine, melted
2 tablespoons honey

1. Mix all ingredients.

TORTA SICILIANA

A frozen ricotta cheesecake, flavored with raisins, glacéed fruit, and anise liqueur.

12 servings

Vanilla Crumb Crust (see p. 133)

1/2 cup coarsely chopped mixed glacéed fruit

1/4 cup golden raisins

1/4 cup anise liqueur *or* 1 teaspoon anise extract

1 carton (15 ounces) reduced-fat ricotta cheese

1 carton (15 ounces) fat-free ricotta cheese

1 cup sugar

2 tablespoons lemon juice

Toasted pine nuts *or* pistachio nuts, as garnish

Per Serving
Calories: 262
% Calories from fat: 19
Fat (gm): 5.5
Saturated fat (gm): 1.8
Cholesterol (mg): 9.4
Sodium (mg): 195
Protein (gm): 10.6
Carbohydrate (gm): 40.8
Exchanges
Milk: 0.0
Vegetable: 0.0
Fruit: 0.0
Bread: 2.5
Meat: 1.0
Fat: 0.5

1. Make Vanilla Crumb Crust, pressing mixture on bottom and 1/2 inch up side of 9-inch springform pan.

2. Combine glacéed fruit, raisins, and liqueur in bowl; let stand 30 minutes.

3. Beat ricotta cheese, sugar, and lemon juice until smooth. Mix in fruit mixture.

4. Pour filling into crust; sprinkle with pine nuts. Freeze until firm, 8 hours or overnight. Let stand at room temperature 30 minutes before serving.

BRANDIED FRUIT CHEESECAKE

A dense cheesecake, filled with candied fruits for the holidays.

12 servings

$^1/_4$ cup brandy *or* apple juice

$1^1/_2$ cups coarsely chopped mixed glacéed fruit

Gingersnap Crumb Crust (see p. 135)

$1^1/_2$ packages (8-ounce size) fat-free cream cheese, softened

$^2/_3$ cup plus 2 tablespoons sugar, divided

$^1/_4$ cup all-purpose flour

$^1/_2$ teaspoon salt

$^1/_3$ cup fat-free milk

3 eggs

1 cup fat-free sour cream

Glacéed fruit, as garnish

Per Serving
Calories: 282
% Calories from fat: 16
Fat (gm): 4.9
Saturated fat (gm): 1.3
Cholesterol (mg): 55.4
Sodium (mg): 375
Protein (gm): 8.1
Carbohydrate (gm): 48.4
Exchanges
Milk: 0.0
Vegetable: 0.0
Fruit: 1.0
Bread: 2.5
Meat: 0.0
Fat: 1.0

1. Pour brandy over glacéed fruit in bowl; let stand 30 minutes.

2. Make Gingersnap Crumb Crust, pressing mixture on bottom and $^1/_2$ inch up side of 9- or 10-inch springform pan.

3. Beat cream cheese until fluffy in large bowl; beat in $^2/_3$ cup sugar, flour, salt, milk, and eggs. Mix in fruit and brandy.

4. Pour filling into crust. Bake at 350 until cheesecake is just set in the center, about 30 minutes. Mix sour cream and 2 tablespoons sugar; spread over top of cheesecake and bake 10 minutes. Cool on wire rack; refrigerate 8 hours or overnight.

5. Remove side of pan and place cheesecake on serving plate. Garnish decoratively with glacéed fruit.

Variations: **Maple-Date Cheesecake**—Omit brandy, glacéed fruit, and Step 1. Substitute Vanilla Crumb Crust (see p. 133) for the Gingersnap Crumb Crust. Make cheesecake, adding 1 cup chopped dates and 1 teaspoon maple extract to the cream cheese mixture. Garnish with whole pitted dates.

Rum Raisin Cheesecake—Make cheesecake as above, substituting Ginger Raisin Crumb Crust (see p. 135) for the Gingersnap Crumb Crust, 1 cup raisins for the glacéed fruit, and light rum for the brandy; add 2 generous pinches ground nutmeg to the filling. Omit glacéed fruit garnish; serve with Warm Rum Sauce (see p. 54).

FOUR

Cream Puffs
AND
Pastries

CREAM PUFFS

These low-fat cream puffs can be baked into many different shapes and sizes to create numerous desserts (see variations and following recipes). Or, simply fill with fat-free ice cream, light whipped topping, or pudding and dust with powdered sugar.

8 servings (1 large or 2 small puffs per serving)

1 cup fat-free milk
3 tablespoons margarine
1 cup all-purpose flour
1 tablespoon sugar
1/2 teaspoon salt
3 eggs
2 egg whites *or* 1/4 cup no-cholesterol real egg product

Per Serving
Calories: 144
% Calories from fat: 40*
Fat (gm): 6.3
Saturated fat (gm): 1.5
Cholesterol (mg): 80.1
Sodium (mg): 249
Protein (gm): 5.9
Carbohydrate (gm): 15.3
Exchanges
Milk: 0.0
Vegetable: 0.0
Fruit: 0.0
Bread: 1.0
Meat: 0.0
Fat: 1.5

1. Heat milk and margarine to boiling in medium saucepan. Add combined flour, sugar, and salt all at once, and stir over medium heat until mixture leaves side of pan and forms a ball, 1 to 2 minutes; remove from heat and allow to cool 5 minutes.

2. Beat in eggs and egg whites 1 at a time, beating until mixture is smooth after each addition. Drop dough by spoonfuls, or pipe with large pastry bag fitted with 1/2-inch plain tip, to form large or mini cream puffs on parchment-lined or greased and floured cookie sheets. Gently smooth tops of cream puffs with pastry brush or fingers dipped in cold water.

3. Bake at 400 degrees 15 minutes for large cream puffs, 10 minutes for small cream puffs; reduce oven temperature to 325 degrees and bake until cream puffs are golden and crisp, 20 to 25 minutes for large cream puffs, 15 to 20 minutes for small cream puffs. Remove from oven; pierce side of each puff with sharp knife and cool on wire rack.

4. Cut top third off cream puffs and remove any soft dough from insides. Return to oven and bake at 325 degrees to dry insides, 3 or 4 minutes.

*Percentage of calories from fat will decrease in servings of actual puffs.

Variations: **Profiteroles au Chocolat**—Make 8 Cream Puffs as above. Fill puffs with vanilla fat-free ice cream. Sprinkle with powdered sugar; serve with Chocolate Sauce (see p. 642).

Autumn Profiteroles—Make 8 Cream Puffs as above. Fill puffs with scoops of Pumpkin Spice Ice Cream (see p. 444); serve with Warm Rum Sauce (see p. 54).

Mandarin Orange Cream Puffs—Make 8 Cream Puffs as above. Fold 1/3 cup toasted coconut into Orange Chantilly (see p. 270) and fill puffs with mixture. Drizzle with Orange Glaze (see p. 47) and sprinkle lightly with additional toasted coconut; garnish with Mandarin orange segments.

Black Forest Cream Puffs—Make 8 Cream Puffs as above. Fill puffs with fat-free cherry ice cream. Serve with Brandied Cherry Sauce (see p. 655); garnish with light whipped topping and chocolate curls.

Cream Puffs Melba—Make 8 Cream Puffs as above. Fill each puff with Pastry Cream (see p. 268) and 1/2 sliced small peach. Serve with Raspberry Sauce (see p. 658).

Tortoni Puffs—Make 8 Cream Puffs as above; fill with Mixed Fruit Tortoni (see p. 455) and freeze until firm, 6 hours or overnight. Drizzle serving plates with 1/2 ounce melted chocolate; place filled puffs on plates. Garnish with light whipped topping and chocolate curls.

CLASSIC CREAM PUFFS

Always a favorite!

8 servings

8 Cream Puffs (see p. 266)
   Pastry Cream (recipe follows)
2 cups light whipped topping
   Powdered sugar, as garnish

Per Serving
Calories: 351
% Calories from fat: 29
Fat (gm): 11
Saturated fat (gm): 4.4
Cholesterol (mg): 187.7
Sodium (mg): 284
Protein (gm): 9.8
Carbohydrate (gm): 50.9
Exchanges
Milk: 0.0
Vegetable: 0.0
Fruit: 0.0
Bread: 3.5
Meat: 0.0
Fat: 2.0

1. Fill each Cream Puff with ¼ cup Pastry Cream; top with ¼ cup whipped topping. Sprinkle with powdered sugar.

Pastry Cream

makes about 2 cups

2 cups fat-free milk
4 egg yolks
1 cup sugar
¼ cup flour
1 tablespoon vanilla

1. Heat milk to boiling in small saucepan. Combine egg yolks and sugar in medium bowl; stir in flour and vanilla. Whisk milk into egg mixture gradually. Return mixture to saucepan. Heat to boiling; boil, whisking constantly until smooth and thick.
2. Transfer Pastry Cream to bowl and cover surface with plastic wrap. Cool. Refrigerate until chilled.

BERRY LEMON CREAM PUFFS

An easy lemon custard with fresh berries fills these golden cream puffs.

8 servings

1 cup fresh raspberries
 Lemon Yogurt Pastry Cream
 (recipe follows)
8 Cream Puffs (see p. 266)
 Powdered sugar, as garnish
 Raspberry Sauce (see p. 658)

Per Serving
Calories: 266
% Calories from fat: 26
Fat (gm): 7.7
Saturated fat (gm): 2.1
Cholesterol (mg): 109.7
Sodium (mg): 282
Protein (gm): 9
Carbohydrate (gm): 40.2
Exchanges
Milk: 0.0
Vegetable: 0.0
Fruit: 0.0
Bread: 2.5
Meat: 0.0
Fat: 1.5

1. Gently stir raspberries into Lemon Yogurt Pastry Cream. Fill Cream Puffs with Lemon Yogurt Pastry Cream and sprinkle with powdered sugar. Serve with Raspberry Sauce.

Lemon Yogurt Pastry Cream

makes about 2¹/₄ cups

 ¹/₄ cup sugar
 2 tablespoons cornstarch
 1 cup fat-free milk
 1 egg yolk, beaten
 ¹/₂ teaspoon vanilla
 1 container (8 ounces) low-fat custard-style
 lemon yogurt

1. Combine sugar and cornstarch in small saucepan; whisk in milk. Whisk over medium-high heat until mixture boils and thickens, 2 to 3 minutes. Whisk ¹/₂ the milk mixture into egg yolk; whisk yolk mixture back into saucepan. Whisk over low heat 1 minute. Transfer to bowl; stir in vanilla. Cover surface of custard with plastic wrap. Cool; refrigerate until chilled, 1 to 2 hours. Stir in yogurt.

ORANGE CHANTILLY CREAM PUFFS

Orange Chantilly can be used as a filling for Fillo Tart Shells (see p. 306), or any baked pastry shells. It's also delicious served with fruit.

8 servings

8 Cream Puffs (see p. 266)
   Orange Chantilly (recipe follows)
¹/₂-1 cup light whipped topping
   Powdered sugar, as garnish
   Orange slices, as garnish

Per Serving
Calories: 283
% Calories from fat: 33
Fat (gm): 10.2
Saturated fat (gm): 4.4
Cholesterol (mg): 133.3
Sodium (mg): 251
Protein (gm): 6.9
Carbohydrate (gm): 39.3
Exchanges
Milk: 0.0
Vegetable: 0.0
Fruit: 0.0
Bread: 2.5
Meat: 0.0
Fat: 2.0

1. Fill Cream Puffs with Orange Chantilly and 1 to 2 tablespoons whipped topping. Sprinkle with powdered sugar; garnish with orange slices.

Orange Chantilly

makes about 2 cups

¹/₂ cup sugar
2 tablespoons cornstarch
1 cup orange juice
¹/₄ cup lemon juice
3 tablespoons grated orange rind
1 tablespoon grated lemon rind
2 egg yolks, beaten
2 cups light whipped topping

1. Combine sugar and cornstarch in small saucepan; whisk in orange and lemon juice, and orange and lemon rind. Whisk over medium-high heat until mixture boils and thickens, 2 to 3 minutes.

2. Whisk about ¹/₂ the orange juice mixture into egg yolks; whisk yolk mixture back into saucepan. Whisk over low heat 1 minute. Cool; refrigerate until chilled. Fold in whipped topping.

MOCHA ECLAIRS

Crisp puffs filled with a quick and easy coffee-flavored filling and generously topped with a chocolate glaze.

8 servings

Cream Puffs (see p. 266)
1 package (3 ounces) vanilla pudding and pie filling
1 1/2 cups fat-free milk
3 tablespoons coffee liqueur *or* strong coffee
2 cups light whipped topping
Chocolate Eclair Glaze (recipe follows)

Per Serving
Calories: 366
% Calories from fat: 26
Fat (gm): 10.8
Saturated fat (gm): 4.8
Cholesterol (mg): 81.2
Sodium (mg): 462
Protein (gm): 8.6
Carbohydrate (gm): 55.9
Exchanges
Milk: 0.0
Vegetable: 0.0
Fruit: 0.0
Bread: 4.0
Meat: 0.0
Fat: 2.0

1. Make Cream Puff dough. Using a large pastry bag fitted with a 1/2-inch plain tip, pipe dough into 8 oval eclair shapes, about 3 1/2 inches long and 1 1/2 inches wide. Bake according to recipe.

2. Make pudding and pie filling according to package directions, using 1 1/2 cups milk. Stir in coffee liqueur; cover and refrigerate until chilled. Fold in whipped topping.

3. Fill eclairs with pudding mixture and frost with Chocolate Eclair Glaze.

Chocolate Eclair Glaze

makes about 3/4 cup

2 ounces semisweet chocolate, chopped
1/4 cup fat-free evaporated milk
1 teaspoon light corn syrup
1 cup powdered sugar
1/2 teaspoon vanilla extract

1. Heat chocolate and evaporated milk in small saucepan over low heat until melted; remove from heat and stir in remaining ingredients until smooth. Use immediately.

Variations: **Banana Split Eclairs**—Make 8 eclairs as above. Make pudding, substituting banana liqueur or 1/2 teaspoon banana extract for the coffee liqueur. Fill each eclair with pudding mixture and 4 to 6 slices banana; frost with glaze.

Rocky Road Eclairs—Make 8 eclairs as above. Substitute chocolate fudge pudding and pie filling for the vanilla pudding. Omit coffee liqueur and whipped topping. Fold 1/2 cup mini-marshmallows and 1/2 cup chopped dry roasted peanuts into pudding. Fill puffs with pudding mixture; frost with glaze.

ALMOND PARIS BREST

Cream puff dough is baked into a large ring and filled. We've used an almond praline custard to fill this rich-tasting dessert.

10 servings

Cream Puffs (see p. 266)
1 egg white, beaten
2 tablespoons sliced almonds
Almond Praline (see p. 224)
Pastry Cream (see p. 268)
1 3/4 cups light whipped topping
Powdered sugar, as garnish

Per Serving
Calories: 375
% Calories from fat: 30
Fat (gm): 12
Saturated fat (gm): 3.6
Cholesterol (mg): 150.1
Sodium (mg): 233
Protein (gm): 9.5
Carbohydrate (gm): 51.6
Exchanges
Milk: 0.0
Vegetable: 0.0
Fruit: 0.0
Bread: 3.5
Meat: 0.0
Fat: 2.5

1. Make Cream Puff dough. Using a large pastry bag fitted with 1/2-inch plain tip, pipe a 9-inch circle on parchment-lined, or greased and floured, cookie sheet. Pipe another circle inside first circle, with edges touching; pipe one more circle, covering seam where bottom rings touch. Brush dough with beaten egg white and sprinkle with almonds.

2. Bake at 400 degrees 20 minutes; reduce temperature to 325 degrees and bake until golden and crisp, 10 to 15 minutes. Cool on wire rack. Slice top third off pastry, and remove any raw dough remaining inside; return pastry to oven to dry, about 3 minutes. Cool on wire rack.

3. At serving time, stir Almond Praline into Pastry Cream; fold in whipped topping. Place bottom of pastry on serving plate; fill with custard. Replace top; sprinkle with powdered sugar.

Variations: **Chocolate Paris Brest**—Make cream puff ring as above. Substitute Chocolate Mousse (see p. 23) for the Pastry Cream; omit Almond Praline and whipped topping. Fill pastry with mousse, sprinkle with powdered sugar, and garnish with chocolate shavings or drizzle with Chocolate Glaze (see p. 76).

Mocha Cheesecake Paris Brest—Make cream puff ring as above. Substitute Mocha Rum Cheesecake Filling (see p. 212) for the Pastry Cream; omit Almond Praline and whipped topping. Chill cheesecake filling until mixture mounds on a spoon, 20 to 30 minutes. Fill pastry and refrigerate 2 to 3 hours; sprinkle with powdered sugar and serve with Bittersweet Chocolate Sauce (see p. 641).

Tropical Paris Brest—Make cream puff ring as above. Substitute Mango Filling (see p. 110) for the Pastry Cream; omit Almond Praline. Fold whipped topping and 1/3 cup toasted coconut into chilled Mango Filling. Fill pastry; sprinkle with powdered sugar. Serve with Pineapple-Rum Sauce (see p. 654).

Fresh Apricot Paris Brest—Make cream puff ring as above. Heat 1/4 cup sugar, 2 tablespoons lemon juice, and 1 tablespoon grated lemon rind over medium heat in medium skillet until sugar is melted. Add 2 cups chopped fresh apricots and cook until tender and slightly thickened; cool. Fold 1 cup light whipped topping and apricot mixture into chilled Pastry Cream. Omit Almond Praline and remaining whipped topping. Fill pastry; sprinkle with powdered sugar.

Paris Brest Noël—Make cream puff ring as above. Substitute Candied Fruit Cream (see p. 304) for the Pastry Cream; omit Almond Praline and whipped topping. Fill pastry; sprinkle with powdered sugar and serve with Warm Rum Sauce (see p. 54).

CREPES

These thin French pancakes can be made ahead. Just cool, stack between layers of waxed paper or plastic wrap, and refrigerate or freeze. Double or triple the recipe if desired.

4 servings (2 per serving)

1/2 cup all-purpose flour
1/2 cup fat-free milk
1 egg
2 egg whites
1 tablespoon margarine, melted
2 tablespoons sugar
1/4 teaspoon salt
Vegetable cooking spray

Per Serving
Calories: 144
% Calories from fat: 27
Fat (gm): 4.3
Saturated fat (gm): 1
Cholesterol (mg): 53.6
Sodium (mg): 238
Protein (gm): 6
Carbohydrate (gm): 20
Exchanges
Milk: 0.0
Vegetable: 0.0
Fruit: 0.0
Bread: 1.5
Meat: 0.0
Fat: 1.0

1. Combine all ingredients, except cooking spray, in small bowl; beat until smooth (batter will be thin).

2. Spray 8-inch crepe pan or small skillet with cooking spray; heat over medium heat until hot. Pour scant 1/4 cup batter into pan, tilting to coat bottom evenly with batter.

3. Cook over medium heat until browned on the bottom, 2 to 3 minutes. Turn crepe and cook until browned on the other side, 2 to 3 minutes. Repeat with remaining batter.

STRAWBERRIES AND CREAM CREPES

The elegant appearance of this dessert belies the ease with which it is made. The crepes can be rolled in advance and refrigerated.

4 servings (2 per serving)

Cream Cheese Filling (recipe follows)
Crepes (see p. 274)
1/3 cup granulated sugar, divided
3 cups sliced strawberries
Light whipped topping, as garnish

Per Serving
Calories: 366
% Calories from fat: 13
Fat (gm): 5.5
Saturated fat (gm): 1.6
Cholesterol (mg): 58.1
Sodium (mg): 566
Protein (gm): 15.9
Carbohydrate (gm): 64.2
Exchanges
Milk: 0.0
Vegetable: 0.0
Fruit: 2.0
Bread: 2.5
Meat: 1.0
Fat: 0.5

1. Spread generous 2 tablespoons Cream Cheese Filling on light side of each crepe and roll. Place crepes on flameproof platter or baking dish. Sprinkle with 2 tablespoons granulated sugar. Broil 6 inches from heat source until the sugar is melted, 2 to 3 minutes.

2. Crush half the strawberries with remaining granulated sugar; stir in remaining berries. Heat in small saucepan just to simmering.

3. Arrange crepes on serving plates; spoon warm berries over. Garnish with dollops of whipped topping.

Cream Cheese Filling

makes about 1 1/3 cups

1 package (8 ounces) fat-free cream cheese, softened
1/4 cup packed light brown sugar
1/4 cup fat-free sour cream

1. Beat all ingredients in small bowl until smooth.

Variation: **Fresh Berry Crepes**—Substitute Sugared Crushed Berries (see p. 249) for the Cream Cheese Filling. Omit granulated sugar and strawberries. Fill crepes with berry mixture and roll up; top with dollops of light whipped topping and sprinkle each with 1 teaspoon chopped pecans.

PINEAPPLE CREPES

Canned pineapple is simmered to enhance the flavor, then folded into a custard filling. These crepes are also delicious served with Warm Rum Sauce (see p. 54).

8 servings

1 can (8 ounces) crushed pineapple in juice
1 tablespoon rum *or* ¹/₂ teaspoon rum extract
  Pastry Cream (see p. 268)
  Crepes (see p. 274)
¹/₂ cup light whipped topping
2 tablespoons chopped toasted macadamia nuts

Per Serving
Calories: 289
% Calories from fat: 25
Fat (gm): 8
Saturated fat (gm): 2.8
Cholesterol (mg): 137.9
Sodium (mg): 154
Protein (gm): 7.1
Carbohydrate (gm): 46.8
Exchanges
Milk: 0.0
Vegetable: 0.0
Fruit: 1.0
Bread: 2.0
Meat: 0.0
Fat: 1.5

1.   Drain pineapple, reserving juice. Boil juice in small saucepan until syrupy, about 5 minutes. Add pineapple and simmer 5 minutes; cool to room temperature.

2.   Stir pineapple and rum into Pastry Cream. Spoon about 3 tablespoons filling on light side of each crepe, and roll. Place on serving plates; spoon 2 tablespoons of whipped topping on each and sprinkle with macadamia nuts.

Variation: **Tropical Fruit Crepes**—Complete Step 1 above. Omit Pastry Cream. Combine pineapple, ¹/₂ cup sliced banana, 1¹/₂ cups kiwi-strawberry low-fat yogurt, and rum. Fill crepes and roll. Top with whipped topping, macadamia nuts, and toasted coconut.

APPLE CREPE CAKE

Crepes are layered with an apple and almond filling, baked, then cut into wedges to serve.

6 servings

4 cups diced, peeled, cored apples
$^1/_4$ cup water
$^1/_3$ cup plus 2 tablespoons sugar, divided
1 tablespoon brandy *or* $^1/_2$ teaspoon brandy extract
$^1/_4$ teaspoon almond extract
Crepes (see p. 274)
Almond Praline (see p. 224)
2 tablespoons slivered almonds
Light whipped topping, as garnish

Per Serving
Calories: 358
% Calories from fat: 24
Fat (gm): 8.8
Saturated fat (gm): 1.2
Cholesterol (mg): 35.7
Sodium (mg): 160
Protein (gm): 6.4
Carbohydrate (gm): 55.9
Exchanges
Milk: 0.0
Vegetable: 0.0
Fruit: 1.0
Bread: 3.0
Meat: 0.0
Fat: 1.5

1. Heat apples and water to boiling in medium saucepan; reduce heat and simmer, covered, until tender, about 15 minutes. Stir in $^1/_3$ cup sugar; boil, uncovered, stirring frequently until mixture measures about 2 cups and is thick enough to mound on spoon. Add brandy and almond extract.

2. Place 1 crepe in greased glass baking dish or on heatproof platter. Spread with about $^1/_4$ cup apple mixture and sprinkle with about $1^1/_2$ tablespoons Almond Praline. Repeat layers, using remaining apple mixture and praline, and ending with a crepe. Sprinkle top with slivered almonds and remaining 2 tablespoons sugar.

3. Bake at 375 degrees 15 to 20 minutes or until cake is warm and top has begun to caramelize. Cut into wedges to serve; garnish with dollops of whipped topping.

DATE TURNOVERS

These small pastries can be served as a part of a pastry assortment for parties.

8 servings (3 per serving)

1¹/₃ cups chopped pitted dates
²/₃ cup water
¹/₂ cup sugar
2 tablespoons grated lemon rind
¹/₃ cup chopped pecans
2 tablespoons rum *or* 1 teaspoon rum extract
1 teaspoon vanilla extract
   Double Pie Crust (see p. 128)
2 egg whites, lightly beaten

Per Serving
Calories: 357
% Calories from fat: 26
Fat (gm): 10.8
Saturated fat (gm): 1.8
Cholesterol (mg): 0
Sodium (mg): 244
Protein (gm): 4.9
Carbohydrate (gm): 61
Exchanges
Milk: 0.0
Vegetable: 0.0
Fruit: 1.0
Bread: 3.0
Meat: 0.0
Fat: 2.0

1. Heat dates, water, sugar, and lemon rind in small saucepan to boiling, stirring constantly; reduce heat and simmer 3 to 4 minutes. Stir in pecans, rum, and vanilla; cool.

2. Roll ¹/₂ of the Double Pie Crust on lightly floured board into rectangle 12 x 9 inches; cut into twelve 3-inch squares. Spoon scant tablespoon date mixture on half of each square. Fold pastry over to form triangle; seal edges with fork. Pierce tops with fork or knife. Repeat with remaining dough and filling.

3. Place turnovers on greased cookie sheets; brush with egg whites. Bake at 400 degrees until golden, 15 to 20 minutes. Cool on wire racks.

BROWN SUGAR PECAN TARTS

A bite-sized tart with the flavor of pecan pie.

12 servings (4 per serving)

1 egg
1 tablespoon fat-free milk
2 tablespoons margarine, melted
1/2 teaspoon vanilla extract
1 cup packed light brown sugar
1/4 cup chopped pecans
   Double Pie Crust (see p. 128)

Per Serving
Calories: 230
% Calories from fat: 34
Fat (gm): 8.8
Saturated fat (gm): 1.6
Cholesterol (mg): 17.7
Sodium (mg): 188
Protein (gm): 2.8
Carbohydrate (gm): 35.4
Exchanges
Milk: 0.0
Vegetable: 0.0
Fruit: 0.0
Bread: 2.5
Meat: 0.0
Fat: 1.0

1. Beat egg, milk, margarine, vanilla, and brown sugar until smooth; stir in pecans.

2. Roll 1/2 of the Double Pie Crust on floured surface to 1/8 inch thickness. Cut into rounds with 2 3/4-inch cutter; press each round into 1 3/4-inch mini-muffin pan. Repeat with remaining dough, re-rolling scraps if necessary. Chill 30 minutes.

3. Spoon 1 teaspoon filling into each tart shell. Bake at 400 degrees until golden brown, about 12 minutes. Cool in pans on wire rack 5 minutes; remove from pans and cool on wire rack.

MACADAMIA NUT TARTS

The spicy pastry enhances the rich flavor of macadamia nuts.

12 servings (4 per serving)

Double Pie Crust (see p. 128)
1 teaspoon ground cinnamon
$^1/_2$ teaspoon ground ginger
$^1/_8$ teaspoon ground nutmeg
1 egg
$^1/_2$ cup light corn syrup
$^2/_3$ cup sugar
1 tablespoon flour
1 teaspoon vanilla
$^1/_2$ teaspoon salt
$^2/_3$ cup reduced-fat granola, lightly crushed
$^1/_2$ cup coarsely chopped macadamia nuts

Per Serving
Calories: 275
% Calories from fat: 31
Fat (gm): 9.8
Saturated fat (gm): 1.8
Cholesterol (mg): 17.7
Sodium (mg): 212
Protein (gm): 3.6
Carbohydrate (gm): 44.8
Exchanges
Milk: 0.0
Vegetable: 0.0
Fruit: 0.0
Bread: 3.0
Meat: 0.0
Fat: 1.5

1. Make Double Pie Crust, adding cinnamon, ginger, and nutmeg. Press about 2 teaspoons dough into each $1^3/_4$-inch tart or mini-muffin pan. Chill 30 minutes.

2. Beat egg, corn syrup, sugar, flour, vanilla, and salt until smooth; stir in granola and macadamia nuts. Spoon 1 teaspoon filling into each tart shell. Bake at 350 degrees until bubbly and golden, about 12 minutes. Cool completely on wire rack; remove from tart pans.

FRUIT EMPAÑADAS

Other dried fruit, such as pears or apples, can be substituted for the apricots or raisins.

8 servings (3 per serving)

$1/2$ cup chopped dried apricots

$1/2$ cup raisins

$1/2$ cup water

$1/4$ cup sugar

$1/2$ teaspoon ground cinnamon

$1/8$ teaspoon ground nutmeg

Basic Pie Crust (All-Purpose Flour) (see p. 126)

Fat-free milk

Sugar

Per Serving
Calories: 204
% Calories from fat: 25
Fat (gm): 6
Saturated fat (gm): 1.2
Cholesterol (mg): 0
Sodium (mg): 141
Protein (gm): 2.7
Carbohydrate (gm): 36.6
Exchanges
Milk: 0.0
Vegetable: 0.0
Fruit: 0.0
Bread: 3.0
Meat: 0.0
Fat: 0.0

1. Heat apricots, raisins, and water to boiling in small saucepan. Reduce heat and simmer, covered, until fruit is very soft, about 5 minutes. Mash fruit with fork until almost smooth; stir in sugar and spices.

2. Roll $1/2$ of the Basic Pie Crust on lightly floured surface to $1/8$ inch thickness; cut into rounds with 3-inch cookie cutters. Spoon slightly rounded teaspoon of fruit mixture in center of each round; fold pastries in half and crimp edges with tines of fork. Make cut in top of each pastry with knife. Repeat with remaining crust and fruit mixture.

3. Bake on greased cookie sheets at 350 degrees until golden, 12 to 15 minutes. Brush pastries lightly with milk and sprinkle generously with sugar; bake 1 to 2 minutes, until glazed. Serve warm.

PEAR TARTLETS

Fresh pears and lemon filling are baked in tart shells, then served with a richly flavored pear sauce.

12 servings

Double Pie Crust (see p. 128)
3 eggs
1 cup sugar
3 tablespoons flour
1/3 cup lemon juice
4 pears, peeled, cored, thinly sliced
Caramel Pear Sauce (recipe follows)

Per Serving
Calories: 373
% Calories from fat: 17
Fat (gm): 7.2
Saturated fat (gm): 1.5
Cholesterol (mg): 53
Sodium (mg): 177
Protein (gm): 4.2
Carbohydrate (gm): 75.9
Exchanges
Milk: 0.0
Vegetable: 0.0
Fruit: 1.0
Bread: 3.5
Meat: 0.0
Fat: 1.5

1. Roll Double Pie Crust on floured surface to 1/8 inch thickness. Cut dough into rounds, using 4- to 5-inch cutter; press into 3-inch tart pans.

2. Beat eggs, sugar, flour, and lemon juice until smooth; spoon about 2 tablespoons mixture into each tart shell. Cut pear slices into halves or thirds; arrange pear pieces on top of filling to cover.

3. Bake at 350 degrees until pears are tender and filling is set, about 35 minutes. Cool on wire rack. Remove from pans. Place on serving plates; spoon Caramel Pear Sauce over tarts.

Caramel Pear Sauce

makes about 2 cups

1 1/3 cups sugar
2 cups diced, peeled pears
3/4 cup apple cider, divided
2 tablespoons cornstarch
2 teaspoons margarine

1. Melt sugar in large heavy saucepan over low heat, stirring occasionally, until melted and golden brown. Add pears and 1/2 cup apple cider, and stir over medium heat until caramel dissolves. Combine remaining 1/4 cup apple cider and cornstarch, and add to caramel mixture; boil until thickened, stirring constantly, about 5 minutes. Stir in margarine.

MINCEMEAT TARTS

An easily made mincemeat fills these tiny tarts—pipe with rosettes of brandy-flavored whipped topping for that special touch!

12 servings (3 per serving)

Cornmeal Double Pie Crust (see p. 128)
Mincemeat (recipe follows)
3/4 cup brandy, optional
Light whipped topping

Per Serving
Calories: 248
% Calories from fat: 19
Fat (gm): 5.2
Saturated fat (gm): 1.1
Cholesterol (mg): 0.4
Sodium (mg): 238
Protein (gm): 4.5
Carbohydrate (gm): 38.2
Exchanges
Milk: 0.0
Vegetable: 0.0
Fruit: 1.0
Bread: 1.5
Meat: 0.0
Fat: 1.5

1. Make Cornmeal Double Pie Crust; refrigerate 1 hour. Press about 2 teaspoons dough into each mini-muffin cup. Pierce lightly with fork. Bake at 400 degrees 5 minutes.

2. Spoon about 2 teaspoons Mincemeat into each tart shell; press lightly with back of spoon. Bake until tarts are golden, about 20 minutes. Cool on wire racks. Drizzle each tart with 1 teaspoon brandy and top with a dollup of whipped topping.

Mincemeat

3/4 cup shredded, peeled tart apple
3/4 cup finely chopped raisins
1/2 cup finely chopped mixed candied fruit
1/4 cup packed light brown sugar
2 tablespoons brandy *or* 2 teaspoons brandy extract
1 tablespoon grated lemon rind
1/4 cup finely chopped, peeled lemon
1/4 teaspoon ground cinnamon
1/8 teaspoon ground ginger
1/8 teaspoon ground mace
Dash salt

1. Mix all ingredients.

STRAWBERRY TARTS

Fresh berries are flavored with a sherry syrup and served in a flaky short-bread crust.

6 servings (2 per serving)

Shortbread Crust (see p. 130)
1/2 cup sugar
5 teaspoons cornstarch
1 cup water
2 tablespoons lemon juice
2 tablespoons dry sherry *or* 1 teaspoon sherry extract
3 cups halved strawberries
Sliced toasted almonds, as garnish

Per Serving
Calories: 343
% Calories from fat: 28
Fat (gm): 10.8
Saturated fat (gm): 2.2
Cholesterol (mg): 35.4
Sodium (mg): 123
Protein (gm): 4.5
Carbohydrate (gm): 56.2
Exchanges
Milk: 0.0
Vegetable: 0.0
Fruit: 2.0
Bread: 2.0
Meat: 0.0
Fat: 2.0

1. Divide Shortbread Crust into 12 equal parts and press into 3-inch fluted tart pans; pierce bottoms with fork. Bake on cookie sheet at 350 degrees until light brown, about 15 minutes.

2. Combine sugar and cornstarch in small saucepan; add water and lemon juice. Heat to boiling; boil, stirring constantly, 1 minute. Stir in sherry. Cool slightly. Gently stir strawberries into sauce. Fill each tart with strawberry mixture and sprinkle with almonds; serve immediately.

Variation: **Orange Glazed Fruit Tarts**—Prepare tart shells as in Step 1 above. Make filling, substituting orange juice for the water and lemon juice and adding 1 tablespoon grated orange rind and 1 tablespoon orange liqueur. Omit sherry and strawberries. Stir in 1 cup sliced bananas, 1 cup diced peaches, and 1 cup raspberries; fill and garnish as above.

SOUR CREAM APPLE TARTLETS

Miniature sour cream apple pies are topped with meringue for a very special presentation. They are also delicious without the meringue—just sprinkle with powdered sugar and serve warm.

8 servings

Basic Pie Crust (All-Purpose Flour) (see p. 126)

2-3 medium baking apples, peeled, thinly sliced

Ground cinnamon

2 eggs

1 cup fat-free sour cream

1/2 cup sugar

1/2 teaspoon vanilla

Dash salt

Two-Egg Meringue (recipe follows)

Per Serving
Calories: 284
% Calories from fat: 23
Fat (gm): 7.2
Saturated fat (gm): 1.6
Cholesterol (mg): 53
Sodium (mg): 194
Protein (gm): 6.6
Carbohydrate (gm): 48
Exchanges
Milk: 0.0
Vegetable: 0.0
Fruit: 0.0
Bread: 3.0
Meat: 0.0
Fat: 1.5

1. Roll Basic Pie Crust on floured surface to 1/8 inch thickness; cut into eight 5-inch rounds. Ease into 4-inch tart pans with removable bottoms; trim.

2. Arrange apples in pastry; sprinkle lightly with cinnamon. Bake at 450 degrees until pastry is golden, about 15 minutes. Remove from oven.

3. Mix eggs, sour cream, sugar, vanilla, and salt; spoon over apples in tart shells, filling almost to rim. Bake until filling is set and golden, about 10 minutes.

4. Make Two-Egg Meringue; pipe or spread about 1/4 cup meringue over each hot tart, sealing to edge of crust. Bake until meringue is brown, about 2 minutes. Cool slightly; remove tarts from pans and serve warm.

Two-Egg Meringue

makes about 2 cups

>   2 egg whites, room temperature
> $1/4$ teaspoon cream of tartar
> $1/4$ cup sugar
> $1/4$ teaspoon vanilla

1. Beat egg whites and cream of tartar in small mixing bowl to soft peaks. Beat to stiff peaks, adding sugar gradually; beat in vanilla.

Variation: **Peach Tartlets**—Complete Step 1 above. Sprinkle bottom of tart shells with 2 teaspoons dry bread crumbs. Substitute sliced ripe peaches for the apples, and brown sugar for the granulated sugar. Complete recipe as above.

APPLE TURNOVERS

Use several varieties of firm cooking apples for the best flavor in these classic turnovers.

12 servings

>   3 cups finely chopped, peeled cooking apples, divided
>   1 tablespoon margarine
> $1/4$ cup apple cider
>   1 tablespoon lemon juice
> $1/4$ cup packed light brown sugar
> $1/4$ cup golden raisins
> $1/2$ teaspoon ground cinnamon
>   Pinch ground nutmeg
>   Cream Cheese Tart Crust (see p. 131)
>   1 egg white, lightly beaten
>   Brown Sugar Glaze (see p. 50)

Per Serving
Calories: 348
% Calories from fat: 28
Fat (gm): 10.9
Saturated fat (gm): 2.9
Cholesterol (mg): 22.9
Sodium (mg): 177
Protein (gm): 4
Carbohydrate (gm): 59.5
Exchanges
Milk: 0.0
Vegetable: 0.0
Fruit: 1.0
Bread: 3.0
Meat: 0.0
Fat: 1.5

1. Saute 2 cups apples in margarine in large skillet until lightly browned, about 5 minutes; add cider, lemon juice, brown sugar, raisins, cinnamon, and nutmeg, and cook until liquid has almost evaporated. Add remaining apples and refrigerate until chilled.

2. Roll Cream Cheese Tart Crust on lightly floured board into rectangle 16 x 12 inches; cut into twelve 4-inch squares. Spoon about 2 tablespoons apple mixture on half of each square. Fold pastry over to form triangles; seal edges with fork. Pierce tops.

3. Place turnovers on ungreased cookie sheet; brush with egg white. Bake at 400 degrees until golden brown, 15 to 20 minutes. Cool on wire rack. Drizzle with Sugar Glaze.

CHOCOLATE MANGO TARTS

A chocolate crust accentuates the sweetness of the mango custard in these unusual tarts.

10 servings

Chocolate Tart Crust (recipe follows)
2¹/₂ cups diced, peeled ripe mango
¹/₂ cup sugar
2 tablespoons lemon juice
¹/₂ teaspoon rum extract
¹/₂ cup no-cholesterol real egg product *or* 4 egg whites
1 cup light whipped topping

Per Serving
Calories: 218
% Calories from fat: 26
Fat (gm): 6.5
Saturated fat (gm): 2.3
Cholesterol (mg): 0
Sodium (mg): 135
Protein (gm): 3.5
Carbohydrate (gm): 37.4
Exchanges
Milk: 0.0
Vegetable: 0.0
Fruit: 0.5
Bread: 2.0
Meat: 0.0
Fat: 1.0

1. Make Chocolate Tart Crust; press dough into 3-inch tart pans. Refrigerate 30 minutes.

2. Process remaining ingredients, except whipped topping, in food processor or blender until smooth. Spoon into tart shells. Bake at 350 degrees until set, about 20 minutes. Cool on wire rack; remove tarts from pans and refrigerate until chilled. Spoon or pipe whipped topping on each tart.

Chocolate Tart Crust

makes 10 tart shells

1¹/₄ cups all-purpose flour
2 tablespoons cocoa
2 tablespoons sugar
¹/₄ teaspoon salt
4-5 tablespoons cold margarine, cut into pieces, *or* vegetable shortening
1 ounce semisweet baking chocolate, melted and slightly cooled
3-5 tablespoons cold coffee

1. Combine flour, cocoa, sugar, and salt in medium bowl. Cut in margarine until mixture resembles coarse crumbs. Pour chocolate over; sprinkle with coffee, 1 tablespoon at a time, mixing lightly with a fork after each addition until pastry just holds together.

CINNAMON SPIRALS

Easy as pie—and even faster!

12 servings (2 per serving)

Cornmeal Double Pie Crust (see p. 128)
1/2 cup sugar
1/2 cup dried fruit bits
1 teaspoon ground cinnamon

Per Serving
Calories: 189
% Calories from fat: 24
Fat (gm): 5.1
Saturated fat (gm): 1
Cholesterol (mg): 0.4
Sodium (mg): 235
Protein (gm): 4.2
Carbohydrate (gm): 31.8
Exchanges
Milk: 0.0
Vegetable: 0.0
Fruit: 0.0
Bread: 2.0
Meat: 0.0
Fat: 1.0

1. Make Cornmeal Double Pie Crust; chill 1 to 2 hours. Roll 1/2 the dough on floured surface into 16 x 8-inch rectangle; sprinkle with 1/4 of the combined remaining ingredients. Fold narrow ends in to meet at center, forming 8-inch square; sprinkle with 1/4 of the fruit mixture. Fold ends in to meet at center, forming 8 x 4-inch rectangle. Pinch open ends together. Fold in half to form 4-inch square; flatten slightly with rolling pin. Fold in half again in the same direction.

2. Cut dough crosswise into twelve 1/2-inch-thick slices; repeat with remaining dough and fruit mixture. Place, cut sides down, on parchment-lined baking sheets; bake at 350 degrees until golden, about 25 minutes.

CHEESE-FILLED PASTRIES

A sweet yeast dough encloses a raisin and cream cheese filling.

12 servings (2 per serving)

1 package active dry yeast
$^1/_4$ cup warm water (110-115 degrees)
$^1/_4$ cup warm milk
$^1/_4$ cup sugar
1 teaspoon ground cinnamon
$^1/_2$ teaspoon salt
1 egg
1 tablespoon grated orange rind
$^1/_4$ cup vegetable shortening
$2^1/_2$-3 cups all-purpose flour
Cream Cheese-Raisin Filling (recipe follows)
Orange Glaze (see p. 47)

Per Serving
Calories: 222
% Calories from fat: 22
Fat (gm): 5.5
Saturated fat (gm): 1.6
Cholesterol (mg): 37.3
Sodium (mg): 212
Protein (gm): 7
Carbohydrate (gm): 36
Exchanges
Milk: 0.0
Vegetable: 0.0
Fruit: 0.0
Bread: 2.5
Meat: 0.0
Fat: 1.0

1. Dissolve yeast in warm water in large bowl. Beat in milk, sugar, cinnamon, salt, egg, orange rind, shortening, and $1^1/_4$ cups flour until smooth. Mix in enough remaining flour to make dough easy to handle.

2. Knead dough on lightly floured surface until smooth and elastic, about 5 minutes; place in greased bowl and cover. Let rise until doubled in size, about $1^1/_2$ hours.

3. Punch down dough; roll on lightly floured surface into 18 x 12-inch rectangle. Cut into twenty-four 3-inch squares. Place 1 tablespoon Cream Cheese-Raisin Filling in center of each square. Bring diagonally opposite corners together and overlap slightly; moisten edges and pinch to seal.

4. Place on greased cookie sheets; let rise until doubled in size. Bake at 375 degrees until golden brown, about 15 minutes. Cool on wire racks; drizzle with Orange Glaze.

Cream Cheese-Raisin Filling

makes about 1¹/₂ cups

- 1 package (8 ounces) fat-free cream cheese, softened
- ¹/₄ cup packed light brown sugar
- 1 egg yolk
- 1 tablespoon grated lemon rind
- ¹/₂ cup golden raisins

1. Beat cream cheese, brown sugar, egg yolk, and lemon rind until light and fluffy; stir in raisins.

PETIT FOURS

These tiny cakes with glossy fondant icing are lovely for a special party, or as part of a pastry assortment.

12 servings (2 per serving)

Classic Sponge Cake (see p. 100)
Fondant Icing (recipe follows)
Colored cake decorating sprinkles, decorating icing, colored jimmies, etc., as garnish

Per Serving
Calories: 368
% Calories from fat: 3
Fat (gm): 1.4
Saturated fat (gm): 0.4
Cholesterol (mg): 53.3
Sodium (mg): 129
Protein (gm): 2.9
Carbohydrate (gm): 87.2
Exchanges
Milk: 0.0
Vegetable: 0.0
Fruit: 0.0
Bread: 5.0
Meat: 0.0
Fat: 0.0

1. Line a 13 x 9-inch pan with parchment and grease lightly. Make Classic Sponge Cake; bake in prepared pan until cake springs back when lightly touched, 25 to 30 minutes. Invert onto wire rack covered with kitchen towel; remove parchment. Invert onto second rack; let stand, uncovered, 24 hours.

2. Make Fondant Icing. Trim off top crust of cake; cut cake into 1¹/₂-inch squares. Pierce bottom side of cake square with fork. Spoon icing over cake on fork, allowing excess to drip into icing pan. Place cake square on wire rack set over a jelly roll pan (excess icing on pan can be reheated and used). Repeat with remaining cake squares. Let stand until icing is set, at least 15 minutes. Decorate with sprinkles, decorating icing, etc.

Fondant Icing

makes about 3 cups

6 cups powdered sugar
$^1/_4$ cup water
$^1/_2$ cup light corn syrup
1 teaspoon vanilla
$^1/_2$ teaspoon lemon extract
Food coloring

1. Sift powdered sugar into top of double boiler; mix in remaining ingredients, except food coloring. Heat over simmering water, stirring occasionally, until warm (110 to 115 degrees). Remove from heat; color with food coloring as desired. Keep warm over hot water and thin if necessary with hot water.

FILLED LADYFINGERS

Ladyfingers can be used for many desserts, such as Tiramisu and Trifle (see pp. 385, 386), or simply served with fresh fruit.

12 servings

3 eggs, separated
$^1/_2$ teaspoon vanilla
Dash salt
$^1/_2$ cup plus 1 to 2 tablespoons powdered sugar, divided
$^1/_2$ cup all-purpose flour
Lemon Curd Filling (recipe follows)

Per Serving
Calories: 98
% Calories from fat: 24
Fat (gm): 2.7
Saturated fat (gm): 0.7
Cholesterol (mg): 70.7
Sodium (mg): 32
Protein (gm): 2.7
Carbohydrate (gm): 15.9
Exchanges
Milk: 0.0
Vegetable: 0.0
Fruit: 0.0
Bread: 1.0
Meat: 0.0
Fat: 0.5

1. Beat egg yolks and vanilla in small bowl at high speed until thick and lemon colored, about 5 minutes. With clean beaters and bowl, beat egg whites and salt until foamy. Add $^1/_4$ cup powdered sugar to whites, 1 tablespoon at a time, beating to stiff peaks.

2. Fold beaten egg yolks into egg white mixture. Fold in $^1/_4$ cup powdered sugar and flour. Pipe batter onto parchment-lined cookie sheets, using large pastry bag with $^1/_2$-inch round tip, into 24 finger shapes, $3^1/_2$ x 1 inch. Sprinkle lightly with remaining 1 to 2 tablespoons powdered sugar.

3. Bake at 350 degrees until edges are barely brown, about 8 minutes. Slide parchment immediately onto wire rack; cool.

4. Spread Lemon Curd Filling on the flat side of half the ladyfingers. Top with remaining ladyfingers, flat side down, to form "sandwiches."

Lemon Curd Filling

makes about 2/3 cup

> 1/4 cup lemon juice
> 1/3 cup sugar
> 1 tablespoon margarine
> 1 egg, beaten
> 1 tablespoon grated lemon rind
> Dash salt

1. Combine all ingredients in small saucepan. Cook over medium heat, stirring constantly, until mixture thickens. Cover and refrigerate.

TUILE "TACOS"

Crisp cookie "tacos" are filled with a sweet orange mixture. The tuiles can be made in advance and stored in an airtight container; fill before serving.

12 servings (3 per serving)

> Almond Tuiles (see p. 347)
> 1/4 cup finely chopped pecans
> 1 teaspoon orange extract
> 4 cups light whipped topping
> 1/2 cup powdered sugar
> 1/2 cup orange marmalade *or* other fruit preserves
> Orange slices, as garnish

Per Serving
Calories: 249
% Calories from fat: 30
Fat (gm): 8.4
Saturated fat (gm): 3.6
Cholesterol (mg): 0
Sodium (mg): 111
Protein (gm): 1.4
Carbohydrate (gm): 42.1
Exchanges
Milk: 0.0
Vegetable: 0.0
Fruit: 0.0
Bread: 3.0
Meat: 0.0
Fat: 1.0

1. Make Almond Tuiles, substituting pecans for the almonds and orange extract for the lemon extract. Remove tuiles from cookie sheet 1 at a time and fold loosely around handle of wooden spoon to make a "taco" shape; transfer to wire rack and cool.

2. Combine whipped topping, powdered sugar, and orange marmalade. Spoon mixture into tuiles, using scant 2 table-spoons mixture for each. Arrange 3 tuiles on each serving plate; garnish with orange slices.

TUILE NAPOLEONS

Delicate lace cookies are drizzled with chocolate and layered with berries for this spectacular dessert.

12 servings

Almond Tuiles (see p. 347)
1 ounce semisweet chocolate, melted
Raspberry Sauce (see p. 658)
4 cups Orange Chantilly (double recipe) (see p. 270)
Light whipped topping, as garnish
3 cups raspberries, blackberries, *or* sliced strawberries

Per Serving
Calories: 370
% Calories from fat: 26
Fat (gm): 10.7
Saturated fat (gm): 4.5
Cholesterol (mg): 71
Sodium (mg): 113
Protein (gm): 3.5
Carbohydrate (gm): 64.7
Exchanges
Milk: 0.0
Vegetable: 0.0
Fruit: 0.0
Bread: 4.0
Meat: 0.0
Fat: 2.0

1. Make Almond Tuiles, leaving cookies flat. Drizzle chocolate over 12 cooled cookies and reserve. Let stand or refrigerate until chocolate is firm.

2. Drizzle about 1 tablespoon Raspberry Sauce on serving plate; place 1 plain cookie on plate. Spread with generous 2 tablespoons Orange Chantilly; top with another plain cookie and spread with generous 2 tablespoons Orange Chantilly. Top with a chocolate drizzled cookie and garnish with a dollop of whipped topping; spoon 1/4 cup berries over. Repeat using remaining ingredients.

HONEY NUT SQUARES

Honey lemon syrup soaks into these Greek-style pastries, making them chewy and delicious.

16 servings

3 cups crushed shredded wheat cereal (9 large biscuits)

1/2 cup finely chopped dates

1/2 cup finely chopped walnuts

1/4 cup sugar

1 teaspoon ground cinnamon

1/4 teaspoon ground cloves

1/8 teaspoon salt

1/2 cup margarine, melted

Honey Lemon Syrup (recipe follows)

Per Serving
Calories: 228
% Calories from fat: 30
Fat (gm): 8.1
Saturated fat (gm): 1.3
Cholesterol (mg): 0
Sodium (mg): 86
Protein (gm): 2.6
Carbohydrate (gm): 39.9
Exchanges
Milk: 0.0
Vegetable: 0.0
Fruit: 0.0
Bread: 2.5
Meat: 0.0
Fat: 1.0

1. Combine all ingredients, except margarine and Honey Lemon Syrup. Press evenly in greased 8-inch square baking pan. Pour margarine evenly over top. Bake at 400 degrees until light brown, 20 to 25 minutes.

2. Immediately pour warm Honey Lemon Syrup over pastry; press down with back of spoon. Let stand at room temperature 4 to 6 hours. Cut into 16 squares.

Honey Lemon Syrup

makes about 1 1/2 cups

1 cup sugar

1/2 cup water

1/2 cup honey

2 tablespoons lemon juice

1. Heat sugar and water in medium saucepan to boiling; reduce heat and simmer 5 minutes. Add remaining ingredients and simmer 5 minutes.

BAKLAVA

The traditional Greek dessert with a fraction of the fat!

9 servings

1 cup barley-wheat cereal (Grape-Nuts)
1/2 cup chopped walnuts
1/4 cup sugar
1 teaspoon ground cinnamon
3 tablespoons vegetable oil
2 egg whites, beaten
19 sheets frozen fillo, thawed
    Butter-flavored vegetable cooking spray
    Baklava Syrup (recipe follows)

Per Serving
Calories: 375
% Calories from fat: 26
Fat (gm): 11
Saturated fat (gm): 1.2
Cholesterol (mg): 0
Sodium (mg): 286
Protein (gm): 7
Carbohydrate (gm): 64.6
Exchanges
Milk: 0.0
Vegetable: 0.0
Fruit: 0.0
Bread: 4.0
Meat: 0.0
Fat: 2.0

1. Combine cereal, walnuts, sugar, and cinnamon. Beat oil and egg whites in small bowl until well blended.

2. Cut fillo into 38, 9-inch squares; cover with damp kitchen towel to prevent drying. Place 2 squares fillo in 9-inch square baking pan, brushing each lightly with oil mixture; sprinkle with 2 tablespoons cereal mixture. Repeat layering until all cereal mixture has been used. Continue layering remaining fillo, brushing each layer with oil mixture. Spray top with cooking spray. Carefully score through top layer with sharp knife into 3 x 3-inch serving pieces.

3. Bake at 350 degrees until golden, about 25 minutes. Cool to lukewarm.

4. Pour hot Baklava Syrup over baklava, allowing syrup to saturate layers. Let stand at room temperature 4 to 6 hours. Cut into pieces.

Baklava Syrup

makes about 1 cup

1 1/2 cups water
1/2 cup sugar
1/2 cup honey
2 sticks cinnamon
1 tablespoon lemon juice

1. Combine all ingredients in large saucepan; boil until syrup reaches 220 degrees on candy thermometer, about 20 minutes. Use immediately.

CRANBERRY APRICOT STRUDEL

Use any dried fruit in this strudel—dried pears and cherries make a delicious combination.

8 servings (2 slices per serving)

¹/₂ cup dried cranberries

¹/₂ cup chopped dried apricots

1 tablespoon chopped crystallized ginger

¹/₃ cup orange juice

¹/₄ cup sugar

¹/₃ cup barley-wheat cereal (Grape-Nuts)

¹/₃ cup reduced-fat semisweet chocolate morsels

6 sheets frozen fillo, thawed

2 tablespoons vegetable oil

1 egg white, beaten

Butter-flavored vegetable cooking spray

Per Serving
Calories: 210
% Calories from fat: 27
Fat (gm): 6.7
Saturated fat (gm): 2.9
Cholesterol (mg): 0
Sodium (mg): 106
Protein (gm): 2.8
Carbohydrate (gm): 38
Exchanges
Milk: 0.0
Vegetable: 0.0
Fruit: 0.0
Bread: 2.5
Meat: 0.0
Fat: 1.0

1. Combine cranberries, apricots, ginger, orange juice, and sugar in medium saucepan; simmer until fruits are soft, about 5 minutes. Cool completely; stir in cereal and chocolate morsels.

2. Place 1 sheet fillo on counter (cover remaining fillo with damp kitchen towel to prevent drying); brush lightly with combined oil and egg white. Top with second sheet fillo and brush with egg white mixture; repeat with remaining fillo and egg white mixture.

3. Spoon cranberry mixture along one long edge of fillo; fold over short edges and roll strudel from long edge. Place on greased baking sheet. Spray generously with cooking spray. Score strudel diagonally into 16 serving pieces.

4. Bake at 350 degrees until golden, about 25 minutes; cool on wire rack.

CHERRY STRUDEL

Thanks to frozen fillo leaves and canned cherries, this dessert couldn't be easier.

8 servings

1/2 cup dry unseasoned bread crumbs

1 tablespoon margarine

6 sheets frozen fillo, thawed

2 tablespoons vegetable oil

1 egg white, beaten

2 cans (16 ounces each) pitted tart pie cherries, drained

1/3 cup sugar

1 teaspoon grated lemon rind

1 teaspoon ground cinnamon
Butter-flavored vegetable cooking spray

Per Serving
Calories: 188
% Calories from fat: 28
Fat (gm): 6.2
Saturated fat (gm): 0.9
Cholesterol (mg): 0
Sodium (mg): 159
Protein (gm): 3.2
Carbohydrate (gm): 31.2
Exchanges
Milk: 0.0
Vegetable: 0.0
Fruit: 1.0
Bread: 1.0
Meat: 0.0
Fat: 1.0

1. Cook bread crumbs in margarine in small skillet over medium heat until light brown, stirring frequently.

2. Place 1 sheet fillo on counter (cover remaining fillo with damp kitchen towel to prevent drying); brush lightly with combined oil and egg white. Top with second sheet fillo and brush with egg white mixture; repeat with remaining fillo and egg white mixture. Sprinkle with toasted bread crumbs, reserving 2 teaspoons.

3. Mound cherries along one long edge of fillo; sprinkle with combined sugar, lemon rind, and cinnamon. Fold over short edges of fillo and roll strudel from long edge. Place on greased baking sheet. Spray generously with cooking spray. Score strudel diagonally into serving pieces. Sprinkle with reserved 2 teaspoons toasted crumbs.

4. Bake at 350 degrees until golden, about 20 minutes; cool on wire rack.

Variations: **Georgia Peach Strudel**—Substitute 5 cups sliced, peeled peaches for the cherries, and 1/4 cup packed light brown sugar for the granulated sugar. Toss peaches with 1 tablespoon lemon juice. Complete recipe as above.

Tropical Fruit Strudel—Substitute 2 cups diced fresh or canned, drained, pineapple, 2 cups diced mango, 1 cup diced, peeled apple, and $^1/_2$ cup golden raisins for the cherries. Toss fruit with 2 tablespoons dark rum. Complete recipe as above. Serve with Mango Coulis (see p. 659).

VIENNESE APPLE STRUDEL

The flavor of apples is accented with apricot and brandy in this classic Old World strudel.

8 servings

$^1/_2$ cup dry unseasoned bread crumbs
1 tablespoon margarine
$^1/_2$ cup apricot preserves
1 tablespoon brandy *or* $^1/_2$ teaspoon brandy extract
6 sheets frozen fillo, thawed
2 tablespoons vegetable oil
1 egg white, beaten
4 cups thinly sliced, peeled tart baking apples
$^1/_3$ cup packed light brown sugar
$^1/_4$ cup chopped walnuts
$^1/_4$ cup raisins
1 tablespoon grated lemon rind
1 teaspoon ground cinnamon
Butter-flavored vegetable cooking spray

Per Serving
Calories: 283
% Calories from fat: 26
Fat (gm): 8.6
Saturated fat (gm): 1.1
Cholesterol (mg): 0
Sodium (mg): 158
Protein (gm): 3.7
Carbohydrate (gm): 49.4
Exchanges
Milk: 0.0
Vegetable: 0.0
Fruit: 1.0
Bread: 2.0
Meat: 0.0
Fat: 1.5

1. Cook bread crumbs in margarine in small skillet over medium heat until light brown, stirring frequently. Melt apricot preserves in small saucepan; add brandy.

2. Place 1 sheet fillo on counter (cover remaining fillo with damp kitchen towel to prevent drying); brush with combined oil and egg white. Top with second sheet fillo and brush with egg white mixture; repeat with remaining fillo and egg white mixture. Brush top of fillo with warm apricot mixture; sprinkle with toasted bread crumbs.

3. Mound combined remaining ingredients, except cooking spray, along one long edge of fillo. Fold over short edges of fillo and roll strudel from long edge. Place on greased baking sheet. Spray generously with cooking spray. Score strudel diagonally into serving pieces.

4. Bake at 350 degrees until apples are tender and strudel is golden, about 45 minutes; cool on wire rack.

RAISIN CHEESE STRUDEL

This flaky dessert is filled with sweetened cottage cheese and raisins; other dried fruits can be substituted for the raisins.

8 servings

1 carton (16-ounce size) 1% low-fat cottage cheese
1/3 cup sugar
1 egg
1 tablespoon grated lemon rind
2 teaspoons vanilla
1 cup dark, *or* golden, raisins
1/4 cup chopped walnuts
6 sheets frozen fillo, thawed
2 tablespoons vegetable oil
1 egg white, beaten
Butter-flavored vegetable cooking spray
Powdered sugar, as garnish

Per Serving
Calories: 239
% Calories from fat: 28
Fat (gm): 7.8
Saturated fat (gm): 1.3
Cholesterol (mg): 29
Sodium (mg): 316
Protein (gm): 10.8
Carbohydrate (gm): 32.8
Exchanges
Milk: 0.0
Vegetable: 0.0
Fruit: 0.0
Bread: 2.0
Meat: 1.0
Fat: 1.0

1. Process cottage cheese, sugar, egg, lemon rind, and vanilla in food processor or blender until smooth. Pour into bowl; stir in raisins and nuts.

2. Place 1 sheet fillo on counter (cover remaining fillo with damp kitchen towel to prevent drying); brush with combined oil and egg white. Top with second sheet fillo and brush with egg white mixture; repeat with remaining fillo and egg white mixture. Spoon cottage cheese mixture along one long edge of fillo. Fold over short edges of fillo and roll strudel from long edge. Place on greased baking sheet. Score strudel diagonally into serving pieces. Spray generously with cooking spray.

3. Bake at 350 degrees until golden, about 25 minutes; cool on wire rack. Sprinkle with powdered sugar.

PEAR FILLO TURNOVERS

With frozen fillo dough, turnovers just became easy!

9 servings

3 tablespoons dry unseasoned bread crumbs

3 tablespoons packed light brown sugar

1½ cups finely chopped, peeled pears

⅓ cup dried cherries *or* cranberries

¼ cup chopped toasted pecans

¼ cup granulated sugar

½ teaspoon ground cinnamon

½ teaspoon almond extract

9 sheets frozen fillo, thawed

2 tablespoons vegetable oil

2 egg whites, beaten
   Butter-flavored vegetable cooking spray

Per Serving
Calories: 199
% Calories from fat: 30
Fat (gm): 6.8
Saturated fat (gm): 0.8
Cholesterol (mg): 0
Sodium (mg): 126
Protein (gm): 3.3
Carbohydrate (gm): 32.8
Exchanges
Milk: 0.0
Vegetable: 0.0
Fruit: 1.0
Bread: 1.0
Meat: 0.0
Fat: 1.5

1. Combine bread crumbs and brown sugar in small bowl. Toss pears with cherries, pecans, granulated sugar, cinnamon, and almond extract.

2. Place 1 sheet fillo on counter (cover remaining fillo with damp kitchen towel to prevent drying); brush with combined oil and egg white. Top with 2 more sheets fillo, brushing each with egg white mixture. Sprinkle with about 2 tablespoons bread crumb mixture. Cut fillo stack lengthwise into three strips, each about 4 inches wide.

3. Spoon about ¼ cup pear mixture about 4 inches from end of each fillo strip. Fold fillo over fruit, forming a triangle; continue folding back and forth, as if folding a flag. Place turnover on greased cookie sheet; repeat with remaining fillo strips. Spray generously with cooking spray. Make 6 more turnovers using remaining ingredients.

4. Bake at 350 degrees until golden, about 15 minutes. Cool on wire rack.

Variation: **Cherry-Apple Fillo Turnovers**—Make recipe as above, substituting 1½ cups pitted dark sweet cherries and 1 cup finely chopped tart apple for the pears, and omitting dried cherries and pecans.

APRICOT CHEESE FILLO TURNOVERS

Tangy apricots in a cream cheese filling give a wonderful flavor to these turnovers.

9 servings

Cream Cheese-Raisin Filling (see p. 290)

1/3 cup chopped dried apricots

3 tablespoons dry unseasoned bread crumbs

3 tablespoons sugar

9 sheets frozen fillo, thawed

2 tablespoons vegetable oil

2 egg whites, beaten

Butter-flavored vegetable cooking spray

Powdered sugar, as garnish

Per Serving
Calories: 206
% Calories from fat: 23
Fat (gm): 5.3
Saturated fat (gm): 1
Cholesterol (mg): 25.7
Sodium (mg): 266
Protein (gm): 6.8
Carbohydrate (gm): 33.7
Exchanges
Milk: 0.0
Vegetable: 0.0
Fruit: 0.0
Bread: 2.0
Meat: 0.0
Fat: 1.0

1. Make Cream Cheese-Raisin Filling, substituting dried apricots for the raisins. Combine bread crumbs and sugar in small bowl.

2. Place 1 sheet fillo on counter (cover remaining fillo with damp kitchen towel to prevent drying); brush with combined oil and egg white. Top with 2 more sheets fillo, brushing each with egg white mixture. Sprinkle with about 2 tablespoons bread-crumb mixture. Cut fillo stack lengthwise into three strips, each about 4 inches wide.

3. Spoon about 1/4 cup cheese mixture about 4 inches from end of each fillo strip. Fold fillo over fruit, forming a triangle; continue folding back and forth, as if folding a flag. Place turnover on greased cookie sheet; repeat with remaining fillo strips. Spray generously with cooking spray. Make 6 more turnovers using remaining ingredients.

4. Bake at 350 degrees until golden, about 15 minutes. Cool on wire rack; sprinkle with powdered sugar.

FILLO NAPOLEONS

An elegant French pastry in low-fat disguise. Fillo Wafers can be baked 2 to 3 weeks in advance and stored in an air-tight container.

8 servings

   2 cups blueberries
     Vanilla Pastry Cream (recipe follows)
     Raspberry Sauce (see p. 658)
     Fillo Wafers (recipe follows)
     Powdered sugar, as garnish

Per Serving
Calories: 273
% Calories from fat: 29
Fat (gm): 8.5
Saturated fat (gm): 1.5
Cholesterol (mg): 108
Sodium (mg): 90
Protein (gm): 6.1
Carbohydrate (gm): 41.4
Exchanges
Milk: 0.0
Vegetable: 0.0
Fruit: 1.0
Bread: 2.0
Meat: 0.0
Fat: 1.5

1. Fold blueberries into chilled Vanilla Pastry Cream. Drizzle about 2 tablespoons Raspberry Sauce on each serving plate. Place 1 Fillo Wafer on each plate; top each with about 1/2 cup pastry cream mixture. Top with remaining Fillo Wafers. Sprinkle with powdered sugar.

Vanilla Pastry Cream

makes about 2 cups

   2 cups fat-free milk
   4 egg yolks
  2/3 cup sugar
  1/4 cup plus 2 tablespoons all-purpose flour
   1 teaspoon vanilla

1. Heat milk to boiling in small saucepan. Combine egg yolks and sugar in medium bowl; stir in flour. Whisk milk into egg mixture gradually. Return mixture to saucepan. Heat to boiling; cook, whisking constantly, until smooth and thick. Stir in vanilla.

2. Transfer to bowl and cover surface with plastic wrap; cool. Refrigerate until chilled.

Fillo Wafers

makes 16

- 1/4 cup ground toasted almonds
- 1/4 cup sugar
- 4 sheets frozen fillo, thawed
- 2 tablespoons vegetable oil
- 1 egg white, beaten
  Butter-flavored vegetable cooking spray

1. Combine almonds and sugar in small bowl. Place 1 sheet fillo on counter (cover remaining fillo with damp kitchen towel to prevent drying); brush lightly with combined oil and egg white. Sprinkle with 1/2 of almond mixture. Top with second fillo sheet.

2. Cut prepared fillo into 8 rectangles, approximately 3 x 4 inches each. Place on parchment-lined cookie sheet; spray generously with cooking spray. Repeat with remaining ingredients. Cover with parchment and another cookie sheet to weight down the fillo during baking.

3. Bake at 350 degrees 10 minutes; remove top baking sheet and parchment and bake until golden brown, about 5 minutes longer. Cool on wire rack.

Variations: **Orange Napoleons**—Make Vanilla Pastry Cream as above, adding 2 tablespoons grated orange rind, and substituting 1/2 teaspoon orange extract for the vanilla; chill. Fold in 2 cups light whipped topping. Omit blueberries and Raspberry Sauce. Assemble as above; serve with Spiced Orange Slices (see p. 509).

Chocolate Caramel Napoleons—Sprinkle 8 Fillo Wafers with 1 teaspoon of sugar each. Broil 3 inches from heat until sugar is caramelized; cool and drizzle with 1 ounce melted semisweet baking chocolate. Substitute raspberries for blueberries; fold into Vanilla Pastry Cream. Assemble as above, using caramelized Fillo Wafers as tops.

CANDIED CREAM NAPOLEONS

Pastry cream, flavored with crushed Italian anisette cookies (such as Stella D'Oro) and candied fruit, is layered between crisp fillo wafers. Use red and green candied cherries for a perfect holiday dessert.

8 servings

Fillo Wafers (see p. 303)
Candied Fruit Cream (recipe follows)
Powdered Sugar, as garnish
Light whipped topping, as garnish
Sliced almonds, as garnish

Per Serving
Calories: 365
% Calories from fat: 24
Fat (gm): 9.8
Saturated fat (gm): 4.1
Cholesterol (mg): 119.3
Sodium (mg): 140
Protein (gm): 6.2
Carbohydrate (gm): 61.6
Exchanges
Milk: 0.0
Vegetable: 0.0
Fruit: 1.0
Bread: 3.5
Meat: 0.0
Fat: 1.5

1. Make Fillo Wafers, omitting almonds. Place 1 Fillo Wafer on each plate; spread with about $1/2$ cup Candied Fruit Cream. Top with second Fillo Wafer. Sprinkle with powdered sugar; garnish with whipped topping and sliced almonds.

Candied Fruit Cream

makes about $4^1/2$ cups

2 cups fat-free milk
4 egg yolks
$2/3$ cup sugar
$1/4$ cup plus 2 tablespoons all-purpose flour
$1/2$ teaspoon rum extract
$1/3$-$1/2$ cup golden raisins
$1/3$-$1/2$ cup chopped candied fruit
1 cup anisette cookie crumbs (about 8 cookies)
$2^2/3$ cups light whipped topping

1. Heat milk to boiling in small saucepan. Combine egg yolks and sugar in medium bowl; stir in flour. Whisk milk into egg mixture gradually. Return mixture to saucepan. Heat just to boiling, whisking constantly, until smooth and thick.

2. Transfer to bowl and cover surface with plastic wrap; cool. Refrigerate until chilled. Stir in rum extract, raisins, candied fruit, and cookie crumbs; fold in whipped topping.

Variations: **Key Lime Napoleons**—Substitute macadamia nuts for the almonds in the Fillo Wafers. Omit Candied Fruit Cream. Make double batch of Lemon Custard (see p. 104), substituting lime juice and rind for the lemon juice. Chill; fold in 2 cups light whipped topping. Assemble napoleons as above. Serve with fresh berries or diced tropical fruits.

Spiced Apple Napoleons—Omit Candied Fruit Cream. To make **Spiced Apple Filling:** Combine 1 cup sugar, 1¹/₂ cups apple cider, 1 teaspoon cinnamon, and ¹/₂ teaspoon allspice in large saucepan. Heat to boiling; reduce heat and simmer, uncovered, 10 minutes. Add 7 cups shredded, unpeeled tart cooking apples, and 1 cup dried cranberries or raisins. Simmer until liquid is almost gone, about 15 minutes. Assemble napoleons as above, spreading wafers with cooled Spiced Apple Filling.

BANANAS FOSTER CHEESECAKE TARTS

The flavors of the French Quarter, in flaky pastry cups!

6 servings

2 tablespoons margarine

¹/₄ cup packed light brown sugar

1 tablespoon rum *or* 1 teaspoon rum extract

1 banana, coarsely chopped

1 package (8 ounces) fat-free cream cheese, softened

¹/₄ cup sweetened flaked coconut

¹/₄ teaspoon coconut extract

Fillo Tart Shells (recipe follows)

Chopped toasted pecans, as garnish

Per Serving
Calories: 256
% Calories from fat: 27
Fat (gm): 7.7
Saturated fat (gm): 2.4
Cholesterol (mg): 3
Sodium (mg): 439
Protein (gm): 8.5
Carbohydrate (gm): 37
Exchanges
Milk: 0.0
Vegetable: 0.0
Fruit: 0.0
Bread: 2.5
Meat: 0.0
Fat: 1.5

1. Cook margarine, brown sugar, and rum in small saucepan over medium high heat until slightly thickened, 1 to 2 minutes. Remove from heat; stir in banana. Let cool to room temperature.

2. Beat cream cheese in bowl until smooth; mix in coconut and extract. Fold in banana mixture. Spoon mixture into Fillo Tart Shells; sprinkle with pecans. Refrigerate until chilled, 1 to 2 hours.

Fillo Tart Shells

makes 6

 12 sheets frozen fillo, thawed
     Butter-flavored vegetable cooking spray

1. Cut fillo into twenty-four 8-inch squares. Cover fillo with damp kitchen towel to prevent drying. Spray 4 squares of fillo with vegetable cooking spray; layer squares, turning each slightly so that corners are staggered. Carefully fit fillo into 8-ounce custard cup, shaping edges to form tart shell. Repeat with remaining fillo squares, lining 6 custard cups. Spray generously with cooking spray. Bake at 350 degrees until golden, about 20 minutes.

MERINGUE SHELLS

Crisp, delicate shells to hold your favorite fillings!

4 servings

 2 egg whites, room temperature
    Pinch salt
 1/4 teaspoon cider vinegar
 1/2 cup sugar

Per Serving
Calories: 105
% Calories from fat: 0
Fat (gm): 0
Saturated fat (gm): 0
Cholesterol (mg): 0
Sodium (mg): 28
Protein (gm): 1.8
Carbohydrate (gm): 25.2
Exchanges
Milk: 0.0
Vegetable: 0.0
Fruit: 0.0
Bread: 1.5
Meat: 0.0
Fat: 0.0

1. Beat egg whites, salt, and vinegar in medium bowl to soft peaks; beat to stiff peaks, adding sugar 2 tablespoons at a time. Continue beating until sugar is dissolved (mixture will feel smooth, with no graininess).

2. Spoon meringue into 4 mounds on parchment-lined cookie sheet; using back of spoon, shape meringue into "nests" with 1-inch sides. Or, shells can be shaped using large pastry bag with 1/2-inch round or star tip.

3. Bake at 225 degrees for 1 1/2 hours or until dry and crisp, but not brown. Cool on cookie sheet on wire rack.

Variations: **Mocha Meringue Shells**—Make meringue shells as in Step 1 above; fold in 2 tablespoons sifted unsweetened cocoa and 1 teaspoon powdered instant coffee. Shape and bake as above. Fill with Pastry Cream (see p. 268) and top each with ¹/₂ cup fresh fruit.

Meringue Fruit Puffs—Complete Step 1 above. Spoon meringue into 8 mounds on parchment-lined cookie sheet. (Do not make "nests.") Bake at 225 degrees until dry and crisp, about 1 hour. Cool on wire rack; hollow out bottoms of meringues with tip of sharp knife. Fill with Orange Chantilly (see p. 270); put cut sides of two shells together. Serve each with ¹/₂ cup sliced strawberries.

PEACH MELBA MERINGUES

Fresh peaches and raspberries are accented with two sauces in this elegant presentation.

4 servings

Buttermilk Crème Anglaise
(recipe follows)
Meringue Shells (see p. 306)
2 cups sliced peaches
1 cup raspberries
Raspberry Sauce (see p. 658)

Per Serving
Calories: 295
% Calories from fat: 11
Fat (gm): 3.6
Saturated fat (gm): 1.3
Cholesterol (mg): 109.7
Sodium (mg): 128
Protein (gm): 7.1
Carbohydrate (gm): 60.8
Exchanges
Milk: 0.0
Vegetable: 0.0
Fruit: 1.5
Bread: 2.5
Meat: 0.0
Fat: 0.5

1. Spoon Buttermilk Crème Anglaise onto serving plates; top with Meringue Shells. Fill with peaches and raspberries; drizzle with Raspberry Sauce.

Buttermilk Crème Anglaise

makes about $1^3/_4$ cups

- $1^1/_2$ cups low-fat buttermilk
- $^1/_3$ cup sugar
- 2 teaspoons cornstarch
- 2 egg yolks
- $^1/_2$ teaspoon vanilla extract

1. Mix buttermilk, sugar, cornstarch, and egg yolks in medium saucepan. Boil 1 minute, whisking constantly. Add vanilla. Chill.

VALENTINE VACHERIN

This dramatic French dessert is surprisingly easy to make—great for practicing with your pastry bag! Fill with Orange Chantilly or Pastry Cream with fresh berries, Strawberry Rhubarb Filling and whipped topping, Chocolate Mousse (pp. 270, 268, 77, 23) or scoops of your favorite sherbet.

6 servings

- 8 egg whites, room temperature
- $^1/_2$ teaspoon cream of tartar
- $^1/_2$ teaspoon salt
- $2^1/_2$ cups sugar
- 2 teaspoons vanilla

Per Serving
Calories: 350
% Calories from fat: 0
Fat (gm): 0
Saturated fat (gm): 0
Cholesterol (mg): 0
Sodium (mg): 268
Protein (gm): 4.7
Carbohydrate (gm): 84.4

Exchanges
Milk: 0.0
Vegetable: 0.0
Fruit: 0.0
Bread: 5.0
Meat: 0.0
Fat: 0.0

1. Beat egg whites, cream of tartar, and salt in large bowl to soft peaks; beat to stiff peaks, adding sugar 2 tablespoons at a time. Continue beating until sugar is dissolved (mixture will feel smooth, with no graininess). Beat in vanilla.

2. Trace two 11-inch heart shapes on parchment; place parchment on cookie sheets. Spoon $^2/_3$ meringue mixture into large pastry bag fitted with $^3/_4$-inch plain tip. On one sheet, pipe meringue mixture in heart shape, filling in heart outline completely to form a base layer; pipe two additional layers of meringue along edges, forming a rim. Pipe remaining meringue mixture into a lattice top, using second heart outline as a guide; outline heart with a shell border.

3. Bake at 200 degrees for about 2^1/$_2$ hours or until dry and crisp, but not brown. Cool on cookie sheets on wire racks. Carefully remove from parchment. Place Vacherin on serving platter. Fill with selected filling; cover with lattice top.

Variations: **Meringue Buttercream Torte**—Make meringue as in Step 1 above. Trace three 9-inch circles on parchment sheets. Pipe or spread meringue into flat disks to fill the circles. Bake and cool as in Step 3 above. Spread each disk with about ^{2}/$_3$ cup Chocolate Buttercream (see p. 74); stack layers and frost side with remaining buttercream. Garnish with chocolate shavings.

Strawberry Meringue Torte—Make meringue as in Step 1 above. Trace three 9-inch circles on parchment sheets. Pipe or spread meringue into flat disks to fill the circles. Bake and cool as in Step 3 above. Combine 1^1/$_2$ cups light whipped topping, 1^1/$_2$ cups low-fat custard-style strawberry yogurt, and 2 cups quartered strawberries. Place one meringue disk on platter; spread with half the strawberry mixture. Top with meringue disk and remaining strawberry mixture; top with remaining meringue disk. Dust with powdered sugar. Garnish with whole strawberries.

FIVE

Cookies

CHOCOLATE CHIP COOKIES

Chocolate chip are no doubt America's favorite cookie—you'll love these.

5 dozen cookies (1 per serving)

  8 tablespoons margarine, softened
  1 cup packed light brown sugar
$^1/_2$ cup granulated sugar
  1 egg
  1 teaspoon vanilla
$2^1/_2$ cups all-purpose flour
$^1/_2$ teaspoon baking soda
$^1/_2$ teaspoon salt
$^1/_3$ cup fat-free milk
$^1/_2$ package (12-ounce size) reduced-fat
    semisweet chocolate morsels

Per Serving
Calories: 66
% Calories from fat: 27
Fat (gm): 2
Saturated fat (gm): 0.7
Cholesterol (mg): 3.6
Sodium (mg): 70
Protein (gm): 0.8
Carbohydrate (gm): 11.2
Exchanges
Milk: 0.0
Vegetable: 0.0
Fruit: 0.0
Bread: 0.5
Meat: 0.0
Fat: 0.5

1. Beat margarine and sugars in medium bowl until fluffy; beat in egg and vanilla. Mix in combined flour, baking soda, and salt alternately with milk, beginning and ending with dry ingredients. Mix in chocolate morsels.

2. Drop cookies by tablespoonfuls onto greased cookie sheets. Bake at 375 degrees until browned, about 10 minutes. Cool on wire racks.

CHOCOLATE CHIP OATMEAL CHEWS

These cookies remain deliciously soft and chewy for days! Cookie sheets with a non-stick surface are best for this recipe.

5 dozen cookies (1 per serving)

6 tablespoons margarine, softened
1/2 cup unsweetened applesauce *or* Prune Puree (see p. 42)
1³/4 cups packed light brown sugar
1 egg
1 teaspoon vanilla
2 cups quick-cooking oats
1³/4 cups all-purpose flour
1 teaspoon baking soda
1/2 teaspoon salt
3/4 teaspoon ground cinnamon
1-1¹/2 cups reduced-fat semisweet chocolate morsels

Per Serving
Calories: 76
% Calories from fat: 26
Fat (gm): 2.4
Saturated fat (gm): 1.2
Cholesterol (mg): 3.5
Sodium (mg): 57
Protein (gm): 1.1
Carbohydrate (gm): 13.8
Exchanges
Milk: 0.0
Vegetable: 0.0
Fruit: 0.0
Bread: 1.0
Meat: 0.0
Fat: 0.0

1. Beat margarine and applesauce in large bowl until smooth; beat in brown sugar, egg, and vanilla. Mix in combined oats, flour, baking soda, salt, and cinnamon. Mix in chocolate morsels.

2. Drop dough by rounded teaspoons, 3 inches apart, onto greased cookie sheets. Bake at 350 degrees until lightly browned, about 10 minutes (cookies will spread and be very soft). Cool completely on wire racks before removing from pan.

RAISIN OATMEAL COOKIES

Moist and chewy, just the way they should be!

2¹/₂ dozen cookies (1 per serving)

   6 tablespoons margarine, softened
  ¹/₄ cup fat-free sour cream
   1 egg
   1 teaspoon vanilla
   1 cup packed light brown sugar
1¹/₂ cups quick-cooking oats
   1 cup all-purpose flour
  ¹/₂ teaspoon baking soda
  ¹/₄ teaspoon baking powder
   1 teaspoon ground cinnamon
  ¹/₂ cup raisins for baking

Per Serving
Calories: 90
% Calories from fat: 27
Fat (gm): 2.7
Saturated fat (gm): 0.5
Cholesterol (mg): 7.1
Sodium (mg): 57
Protein (gm): 1.5
Carbohydrate (gm): 15.3
Exchanges
Milk: 0.0
Vegetable: 0.0
Fruit: 0.0
Bread: 1.0
Meat: 0.0
Fat: 0.5

1. Mix margarine, sour cream, egg, and vanilla in large bowl; beat in brown sugar. Mix in combined oats, flour, baking soda, baking powder, and cinnamon. Mix in raisins.

2. Drop dough onto greased cookie sheets, using 2 tablespoons for each cookie. Bake at 350 degrees until browned, 12 to 15 minutes. Cool on wire racks.

Variation: **Cherry Chocolate Chip Oatmeal Cookies**—Make cookies as above, omitting raisins, mixing ¹/₃ cup each dried cherries and reduced-fat semisweet chocolate morsels and ¹/₄ cup chopped toasted almonds into the dough, and substituting almond extract for the vanilla.

SOFT MOLASSES COOKIES

Fill your home with the scent of spices when you bake these cookies.

3 dozen cookies (1 per serving)

- 1/4 cup vegetable shortening
- 1/2 cup packed dark brown sugar
- 1 egg yolk
- 1 1/4 cups all-purpose flour
- 2 teaspoons baking soda
- 1/2 teaspoon ground cinnamon
- 1/2 teaspoon ground ginger
- 1/4 teaspoon ground nutmeg
- 1/4 teaspoon salt
- 1/4 cup light molasses
- 2 tablespoons water
- 1/2 cup currants *or* chopped raisins

Per Serving
Calories: 53
% Calories from fat: 25
Fat (gm): 1.5
Saturated fat (gm): 0.4
Cholesterol (mg): 6
Sodium (mg): 89
Protein (gm): 0.6
Carbohydrate (gm): 9.3
Exchanges
Milk: 0.0
Vegetable: 0.0
Fruit: 0.0
Bread: 0.5
Meat: 0.0
Fat: 0.0

1. Beat shortening, brown sugar, and egg yolk in bowl until blended. Mix in combined flour, baking soda, spices, and salt alternately with combined molasses and water, beginning and ending with dry ingredients. Mix in currants.

2. Drop mixture by rounded teaspoons onto greased cookie sheets. Bake at 350 degrees until lightly browned on the bottoms (cookies will be soft), 8 to 10 minutes. Cool on wire racks.

CHOCOLATE CHEWS

Moist and chewy, these cookies will satisfy any chocolate craving.

4 dozen cookies (1 per serving)

1¹/₄ cups reduced-fat semisweet chocolate morsels, divided
4 tablespoons margarine, softened
1 cup packed light brown sugar
1 egg
2 egg whites
2 tablespoons light corn syrup
1 tablespoon water
1 teaspoon vanilla
1³/₄ cups all-purpose flour
³/₄ cup powdered sugar
¹/₃ cup unsweetened cocoa
2 teaspoons baking powder
¹/₄ teaspoon salt

Per Serving
Calories: 80
% Calories from fat: 26
Fat (gm): 2.6
Saturated fat (gm): 1.7
Cholesterol (mg): 4.4
Sodium (mg): 51
Protein (gm): 1
Carbohydrate (gm): 14.9
Exchanges
Milk: 0.0
Vegetable: 0.0
Fruit: 0.0
Bread: 1.0
Meat: 0.0
Fat: 0.5

1. Heat chocolate morsels and margarine in small saucepan until chocolate is melted; transfer to large bowl and cool several minutes. Mix in brown sugar, egg, egg whites, corn syrup, water, and vanilla; mix in combined remaining ingredients.

2. Drop dough by tablespoons, 2 inches apart, onto greased cookie sheets. Bake at 350 degrees until browned on the bottoms, 8 to 10 minutes. Cool on wire racks.

MINCEMEAT COOKIES

Great at any time of the year!

2¹/₂ dozen cookies (1 per serving)

10	tablespoons margarine, softened
²/₃	cup packed dark brown sugar
2	eggs
2	tablespoons brandy *or* water
2	cups all-purpose flour
¹/₂	teaspoon baking soda
1	teaspoon ground cinnamon
¹/₄	teaspoon ground nutmeg
¹/₄	teaspoon ground ginger
¹/₄	teaspoon salt
1¹/₂	cups prepared mincemeat

Per Serving
Calories: 126
% Calories from fat: 3.3
Fat (gm): 4.7
Saturated fat (gm): 1.2
Cholesterol (mg): 14.1
Sodium (mg): 133
Protein (gm): 1.4
Carbohydrate (gm): 19.9
Exchanges
Milk: 0.0
Vegetable: 0.0
Fruit: 0.0
Bread: 1.0
Meat: 0.0
Fat: 1.0

1. Beat margarine and brown sugar in large bowl until blended; beat in eggs and brandy. Mix in combined remaining ingredients, except mincemeat; mix in mincemeat.

2. Drop dough by tablespoons, 2 to 3 inches apart, onto greased cookie sheets. Bake at 375 degrees until browned on bottoms, 10 to 12 minutes. Cool on wire racks.

CRUNCHY FRUIT DROPS

Made with fortified cereal and dried fruit, these cookies offer a nutritional bonus.

4 dozen cookies (1 per serving)

²/₃	cup vegetable shortening
1	cup packed light brown sugar
1	egg
¹/₄	cup honey
1	teaspoon vanilla
1²/₃	cups all-purpose flour
1	teaspoon baking soda
¹/₄	teaspoon salt
³/₄	teaspoon ground cinnamon
1	cup chopped mixed dried fruit
4	cups fortified whole grain cereal flakes (Total)

Per Serving
Calories: 85
% Calories from fat: 31
Fat (gm): 2.9
Saturated fat (gm): 0.7
Cholesterol (mg): 4.4
Sodium (mg): 64
Protein (gm): 0.9
Carbohydrate (gm): 14.1
Exchanges
Milk: 0.0
Vegetable: 0.0
Fruit: 0.0
Bread: 1.0
Meat: 0.0
Fat: 0.5

1. Mix shortening, brown sugar, egg, honey, and vanilla in large bowl until well blended. Mix in combined flour, baking soda, salt, and cinnamon. Mix in dried fruit and cereal.

2. Drop dough by rounded teaspoons, 2 inches apart, onto greased cookie sheets. Bake at 375 degrees until lightly browned on bottoms, 8 to 10 minutes. Cool on wire racks.

GLACÉED FRUIT GEMS

One cup chopped mixed dried fruit can be substituted for the glacéed pine-apple and cherries.

5 dozen cookies (1 per serving)

1 cup golden raisins
$^1/_2$ cup chopped dates
$^1/_2$ cup glacéed pineapple wedges, chopped
$^1/_2$ cup glacéed cherries, chopped
$^1/_3$ cup apple juice
$^1/_2$ cup margarine, softened
1 cup packed light brown sugar
$^1/_2$ cup granulated sugar
2 eggs
$2^1/_2$ cups all-purpose flour
1 teaspoon baking powder
$^1/_2$ teaspoon salt
$^3/_4$ teaspoon ground cinnamon
$^1/_4$ teaspoon ground nutmeg
$^1/_4$ teaspoon ground ginger
$^1/_2$ cup coarsely chopped walnuts

Per Serving
Calories: 83
% Calories from fat: 25
Fat (gm): 2.3
Saturated fat (gm): 0.4
Cholesterol (mg): 7.1
Sodium (mg): 51
Protein (gm): 1.1
Carbohydrate (gm): 15
Exchanges
Milk: 0.0
Vegetable: 0.0
Fruit: 0.0
Bread: 1.0
Meat: 0.0
Fat: 0.5

1. Combine fruit and apple juice in large bowl; let stand 20 to 30 minutes. Beat margarine, sugars, and eggs until well blended in large bowl; beat 2 minutes at high speed. Mix in combined remaining ingredients; mix in fruit and juice.

2. Drop dough by teaspoons, 2 inches apart, onto greased cookie sheets. Bake at 350 degrees until lightly browned, 12 to 15 minutes. Cool on wire racks.

CRY BABIES

This low-fat version of Cry Babies is the best we've tasted!

4 dozen cookies (1 per serving)

$^1/_2$ cup vegetable shortening
$^1/_2$ cup sugar
$^1/_4$ cup light molasses
$^1/_4$ cup honey
  1 egg
  2 cups all-purpose flour
  1 teaspoon baking soda
$^1/_4$ teaspoon salt
$^1/_2$ teaspoon ground ginger
$^1/_2$ cup buttermilk
     Citrus Glaze (see p. 63)

Per Serving
Calories: 68
% Calories from fat: 28
Fat (gm): 2.2
Saturated fat (gm): 0.6
Cholesterol (mg): 4.5
Sodium (mg): 43
Protein (gm): 0.8
Carbohydrate (gm): 11.4
Exchanges
Milk: 0.0
Vegetable: 0.0
Fruit: 0.0
Bread: 1.0
Meat: 0.0
Fat: 0.0

1. Beat shortening, sugar, molasses, honey, and egg in large bowl until well blended. Mix in combined flour, baking soda, salt, and ginger alternately with buttermilk, beginning and ending with dry ingredients.

2. Drop dough by teaspoons, 2 inches apart, onto greased cookie sheets. Bake at 375 degrees until lightly browned and set enough that almost no imprint remains when touched with a finger, about 10 minutes. Cool on wire racks. Drizzle with Citrus Glaze.

CARAMEL APPLE COOKIES

A caramel flavored frosting tops these moist apple cookies.

5 dozen cookies (1 per serving)

$^1/_2$	cup vegetable shortening
$1^1/_4$	cups packed light brown sugar
1	egg
$^1/_2$	cup apple juice, divided
$2^1/_4$	cups all-purpose flour
1	teaspoon baking soda
$^1/_4$	teaspoon salt
1	teaspoon ground cinnamon
$^1/_4$	teaspoon ground cloves
1	cup shredded, peeled apples
$^3/_4$	cup golden raisins
	Caramel Frosting (recipe follows)
$2^1/_2$-5	tablespoons finely chopped walnuts

Per Serving
Calories: 81
% Calories from fat: 25
Fat (gm): 2.3
Saturated fat (gm): 0.5
Cholesterol (mg): 3.5
Sodium (mg): 39
Protein (gm): 0.8
Carbohydrate (gm): 14.5
Exchanges
Milk: 0.0
Vegetable: 0.0
Fruit: 0.0
Bread: 1.0
Meat: 0.0
Fat: 0.0

1. Beat shortening and brown sugar in medium bowl until blended; beat in egg. Mix in $^1/_4$ cup apple juice, combined flour, baking soda, salt, and spices; mix in remaining $^1/_4$ cup apple juice, apples, and raisins.

2. Drop dough by teaspoons, 2 inches apart, onto greased cookie sheets. Bake at 350 degrees until browned, 10 to 12 minutes. Cool on wire racks. Spread with Caramel Frosting and sprinkle each cookie with $^1/_8$ to $^1/_4$ teaspoon walnuts.

Caramel Frosting

makes about $^3/_4$ cup

2-3	tablespoons margarine, softened
$^1/_3$	cup packed light brown sugar
2	tablespoons water
$1^1/_2$	cups powdered sugar
2-4	tablespoons fat-free milk

1. Heat margarine, brown sugar, and water over medium-high heat in saucepan, stirring until sugar dissolves. Remove from heat; beat in powdered sugar and enough milk to make spreadable consistency; use immediately. If frosting begins to harden, return to low heat and stir in more milk.

CINNAMON DROPS

Cardamom can be substituted for cinnamon in these moist cookies. Flavor is best if cookies are stored in an airtight container with a piece of bread for one week.

4 dozen cookies (1 per serving)

   3 eggs
  ³/₄ cup granulated sugar
  ³/₄ cup packed light brown sugar
  2 cups all-purpose flour
  ¹/₄ teaspoon salt
 1-2 teaspoons ground cinnamon
      Non-pareils *or* other small candy
      decorations

Per Serving
Calories: 49
% Calories from fat: 6
Fat (gm): 0.4
Saturated fat (gm): 0.1
Cholesterol (mg): 13.3
Sodium (mg): 18
Protein (gm): 0.9
Carbohydrate (gm): 10.5
Exchanges
Milk: 0.0
Vegetable: 0.0
Fruit: 0.0
Bread: 0.5
Meat: 0.0
Fat: 0.0

1. Beat eggs in medium bowl until thick and lemon colored, about 5 minutes; beat in sugars, beating 1 to 2 minutes. Mix in flour, salt, and cinnamon.

2. Drop dough by teaspoons, 2 inches apart, onto greased cookie sheets. Sprinkle with non-pareils. Refrigerate, uncovered, until dough appears dry, at least 6 to 8 hours, no longer than 24 hours.

3. Bake cookies at 300 degrees until set and browned on the bottom, about 20 minutes. Cool on wire racks. Store at least 1 week in airtight container with piece of bread before eating.

BEANY BITES

No one will guess that the secret to these moist cookies is pureed beans—a nutritional bonus too!

4 dozen cookies (1 per serving)

 1 can (15 ounces) garbanzo beans, rinsed, drained
 1/4 cup orange juice
 1/2 cup margarine, softened
 2/3 cup packed light brown sugar
 1 egg
 1/2 teaspoon vanilla
 1 1/2 cups all-purpose flour
 2 teaspoons baking powder
 1/4 teaspoon salt
 1/2 teaspoon ground cinnamon
 1/4 teaspoon ground nutmeg
 1/3 cup fat-free milk
   Orange, *or* Lemon, Glaze
   (see pp. 47, 62)
   Ground nutmeg, as garnish

Per Serving
Calories: 59
% Calories from fat: 33
Fat (gm): 2.2
Saturated fat (gm): 0.4
Cholesterol (mg): 4.4
Sodium (mg): 93
Protein (gm): 1
Carbohydrate (gm): 9
Exchanges
Milk: 0.0
Vegetable: 0.0
Fruit: 0.0
Bread: 0.5
Meat: 0.0
Fat: 0.5

1. Process beans and orange juice in food processor or blender until smooth. Beat margarine, brown sugar, egg, and vanilla in large bowl until blended; mix in bean mixture. Mix in combined flour, baking powder, salt, and spices alternately with milk, beginning and ending with dry ingredients.

2. Drop dough by scant tablespoons onto greased cookie sheets. Bake at 375 degrees until lightly browned, 12 to 15 minutes. Cool on wire racks; drizzle with glaze and sprinkle very lightly with nutmeg.

FROSTED SUGAR COOKIES

Rich, crisp, and generously frosted, these cookies will flatter any holiday or special occasion.

6 dozen cookies (1 per serving)

10 tablespoons margarine, softened
2 tablespoons fat-free sour cream
1 egg
1 teaspoon lemon extract
1 cup powdered sugar
2 cups all-purpose flour
1 teaspoon baking powder
1/4 teaspoon salt
Sugar Frosting (recipe follows)
Ground cinnamon, as garnish

Per Serving
Calories: 48
% Calories from fat: 31
Fat (gm): 1.7
Saturated fat (gm): 0.3
Cholesterol (mg): 3
Sodium (mg): 45
Protein (gm): 0.5
Carbohydrate (gm): 7.7
Exchanges
Milk: 0.0
Vegetable: 0.0
Fruit: 0.0
Bread: 0.5
Meat: 0.0
Fat: 0.5

1. Beat margarine, sour cream, egg, and lemon extract in medium bowl until smooth; mix in sugar. Mix in combined flour, baking powder, and salt. Refrigerate dough 4 to 6 hours.

2. Roll dough on floured surface to 1/4 inch thickness. Cut cookies into decorative shapes with 2-inch cookie cutters. Bake at 375 degrees on greased cookie sheets until lightly browned, 8 to 10 minutes. Cool on wire racks.

3. Frost cookies with Sugar Frosting; sprinkle very lightly with cinnamon.

Sugar Frosting

makes about 3/4 cup

    2 cups powdered sugar
    1/2 teaspoon lemon extract *or* vanilla
    2-3 tablespoons fat-free milk

1. Mix powdered sugar, lemon extract, and enough milk to make spreadable consistency.

Variation: **Italian-Style Sugar Cookies**—Make cookie dough as above, substituting orange extract for the lemon extract, 1/2 cup yellow cornmeal for 1/2 cup of the flour, granulated sugar for the powdered sugar, and Citrus Glaze (see p. 63) for the Sugar Frosting. Garnish with pieces of glacéed orange rind, if desired.

CARDAMOM CUT-OUTS

Intensely flavored with cardamom, these delicate cookies are also delicious made with cinnamon. Cut into tiny 1-inch rounds for tea cookies.

5 dozen cookies (1 per serving)

1/2 cup vegetable shortening
1 cup plus 2 tablespoons sugar, divided
3 tablespoons fat-free milk
1 egg yolk
3/4 teaspoon ground cardamom, divided
2 cups all-purpose flour
1/4 teaspoon salt

Per Serving
Calories: 46
% Calories from fat: 34
Fat (gm): 1.7
Saturated fat (gm): 0.4
Cholesterol (mg): 3.6
Sodium (mg): 10
Protein (gm): 0.5
Carbohydrate (gm): 7
Exchanges
Milk: 0.0
Vegetable: 0.0
Fruit: 0.0
Bread: 0.5
Meat: 0.0
Fat: 0.0

1. Beat shortening, 1 cup sugar, milk, egg yolk, and 1/2 teaspoon cardamom in bowl until well blended; mix in flour and salt.

2. Roll 1/2 the dough on floured surface to scant 1/4 inch thickness; cut into rounds or decorative shapes with 2-inch cutter. Repeat with remaining dough.

3. Bake on greased baking sheets at 375 degrees until browned, 8 to 10 minutes. Combine remaining 2 tablespoons sugar and 1/4 teaspoon cardamom; sprinkle over warm cookies. Cool on wire racks.

TART LEMON DAINTIES

Enjoy the subtle lemon flavor of these tiny crisp cookies—perfect with coffee or tea.

4 dozen cookies (1 per serving)

4	tablespoons margarine, softened
1	cup granulated sugar
1	egg
3	tablespoons fat-free milk
2	teaspoons lemon juice
1	teaspoon finely grated lemon rind
2	cups all-purpose flour
1	teaspoon baking powder
1/4	teaspoon salt

Per Serving
Calories: 46
% Calories from fat: 22
Fat (gm): 1.1
Saturated fat (gm): 0.2
Cholesterol (mg): 4.4
Sodium (mg): 35
Protein (gm): 0.7
Carbohydrate (gm): 8.2
Exchanges
Milk: 0.0
Vegetable: 0.0
Fruit: 0.0
Bread: 0.5
Meat: 0.0
Fat: 0.0

1. Beat margarine, sugar, egg, milk, lemon juice, and lemon rind in bowl until blended. Mix in combined flour, baking powder, and salt. Refrigerate until chilled, 2 to 3 hours.

2. Roll 1/2 the dough on floured surface to 1/4 inch thickness; cut into rounds or decorative shapes with 1 1/2-inch cutter. Repeat with remaining dough.

3. Bake on greased cookie sheet at 375 degrees until lightly browned, 7 to 8 minutes. Cool on wire racks.

ORANGE MOLASSES CUT-OUTS

Frosted, decorated, and ready for any special occasion!

3 dozen cookies (1 per serving)

 10 tablespoons margarine, softened
 1/2 cup sugar
 1/2 cup light molasses
 1/4 cup hot strong coffee
3-3 1/2 cups all-purpose flour
  1 teaspoon ground cinnamon
  1 teaspoon ground ginger
  1 tablespoon finely grated orange rind
 1/4 teaspoon salt
    Snow Cap Frosting (recipe follows)
    Cake decorations, as garnish

Per Serving
Calories: 109
% Calories from fat: 27
Fat (gm): 3.2
Saturated fat (gm): 0.6
Cholesterol (mg): 0
Sodium (mg): 57
Protein (gm): 1.2
Carbohydrate (gm): 18.9
Exchanges
Milk: 0.0
Vegetable: 0.0
Fruit: 0.0
Bread: 1.0
Meat: 0.0
Fat: 0.5

1. Beat margarine and sugar in large bowl until fluffy. Beat in molasses and coffee. Mix in 3 cups flour and remaining ingredients, except Snow Cap Frosting and cake decorations. Knead dough on lightly floured surface until smooth, 2 to 3 minutes, adding more flour if needed. Refrigerate 2 to 3 hours.

2. Roll 1/2 the dough on floured surface to 1/4 inch thickness; cut into decorative shapes with 2- or 3-inch cutters. Repeat with remaining dough.

3. Bake on ungreased cookie sheets at 375 degrees until firm to touch and lightly browned, about 10 minutes. Cool on wire racks.

4. Spread Snow Cap Frosting on cookies, or pipe onto cookies using medium star tip; sprinkle with decorations.

Snow Cap Frosting

makes about 3/4 cup

  2 tablespoons no-cholesterol real egg
    product
1 1/2 cups powdered sugar
    Water

1. Beat egg product and powdered sugar with enough water to make thick, smooth frosting.

SCANDINAVIAN SPICE COOKIES

Serve these nicely spiced cookies with warm cider or a favorite coffee or tea.

3 dozen cookies (1 per serving)

5	tablespoons margarine, softened
1/4	cup packed dark brown sugar
1/4	cup fat-free milk
1/4	cup light molasses
1 1/2	cups all-purpose flour
1/2	teaspoon baking powder
1 1/2	teaspoons ground ginger
1	teaspoon ground allspice
1/8	teaspoon salt

Per Serving
Calories: 46
% Calories from fat: 32
Fat (gm): 1.6
Saturated fat (gm): 0.3
Cholesterol (mg): 0
Sodium (mg): 36
Protein (gm): 0.6
Carbohydrate (gm): 7.2
Exchanges
Milk: 0.0
Vegetable: 0.0
Fruit: 0.0
Bread: 0.5
Meat: 0.0
Fat: 0.0

1. Beat margarine, brown sugar, milk, and molasses in bowl until blended. Mix in combined remaining ingredients. Refrigerate until firm, 3 to 4 hours.

2. Roll 1/2 the dough on floured surface to 1/4 inch thickness. Cut into rounds or decorative shapes with 2 1/2-inch cutter. Place 1 inch apart on greased cookie sheets. Repeat with remaining dough.

3. Bake at 375 degrees until lightly browned, 8 to 10 minutes. Cool on wire racks.

LEMON SLICES

Keep this slice-and-bake cookie dough in the refrigerator or freezer for fresh-baked cookies at any time.

4 dozen cookies (1 per serving)

₁/2 cup margarine, softened
1 cup granulated sugar
1 egg
1 tablespoon finely grated lemon rind
2 cups all-purpose flour
1/4 teaspoon salt
Lemon Glaze (see p. 62)

Per Serving
Calories: 59
% Calories from fat: 31
Fat (gm): 2
Saturated fat (gm): 0.4
Cholesterol (mg): 4.4
Sodium (mg): 36
Protein (gm): 0.7
Carbohydrate (gm): 9.5
Exchanges
Milk: 0.0
Vegetable: 0.0
Fruit: 0.0
Bread: 0.5
Meat: 0.0
Fat: 0.5

1. Beat margarine, sugar, egg, and lemon rind in medium bowl until well blended. Mix in flour and salt. Roll dough into 12-inch log and refrigerate 3 to 4 hours.

2. Cut dough into 1/4-inch slices. Bake at 350 degrees on greased cookie sheets until beginning to brown at the edges, about 10 minutes. Cool on wire racks. Drizzle with Lemon Glaze.

Variation: **Maple Spice Slices**—Make cookies as above, substituting 1/2 cup packed light brown sugar for 1/2 cup of the granulated sugar, omitting lemon rind, and adding 1/2 teaspoon maple extract and 1/2 teaspoon ground cinnamon. Substitute Maple Glaze (see p. 60) for the Lemon Glaze.

GINGERSNAPPERS

Dry mustard and black pepper are the "secret" ingredients that add the zesty flavor to these ginger favorites.

4¹/₂ dozen cookies (1 per serving)

9 tablespoons margarine, softened
³/₄ cup packed light brown sugar
¹/₄ cup light molasses
1 egg
2 cups all-purpose flour
1 teaspoon baking soda
1 teaspoon ground cinnamon
1 teaspoon ground ginger
¹/₂ teaspoon ground cloves
¹/₂ teaspoon dry mustard
¹/₄ teaspoon ground black pepper
3 tablespoons granulated sugar

Per Serving
Calories: 54
% Calories from fat: 34
Fat (gm): 2
Saturated fat (gm): 0.4
Cholesterol (mg): 4
Sodium (mg): 49
Protein (gm): 0.6
Carbohydrate (gm): 8.3
Exchanges
Milk: 0.0
Vegetable: 0.0
Fruit: 0.0
Bread: 0.5
Meat: 0.0
Fat: 0.5

1. Beat margarine and brown sugar until fluffy in large bowl; mix in molasses and egg. Mix in combined flour, baking soda, spices, dry mustard, and pepper. Refrigerate, covered, 2 to 3 hours.

2. Measure granulated sugar into pie pan or shallow bowl. Drop dough by teaspoons into sugar and roll into balls (dough will be sticky). Place cookies on greased cookie sheets; flatten with fork or bottom of glass. Bake at 350 degrees until firm to touch, 8 to 10 minutes. Cool on wire racks.

KRINGLA

Most often considered a holiday cookie, these lovely cookies are good at any time of the year. Sprinkle cookies with powdered sugar instead of frosting with Snow Cap Frosting, if desired.

4 dozen cookies (1 per serving)

$1/2$ cup fat-free sour cream

4 tablespoons margarine, softened

$1/2$ cup sugar

$1^3/4$ cups all-purpose flour

$1/2$ teaspoon baking powder

$1/4$ teaspoon baking soda

$1/2$ teaspoon salt

$1/2$ teaspoon anise seeds, crushed

$1/4$ teaspoon ground nutmeg

Snow Cap Frosting (see p. 327)

Per Serving
Calories: 51
% Calories from fat: 17
Fat (gm): 0.1
Saturated fat (gm): 0.2
Cholesterol (mg): 0
Sodium (mg): 50
Protein (gm): 0.7
Carbohydrate (gm): 9.9
Exchanges
Milk: 0.0
Vegetable: 0.0
Fruit: 0.0
Bread: 0.5
Meat: 0.0
Fat: 0.0

1. Beat sour cream and margarine until smooth in medium bowl; beat in sugar. Mix in combined remaining ingredients, except Snow Cap Frosting, until well blended. Refrigerate dough 2 to 3 hours.

2. Roll 1 tablespoon dough on floured surface to 12-inch rope; cut into 3 equal pieces. Shape each piece on ungreased cookie sheet into circle, overlapping ends at the top to form a "knot." Repeat with remaining dough.

3. Bake at 350 degrees until cookies are lightly browned on the bottoms, about 10 minutes. Cool on wire racks. Frost with Snow Cap Frosting.

SWEET FENNEL COOKIES

The flavor of the cookies mellows if stored for about 1 week in an airtight container with a slice of bread.

5 dozen cookies (1 per serving)

3 eggs
1¹/₂ cups sugar
2 cups all-purpose flour
¹/₄ teaspoon salt
1 tablespoon fennel *or* anise seeds, lightly crushed

Per Serving
Calories: 39
% Calories from fat: 7
Fat (gm): 0.3
Saturated fat (gm): 0
Cholesterol (mg): 10.6
Sodium (mg): 13
Protein (gm): 0.8
Carbohydrate (gm): 8.3
Exchanges
Milk: 0.0
Vegetable: 0.0
Fruit: 0.0
Bread: 0.5
Meat: 0.0
Fat: 0.0

1. Beat eggs and sugar in large bowl until mixture is thick and lemon colored, about 5 minutes. Mix in combined flour, salt, and fennel seeds gradually, adding ¹/₄ cup mixture at a time. Beat 3 minutes at high speed after last addition.

2. Using large pastry bag with ¹/₂-inch plain tip, pipe dough into 1¹/₂-inch rounds on greased cookie sheets. Refrigerate, uncovered, until dough appears dry, at least 6 hours, no longer than 24 hours.

3. Bake cookies at 300 degrees until firm, about 20 minutes (cookies will separate into 2 layers while baking). Cool on wire racks. Store at least 1 week in airtight container with piece of bread before eating.

CHOCOLATE CRINKLES

These cookies have crinkled, crisp tops and are soft inside.

4¹/₂ dozen cookies (1 per serving)

8 tablespoons margarine, softened
1¹/₄ cups packed light brown sugar
¹/₃ cup reduced-fat sour cream
1 egg
1-2 ounces semisweet baking chocolate, melted
1 teaspoon vanilla
1³/₄ cups all-purpose flour
³/₄ cup unsweetened cocoa
1 teaspoon baking soda
1 teaspoon ground cinnamon
¹/₄ cup granulated sugar

Per Serving
Calories: 60
% Calories from fat: 31
Fat (gm): 2.1
Saturated fat (gm): 0.6
Cholesterol (mg): 4.5
Sodium (mg): 49
Protein (gm): 0.8
Carbohydrate (gm): 9.8
Exchanges
Milk: 0.0
Vegetable: 0.0
Fruit: 0.0
Bread: 0.5
Meat: 0.0
Fat: 0.5

1. Beat margarine and brown sugar in large bowl until fluffy. Mix in sour cream, egg, chocolate, and vanilla. Mix in combined flour, cocoa, baking soda, and cinnamon. Refrigerate, covered, 2 to 3 hours.

2. Measure granulated sugar into pie pan or shallow bowl. Drop dough by tablespoons into sugar and roll into balls. (Dough will be soft.) Place cookies on greased cookie sheets; flatten with fork or bottom of glass. Bake at 350 degrees until firm to touch, 10 to 12 minutes. Cool on wire racks.

PEANUT BUTTER COOKIES

Yes, peanut butter cookies can be low in fat! Store in an airtight container 2 to 3 days for flavor and texture to mellow.

4 dozen cookies (1 per serving)

- 1/2 cup reduced-fat peanut butter
- 1/4 cup vegetable shortening
- 3/4 cup packed light brown sugar
- 1 egg
- 2-3 tablespoons fat-free milk
- 1 tablespoon honey
- 1 teaspoon vanilla
- 1 2/3 cups all-purpose flour
- 1 teaspoon baking soda
- 1/4 teaspoon salt

Per Serving
Calories: 57
% Calories from fat: 34
Fat (gm): 2.2
Saturated fat (gm): 0.5
Cholesterol (mg): 4.4
Sodium (mg): 58
Protein (gm): 1.4
Carbohydrate (gm): 8.1
Exchanges
Milk: 0.0
Vegetable: 0.0
Fruit: 0.0
Bread: 0.5
Meat: 0.0
Fat: 0.5

1. Beat peanut butter and shortening until blended; beat in brown sugar. Beat in egg, milk, honey, and vanilla. Mix in combined flour, baking soda, and salt.

2. Roll dough into 48 balls and place on greased cookie sheets; flatten with fork dipped in sugar. Bake at 350 degrees just until browned, about 10 minutes. Cool on wire racks.

TUSCAN CORNMEAL COOKIES

Cornmeal adds a delightful crispness to these sweet morsels.

4 dozen cookies (1 per serving)

- 6 tablespoons margarine, softened
- 2/3 cup packed light brown sugar
- 1/2 cup granulated sugar
- 1 egg
- 1 teaspoon vanilla
- 1 1/3 cups all-purpose flour
- 2/3 cup yellow, *or* white, cornmeal
- 1/4 cup finely ground toasted almonds
- 1 teaspoon baking powder
- 1/4 teaspoon ground nutmeg

Per Serving
Calories: 58
% Calories from fat: 30
Fat (gm): 1.9
Saturated fat (gm): 0.4
Cholesterol (mg): 4.4
Sodium (mg): 30
Protein (gm): 0.8
Carbohydrate (gm): 9.1
Exchanges
Milk: 0.0
Vegetable: 0.0
Fruit: 0.0
Bread: 0.5
Meat: 0.0
Fat: 0.5

1. Beat margarine in large bowl until fluffy; mix in brown sugar, granulated sugar, egg, and vanilla, blending well. Mix in combined remaining ingredients. Refrigerate dough 2 to 3 hours (dough will be soft and easy to handle).

2. Roll dough into 48 balls and place 2 to 3 inches apart on greased cookie sheets; flatten cookies with fork dipped in sugar. Bake at 350 degrees until lightly browned, 10 to 12 minutes. Cool on wire racks.

NUTMEG SUGAR COOKIES

Moist and slightly chewy—please don't overbake! Ground cinnamon can be substituted for the nutmeg if you like.

3 dozen cookies (1 per serving)

6	tablespoons margarine, softened
2/3	cup sugar
1	egg
1 1/2	tablespoons lemon juice
1 1/2	cups all-purpose flour
1/2	teaspoon baking soda
1/4	teaspoon ground nutmeg
	Granulated sugar

Per Serving
Calories: 53
% Calories from fat: 35
Fat (gm): 2.1
Saturated fat (gm): 0.4
Cholesterol (mg): 5.9
Sodium (mg): 42
Protein (gm): 0.7
Carbohydrate (gm): 7.8
Exchanges
Milk: 0.0
Vegetable: 0.0
Fruit: 0.0
Bread: 0.5
Meat: 0.0
Fat: 0.5

1. Beat margarine in large bowl until fluffy. Beat in 2/3 cup sugar, egg, and lemon juice. Mix in combined flour, baking soda, and nutmeg.

2. Roll dough into 3/4-inch balls; roll balls in granulated sugar and place on ungreased cookie sheets. Flatten to 2 inch diameter with bottom of glass.

3. Bake at 375 degrees until beginning to brown, about 10 minutes. Cool on wire racks.

ORANGE GRANOLA NUGGETS

Pieces of dried fruit or a few slivered almonds can be substituted for the glacéed cherries.

3 dozen cookies (1 per serving)

  6 tablespoons margarine, softened
 1/3 cup packed light brown sugar
  1 egg white
  1 tablespoon finely grated orange rind
  1 tablespoon finely grated lemon rind
  2 teaspoons lemon juice
 1/4 teaspoon salt
  1 cup all-purpose flour
  1 cup reduced-fat granola, divided
  1 egg white
  2 tablespoons water
 18 glacéed cherries, cut into halves

Per Serving
Calories: 55
% Calories from fat: 34
Fat (gm): 2.1
Saturated fat (gm): 0.4
Cholesterol (mg): 0
Sodium (mg): 50
Protein (gm): 0.9
Carbohydrate (gm): 8.3
Exchanges
Milk: 0.0
Vegetable: 0.0
Fruit: 0.0
Bread: 0.5
Meat: 0.0
Fat: 0.5

1. Beat margarine, brown sugar, egg white, citrus rinds, lemon juice, and salt until well blended; beat at medium speed 2 minutes. Mix in flour and 1/2 cup granola.

2. Beat egg white and water until foamy in shallow bowl. Roll dough into 1/2-inch balls; roll in egg white mixture; roll in remaining 1/2 cup granola and place on greased cookie sheet. Press cherry halves in tops of cookies.

3. Bake at 325 degrees until cookies are lightly browned, 25 to 30 minutes. Cool on wire racks.

JAM BUTTONS

Use several flavors and colors of jam for these jewel-tone cookies.

4 dozen cookies (1 per serving)

  8 tablespoons margarine, softened

$1/2$ cup sugar

  1 egg

  1 teaspoon vanilla

  2 cups all-purpose flour

$1/4$ cup cornstarch

$1/2$ teaspoon baking powder

$1/4$ teaspoon baking soda

  2 generous pinches ground nutmeg

$1/4$ teaspoon salt

$1/2$ cup jam (apricot, peach, strawberry, raspberry, etc.)

    Powdered sugar, as garnish

Per Serving
Calories: 54
% Calories from fat: 33
Fat (gm): 2
Saturated fat (gm): 0.4
Cholesterol (mg): 4.4
Sodium (mg): 49
Protein (gm): 0.7
Carbohydrate (gm): 8.4
Exchanges
Milk: 0.0
Vegetable: 0.0
Fruit: 0.0
Bread: 0.5
Meat: 0.0
Fat: 0.5

1. Beat margarine and sugar in large bowl until blended; beat in egg and vanilla. Mix in combined remaining ingredients, except jam and powdered sugar. Refrigerate dough 3 to 4 hours (dough will be soft and easy to handle).

2. Roll dough into 48 balls and place 2 inches apart on greased cookie sheets. Make deep indentation in center of each cookie with thumb. Bake at 375 degrees until lightly browned, about 10 minutes. If indentations have puffed up, press down gently with spoon. Cool on wire racks. Fill center of each cookie with about $1/2$ teaspoon jam. Sprinkle with powdered sugar before serving.

ORANGE MARMALADE COOKIES

Peach or apricot preserves or spreadable fruit can be substituted for the orange marmalade.

5 dozen cookies (1 per serving)

9 tablespoons vegetable shortening
1 cup orange marmalade
1 egg
1 teaspoon vanilla
2 cups all-purpose flour
1 teaspoon baking soda
1/2 teaspoon salt
1/2 cup currants *or* chopped raisins

Per Serving
Calories: 50
% Calories from fat: 34
Fat (gm): 1.9
Saturated fat (gm): 0.5
Cholesterol (mg): 3.5
Sodium (mg): 42
Protein (gm): 0.6
Carbohydrate (gm): 7.8
Exchanges
Milk: 0.0
Vegetable: 0.0
Fruit: 0.0
Bread: 0.5
Meat: 0.0
Fat: 0.5

1. Beat shortening and marmalade in large bowl until blended; beat in egg and vanilla. Mix in remaining ingredients.

2. Drop dough by tablespoons, 2 to 3 inches apart, on ungreased cookie sheets. Bake at 375 degrees until browned, 10 to 12 minutes. Cool on wire racks.

JAM PINWHEELS

This cookie dough can be kept in the freezer, ready to slice and bake whenever warm cookies are needed.

4 dozen cookies (1 per person)

8 tablespoons margarine, softened
1 cup granulated sugar
1/2 cup packed light brown sugar
1 egg
1 teaspoon vanilla
3 cups all-purpose flour
3/4 teaspoon baking powder
1/4 teaspoon baking soda
1/4 teaspoon salt
Jam Filling (recipe follows)

Per Serving
Calories: 93
% Calories from fat: 19
Fat (gm): 2.1
Saturated fat (gm): 0.4
Cholesterol (mg): 4.4
Sodium (mg): 54
Protein (gm): 1.1
Carbohydrate (gm): 18
Exchanges
Milk: 0.0
Vegetable: 0.0
Fruit: 0.0
Bread: 1.0
Meat: 0.0
Fat: 0.5

1. Beat margarine and sugars in large bowl until blended; beat in egg and vanilla. Mix in combined flour, baking powder, baking soda, and salt. Refrigerate 3 to 4 hours.

2. Press ¹/₂ the dough into 6-inch square on waxed paper; cover with second sheet of waxed paper and roll dough into 10-inch square. Slide onto cookie sheet and refrigerate 30 minutes; repeat with remaining dough.

3. Remove top sheet of waxed paper from dough. Spread ¹/₂ the Jam Filling on each piece of dough, spreading to within ¹/₂ inch of the edges. Carefully roll up dough, wrap in plastic wrap, and freeze 3 to 4 hours.

4. Slice each roll into 24 cookies and place 1 inch apart on greased cookie sheets. Bake at 350 degrees until lightly browned, 10 to 12 minutes. Cool on wire racks.

Jam Filling

makes about 1¹/₂ cups

- 1 cup (total) peach, apricot, *or* strawberry preserves
- ³/₄ cup very finely chopped dried apricots *or* raisins
- 2 tablespoons water

1. Heat all ingredients to boiling in small saucepan; reduce heat to medium-low and simmer 8 to 10 minutes, stirring occasionally. Cool completely.

Variation: **Date Pinwheels**—Make cookie dough as above, adding ¹/₂ teaspoon ground cinnamon and 1 tablespoon finely chopped orange rind; omit Jam Filling. To make **Orange-Date Filling:** Heat 1¹/₂ cups chopped dates, ¹/₃ cup orange marmalade, ¹/₃ cup orange juice, and ¹/₂ teaspoon cinnamon to boiling in medium saucepan; reduce heat and simmer, stirring frequently, until thickened, 2 to 3 minutes. Cool. Complete cookies as above.

SPICED RAISIN-RUM COOKIES

Generously flavored with spices and rum, these glazed raisin cookies will soon disappear from your cookie jar.

4 dozen cookies (1 per serving)

Per Serving
Calories: 126
% Calories from fat: 16
Fat (gm): 2.2
Saturated fat (gm): 0.6
Cholesterol (mg): 4.4
Sodium (mg): 83
Protein (gm): 1.4
Carbohydrate (gm): 25.6
Exchanges
Milk: 0.0
Vegetable: 0.0
Fruit: 0.0
Bread: 1.5
Meat: 0.0
Fat: 0.5

 1/2 cup vegetable shortening
   1 cup packed light brown sugar
 1/2 cup light molasses
   1 egg
   2 tablespoons dark rum *or* 1 teaspoon rum extract
   1 tablespoon vanilla
   2 cups golden raisins
   2 cups dark raisins
   3 cups all-purpose flour
   2 teaspoons baking soda
 1/2 teaspoon salt
 1/2 teaspoon ground cinnamon
 1/2 teaspoon ground nutmeg
 1/8 teaspoon ground cloves
 1/2 cup Rum Glaze (double recipe) (see p. 43)

1. Beat shortening, brown sugar, molasses, egg, rum, and vanilla in large bowl until well blended. Process raisins in food processor until very finely chopped, using pulse technique, or chop finely by hand; mix into shortening mixture. Mix in combined flour, baking soda, salt, and spices. Refrigerate dough 2 to 3 hours.

2. Shape dough into "logs" about 2 inches long, using 1 tablespoon for each. Bake cookies, 2 inches apart, on greased cookie sheets at 375 degrees until browned, about 10 minutes. Cool on wire racks. Drizzle with Rum Glaze.

FRUIT NEWTONS

Chewy, dense, and oh, so good! A fruit bar at its best.

2¹/₂ dozen bars (1 per serving)

³/₄ cup dried figs, chopped
³/₄ cup dried pears, chopped
¹/₂ cup water
2 tablespoons packed light brown sugar
5 tablespoons margarine, softened
2 tablespoons granulated sugar
3 egg whites
1 teaspoon vanilla
1³/₄ cups all-purpose flour
¹/₂ teaspoon baking soda
¹/₄ teaspoon salt
2 tablespoons 2% reduced-fat milk

Per Serving
Calories: 77
% Calories from fat: 23
Fat (gm): 2.1
Saturated fat (gm): 0.4
Cholesterol (mg): 0.1
Sodium (mg): 70
Protein (gm): 1.4
Carbohydrate (gm): 13.8
Exchanges
Milk: 0.0
Vegetable: 0.0
Fruit: 1.0
Bread: 0.0
Meat: 0.0
Fat: 0.5

1. Heat figs, pears, water, and brown sugar to boiling in small saucepan. Reduce heat and simmer, uncovered, until fruit is softened and mixture is thick, about 20 minutes. Process mixture in food processor or blender until smooth. Cool.

2. Beat margarine and granulated sugar in medium bowl until fluffy; beat in egg whites and vanilla. Mix in combined flour, baking soda, and salt. Shape dough into 4 logs, each about 5 x 2 x ¹/₂ inches. Wrap each in plastic wrap and refrigerate about 1 hour.

3. Roll 1 log on floured surface into 12 x 5-inch rectangle. Spread ¹/₄ of the fruit mixture in a 1-inch strip down center of dough. Fold sides of dough over the filling, pressing edges to seal. Cut log in half and place, seam side down, on greased cookie sheet. Repeat with remaining dough logs and filling. Brush top of logs with milk.

4. Bake at 400 degrees until lightly browned, about 12 minutes. Cool on wire racks; cut into 1¹/₂-inch bars.

Variation: **Date and Prune Newtons**—Make cookie filling as above, substituting dates and orange-essence pitted prunes for the figs and pears; increase brown sugar to ¹/₄ cup and add 1 tablespoon finely grated orange rind. Complete recipe as above. Dust cooled cookies with powdered sugar.

FRUIT-FILLED COOKIES

Fruit preserves, raisins, walnuts, and sweet spices combine in a fragrant filling for these wonderful cookies. Store in an airtight tin.

4 dozen cookies (1 per serving)

6	tablespoons vegetable shortening
3/4	cup granulated sugar
1	egg
1	egg yolk
2	teaspoons vanilla
2	cups all-purpose flour
1	tablespoon baking powder
1/8	teaspoon salt
	Fruit Filling (recipe follows)
	Powdered sugar, as garnish

Per Serving
Calories: 63
% Calories from fat: 32
Fat (gm): 2.3
Saturated fat (gm): 0.5
Cholesterol (mg): 8.9
Sodium (mg): 39
Protein (gm): 1
Carbohydrate (gm): 9.7
Exchanges
Milk: 0.0
Vegetable: 0.0
Fruit: 0.0
Bread: 0.5
Meat: 0.0
Fat: 0.5

1. Beat shortening and sugar in bowl until blended; beat in egg, egg yolk, and vanilla. Mix in combined flour, baking powder, and salt (dough will be stiff).

2. Roll 1/2 the dough on floured surface into 12 x 8-inch rectangle; cut into 48 pieces, 1 x 2 inches. Place scant teaspoon Fruit Filling in center of 24 pieces of dough; top with remaining pieces of dough and press edges together to seal. Repeat with remaining dough and Fruit Filling.

3. Bake cookies on ungreased cookie sheets until browned, 10 to 12 minutes. Cool on wire racks. Sprinkle with powdered sugar.

Fruit Filling

makes about 1 cup

1/3 cup peach, *or* strawberry, preserves
1/3 cup golden raisins
1/3 cup finely chopped walnuts
1/2 teaspoon ground cinnamon
1/8 teaspoon ground nutmeg

1. Mix all ingredients.

MINCEMEAT MOONS

Holiday perfect—enjoy the date or jam variations year-round.

3 dozen cookies (1 per serving)

$^1/_2$ cup margarine, softened	
$^1/_2$ cup granulated sugar	
$^1/_2$ cup packed light brown sugar	
$^1/_2$ cup fat-free milk	
1 egg	
1 teaspoon vanilla	
$3^1/_2$ cups all-purpose flour	
1 tablespoon baking powder	
$^1/_4$ teaspoon salt	
Mince Filling (recipe follows)	

Per Serving
Calories: 125
% Calories from fat: 22
Fat (gm): 3.2
Saturated fat (gm): 0.8
Cholesterol (mg): 6
Sodium (mg): 126
Protein (gm): 1.7
Carbohydrate (gm): 23.1
Exchanges
Milk: 0.0
Vegetable: 0.0
Fruit: 0.0
Bread: 1.5
Meat: 0.0
Fat: 0.5

1. Beat margarine and sugars until blended in large bowl; beat in milk, egg, and vanilla. Mix in combined flour, baking powder, and salt. Refrigerate dough 4 to 5 hours.

2. Roll $^1/_3$ the dough on floured surface to scant $^1/_8$ inch thickness; cut into $2^1/_2$-inch rounds. Cut small crescent moons or other decorative shapes in centers of half the rounds, using tiny cutters or sharp knife. Spoon about 1 tablespoon filling on each of the remaining rounds; top with decorative rounds and seal edges with tines of fork. Repeat with remaining dough and filling.

3. Bake at 375 degrees until beginning to brown at the edges, 10 to 12 minutes. Cool on wire racks.

Mince Filling

makes about 2 cups

- $1^1/_2$ cups prepared mincemeat
- 1 large apple, peeled, cored, finely chopped
- 1 tablespoon grated orange, *or* lemon, rind
- 1 teaspoon ground cinnamon

1. Mix all ingredients.

Variations: **Date Moons**—Make cookie dough as above; omit Mince Filling. To make **Date Filling:** Heat 2 cups chopped dates, 1 cup water, $^1/_4$ cup packed light brown sugar, 1 tablespoon flour, and 1 teaspoon lemon juice to boiling in saucepan; reduce heat and simmer, uncovered, until thickened, about 5 minutes. Cool. Complete cookies as above.

Jam Ravioli Cookies—Make cookies, substituting granulated sugar for the brown sugar and butter extract for the vanilla and adding ¹/₂ teaspoon ground cinnamon. Substitute 2 cups desired flavor jam for the Mince Filling. Brush tops of cookies with fat-free milk and sprinkle generously with sugar; bake as above.

FRUIT AND COCONUT BITES

Keep these healthy no-bake cookies in an airtight tin to retain moistness.

5 dozen cookies (1 per serving)

2	cups mixed dried fruit *or* fruit bits
1	cup golden raisins
1	cup dark raisins
³/₄	cup flaked coconut
¹/₂	cup wheat germ *or* crushed reduced-fat granola
2	teaspoons finely grated orange, *or* lemon, rind
2-3	tablespoons honey
2-3	tablespoons orange juice
¹/₂	cup chopped almonds
¹/₂	teaspoon salt
	Crushed reduced-fat granola *or* toasted coconut

Per Serving
Calories: 47
% Calories from fat: 16
Fat (gm): 0.9
Saturated fat (gm): 0.3
Cholesterol (mg): 0
Sodium (mg): 21
Protein (gm): 0.8
Carbohydrate (gm): 9.2
Exchanges
Milk: 0.0
Vegetable: 0.0
Fruit: 0.5
Bread: 0.0
Meat: 0.0
Fat: 0.0

1. Process dried fruit, raisins, and coconut in food processor until very finely chopped, using pulse technique, or chop fruit and raisins very finely by hand. Combine fruit with remaining ingredients, except granola, mixing until well blended.

2. Roll fruit mixture into scant 1-inch balls; roll in granola or coconut. Store in airtight containers.

TURKISH COOKIES

Warm cookies are dipped in a sweet sugar syrup before cooling—irresistible!

3 dozen cookies (1 per serving)

14 tablespoons margarine, softened
1 cup powdered sugar
3 eggs
3$^1/_2$ cups all-purpose flour
1 tablespoon baking powder
$^1/_4$ teaspoon salt
18 blanched whole almonds, halved
    Lemon Scented Syrup (recipe follows)

Per Serving
Calories: 139
% Calories from fat: 34
Fat (gm): 5.3
Saturated fat (gm): 1.1
Cholesterol (mg): 17.7
Sodium (mg): 87
Protein (gm): 2
Carbohydrate (gm): 21.2
Exchanges
Milk: 0.0
Vegetable: 0.0
Fruit: 0.0
Bread: 1.5
Meat: 0.0
Fat: 1.0

1. Beat margarine and powdered sugar in bowl until fluffy; beat in eggs. Mix in combined flour, baking powder, and salt. Refrigerate 2 hours.

2. Shape dough into scant 1$^1/_2$-inch balls and place 2 inches apart on greased cookie sheets. Press an almond half into each cookie; brush tops of cookies lightly with Lemon Scented Syrup.

3. Bake at 350 degrees until browned, 15 to 20 minutes. Dip warm cookies in remaining Lemon Scented Syrup. Cool on wire racks.

Lemon Scented Syrup

makes about 1$^1/_2$ cups

1$^2/_3$ cups sugar
1 cup water
2 teaspoons lemon juice

1. Heat all ingredients to boiling; reduce heat and simmer 10 minutes, stirring occasionally.

GRANOLA LACE COOKIES

When cookies are still warm, they can be rolled or folded over the handle of a wooden spoon, or "pinched" in the center to form bow shapes; see recipe for Almond Tuiles, p. 347, for shaping directions. Bake only 4 to 6 cookies at a time as they must be handled quickly and carefully before cooling.

4 dozen cookies (1 per serving)

4	tablespoons margarine, softened
1/4	cup granulated sugar
1/4	cup packed light brown sugar
2	egg whites
1	tablespoon orange juice
1/4-1/2	teaspoon orange extract
1/2	cup finely crushed reduced-fat granola without raisins
1/2	cup all-purpose flour
1/4	teaspoon baking soda
2	teaspoons finely grated orange rind
1/4	teaspoon salt

Per Serving
Calories: 27
% Calories from fat: 33
Fat (gm): 1
Saturated fat (gm): 0.2
Cholesterol (mg): 0
Sodium (mg): 35
Protein (gm): 0.4
Carbohydrate (gm): 4.1
Exchanges
Milk: 0.0
Vegetable: 0.0
Fruit: 0.0
Bread: 0.5
Meat: 0.0
Fat: 0.0

1. Beat all ingredients in large bowl until smooth.

2. Drop rounded 1/2 teaspoons dough 3 inches apart on parchment-lined cookie sheets, making 4 to 6 cookies per pan. Bake at 400 degrees until lightly browned, about 3 minutes. Let stand until firm enough to remove from pans, about 1 minute. Cool on wire racks.

ALMOND TUILES

These lacy cookies are crisp and delicate. They can be folded, rolled, or formed into small basket shapes for ice cream or other fillings (see Variations below).

3 dozen cookies (1 per serving)

- 1/2 cup quick-cooking oats
- 1/4 cup finely chopped blanched almonds
- 4 tablespoons margarine, melted
- 1/2 cup light corn syrup
- 1/3 cup sugar
- 1 teaspoon almond extract
- 1/2 cup all-purpose flour
- 1/4 teaspoon salt

Per Serving
Calories: 49
% Calories from fat: 33
Fat (gm): 1.7
Saturated fat (gm): 0.3
Cholesterol (mg): 0
Sodium (mg): 36
Protein (gm): 0.5
Carbohydrate (gm): 7.5
Exchanges
Milk: 0.0
Vegetable: 0.0
Fruit: 0.0
Bread: 0.5
Meat: 0.0
Fat: 0.5

1. Place oats and almonds in separate pie pans. Bake at 350 degrees until toasted, 5 to 8 minutes for the almonds and about 10 minutes for the oats. Cool.

2. Mix margarine and corn syrup in bowl; mix in sugar and almond extract. Mix in combined oats, almonds, flour, and salt.

3. Drop batter by well-rounded teaspoons, 3 inches apart, onto parchment-lined cookie sheets (4 to 6 cookies per pan). Bake at 350 degrees until golden and bubbly, 7 to 10 minutes. Let cookies cool just until firm enough to remove from pan, about 1 minute. Working quickly, remove each cookie and roll or fold over the handle of a wooden spoon, or leave flat; cool on wire rack. If cookies have cooled too much to shape, return to warm oven for about 1 minute to soften.

Variations: **Cream-Filled Tuiles**—Remove warm tuiles from cookie sheet 1 at a time and roll loosely around handle of wooden spoon; transfer to wire rack and cool. Mix 3 cups light whipped topping and 1/3 cup powdered sugar. Using pastry bag with medium star tip, fill cookies with mixture. Drizzle cookies with 1 ounce melted semisweet baking chocolate.

Florentines—Make tuiles, leaving them flat. Make 1/2 recipe Buttercream Frosting (see p. 542); spread 1/2 the tuiles with frosting, using about 1 tablespoon for each. Top with remaining tuiles and drizzle with 1 ounce melted semisweet baking chocolate.

MAPLE SQUARES

A richly flavored cookie that will satisfy any sweet tooth.

3 dozen cookies (1 per serving)

¹/₂ cup margarine, softened
1¹/₄ cups packed light brown sugar
1 egg
1-1¹/₂ teaspoons maple extract
2 cups all-purpose flour
1¹/₂ teaspoons baking soda
¹/₄ teaspoon salt
1 cup buttermilk
Maple Glaze (see p. 60)
2-4 tablespoons very finely chopped pecans

Per Serving
Calories: 98
% Calories from fat: 28
Fat (gm): 3.1
Saturated fat (gm): 0.6
Cholesterol (mg): 6.1
Sodium (mg): 110
Protein (gm): 1.2
Carbohydrate (gm): 16.1
Exchanges
Milk: 0.0
Vegetable: 0.0
Fruit: 0.0
Bread: 1.0
Meat: 0.0
Fat: 0.5

1. Beat margarine and brown sugar in medium bowl until blended; beat in egg and maple extract. Mix in combined flour, baking soda, salt, and buttermilk.

2. Pour batter into greased jelly roll pan, 15 x 10 inches. Bake at 350 degrees until browned, about 25 minutes. Cool on wire rack. Drizzle with Maple Glaze, sprinkle with pecans, and cut into squares while slightly warm.

Variation: **Toffee Bars**—Make cookies as above, substituting vanilla for the maple extract, and omitting Maple Glaze. Sprinkle English Toffee bits over dough; press lightly into dough. Bake as above.

GLAZED CHOCOLATE SHORTBREAD SQUARES

Rich, chocolatey, and crisp!

5 dozen cookies (1 per serving)

1½ cups all-purpose flour
¼ cup unsweetened cocoa
⅔ cup sugar
¼ teaspoon salt
8 tablespoons margarine, softened
1 egg
2 teaspoons vanilla
Sugar Glaze (recipe follows)

Per Serving
Calories: 44
% Calories from fat: 33
Fat (gm): 1.6
Saturated fat (gm): 0.3
Cholesterol (mg): 3.6
Sodium (mg): 29
Protein (gm): 0.5
Carbohydrate (gm): 6.8
Exchanges
Milk: 0.0
Vegetable: 0.0
Fruit: 0.0
Bread: 0.5
Meat: 0.0
Fat: 0.0

1. Combine flour, cocoa, sugar, and salt in medium bowl; cut in margarine with pastry blender or 2 knives until mixture resembles coarse crumbs. Mix in egg and vanilla, stirring just enough to form a soft dough.

2. Place dough in bottom of greased jelly roll pan, 15 x 10 inches. Pat and spread dough, using fingers and small spatula, until bottom of pan is evenly covered. Pierce dough with tines of fork.

3. Bake at 350 degrees until firm to touch, 20 to 25 minutes. Cool on wire rack. Drizzle Sugar Glaze over shortbread and cut into squares while warm.

Sugar Glaze

makes about 1 cup

1 cup powdered sugar
1-2 tablespoons fat-free milk

1. Mix powdered sugar and enough milk to make glaze consistency.

CARDAMOM CRISPS

For flavor variations, ground cinnamon or allspice can be substituted for the cardamom. These cookies require some care in spreading in the pan but are well worth the effort!

5 dozen cookies (1 per serving)

1³/₄	cups all-purpose flour
²/₃	cup sugar
1¹/₂	teaspoons ground cardamom
¹/₄	teaspoon salt
8	tablespoons margarine, softened
1	egg
1	teaspoon vanilla
1	egg white, lightly beaten
	Vanilla Glaze (recipe follows)

Per Serving
Calories: 45
% Calories from fat: 32
Fat (gm): 1.6
Saturated fat (gm): 0.3
Cholesterol (mg): 3.5
Sodium (mg): 30
Protein (gm): 0.6
Carbohydrate (gm): 7.1
Exchanges
Milk: 0.0
Vegetable: 0.0
Fruit: 0.0
Bread: 0.5
Meat: 0.0
Fat: 0.5

1. Combine flour, sugar, cardamom, and salt in medium bowl; cut in margarine with pastry blender or 2 knives until mixture resembles coarse crumbs. Mix in whole egg and vanilla, stirring just enough to form a soft dough.

2. Place dough in bottom of greased jelly roll pan, 15 x 10 inches. Pat and spread dough, using fingers and small spatula or knife, until bottom of pan is evenly covered. Brush dough with beaten egg white.

3. Bake at 350 degrees until edges are lightly browned, 20 to 25 minutes. Cool on wire rack. Drizzle with Vanilla Glaze and cut into squares while warm.

Vanilla Glaze

makes about ¹/₂ cup

1	cup powdered sugar
1	teaspoon vanilla
1-2	tablespoons fat-free milk

1. Mix powdered sugar, vanilla, and enough milk to make glaze consistency.

COCOA-GLAZED COOKIE CRISPS

Bake cookie crisps only until beginning to brown, and cut while warm for best results.

5 dozen cookies (1 per serving)

1³/₄ cups all-purpose flour
²/₃ cup packed light brown sugar
¹/₄ teaspoon salt
8 tablespoons margarine, softened
1 egg
1 teaspoon vanilla
1 egg white, lightly beaten
Cocoa Drizzle (recipe follows)

Per Serving
Calories: 45
% Calories from fat: 32
Fat (gm): 1.6
Saturated fat (gm): 0.3
Cholesterol (mg): 3.5
Sodium (mg): 31
Protein (gm): 0.6
Carbohydrate (gm): 7.3
Exchanges
Milk: 0.0
Vegetable: 0.0
Fruit: 0.0
Bread: 0.5
Meat: 0.0
Fat: 0.5

1. Combine flour, brown sugar, and salt in medium bowl; cut in margarine with pastry blender or 2 knives until mixture resembles coarse crumbs. Mix in whole egg and vanilla, stirring just enough to form a soft dough.

2. Place dough in bottom of greased jelly roll pan, 15 x 10 inches. Pat and spread dough, using fingers and small spatula or knife, until bottom of pan is evenly covered. Brush dough with beaten egg white.

3. Bake dough at 350 degrees until edges are lightly browned, 20 to 25 minutes. Cool on wire rack. Drizzle with Cocoa Drizzle and cut into squares while warm.

Cocoa Drizzle

makes about ¹/₂ cup

1 cup powdered sugar
2 tablespoons unsweetened cocoa
1-2 tablespoons skim milk

1. Mix powdered sugar and cocoa in small bowl. Mix in enough milk to make glaze consistency.

CHOCOLATE FUDGE MERINGUES

Better bake several batches—these won't last long!

2 dozen cookies (1 per serving)

  3 egg whites

$1/2$ teaspoon cream of tartar

$1/4$ teaspoon salt

  2 cups powdered sugar

$1/2$ cup unsweetened cocoa

$1/2$ package (6-ounce size) reduced-fat semisweet chocolate morsels, chopped

Per Serving
Calories: 58
% Calories from fat: 12
Fat (gm): 0.8
Saturated fat (gm): 0.8
Cholesterol (mg): 0
Sodium (mg): 34
Protein (gm): 0.7
Carbohydrate (gm): 12.8
Exchanges
Milk: 0.0
Vegetable: 0.0
Fruit: 0.0
Bread: 1.0
Meat: 0.0
Fat: 0.0

1. Beat egg whites, cream of tartar, and salt to soft peaks in medium bowl. Beat to stiff peaks, adding sugar gradually. Fold in cocoa; fold in chopped chocolate.

2. Drop mixture by tablespoons onto parchment or aluminum foil-lined cookie sheets. Bake at 300 degrees until cookies feel crisp when touched, 20 to 25 minutes. Cool on pans on wire racks.

ORANGE-ALMOND MERINGUES

Party perfect!

2 dozen cookies (1 per serving)

  3 egg whites

$1/2$ teaspoon orange extract

$1/2$ teaspoon cream of tartar

$1/4$ teaspoon salt

$3/4$ cup sugar

$1/2$ cup chopped toasted almonds

Per Serving
Calories: 34
% Calories from fat: 21
Fat (gm): 0.8
Saturated fat (gm): 0.1
Cholesterol (mg): 0.0
Sodium (mg): 29
Protein (gm): 0.8
Carbohydrate (gm): 6.4
Exchanges
Milk: 0.0
Vegetable: 0.0
Fruit: 0.0
Bread: 0.5
Meat: 0.0
Fat: 0.0

1. Beat egg whites, orange extract, cream of tartar, and salt to soft peaks in medium bowl. Beat to stiff peaks, adding sugar gradually. Fold in almonds.

2. Drop mixture by tablespoons onto parchment or aluminum foil-lined cookie sheets. Bake at 300 degrees until cookies begin to brown and feel crisp when touched, 20 to 25 minutes. Cool on pans on wire racks.

Variations: **Lemon-Poppy Seed Meringues**—Make cookies, substituting lemon extract for the orange extract and omitting almonds. Fold 2 teaspoons finely chopped lemon rind and 2 tablespoons poppy seeds into meringue mixture.

Black Walnut Meringues—Make cookies as above, substituting $1/4$ teaspoon black walnut extract for the orange extract and $1/2$ cup finely chopped black or English walnuts for the almonds.

PEPPERMINT CLOUDS

Although wonderful cookies for any season, peppermint always reminds me of Christmas holidays.

2 dozen cookies (1 per serving)

3 egg whites
$1/2$ teaspoon cream of tartar
$1/4$ teaspoon salt
$3/4$ cup sugar
$1/3$ cup (2 ounces) crushed peppermint candies, divided

Per Serving
Calories: 34
% Calories from fat: 0
Fat (gm): 0
Saturated fat (gm): 0
Cholesterol (mg): 0
Sodium (mg): 30
Protein (gm): 0.4
Carbohydrate (gm): 8.4
Exchanges
Milk: 0.0
Vegetable: 0.0
Fruit: 0.0
Bread: 0.5
Meat: 0.0
Fat: 0.0

1. Beat egg whites, cream of tartar, and salt to soft peaks in medium bowl. Beat to stiff peaks, adding sugar gradually. Reserve 2 tablespoons peppermint candy; fold in remaining candy.

2. Drop mixture by tablespoons onto parchment or aluminum foil-lined cookie sheets. Sprinkle tops of cookies with reserved candy. Bake at 300 degrees until cookies begin to brown and feel crisp when touched, 20 to 25 minutes. Cool on pans on wire racks.

Variations: **Brown Sugar Pecan Kisses**—Make cookies as above, adding ¹/₄ teaspoon maple extract and substituting packed brown sugar for the granulated sugar and ¹/₄ cup finely chopped toasted pecans for the peppermint candies.

Meringue Mushrooms—Make cookies as above, increasing sugar to 1 cup and omitting peppermint candies. Reserve ¹/₄ cup meringue mixture. Pipe ³/₄ of the remaining mixture into 1- to 1¹/₂-inch "mushroom caps" onto parchment-lined cookie sheets, using pastry bag and ¹/₂-inch plain tip. Pipe remaining mixture into upright "stems," using ¹/₄-inch plain tip. Bake until crisp, 15 to 20 minutes; cool. With tip of paring knife, make a small indentation on bottom of each "cap." Pipe a tiny amount of reserved meringue into the indentations and attach the "stems." Return to oven for 2 to 3 minutes. Makes about 4 dozen.

HAZELNUT MACAROONS

Use any favorite nuts in these moist and crunchy macaroons.

1¹/₂ dozen cookies (1 per serving)

4 egg whites
¹/₈ teaspoon cream of tartar
¹/₄ teaspoon salt
1 cup sugar
1 cup flaked coconut
¹/₄ cup finely chopped hazelnuts *or* pecans

Per Serving
Calories: 44
% Calories from fat: 28
Fat (gm): 1.4
Saturated fat (gm): 0.8
Cholesterol (mg): 0.0
Sodium (mg): 25.6
Protein (gm): 0.7
Carbohydrate (gm): 7.6
Exchanges
Milk: 0.0
Vegetable: 0.0
Fruit: 0.0
Bread: 0.5
Meat: 0.0
Fat: 0.5

1. Beat egg whites, cream of tartar, and salt to soft peaks in medium bowl. Beat to stiff peaks, adding sugar gradually. Fold in coconut and hazelnuts.

2. Drop mixture by tablespoons onto parchment or aluminum foil-lined cookie sheets. Bake at 300 degrees until cookies begin to brown and feel crisp when touched, 20 to 25 minutes. Cool on pans on wire racks.

Variation: **Island Dreams**—Make cookies as above, adding ¹/₂ teaspoon pineapple extract, reducing coconut to ¹/₂ cup, and substituting macadamia nuts for the hazelnuts. Fold in ¹/₂ cup chopped dried pineapple or mango; bake as above.

CHERRY PECAN MERINGUES

A colorful holiday offering—use red cherries for February sweethearts.

3¹/₂ dozen cookies (1 per serving)

3 egg whites
¹/₈ teaspoon cream of tartar
¹/₄ teaspoon salt
1 cup sugar
¹/₄ cup finely chopped toasted pecans
³/₄ cup finely chopped glacéed red and green cherries

Per Serving
Calories: 33
% Calories from fat: 13
Fat (gm): 0.5
Saturated fat (gm): 0
Cholesterol (mg): 0
Sodium (mg): 20
Protein (gm): 0.3
Carbohydrate (gm): 7
Exchanges
Milk: 0.0
Vegetable: 0.0
Fruit: 0.0
Bread: 0.5
Meat: 0.0
Fat: 0.0

1. Beat egg whites, cream of tartar, and salt to soft peaks in large bowl. Beat to stiff peaks, adding sugar gradually. Fold in pecans and glacéed cherries.

2. Drop mixture by tablespoons onto parchment or aluminum foil-lined cookie sheets. Bake at 300 degrees until cookies begin to brown and feel crisp when touched, 15 to 20 minutes. Cool on pans on wire racks.

Variation: **Glacéed Orange Meringues**—Make cookies as above, adding ¹/₂ teaspoon orange extract and substituting ¹/₃ cup almonds for the pecans and finely chopped glacéed orange peel for the cherries.

ANISE-ALMOND BISCOTTI

Crisp biscotti are perfect for dunking into coffee, tea, or Vin Santo, the Italian way!

5 dozen biscotti (1 per serving)

4	tablespoons margarine, softened
3/4	cup sugar
2	eggs
2	egg whites
2 1/2	cups all-purpose flour
2	teaspoons crushed anise seeds
1 1/2	teaspoons baking powder
1/2	teaspoon baking soda
1/4	teaspoon salt
1/3	cup whole blanched almonds

Per Serving
Calories: 43
% Calories from fat: 28
Fat (gm): 1.4
Saturated fat (gm): 0.3
Cholesterol (mg): 7.1
Sodium (mg): 45
Protein (gm): 1
Carbohydrate (gm): 6.7
Exchanges
Milk: 0.0
Vegetable: 0.0
Fruit: 0.0
Bread: 0.5
Meat: 0.0
Fat: 0.0

1. Beat margarine, sugar, eggs, and egg whites until smooth in large bowl. Mix in combined flour, anise seeds, baking powder, baking soda, and salt. Mix in almonds.

2. Shape dough on greased cookie sheets into 4 slightly flattened rolls 1 1/2 inches in diameter. Bake at 350 degrees until lightly browned, about 20 minutes. Let stand on wire rack until cool enough to handle; cut rolls into 1/2-inch slices. Arrange slices, cut sides down, on ungreased cookie sheets.

3. Bake biscotti at 350 degrees until toasted on the bottoms, 7 to 10 minutes; turn and bake until biscotti are golden on the bottoms and feel almost dry, 7 to 10 minutes. Cool on wire racks.

Variations: **Chocolate-Walnut Biscotti**—Make biscotti as above, omitting anise seeds, substituting walnuts for the almonds, adding 1 teaspoon vanilla, and adding 1/2 cup reduced-fat semisweet chocolate morsels *or* 1/3 cup semisweet mini-morsels.

GRANOLA BISCOTTI

This cookie will find its way to the breakfast table for coffee dunking.

5 dozen biscotti (1 per serving)

1 cup all-purpose flour

3/4 teaspoon baking powder

3/4 cup packed light brown sugar

3 tablespoons cold margarine, cut into pieces

2 eggs, lightly beaten

1 teaspoon vanilla

1 tablespoon finely grated orange rind

2 cups lightly crushed reduced-fat granola

1/4 cup currants *or* chopped raisins

Per Serving
Calories: 42
% Calories from fat: 20
Fat (gm): 1
Saturated fat (gm): 0.2
Cholesterol (mg): 7.1
Sodium (mg): 24
Protein (gm): 0.8
Carbohydrate (gm): 7.7
Exchanges
Milk: 0.0
Vegetable: 0.0
Fruit: 0.0
Bread: 0.5
Meat: 0.0
Fat: 0.0

1. Combine flour, baking powder, and brown sugar in large bowl; cut in margarine until mixture resembles small crumbs. Mix in eggs, vanilla, and orange rind; mix in granola and currants.

2. Divide mixture into 4 equal pieces. Shape each piece on greased cookie sheet into 6 x 1-inch roll; flatten rolls slightly, tapering sides. Bake at 350 degrees until browned and almost firm, about 20 minutes; cool on wire racks. Carefully slice rolls into 1/2-inch slices, using serrated knife. Arrange slices, cut sides down, on ungreased cookie sheets.

3. Bake biscotti at 350 degrees until toasted on the bottoms, 5 to 6 minutes; turn and bake until biscotti are golden on the bottoms and feel almost dry, 5 to 6 minutes. Cool on wire racks.

APRICOT-SESAME BISCOTTI

Bake biscotti until almost dry, as they become crisper as they cool.

5 dozen biscotti (1 per serving)

2¹/₂ cups all-purpose flour

1 teaspoon baking powder

¹/₂ teaspoon baking soda

³/₄ cup packed light brown sugar

2 tablespoons grated orange rind

2 tablespoons sesame seeds, toasted

2 eggs

2 egg whites

¹/₂ cup finely chopped dried apricots

Per Serving
Calories: 37
% Calories from fat: 8
Fat (gm): 0.4
Saturated fat (gm): 0
Cholesterol (mg): 7.1
Sodium (mg): 24
Protein (gm): 1
Carbohydrate (gm): 7.4
Exchanges
Milk: 0.0
Vegetable: 0.0
Fruit: 0.0
Bread: 0.5
Meat: 0.0
Fat: 0.0

1. Combine flour, baking powder, baking soda, brown sugar, orange rind, and sesame seeds in large bowl. Mix eggs and egg whites; stir into flour mixture until smooth. Mix in the dried apricots.

2. Shape dough on greased cookie sheets into 4 slightly flattened rolls, 1¹/₂ inches in diameter. Bake at 350 degrees until lightly browned, about 20 minutes. Let stand on wire rack until cool enough to handle; cut rolls into ¹/₂-inch slices.

3. Arrange slices, cut sides down, on ungreased cookie sheets. Bake biscotti until toasted on the bottoms, 7 to 10 minutes; turn and bake until biscotti are golden on the bottoms and feel almost dry, 7 to 10 minutes. Cool on wire racks.

Variation: **Crunchy Peanut Butter Biscotti**—Make biscotti as above, omitting orange rind, sesame seeds, and dried apricots and adding ¹/₂ cup reduced-fat crunchy peanut butter. If desired, drizzle baked biscotti with ¹/₃ cup melted semisweet chocolate morsels.

ALMOND MERINGUE BISCOTTI

This unusual biscotti is made with meringue.

2 dozen cookies (1 per serving)

4 egg whites
1/8 teaspoon cream of tartar
Pinch salt
3/4 cup sugar
1/2 teaspoon almond extract
3/4 cup all-purpose flour
1/3 cup chopped almonds

Per Serving
Calories: 55
% Calories from fat: 14
Fat (gm): 0.8
Saturated fat (gm): 0.1
Cholesterol (mg): 0
Sodium (mg): 9
Protein (gm): 1.3
Carbohydrate (gm): 9.6
Exchanges
Milk: 0.0
Vegetable: 0.0
Fruit: 0.0
Bread: 0.5
Meat: 0.0
Fat: 0.0

1. Beat egg whites, cream of tartar, and salt to soft peaks in large bowl; beat to stiff peaks, adding sugar gradually. Beat in almond extract. Sprinkle 1/2 the flour over the egg whites and fold in; repeat with remaining flour and almonds.

2. Line bottom and 2 sides of 9 x 5-inch loaf pan with parchment paper or aluminum foil. Spoon meringue mixture into pan and smooth top. Bake at 350 degrees until golden, 25 to 30 minutes. Cool in pan on wire rack 15 minutes; remove from pan and cool.

3. Cut loaf into 1/2-inch slices and arrange on ungreased cookie sheet. Bake at 325 degrees until toasted on the bottoms, 7 to 10 minutes; turn and bake until biscotti are golden on the bottoms and feel almost dry, 7 to 10 minutes. Cool on wire racks.

FROSTED COCOA BROWNIES

Very chocolatey and slightly chewy, you'll never guess these brownies are low in fat.

25 brownies (1 per serving)

1	cup all-purpose flour
1	cup sugar
1/4	cup unsweetened cocoa
5	tablespoons margarine, melted
1/4	cup fat-free milk
1	egg
2	egg whites
1/4	cup honey
1	teaspoon vanilla
	Sweet Cocoa Frosting (recipe follows)

Per Serving
Calories: 111
% Calories from fat: 24
Fat (gm): 3.1
Saturated fat (gm): 0.6
Cholesterol (mg): 8.6
Sodium (mg): 42
Protein (gm): 1.5
Carbohydrate (gm): 20.4
Exchanges
Milk: 0.0
Vegetable: 0.0
Fruit: 1.5
Bread: 0.0
Meat: 0.0
Fat: 0.5

1. Combine flour, sugar, and cocoa in medium bowl; add margarine, milk, egg, egg whites, honey, and vanilla, mixing until smooth. Pour batter into greased and floured 8-inch square baking pan.

2. Bake at 350 degrees until brownies spring back when touched, about 30 minutes. Cool in pan on wire rack; spread with Sweet Cocoa Frosting.

Sweet Cocoa Frosting

makes about 1/2 cup

1	cup powdered sugar
2-3	tablespoons unsweetened cocoa
1	tablespoon margarine, softened
2-3	tablespoons fat-free milk

1. In small bowl, beat powdered sugar, cocoa, margarine, and enough milk to make spreading consistency.

Variation: **Cappuccino Brownies**—Make brownies as above, adding 1 to 2 tablespoons instant coffee crystals; omit Sweet Cocoa Frosting and make **Cinnamon Cream Cheese Topping:** Beat 8 ounces softened reduced-fat cream cheese, 3/4 cup powdered sugar, 1/2 teaspoon ground cinnamon, and 1/2 teaspoon vanilla; spread over cooled brownies. Drizzle with 1 ounce melted semisweet baking chocolate.

CHOCOLATE INDULGENCE BROWNIES

Dark chocolate, moist and gooey—a low-fat brownie that's too good to be true!

2 dozen brownies (1 per serving)

3 eggs
³/4 cup packed light brown sugar
2 teaspoons vanilla
2 cups chocolate cookie crumbs
3 tablespoons unsweetened cocoa
¹/4 teaspoon salt
²/3 cup chopped dates
¹/2 cup reduced-fat semisweet chocolate morsels

Per Serving
Calories: 124
% Calories from fat: 26
Fat (gm): 3.8
Saturated fat (gm): 1.7
Cholesterol (mg): 26.5
Sodium (mg): 129
Protein (gm): 1.8
Carbohydrate (gm): 22.7
Exchanges
Milk: 0.0
Vegetable: 0.0
Fruit: 0.0
Bread: 1.5
Meat: 0.0
Fat: 0.5

1. Beat eggs, brown sugar, and vanilla in large bowl until thick, about 2 minutes. Fold in cookie crumbs, cocoa, and salt; fold in dates and chocolate morsels.

2. Spread batter evenly in greased 11 x 7-inch baking pan. Bake at 300 degrees until top springs back when touched and brownie begins to pull away from sides of pan, about 40 minutes. Cool on wire rack.

MARBLED CHEESECAKE BROWNIES

Cheesecake and brownies—an unbeatable combination!

2 dozen brownies (1 per serving)

1¹/2 cups packed light brown sugar
5 tablespoons margarine, melted
¹/4 cup buttermilk
2 eggs
1 teaspoon vanilla
1 cup all-purpose flour
¹/2 cup Dutch process cocoa
¹/2 teaspoon salt
Cheesecake Topping (recipe follows)

Per Serving
Calories: 132
% Calories from fat: 22
Fat (gm): 3.2
Saturated fat (gm): 0.8
Cholesterol (mg): 27.4
Sodium (mg): 147
Protein (gm): 3
Carbohydrate (gm): 23.1
Exchanges
Milk: 0.0
Vegetable: 0.0
Fruit: 0.0
Bread: 1.5
Meat: 0.0
Fat: 0.5

1. Beat brown sugar, margarine, buttermilk, eggs, and vanilla until smooth. Mix in combined flour, cocoa, and salt.

2. Spread ¹/₂ the batter in greased 11 x 7-inch baking pan. Pour Cheesecake Topping evenly over chocolate batter; dollop remaining chocolate batter over Cheesecake Topping. Swirl knife through mixtures to create marbled effect.

3. Bake at 350 degrees until brownies are set and firm to touch, 45 to 55 minutes. Cool on wire rack.

Cheesecake Topping

makes about 1¹/₂ cups

> 1 package (8 ounces) fat-free cream cheese, softened
> ¹/₂ cup sugar
> 1 tablespoon flour
> 1 egg
> 1 teaspoon vanilla

1. Beat cream cheese, sugar, and flour in large bowl until smooth; beat in egg and vanilla.

Variation: **Banana Split Brownies**—Make brownies as above, mixing ¹/₂ cup mashed banana into the Cheesecake Topping and substituting ¹/₄ teaspoon banana extract for the vanilla in both the brownies and topping recipes. Serve brownies with fat-free vanilla ice cream, banana slices, and Chocolate Sauce (see p. 642).

CARROT SNACK BARS

When you crave a snack, this is a delicious low-fat way to indulge!

1¹/₂ dozen bars (1 per serving)

4 tablespoons margarine, softened
³/₄ cup packed light brown sugar
³/₄ cup fat-free milk
1 egg
1 tablespoon lemon juice
1 teaspoon vanilla
1¹/₄ cups quick-cooking oats
¹/₂ cup all-purpose flour
¹/₄ cup whole wheat flour
2 teaspoons baking powder
¹/₄ teaspoon baking soda
1 teaspoon ground cinnamon
¹/₄ teaspoon salt
1 cup shredded carrots
¹/₂ cup raisins
¹/₂ cup chopped pecans *or* walnuts
Orange Glaze (see p. 47)

Per Serving
Calories: 155
% Calories from fat: 31
Fat (gm): 5.5
Saturated fat (gm): 0.8
Cholesterol (mg): 12
Sodium (mg): 149
Protein (gm): 2.8
Carbohydrate (gm): 25.1
Exchanges
Milk: 0.0
Vegetable: 0.0
Fruit: 0.0
Bread: 1.5
Meat: 0.0
Fat: 1.0

1. Beat margarine and brown sugar in large bowl until blended; beat in milk, egg, lemon juice, and vanilla. Mix in combined oats, flours, baking powder, baking soda, cinnamon, and salt; mix in carrots, raisins, and pecans.

2. Pour batter into greased 11 x 7-inch baking pan. Bake at 350 degrees until toothpick inserted in center comes out clean, about 30 minutes. Cool on wire rack. Drizzle with Orange Glaze.

OATMEAL DATE SQUARES

The oats lend a texture and flavor similar to coconut.

2 dozen bars (1 per serving)

$^3/_4$ cup chopped dates
$^1/_2$ cup boiling water
  6 tablespoons margarine, softened
$^3/_4$ cup packed light brown sugar
  2 eggs
  2 tablespoons honey
  1 teaspoon vanilla
$1^1/_2$ cups quick-cooking oats
  1 cup all-purpose flour
$^1/_2$ teaspoon baking soda
$^1/_2$ teaspoon salt
  1 teaspoon ground cinnamon
$^1/_8$ teaspoon ground nutmeg
     Brown Sugar Glaze (see p. 50)

Per Serving
Calories: 131
% Calories from fat: 26
Fat (gm): 3.8
Saturated fat (gm): 0.8
Cholesterol (mg): 17.7
Sodium (mg): 119
Protein (gm): 2
Carbohydrate (gm): 22.8
Exchanges
Milk: 0.0
Vegetable: 0.0
Fruit: 0.0
Bread: 1.5
Meat: 0.0
Fat: 0.5

1. Process dates and boiling water in food processor or blender until smooth. Beat margarine and brown sugar in large bowl until blended; beat in eggs, honey, vanilla, and date mixture. Mix in combined remaining ingredients, except Brown Sugar Glaze.

2. Pour batter into greased 13 x 9-inch baking pan. Bake at 375 degrees until wooden pick inserted in center comes out clean, 15 to 18 minutes. Cool on wire rack. Drizzle with Brown Sugar Glaze.

CHOCOLATE CARAMEL BLONDIES

Blonde brownies with a rich swirl of chocolate-flavored caramel—they are irresistible!

3 dozen brownies (1 per serving)

 $^1/_2$ cup margarine
1$^1/_2$ cups packed dark brown sugar
 2 eggs
 1 teaspoon vanilla
1$^1/_2$ cups all-purpose flour
 2 teaspoons baking powder
 $^1/_2$ teaspoon salt
 1 package (14 ounces) chocolate cara-
    mels (about 50 caramels)
 $^1/_4$ cup fat-free milk
 $^1/_2$ cup walnut pieces

Per Serving
Calories: 131
% Calories from fat: 27
Fat (gm): 4.1
Saturated fat (gm): 0.7
Cholesterol (mg): 11.8
Sodium (mg): 100
Protein (gm): 1.6
Carbohydrate (gm): 23
Exchanges
Milk: 0.0
Vegetable: 0.0
Fruit: 0.0
Bread: 1.5
Meat: 0.0
Fat: 0.5

1. Melt margarine in medium saucepan; remove from heat and stir in brown sugar, eggs, and vanilla. Mix in combined flour, baking powder, and salt.

2. Reserve 1 cup batter; spread remaining batter in greased 13 x 9-inch baking pan. Bake at 350 degrees until firm to touch, about 15 minutes.

3. Heat caramels and milk in small saucepan on medium to medium-low heat until melted, stirring frequently. Pour mixture over baked brownies, spreading to within $^1/_2$ inch of edges.

4. Spoon reserved batter over caramel layer and sprinkle with walnuts; swirl together with knife. Bake at 350 degrees until firm to touch, 15 to 18 minutes. Cool on wire rack; cut into squares.

SUGARED LEMON SQUARES

Just like the favorites you remember, but low-fat and healthy!

1 dozen squares (1 per serving)

Sour Cream Crust (recipe follows)
1 cup granulated sugar
2 eggs
2 egg whites
1 tablespoon grated lemon rind
3 tablespoons lemon juice
1/2 teaspoon baking powder
1/4 teaspoon salt
Powdered sugar, as garnish

Per Serving
Calories: 152
% Calories from fat: 29
Fat (gm): 4.9
Saturated fat (gm): 1.2
Cholesterol (mg): 36.2
Sodium (mg): 126
Protein (gm): 2.1
Carbohydrate (gm): 25.5
Exchanges
Milk: 0.0
Vegetable: 0.0
Fruit: 0.0
Bread: 1.5
Meat: 0.0
Fat: 1.0

1. Press Sour Cream Crust into bottom and 1/4 inch up sides of 8-inch square baking pan. Bake at 350 degrees until lightly browned, about 20 minutes. Cool on wire rack.

2. Mix remaining ingredients, except powdered sugar, in small bowl; pour over baked pastry. Bake at 350 degrees until set and no indentation remains when touched in the center, 20 to 25 minutes. Cool on wire rack; cut into squares. Sprinkle lightly with powdered sugar.

Sour Cream Crust

3/4 cup all-purpose flour
4 tablespoons margarine, softened
2 tablespoons reduced-fat sour cream
2 tablespoons sugar

1. Mix flour, margarine, sour cream, and 2 tablespoons granulated sugar in small bowl to form soft dough.

Variations: **Key Lime Squares**—Make Sour Cream Crust as above, adding 1/4 cup coconut to the mixture. Make filling, substituting lime juice and rind for the lemon juice and rind, and adding 1/4 cup coconut. Bake as above; sprinkle with powdered sugar.

Orange Almond Squares—Make Sour Cream Crust as above, adding 1/4 cup finely chopped almonds. Make filling, substituting orange juice and rind for the lemon juice and rind, and reducing sugar to 3/4 cup. Bake as above; sprinkle with powdered sugar.

MISSISSIPPI MUD BARS

A favorite with kids of all ages—serve with ice cream and warm Chocolate Sauce (see p. 642) for an ultimate treat.

2 dozen bars (1 per serving)

5 tablespoons margarine, softened
1/2 cup granulated sugar
1/2 cup packed light brown sugar
1 teaspoon vanilla
3 eggs
1 cup all-purpose flour
1/3 cup unsweetened cocoa
1/2 teaspoon baking powder
1/4 teaspoon salt
3 cups miniature marshmallows
1/3 cup chopped pecans
1/2 cup melted reduced-fat semisweet
chocolate morsels

Per Serving
Calories: 140
% Calories from fat: 32
Fat (gm): 5.2
Saturated fat (gm): 1.9
Cholesterol (mg): 26.6
Sodium (mg): 81
Protein (gm): 1.9
Carbohydrate (gm): 22.9
Exchanges
Milk: 0.0
Vegetable: 0.0
Fruit: 0.0
Bread: 1.5
Meat: 0.0
Fat: 1.0

1. Beat margarine, sugars, and vanilla until blended; beat in eggs, 1 at a time. Mix in combined flour, cocoa, baking powder, and salt.

2. Pour batter into greased 13 x 9-inch baking pan. Bake at 325 degrees until toothpick inserted in center comes out clean, 18 to 20 minutes. Sprinkle top of cake with marshmallows and pecans; bake until marshmallows are lightly browned, 2 to 3 minutes. Cool on wire rack. Drizzle melted chocolate over marshmallows. Cut into bars.

PEACH STREUSEL BARS

Any flavor preserves can be used in these crunchy bars.

3 dozen bars (1 per serving)

1³/₄ cups all-purpose flour

2 cups quick-cooking oats

¹/₂ cup packed light brown sugar

¹/₂ cup granulated sugar

12 tablespoons cold margarine, cut into pieces

2 tablespoons honey

1¹/₂ cups peach preserves

Per Serving
Calories: 131
% Calories from fat: 28
Fat (gm): 4.1
Saturated fat (gm): 0.8
Cholesterol (mg): 0
Sodium (mg): 51
Protein (gm): 1.5
Carbohydrate (gm): 23
Exchanges
Milk: 0.0
Vegetable: 0.0
Fruit: 0.0
Bread: 1.5
Meat: 0.0
Fat: 0.5

1. Combine flour, oats, and sugars in large bowl; cut in margarine until mixture resembles coarse crumbs. Reserve ¹/₃ mixture. Mix honey into remaining mixture; pat evenly in bottom of greased 13 x 9-inch baking pan.

2. Spread preserves over mixture in pan; sprinkle with reserved crumb mixture. Bake at 350 degrees until bubbly and golden, about 35 minutes. Cool on wire rack.

APPLE CRANBERRY BARS

Moist and chewy, with old-fashioned flavor. Substitute dried cherries or blueberries for the cranberries another time.

1½ dozen bars (1 per serving)

6 tablespoons margarine, softened
¾ cup packed light brown sugar
2 eggs
2 tablespoons honey
1 teaspoon vanilla
1 cup all-purpose flour
⅔ cup quick-cooking oats
¾ teaspoon baking powder
¼ teaspoon baking soda
¾ teaspoon ground allspice
¼ teaspoon salt
1 cup finely chopped peeled apple
½ cup chopped dried cranberries
Powdered sugar, as garnish

Per Serving
Calories: 137
% Calories from fat: 30
Fat (gm): 4.6
Saturated fat (gm): 1
Cholesterol (mg): 23.6
Sodium (mg): 126
Protein (gm): 2
Carbohydrate (gm): 22.2
Exchanges
Milk: 0.0
Vegetable: 0.0
Fruit: 0.0
Bread: 1.5
Meat: 0.0
Fat: 0.5

1. Beat margarine and brown sugar until well blended in large bowl; beat in eggs, honey, and vanilla. Mix in combined flour, oats, baking powder, baking soda, allspice, and salt. Mix in apple and cranberries.

2. Pour batter in greased 8- or 9-inch square baking pan. Bake at 350 degrees until a wooden pick inserted in center comes out clean, 35 to 40 minutes. Cool on wire rack; sprinkle with powdered sugar.

CRANBERRY CHEESECAKE BARS

A delicious combination of layers—rich crust, creamy cheesecake, and moist cranberries.

3 dozen bars (1 per serving)

Per Serving
Calories: 143
% Calories from fat: 30
Fat (gm): 4.8
Saturated fat (gm): 1
Cholesterol (mg): 1
Sodium (mg): 131
Protein (gm): 3.5
Carbohydrate (gm): 21.8
Exchanges
Milk: 0.0
Vegetable: 0.0
Fruit: 0.0
Bread: 1.5
Meat: 0.0
Fat: 1.0

2 cups all-purpose flour
1³/₄ cups quick-cooking oats
³/₄ cup packed light brown sugar
14 tablespoons cold margarine, cut into pieces
2 packages (8 ounces each) fat-free cream cheese, softened
³/₄ cup granulated sugar
4 egg whites *or* ¹/₂ cup no-cholesterol real egg product
2 tablespoons frozen orange juice concentrate
2 teaspoons grated orange rind
¹/₂ teaspoon orange extract *or* vanilla
1 can (16 ounces) whole berry cranberry sauce
2 teaspoons cornstarch

1. Combine flour, oats, and brown sugar in large bowl; cut in margarine until mixture resembles coarse crumbs. Reserve 1 cup mixture; pat remaining mixture evenly on bottom of greased 13 x 9-inch baking pan.

2. Beat cream cheese in large bowl until fluffy; beat in granulated sugar, egg whites, orange juice concentrate, orange rind, and orange extract, mixing well.

3. Pour mixture over crust in pan. Mix cranberry sauce and cornstarch; spoon carefully over cream cheese mixture and sprinkle with reserved crumb mixture. Bake at 350 degrees until browned and bubbly. Cool on wire rack.

PUTTING ON THE RITZ BARS

Never have these rice cereal treats been quite so glamorous!

2¹/₂ dozen bars (1 per serving)

   1 package (10 ounces) marshmallows
   4 tablespoons margarine
   3 cups rice cereal (Rice Crispies)
¹/₂ cup flaked coconut
   1 cup dried cranberries *or* raisins
   1 cup chopped dried mixed fruit
¹/₂-³/₄ cup coarsely chopped walnuts
   2 ounces semisweet baking chocolate, melted

Per Serving
Calories: 108
% Calories from fat: 30
Fat (gm): 3.7
Saturated fat (gm): 1.1
Cholesterol (mg): 0
Sodium (mg): 59
Protein (gm): 1.2
Carbohydrate (gm): 18.7
Exchanges
Milk: 0.0
Vegetable: 0.0
Fruit: 0.0
Bread: 1.0
Meat: 0.0
Fat: 1.0

1. Heat marshmallows and margarine in large saucepan over low heat until melted, stirring frequently. Stir in remaining ingredients, except chocolate, mixing well.

2. Spoon mixture into greased 15 x 10-inch jelly roll pan, pressing into an even layer. Refrigerate 1 hour.

3. Drizzle top with chocolate; refrigerate until set, about 15 minutes. Cut into bars.

SIX

Puddings
AND
Custards

RICH CHOCOLATE PUDDING

Unbelievably rich in flavor, smooth in texture. Use Dutch or European process cocoa for fullest flavor. Offer Hazelnut Macaroons (see p. 354) as an accompaniment to this dessert.

4 servings

1/2 cup sugar
1/3 cup unsweetened cocoa
2 tablespoons cornstarch
1/8 teaspoon salt
2 cups 2% reduced-fat milk
2 egg yolks, slightly beaten
2 teaspoons vanilla

Per Serving
Calories: 219
% Calories from fat: 24
Fat (gm): 5.8
Saturated fat (gm): 2.3
Cholesterol (mg): 116
Sodium (mg): 133
Protein (gm): 7.3
Carbohydrate (gm): 34.4
Exchanges
Milk: 0.5
Vegetable: 0.0
Fruit: 1.5
Bread: 0.0
Meat: 0.5
Fat: 1.0

1. Mix sugar, cocoa, cornstarch, and salt in medium saucepan; stir in milk. Whisk over medium heat until mixture boils and thickens.

2. Whisk about 1/2 cup milk mixture into egg yolks; whisk egg yolk mixture back into saucepan. Whisk over medium heat 1 to 2 minutes. Stir in vanilla.

3. Spoon pudding into dessert bowls. Refrigerate, covered with plastic wrap, until chilled, 1 to 2 hours.

LEMON VELVET PUDDING

Top this velvet-textured custard with fresh peaches, strawberries, or other seasonal fruit. Serve a plate of Apricot-Sesame Biscotti (see p.358) on the side.

4 servings

1/2 cup sugar

2 tablespoons cornstarch

1/8 teaspoon salt

2 cups 2% reduced-fat milk

2 egg yolks, slightly beaten

2 tablespoons lemon juice

1 teaspoon lemon extract

Per Serving
Calories: 201
% Calories from fat: 22
Fat (gm): 4.9
Saturated fat (gm): 2.2
Cholesterol (mg): 116
Sodium (mg): 132
Protein (gm): 5.5
Carbohydrate (gm): 34.7
Exchanges
Milk: 0.5
Vegetable: 0.0
Fruit: 1.5
Bread: 0.0
Meat: 0.5
Fat: 1.0

1. Heat sugar, cornstarch, salt, and milk to boiling in medium saucepan, whisking constantly until thickened, about 1 minute.

2. Whisk about 1/2 cup milk mixture into egg yolks; whisk egg yolk mixture back into saucepan. Whisk in lemon juice and extract. Whisk over low heat 1 to 2 minutes.

3. Spoon pudding into dessert dishes. Refrigerate until chilled, 1 to 2 hours.

FRESH APRICOT CUSTARD

A delicate custard with fresh apricots gently folded throughout. Serve with cookies—Cardamom Crisps (see p. 350) would be nice.

6 servings

$^1/_2$ cup sugar

3 tablespoons cornstarch

2 cups fat-free milk

$^1/_2$ cup apricot nectar

2 egg yolks, slightly beaten

2 tablespoons margarine

1$^1/_2$ cups fresh apricots (7 medium), peeled, coarsely chopped

Per Serving
Calories: 193
% Calories from fat: 26
Fat (gm): 5.8
Saturated fat (gm): 1.4
Cholesterol (mg): 72.5
Sodium (mg): 90
Protein (gm): 4.4
Carbohydrate (gm): 32
Exchanges
Milk: 0.0
Vegetable: 0.0
Fruit: 0.0
Bread: 2.0
Meat: 0.0
Fat: 1.0

1. Mix sugar, cornstarch, milk, and apricot nectar in medium saucepan; whisk over medium heat until mixture boils and thickens.

2. Whisk about $^1/_2$ cup milk mixture into egg yolks; whisk egg yolk mixture back into saucepan. Whisk over low heat until thickened, 2 to 3 minutes. Remove from heat; stir in margarine. Refrigerate until chilled, 1 to 2 hours.

3. Whisk custard until fluffy; stir in apricots. Spoon into dessert dishes.

FLOATING ISLANDS

Poached meringue "islands" float in a delicate custard sauce in this classic dessert. An Almond Praline garnish adds extra flavor.

12 servings

4 eggs, separated
Dash salt
1 cup sugar, divided
1 teaspoon almond extract
2-2¼ cups 2% reduced-fat milk
1 teaspoon vanilla
Almond Praline (see p. 224)

Per Serving
Calories: 183
% Calories from fat: 25
Fat (gm): 4.7
Saturated fat (gm): 1.2
Cholesterol (mg): 73.7
Sodium (mg): 42
Protein (gm): 4.3
Carbohydrate (gm): 28.2
Exchanges
Milk: 0.0
Vegetable: 0.0
Fruit: 0.0
Bread: 2.0
Meat: 0.0
Fat: 1.0

1. Beat egg whites and salt to soft peaks in large bowl; beat to stiff peaks, gradually adding ½ cup sugar and almond extract.

2. Heat milk to simmering in large skillet. With a large serving spoon, scoop out an egg-shaped portion of meringue. Round the top with another spoon and drop into simmering milk; poach for 3 to 4 minutes, carefully turning once. Remove with slotted spoon and drain on paper toweling. Repeat with remaining meringue mixture, forming 12 meringues and cooking several at a time. Refrigerate, loosely covered with plastic wrap.

3. Beat egg yolks with remaining ½ cup sugar in medium bowl until fluffy; add vanilla. Strain the hot milk, adding additional milk, if necessary, to make 2 cups. Slowly whisk milk into egg yolk mixture. Cook in medium saucepan over medium-low heat, stirring with a wooden spoon, until custard is thick enough to coat the back of spoon; do not boil. Pour into shallow serving bowl and refrigerate until chilled, 3 to 4 hours.

4. To serve, arrange poached meringues on custard and sprinkle with Almond Praline.

Variation: **Boules sur Chocolat**—Make recipe as above, adding ⅓ cup unsweetened cocoa to the egg yolk and sugar mixture in Step 3. Omit Almond Praline. Sprinkle chilled meringues and custard with grated semisweet chocolate.

CARAMEL FLAN

Unbelievably delicate and fine in texture, this flan is one you'll serve over and over again.

8 servings

2/3 cup sugar, divided
4 cups fat-free milk
5 eggs, lightly beaten
2 teaspoons vanilla

Per Serving
Calories: 146
% Calories from fat: 21
Fat (gm): 3.4
Saturated fat (gm): 1.1
Cholesterol (mg): 135
Sodium (mg): 103
Protein (gm): 8.1
Carbohydrate (gm): 20.7
Exchanges
Milk: 0.5
Vegetable: 0.0
Fruit: 1.0
Bread: 0.0
Meat: 0.5
Fat: 0.5

1. Heat 1/3 cup sugar in small skillet over medium-high heat until sugar melts and turns golden, stirring occasionally (watch carefully as the sugar can burn easily!). Quickly pour syrup into bottom of 2-quart soufflé dish or casserole and tilt bottom to spread caramel. Set aside to cool.

2. Heat milk and remaining 1/3 cup sugar until steaming and just beginning to bubble at edges. Whisk into eggs; add vanilla. Strain into soufflé dish over caramel.

3. Place soufflé dish in roasting pan on middle oven rack. Cover soufflé dish with lid or aluminum foil. Pour 2 inches hot water into roasting pan. Bake at 350 degrees 1 hour or until sharp knife inserted halfway between center and edge of custard comes out clean. Remove soufflé dish from roasting pan and cool on wire rack. Refrigerate 8 hours or overnight.

4. To unmold, loosen edge of custard with sharp knife. Place rimmed serving dish over soufflé dish and invert.

Variation: **Pumpkin Flan**—Make flan as above, reducing milk to 2 cups, and mixing 1 cup canned pumpkin puree and 1 teaspoon cinnamon into milk mixture.

DOUBLE CARAMEL FLAN

Caramelized sugar both flavors the custard and coats the custard cups.

6 servings

1¹/₄ cups sugar, divided
2³/₄ cups fat-free milk
1 tablespoon vanilla
2 eggs
6 egg whites *or* ³/₄ cup no-cholesterol real egg product

Per Serving
Calories: 249
% Calories from fat: 7
Fat (gm): 1.9
Saturated fat (gm): 0.7
Cholesterol (mg): 72.7
Sodium (mg): 134
Protein (gm): 9.4
Carbohydrate (gm): 48.4
Exchanges
Milk: 0.0
Vegetable: 0.0
Fruit: 0.0
Bread: 3.0
Meat: 0.5
Fat: 0.0

1. Place six 6-ounce custard cups in small roasting pan. Heat ¹/₂ cup sugar over medium heat in small skillet, stirring occasionally, until sugar melts and is golden (watch carefully, as sugar can burn easily!). Quickly pour into custard cups, tilting cups to coat bottoms evenly.

2. Heat remaining ³/₄ cup sugar in large saucepan over medium heat, stirring occasionally, until sugar melts and is golden. Stir in milk slowly (mixture will spatter). Cook over medium heat, stirring frequently, until all bits of caramel are melted and mixture just comes to a boil; stir in vanilla.

3. Whisk hot milk mixture into combined eggs and egg whites in large bowl. Strain and pour into custard cups.

4. Place roasting pan with custard cups on middle oven rack; pour 1 inch hot water into pan. Bake, uncovered, at 300 degrees until custards are just set in the center and a sharp knife inserted halfway between center and edge of custards comes out clean, about 45 minutes. Remove custard cups from roasting pan; cool on wire rack. Refrigerate until chilled, 3 to 4 hours.

5. Loosen sides of custards with sharp knife and invert on dessert plates.

PINEAPPLE FLAN

Another wonderful flan variation; serve with fresh pineapple chunks and dollops of whipped topping.

8 servings

²/₃ cup sugar, divided
3 cups unsweetened pineapple juice
1 cup 2% reduced-fat milk
3 eggs
4 egg whites *or* ¹/₂ cup no-cholesterol real egg product
Mint leaves, as garnish

Per Serving
Calories: 168
% Calories from fat: **13**
Fat (gm): 2.5
Saturated fat (gm): 1
Cholesterol (mg): 81.8
Sodium (mg): 67
Protein (gm): 5.4
Carbohydrate (gm): 31.5
Exchanges
Milk: 0.0
Vegetable: 0.0
Fruit: 1.0
Bread: 0.0
Meat: 1.0
Fat: 0.0

1. Heat ¹/₃ cup sugar in small skillet over medium-high heat until sugar melts and turns golden, stirring occasionally (watch carefully as the sugar can burn easily!). Quickly pour syrup into bottom of 2-quart soufflé dish or casserole and tilt bottom to spread caramel. Set aside to cool.

2. Heat pineapple juice, milk, and remaining ¹/₃ cup sugar until steaming and just beginning to bubble at edges. Whisk into combined eggs and egg whites in large bowl; strain into soufflé dish.

3. Place soufflé dish in roasting pan on middle oven rack. Cover soufflé dish with lid or aluminum foil. Pour 2 inches hot water into roasting pan. Bake at 350 degrees 1 hour or until sharp knife inserted halfway between center and edge of custard comes out clean. Remove soufflé dish from roasting pan and cool on wire rack. Refrigerate 8 hours or overnight.

4. To unmold, loosen edge of custard with sharp knife. Place rimmed serving dish over soufflé dish and invert. Garnish with mint leaves.

Variation: **Raspberry Flan**—Make recipe as above, substituting Raspberry Puree for the pineapple juice, and increasing milk to 1¹/₂ cups. To make **Raspberry Puree,** process 2 packages (10 ounces each) frozen, thawed raspberries in syrup in food processor or blender; strain and discard seeds. Stir in 2 to 3 drops red food color, if desired. Garnish flan with fresh raspberries.

ORANGE FLAN

This flan is scented with orange for a subtle flavor accent.

8 servings

$^2/_3$ cup sugar
3$^3/_4$ cups fat-free milk
$^1/_4$ cup frozen orange juice concentrate
6 eggs, lightly beaten
$^1/_8$-$^1/_4$ teaspoon orange extract

Per Serving
Calories: 161
% Calories from fat: 22
Fat (gm): 4
Saturated fat (gm): 1.3
Cholesterol (mg): 162
Sodium (mg): 107
Protein (gm): 8.8
Carbohydrate (gm): 22.7
Exchanges
Milk: 0.5
Vegetable: 0.0
Fruit: 1.0
Bread: 0.0
Meat: 1.0
Fat: 0.5

1. Heat $^1/_3$ cup sugar in small skillet over medium-high heat until sugar melts and turns golden, stirring occasionally (watch carefully as the sugar can burn easily!). Quickly pour syrup into bottom of 2-quart soufflé dish or casserole and tilt bottom to spread caramel. Set aside to cool.

2. Heat milk, orange juice concentrate, and remaining $^1/_3$ cup sugar in medium saucepan until steaming and just beginning to bubble at edges. Whisk hot milk mixture into eggs; add orange extract. Strain into soufflé dish.

3. Place soufflé dish in roasting pan on middle oven rack. Cover soufflé dish with lid or aluminum foil. Pour 2 inches hot water into roasting pan. Bake at 350 degrees 1 hour or until sharp knife inserted halfway between center and edge of custard comes out clean. Remove soufflé dish from roasting pan and cool to room temperature on wire rack. Refrigerate 8 hours or overnight.

4. To unmold, loosen edge of custard with sharp knife. Place rimmed serving dish over soufflé dish and invert.

HERBED CUSTARD BRULÉE

Scented with herbs, the delicate custard is topped with a sprinkling of caramelized brown sugar.

6 servings

3 cups fat-free milk

2 tablespoons minced fresh, *or* ¹/₂ teaspoon dried, basil leaves

2 tablespoons minced fresh, *or* ¹/₂ teaspoon dried, cilantro leaves

2 tablespoons minced fresh, *or* ¹/₂ teaspoon dried, tarragon leaves

5 eggs

¹/₂ cup granulated sugar

¹/₄ cup packed light brown sugar

Per Serving
Calories: 192
% Calories from fat: 20
Fat (gm): 4.4
Saturated fat (gm): 1.5
Cholesterol (mg): 180
Sodium (mg): 117
Protein (gm): 9.4
Carbohydrate (gm): 29.2
Exchanges
Milk: 1.0
Vegetable: 0.0
Fruit: 0.0
Bread: 1.0
Meat: 0.0
Fat: 1.0

1. Heat milk and herbs to boiling in medium saucepan. Remove from heat, cover, and let stand 10 minutes. Strain; discard herbs.

2. Beat eggs and granulated sugar in medium bowl until thick and lemon-colored, about 5 minutes. Gradually whisk milk mixture into eggs; strain mixture and pour into eight 6-ounce custard cups.

3. Place custard cups in roasting pan on center oven rack; pour 2 inches hot water into pan. Bake at 350 degrees 20 minutes or until knife inserted halfway between center and edge of custards comes out clean. Remove cups from roasting pan and cool on wire rack. Refrigerate until chilled, 2 to 4 hours.

4. Press brown sugar through a strainer evenly over chilled custards. Place on cookie sheet and broil, 4 inches from heat source, until sugar is melted and caramelized, 2 to 3 minutes. Serve immediately.

Variations: **Maple Crème Brulée**—Make recipe as above, reducing milk to 2 cups, granulated sugar to ¹/₄ cup, and omitting herbs. Boil 1 cup pure maple syrup until reduced to ¹/₃ cup; add to milk in Step 1.

Coconut Crème Brulée—Make recipe as above, substituting $1/2$ cup toasted flaked coconut for the herbs in Step 1 and adding 1 teaspoon vanilla and $3/4$ teaspoon coconut extract to the strained milk mixture. Complete recipe as above.

Coffee Crème Brulée—Make recipe as above, omitting herbs. Heat 1 tablespoon instant espresso or coffee powder with milk in Step 1, stirring until dissolved. Increase granulated sugar to $2/3$ cup, and add 2 tablespoons coffee liqueur in Step 2.

BLUEBERRY CRÈME BRULÉE

A delicate custard enhances the flavor of fresh blueberries.

4 servings

$1/2$ cup granulated sugar
3 tablespoons cornstarch
2 cups fat-free milk
2 eggs, lightly beaten
$1/4$ cup fat-free sour cream
$1/2$ teaspoon lemon extract
$1^1/3$ cups blueberries
$1/4$ cup packed light brown sugar

Per Serving
Calories: 298
% Calories from fat: 9
Fat (gm): 2.9
Saturated fat (gm): 0.9
Cholesterol (mg): 108.2
Sodium (mg): 116
Protein (gm): 8.6
Carbohydrate (gm): 60.1
Exchanges
Milk: 0.0
Vegetable: 0.0
Fruit: 0.0
Bread: 4.0
Meat: 0.0
Fat: 0.5

1. Combine sugar, cornstarch, and milk in medium saucepan; whisk until boiling and thickened over medium heat. Whisk $1/2$ the milk mixture into eggs; whisk egg mixture back into saucepan. Whisk constantly over low heat until thickened, about 2 minutes; whisk in sour cream and lemon extract.

2. Divide blueberries among four 6-ounce custard cups; pour custard over. Refrigerate until chilled, 2 to 4 hours.

3. Press brown sugar through a strainer evenly over chilled custards. Place on cookie sheet and broil, 4 inches from heat source, until the sugar is melted and caramelized, 2 to 3 minutes. Serve immediately.

BLUEBERRY CHEESECAKE PARFAITS

Luscious cheesecake, layered with fresh blueberries in a parfait!

4 servings

3/4	cup reduced-fat ricotta cheese
1	package (8 ounces) fat-free cream cheese, softened
1/4	cup sugar
1/2	teaspoon almond extract
1	teaspoon grated lemon rind
1/3	cup blueberry spreadable fruit
1	cup fresh blueberries
1/4	cup vanilla wafer, *or* gingersnap, crumbs, divided
	Light whipped topping, as garnish

Per Serving
Calories: 227
% Calories from fat: 13
Fat (gm): 3.3
Saturated fat (gm): 1.6
Cholesterol (mg): 16.3
Sodium (mg): 431
Protein (gm): 15.6
Carbohydrate (gm): 34.5
Exchanges
Milk: 0.0
Vegetable: 0.0
Fruit: 0.0
Bread: 2.5
Meat: 1.0
Fat: 0.0

1. Process cheeses, sugar, almond extract, and lemon rind in food processor until smooth. Gently combine spreadable fruit and blueberries.

2. Spoon about 3 tablespoons cheese mixture into each parfait glass. Spoon berry mixture over cheese mixture; sprinkle each with 2 teaspoons vanilla wafer crumbs. Spoon remaining cheese mixture over crumbs; sprinkle with remaining crumbs. Refrigerate 2 to 3 hours or until set. Garnish with whipped topping.

TIRAMISU

An Italian favorite made low fat—especially good with homemade Lady-fingers (see p. 291).

9 servings

3³/₄ cups Mock Mascarpone (triple recipe, see p. 161)

¹/₂ cup sugar

2 tablespoons dark rum *or* 1 teaspoon rum extract

3 packages (3 ounces each) ladyfingers (36)

1 cup cold espresso *or* strong coffee Chocolate shavings, as garnish

Per Serving
Calories: 309
% Calories from fat: 19
Fat (gm): 6.5
Saturated fat (gm): 3
Cholesterol (mg): 172.2
Sodium (mg): 493
Protein (gm): 16.9
Carbohydrate (gm): 43.4
Exchanges
Milk: 0.0
Vegetable: 0.0
Fruit: 0.0
Bread: 3.0
Meat: 2.0
Fat: 0.0

1. Mix Mock Mascarpone, sugar, and rum. Split ladyfingers in half lengthwise. Quickly dip cut sides of 18 ladyfinger halves into espresso and arrange, cut sides up, in bottom of 9-inch square glass baking dish; repeat with 18 more ladyfinger halves. Spread with half the mascarpone mixture. Repeat with remaining ladyfingers, espresso, and mascarpone mixture. Sprinkle with chocolate shavings.

2. Refrigerate, loosely covered, until chilled, 3 to 4 hours. Cut into squares to serve.

TRIFLE ST. TROPEZ

A dessert with Riviera flair; fruit can be varied according to the season.

10 servings

1/4 cup sugar

2 tablespoons water

1 tablespoon dark rum *or* 1/2-1 teaspoon rum extract

1 pound cake (10³/4 ounces)

1/4 cup apricot preserves

2 cups cubed tropical fruit (mango, pineapple, papaya, kiwi, banana, etc.)

Mallow Crème Custard (recipe follows)

1-1¹/2 cups light whipped topping

Chopped macadamia nuts, as garnish

Toasted coconut, as garnish

Per Serving
Calories: 311
% Calories from fat: 24
Fat (gm): 8.6
Saturated fat (gm): 4.7
Cholesterol (mg): 131.6
Sodium (mg): 170
Protein (gm): 5.4
Carbohydrate (gm): 53.1
Exchanges
Milk: 0.0
Vegetable: 0.0
Fruit: 0.5
Bread: 3.0
Meat: 0.0
Fat: 1.5

1. Heat sugar and water to boiling, stirring to dissolve sugar; stir in rum and cool.

2. Cut cake horizontally into 3 layers; drizzle layers with sugar syrup. Spread preserves on cake layers; cut into 1-inch cubes.

3. Place 1/2 of the cake cubes in 2-quart glass bowl; spoon 1/2 of the fruit and Mallow Crème Custard over cake. Repeat layering. Refrigerate until chilled, 2 to 3 hours.

4. Spread top of trifle with whipped topping; sprinkle with macadamia nuts and toasted coconut.

Mallow Crème Custard

makes about 2¹/2 cups

1¹/2 cups fat-free milk

1/4 cup cornstarch

1 jar (7 ounces) marshmallow crème

3 eggs, lightly beaten

1 tablespoon dark rum *or* 1/4 teaspoon rum extract

1. Whisk milk and cornstarch in medium saucepan until boiling; whisk until thickened, about 1 minute. Add marshmallow crème, whisking until smooth.

2. Whisk about ¹/₂ cup milk mixture into eggs; whisk egg mixture back into saucepan. Whisk over low heat until thickened, 1 to 2 minutes. Stir in rum; cool.

BERRY LEMON TRIFLE

Layers of sponge cake, sherry, and the fresh berries of summer make this trifle especially good.

10 servings

    Classic Sponge Cake (see p. 100)
3 tablespoons dry sherry
¹/₄ cup strawberry preserves
4 cups assorted fresh berries (sliced strawberries, blueberries, raspberries, etc.)
    Lemon Yogurt Pastry Cream (see p. 269)
1-1¹/₂ cups light whipped topping
    Whole berries, as garnish

Per Serving
Calories: 279
% Calories from fat: 12
Fat (gm): 3.6
Saturated fat (gm): 1.8
Cholesterol (mg): 87.7
Sodium (mg): 169
Protein (gm): 6.1
Carbohydrate (gm): 54.5
Exchanges
Milk: 0.0
Vegetable: 0.0
Fruit: 1.0
Bread: 2.5
Meat: 0.0
Fat: 0.5

1. Bake Classic Sponge Cake in 13 x 9-inch pan; cool. Slice cake into 2 layers horizontally. Drizzle cut sides of cake layers with sherry; spread with preserves and cut into 1-inch cubes.

2. Place ¹/₂ of the cake cubes in 2-quart glass bowl; spoon ¹/₂ of the fruit and Lemon Yogurt Pastry Cream over cake. Repeat layering. Refrigerate until chilled, 2 to 3 hours.

3. Spread top of trifle with whipped topping; decorate with whole berries.

BAKED CEREAL PUDDING

Eat pudding warm from the oven, or refrigerate for a chilled dessert. Either way, this comfort food is just delicious.

6 servings (¹/₂ cup each)

2 eggs
2 egg whites
¹/₄ cup sugar
¹/₄ cup packed light brown sugar
³/₄ cup natural wheat and barley cereal
   (Grape-Nuts)
2 cups fat-free milk
2 tablespoons margarine, melted
1 teaspoon vanilla
¹/₈ teaspoon salt

Per Serving
Calories: 214
% Calories from fat: 24
Fat (gm): 5.8
Saturated fat (gm): 1.4
Cholesterol (mg): 72.3
Sodium (mg): 262
Protein (gm): 7.9
Carbohydrate (gm): 33.2
Exchanges
Milk: 0.0
Vegetable: 0.0
Fruit: 0.0
Bread: 2.0
Meat: 0.5
Fat: 1.0

1. Beat eggs, egg whites, and sugars in medium bowl; mix in remaining ingredients.

2. Pour mixture into 1-quart soufflé dish or casserole. Place dish in roasting pan on middle oven rack; pour 2 inches hot water into pan. Bake, uncovered, at 375 degrees until pudding is set, about 50 minutes, stirring halfway through baking time.

3. Remove soufflé dish from pan; cool on wire rack. Serve warm, or refrigerate and serve chilled.

WARM INDIAN PUDDING

Molasses and sweet spices signal the welcome flavors of the fall season.

6 servings

1/4 cup yellow cornmeal

3 cups fat-free milk, divided

3/4 cup light molasses

1/3 cup packed light brown sugar

1/4 teaspoon salt

3 tablespoons margarine

1/4 cup dark raisins

1/2 teaspoon ground cinnamon

1/4 teaspoon ground nutmeg

1/8 teaspoon ground cloves

1/8 teaspoon ground ginger

Per Serving
Calories: 277
% Calories from fat: 19
Fat (gm): 6.1
Saturated fat (gm): 1.3
Cholesterol (mg): 2
Sodium (mg): 143
Protein (gm): 5.3
Carbohydrate (gm): 35
Exchanges
Milk: 0.5
Vegetable: 0.0
Fruit: 0.5
Bread: 2.5
Meat: 0.0
Fat: 0.5

1. Combine cornmeal and 1 cup milk in a small bowl; set aside.

2. Heat 1 3/4 cups milk in a medium saucepan until steaming. Stir in cornmeal mixture and cook until thickened, about 15 minutes, stirring occasionally. Stir in molasses, sugar, and salt. Cook 2 to 3 minutes to dissolve sugar. Remove from heat; stir in margarine, raisins, and spices.

3. Spoon mixture into greased 1 1/2-quart casserole. Pour remaining 1/4 cup milk over mixture; bake, uncovered, 1 1/4 hours or until knife inserted near center comes out clean. Serve warm.

BAKED STRAWBERRY PUDDING

Fresh or frozen strawberries can be used for this refreshing pudding. Decorate with sliced fresh strawberries or other berries if desired.

8 servings

1 cup sugar, divided
$^1/_4$ cup all-purpose flour
$^1/_8$ teaspoon salt
$1^1/_2$ cups pureed strawberries (about $1^1/_2$ pints)
$^1/_4$ cup fat-free milk
1 tablespoon lemon juice
$^1/_3$ cup flaked coconut
3 egg whites

Per Serving
Calories: 151
% Calories from fat: 7
Fat (gm): 1.3
Saturated fat (gm): 0.9
Cholesterol (mg): 0.1
Sodium (mg): 62
Protein (gm): 2.4
Carbohydrate (gm): 33.9
Exchanges
Milk: 0.0
Vegetable: 0.0
Fruit: 0.0
Bread: 2.0
Meat: 0.0
Fat: 0.0

1. Mix $^3/_4$ cup sugar, flour, and salt in large bowl. Stir in strawberries, milk, lemon juice, and coconut.

2. Beat egg whites in medium bowl until foamy; beat to stiff peaks, adding remaining $^1/_4$ cup sugar gradually. Fold in strawberry mixture.

3. Spoon mixture into eight 6-ounce custard cups. Place cups in baking pan. Pour in 1 inch of hot water. Bake at 350 degrees until golden brown around the edges, about 35 minutes. Serve warm or cold.

BROWN SUGAR APPLE PUDDING

Topped and baked with a batter and brown sugar syrup, this is the best apple pudding you'll ever eat!

10 servings

8 cups sliced, peeled tart baking apples
1/2 cup packed light brown sugar
1/4 cup margarine, softened
1 1/2 teaspoons ground cinnamon
1 egg
1/2 teaspoon vanilla
3/4 cup all-purpose flour
2 teaspoons baking powder
1/4 teaspoon salt
1/2 cup fat-free milk
Brown Sugar Syrup (recipe follows)

Per Serving
Calories: 241
% Calories from fat: 22
Fat (gm): 6
Saturated fat (gm): 1.2
Cholesterol (mg): 21.4
Sodium (mg): 236
Protein (gm): 2.5
Carbohydrate (gm): 46.5
Exchanges
Milk: 0.0
Vegetable: 0.0
Fruit: 1.0
Bread: 2.0
Meat: 0.0
Fat: 1.0

1. Arrange apple slices in lightly greased 2-quart casserole.

2. Combine brown sugar, margarine, and cinnamon in medium bowl; stir in egg and vanilla. Mix in combined flour, baking powder, and salt alternately with milk, stirring only until blended. Spread batter over apple slices.

3. Pour Brown Sugar Syrup over batter. Bake, uncovered, at 375 degrees, 50 to 55 minutes or until apples are tender. Serve warm or at room temperature.

Brown Sugar Syrup

1/2 cup packed light brown sugar
2 tablespoons flour
1 teaspoon margarine
1 cup water
1/2 teaspoon vanilla

1. Combine brown sugar, flour, and margarine in small saucepan. Stir in water and heat to boiling, stirring constantly. Boil 2 to 3 minutes, stirring constantly. Remove from heat and stir in vanilla.

BAKED PUMPKIN PUDDING

This is a dramatic presentation for a delicately spiced pudding—great for a special autumn feast! Steam the pumpkin well ahead of time for your convenience.

6 servings

1 small pumpkin (about 5 pounds)
1¹/₂ teaspoons pumpkin pie spice, divided
6 tablespoons quick-cooking tapioca
1 cup sugar
¹/₂ teaspoon salt
4 eggs, beaten
4 cups fat-free milk
2 teaspoons vanilla

Per Serving
Calories: 351
% Calories from fat: 9
Fat (gm): 4
Saturated fat (gm): 1.4
Cholesterol (mg): 144.3
Sodium (mg): 323
Protein (gm): 12.4
Carbohydrate (gm): 69.6
Exchanges
Milk: 0.0
Vegetable: 0.0
Fruit: 0.0
Bread: 4.5
Meat: 0.0
Fat: 0.5

1. Cut top off pumpkin; set aside. Remove seeds and fibers from shell. Sprinkle inside of pumpkin with 1 teaspoon pumpkin pie spice.

2. Pour 1 inch water into large saucepan; place pumpkin on rack in saucepan and replace pumpkin top. Heat to boiling; reduce heat and simmer, covered, until inside of pumpkin is tender when pierced with a fork, about 50 minutes. Remove pumpkin from saucepan and drain excess moisture from inside.

3. Mix tapioca, sugar, salt, eggs, and milk in saucepan; let stand 10 minutes. Heat to boiling, stirring constantly. Remove from heat; stir in vanilla.

4. Place pumpkin shell (without top) in roasting pan on middle oven rack. Pour tapioca mixture into pumpkin and sprinkle with remaining ¹/₂ teaspoon pumpkin pie spice. Pour 1 inch hot water into pan.

5. Bake, uncovered, until set, about 30 minutes. Cut around top of pumpkin to loosen baked pumpkin from outer shell. Serve pudding with spoonfuls of baked pumpkin.

CREAMY RICE PUDDING

This stove-top rice pudding can be made with 2¹/₂ cups leftover, unseasoned rice, if you like. In that case, start with Step 2 in the recipe.

6 servings

³/₄ cup uncooked rice

2 cups water

4 cups fat-free milk, divided

¹/₂ cup sugar

¹/₂ teaspoon salt

1¹/₂ tablespoons cornstarch

Ground cinnamon, as garnish

Per Serving
Calories: 214
% Calories from fat: 1
Fat (gm): 0.4
Saturated fat (gm): 0.2
Cholesterol (mg): 2.9
Sodium (mg): 279
Protein (gm): 7.2
Carbohydrate (gm): 44.9
Exchanges
Milk: 0.0
Vegetable: 0.0
Fruit: 0.0
Bread: 3.0
Meat: 0.0
Fat: 0.0

1. Heat rice and water in small saucepan over medium heat to boiling; reduce heat and simmer, uncovered, until rice is tender and water is absorbed, about 20 minutes. Reserve.

2. Heat 3 cups milk, sugar, and salt to boiling in medium saucepan. Stir in reserved rice and combined remaining 1 cup milk and cornstarch. Reduce heat and simmer, uncovered, stirring occasionally, until thick, about 20 minutes. Cool slightly; spoon into serving dishes or bowl. Sprinkle with cinnamon. Refrigerate, covered, until chilled.

Variations: **Apple Rice Pudding**—Make recipe as above, substituting brown sugar for the granulated sugar. Saute 1 cup coarsely chopped, unpeeled apple in 1 tablespoon margarine in large skillet until lightly browned. Stir apples and 1 teaspoon vanilla into rice pudding at the end of cooking time.

Almond Rice Pudding—Make recipe as above, simmering rice with 1 cinnamon stick, and reducing sugar to ¹/₄ cup. Stir ²/₃ cup finely chopped toasted almonds, 2 teaspoons vanilla, and 1 teaspoon almond extract into pudding at the end of cooking time. Cool to room temperature; fold in 2 cups light whipped topping. Spoon into serving dishes and chill. Serve with Raspberry Sauce or Cranberry Coulis (see pp. 658, 251).

OLD-FASHIONED BAKED RICE PUDDING

Serve warm with Tart Lemon Sauce or Raspberry Sauce (see pp. 650, 658).

6 servings

$^1/_2$ cup uncooked rice

3 cups fat-free milk

$^1/_3$ cup sugar

$^1/_4$ cup golden raisins

$^1/_2$ teaspoon ground cinnamon

2 dashes ground nutmeg

Per Serving
Calories: 158
% Calories from fat: 2
Fat (gm): 0.3
Saturated fat (gm): 0.2
Cholesterol (mg): 2
Sodium (mg): 65
Protein (gm): 5.4
Carbohydrate (gm): 34
Exchanges
Milk: 0.5
Vegetable: 0.0
Fruit: 0.5
Bread: 1.0
Meat: 0.0
Fat: 0.0

1. Combine all ingredients in 2-quart casserole.

2. Bake, uncovered, at 350 degrees until rice is tender and milk is absorbed, about $1^1/_2$ hours, stirring occasionally. Serve warm or chilled.

BROWN RICE PUDDING

This pudding is soft when it comes from the oven but becomes firm, with a delicately crusted top, after chilling.

6 servings

$^1/_2$ cup uncooked brown rice

3 cups fat-free milk

4 eggs, beaten

4 tablespoons margarine, softened

$^1/_2$ cup sugar

$^1/_4$ cup raisins

1 teaspoon ground cinnamon

$^1/_4$ teaspoon ground mace

Dash salt

Per Serving
Calories: 301
% Calories from fat: 34
Fat (gm): 11.6
Saturated fat (gm): 2.8
Cholesterol (mg): 143.5
Sodium (mg): 196
Protein (gm): 9.9
Carbohydrate (gm): 40.2
Exchanges
Milk: 0.0
Vegetable: 0.0
Fruit: 0.0
Bread: 2.5
Meat: 0.0
Fat: 2.5

1. Heat rice and milk in medium saucepan to boiling; reduce heat and simmer, covered, until most of the milk has been absorbed, 1 to 1¹/₂ hours; cool to lukewarm.

2. Add remaining ingredients to rice mixture. Spoon into greased 1¹/₂-quart casserole. Bake, uncovered, 30 minutes at 350 degrees; cool. Refrigerate, covered, until chilled and firm, 4 to 5 hours.

Variation: **Raspberry Rice Pudding**—Make pudding as above, omitting spices and raisins. Instead of using casserole, spoon ¹/₄ cup raspberries into each of six 6-ounce custard cups. Spoon rice mixture over raspberries and stir gently to combine. Place custard cups in baking pan; pour boiling water into pan to come halfway up sides of cups. Bake 45 to 60 minutes. Serve with Raspberry Sauce (see p. 658), if desired.

RISOTTO PUDDING

This creamy wine-flavored rice pudding is a special treat. Arborio rice is available in large supermarkets or specialty food stores. Long-grain rice can be substituted if necessary, but the pudding will be less creamy in texture.

6 servings

   2 cups sweet white wine (Chablis or Sauterne)
1¹/₂ cups water
   2 teaspoons ground cinnamon
   1 tablespoon grated orange rind
   1 cup arborio rice
 ¹/₄ cup sugar
¹/₄-¹/₂ cup coarsely chopped toasted walnuts
1¹/₂ cups Sugared Crushed Berries
    (¹/₂ recipe) (see p. 249)

Per Serving
Calories: 277
% Calories from fat: 10
Fat (gm): 3.3
Saturated fat (gm): 0.3
Cholesterol (mg): 0
Sodium (mg): 6
Protein (gm): 3.9
Carbohydrate (gm): 46.1
Exchanges
Milk: 0.0
Vegetable: 0.0
Fruit: 0.0
Bread: 3.0
Meat: 0.0
Fat: 1.0

1. Heat wine, water, cinnamon, and orange rind to boiling in medium saucepan; reduce heat and simmer, covered, 5 minutes. Add rice and sugar. Heat to boiling; reduce heat and simmer, uncovered, stirring frequently, until rice is tender and liquid is absorbed, 18 to 20 minutes. Stir in walnuts. Serve immediately with Sugared Crushed Berries.

FRUITED TAPIOCA

Tapioca pudding is so easy, and this fruity version is delicious.

6 servings

3 tablespoons quick-cooking tapioca

$1/8$ teaspoon salt

1 egg, beaten

$2^3/4$ cups fat-free milk

$2/3$ cup sugar

$2/3$ cup drained pineapple tidbits

$1/3$ cup golden raisins

$1/3$ cup dried cranberries

Ground cinnamon and nutmeg, as garnish

Per Serving
Calories: 224
% Calories from fat: 4
Fat (gm): 1.1
Saturated fat (gm): 0.4
Cholesterol (mg): 37.4
Sodium (mg): 118
Protein (gm): 5.3
Carbohydrate (gm): 49.9
Exchanges
Milk: 0.0
Vegetable: 0.0
Fruit: 1.5
Bread: 2.0
Meat: 0.0
Fat: 0.0

1. Mix all ingredients except cinnamon and nutmeg in medium saucepan. Let stand 5 minutes. Heat to boiling, stirring constantly. Remove from heat; let stand 20 minutes. Stir and pour into serving dishes.

2. Refrigerate until chilled; sprinkle with cinnamon and nutmeg.

Variation: **Butterscotch Tapioca**—Make recipe as above, omitting fruit, substituting $1/2$ cup packed brown sugar for the granulated sugar, and adding $1/2$ teaspoon maple extract.

BLUEBERRY BREAD PUDDING WITH TART LEMON SAUCE

For a double berry treat, try this pudding with Raspberry Sauce (see p. 658) too.

8 servings

3 tablespoons margarine, softened

6 slices whole wheat bread

1 egg

2 egg whites

$1/2$ cup sugar

$1/4$ teaspoon salt

2 cups fat-free milk

1 teaspoon vanilla

1 cup fresh, *or* frozen, blueberries

Tart Lemon Sauce (see p. 650)

Per Serving
Calories: 295
% Calories from fat: 29
Fat (gm): 9.9
Saturated fat (gm): 2.2
Cholesterol (mg): 80.6
Sodium (mg): 325
Protein (gm): 7.4
Carbohydrate (gm): 46.5
Exchanges
Milk: 0.0
Vegetable: 0.0
Fruit: 0.0
Bread: 3.0
Meat: 0.0
Fat: 2.0

1. Spread margarine on one side of each slice of bread; cut into 2-inch squares and place in greased 9-inch baking dish or 1-quart casserole.

2. Combine egg, egg whites, sugar, and salt in medium bowl. Heat milk in small saucepan until just boiling; whisk milk into egg mixture. Stir in vanilla and blueberries; pour over bread cubes and toss.

3. Place baking dish in roasting pan on middle oven rack; pour 1 inch hot water into pan. Bake, uncovered, at 350 degrees 35 to 40 minutes or until knife inserted near center comes out clean. Serve warm or at room temperature with Tart Lemon Sauce

Variations: **Rum-Raisin Bread Pudding**—Make recipe as above, substituting 1/3 cup raisins for the blueberries. Add 1 tablespoon grated orange rind, 1 tablespoon dark rum *or* 1 teaspoon rum extract, and 1 teaspoon ground cinnamon to the milk mixture. Serve with Warm Rum Sauce (see p. 54).

Dark Chocolate Bread Pudding—Make recipe as above omitting blueberries, increasing sugar to 3/4 cup, and also melting 2 ounces unsweetened chocolate with milk in Step 2. Serve with Crème Anglaise or Bittersweet Chocolate Sauce (see pp. 640, 641).

Dried Cherry-Apricot Bread Pudding—Make recipe as above, substituting white bread for the whole wheat and omitting blueberries. Simmer 1/3 cup each sliced dried apricots and dried cherries in 1/2 cup orange juice until fruit is soft and juice absorbed; combine with milk mixture, spoon over bread cubes, and toss. Bake as above. Serve with Orange Sauce (see p. 652).

Sourdough Bread Pudding with Caramelized Pears—Make Step 1 as above, substituting sourdough bread for the whole wheat bread and placing cubes in large bowl; omit blueberries. To make Caramelized Pears: Melt 2 tablespoons margarine in medium skillet; sprinkle with 1/2 cup sugar. Arrange 2 large, sliced pears evenly over sugar in skillet. Cook over medium-high heat until bubbly and browned, about 20 minutes. Arrange pears in bottom of casserole dish, scraping syrup over. Spoon bread mixture over pears and bake as above. Invert onto serving platter.

BLUSHING BREAD PUDDING

*This unusual Welsh-style bread pudding is soufflé-like in texture and fla-
vored with raspberries and sherry. Use a firm white bread for the best texture.*

10 servings

2/3 cup fat-free milk

12 cups fresh white bread crumbs (about 1
pound loaf)

1/4 cup sugar

2 tablespoons margarine, melted

4 egg whites

1 1/2 cups seedless raspberry preserves

2 tablespoons sweet sherry

Light whipped topping, as garnish

Per Serving
Calories: 331
% Calories from fat: 13
Fat (gm): 4.7
Saturated fat (gm): 1.2
Cholesterol (mg): 0.3
Sodium (mg): 340
Protein (gm): 7.1
Carbohydrate (gm): 66.2
Exchanges
Milk: 0.0
Vegetable: 0.0
Fruit: 0.0
Bread: 4.0
Meat: 0.0
Fat: 1.0

1. Heat milk to boiling; pour over bread crumbs in large bowl
and toss lightly. Let stand 20 minutes. Stir in sugar and margarine. Beat egg whites until stiff, but not dry; fold into the crumb
mixture.

2. Mix preserves and sherry. Spread half the preserves mixture
over bottom of greased 11 x 7-inch baking dish. Spoon half the
bread crumb mixture over preserves; repeat layering.

3. Bake, uncovered, at 300 degrees until set, about 25 minutes.
Serve hot, with whipped topping.

CARAMEL APPLE BREAD PUDDING

Two of America's favorite flavors combine in this richly flavored pudding. Serve warm with scoops of fat-free frozen yogurt or ice cream.

8 servings

2¹/₂ cups fat-free milk

¹/₂ package (14-ounce size) caramels (about 25)

¹/₂ teaspoon ground cinnamon

¹/₄ teaspoon ground nutmeg

3 eggs, lightly beaten

6 cups cubed day-old bread (³/₄-inch cubes)

¹/₂ cup chopped dried apple

¹/₄ cup raisins

¹/₄ cup chopped walnuts

Per Serving
Calories: 255
% Calories from fat: 19
Fat (gm): 5.7
Saturated fat (gm): 1.3
Cholesterol (mg): 80.9
Sodium (mg): 190
Protein (gm): 8.1
Carbohydrate (gm): 44.6
Exchanges
Milk: 0.0
Vegetable: 0.0
Fruit: 0.0
Bread: 3.0
Meat: 0.0
Fat: 1.0

1. Heat milk, caramels, cinnamon, and nutmeg in medium saucepan over medium heat until caramels are melted, stirring frequently. Whisk milk mixture into eggs in small bowl.

2. Toss bread cubes, dried apple, raisins, and walnuts in 2-quart casserole; pour milk mixture over and toss. Place casserole in roasting pan on middle oven rack; pour 1¹/₂ inches hot water into roasting pan.

3. Bake, uncovered, at 350 degrees until set, 40 to 45 minutes. Serve warm.

OLD-FASHIONED DATE PUDDING

Marcie's date pudding is a family favorite—it's delicious warm from the oven.

8 servings

1 cup cubed firm white bread (³/₄-inch cubes)

1 cup sugar

¹/₂ cup coarsely chopped pecans *or* walnuts

1 cup chopped dates

2 tablespoons flour

1 teaspoon baking powder

2 tablespoons water

2 eggs, beaten

Light whipped topping, as garnish

Per Serving
Calories: 242
% Calories from fat: 23
Fat (gm): 6.5
Saturated fat (gm): 0.9
Cholesterol (mg): 53
Sodium (mg): 97
Protein (gm): 3.2
Carbohydrate (gm): 46.1
Exchanges
Milk: 0.0
Vegetable: 0.0
Fruit: 0.0
Bread: 3.0
Meat: 0.0
Fat: 1.0

1. Combine bread, sugar, pecans, dates, flour, and baking powder in large bowl and toss well. Stir in combined water and eggs. Pour into greased 11 x 7-inch baking pan.

2. Bake at 300 degrees until set, about 45 minutes. Serve with dollops of whipped topping.

HUNGARIAN NOODLE PUDDING

A dessert kugel, flavored with raspberry preserves and almonds.

8 servings

4 eggs, separated
1/2 cup sugar
1 cup fat-free sour cream
1 tablespoon grated orange rind
2 teaspoons ground cinnamon
1 package (8 ounces) egg noodles, cooked, warm
2 tablespoons margarine
2 tablespoons unseasoned dry bread crumbs
1/2 cup seedless raspberry preserves, melted
1/2 cup chopped almonds

Per Serving
Calories: 367
% Calories from fat: 26
Fat (gm): 9.9
Saturated fat (gm): 1.9
Cholesterol (mg): 130.5
Sodium (mg): 112
Protein (gm): 10.4
Carbohydrate (gm): 54.3
Exchanges
Milk: 0.0
Vegetable: 0.0
Fruit: 0.0
Bread: 4.0
Meat: 0.0
Fat: 2.0

1. Beat egg yolks and sugar in small bowl until thick and lemon-colored, about 5 minutes. Beat in sour cream, orange rind, and cinnamon. Beat egg whites in large bowl until stiff peaks form. Fold yolk mixture into egg whites.

2. Mix noodles and margarine in large bowl; mix in egg mixture. Sprinkle bread crumbs in greased 1 1/2-quart casserole. Layer half the noodle mixture in casserole; spread with preserves and sprinkle with 1/2 the almonds. Top with remaining noodle mixture and sprinkle with remaining almonds.

3. Bake, uncovered, at 350 degrees until set, about 30 minutes. Let stand 10 minutes before serving.

Variation: **Cherry-Peach Kugel**—Make recipe as above, stirring 1 cup 1% low-fat cottage cheese, 1 can (8 ounces) drained, chopped peaches, and 1/2 cup dried cherries into noodle mixture. Spoon entire noodle mixture over bread crumbs in prepared casserole, omitting raspberry preserves. Sprinkle with almonds and bake as above.

STEAMED MARMALADE PUDDING

Steamed puddings are traditional celebration desserts in England. They can be made in any 1-quart casserole or soufflé dish if you don't have a pudding mold.

8 servings

1/2 cup sugar
5 tablespoons margarine, softened
2 eggs, slightly beaten
1 1/3 cups all-purpose flour
1 1/2 teaspoons baking powder
2 tablespoons fat-free milk
3/4 cup orange marmalade
Orange Marmalade Sauce (see p. 653)

Per Serving
Calories: 365
% Calories from fat: 20
Fat (gm): 8.6
Saturated fat (gm): 1.8
Cholesterol (mg): 53.1
Sodium (mg): 201
Protein (gm): 4.2
Carbohydrate (gm): 71.7
Exchanges
Milk: 0.0
Vegetable: 0.0
Fruit: 1.5
Bread: 3.0
Meat: 0.0
Fat: 1.5

1. Cream sugar and margarine in mixing bowl until light and fluffy. Beat in eggs gradually. Stir in combined flour and baking powder; stir in milk.

2. Spread marmalade in bottom of greased 1-quart pudding mold or soufflé dish. Spread batter over marmalade, spreading to side of mold. Cover tightly with cover, or greased aluminum foil tied securely with string.

3. Place mold on rack in Dutch oven or large saucepan. Pour boiling water into pan to come about 2/3 up side of mold. Heat to boiling; reduce heat and simmer, covered, until toothpick inserted in center of pudding comes out clean, about 1 1/2 hours.

4. Remove mold from water; remove cover. Cool pudding on wire rack about 30 minutes. Run knife around edge of mold; invert pudding onto serving platter. Serve warm with Orange Marmalade Sauce.

CHOCOLATE STEAMED PUDDING

Warm chocolate steamed pudding is a special treat! This goes together quickly and can cook while you prepare and eat the rest of your dinner.

6 servings

2 ounces unsweetened chocolate, melted, cooled

1 cup all-purpose flour

$^1/_2$ cup sugar

$^1/_2$ cup fat-free milk

1 egg

1 teaspoon baking powder

$^1/_2$ teaspoon ground cinnamon

$^1/_4$ teaspoon salt

$^1/_4$ cup chopped walnuts

Crème Anglaise (see p. 640)

Per Serving
Calories: 275
% Calories from fat: 30
Fat (gm): 9.7
Saturated fat (gm): 3.9
Cholesterol (mg): 71.9
Sodium (mg): 222
Protein (gm): 8.1
Carbohydrate (gm): 42.3
Exchanges
Milk: 0.0
Vegetable: 0.0
Fruit: 0.0
Bread: 2.5
Meat: 0.0
Fat: 2.0

1. Combine all ingredients except walnuts and Crème Anglaise in large mixing bowl. Beat on low speed until blended; beat 1 minute on high speed. Fold in walnuts.

2. Spoon batter into greased 1-quart pudding mold or soufflé dish. Cover tightly with cover, or greased aluminum foil tied securely with string.

3. Place mold on rack in Dutch oven or large saucepan. Pour boiling water into pan to come about $^2/_3$ up side of mold. Heat to boiling; reduce heat and simmer, covered, until toothpick inserted in center of pudding comes out clean, about $1^1/_2$ hours.

4. Remove mold from water; remove lid. Cool pudding on wire rack about 10 minutes. Run knife around edge of mold; invert pudding onto serving platter. Serve warm with Crème Anglaise.

SEVEN

Soufflés, Mousses
AND
Gelatins

PEACH-ALLSPICE SOUFFLÉS

The soufflé can also be baked in a 1-quart soufflé dish. Bake at 450 degrees for 10 minutes; reduce heat to 425 degrees and bake another 10 minutes or until sharp knife inserted near center comes out clean.

6 servings

Vegetable cooking spray

1¹/₂ cups chopped fresh *or* frozen, thawed *or* drained, canned peaches

2 teaspoons lemon juice

1 teaspoon vanilla

¹/₄ cup plus 1 teaspoon sugar, divided

¹/₈ teaspoon ground allspice

2 egg yolks

4 egg whites

¹/₈ teaspoon cream of tartar

Powdered sugar, as garnish

Per Serving
Calories: 93
% Calories from fat: 17
Fat (gm): 1.7
Saturated fat (gm): 0.5
Cholesterol (mg): 71
Sodium (mg): 39
Protein (gm): 3.6
Carbohydrate (gm): 15.9
Exchanges
Milk: 0.0
Vegetable: 0.0
Fruit: 1.0
Bread: 0.0
Meat: 0.5
Fat: 0.0

1. Spray six 1-cup soufflé dishes or custard cups with cooking spray; place dishes on baking sheet.

2. Process peaches, lemon juice, vanilla, 1 teaspoon sugar, and allspice in food processor or blender until smooth. Add egg yolks, one at a time, processing until smooth.

3. Beat egg whites and cream of tartar in large bowl until soft peaks form. Gradually beat in remaining ¹/₄ cup sugar, beating to stiff peaks. Fold in peach mixture. Spoon into prepared dishes.

4. Bake at 450 degrees 7 minutes; reduce heat to 425 degrees and bake 7 minutes or until soufflés are lightly browned and sharp knife inserted near centers comes out clean. Sprinkle with powdered sugar, and serve immediately.

BAKED BANANA SOUFFLÉS

For perfect flavor and texture, select bananas that are ripe and soft, but not overripe. The soufflé can also be baked in a 1-quart soufflé dish. Bake at 450 degrees for 10 minutes, then at 425 degrees about 10 additional minutes.

6 servings

2 ripe bananas, peeled
2 teaspoons lemon juice
1 teaspoon vanilla
1/4 cup sugar, divided
1/4 teaspoon ground nutmeg
2 egg yolks
4 egg whites
1/2 teaspoon cream of tartar
Powdered sugar, as garnish

Per Serving
Calories: 102
% Calories from fat: 17
Fat (gm): 1.9
Saturated fat (gm): 0.6
Cholesterol (mg): 71
Sodium (mg): 39
Protein (gm): 3.7
Carbohydrate (gm): 18.1
Exchanges
Milk: 0.0
Vegetable: 0.0
Fruit: 0.0
Bread: 1.0
Meat: 0.0
Fat: 0.5

1. Process bananas, lemon juice, vanilla, 1 tablespoon sugar, and nutmeg in food processor or blender until smooth. Add egg yolks, one at a time, blending until smooth.

2. Beat egg whites and cream of tartar in medium bowl to soft peaks; gradually beat in remaining 3 tablespoons sugar, beating to stiff peaks. Fold in banana mixture. Spoon into 6 lightly greased 1-cup soufflé dishes or custard cups. Place dishes on cookie sheet.

3. Bake at 450 degrees 7 minutes; reduce heat to 425 degrees and bake until soufflés are lightly browned and sharp knife inserted near centers comes out clean, about 7 minutes. Remove from oven; sprinkle with powdered sugar and serve immediately.

VANILLA DOLCE SOUFFLÉ

For the purest vanilla flavor, use a whole vanilla bean as the recipe directs. The pod can be buried in a jar of sugar to make vanilla sugar for baking, over fruit, or in beverages. Two teaspoons vanilla can be substituted for the vanilla bean; add it after cooking the egg yolk mixture.

6 servings

1 tablespoon rum *or* 1 teaspoon rum extract
¹/₄ cup finely chopped mixed candied fruit
1 vanilla bean (about 4 inches long)
1 cup fat-free milk
3 egg yolks
¹/₃ cup granulated sugar
2 tablespoons flour
6 egg whites
Pinch salt
2 tablespoons powdered sugar, divided

Per Serving
Calories: 153
% Calories from fat: 16
Fat (gm): 2.7
Saturated fat (gm): 0.8
Cholesterol (mg): 107.2
Sodium (mg): 80
Protein (gm): 6.6
Carbohydrate (gm): 24.2
Exchanges
Milk: 0.0
Vegetable: 0.0
Fruit: 0.0
Bread: 2.0
Meat: 0.0
Fat: 0.5

1. Grease a 1¹/₂-quart soufflé dish; sprinkle lightly with sugar. Refrigerate dish.

2. Sprinkle rum over candied fruit; let stand 5 minutes. Split vanilla bean lengthwise; scrape seeds into milk in small saucepan. Heat over low heat until simmering.

3. Beat egg yolks and granulated sugar in small bowl until thick and lemon colored, about 5 minutes; stir in flour. Whisk half the warm milk into egg mixture; whisk mixture into saucepan. Whisk over medium heat until boiling and thickened. Stir in candied fruit mixture.

3. Beat egg whites and salt in large bowl until soft peaks form. Add 1 tablespoon powdered sugar, and continue beating to stiff peaks. Fold in egg yolk mixture. Spoon into prepared dish.

4. Bake at 400 degrees 20 minutes or until soufflé is golden brown. Sprinkle with remaining 1 tablespoon powdered sugar, and serve immediately.

Variations: **Ginger-Orange Soufflé**—Make recipe as above, omitting candied fruit, rum, and vanilla bean. Simmer milk with 2 tablespoons chopped fresh ginger; strain before adding to yolks. Stir ¹/₄ cup chopped crystallized ginger and 1 tablespoon grated orange rind into cooked egg yolk mixture in Step 3. Serve with Orange Sauce (see p. 652).

Rum Raisin Soufflé—Make recipe as above, omitting vanilla bean, substituting $1/2$ cup chopped golden raisins for the candied fruit, increasing rum to $1/4$ cup or 1 to 2 teaspoons rum extract, and adding $1/8$ teaspoon ground nutmeg. Serve with Rum Raisin Sauce (see p. 645), substituting golden raisins for the dark raisins.

TANGERINE SOUFFLÉ

Fresh tangerines give an intense flavor to this lovely soufflé.

8 servings

3 medium tangerines
$1/2$ cup frozen tangerine concentrate
$1/2$ cup water
$1^1/2$ cups sugar, divided
5 egg whites
1 cup light whipped topping
2 tablespoons orange liqueur, optional

Per Serving
Calories: 196
% Calories from fat: 5
Fat (gm): 1.1
Saturated fat (gm): 1
Cholesterol (mg): 0
Sodium (mg): 35
Protein (gm): 2.5
Carbohydrate (gm): 44.9
Exchanges
Milk: 0.0
Vegetable: 0.0
Fruit: 2.0
Bread: 1.0
Meat: 0.0
Fat: 0.0

1. Peel and slice tangerines, removing seeds, and reserving rind from 1 tangerine. Chop rind coarsely.

2. Heat tangerines, chopped rind, frozen tangerine concentrate, water, and 1 cup sugar to boiling in large saucepan; reduce heat and simmer, covered, until rind is very tender, about 35 minutes. Uncover and boil until juices are very thick and form large bubbles. Process tangerine mixture in food processor or blender until rind is very finely chopped; pour into large bowl.

3. Beat egg whites to soft peaks in large bowl; beat to stiff peaks, gradually adding remaining $1/2$ cup sugar. Fold $1/4$ of the egg whites into tangerine mixture; fold tangerine mixture into whites. Pour soufflé mixture into 2-quart soufflé dish that has been lightly greased and sprinkled with sugar.

4. Bake at 350 degrees until puffed and set, about 40 minutes. Mix whipped topping and orange liqueur. Serve soufflé immediately with dollops of whipped topping mixture.

CHOCOLATE SOUFFLÉ WITH PEANUT SAUCE

Make sure everyone is at the table, ready to view this dramatic dessert as it comes from the oven!

8 servings

1¹/₂ cups fat-free milk, divided
1 ounce unsweetened chocolate
³/₄ cup sugar
¹/₄ cup unsweetened cocoa
2¹/₂ tablespoons cornstarch
2 teaspoons vanilla
4 egg yolks
6 egg whites
¹/₂ teaspoon salt
Peanut Sauce (recipe follows)

Per Serving
Calories: 239
% Calories from fat: 25
Fat (gm): 6.7
Saturated fat (gm): 2.3
Cholesterol (mg): 107.4
Sodium (mg): 293
Protein (gm): 7.3
Carbohydrate (gm): 34.6
Exchanges
Milk: 0.0
Vegetable: 0.0
Fruit: 0.0
Bread: 2.0
Meat: 0.0
Fat: 2.0

1. Grease a 2-quart soufflé dish; sprinkle generously with sugar.

2. Heat ³/₄ cup milk and chocolate in medium saucepan over medium heat, whisking until chocolate is melted. Mix sugar, cocoa, cornstarch, and remaining ³/₄ cup milk in small bowl until smooth; whisk into mixture in saucepan. Whisk over medium heat until mixture boils and thickens. Remove from heat; stir in vanilla.

3. Beat egg yolks in small bowl until thick and lemon colored, about 5 minutes. Fold into chocolate mixture. Beat egg whites and salt in large bowl to stiff peaks. Fold chocolate mixture into egg whites. Pour into prepared dish.

4. Bake at 350 degrees until knife inserted halfway between edge and center comes out clean, 1 to 1¹/₄ hours. Serve immediately with Peanut Sauce.

Peanut Sauce

makes about 1¹/₂ cups

  2 tablespoons sugar
  2 tablespoons cornstarch
¹/₈ teaspoon salt
  1 cup water
¹/₄ cup coffee liqueur *or* strong coffee
¹/₄-¹/₃ cup chopped dry-roasted peanuts

1. Mix sugar, cornstarch, and salt in small saucepan. Stir in water gradually. Whisk over medium heat until mixture boils and thickens. Remove from heat; stir in liqueur and peanuts.

Variations: **Chocolate Banana Soufflé**—Make recipe as above, mixing ¹/₂ cup mashed ripe banana and 1 tablespoon dark rum into egg yolks before folding into chocolate mixture. Complete and bake as above; serve with Peanut Sauce (above), Warm Rum Sauce, or Bittersweet Chocolate Sauce (see pp. 54, 641).

Chocolate Mint Soufflé—Make the recipe as above, substituting ¹/₃ cup mint chocolate morsels for the unsweetened chocolate and 2 teaspoons mint liqueur or ¹/₂ teaspoon mint extract for the vanilla. Omit Peanut Sauce. Serve soufflé with Chocolate Sauce (see p. 642), adding ¹/₄ to ¹/₂ teaspoon mint extract.

DOUBLE CHOCOLATE SOUFFLÉ

This fabulously rich chocolate soufflé is accented by White Chocolate Sauce. Melt the white chocolate very carefully, as it can easily become grainy.

8 servings

¹/₂ cup Prune Puree (see p. 42)
  3 ounces semisweet chocolate, grated
  2 tablespoons unsweetened cocoa
  2 teaspoons instant espresso powder *or* instant coffee granules
  1 egg yolk
  5 egg whites
¹/₄ cup granulated sugar
  1 tablespoon powdered sugar
      White Chocolate Sauce (recipe follows)

Per Serving
Calories: 254
% Calories from fat: 25
Fat (gm): 7.6
Saturated fat (gm): 4.4
Cholesterol (mg): 28.7
Sodium (mg): 58
Protein (gm): 5.2
Carbohydrate (gm): 46
Exchanges
Milk: 0.0
Vegetable: 0.0
Fruit: 2.0
Bread: 1.0
Meat: 0.0
Fat: 1.5

1. Mix Prune Puree, chocolate, cocoa, espresso, and egg yolk until well blended.

2. Beat egg whites in large bowl to soft peaks; beat to stiff peaks, adding granulated sugar gradually. Fold $1/4$ of the egg white mixture into chocolate mixture. Fold chocolate mixture into egg white mixture. Pour into $1^1/2$-quart soufflé dish that has been lightly greased and sprinkled with sugar.

3. Place soufflé dish in square baking pan on middle shelf of oven. Pour 2 inches boiling water into pan. Bake at 350 degrees until puffed and set, about 55 minutes. Sprinkle with powdered sugar. Serve immediately with White Chocolate Sauce.

White Chocolate Sauce

makes about $1/2$ cup

> 2 tablespoons fat-free milk
> 3 ounces white chocolate, chopped
> 1 tablespoon coffee *or* chocolate liqueur, optional

1. Heat milk over low heat in small saucepan to simmering; add white chocolate and whisk over very low heat until melted. Remove from heat; stir in coffee or liqueur.

BREAD PUDDING SOUFFLÉ WITH WHISKEY SAUCE

A soufflé of bread pudding with figs is enhanced with a flavorful sauce.

6 servings

> 6 cups cubed day-old egg bread ($1/2$-inch cubes)
> $2/3$ cup fat-free milk
> 2 egg yolks
> $1/2$ cup sugar
> $1/4$ teaspoon ground cinnamon
> Pinch ground nutmeg
> $1/4$ cup chopped dried figs
> 4 egg whites
> Whiskey Sauce (see p. 646)

Per Serving
Calories: 349
% Calories from fat: 16
Fat (gm): 6.3
Saturated fat (gm): 1.6
Cholesterol (mg): 71.5
Sodium (mg): 201
Protein (gm): 5.8
Carbohydrate (gm): 67.4
Exchanges
Milk: 0.0
Vegetable: 0.0
Fruit: 2.0
Bread: 2.5
Meat: 0.0
Fat: 1.0

1. Toss bread cubes with milk in large bowl, breaking up bread slightly. Beat egg yolks, sugar, and spices until thick and pale, about 5 minutes; fold into bread mixture. Stir in figs.

2. Beat egg whites in large bowl to stiff peaks; fold into bread mixture. Spoon into 1-quart soufflé dish that has been greased and sprinkled with sugar.

3. Bake at 350 degrees until puffed and set, about 40 minutes. Serve immediately with Whiskey Sauce.

STRAWBERRY ANGEL SOUFFLÉ

Angel food cake forms the base for this very easy soufflé. Use leftover homemade cake, or half of a purchased 10-ounce angel food cake. Any type of cake crumbs can be substituted for the angel food.

6 servings

2 cups angel food cake crumbs

1 package (16 ounces) frozen strawberries in syrup, thawed, pureed, divided

1 tablespoon orange liqueur *or* 1 teaspoon orange extract

5 egg whites

¹/₂ cup sugar

Per Serving
Calories: 245
% Calories from fat: 1
Fat (gm): 0.4
Saturated fat (gm): 0.1
Cholesterol (mg): 0
Sodium (mg): 298
Protein (gm): 5.3
Carbohydrate (gm): 56.8
Exchanges
Milk: 0.0
Vegetable: 0.0
Fruit: 2.0
Bread: 2.0
Meat: 0.0
Fat: 0.0

1. Combine cake crumbs, 1¹/₂ cups strawberry puree, and orange liqueur in large bowl. Pour remaining ¹/₂ cup strawberry puree into bottom of 2-quart soufflé dish that has been greased and sprinkled with sugar.

2. Beat egg whites to stiff peaks in large bowl, adding sugar gradually; fold into cake mixture. Pour into soufflé dish. Bake at 350 degrees until puffed and set, about 35 minutes.

CHOCOLATE BOURBON SOUFFLÉ PIE

An easy soufflé, baked in a chocolate pie crust.

8 servings

Chocolate Cookie Crumb Crust
(see p. 134)
3 eggs, separated
Pinch salt
1/3 cup granulated sugar
1²/3 cups chocolate-flavored syrup, divided
2 teaspoons vanilla
3 tablespoons bourbon *or* 1-2 teaspoons brandy extract
2 tablespoons powdered sugar
Light whipped topping, as garnish

Per Serving
Calories: 324
% Calories from **fat: 27**
Fat (gm): 9.9
Saturated fat (gm): 2
Cholesterol (mg): 79.5
Sodium (mg): 309
Protein (gm): 3.6
Carbohydrate (gm): 52.4
Exchanges
Milk: 0.0
Vegetable: 0.0
Fruit: 0.0
Bread: 3.5
Meat: 0.0
Fat: 2.0

1. Make Chocolate Cookie Crumb Crust, using an 8-inch pie pan.

2. Beat egg yolks with salt, granulated sugar, ²/3 cup chocolate syrup, vanilla, and bourbon. Beat egg whites to soft peaks; add powdered sugar gradually, beating to stiff peaks. Fold into chocolate mixture. Pour into crust.

3. Bake at 350 degrees 25 to 30 minutes or until knife inserted near center comes out clean. Cool on wire rack before serving. Top each slice with dollop of whipped topping and 2 tablespoons of remaining chocolate syrup.

SEMOLINA SOUFFLÉ WITH FIGS

Semolina, often used for making homemade pasta, is now available in most grocery stores or in Italian specialty stores.

10 servings

1 pound dried figs
2 cups dry red wine *or* orange juice
3 tablespoons honey
1/2 teaspoon dried thyme leaves
1 cup water
1 cup white wine *or* water
1/2 cup fine semolina
3/4 cup sugar
1/4 teaspoon salt
1 egg
3 egg whites

Per Serving
Calories: 286
% Calories from fat: 3
Fat (gm): 1.1
Saturated fat (gm): 0.3
Cholesterol (mg): 21.2
Sodium (mg): 90
Protein (gm): 4.3
Carbohydrate (gm): 57.1
Exchanges
Milk: 0.0
Vegetable: 0.0
Fruit: 1.5
Bread: 2.0
Meat: 0.0
Fat: 1.0

1. Heat figs, red wine, honey, and thyme to boiling in medium saucepan; reduce heat and simmer, covered, over low heat, stirring occasionally, 1 hour. Remove figs with slotted spoon. Boil cooking liquid, uncovered, over high heat until thick and syrupy. Pour over figs and reserve.

2. Heat water and white wine in medium saucepan to boiling; pour in semolina in a steady stream, whisking constantly to prevent lumps. Reduce heat; simmer, covered, whisking occasionally, 25 minutes. Remove from heat; stir in sugar and salt. Cool, whisking occasionally; stir in egg.

3. Beat egg whites in large bowl to stiff peaks; fold into semolina mixture. Spoon into greased 1-quart soufflé dish. Cover surface with greased parchment or waxed paper. Set dish in roasting pan on middle oven rack; pour 2 inches boiling water into pan.

4. Bake at 350 degrees until top is golden and puffy, about 1 hour. Let stand in dish until ready to serve. Invert onto dinner plate; invert again onto rimmed serving plate and remove parchment. Arrange figs around soufflé; pour syrup over soufflé and figs. Serve hot, at room temperature, or chilled.

COFFEE CUP SOUFFLÉS

A clever presentation for delicious soufflés!

8 servings

1/2 cup all-purpose flour

1 1/2 cups fat-free milk

1 tablespoon instant coffee granules

2-3 tablespoons margarine

5 egg yolks

8 egg whites

3/4 cup sugar

Cinnamon, cocoa, *or* powdered sugar, as garnish

Per Serving
Calories: 198
% Calories from fat: 28
Fat (gm): 6.2
Saturated fat (gm): 1.6
Cholesterol (mg): 134
Sodium (mg): 117
Protein (gm): 7.7
Carbohydrate (gm): 27.8
Exchanges
Milk: 0.0
Vegetable: 0.0
Fruit: 0.0
Bread: 1.5
Meat: 1.0
Fat: 0.5

1. Grease eight 12-ounce oven-proof coffee mugs; sprinkle lightly with sugar.

2. Whisk flour, milk, and coffee granules until smooth in medium saucepan; whisk over medium heat until boiling and thickened. Stir in margarine. Cool to lukewarm; stir in egg yolks.

3. Beat egg whites in large bowl to soft peaks. Beat to stiff peaks, adding sugar gradually. Fold into yolk mixture.

4. Pour soufflé mixture into prepared mugs; bake at 425 degrees until puffed and set, about 15 minutes. Sprinkle with cinnamon and serve immediately.

SOUFFLÉ CREPES

A crepe filled with chocolate soufflé makes a most elegant dessert. These are delicious with Bittersweet Chocolate Sauce (see p. 641).

8 servings

- 4 tablespoons granulated sugar, divided
- 3 tablespoons unsweetened cocoa
- 1 tablespoon flour
- 1/3 cup 1% low-fat milk
- 2 egg yolks
- 1 tablespoon coffee liqueur *or* strong coffee
- 2 teaspoons vanilla
- 4 egg whites
  Crepes (see p. 274)
- 2 tablespoons powdered sugar

Per Serving
Calories: 148
% Calories from fat: 22
Fat (gm): 3.5
Saturated fat (gm): 1
Cholesterol (mg): 80.5
Sodium (mg): 157
Protein (gm): 6.1
Carbohydrate (gm): 21.2
Exchanges
Milk: 0.0
Vegetable: 0.0
Fruit: 0.0
Bread: 1.5
Meat: 0.0
Fat: 0.5

1. Mix 3 tablespoons granulated sugar, cocoa, and flour in small saucepan; whisk in milk and egg yolks. Whisk over low heat, stirring constantly until thick, about 5 minutes. Remove from heat; stir in liqueur and vanilla.

2. Beat egg whites to soft peaks in large bowl; gradually add remaining 1 tablespoon granulated sugar, beating to stiff peaks. Fold into chocolate mixture.

3. Place crepes on greased baking sheet; spoon about 1/3 cup soufflé mixture in center of each crepe. Fold in half. Bake at 350 degrees until puffed, about 10 minutes. Sprinkle with powdered sugar; serve immediately.

Variation: **Lemon Soufflé Crepes**—Make recipe as above, omitting cocoa, coffee liqueur, and vanilla. Add 1 tablespoon grated lemon rind, 1 tablespoon lemon juice, and 1/2 teaspoon lemon extract to yolk mixture. Complete recipe as above. Serve with Tart Lemon Sauce or Sugared Crushed Berries (see pp. 650, 249).

RHUBARB MOUSSE

A new use for rhubarb! Try this with assorted fresh berries along with the Rhubarb Sauce.

8 servings

3-4 pounds fresh *or* frozen, rhubarb, cut into 1-inch pieces
2³/₄-3 cups sugar
³/₄ cup water
1 envelope unflavored gelatin
¹/₄ cup orange juice
2 cups light whipped topping
Rhubarb Sauce (recipe follows)
Whole strawberries, as garnish

Per Serving
Calories: 364
% Calories from fat: 6
Fat (gm): 2.4
Saturated fat (gm): 2
Cholesterol (mg): 0
Sodium (mg): 10
Protein (gm): 1.7
Carbohydrate (gm): 86
Exchanges
Milk: 0.0
Vegetable: 0.0
Fruit: 5.5
Bread: 0.0
Meat: 0.0
Fat: 0.5

1. Simmer rhubarb, sugar, and water in large saucepan, covered, until tender, about 20 minutes. Reserve ¹/₂ cup cooked rhubarb pieces. Drain remaining rhubarb, reserving 2 tablespoons juice; process rhubarb in food processor or blender until smooth. Reserve 1 cup puree for sauce.

2. Sprinkle gelatin over orange juice in small saucepan; let stand 2 minutes. Dissolve over low heat. Mix with 2 cups rhubarb puree. Refrigerate until mixture mounds when dropped from spoon. Fold in the reserved rhubarb pieces; fold in whipped topping. Pour into 6-cup mold; refrigerate until firm, about 4 hours.

3. Unmold mousse onto serving plate with raised edge. Pour Rhubarb Sauce over. Garnish with strawberries.

Rhubarb Sauce

makes about 1 cup

¹/₄ cup orange juice
2 tablespoons sugar
1 cup reserved rhubarb puree
2 tablespoons reserved cooking liquid
Few drops red food coloring

1. Mix orange juice and sugar in small saucepan. Heat to boiling; boil 3 minutes. Pour into food processor or blender container with remaining ingredients; process until smooth. Refrigerate 30 minutes or longer.

STRAWBERRY-RASPBERRY MOUSSE

As easy to make as it is delicious to eat.

8 servings (about 1 cup each)

- 3 envelopes unflavored gelatin
- 1/2 cup orange liqueur *or* 1/2 cup water and 1/2 teaspoon orange extract
- 1 jar (7 ounces) marshmallow crème
- 1 package (14 ounces) frozen unsweetened raspberries, thawed
- 1 package (16 ounces) frozen unsweetened strawberries, thawed
- 4 cups light whipped topping
  Strawberries *or* raspberries, as garnish
  Mint sprigs, as garnish

Per Serving
Calories: 255
% Calories from fat: 15
Fat (gm): 4.1
Saturated fat (gm): 4
Cholesterol (mg): 0
Sodium (mg): 20
Protein (gm): 1.1
Carbohydrate (gm): 45.4
Exchanges
Milk: 0.0
Vegetable: 0.0
Fruit: 3.0
Bread: 0.0
Meat: 0.0
Fat: 1.5

1. Sprinkle gelatin over liqueur in medium saucepan; let stand 3 to 4 minutes. Whisk over low heat until gelatin is dissolved. Add marshmallow crème, whisking over low heat until smooth. Remove from heat.

2. Process raspberries and strawberries in food processor or blender until smooth; strain and discard seeds. Stir pureed fruit into marshmallow mixture. Refrigerate, stirring occasionally, until mixture mounds slightly when dropped from spoon.

3. Fold whipped topping into fruit mixture. Spoon into stemmed serving dishes or serving bowl. Refrigerate until set, about 4 hours. Garnish each serving with berries and mint sprigs.

BLUEBERRY WINE MOUSSE

This mousse is made in a soufflé dish with a foil "collar" attached to make it taller. When the foil is removed, the mousse rises above the rim of the dish and looks quite spectacular. Of course the mousse can be chilled in a 2-quart bowl, or individual serving dishes, if you prefer.

8 servings

Vegetable cooking spray
2 envelopes unflavored gelatin
1/4 cup lemon juice
1 cup sugar
1 cup white wine *or* orange juice
1/8 teaspoon ground nutmeg
4 egg yolks
1 tablespoon grated lemon rind
1 teaspoon vanilla
3 cups fresh blueberries, divided
3 tablespoons meringue powder
1/2 cup water
3 cups light whipped topping

Per Serving
Calories: 257
% Calories from fat: 21
Fat (gm): 5.8
Saturated fat (gm): 3.8
Cholesterol (mg): 106.5
Sodium (mg): 42
Protein (gm): 3.9
Carbohydrate (gm): 41.7
Exchanges
Milk: 0.0
Vegetable: 0.0
Fruit: 1.0
Bread: 1.5
Meat: 0.0
Fat: 2.0

1. Secure a 3-inch-wide band of double-thickness aluminum foil around rim of 1 1/2-quart soufflé dish. Spray foil lightly with cooking spray.

2. Sprinkle gelatin over lemon juice in medium saucepan; whisk in sugar, wine, nutmeg, and egg yolks. Stir constantly with wooden spoon, over low heat, until mixture coats the back of spoon. Stir in lemon rind and vanilla. Refrigerate, stirring occasionally, until mixture mounds on spoon; fold in 2 cups blueberries.

3. Beat meringue powder and water to stiff peaks. Fold into yolk mixture; fold in whipped topping. Mound mixture in prepared soufflé dish. Refrigerate until firm, about 4 hours. Carefully remove collar. Serve with remaining 1 cup blueberries.

Variations: **Strawberry Mousse**—Make recipe as above, increasing gelatin to 3 envelopes, omitting wine and nutmeg, and substituting 3 cups pureed strawberries for the blueberries. Add 1 1/2 cups strawberry puree to the gelatin mixture with the sugar and egg yolks; add remaining strawberry puree after chilling gelatin mixture.

Lemon Mousse—Make recipe as above, increasing sugar to 1¹/₂ cups, substituting lemon juice for the wine, and substituting 2 tablespoons orange liqueur, or 1 teaspoon orange extract, for the vanilla. Garnish with strips of lemon peel and toasted sliced almonds.

PEACH AMARETTO MOUSSE

Ripe peaches are the base for this delicate mousse. Frozen or canned may be substituted when peaches are not in season. Dip peaches in boiling water for 30 to 40 seconds to loosen skins for easy peeling. Substitute 3 tablespoons orange juice mixed with 2 teaspoons almond extract for the liqueur, if desired.

12 servings

- ¹/₂ cup granulated sugar
- 1 tablespoon cornstarch
- ¹/₂ cup orange juice, divided
- ¹/₄ cup almond liqueur (Amaretto), divided
- 1 tablespoon grated orange rind
- 3 medium ripe peaches, peeled, pitted, chopped, divided
- 1 envelope unflavored gelatin
- ¹/₄ cup powdered sugar
- 3 tablespoons meringue powder
- ¹/₂ cup water
- 1 cup Pastry Cream (¹/₂ recipe) (see p. 268)
- 2 cups light whipped topping
  Peach slices, as garnish
  Fresh mint sprigs, as garnish

Per Serving
Calories: 167
% Calories from fat: 14
Fat (gm): 2.6
Saturated fat (gm): 1.8
Cholesterol (mg): 37
Sodium (mg): 33
Protein (gm): 2.8
Carbohydrate (gm): 30.7
Exchanges
Milk: 0.0
Vegetable: 0.0
Fruit: 0.0
Bread: 2.0
Meat: 0.0
Fat: 0.5

1. Mix granulated sugar and cornstarch in small saucepan. Whisk in ¹/₄ cup orange juice, 2 tablespoons liqueur, and orange rind; stir in ¹/₂ cup peaches. Stir over medium heat until thick, about 5 minutes; cool to lukewarm.

2. Sprinkle gelatin over remaining ¹/₄ cup orange juice in small saucepan; let stand 2 minutes. Whisk over low heat until gelatin is dissolved. Stir in remaining peaches, liqueur, and powdered sugar. Refrigerate, covered, 15 minutes.

3. Beat meringue powder and water in large bowl until mixture forms stiff peaks. Whisk refrigerated peach mixture to remove any lumps; fold in cooked peach mixture and Pastry Cream. Fold in meringue mixture; fold in whipped topping. Pour into 2-quart serving bowl. Refrigerate until firm, about 6 hours. Garnish with peach slices and mint sprigs.

FRENCH MOCHA MOUSSE

Made with the best quality bittersweet (not unsweetened) chocolate, and lightened with meringue, this mousse is comparable in flavor and texture to the very best!

6 servings

1 envelope unflavored gelatin
1/4 cup cold espresso *or* strong coffee
1 cup sugar, divided
1/2 cup Dutch process cocoa
1 1/4 cups 1% low-fat milk
2 egg yolks, lightly beaten
4 ounces bittersweet chocolate, finely chopped
2 tablespoons coffee liqueur *or* 2 teaspoons vanilla
2 egg whites
1/8 teaspoon cream of tartar
Light whipped topping, as garnish
Chocolate curls, as garnish

Per Serving
Calories: 318
% Calories from fat: 25
Fat (gm): 9.5
Saturated fat (gm): 5.2
Cholesterol (mg): 73
Sodium (mg): 55
Protein (gm): 6.8
Carbohydrate (gm): 53.3
Exchanges
Milk: 0.0
Vegetable: 0.0
Fruit: 0.0
Bread: 3.0
Meat: 0.0
Fat: 2.0

1. Sprinkle gelatin over espresso in medium saucepan; let stand 3 to 4 minutes. Heat over low heat until gelatin is dissolved, stirring constantly.

2. Mix 1/2 cup sugar and cocoa in medium saucepan; whisk in milk. Heat to boiling over medium-high heat; reduce heat and simmer briskly, whisking constantly, until thickened, 3 to 4 minutes. Whisk about 1/2 of the milk mixture into egg yolks; whisk yolk mixture into milk mixture in saucepan. Cook over low heat 1 to 2 minutes, whisking constantly. Remove from heat; add gelatin mixture, chocolate, and liqueur, whisking until chocolate is melted. Refrigerate until cool, but not set, about 20 minutes.

3. Beat egg whites, remaining ¹/₂ cup sugar, and cream of tartar until foamy in medium bowl; place bowl over pan of simmering water and beat at medium speed until temperature of egg whites reaches 160 degrees on candy thermometer. Remove from heat and beat at high speed until very thick and cool, about 5 minutes. Mix ¹/₄ of the egg white mixture into chocolate mixture; fold chocolate mixture into remaining egg white mixture. Pour into serving dishes or large glass bowl. Refrigerate until firm, about 4 hours. Serve with dollops of whipped topping and chocolate curls.

Variation: **Orange Pumpkin Mousse**—Make Step 1 of recipe, substituting ¹/₂ cup orange juice for the coffee. Make Step 2, substituting ³/₄ cup brown sugar for the 1 cup granulated sugar, orange liqueur for the coffee liqueur, reducing milk to ³/₄ cup, and omitting cocoa and bittersweet chocolate. Stir 1 can (16 ounces) pumpkin into custard mixture after removing from heat. Complete recipe as above.

EGGNOG MOUSSE

This is a large recipe—perfect for holiday meals. Simply halve the recipe if you prefer a smaller dessert. The mousse can be prepared one day in advance; remove "collar" and garnish just before serving.

12 servings

3 envelopes unflavored gelatin
¹/₄ cup light rum *or* 3 tablespoons water and 1 tablespoon rum extract
1 cup sugar
3 cups fat-free milk, hot
¹/₈ teaspoon ground nutmeg
4 egg yolks
1 teaspoon vanilla
1 teaspoon brandy extract
3 tablespoons meringue powder
¹/₂ cup water
4 cups light whipped topping, divided
Ground nutmeg, as garnish

Per Serving
Calories: 185
% Calories from fat: 23
Fat (gm): 4.5
Saturated fat (gm): 3.3
Cholesterol (mg): 72.1
Sodium (mg): 58
Protein (gm): 4.4
Carbohydrate (gm): 27
Exchanges
Milk: 0.0
Vegetable: 0.0
Fruit: 0.0
Bread: 2.0
Meat: 0.0
Fat: 1.0

1. Secure a 3-inch-wide band of double-thickness aluminum foil around rim of 2-quart soufflé dish.

2. Sprinkle gelatin on rum in medium saucepan. Whisk in sugar, milk, nutmeg, and egg yolks. Stir constantly with wooden spoon, over low heat, until mixture coats the back of spoon. Stir in vanilla and brandy extract. Refrigerate, stirring occasionally, until mixture mounds on spoon.

3. Beat meringue powder and water to stiff peaks. Fold into milk mixture; fold in 3 cups whipped topping. Spoon mixture into prepared dish. Refrigerate until firm, about 6 hours. Carefully remove foil "collar." Top with remaining 1 cup whipped topping and sprinkle with nutmeg.

Variation: **Autumn Apple Mousse**—Make recipe through Step 2, reducing sugar to 3/4 cup, milk to 1 1/2 cups, and gelatin to 2 envelopes. Combine 4 cups coarsely chopped, peeled tart cooking apples, 1 tablespoon grated orange rind, 1/2 teaspoon cinnamon, and 1/3 cup apricot preserves in medium saucepan; cook, covered, over medium heat until apples are very soft. Puree in food processor or blender. Cool; stir into chilled milk mixture. Complete recipe as in Step 3 above. Serve with Warm Rum Sauce (see p. 54).

ORANGE BAVARIAN

This dessert can also be served in individual dishes if you prefer—it will chill much faster that way.

6 servings

3/4 cup fresh orange juice
1 envelope unflavored gelatin
3/4 cup sugar, divided
1 tablespoon grated orange rind
2 eggs
2 cups light whipped topping
Orange Sauce (see p. 652)
Orange segments, as garnish

Per Serving
Calories: 311
% Calories from fat: 18
Fat (gm): 6.2
Saturated fat (gm): 3.7
Cholesterol (mg): 141.7
Sodium (mg): 28
Protein (gm): 3.7
Carbohydrate (gm): 59.7
Exchanges
Milk: 0.0
Vegetable: 0.0
Fruit: 2.0
Bread: 2.0
Meat: 0.0
Fat: 1.0

1. Heat orange juice, gelatin, 2 tablespoons sugar, and orange rind in small saucepan over medium heat, stirring constantly, until gelatin is dissolved.

2. Beat eggs and remaining 10 tablespoons sugar in medium bowl until light and fluffy. Whisk small amount of orange juice mixture into eggs; whisk egg mixture into saucepan. Stir constantly with a wooden spoon, over low heat, until mixture coats the back of spoon. Remove from heat; refrigerate until mixture mounds slightly when dropped from spoon.

3. Fold in whipped topping; spoon mixture into lightly oiled 1-quart ring mold. Refrigerate until set, about 4 hours. Unmold onto serving plate; serve with Orange Sauce and garnish with orange segments.

COFFEE ALMOND BAVARIAN

This delicate coffee-flavored custard is lovely served in stemmed parfait or sorbet glasses. It can also be spooned from a serving bowl.

4 servings

2 cups fat-free milk

1 envelope unflavored gelatin

1/4 cup sugar

1 tablespoon instant coffee granules

2 egg yolks, beaten

1/2 teaspoon vanilla

1/4 teaspoon almond extract

1 1/2 cups light whipped topping, divided
   Sliced almonds, as garnish
   Chocolate-covered coffee beans, as garnish

Per Serving
Calories: 193
% Calories from fat: 28
Fat (gm): 5.8
Saturated fat (gm): 3.9
Cholesterol (mg): 108.7
Sodium (mg): 72
Protein (gm): 5.9
Carbohydrate (gm): 27
Exchanges
Milk: 0.0
Vegetable: 0.0
Fruit: 0.0
Bread: 2.0
Meat: 0.0
Fat: 1.0

1. Whisk milk, gelatin, sugar, and coffee granules in small saucepan over medium heat until almost simmering. Whisk small amount of milk mixture into egg yolks; whisk yolk mixture into saucepan. Stir constantly with wooden spoon, over low heat, until mixture coats the back of spoon. Remove from heat; stir in vanilla and almond extract. Refrigerate until mixture mounds slightly when dropped from spoon.

2. Fold in 1 1/4 cups whipped topping; spoon mixture into serving glasses. Refrigerate until serving time. Top with remaining 1/4 cup whipped topping and garnish with almonds and chocolate-covered coffee beans.

CHILLED RASPBERRY CHIFFON

Serve this delicate soufflé with Raspberry Sauce (see p. 658).

6 servings (about ¹/₂ cup each)

¹/₃ cup sugar
¹/₂ cup water
1 tablespoon lemon juice
1 envelope unflavored gelatin
2 cups fresh, *or* frozen, thawed, raspberries
2 envelopes (1.3 ounces each) low-fat
   whipped topping mix
1 cup 2% reduced-fat milk
   Fresh raspberries, as garnish
   Mint sprigs, as garnish

Per Serving
Calories: 69
% Calories from fat: 14
Fat (gm): 1
Saturated fat (gm): 0.5
Cholesterol (mg): 3
Sodium (mg): 30
Protein (gm): 2.7
Carbohydrate (gm): 10.9
Exchanges
Milk: 0.0
Vegetable: 0.0
Fruit: 1.5
Bread: 0.0
Meat: 0.0
Fat: 1.0

1. Combine sugar, water, and lemon juice in small saucepan; sprinkle gelatin over and let stand 2 to 3 minutes. Heat to simmering over medium heat, stirring constantly until sugar and gelatin are dissolved. Cool; refrigerate until mixture is consistency of unbeaten egg whites.

2. Process 2 cups raspberries in food processor or blender until smooth; strain and discard seeds. Blend whipped topping mix and milk in large bowl; beat at high speed until topping forms soft peaks, about 4 minutes. Stir raspberry puree into gelatin mixture; fold into whipped topping.

3. Spoon soufflé mixture into serving dish or individual stemmed dishes. Chill 2 to 4 hours or until set. Garnish with fresh raspberries and mint.

APRICOT CHIFFON

This dessert uses canned fruit, making it a good choice for winter when fresh fruit is not readily available.

6 servings

- 1 can (8 ounces) apricot halves, undrained
- 3 egg yolks
- 2/3 cup sugar
- 1 envelope unflavored gelatin
- 1/4 cup orange juice
- 1/2 teaspoon ground nutmeg
- 2 1/2 tablespoons meringue powder
- 1/3 cup water
- 6 tablespoons light whipped topping
  Ground nutmeg, as garnish

Per Serving
Calories: 164
% Calories from fat: 17
Fat (gm): 3.2
Saturated fat (gm): 1.3
Cholesterol (mg): 106.5
Sodium (mg): 41
Protein (gm): 3.9
Carbohydrate (gm): 30.4
Exchanges
Milk: 0.0
Vegetable: 0.0
Fruit: 1.0
Bread: 1.0
Meat: 0.0
Fat: 0.5

1. Process apricots with juice in food processor or blender until smooth. Blend egg yolks, sugar, and apricots in medium saucepan. Soften gelatin in orange juice in small bowl; stir into apricot mixture. Stir in nutmeg. Cook over medium heat, stirring constantly, until mixture is beginning to simmer. Refrigerate, stirring occasionally, until mixture mounds when dropped from spoon.

2. Beat meringue powder and water until stiff peaks form. Fold into apricot mixture. Spoon into serving dishes. Refrigerate until chilled, 2 to 3 hours. Top each with 1 tablespoon whipped topping; sprinkle with nutmeg.

CHARLOTTE RUSSE

Russian in origin, this dessert features a custard molded in a ladyfinger-lined soufflé dish or charlotte mold. Vanilla is the traditional flavoring, but we've used sherry. To use vanilla, increase milk to 1 cup and add 2 teaspoons vanilla extract.

6 servings

1 package (3 ounces) ladyfingers (12), split into halves lengthwise

⅓ cup sugar

1 envelope unflavored gelatin

Pinch salt

4 egg yolks

¾ cup fat-free milk

¼ cup cream sherry

2 tablespoons meringue powder

⅓ cup water

1 cup light whipped topping

Candied cherries, as garnish

Per Serving
Calories: 226
% Calories from fat: 28
Fat (gm): 6.8
Saturated fat (gm): **3**
Cholesterol (mg): 222.8
Sodium (mg): 82
Protein (gm): 7.1
Carbohydrate (gm): 30.5
Exchanges
Milk: 0.0
Vegetable: 0.0
Fruit: 0.0
Bread: 2.0
Meat: 0.0
Fat: 2.0

1. Cut several split ladyfingers diagonally in half to form triangles. Arrange triangles cut sides up in bottom of ungreased 5-cup charlotte mold or soufflé dish, placing points of triangles toward center of mold and completely covering bottom of mold. If points don't meet in the center, cut a small circle of ladyfinger to fill gap. Line side of dish with remaining ladyfinger halves, placing uncut sides against dish.

2. Mix sugar, gelatin, and salt in medium saucepan. Beat egg yolks and milk; whisk into sugar mixture. Stir constantly with wooden spoon, over medium heat, until mixture coats the back of spoon. Remove from heat; stir in sherry. Refrigerate, stirring occasionally, until mixture mounds slightly when dropped from spoon.

3. Beat meringue powder and water until stiff peaks form. Fold into yolk mixture. Fold in whipped topping. Spoon mixture into ladyfinger-lined dish. Cover; refrigerate until set, about 6 hours.

4. Unmold onto serving plate; decorate with candied cherries.

CHOCOLATE CHARLOTTE

A chocolate mousse, molded in a ladyfinger-lined soufflé dish.

4 servings

1 package (3 ounces) ladyfingers (12), split into halves lengthwise

2 ounces semisweet chocolate

1 tablespoon coffee liqueur *or* strong coffee

1 tablespoon meringue powder

3 tablespoons water

3/4 teaspoon rum extract

1 envelope (1.3 ounces) whipped topping mix

1/2 cup fat-free milk

1/2 teaspoon vanilla

Per Serving
Calories: 240
% Calories from fat: 31
Fat (gm): 8.6
Saturated fat (gm): 4.4
Cholesterol (mg): 120.3
Sodium (mg): 68
Protein (gm): 5.8
Carbohydrate (gm): 34.2
Exchanges
Milk: 0.0
Vegetable: 0.0
Fruit: 0.0
Bread: 2.0
Meat: 0.0
Fat: 2.0

1. Line side of ungreased 1-quart charlotte mold or soufflé dish with ladyfingers, placing uncut sides against dish. Break remaining ladyfingers into small pieces. Heat chocolate and coffee liqueur in small saucepan over low heat until chocolate is melted. Cool slightly.

2. Beat meringue powder, water, and rum extract until stiff peaks form. Fold chocolate mixture into meringue. Beat whipped topping mix with milk and vanilla according to package directions. Fold into chocolate mixture.

3. Layer chocolate mixture and broken ladyfingers in mold, beginning and ending with chocolate mixture. Refrigerate until set, about 3 hours. Unmold onto serving dish.

WHITE CHOCOLATE BERRY PARFAITS

White chocolate mousse layered with fresh berries makes a beautiful presentation. Try it with fresh sweet cherries for a delicious variation.

6 servings

2 cups fat-free milk

1 envelope unflavored gelatin

1/4 cup sugar

2 egg yolks, beaten

3 ounces white chocolate, finely chopped

1/2 teaspoon vanilla

1 1/2 cups light whipped topping, divided

3 cups fresh raspberries *or* other berries, divided

Mint leaves, as garnish

Per Serving
Calories: 237
% Calories from fat: 34
Fat (gm): 8.7
Saturated fat (gm): 5.7
Cholesterol (mg): 75
Sodium (mg): 60
Protein (gm): 5.4
Carbohydrate (gm): 33.3
Exchanges
Milk: 0.0
Vegetable: 0.0
Fruit: 1.0
Bread: 1.5
Meat: 0.0
Fat: 1.5

1. Whisk milk, gelatin, and sugar in medium saucepan to simmering over medium heat. Whisk about 1/2 cup of milk mixture into egg yolks; whisk yolk mixture into saucepan. Stir constantly with wooden spoon, over low heat, until mixture coats back of spoon. Remove from heat; add white chocolate and vanilla, stirring until chocolate melts. Refrigerate until mixture mounds slightly when dropped from spoon. Fold in 1 1/4 cups whipped topping.

2. Spoon 1/4 cup raspberries into each of 6 parfait glasses; top each with about 1/3 cup mousse. Repeat with remaining berries and mousse, forming 4 layers. Refrigerate until set, about 2 hours. Top with remaining 1/4 cup whipped topping and garnish with mint leaves.

LEMON BLACKBERRY PARFAIT

Fresh blackberries and lemonade combine in this beautiful and flavorful parfait. Use frozen blackberries or other berries if you like. This is also lovely layered in a glass serving dish.

8 servings

9 cups fresh, *or* 3 packages (14 ounces each) frozen unsweetened, thawed, blackberries, divided

1¹/₂ cups lemonade, divided

1 cup sugar

1 teaspoon grated lemon rind

2 envelopes unflavored gelatin

Lemon Custard Cream (recipe follows)

Mint sprigs, as garnish

Per Serving
Calories: 276
% Calories from fat: 8
Fat (gm): 2.7
Saturated fat (gm): 1.9
Cholesterol (mg): 2.8
Sodium (mg): 36
Protein (gm): 3.2
Carbohydrate (gm): 62.1
Exchanges
Milk: 0.0
Vegetable: 0.0
Fruit: 3.0
Bread: 1.0
Meat: 0.0
Fat: 0.5

1. Puree 6 cups blackberries in blender or food processor until smooth. Strain and discard seeds. Pour puree into large bowl; mix in 1 cup lemonade, sugar, and lemon rind.

2. Sprinkle gelatin over remaining ¹/₂ cup lemonade in small saucepan; let stand 2 to 3 minutes to soften. Stir over medium heat until gelatin dissolves; whisk into blackberry mixture. Refrigerate, stirring occasionally, until mixture mounds when dropped from spoon.

3. Spoon half the blackberry mixture into 8 parfait glasses; top with half the Lemon Custard Cream, and 1¹/₂ cups blackberries; repeat layers. Refrigerate until set, about 3 hours. Garnish with mint sprigs.

Lemon Custard Cream

makes about 3 cups

1¹/₂ cups light whipped topping

1¹/₂ cups lemon custard-style low-fat yogurt

2 teaspoons lemon juice

1. Combine all ingredients, whisking until smooth.

COFFEE CRÈME

This dessert can be made in any decorative mold you have—the prettier the better—or chill it in a glass serving bowl.

8 servings

2 envelopes unflavored gelatin

²/₃ cup sugar

¹/₄ teaspoon salt

1 cup water

1 quart fat-free coffee ice cream, softened

2 tablespoons lemon juice

¹/₄ cup dark rum *or* 1 tablespoon rum extract

Light whipped topping, as garnish

Chocolate curls, as garnish

Per Serving
Calories: 178
% Calories from fat: 0
Fat (gm): 0
Saturated fat (gm): 0
Cholesterol (mg): 0
Sodium (mg): 147
Protein (gm): 4.2
Carbohydrate (gm): 38.6

Exchanges
Milk: 0.0
Vegetable: 0.0
Fruit: 0.0
Bread: 2.5
Meat: 0.0
Fat: 0.0

1. Mix gelatin, sugar, and salt in medium saucepan. Gradually stir in water. Whisk over medium heat until gelatin is dissolved; remove from heat.

2. Add ice cream, lemon juice, and rum, stirring until ice cream is melted. Pour into lightly oiled 5- or 6-cup mold. Refrigerate until set, about 6 hours.

3. Unmold onto serving plate; garnish with dollops of whipped topping and chocolate curls.

ORANGE PINEAPPLE CREAM

This creamy dessert is also pretty made in parfait glasses.

4 servings

1 can (8³/₄ ounces) crushed pineapple in juice, undrained

1 package (3 ounces) orange-flavored gelatin

1¹/₄ cups boiling water

¹/₂ package (8-ounce size) reduced-fat cream cheese

1 tablespoon grated orange rind

3 tablespoons sugar

1 teaspoon vanilla

1 cup fat-free sour cream

Per Serving
Calories: 288
% Calories from fat: 14
Fat (gm): 4.5
Saturated fat (gm): 3.1
Cholesterol (mg): 13.3
Sodium (mg): 232
Protein (gm): 8.9
Carbohydrate (gm): 52
Exchanges
Milk: 0.0
Vegetable: 0.0
Fruit: 0.0
Bread: 3.5
Meat: 0.0
Fat: 1.0

1. Drain pineapple, reserving juice. Dissolve gelatin in boiling water. Add reserved pineapple juice and cool slightly. Stir ¹/₂ cup gelatin mixture into drained pineapple; reserve, covered, at room temperature.

2. Beat cream cheese, orange rind, sugar, and vanilla until smooth. Gradually mix in remaining gelatin mixture; fold in sour cream. Pour cream cheese mixture into glass serving bowl. Refrigerate until set, but not firm, about 45 minutes. Carefully spoon pineapple mixture over cream cheese mixture. Refrigerate until firm, about 2 hours.

Variation: **Lemon Pineapple Cream Pie**—Make Graham Cracker Crumb Crust (see p. 132), using 9-inch pie pan. Make recipe as above, doubling amounts of ingredients, and substituting lemon gelatin for the orange gelatin. Fold pineapple mixture into cream cheese mixture and spoon into crust. Refrigerate until set, about 3 hours. Garnish with rosettes or dollops of light whipped topping.

POSSET PUDDING

*Posset was originally a warm milk drink of medieval England. We've trans-
formed it into a fluffy port-and-sherry-flavored pudding.*

8 servings

  4 egg yolks
²/₃ cup lemon juice
¹/₃ cup sugar
  3 tablespoons grated lemon rind
¹/₄ teaspoon salt
  1 envelope unflavored gelatin
¹/₃ cup dry sherry, divided
¹/₃ cup white port *or* dry sherry
  1 cup light whipped topping
  2 tablespoons meringue powder
¹/₃ cup water

Per Serving
Calories: 125
% Calories from fat: 26
Fat (gm): 3.6
Saturated fat (gm): 1.8
Cholesterol (mg): 106.5
Sodium (mg): 99
Protein (gm): 2.9
Carbohydrate (gm): 15.5
Exchanges
Milk: 0.0
Vegetable: 0.0
Fruit: 0.0
Bread: 1.0
Meat: 0.0
Fat: 1.0

1. Whisk egg yolks, lemon juice, sugar, lemon rind, and salt in
medium saucepan. Stir constantly with wooden spoon, over
medium heat, until mixture coats the back of spoon. Remove
from heat; cool to lukewarm, stirring occasionally.

2. Sprinkle gelatin over 2 tablespoons sherry in small saucepan.
Stir over low heat until gelatin is dissolved. Stir into lemon mixture; stir in remaining sherry and port. Refrigerate until mixture
has the consistency of egg whites.

3. Fold whipped topping into lemon mixture. Beat meringue
powder and water to soft peaks; fold into lemon mixture. Pour
into 2-quart serving bowl. Refrigerate until set, about 2 hours.

PEACH ALMOND CREAM

This shimmery, delicate gelatin custard is reminiscent of the oriental dessert often made with Mandarin oranges and lychee fruit.

6 servings

2 envelopes unflavored gelatin
1/2 cup sugar
1 quart 2% reduced-fat milk
1/2 teaspoon almond extract
1 cup sliced canned peaches packed in juice, drained
Light whipped topping, as garnish
Ground nutmeg, as garnish

Per Serving
Calories: 173
% Calories from fat: 16
Fat (gm): 3.1
Saturated fat (gm): 1.9
Cholesterol (mg): 12.2
Sodium (mg): 89
Protein (gm): 5.9
Carbohydrate (gm): 31.5
Exchanges
Milk: 1.0
Vegetable: 0.0
Fruit: 1.0
Bread: 0.0
Meat: 0.0
Fat: 0.5

1. Sprinkle gelatin and sugar over milk in medium saucepan; let stand 2 to 3 minutes. Whisk over medium heat just to simmering; stir in almond extract.

2. Pour mixture into medium bowl; refrigerate until the consistency of unbeaten egg whites, about 1 hour. Stir in peaches; spoon into individual dishes. Refrigerate until set, 2 to 3 hours. Garnish with dollops of light whipped topping and sprinkle with nutmeg.

COEUR À LA CRÈME

This dessert is perfect for Valentine's Day. The traditional Coeur à la Crème (Cream Heart) mold is porcelain, with holes in the bottom to drain the excess liquid from the cheeses. With this recipe, any 5-cup mold can be used.

6 servings

2 envelopes unflavored gelatin

3/4 cup fat-free milk

2 cups 1% low-fat cottage cheese

1 package (8 ounces) reduced-fat cream cheese

3 tablespoons sugar

1 teaspoon vanilla

Whole strawberries, as garnish

3 cups sliced strawberries *or* fresh raspberries

Per Serving
Calories: 206
% Calories from fat: 31
Fat (gm): 7
Saturated fat (gm): 4.7
Cholesterol (mg): 21.6
Sodium (mg): 506
Protein (gm): 14.6
Carbohydrate (gm): 19.7
Exchanges
Milk: 0.0
Vegetable: 0.0
Fruit: 1.0
Bread: 0.0
Meat: 2.0
Fat: 0.5

1. Sprinkle gelatin over milk in small saucepan; let stand 1 minute. Stir over low heat just to simmering.

2. Process cottage cheese in food processor until smooth. Add cream cheese, sugar, vanilla, and gelatin mixture and process until smooth. Pour cheese mixture into lightly greased 5-cup heart mold or cake pan. Cover; refrigerate until firm, 3 to 4 hours.

3. Unmold onto serving platter. Garnish with whole strawberries; serve with sliced strawberries.

MOLDED BERRIES AND MINT

Cool and refreshing on a hot summer day!

4 servings

3/4 cup water, divided
1/2 cup sugar
2/3 cup chopped fresh mint leaves
1 1/2 teaspoons unflavored gelatin
1 cup sliced strawberries
1 cup raspberries
Mint sprigs, as garnish

Per Serving
Calories: 131
% Calories from fat: 2
Fat (gm): 0.4
Saturated fat (gm): 0
Cholesterol (mg): 0
Sodium (mg): 3
Protein (gm): 1.6
Carbohydrate (gm): 31.7
Exchanges
Milk: 0.0
Vegetable: 0.0
Fruit: 2.0
Bread: 0.0
Meat: 0.0
Fat: 0.0

1. Heat 1/2 cup water, sugar, and mint leaves to boiling in small saucepan, stirring until sugar is dissolved; reduce heat and simmer 3 to 4 minutes. Strain into medium bowl, pressing hard on solids; discard mint. Add water if necessary for syrup to measure 3/4 cup.

2. Sprinkle gelatin over remaining 1/4 cup water; let stand 2 to 3 minutes to soften. Stir into hot mint syrup and stir until dissolved. Refrigerate until mixture mounds on spoon; stir in berries. Divide mixture among four 6-ounce molds. Refrigerate until firm.

3. Unmold onto serving plates; garnish with mint sprigs.

SPRING FRUIT GELATIN

This adult version of the popular children's dessert is homemade with fresh fruit and orange juice. The reserved fruit can be made into a baked soufflé for another wonderful springtime dessert (see Variation below for Berry Rhubarb Soufflé).

4 servings

3 cups sliced rhubarb
3 cups sliced strawberries
1¹/₂ cups water
1¹/₄ cups sugar
2 tablespoons lemon juice
2 envelopes unflavored gelatin
¹/₂ cup orange juice
Light whipped topping, as garnish
Sliced strawberries, as garnish

Per Serving
Calories: 276
% Calories from fat: 0
Fat (gm): 0.1
Saturated fat (gm): 0
Cholesterol (mg): 0
Sodium (mg): 10
Protein (gm): 0.7
Carbohydrate (gm): 70.8
Exchanges
Milk: 0.0
Vegetable: 0.0
Fruit: 4.5
Bread: 0.0
Meat: 0.0
Fat: 0.0

1. Heat rhubarb, 3 cups strawberries, water, sugar, and lemon juice to boiling in large saucepan; reduce heat and simmer, covered, until fruit is very soft, about 10 minutes. Strain fruit, reserving juice, and reserving cooked fruit for another use.

2. Sprinkle gelatin over orange juice in small saucepan; let stand 2 to 3 minutes to soften. Stir over low heat until gelatin is dissolved; stir into reserved fruit juice. Pour into 4 large goblets or serving bowls; refrigerate until set, 2 to 3 hours. Garnish with whipped topping and sliced strawberries.

Variation: **Berry Rhubarb Soufflé**—Beat 2 egg whites to soft peaks; beat to stiff peaks, adding 3 tablespoons sugar gradually. Fold egg whites and generous pinch each of ground ginger and cinnamon into reserved fruit from Step 1. Spoon into 4 greased 6-ounce soufflé dishes. Bake at 375 degrees until puffed and set, about 10 minutes.

MINTED PEACH TEA GELÉE

This light and elegant dessert is also delicious made with other flavored teas—try raspberry, mint, or ginger.

6 servings

3 cups water, divided

1/2 cup sugar

4 orange-spice tea bags

2 envelopes unflavored gelatin

2 tablespoons lemon juice

1 1/2 cups diced peaches

1 1/2 cups mixed berries

1/4 cup chopped mint leaves

Mint sprigs, as garnish

Per Serving
Calories: 106
% Calories from fat: 1
Fat (gm): 0.2
Saturated fat (gm): 0
Cholesterol (mg): 0
Sodium (mg): 10
Protein (gm): 0.7
Carbohydrate (gm): 27.1
Exchanges
Milk: 0.0
Vegetable: 0.0
Fruit: 1.5
Bread: 0.0
Meat: 0.0
Fat: 0.0

1. Heat 2 cups water and the sugar to boiling in medium saucepan; add tea bags and let steep, covered, 5 minutes. Remove tea bags, squeezing out liquid.

2. Sprinkle gelatin over 1/3 cup water; let stand 2 to 3 minutes to soften. Stir gelatin mixture into hot tea and stir to dissolve gelatin. Stir in remaining 2/3 cup water and lemon juice. Refrigerate, stirring occasionally, until mixture mounds when dropped from spoon. Stir in fruit and mint; pour into 6-cup ring mold. Refrigerate until set.

3. Unmold onto serving plate; garnish with mint sprigs.

EIGHT

Frozen Desserts

FRENCH VANILLA ICE CREAM

This delicious ice cream is rich in flavor and smooth in texture.

4 servings

2 egg yolks
$1/3$ cup sugar
1 tablespoon cornstarch
2 cups fat-free milk, divided
1 envelope (1.3 ounces) whipped topping mix
1 teaspoon vanilla

Per Serving
Calories: 208
% Calories from fat: 22
Fat (gm): 4.8
Saturated fat (gm): 2.9
Cholesterol (mg): 108.7
Sodium (mg): 67
Protein (gm): 5.6
Carbohydrate (gm): 32.9
Exchanges
Milk: 0.0
Vegetable: 0.0
Fruit: 0.0
Bread: 2.0
Meat: 0.0
Fat: 1.0

1. Whisk egg yolks, sugar, and cornstarch in small bowl until smooth; heat 1 cup milk to boiling in small saucepan. Whisk small amount of milk into egg yolk mixture; whisk yolk mixture into saucepan. Whisk mixture constantly over medium heat until boiling; pour into medium bowl. Refrigerate until chilled.

2. Beat whipped topping mix with remaining 1 cup milk until fluffy and thickened, about 5 minutes. Fold into chilled yolk mixture; stir in vanilla.

3. Freeze mixture in ice cream maker according to manufacturer's directions. Or pour mixture into 9-inch square baking dish and freeze until slushy, about 2 hours; spoon into bowl and beat until fluffy. Return to pan and freeze until firm, 6 hours or overnight.

Variations: **Grape-Nuts Ice Cream**—Make recipe as above, adding $1/3$ cup Grape-Nuts cereal after adding vanilla.

Creamy Chocolate Ice Cream—Whisk 1 tablespoon unsweetened cocoa into the egg yolks, sugar, and cornstarch mixture in Step 1, and cook as above. Stir 1 ounce chopped semisweet chocolate into hot yolk mixture until melted; refrigerate until chilled. Complete recipe as above.

Fresh Peach Ice Cream—Combine 1 cup peeled, mashed, ripe peaches with $^1/_2$ cup sugar. Let stand, covered, at room temperature 1 hour. Make recipe as above, reducing sugar to $^1/_4$ cup, and vanilla to $^1/_2$ teaspoon. Fold in peach mixture and $^1/_2$ teaspoon almond extract with whipped topping in Step 2.

Rum-Raisin Ice Cream—Soak $^1/_3$ cup dark raisins in $^1/_4$ cup dark rum, covered, several hours or overnight. Make recipe as above, adding raisin mixture before freezing.

TANGERINE COCONUT FROZEN CUSTARD

Tropical flavors and a wonderful creamy texture.

6 servings

- 1 egg yolk
- $^1/_4$ cup sugar
- 2 teaspoons cornstarch
- $1^1/_2$ cups 2% reduced-fat milk, divided
- 1 can (6 ounces) frozen tangerine concentrate
- 1 envelope (1.3 ounces) whipped topping mix
- $^1/_2$ teaspoon coconut extract
- Toasted coconut, as garnish

Per Serving
Calories: 169
% Calories from fat: 19
Fat (gm): 3.5
Saturated fat (gm): 2.3
Cholesterol (mg): 40.1
Sodium (mg): 33
Protein (gm): 3
Carbohydrate (gm): 30.1
Exchanges
Milk: 0.0
Vegetable: 0.0
Fruit: 0.0
Bread: 2.0
Meat: 0.0
Fat: 0.5

1. Whisk egg yolk, sugar, and cornstarch in small bowl until smooth; heat $^1/_2$ cup milk to boiling in small saucepan. Whisk small amount of milk into egg yolk mixture; whisk yolk mixture into saucepan. Whisk mixture constantly over medium heat until boiling; pour into medium bowl. Stir in tangerine concentrate; refrigerate until chilled.

2. Beat whipped topping mix with remaining 1 cup milk until fluffy and thickened, about 5 minutes. Fold into chilled tangerine mixture; stir in coconut extract.

3. Freeze mixture in ice cream maker according to manufacturer's directions. Or pour mixture into 9-inch square baking dish and freeze until slushy, about 2 hours; spoon into bowl and beat until fluffy. Return to pan and freeze until firm, 6 hours or overnight. Scoop into bowls; sprinkle with toasted coconut.

GINGER-ORANGE ICE CREAM

Very light, very flavorful, and very easy!

8 servings

2 cartons (16 ounces each) fat-free sour cream
1 carton (8 ounces) fat-free orange yogurt
³/4 cup lightly packed light brown sugar
3 tablespoons honey
3 tablespoons minced crystallized ginger
2 teaspoons lemon juice
¹/8 teaspoon salt
Finely grated rind of 1 orange
Pinch nutmeg

Per Serving
Calories: 266
% Calories from fat: 0
Fat (gm): 0
Saturated fat (gm): 0
Cholesterol (mg): 0
Sodium (mg): 150
Protein (gm): 8.3
Carbohydrate (gm): 57.2
Exchanges
Milk: 0.0
Vegetable: 0.0
Fruit: 0.0
Bread: 3.5
Meat: 0.0
Fat: 0.0

1. Process all ingredients in blender or food processor until smooth.

2. Freeze mixture in ice cream maker according to manufacturer's directions. Or pour mixture into 9-inch square baking dish and freeze until slushy, about 2 hours; spoon into bowl and beat until fluffy. Return to pan and freeze until firm, 6 hours or overnight.

Variation: **Pumpkin Spice Ice Cream**—Make recipe as above, reducing sour cream to 1 carton, omitting ginger, and adding ³/4 cup canned pumpkin, ¹/4 cup chopped walnuts, 2 tablespoons dark rum *or* 1 teaspoon rum extract, and 1 teaspoon pumpkin pie spice to mixture before freezing. Mix all ingredients in large bowl; freeze as above.

ORANGE-PINEAPPLE SHERBET

Use an ice cream maker to produce the smoothest texture in sherbets and ices. To keep orange segments whole, add them just before freezing is completed.

8 servings (about 1/2 cup each)

1/2 cup sugar

1/3 cup water

1 can (15 1/4 ounces) unsweetened crushed pineapple, undrained

1 1/4 cups reduced-fat buttermilk

1/4 cup orange juice

1 can (11 ounces) Mandarin orange segments, drained

Per Serving
Calories: 114
% Calories from fat: 3
Fat (gm): 0.4
Saturated fat (gm): 0.2
Cholesterol (mg): 1.3
Sodium (mg): 43
Protein (gm): 1.8
Carbohydrate (gm): 27.3
Exchanges
Milk: 0.0
Vegetable: 0.0
Fruit: 2.0
Bread: 0.0
Meat: 0.0
Fat: 0.0

1. Heat sugar and water to boiling in medium saucepan, stirring until sugar is dissolved. Cool to room temperature.

2. Process pineapple, buttermilk, sugar syrup, and orange juice in food processor or blender until smooth. Freeze in ice cream maker according to manufacturer's directions, adding oranges just before sherbet is frozen. Or pour into 8-inch square baking dish and freeze until slushy, about 2 hours; spoon into bowl and beat until fluffy. Stir in oranges and return to pan; freeze until firm, 6 hours or overnight.

Variations: **Strawberry-Banana Buttermilk Sherbet**—Make recipe as above, substituting 2 cups fresh, *or* frozen, thawed, strawberries and 1 small banana for the pineapple in the recipe. Add 1/2 teaspoon banana, *or* lemon, extract, and omit Mandarin oranges.

Piña Colada Sherbet—Make recipe as above, substituting 1/3 cup light cream of coconut for the water, 1/4 cup rum *or* 1/4 cup water and 1 teaspoon rum extract for the orange juice, and 1/2 cup sweetened flaked coconut for the Mandarin orange segments.

RASPBERRY CHEESECAKE SHERBET

Only three ingredients in this delicious sherbet—the buttermilk gives a flavor reminiscent of cheesecake. Garnish with fresh berries, if you like.

16 servings

1 can (12 ounces) frozen raspberry-orange juice concentrate, thawed
1 quart reduced-fat buttermilk
1¹/₂ cups sugar

Per Serving
Calories: 131
% Calories from fat: 3
Fat (gm): 0.6
Saturated fat (gm): 0.3
Cholesterol (mg): 2.1
Sodium (mg): 65
Protein (gm): 2.5
Carbohydrate (gm): 29.8
Exchanges
Milk: 0.0
Vegetable: 0.0
Fruit: 0.0
Bread: 2.0
Meat: 0.0
Fat: 0.0

1. Mix all ingredients until sugar dissolves. Freeze in ice cream maker according to manufacturer's directions. Or pour into 8-inch square baking dish and freeze until slushy, about 2 hours; spoon into bowl and beat until fluffy. Return to pan, and freeze until firm, 6 hours or overnight.

GINGER-CITRUS SORBET

Slightly tart, slightly zesty, very refreshing!

6 servings

3¹/₂ cups water
1¹/₂ cups sugar
¹/₄ cup peeled, minced gingerroot
2 teaspoons grated orange rind
¹/₃ cup orange juice
2 tablespoons lemon juice

Per Serving
Calories: 190
% Calories from fat: 0
Fat (gm): 0.1
Saturated fat (gm): 0.0
Cholesterol (mg): 0.0
Sodium (mg): 1
Protein (gm): 0.2
Carbohydrate (gm): 50.6
Exchanges
Milk: 0.0
Vegetable: 0.0
Fruit: 3.0
Bread: 0.0
Meat: 0.0
Fat: 0.0

1. Combine water, sugar, gingerroot, and orange rind in medium saucepan. Heat to boiling over medium-high heat, stirring until sugar is dissolved; reduce heat and simmer 7 to 10 minutes. Cool to room temperature; stir in orange juice and lemon juice.

2. Freeze mixture in ice cream maker according to manufacturer's directions. Or pour into 8-inch square baking dish and freeze until slushy, 2 to 4 hours; spoon into bowl and beat until fluffy. Return to pan and freeze until firm, 6 hours.

LEMON ICE

Serve this sweet-and-tart ice as a dessert or as a refreshing palate cleanser between dinner courses.

8 servings

2 cups water
1 cup sugar
1 cup fresh lemon juice
1/2 cup grated lemon rind

Per Serving
Calories: 101
% Calories from fat: 0.0
Fat (gm): 0.0
Saturated fat (gm): 0.0
Cholesterol (mg): 0.0
Sodium (mg): 1.3
Protein (gm): 0.2
Carbohydrate (gm): 27.6
Exchanges
Milk: 0.0
Vegetable: 0.0
Fruit: 0.0
Bread: 1.5
Meat: 0.0
Fat: 0.0

1. Combine water and sugar in medium saucepan. Heat to boiling over medium-high heat, stirring until sugar is dissolved. Reduce heat and simmer, uncovered, 5 minutes. Remove from heat; cool to room temperature. Stir in lemon juice and lemon rind.

2. Freeze mixture in ice cream maker according to manufacturer's directions. Or pour into 8-inch square baking dish and freeze until slushy, about 2 hours; spoon into bowl and beat until fluffy. Return to pan and freeze until firm, 6 hours or overnight.

WATERMELON STRAWBERRY ICE

Nothing is as refreshing as watermelon on a hot summer day! Combined with strawberries, this is a sure winner.

6 servings

2 cups cubed, seeded watermelon
2 cups sliced strawberries
1/2 cup sugar
2 tablespoons lemon juice
1 teaspoon balsamic vinegar, optional

Per Serving
Calories: 98
% Calories from fat: 3
Fat (gm): 0.4
Saturated fat (gm): 0
Cholesterol (mg): 0
Sodium (mg): 2
Protein (gm): 0.7
Carbohydrate (gm): 24.4
Exchanges
Milk: 0.0
Vegetable: 0.0
Fruit: 1.5
Bread: 0.0
Meat: 0.0
Fat: 0.0

1. Puree all ingredients in food processor or blender until smooth. Freeze mixture in ice cream maker according to manufacturer's directions. Or pour into 8-inch square baking dish and freeze until slushy, about 2 hours; spoon into bowl and beat until fluffy. Return to pan and freeze until firm, 6 hours or overnight.

PINEAPPLE-CHAMPAGNE ICE

Champagne-inspired for a touch of elegance.

8 servings

1 envelope unflavored gelatin
2 1/2 cups unsweetened pineapple juice
1/2 cup dry champagne *or* sparkling wine
1/4 teaspoon ground nutmeg
8 slices fresh pineapple (1/2 inch thick)
Mint sprigs, as garnish

Per Serving
Calories: 66
% Calories from fat: 2
Fat (gm): 0.1
Saturated fat (gm): 0.0
Cholesterol (mg): 0.0
Sodium (mg): 2
Protein (gm): 1.8
Carbohydrate (gm): 57.6
Exchanges
Milk: 0.0
Vegetable: 0.0
Fruit: 1.0
Bread: 0.0
Meat: 0.0
Fat: 0.0

1. Sprinkle gelatin over pineapple juice in medium saucepan; let stand 2 to 3 minutes. Cook over low heat, stirring constantly, until gelatin is dissolved. Cool to room temperature. Stir in champagne and nutmeg.

2. Freeze mixture in ice cream maker according to manufacturer's directions. Or pour mixture into 9-inch square baking dish and freeze until slushy, about 2 hours; spoon into bowl and beat until fluffy. Return to pan and freeze until firm, 6 hours or overnight.

3. To serve, place pineapple slices on dessert plates. Top each with a scoop of Pineapple-Champagne Ice. Garnish with mint.

LIME CHIFFON ICE

Meringue is folded into the lime mixture, giving an exceptional smoothness to this dessert.

6 servings

1 cup sugar
$3^1/2$ cups water, divided
$^1/2$ cup light corn syrup
$^1/8$ teaspoon salt
1 envelope unflavored gelatin
$^3/4$ cup lime juice
1 teaspoon grated lime rind
1 tablespoon meringue powder

Per Serving
Calories: 221
% Calories from fat: 0
Fat (gm): 0
Saturated fat (gm): 0
Cholesterol (mg): 0
Sodium (mg): 97
Protein (gm): 1.1
Carbohydrate (gm): 57.7
Exchanges
Milk: 0.0
Vegetable: 0.0
Fruit: 3.5
Bread: 0.0
Meat: 0.0
Fat: 0.0

1. Heat sugar, 3 cups water, corn syrup, and salt to boiling in large saucepan, stirring to dissolve sugar; boil uncovered 5 minutes. Sprinkle gelatin over $^1/4$ cup water; let stand to soften 2 to 3 minutes. Stir gelatin into sugar syrup and stir until dissolved. Add lime juice and rind; cool. Freeze, uncovered, in shallow bowl or baking pan until slushy, about 2 hours

2. Beat meringue powder and remaining $^1/4$ cup water to stiff peaks. Remove lime mixture from freezer and beat until smooth; fold in meringue mixture. Freeze mixture in ice cream maker according to manufacturer's directions. Or return mixture to bowl and freeze until slushy, about 2 hours; remove from freezer and beat until fluffy. Freeze until firm, 6 hours or overnight.

STRAWBERRY RHUBARB SORBET

Delicious, and virtually fat-free too!

8 servings

3 cups sliced fresh, *or* frozen, rhubarb (about 1 pound)

1 cup sugar

¹/₃ cup water

1 pint strawberries, hulled

²/₃ cup orange juice

1 tablespoon grated orange rind

Per Serving
Calories: 129
% Calories from fat: 2
Fat (gm): 0.3
Saturated fat (gm): 0
Cholesterol (mg): 0
Sodium (mg): 3
Protein (gm): 0.8
Carbohydrate (gm): 32.3
Exchanges
Milk: 0.0
Vegetable: 0.0
Fruit: 2.0
Bread: 0.0
Meat: 0.0
Fat: 0.0

1. Combine rhubarb, sugar, and water in large saucepan; heat to boiling. Reduce heat and simmer, uncovered, until rhubarb is very tender, 10 to 15 minutes; cool.

2. Process rhubarb mixture, strawberries, orange juice, and rind in food processor or blender until smooth.

3. Freeze mixture in ice cream maker according to manufacturer's directions. Or pour mixture into 9-inch square baking dish and freeze until slushy, about 2 hours; spoon into bowl and beat until fluffy. Return to pan and freeze until firm, 6 hours or overnight.

CRANBERRY SORBET WITH SUGARED CRANBERRIES

Party perfect, especially when served with Granola Lace Cookies or Almond Tuiles (see pp. 346, 347).

8 servings

2/3 cup sugar
1/3 cup water
2 tablespoons light corn syrup
1 cup fresh, *or* frozen, cranberries
1 small navel orange, peeled, cut into 1-inch pieces
1 tablespoon chopped gingerroot
3 1/2 cups cranberry juice
Sugared Cranberries (recipe follows)
Mint sprigs, as garnish

Per Serving
Calories: 264
% Calories from fat: 2
Fat (gm): 0.7
Saturated fat (gm): 0.2
Cholesterol (mg): 17.8
Sodium (mg): 26
Protein (gm): 0.9
Carbohydrate (gm): 66.2
Exchanges
Milk: 0.0
Vegetable: 0.0
Fruit: 4.5
Bread: 0.0
Meat: 0.0
Fat: 0.0

1. Heat sugar, water, and corn syrup in small saucepan over medium-high heat until sugar is dissolved, 2 to 3 minutes, stirring constantly. Process sugar syrup, cranberries, orange pieces, and gingerroot in food processor or blender until coarsely chopped; refrigerate until cold.

2. In ice cream maker, combine cranberry mixture and cranberry juice; freeze according to manufacturer's directions. Stir sorbet well to mix cranberries throughout; freeze until firm, 8 hours or overnight. Or pour mixture into 9-inch square baking dish and freeze until slushy, about 2 hours; spoon into bowl and beat until fluffy. Return to pan and freeze until firm, 6 hours or overnight.

3. Scoop sorbet into small stemmed dishes; top with Sugared Cranberries and mint.

Sugared Cranberries

makes 40

40 fresh, *or* frozen, cranberries
1/4 cup pasteurized egg product
1 cup sugar

In a small bowl, roll cranberries in egg product; drain slightly and roll in sugar to coat generously. Refrigerate on a plate until sugar crust forms, about 1 hour.

CREAMY RASPBERRY-GRAPE SHERBET

This easy sherbet can be made with other fruits and juices—try substituting peaches and white grape juice.

8 servings

2 packages (10 ounces each) frozen sweetened raspberries, thawed
1 can (6 ounces) frozen grape juice concentrate, thawed
4 cups light whipped topping

Per Serving
Calories: 191
% Calories from fat: 20
Fat (gm): 4.2
Saturated fat (gm): 4
Cholesterol (mg): 0
Sodium (mg): 2
Protein (gm): 0.6
Carbohydrate (gm): 36
Exchanges
Milk: 0.0
Vegetable: 0.0
Fruit: 2.5
Bread: 0.0
Meat: 0.0
Fat: 1.0

1. Process raspberries in food processor or blender until smooth; strain and discard seeds. Combine raspberry puree and grape juice concentrate; fold in whipped topping.

2. Freeze in ice cream maker according to manufacturer's directions. Or pour into 8-inch square baking dish and freeze until slushy, about 2 hours; spoon into bowl and beat until fluffy. Return to pan, and freeze until firm, 6 hours or overnight.

CRANBERRY WINE ICE

Rose wine lends an elegant flavor to this ice. Substitute cranberry or orange juice if you prefer.

8 servings

1 can (16 ounces) whole-berry cranberry sauce
1 can (15$^1/_4$ ounces) crushed pineapple in juice, undrained
$^1/_3$ cup sugar
1 cup rose wine
$^1/_4$ cup lime juice

Per Serving
Calories: 169
% Calories from fat: 0
Fat (gm): 0.1
Saturated fat (gm): 0
Cholesterol (mg): 0
Sodium (mg): 14
Protein (gm): 0.3
Carbohydrate (gm): 39
Exchanges
Milk: 0.0
Vegetable: 0.0
Fruit: 2.5
Bread: 0.0
Meat: 0.0
Fat: 0.0

1. Process cranberry sauce, pineapple and juice, and sugar in blender or food processor until smooth. Combine with remaining ingredients, and freeze in ice cream maker according to manufacturer's directions. Or pour into 8-inch square baking dish and freeze until slushy, about 2 hours; spoon into bowl and beat until fluffy. Return to pan and freeze until firm, 6 hours or overnight.

FROZEN LEMON SOUFFLÉ

This luscious soufflé can be made several days before serving. Cover soufflé after it is frozen.

8 servings

1 egg yolk
3 tablespoons sugar
1¹/₂ tablespoons flour
¹/₂ cup fat-free milk
¹/₃ cup lemon juice
2 tablespoons grated lemon rind
2 tablespoons meringue powder
¹/₃ cup water
3 cups light whipped topping
Candied lemon rind, as garnish

Per Serving
Calories: 105
% Calories from fat: 34
Fat (gm): 3.7
Saturated fat (gm): 3.2
Cholesterol (mg): 26.9
Sodium (mg): 28
Protein (gm): 2.4
Carbohydrate (gm): 13.8
Exchanges
Milk: 0.0
Vegetable: 0.0
Fruit: 0.0
Bread: 1.0
Meat: 0.0
Fat: 1.0

1. Whisk egg yolk and sugar in small bowl until smooth; whisk in flour. Heat milk to boiling in small saucepan. Whisk small amount of hot milk into yolk mixture; whisk yolk mixture into saucepan. Whisk constantly over medium heat until thick, about 3 minutes. Stir in lemon juice and rind. Cool to room temperature.

2. Beat meringue powder and water to stiff peaks; fold into lemon mixture. Fold in whipped topping. Pour into 2-quart soufflé dish or serving bowl. Freeze until firm, about 6 hours. Garnish with candied lemon rind.

Variations: **Frozen Orange Soufflés**—Make recipe as above, substituting orange juice and rind for the lemon juice and rind, and adding 1 tablespoon orange liqueur *or* ¹/₂ teaspoon orange extract with the juice in Step 1. Cut the top quarter off 8 large navel oranges. Remove fruit from shells, using a grapefruit spoon or knife (reserve fruit for another use). Dry insides of shells. Spoon soufflé mixture into shells and freeze until firm, about 4 hours.

Frozen Pear Soufflé—Heat 1¹/₂ cups water, ¹/₂ cup sugar, and ¹/₃ cup lemon juice to boiling in medium saucepan. Add 2 medium pears, peeled, cored, and quartered, and simmer until tender, about 10 minutes. Remove pears; cool and dice finely. Make recipe as above, substituting ¹/₃ cup pear cooking liquid for the lemon juice in the recipe, and folding in diced pears, 1 teaspoon vanilla, and ¹/₃ cup pear liqueur (optional).

Peach Amaretti Soufflé—Heat 2 cups peeled, diced fresh peaches, ¹/₄ cup sugar, and 1 teaspoon brandy in small saucepan, stirring until sugar is melted; cook on low heat until peaches are tender. Puree until smooth; cool. Make recipe as above, omitting lemon juice and folding in peach puree and ¹/₃ cup crushed almond macaroons in Step 2.

FROZEN BRANDY MOUSSE

A spirited dish, for spirited occasions! If you prefer, substitute ¹/₂ cup water and 1 tablespoon brandy extract for the brandy in the recipe. It's also delicious with other liqueurs or extracts.

16 servings

2 packages (8 ounces each) fat-free cream cheese
1 can (14 ounces) reduced-fat sweetened condensed milk
¹/₄ teaspoon ground nutmeg
¹/₂ cup brandy
¹/₂ cup water
3 cups light whipped topping
Chocolate shavings, as garnish

Per Serving
Calories: 151
% Calories from fat: 22
Fat (gm): 3.6
Saturated fat (gm): 2
Cholesterol (mg): 9.1
Sodium (mg): 186
Protein (gm): 6
Carbohydrate (gm): 18.1
Exchanges
Milk: 0.0
Vegetable: 0.0
Fruit: 0.0
Bread: 1.0
Meat: 0.5
Fat: 1.0

1. Beat cream cheese in medium bowl until smooth; mix in sweetened condensed milk, nutmeg, brandy, and water. Fold in whipped topping; pour into lightly oiled 8-cup ring mold. Freeze until firm, about 6 hours.

2. Unmold onto serving plate; garnish with chocolate shavings.

MIXED FRUIT TORTONI

Traditionally made with heavy cream and candied fruits, our version of this Italian favorite uses fresh seasonal fruits and low-fat topping.

12 servings

1¹/₂ cups fresh, *or* frozen, thawed, raspberries

3 envelopes (1.3 ounces each) light whipped topping mix

1¹/₂ cups 2% reduced-fat milk

¹/₂ teaspoon sherry extract, optional

¹/₂ cup sweet cherries, pitted, cut into halves, divided

¹/₃ cup peeled, cubed apricots

¹/₃ cup peeled, cubed pineapple

4 tablespoons sugar

¹/₄ cup chopped pistachio nuts *or* slivered almonds, divided

Per Serving
Calories: 126
% Calories from fat: 28
Fat (gm): 3.5
Saturated fat (gm): 0.7
Cholesterol (mg): 2
Sodium (mg): 32
Protein (gm): 2.1
Carbohydrate (gm): 18.2
Exchanges
Milk: 0.0
Vegetable: 0.0
Fruit: 1.5
Bread: 0.0
Meat: 0.0
Fat: 0.5

1. Process raspberries in food processor or blender until smooth; strain and discard seeds.

2. Mix whipped topping, milk, and sherry extract in large bowl; beat at high speed until topping forms soft peaks, about 4 minutes. Fold raspberry puree into whipped topping.

3. Reserve 12 cherry halves. Combine remaining cherries, apricots, and pineapple in small bowl; sprinkle with sugar and stir. Fold fruit and 2 tablespoons nuts into whipped topping mixture.

4. Spoon about ¹/₂ cup mixture into each of 12 foil or paper cupcake liners; garnish tops of each with reserved cherry halves and remaining 2 tablespoons nuts. Place cupcake liners in muffin or baking pan; freeze until firm, 6 hours or overnight.

STRAWBERRY FREEZE

This easy dessert can also be made with other fruit.

9 servings

2 packages (10-ounce size) frozen, thawed, sweetened strawberries

1 can (20 ounces) crushed pineapple in juice, undrained

1 can (11 ounces) reduced-fat sweetened condensed milk

1 container (9 ounces) light whipped topping

Per Serving
Calories: 275
% Calories from fat: 20
Fat (gm): 6.1
Saturated fat (gm): 3.9
Cholesterol (mg): 9.6
Sodium (mg): 47
Protein (gm): 3.3
Carbohydrate (gm): 52.1
Exchanges
Milk: 0.0
Vegetable: 0.0
Fruit: 4.0
Bread: 0.0
Meat: 0.0
Fat: 1.0

1. Stir together strawberries, pineapple and juice, and condensed milk until smooth. Fold in whipped topping. Pour into 13 x 9-inch baking pan. Freeze until firm, 4 to 6 hours. Remove from freezer 10 minutes before serving; cut into squares.

CREAMY CRANBERRY FREEZE

This dessert can be made in any season, since it uses canned fruit.

8 servings

1 package (8 ounces) reduced-fat cream cheese

2 tablespoons sugar

1 tablespoon orange juice

2 teaspoons grated orange rind

1 can (16 ounces) whole-berry cranberry sauce

1 can (8³/₄ ounces) crushed pineapple in juice, drained

1 envelope (1.3 ounces) whipped topping mix

¹/₂ cup fat-free milk

¹/₄ cup chopped walnuts

Orange Sauce (see p. 652)

Per Serving
Calories: 322
% Calories from fat: 25
Fat (gm): 9
Saturated fat (gm): 4.7
Cholesterol (mg): 66.8
Sodium (mg): 156
Protein (gm): 5.2
Carbohydrate (gm): 54.9
Exchanges
Milk: 0.0
Vegetable: 0.0
Fruit: 0.0
Bread: 3.5
Meat: 0.0
Fat: 1.5

1. Beat cream cheese, sugar, orange juice, and orange rind until smooth. Stir in cranberry sauce and drained pineapple.

2. Beat whipped topping mix and milk according to package directions. Fold into fruit mixture. Pour into 8-inch springform pan; sprinkle with walnuts. Freeze until firm, about 4 hours. Remove side of pan; cut into wedges. Serve with Orange Sauce.

PUMPKIN CARDAMOM DESSERT

Pumpkin ice cream on a spicy oat crust—substitute homemade Pumpkin Spice Ice Cream (see p. 444), if you prefer.

9 servings

- 2 cups quick-cooking oats
- 6 tablespoons margarine, melted
- 1/2 cup packed light brown sugar
- 1/4 cup hot water
- 1 1/2 teaspoons ground cinnamon, divided
- 1 1/4 teaspoons ground cardamom, divided
- 1/2 teaspoon salt
- 1 quart low-fat coffee, *or* vanilla, ice cream, softened
- 1 cup canned pumpkin
  Pinch ground cloves
  Light whipped topping, as garnish

Per Serving
Calories: 283
% Calories from fat: 32
Fat (gm): 10.6
Saturated fat (gm): 2.6
Cholesterol (mg): 8.9
Sodium (mg): 260
Protein (gm): 6
Carbohydrate (gm): 43.6
Exchanges
Milk: 0.0
Vegetable: 0.0
Fruit: 0.0
Bread: 2.5
Meat: 0.0
Fat: 2

1. Mix oats, margarine, brown sugar, hot water, 1 teaspoon cinnamon, 1/2 teaspoon cardamom, and salt in medium bowl. Press mixture evenly on bottom of greased 11 x 7-inch baking dish. Bake at 325 degrees until lightly browned and set, about 30 minutes; cool.

2. Mix ice cream, pumpkin, remaining 1/2 teaspoon cinnamon, remaining 3/4 teaspoon cardamom, and cloves in large bowl until smooth. Pour into crust; cover. Freeze until firm, about 6 hours. Remove from freezer 10 minutes before serving. Cut into squares; top with whipped topping.

PARADISE COUPE

This easy dessert can also be frozen in a springform pan, or use a Graham Cracker Crumb Crust (see p. 132) for another easy, and pretty, dessert.

8 servings

 2 cups low-fat vanilla ice cream, softened
 2 cups orange sherbet, softened
 1 can (8 ounces) crushed pineapple in juice, undrained
 1/2 cup frozen, thawed, pineapple juice concentrate
 8 Meringue Shells (see p. 306) (double recipe)
 Light whipped topping, as garnish
 Chopped macadamia nuts, as garnish

Per Serving
Calories: 369
% Calories from fat: 5
Fat (gm): 2
Saturated fat (gm): 1.1
Cholesterol (mg): 8.5
Sodium (mg): 71
Protein (gm): 4.2
Carbohydrate (gm): 86.9
Exchanges
Milk: 0.0
Vegetable: 0.0
Fruit: 0.0
Bread: 5.0
Meat: 0.0
Fat: 0.0

1. Beat ice cream, sherbet, pineapple and juice, and pineapple concentrate in large chilled bowl until smooth. Pour mixture into 9-inch square baking dish; freeze until firm, about 4 hours.

2. Scoop mixture into Meringue Shells. Serve with dollops of whipped topping and macadamia nuts.

MERINGUE ICE CREAM TORTE

Layers of crispy meringue, frozen with ice cream, and fresh berries—it's heaven!

8 servings

 Meringue Layers (see p. 83)
 1 quart low-fat vanilla ice cream, softened
 2 cups light whipped topping
 Sugared Crushed Berries (see p. 249)

Per Serving
Calories: 301
% Calories from fat: 12
Fat (gm): 4.3
Saturated fat (gm): 3
Cholesterol (mg): 10
Sodium (mg): 70
Protein (gm): 5.2
Carbohydrate (gm): 62.2
Exchanges
Milk: 0.0
Vegetable: 0.0
Fruit: 1.0
Bread: 3.0
Meat: 0.0
Fat: 0.5

1. Place 1 meringue layer on serving plate; spread with half the ice cream. Top with another meringue layer; spread with remaining ice cream. Freeze until firm, about 4 hours.

2. Spread side of torte with whipped topping; spoon about ¹/₂ cup Sugared Crushed Berries over top of torte. Cut into wedges; serve with remaining berries.

Variation: **Chocolate Meringue Torte**—Make recipe as above, folding ¹/₄ cup unsweetened cocoa into beaten egg whites and substituting low-fat chocolate fudge ice cream for the vanilla ice cream. Drizzle top of torte with 2 ounces melted semisweet chocolate after freezing. Omit Sugared Crushed Berries and serve with Chocolate Sauce (see p. 642).

SKY HIGH LEMON PIE

Lemony ice cream and fruit served in a beautiful meringue crust—what could be better?

8 servings

1¹/₂ quarts low-fat vanilla ice cream, slightly softened	**Per Serving**
	Calories: 370
	% Calories from fat: 8
	Fat (gm): 3.2
³/₄ cup fresh lemon juice	Saturated fat (gm): 1.6
1¹/₂ tablespoons grated lemon rind	Cholesterol (mg): 15
	Sodium (mg): 97
³/₄ teaspoon ground nutmeg	Protein (gm): 6.6
Few drops yellow food color	Carbohydrate (gm): 81.4
Meringue Pie Crust (see p. 132)	**Exchanges**
	Milk: 0.0
	Vegetable: 0.0
1 cup blueberries	Fruit: 0.0
1 cup raspberries	Bread: 5.0
	Meat: 0.0
1¹/₂ cups strawberry ice cream sauce	Fat: 0.5

1. Mix ice cream, lemon juice, rind, and nutmeg in medium bowl; add food color to make a deep yellow color.

2. Cover bowl with aluminum foil; freeze until ice cream is hard, 8 hours or overnight.

3. At serving time, scoop ice cream into pie crust and sprinkle with berries. Serve with strawberry sauce.

CHOCOLATE CHERRY ICE CREAM PIE

The perfect combination for lovers of chocolate-covered cherries!

8 servings

Meringue Pie Crust (see p. 132)

3 tablespoons cocoa

1 can (16 ounces) pitted dark sweet cherries

1 tablespoon sugar

1 tablespoon cornstarch

1 teaspoon rum extract

1 quart reduced-fat vanilla ice cream

Chocolate curls, as garnish

Per Serving
Calories: 251
% Calories from fat: 7
Fat (gm): 2
Saturated fat (gm): 1
Cholesterol (mg): 10.1
Sodium (mg): 73
Protein (gm): 5.5
Carbohydrate (gm): 55.3
Exchanges
Milk: 0.0
Vegetable: 0.0
Fruit: 0.0
Bread: 3.5
Meat: 0.0
Fat: 0.0

1. Make Meringue Pie Crust, folding cocoa into beaten egg whites.

2. Drain cherries, reserving 1/2 cup juice. Mix sugar, cornstarch, and reserved juice in medium saucepan. Heat to boiling, stirring constantly; cool. Stir in rum extract and cherries.

3. Scoop ice cream into pie shell; top with cherry mixture. Garnish with chocolate curls and serve immediately.

CARAMEL ICE CREAM PIE

10 servings

Graham Cracker Crumb Crust (see p. 132)

1 quart low-fat banana chocolate chip ice cream, slightly softened

1 large banana, sliced

Quick and Easy Caramel Sauce (see p. 644)

Per Serving
Calories: 361
% Calories from fat: 21
Fat (gm): 8.7
Saturated fat (gm): 2.5
Cholesterol (mg): 4.7
Sodium (mg): 163
Protein (gm): 4.6
Carbohydrate (gm): 69
Exchanges
Milk: 0.0
Vegetable: 0.0
Fruit: 0.0
Bread: 4.5
Meat: 0.0
Fat: 1.0

1. Make Graham Cracker Crumb Crust, using 9-inch pie pan.

2. Spoon ice cream into pie crust, spreading evenly; freeze until very hard, 8 hours or overnight.

3. Top with banana slices. Drizzle $^1/_3$ cup Quick and Easy Caramel Sauce over pie; serve slices with remaining caramel sauce.

ORANGE BAKED ALASKA PIE

Create any desired flavor of frozen yogurt by substituting another liqueur for the orange. Try cherry, raspberry, or a non-fruit flavor such as almond, hazelnut, or coffee.

8 servings

Gingersnap Crumb Crust (see p. 135)
$^1/_2$ cup graham cracker crumbs
  1 tablespoon margarine
  4 cups frozen low-fat vanilla yogurt, slightly softened
  2 tablespoons orange-flavor liqueur *or* orange juice concentrate
$^1/_4$ teaspoon ground nutmeg
  3 egg whites
$^1/_8$ teaspoon cream of tartar
$^1/_4$ cup sugar

Per Serving
Calories: 289
% Calories from fat: 28
Fat (gm): 9
Saturated fat (gm): 2.5
Cholesterol (mg): 10
Sodium (mg): 267
Protein (gm): 6.9
Carbohydrate (gm): 44.2
Exchanges
Milk: 0.0
Vegetable: 0.0
Fruit: 0.0
Bread: 3.0
Meat: 0.0
Fat: 1.5

1. Make Gingersnap Crumb Crust, adding $^1/_2$ cup graham cracker crumbs and 1 tablespoon margarine to recipe and using 8-inch pie pan.

2. Mix frozen yogurt, liqueur, and nutmeg; spoon into cooled pie crust. Cover with plastic wrap and freeze until firm, 8 hours or overnight.

3. In medium bowl, beat egg whites with cream of tartar to soft peaks. Gradually add sugar, beating to stiff peaks. Spread meringue over frozen pie, carefully sealing to edge of crust. Bake at 500 degrees 3 to 5 minutes or until meringue is golden. Serve immediately.

Variation: **Chocolate Baked Alaska Pie**—Make recipe as above, substituting Vanilla Crumb Crust (see p. 133) and vanilla wafer crumbs for the Gingersnap Crumb Crust and graham cracker crumbs, and low-fat chocolate yogurt for the vanilla yogurt. Omit orange liqueur and nutmeg. Serve with Bittersweet Chocolate Sauce (see p. 641).

BAKED ALASKA

It's a 50s' classic revisited in low-fat style. Baked Alaska can be completely assembled, and frozen up to 24 hours before baking. Serve with Chocolate Sauce or Rich Caramel Sauce (see pp. 642, 643) if you like.

10 servings

1 quart low-fat vanilla ice cream, softened
Raspberry Jam Cake (see p. 85)
5 egg whites
1/2 teaspoon cream of tartar
3/4 cup sugar

Per Serving
Calories: 326
% Calories from fat: 14
Fat (gm): 5.3
Saturated fat (gm): 1.7
Cholesterol (mg): 51.5
Sodium (mg): 193
Protein (gm): 6.9
Carbohydrate (gm): 65.5
Exchanges
Milk: 0.0
Vegetable: 0.0
Fruit: 0.0
Bread: 4.0
Meat: 0.0
Fat: 1.0

1. Spoon ice cream into 8-inch-diameter bowl; pack down firmly. Cover and freeze until very firm, about 4 hours.

2. Bake Raspberry Jam Cake in 9-inch round pan; omit Marshmallow Frosting. Place cake on heat-proof serving platter. Dip bowl of ice cream into warm water to loosen, and invert it on top of cake. Place platter in freezer for at least 15 minutes.

3. Beat egg whites with cream of tartar in large bowl to soft peaks. Gradually add sugar, beating to stiff peaks. Spread meringue over ice cream and cake, carefully sealing to platter. Bake at 500 degrees 3 to 5 minutes or until meringue is golden. Serve immediately.

Variation: **Pumpkin-Spiced Baked Alaska**—Make recipe as above, substituting Pumpkin Spice Ice Cream (see p. 444) for the vanilla ice cream, and Pumpkin Ginger Cake with Warm Rum Sauce, baked in parchment-lined 9-inch round pan (see p. 54), for the Raspberry Jam Cake.

LEMON BLUEBERRY ICE CREAM CAKE

Cake layers filled with lemony ice cream and blueberry filling compose this great make-ahead dessert.

12 servings

Classic Sponge Cake (see p. 100)
6 cups blueberries, divided
³/₄ cup sugar
¹/₄ cup light corn syrup
1 quart low-fat vanilla ice cream, slightly softened
³/₄ cup lemon juice, divided
2 teaspoons grated lemon rind
2 cups light whipped topping

Per Serving
Calories: 327
% Calories from fat: 12
Fat (gm): 4.3
Saturated fat (gm): 2.4
Cholesterol (mg): 59.9
Sodium (mg): 154
Protein (gm): 5.5
Carbohydrate (gm): 68.9
Exchanges
Milk: 0.0
Vegetable: 0.0
Fruit: 0.0
Bread: 3.0
Meat: 0.0
Fat: 1.0

1. Bake Classic Sponge Cake, using 9-inch springform pan; cool.

2. Heat 4 cups blueberries, sugar, and corn syrup to boiling in large saucepan; simmer, uncovered, stirring occasionally, until reduced to 2 cups, about 20 minutes. Cool; refrigerate, covered, until chilled, about 1 hour.

3. Mix ice cream, ¹/₂ cup lemon juice, and lemon rind in large chilled bowl until smooth.

4. Slice cake in half horizontally. Place bottom half, cut side up, in bottom of 9-inch springform pan. Brush with 2 tablespoons lemon juice; top with ¹/₂ of the blueberry mixture, spreading to within ¹/₂ inch of edge. Top with ¹/₂ of the ice cream mixture, spreading evenly. Top with remaining cake layer, cut side up, and sprinkle with remaining 2 tablespoons lemon juice; spread with remaining blueberry and ice cream mixtures. Freeze, covered, until firm, about 8 hours.

5. To serve, remove side of pan, loosen cake from bottom, and transfer to serving plate. Frost side of cake with whipped topping; serve with remaining 2 cups blueberries.

ICE CREAM JELLY ROLL CAKE

A versatile cake that can be filled with your flavor choice of fat-free ice cream or frozen yogurt; or even use light whipped topping and sliced fruit.

8 servings

3 egg yolks
$^1/_2$ teaspoon vanilla
$^3/_4$ cup sugar, divided
3 egg whites
$^3/_4$ cup cake flour
1 teaspoon baking powder
$^1/_4$ teaspoon salt
1-1$^1/_2$ quarts strawberry, *or* other flavor, fat-free ice cream, slightly softened
Powdered sugar, as garnish
Whole strawberries, as garnish

Per Serving
Calories: 229
% Calories from fat: 8
Fat (gm): 2
Saturated fat (gm): 0.6
Cholesterol (mg): 79.9
Sodium (mg): 197
Protein (gm): 7.2
Carbohydrate (gm): 47.2
Exchanges
Milk: 0.0
Vegetable: 0.0
Fruit: 0.0
Bread: 2.5
Meat: 0.0
Fat: 0.0

1. Grease jelly roll pan, 15 x 10 x 1 inch. Line bottom of pan with parchment paper; grease and flour parchment.

2. Beat egg yolks and vanilla in medium bowl until thick and lemon colored, 3 to 5 minutes. Gradually beat in $^1/_4$ cup sugar, beating 2 minutes longer.

3. Using clean beaters and large bowl, beat egg whites to soft peaks; gradually beat in remaining $^1/_2$ cup granulated sugar, beating to stiff, glossy peaks. Fold egg yolks into whites; sprinkle combined flour, baking powder, and salt over mixture and fold in. Spread batter evenly in prepared pan, using metal spatula.

4. Bake at 375 degrees until cake is golden and springs back when touched, 10 to 12 minutes. Immediately invert cake onto large kitchen towel sprinkled with powdered sugar; remove parchment. Roll cake up in towel, beginning at short end. Cool on wire rack 30 to 60 minutes.

5. Unroll cake; spread with ice cream. Reroll cake and freeze until ice cream is firm, 6 to 8 hours.

6. Trim ends from cake and place cake on serving plate. Sprinkle cake generously with powdered sugar and garnish with strawberries.

Variation: **Chocolate Ice Cream Jelly Roll Cake**—Make cake as above, adding ¹/₄ cup unsweetened cocoa to the flour mixture. Fill cake with chocolate chip or chocolate fudge fat-free ice cream.

FROZEN PEPPERMINT CAKE ROLLS

This beautiful dessert is deceptively easy to prepare, using cake mix. The cake rolls can be frozen, securely wrapped in aluminum foil, up to 1 month.

16 servings

4 eggs
1 package (18³/₄ ounces) yellow cake mix
¹/₂ cup water
   Powdered sugar
³/₄ cup crushed peppermint candies
1¹/₂ quarts frozen low-fat vanilla yogurt, slightly softened
   Bittersweet Chocolate Sauce (see p. 641)

Per Serving
Calories: 317
% Calories from fat: 22
Fat (gm): 8.1
Saturated fat (gm): 2
Cholesterol (mg): 61.6
Sodium (mg): 321
Protein (gm): 6.8
Carbohydrate (gm): 55.1
Exchanges
Milk: 0.0
Vegetable: 0.0
Fruit: 0.0
Bread: 3.5
Meat: 0.0
Fat: 1.5

1. Lightly grease 2 jelly roll pans, 15 x 10 inches, and line with parchment paper; grease and flour parchment.

2. Beat eggs in large bowl at high speed until thick and lemon colored, about 5 minutes. Mix in cake mix and water on low speed. Pour batter into prepared pans; bake 15 minutes or until cakes spring back when touched. Immediately invert cakes onto clean kitchen towels sprinkled with powdered sugar. Remove parchment and roll cakes up in towels, starting at short ends. Cool on wire racks 15 minutes (no longer, or cakes will be too cool to fill and roll easily).

3. Fold peppermint candies into frozen yogurt. Unroll cakes; spread with frozen yogurt mixture. Roll cakes up and wrap in plastic wrap; freeze until firm, 8 hours or overnight.

4. Arrange cakes on serving platters; sprinkle with powdered sugar. Cut into slices; drizzle with Bittersweet Chocolate Sauce.

ALMOND CRUNCH TORTE

A nutty crust holds an easy-to-make chocolate filling. This dessert can be made up to 2 weeks ahead of time.

12 servings

4 tablespoons margarine
1 cup all-purpose flour
1/3 cup sugar
1/3 cup chopped toasted almonds
6 tablespoons honey, divided
1 quart low-fat chocolate ice cream, slightly softened
2 cups light whipped topping
1/4 cup rum *or* 1 tablespoon rum extract

Per Serving
Calories: 262
% Calories from fat: 33
Fat (gm): 9.4
Saturated fat (gm): 3.9
Cholesterol (mg): 16.7
Sodium (mg): 72
Protein (gm): 3.7
Carbohydrate (gm): 36.7
Exchanges
Milk: 0.0
Vegetable: 0.0
Fruit: 0.0
Bread: 2.5
Meat: 0.0
Fat: 2.0

1. Melt margarine in large skillet; add combined flour, sugar, and almonds. Stir constantly over medium heat until mixture is golden brown and crumbly, 6 to 8 minutes. Stir in 1/4 cup honey. Reserve 3/4 cup of crumb mixture. Stir remaining 2 tablespoons honey into remaining crumb mixture; pat onto bottom and 1 inch up side of greased 9-inch springform pan. Freeze 1 hour.

2. Beat ice cream in large chilled bowl until smooth; fold in whipped topping and rum. Spoon into crumb-lined pan and sprinkle with reserved crumb mixture; freeze until firm, about 6 hours.

Variation: **Citrus Grape Torte**—Make recipe as above, substituting vanilla ice cream for the chocolate ice cream. Serve with **Citrus Grape Sauce.** To make Citrus Grape Sauce, heat 1/3 cup sugar, 1 tablespoon cornstarch, 1/2 cup each lemon and orange juice, and pinch nutmeg to boiling in medium saucepan, stirring constantly until thickened. Stir in 3/4 cup halved red seedless grapes and heat just until warm. Serve immediately.

BANANA SPICE ICE CREAM TORTE

Cinnamon ice cream is molded in a springform pan and served with bananas and a caramel sauce.

12 servings

1/2 gallon low-fat vanilla ice cream, softened

2 tablespoons ground cinnamon

2 bananas, sliced

1 tablespoon sliced toasted almonds
  Rich Caramel Sauce (see p. 543)

Per Serving
Calories: 299
% Calories from fat: 22
Fat (gm): 7.8
Saturated fat (gm): 2.5
Cholesterol (mg): 49.1
Sodium (mg): 126
Protein (gm): 5.7
Carbohydrate (gm): 54.7
Exchanges
Milk: 0.0
Vegetable: 0.0
Fruit: 0.0
Bread: 3.5
Meat: 0.0
Fat: 1.0

1. Line an 8-inch springform pan with aluminum foil. Stir ice cream with cinnamon in large chilled bowl until well mixed. Pack ice cream mixture into pan; freeze, covered, until solid, about 6 hours.

2. Invert ice cream onto serving plate; remove foil. Arrange bananas over top of ice cream; sprinkle with almonds. Cut into wedges; serve with Rich Caramel Sauce.

ICE CREAM CHARLOTTE

This presentation turns ordinary ice cream into a special dessert. Use your favorite flavor purchased ice cream, or make an ice cream from this chapter.

8 servings

1 package (3 ounces) ladyfingers, split lengthwise

1 quart low-fat strawberry ice cream, softened

Glazed Strawberry Sauce (see p. 116)

Light whipped topping, as garnish

Per Serving
Calories: 221
% Calories from fat: 12
Fat (gm): 3.2
Saturated fat (gm): 1.3
Cholesterol (mg): 48.8
Sodium (mg): 61
Protein (gm): 4.5
Carbohydrate (gm): 42.1
Exchanges
Milk: 0.0
Vegetable: 0.0
Fruit: 1.0
Bread: 2.0
Meat: 0.0
Fat: 0.5

1. Line side of greased 1-quart soufflé dish with ladyfingers, cut sides toward center of dish. Spoon ice cream into dish, smoothing top with spatula. Freeze until firm, about 4 hours.

2. Unmold charlotte onto serving plate; spoon 1 cup Glazed Strawberry Sauce over. Cut into wedges, and serve with remaining sauce and dollops of whipped topping.

COLOSSAL COOKIE SANDWICH

This deliciously chewy oatmeal cookie, layered with ice cream and topped with peaches, makes a fabulous dessert.

16 servings

10	tablespoons margarine, softened
1¹/₄	cups packed light brown sugar
¹/₂	cup granulated sugar
2	eggs
2	teaspoons vanilla
1³/₄	cups all-purpose flour
1¹/₄	cups quick-cooking oats
1	teaspoon baking powder
¹/₂	teaspoon baking soda
³/₄	teaspoon salt
¹/₂	cup chopped pecans
1¹/₂-2	quarts fat-free butter pecan ice cream, slightly softened
	Light whipped topping, as garnish
24	fresh, *or* canned, peach slices

Per Serving
Calories: 365
% Calories from fat: 30
Fat (gm): 12.3
Saturated fat (gm): 2.6
Cholesterol (mg): 28.4
Sodium (mg): 322
Protein (gm): 6.2
Carbohydrate (gm): 58.6
Exchanges
Milk: 0.0
Vegetable: 0.0
Fruit: 0.0
Bread: 4.0
Meat: 0.0
Fat: 2.0

1. Beat margarine and sugars in large bowl until fluffy; beat in eggs and vanilla. Mix in combined flour, oats, baking powder, baking soda, and salt; mix in pecans.

2. Line two 12-inch pizza pans with aluminum foil and grease. Spread half the dough on each pan, using spatula or lightly floured fingertips.

3. Bake cookies at 350 degrees until browned, 12 to 15 minutes. Cool in pans on wire racks until firm enough to remove from pans, about 15 minutes. Using foil, slide cookies off pans; remove foil.

4. Place 1 cookie flat side up on serving plate or pizza pan; spread with ice cream and top with second cookie, flat side down. Freeze until firm, 4 to 6 hours.

5. Cut into wedges; garnish with whipped topping and peach slices.

CARAMEL CHOCOLATE CHIP ICE CREAM SANDWICH

Perfect for birthdays—or any other time. The sandwich is easier to cut if the caramel-coated cookie is on the bottom, so invert before serving.

20 servings

2 packages (1 pound, 2 ounces each) reduced-fat refrigerated chocolate chip cookie dough

1/2 package (14-ounce size) caramels (about 25)

2 tablespoons fat-free milk

1 quart fat-free vanilla, *or* chocolate, ice cream, slightly softened

Quick and Easy Caramel Sauce (see p. 644)

Per Serving
Calories: 372
% Calories from fat: 26
Fat (gm): 11.2
Saturated fat (gm): 3.8
Cholesterol (mg): 12.6
Sodium (mg): 145
Protein (gm): 4.6
Carbohydrate (gm): 65.6
Exchanges
Milk: 0.0
Vegetable: 0.0
Fruit: 0.0
Bread: 4.0
Meat: 0.0
Fat: 2.0

1. Line two 12-inch pizza pans with aluminum foil and grease lightly. Spread a package of cookie dough on each pan, spreading to edges. Bake at 325 degrees until browned, 17 to 20 minutes. Cool on wire racks. Invert cookies onto cookie sheets or pizza pans; peel off aluminum foil.

2. Heat caramels and milk in small saucepan over medium heat until melted, stirring constantly. Cool 2 to 3 minutes. Place 1 cookie, flat side up, on serving plate or pizza pan; pour caramel on cookie, spreading almost to the edge. Let stand, or refrigerate, until caramel is firm.

3. Spread ice cream evenly on flat side of second cookie; carefully invert caramel-covered cookie over ice cream. Freeze, covered with aluminum foil, until firm, 4 to 6 hours.

4. Invert ice cream sandwich onto serving plate; cut into wedges and serve with Quick and Easy Caramel Sauce.

ICE CREAM PIZZA

This dessert pizza can be made up to 1 week ahead of serving; decorate before serving. Try different combinations of ice cream, sherbets, and toppings.

12 servings

2¹/₂ cups graham cracker crumbs

1¹/₄ cups crushed low-fat granola

¹/₃ cup ground pecans

¹/₂ cup packed light brown sugar

1 teaspoon cinnamon

4 tablespoons margarine, melted

3 tablespoons honey

1-1¹/₂ quarts fat-free vanilla ice cream, softened

Garnishes: Pecan halves, semisweet chocolate morsels, maraschino cherry halves, toasted flaked coconut, marshmallow crème, sliced fruit, etc.

Raspberry Sauce (see p. 658)

Per Serving
Calories: 350
% Calories from fat: 28
Fat (gm): 11.5
Saturated fat (gm): 2.1
Cholesterol (mg): 0
Sodium (mg): 220
Protein (gm): 6
Carbohydrate (gm): 59.6
Exchanges
Milk: 0.0
Vegetable: 0.0
Fruit: 0.0
Bread: 3.5
Meat: 0.0
Fat: 2.0

1. Combine graham cracker crumbs, granola, pecans, brown sugar, and cinnamon. Stir in margarine and honey; press mixture onto bottom and side of 12-inch pizza pan, forming a ridge around edge of pan. Bake at 350 degrees 10 to 12 minutes. Cool on wire rack.

2. Spread ice cream on crust with metal spatula. Freeze until firm, about 3 hours.

3. Arrange desired garnishes over ice cream; drizzle with Raspberry Sauce.

PRALINE SUNDAES

Fresh peach slices would make a flavorful addition to the sundaes, or se-lect one of the cookies from the cookie chapter.

4 servings

- ¹/₄ cup packed light brown sugar
- 1¹/₂ teaspoons cornstarch
- ¹/₂ cup water
- 1 tablespoon bourbon *or* brandy, optional
- 1 teaspoon margarine
- ¹/₂ teaspoon vanilla
- 2 tablespoons chopped pecans
- 1 pint frozen low-fat vanilla yogurt

Per Serving
Calories: 208
% Calories from fat: 22
Fat (gm): 5.2
Saturated fat (gm): 1.4
Cholesterol (mg): 10
Sodium (mg): 92
Protein (gm): 4.3
Carbohydrate (gm): 37.1
Exchanges
Milk: 0.0
Vegetable: 0.0
Fruit: 0.0
Bread: 2.5
Meat: 0.0
Fat: 0.5

1. Mix sugar and cornstarch in small saucepan; stir in water. Heat to boiling over medium heat, stirring constantly until thickened, about 1 minute.

2. Stir in bourbon; cook 10 to 15 seconds. Remove from heat; stir in margarine, vanilla, and pecans. Serve warm over frozen yogurt.

TROPICAL SUNDAES

Exotic new flavors for an old-fashioned favorite sundae.

6 servings

3 cups cubed tropical fruit (pineapple, mango, papaya, banana, kiwi, etc.)
1¹/₂ pints low-fat vanilla ice cream
Kiwi Coulis (see p. 660)
¹/₄ cup coarsely chopped toasted macadamia nuts *or* almonds
Toasted coconut, as garnish

Per Serving
Calories: 261
% Calories from fat: 22
Fat (gm): 6.9
Saturated fat (gm): 1.7
Cholesterol (mg): 10
Sodium (mg): 43
Protein (gm): 4.6
Carbohydrate (gm): 49.7
Exchanges
Milk: 0.0
Vegetable: 0.0
Fruit: 1.5
Bread: 1.5
Meat: 0.0
Fat: 1.0

1. Spoon fruit into 6 stemmed serving dishes; top with scoops of ice cream. Spoon Kiwi Coulis over; sprinkle with macadamia nuts and toasted coconut.

NINE

Cobblers, Crisps, Coffee Cakes AND Kuchens

FRAN'S RHUBARB CRUNCH

Recipes from neighbors are the best. With a crunchy sweet crust on top and bottom, you'll lick your bowl clean and ask for more! The recipe can be halved and baked in a 9-inch square baking pan, if desired.

16 servings

1 cup all-purpose flour
1 cup whole wheat flour
1¹/₂ cups packed light brown sugar
1 cup quick-cooking oats
¹/₂ cup bran *or* quick-cooking oats
2 teaspoons ground cinnamon
10 tablespoons margarine, melted
2 pounds fresh, *or* frozen, thawed, rhubarb, cut into 1-inch pieces (8 cups)
2 cups granulated sugar
¹/₄ cup cornstarch
2 cups water
2 teaspoons vanilla

Per Serving
Calories: 327
% Calories from fat: 20
Fat (gm): 7.6
Saturated fat (gm): 1.5
Cholesterol (mg): 0
Sodium (mg): 95
Protein (gm): 3.1
Carbohydrate (gm): 64.1
Exchanges
Milk: 0.0
Vegetable: 0.0
Fruit: 0.0
Bread: 4.0
Meat: 0.0
Fat: 1.0

1. Combine flours, brown sugar, oats, bran, and cinnamon in large bowl; stir in margarine to make a crumbly mixture. Press half the mixture evenly on bottom of 13 x 9-inch baking pan. Arrange rhubarb evenly over crust.

2. Whisk granulated sugar, cornstarch, and water over high heat in medium saucepan until mixture boils and thickens, 3 to 4 minutes. Stir in vanilla and pour mixture over rhubarb.

3. Sprinkle remaining crumb mixture over rhubarb. Bake, uncovered, until bubbly around the edges, 55 to 60 minutes.

APPLE BROWN BETTY WITH HARD SAUCE

An old favorite with a classic brandy-flavored sauce.

6 servings

Per Serving
Calories: 319
% Calories from fat: 25
Fat (gm): 9
Saturated fat (gm): 1.8
Cholesterol (mg): 0
Sodium (mg): 246
Protein (gm): 2.8
Carbohydrate (gm): 58
Exchanges
Milk: 0.0
Vegetable: 0.0
Fruit: 2.0
Bread: 1.5
Meat: 0.0
Fat: 2.0

4	cups sliced, peeled tart baking apples
2	tablespoons lemon juice
1/4	cup raisins
1/2	cup sugar
3/4	teaspoon ground cinnamon
1/4	teaspoon ground nutmeg
1	cup unseasoned dry bread crumbs
3-4	teaspoons melted margarine
	Hard Sauce (recipe follows)

1. Arrange 1/2 the apples in 9-inch baking pan; sprinkle with 1/2 each of the lemon juice, raisins, combined sugar, cinnamon, and nutmeg, and combined bread crumbs and margarine; repeat the layers.

2. Bake at 350 degrees until apples are tender and bread crumbs browned, 45 to 55 minutes. Cool 10 to 15 minutes on wire rack; serve warm with Hard Sauce.

Hard Sauce

makes about 3/4 cup

1/2	cup powdered sugar
3	tablespoons margarine, softened
1-2	tablespoons brandy *or* 2 tablespoons milk and 1/2 teaspoon brandy extract

1. Beat powdered sugar, margarine, and brandy until smooth, adding a few drops water if necessary (mixture will be stiff); refrigerate until serving time.

Variation: **Plum Betty**—Make recipe as above, substituting plums for the apples, omitting raisins, 1/2 cup bread crumbs, and Hard Sauce, and increasing margarine to 3 tablespoons. Crumble enough reduced-fat oatmeal-raisin cookies to make 1 cup; toss with 1/2 cup bread crumbs and margarine; assemble and bake as above. Serve warm with fat-free ice cream or frozen yogurt.

APPLE-CRANBERRY CRISP

Apples and cranberries are happy companions in this streusel-topped fruit crisp.

6 servings

2¹/₂ pounds baking apples, peeled, sliced
 1 cup fresh, *or* frozen, cranberries, thawed
¹/₂ cup packed light brown sugar
 2 tablespoons flour
 1 teaspoon finely chopped crystallized ginger
 Streusel Topping (see pg. 480)

Per Serving
Calories: 300
% Calories from fat: 11
Fat (gm): 4.2
Saturated fat (gm): 0.8
Cholesterol (mg): 0
Sodium (mg): 46
Protein (gm): 2.1
Carbohydrate (gm): 68.2
Exchanges
Milk: 0.0
Vegetable: 0.0
Fruit: 2.0
Bread: 2.5
Meat: 0.0
Fat: 0.0

1. Combine apples, cranberries, brown sugar, flour, and ginger in a 1-quart glass casserole.

2. Sprinkle Streusel Topping over fruit. Bake, uncovered, at 350 degrees 30 to 40 minutes or until apples are tender. Serve warm.

Variations: **Gingered Pear and Cranberry Crisp**—Make recipe as above, substituting sliced ripe pears for the apples and increasing ginger to 1 tablespoon. Add ¹/₄ cup crushed gingersnap crumbs to Streusel Topping and increase margarine to 3 tablespoons. Bake as above.

Apple-Quince Crisp—Make recipe as above, substituting 1¹/₂ cups sliced peeled quince for the cranberries, and omitting crystallized ginger. Sprinkle apples and quince with 1 tablespoon each lemon juice and finely grated lemon rind, then toss with brown sugar, flour, and ¹/₂ teaspoon ground cinnamon. Complete as above.

APPLE GINGER CRISP

Layers of apples and gingersnap crumbs bake into one of our favorite desserts.

4 servings

3/4 cup gingersnap crumbs

2/3 cup packed light brown sugar

3-4 tablespoons margarine, softened

4 cups thinly sliced, peeled tart baking apples

2 tablespoons lemon juice, divided

Light whipped topping *or* fat-free ice cream

Per Serving
Calories: 369
% Calories from fat: 25
Fat (gm): 10.9
Saturated fat (gm): 2.1
Cholesterol (mg): 0
Sodium (mg): 238
Protein (gm): 1.5
Carbohydrate (gm): 70.1
Exchanges
Milk: 0.0
Vegetable: 0.0
Fruit: 2.0
Bread: 2.0
Meat: 0.0
Fat: 2.0

1. Mix gingersnap crumbs, brown sugar, and margarine until crumbly. Layer 1/2 the apples in 8-inch square baking pan; sprinkle with 1 tablespoon lemon juice and 1/2 of the gingersnap mixture. Repeat layers.

2. Bake, uncovered, at 375 degrees until apples are tender, about 30 minutes. Serve warm with light whipped topping.

AUTUMN FRUIT CRISP

Late harvest peaches and tart apples combine for flavors of fall.

6 servings

2 cups sliced fresh, *or* frozen, thawed, peaches

2 cups sliced, peeled Granny Smith, *or* other tart, baking apples

$1/3$ cup raisins

$1/4$ cup honey

$1/2$ teaspoon rum extract

Brown Sugar-Granola Streusel (recipe follows)

Per Serving
Calories: 287
% Calories from fat: 19
Fat (gm): 6.5
Saturated fat (gm): 1.3
Cholesterol (mg): 0
Sodium (mg): 142
Protein (gm): 2.8
Carbohydrate (gm): 57.9
Exchanges
Milk: 0.0
Vegetable: 0.0
Fruit: 2.0
Bread: 1.5
Meat: 0.0
Fat: 1.0

1. Combine peaches, apples, and raisins in $1^1/2$-quart casserole; drizzle combined honey and rum extract over.

2. Sprinkle Brown Sugar-Granola Streusel over fruit.

3. Bake at 375 degrees until browned and bubbly, about 30 minutes.

Brown Sugar-Granola Streusel

$1/2$ cup all-purpose flour

$1/3$ cup packed light brown sugar

$1/2$ teaspoon ground cinnamon

$1/8$ teaspoon salt

3 tablespoons cold margarine, cut into pieces

$1/2$ cup low-fat granola

1. Combine flour, brown sugar, cinnamon, and salt in small bowl; cut in margarine until pieces resemble coarse crumbs. Add granola and toss.

APRICOT CRUMBLE

Crisp cereal gives the crumble its pleasing "crunch."

8 servings

6 cups thickly sliced pitted apricots
³/₄ cup sugar
¹/₃ cup apricot spreadable fruit
1 teaspoon grated orange rind
Crumble Topping (recipe follows)

Per Serving
Calories: 324
% Calories from fat: 17
Fat (gm): 6.4
Saturated fat (gm): 1.2
Cholesterol (mg): 0
Sodium (mg): 129
Protein (gm): 4
Carbohydrate (gm): 65.1
Exchanges
Milk: 0.0
Vegetable: 0.0
Fruit: 1.0
Bread: 3.0
Meat: 0.0
Fat: 1.0

1. Toss apricots and sugar in large bowl; add spreadable fruit and orange rind and toss. Arrange fruit in greased 2-quart casserole. Sprinkle with Crumble Topping.

2. Bake at 375 degrees until browned and bubbly, 30 to 40 minutes.

Crumble Topping

¹/₂ cup all-purpose flour
¹/₃ cup natural wheat and barley cereal (Grape-Nuts)
¹/₃ cup quick-cooking oats
²/₃ cup packed light brown sugar
¹/₄ teaspoon ground nutmeg
4 tablespoons cold margarine, cut into pieces
1 egg white, slightly beaten
1 teaspoon orange extract

1. Combine flour, cereals, brown sugar, and nutmeg in medium bowl; cut in margarine until mixture resembles coarse crumbs. Mix in egg white and orange extract.

Variation: **Honey-Plum Crumble**—Combine 6 cups thickly sliced pitted red or purple plums, ¹/₂ cup packed light brown sugar, generous pinch ground nutmeg, and 1 teaspoon grated lemon rind in greased 2-quart casserole; drizzle with ¹/₄ cup honey. Make Crumble Topping as above and sprinkle over fruit. Bake as above.

BERRY-CHERRY GRUNT

A wonderful blueberry campfire dessert brought indoors and given a cherry accent.

4 to 6 servings

1/4	cup all-purpose flour
5	tablespoons sugar, divided
1	teaspoon baking powder
1/4	teaspoon salt
3	tablespoons margarine
3	tablespoons fat-free milk
1 1/2	cups dark sweet cherries, pitted
1 1/2	cups blueberries
1	tablespoon lemon juice
1	tablespoon grated lemon rind
1/4	teaspoon ground cinnamon

Per Serving
Calories: 245
% Calories from fat: 31
Fat (gm): 8.9
Saturated fat (gm): 1.7
Cholesterol (mg): 0.2
Sodium (mg): 378
Protein (gm): 2.4
Carbohydrate (gm): 41.9
Exchanges
Milk: 0.0
Vegetable: 0.0
Fruit: 2.0
Bread: 1.0
Meat: 0.0
Fat: 1.5

1. Combine flour, 2 tablespoons sugar, baking powder, and salt in medium bowl. Cut in margarine until mixture resembles coarse crumbs. Mix in milk, stirring just enough to form a soft dough.

2. Combine cherries, blueberries, remaining 3 tablespoons sugar, lemon juice, lemon rind, and cinnamon in medium skillet. Heat to boiling; reduce heat and simmer, uncovered, 5 minutes.

3. Drop dough by rounded tablespoonfuls onto berry mixture. Cook, uncovered, 10 minutes; cover and cook an additional 10 minutes. Serve warm.

Variation: **Tart Cherry Slump**—Make Step 1 as above. Make Step 2, substituting pitted tart cherries for the sweet cherries and blueberries, increasing the sugar to 1/2 cup, substituting 1/4 to 1/2 teaspoon almond extract for the lemon juice and rind, and omitting the cinnamon. Sprinkle top of dough with 1/4 cup slivered almonds and cook as above.

BLUEBERRY BOWLS

The season's freshest blueberries baked in bowls atop a rich shortcake.

4 servings

1/2 cup all-purpose flour
1/2 cup sugar
1 teaspoon baking powder
1/8 teaspoon salt
1/2 cup fat-free milk
1/4 cup melted margarine
2 generous pinches ground nutmeg
2 cups blueberries
4 tablespoons sugar
4 tablespoons light whipped topping

Per Serving
Calories: 366
% Calories from fat: 29
Fat (gm): 12.3
Saturated fat (gm): 2.8
Cholesterol (mg): 0.6
Sodium (mg): 348
Protein (gm): 3.3
Carbohydrate (gm): 62.6
Exchanges
Milk: 0.0
Vegetable: 0.0
Fruit: 2.0
Bread: 2.0
Meat: 0.0
Fat: 2.0

1. Combine flour, sugar, baking powder, and salt in small bowl; add milk, margarine, and nutmeg, mixing just until blended. Spoon batter into 4 lightly greased 8-ounce soufflé or custard cups. Spoon 1/2 cup blueberries into each and sprinkle with 1 tablespoon sugar.

2. Bake at 350 degrees until berries are bubbly and cake is browned, about 30 minutes. Serve warm with dollops of whipped topping.

BLUEBERRY COBBLER

The cobbler topping has a tender cakelike texture.

6 servings

4 cups fresh, *or* frozen, blueberries
2/3 cup packed light brown sugar
1 cup all-purpose flour
1/3 cup granulated sugar
1 1/2 teaspoons baking powder
1/2 teaspoon ground cinnamon
1/4 teaspoon ground allspice
1/4 teaspoon salt
4 tablespoons cold margarine, cut into pieces
1 egg
2/3 cup fat-free milk
6 tablespoons light whipped topping

Per Serving
Calories: 366
% Calories from fat: 23
Fat (gm): 9.5
Saturated fat (gm): 2.3
Cholesterol (mg): 35.8
Sodium (mg): 348
Protein (gm): 4.9
Carbohydrate (gm): 67.6
Exchanges
Milk: 0.0
Vegetable: 0.0
Fruit: 4.0
Bread: 0.5
Meat: 0.0
Fat: 1.5

1. Arrange blueberries in 8-inch square baking dish and sprinkle with brown sugar.

2. Combine flour, granulated sugar, baking powder, spices, and salt in medium bowl; cut in margarine until mixture resembles coarse crumbs. Whisk egg into milk; add to flour mixture, mixing until smooth. Pour mixture over berries.

3. Bake at 350 degrees 30 minutes; increase oven temperature to 400 degrees and bake until batter is browned and puffed, about 15 minutes. Serve warm with whipped topping.

Variation: **Pear Cobbler**—Make recipe as above, substituting sliced, peeled ripe, but firm, pears for the blueberries, decreasing brown sugar to 1/3 cup, substituting 1/2 cup whole wheat flour for 1/2 cup of the all-purpose flour, and substituting 2 generous pinches ground nutmeg for the allspice.

BLUEBERRY PEACH COBBLER

Sour cream adds richness to the sugary glazed cobbler topping.

6 servings

2 pounds peaches, peeled, pitted, thickly sliced
2 cups blueberries
1 tablespoon lemon juice
¹/₂ cup plus 2 tablespoons sugar, divided
2 tablespoons cornstarch
¹/₂ teaspoon ground cinnamon
Generous pinch ground nutmeg
Sour Cream Cobbler Topping (recipe follows)
Fat-free milk

Per Serving
Calories: 376
% Calories from fat: 14
Fat (gm): 6.2
Saturated fat (gm): 1.2
Cholesterol (mg): 0
Sodium (mg): 298
Protein (gm): 5.7
Carbohydrate (gm): 76.8
Exchanges
Milk: 0.0
Vegetable: 0.0
Fruit: 3.0
Bread: 2.0
Meat: 0.0
Fat: 1.0

1. Combine peaches and blueberries in 3-quart casserole; sprinkle with lemon juice. Toss with combined ¹/₂ cup sugar, cornstarch, and spices.

2. Place Sour Cream Cobbler Topping over casserole; cut several vents. Brush with milk and sprinkle with remaining 2 tablespoons sugar.

3. Bake at 375 degrees until toothpick inserted in cobbler topping comes out clean, 35 to 45 minutes.

Sour Cream Cobbler Topping

1¹/₃ cups all-purpose flour
2 tablespoons sugar
³/₄ teaspoon baking powder
¹/₄ teaspoon baking soda
¹/₄ teaspoon salt
3 tablespoons cold margarine, cut into pieces
¹/₂ cup fat-free sour cream
3-4 tablespoons water

1. Combine flour, sugar, baking powder, baking soda, and salt; cut in margarine until mixture resembles coarse crumbs. Whisk sour cream and water until smooth; add to flour mixture and mix to form dough. Knead several times until smooth on floured surface; let stand 5 minutes.

2. Roll dough on floured surface, or between sheets of waxed paper, into circle to fit top of casserole.

DEEP DISH BLACKBERRY COBBLER WITH LEMON HARD SAUCE

Fortunately, frozen blackberries are readily available, as the season for fresh blackberries is very short.

12 servings

8 cups fresh, *or* frozen, slightly thawed, blackberries

1 cup sugar

1/3 cup all-purpose flour

1/8 teaspoon ground nutmeg

1 teaspoon grated lemon rind

1-2 tablespoons margarine

Basic Pie Crust (All-Purpose Flour) (see p. 126)

3-4 tablespoons vegetable shortening

Lemon Hard Sauce (recipe follows)

Per Serving
Calories: 347
% Calories from fat: 35
Fat (gm): 13.9
Saturated fat (gm): 2.9
Cholesterol (mg): 0
Sodium (mg): 177
Protein (gm): 2.5
Carbohydrate (gm): 55.2
Exchanges
Milk: 0.0
Vegetable: 0.0
Fruit: 1.5
Bread: 2.0
Meat: 0.0
Fat: 2.5

1. Toss blackberries with combined sugar, flour, nutmeg, and lemon rind; arrange in 11 x 7-inch baking dish. Dot with margarine

2. Make Basic Pie Crust, reducing flour to 1 cup and substituting vegetable shortening for the margarine. Roll pastry on floured surface into rectangle to fit baking dish, trimming edges if necessary. Place pastry over fruit; cut several slits near center.

3. Bake at 400 degrees until fruit is bubbly and crust browned, about 50 minutes. Serve warm with Lemon Hard Sauce.

Lemon Hard Sauce

makes about 1 1/4 cups

1 cup powdered sugar

6 tablespoons margarine, softened

2 teaspoons finely grated lemon rind

2-3 teaspoons lemon juice

1. Beat powdered sugar, margarine, lemon rind, and lemon juice until smooth, adding few drops water if necessary (mixture will be stiff); refrigerate until serving time.

NECTARINE-BLUEBERRY UPSIDE-DOWN COBBLER

Something a little different—the fruit is baked on top of the cobbler. The season for nectarines is brief, so take advantage of this beautiful fruit, or substitute peaches.

8 servings

1 cup all-purpose flour
1/2 cup quick-cooking oats
1/2 cup packed light brown sugar
1/2 cup fat-free milk
1/3 cup melted margarine
1 teaspoon vanilla
1 1/2 pounds nectarines, pitted, sliced
2 cups blueberries
1/2 cup granulated sugar

Per Serving
Calories: 313
% Calories from fat: 24
Fat (gm): 8.6
Saturated fat (gm): 1.6
Cholesterol (mg): 0.3
Sodium (mg): 105
Protein (gm): 4.1
Carbohydrate (gm): 57.3
Exchanges
Milk: 0.0
Vegetable: 0.0
Fruit: 1.0
Bread: 2.5
Meat: 0.0
Fat: 1.5

1. Combine flour, oats, and brown sugar in large bowl. Mix in milk, margarine, and vanilla. Pour batter into greased 8-inch square baking dish.

2. Toss nectarines and blueberries with granulated sugar; arrange over batter.

3. Bake at 400 degrees until bottom crust is browned, 35 to 45 minutes.

BING CHERRY AND BERRY COBBLER

Use one or more kinds of berries, depending upon availability. For cherries, our choice is Bing.

8 servings

3/4 cup plus 1 1/2 tablespoons sugar, divided
3 tablespoons cornstarch
2 cups pitted Bing cherries
5 cups assorted berries (raspberries, blueberries, blackberries, strawberries)
1 tablespoon grated orange, *or* lemon, rind
Cobbler Topping (recipe follows)
1 egg white, beaten

Per Serving
Calories: 327
% Calories from fat: 17
Fat (gm): 6.5
Saturated fat (gm): 1.3
Cholesterol (mg): 0.7
Sodium (mg): 256
Protein (gm): 4.8
Carbohydrate (gm): 64.8
Exchanges
Milk: 0.0
Vegetable: 0.0
Fruit: 2.0
Bread: 2.0
Meat: 0.0
Fat: 1.5

1. Combine 3/4 cup sugar and cornstarch in large saucepan. Add cherries, berries, and orange rind. Heat over medium heat to simmering, stirring frequently. Simmer until liquid is thickened, stirring constantly; pour into 3-quart casserole.

2. Place Cobbler Topping over hot filling; cut vents in dough. Brush with egg white and sprinkle with remaining 1 1/2 tablespoons sugar.

3. Bake at 375 degrees until toothpick inserted in Cobbler Topping comes out clean, about 35 minutes.

Cobbler Topping

1 1/2 cups all-purpose flour
3 tablespoons sugar
3/4 teaspoon baking powder
1/4 teaspoon baking soda
1/4 teaspoon salt
4 tablespoons cold margarine, cut into pieces
2/3 cup reduced-fat buttermilk

1. Combine flour, sugar, baking powder, baking soda, and salt in bowl; cut in margarine until mixture resembles coarse crumbs. Add buttermilk, mixing just until dough forms. Knead several times until smooth on floured surface; let stand 5 minutes.

2. Roll dough on floured surface, or between sheets of waxed paper, into circle to fit top of casserole.

PEACH AND TART APPLE COBBLER

A lovely blending of fruit and spice flavors. Serve with generous dollops of whipped topping or scoops of fat-free vanilla ice cream.

8 servings

4 cups sliced, peeled, fresh *or* frozen, partially thawed, peaches
4 cups sliced, peeled tart baking apples
²/₃ cup granulated sugar
²/₃ cup packed light brown sugar
2 tablespoons flour
¹/₂ teaspoon ground cinnamon
¹/₄ teaspoon ground nutmeg
2 generous pinches ground cloves
2 tablespoons margarine, cut into pieces
Biscuit Topping (recipe follows)

Per Serving
Calories: 372
% Calories from fat: 21
Fat (gm): 9.1
Saturated fat (gm): 1.8
Cholesterol (mg): 0.3
Sodium (mg): 353
Protein (gm): 3.2
Carbohydrate (gm): 72.8
Exchanges
Milk: 0.0
Vegetable: 0.0
Fruit: 2.0
Bread: 2.5
Meat: 0.0
Fat: 1.5

1. Toss fruit with combined granulated sugar, brown sugar, flour, and spices; arrange in 2¹/₂-quart casserole and dot with margarine.

2. Spoon Biscuit Topping into mounds on fruit. Bake at 400 degrees until fruit is tender and bubbly and topping browned, about 35 to 45 minutes.

Biscuit Topping

1 cup all-purpose flour
3 tablespoons sugar
1¹/₂ teaspoons baking powder
¹/₂ teaspoon salt
4 tablespoons cold margarine, cut into pieces
¹/₂ cup fat-free milk

1. Combine flour, sugar, baking powder, and salt in bowl; cut in margarine until mixture resembles coarse crumbs. Mix in milk, forming a soft dough.

Variations: **Peach and Pear Cornmeal Cobbler**—Make Step 1 as above, using 3 cups peaches, substituting 3 cups sliced, peeled pears for the apples, and reducing amount of granulated sugar to ¹/₃ cup. Make Biscuit Topping, substituting ¹/₄ cup yellow cornmeal for ¹/₂ cup of the flour and increasing sugar to ¹/₄ cup.

Sweet Mango Cobbler—Make Step 1 as above, substituting 8 cups sliced, peeled mangoes for the peaches and apples, reducing amount of granulated and brown sugar to 2 tablespoons each, and omitting cinnamon and nutmeg. Complete recipe as above.

APPLE CRUMB COBBLER

A comforting apple dessert that is a blending of a crisp and a cobbler.

10 servings

8 cups sliced, peeled baking apples
2 cups sugar, divided
1/2 teaspoon cinnamon
1/4 teaspoon ground allspice
1/8 teaspoon ground mace
1 cup all-purpose flour
6 tablespoons margarine, melted
1 egg
1 teaspoon baking powder
1/2 teaspoon salt

Per Serving
Calories: 329
% Calories from fat: 20
Fat (gm): 7.9
Saturated fat (gm): 1.6
Cholesterol (mg): 21.2
Sodium (mg): 253
Protein (gm): 2.3
Carbohydrate (gm): 65.3
Exchanges
Milk: 0.0
Vegetable: 0.0
Fruit: 2.0
Bread: 2.0
Meat: 0.0
Fat: 1.5

1. Arrange apples in 11 x 7-inch baking dish. Combine 1 cup sugar and the spices; sprinkle over the apples. Combine remaining 1 cup sugar and remaining ingredients in bowl (mixture will be dry) and sprinkle over apples.

2. Bake at 350 until apples are tender and topping is browned, about 1 hour.

BLUEBERRY CLAFOUTI

Blender-easy, this recipe combines plump blueberries with a custard-like cake.

6 servings

3 cups fresh, *or* frozen, blueberries
1 cup granulated sugar
2¹/₄ cups fat-free sour cream
3 eggs
¹/₂ teaspoon lemon extract
¹/₃ cup all-purpose flour
¹/₄ teaspoon salt
   Powdered sugar, as garnish

Per Serving
Calories: 338
% Calories from fat: 8
Fat (gm): 2.8
Saturated fat (gm): 0.8
Cholesterol (mg): 106
Sodium (mg): 208
Protein (gm): 10.3
Carbohydrate (gm): 67.3
Exchanges
Milk: 0.0
Vegetable: 0.0
Fruit: 2.0
Bread: 2.5
Meat: 0.0
Fat: 0.5

1. Arrange blueberries in greased 8-inch square baking dish.

2. Process remaining ingredients, except powdered sugar, in blender or food processor until smooth; pour over berries.

3. Bake at 350 degrees until browned and puffed, about 55 minutes. Sprinkle generously with powdered sugar and serve warm.

FRESH CHERRY CLAFOUTI

Don't despair—frozen or canned sweet cherries can be used so this dessert can be enjoyed year round.

6 servings

3 cups pitted sweet cherries
2 cups fat-free milk
³/₄ cup granulated sugar
²/₃ cup all-purpose flour
1 teaspoon almond extract
2 eggs
1 tablespoon melted margarine
   Powdered sugar, as garnish

Per Serving
Calories: 277
% Calories from fat: 13
Fat (gm): 4
Saturated fat (gm): 1
Cholesterol (mg): 72.1
Sodium (mg): 87
Protein (gm): 7.3
Carbohydrate (gm): 54.6
Exchanges
Milk: 0.5
Vegetable: 0.0
Fruit: 1.0
Bread: 2.5
Meat: 0.0
Fat: 0.0

1. Arrange cherries in greased 8-inch square baking dish.

2. Whisk remaining ingredients, except powdered sugar, in medium bowl until smooth; pour over cherries.

3. Bake at 350 degrees until browned and puffed, 50 to 60 minutes. Sprinkle generously with powdered sugar and serve warm.

FRESH PLUM CLAFOUTI

A rustic pudding-cake that has its origins in the French countryside.

4 servings

8 ripe purple, *or* red, plums, pitted, sliced
1¹/2 cups fat-free milk
¹/3 cup granulated sugar
¹/4 cup all-purpose flour
2 eggs
1 teaspoon vanilla
¹/2 teaspoon ground cinnamon
¹/4 teaspoon ground nutmeg
2 teaspoons grated orange rind
¹/8 teaspoon salt
Powdered sugar, as garnish

Per Serving
Calories: 208
% Calories from fat: 12
Fat (gm): 2.8
Saturated fat (gm): 0.9
Cholesterol (mg): 107.7
Sodium (mg): 152
Protein (gm): 7.1
Carbohydrate (gm): 40.3
Exchanges
Milk: 0.0
Vegetable: 0.0
Fruit: 1.0
Bread: 1.5
Meat: 0.0
Fat: 0.5

1. Arrange plums in greased 8-inch square baking dish.

2. Beat remaining ingredients, except powdered sugar, in large bowl until well blended; pour over plums.

3. Bake at 350 degrees until center is set and browned, 40 to 45 minutes. Sprinkle generously with powdered sugar and serve warm.

Variation: **Apricot-Ginger Clafouti**—Make recipe as above, substituting 1 can (16 ounces) well-drained apricot halves for the plums and packed light brown sugar for the granulated sugar; omit spices. Mix ¹/4 cup chopped crystallized ginger into the batter, pour over apricots, and sprinkle with ¹/4 cup sliced almonds. Bake as above.

TWO-BERRY SUMMER PUDDING

A luscious bread pudding with origins in England. Most often made with raspberries, our version uses blueberries too.

8 servings

1 pound day-old firm white bread, sliced

3 cups raspberries

3 cups blueberries

$1/2$ cup granulated sugar

$1/3$ cup red currant jelly

2 tablespoons lemon juice

1 cup light whipped topping

$1/4$ cup powdered sugar

Per Serving
Calories: 323
% Calories from fat: 9
Fat (gm): 3.5
Saturated fat (gm): 1.5
Cholesterol (mg): 0.6
Sodium (mg): 312
Protein (gm): 5.5
Carbohydrate (gm): 68.7
Exchanges
Milk: 0.0
Vegetable: 0.0
Fruit: 1.0
Bread: 3.5
Meat: 0.0
Fat: 0.5

1. Line $1^{1}/_{2}$-quart soufflé dish or casserole with plastic wrap, overlapping sides by 6 to 8 inches. Cut 6 to 8 slices of bread into $1^{1}/_{2}$-inch-wide slices; line side and bottom of dish with bread slices, cutting as necessary to fit.

2. Heat berries, sugar, jelly, and lemon juice in large saucepan over medium heat, stirring frequently until sugar dissolves. Reduce heat and simmer, uncovered, until berries release juices, about 5 minutes. Cool 5 to 10 minutes; drain off $1/2$ cup juice and reserve.

3. Spoon $1/2$ of berry mixture into dish; cover with single layer of bread slices, cutting to fit. Spoon remaining berry mixture over and top with remaining bread; spoon reserved berry juice over bread. Bring sides of plastic wrap over top of pudding; top with plate and weight down with 1 or 2 cans. Refrigerate overnight.

4. Unwrap top of pudding and invert onto serving plate; remove plastic wrap. Mix whipped topping and powdered sugar; serve with pudding.

MOIST PEACH COFFEE CAKE

Canned or frozen, thawed peaches can be substituted for the fresh; drain well on paper toweling before using.

10 servings

6 tablespoons margarine, softened
1 cup granulated sugar
1/2 cup packed light brown sugar
1 cup reduced-fat buttermilk
2 egg whites
1 teaspoon vanilla
2 cups all-purpose flour
1/2 teaspoon baking soda
1/2 teaspoon salt
2 cups cubed (1/2 inch) peaches
Cinnamon Streusel (recipe follows)

Per Serving
Calories: 371
% Calories from fat: 23
Fat (gm): 9.6
Saturated fat (gm): 2
Cholesterol (mg): 0.9
Sodium (mg): 332
Protein (gm): 4.8
Carbohydrate (gm): 67.6
Exchanges
Milk: 0.0
Vegetable: 0.0
Fruit: 1.5
Bread: 3.0
Meat: 0.0
Fat: 2.0

1. Beat margarine and sugars in large bowl until well blended; mix in buttermilk, egg whites, and vanilla. Mix in combined flour, baking soda, and salt; gently stir in peaches.

2. Spread batter in greased 11 x 7-inch baking dish; sprinkle with Cinnamon Streusel. Bake at 350 degrees until toothpick inserted in center of cake comes out clean, 50 to 55 minutes. Cool on wire rack.

Cinnamon Streusel

makes about 3/4 cup

1/2 cup packed light brown sugar
2 tablespoons quick-cooking oats
2 tablespoons flour
1/4 teaspoon ground cinnamon
1/8 teaspoon ground nutmeg
2 tablespoons cold margarine, cut into pieces

1. Combine brown sugar, oats, flour, and spices in small bowl; cut in margarine with pastry blender to form crumbly mixture.

GRANOLA APPLE COFFEE CAKE

Use baking apples as they retain their shape—Granny Smith, Rome, McIntosh, and Jonathan are all excellent choices.

12 servings

2 pounds tart cooking apples, peeled, cored, coarsely chopped

1½ teaspoons ground cinnamon

1¾ cups all-purpose flour

¼ cup whole wheat flour

2 teaspoons baking powder

½ teaspoon salt

¼ cup fat-free milk

4 eggs, lightly beaten

½ cup packed light brown sugar

¼ cup melted margarine

2 tablespoons maple syrup

Granola Topping (recipe follows)

Per Serving
Calories: 322
% Calories from fat: 25
Fat (gm): 9.5
Saturated fat (gm): 3.3
Cholesterol (mg): 78.9
Sodium (mg): 315
Protein (gm): 6.3
Carbohydrate (gm): 55.2
Exchanges
Milk: 0.0
Vegetable: 0.0
Fruit: 1.0
Bread: 2.5
Meat: 0.0
Fat: 2.0

1. Sprinkle apples with cinnamon and toss. Combine flours, baking powder, and salt in large bowl. Mix in milk, eggs, brown sugar, margarine, and maple syrup; beat at medium speed 2 minutes. Gently stir in apples.

2. Pour batter into greased 13 x 9-inch baking pan. Bake at 325 degrees until golden, about 45 minutes. Spoon Granola Topping evenly over cake; bake until Granola Topping is bubbly, about 10 minutes.

Granola Topping

¾ cup low-fat granola cereal

½ cup packed light brown sugar

3 egg whites, lightly beaten

3 tablespoons melted butter

1. Mix all ingredients.

CRANBERRY COFFEE CAKE

Quick and easy to make, this sweet-tart coffee cake can be ready to bake in less than 10 minutes.

6 to 8 servings

1¹/₂ cups fresh, *or* frozen, thawed, cranberries
 1 cup sugar, divided
 1 teaspoon grated orange rind
1¹/₂ cups all-purpose flour
 2 teaspoons baking powder
 ¹/₂ teaspoon salt
 1 egg
 ¹/₄ cup orange juice
 ¹/₄ cup fat-free milk
 3 tablespoons margarine, softened
¹/₄-¹/₂ cup chopped pecans

Per Serving
Calories: 360
% Calories from fat: 25
Fat (gm): 10.2
Saturated fat (gm): 1.7
Cholesterol (mg): 35.5
Sodium (mg): 440
Protein (gm): 5.4
Carbohydrate (gm): 63.5
Exchanges
Milk: 0.0
Vegetable: 0.0
Fruit: 0.0
Bread: 4.0
Meat: 0.0
Fat: 2.0

1. Arrange cranberries in greased 8-inch square baking dish; sprinkle with ¹/₂ cup sugar and the orange rind. Mix remaining ingredients in medium bowl until just moistened; drop by spoonfuls onto cranberries, spreading batter evenly to sides of pan.

2. Bake coffee cake at 400 degrees until wooden pick inserted in center comes out clean, 25 to 30 minutes. Immediately invert coffee cake onto serving plate. Serve warm.

SOUR CREAM BRUNCH CAKE WITH APPLE-DATE FILLING

An irresistible offering, this moist cake is filled with apples, dates, sugar, and spices. Serve warm, if desired.

16 servings

1/2 cup margarine, softened
1/4 cup unsweetened applesauce
1 cup granulated sugar
1/2 cup packed light brown sugar
3 eggs
1 1/2 teaspoons vanilla
3 cups all-purpose flour
1 1/2 teaspoons baking powder
1 1/2 teaspoons baking soda
1 teaspoon ground cinnamon
1/2 teaspoon salt
1 1/2 cups fat-free sour cream
Apple-Date Filling (recipe follows)
Cream Cheese Glaze (recipe follows)

Per Serving
Calories: 306
% Calories from fat: 20
Fat (gm): 6.9
Saturated fat (gm): 1.4
Cholesterol (mg): 39.9
Sodium (mg): 353
Protein (gm): 5.7
Carbohydrate (gm): 56.4
Exchanges
Milk: 0.0
Vegetable: 0.0
Fruit: 1.0
Bread: 2.5
Meat: 0.0
Fat: 1.5

1. Beat margarine, applesauce, and sugars until smooth. Beat in eggs, 1 at a time; beat in vanilla. Mix in combined flour, baking powder, baking soda, cinnamon, and salt alternately with sour cream, beginning and ending with dry ingredients.

2. Spoon 1/3 of batter into greased and floured 12-cup fluted cake pan; spoon 1/3 of Apple-Date Filling over batter. Repeat layers, ending with batter.

3. Bake at 325 degrees until toothpick inserted in center of cake comes out clean, about 1 hour. Cool in pan on wire rack 10 minutes; remove from pan and cool to room temperature. Drizzle with Cream Cheese Glaze.

Apple-Date Filling

makes about 1 cup

- $^1/_2$ cup dried apples, coarsely chopped
- $^1/_4$ cup chopped dates
- $^2/_3$ cup water
- $^1/_3$ cup packed light brown sugar
- 1 tablespoon flour
- $^1/_4$ teaspoon ground nutmeg
- $^1/_8$ teaspoon salt

1. Combine all ingredients in small saucepan and heat to boiling; reduce heat and simmer, uncovered, until apples are tender and mixture is thick, 5 to 8 minutes. Cool.

Cream Cheese Glaze

makes $^1/_2$ cup

- 2 ounces fat-free cream cheese, room temperature
- 1 cup powdered sugar

1. Beat cream cheese and powdered sugar until smooth; refrigerate until ready to use.

APPLE HONEY KUCHEN

Use your favorite baking apple, tart or sweet, for this special brunch bread.

2 kuchen (8 to 10 servings each)

- 1 package active dry yeast
- $^3/_4$ cup warm fat-free milk (110-115 degrees)
- 6 tablespoons granulated sugar, divided
- 4 tablespoons margarine, divided
- 1 egg
- 2-3 cups all-purpose flour, divided
- $^3/_4$ teaspoon salt
- 1 pound tart or sweet baking apples, peeled, sliced

Per Serving
Calories: 165
% Calories from fat: 18
Fat (gm): 3.5
Saturated fat (gm): 0.7
Cholesterol (mg): 13.5
Sodium (mg): 155
Protein (gm): 2.9
Carbohydrate (gm): 31.6
Exchanges
Milk: 0.0
Vegetable: 0.0
Fruit: 0.0
Bread: 2.0
Meat: 0.0
Fat: 0.5

$1/2$ cup raisins
$1/4$ cup light brown sugar
2 tablespoons grated orange rind
$1/4$ teaspoon ground cinnamon
$1/8$ teaspoon ground nutmeg
2-4 tablespoons honey
Fat-free milk
Powdered sugar, as garnish

1. Mix yeast, milk, and 2 tablespoons granulated sugar in large bowl; let stand 5 minutes. Add 2 tablespoons margarine, egg, 2 cups flour, and salt, mixing until smooth. Mix in enough remaining 1 cup flour to make smooth dough.

2. Knead dough on floured surface until smooth and elastic, about 5 minutes. Place dough in greased bowl; let rise, covered, in warm place until double in size, 1 to $1^{1}/2$ hours. Punch down dough.

3. Heat remaining 2 tablespoons margarine in large skillet until melted; add apples and cook over medium heat until apples are tender, 5 to 8 minutes. Stir in raisins; remove from heat. Mix brown sugar, orange rind, cinnamon, and nutmeg; sprinkle over apple mixture and toss. Cool.

4. Divide dough into 2 equal pieces. Roll each piece of dough on floured surface into 12-inch round. Arrange apple mixture on half of each round; drizzle each with 1 to 2 tablespoons honey. Brush edges of dough with water; fold dough over filling and press edges with tines of fork to seal.

5. Transfer kuchens to greased cookie sheets; brush with milk and sprinkle with remaining 4 tablespoons granulated sugar. Let rise, loosely covered, until impression of finger remains in dough when touched, about 1 hour. Reseal edges of kuchen, if necessary.

6. Bake kuchens at 375 degrees until golden, about 20 minutes. Slide onto wire racks to cool; sprinkle with powdered sugar and serve warm.

CARAMEL APPLE STREUSEL KUCHEN

Apples are baked with brown sugar and topped with a brown sugar streusel in this apple treat.

12 servings

Butter-flavored vegetable cooking spray

5 cups chopped peeled Granny Smith, *or* other tart, baking apples

3/4 cup packed light brown sugar, divided

1 1/2 cups all-purpose flour

1 1/4 teaspoons baking powder

1/4 teaspoon baking soda

1/4 teaspoon salt

1/2 teaspoon ground cardamom

1/8 teaspoon ground nutmeg

3/4 cup reduced-fat buttermilk

1 egg

3 tablespoons vegetable oil

2 teaspoons grated lemon rind

1/2 cup raisins

Brown Sugar-Granola Streusel (see p. 480)

Per Serving
Calories: 281
% Calories from fat: 26
Fat (gm): 8.3
Saturated fat (gm): 1.4
Cholesterol (mg): 18.2
Sodium (mg): 214
Protein (gm): 4.1
Carbohydrate (gm): 49.3
Exchanges
Milk: 0.0
Vegetable: 0.0
Fruit: 1.0
Bread: 2.0
Meat: 0.0
Fat: 1.5

1. Line jelly roll pan with aluminum foil and spray with cooking spray. Arrange apples on pan; spray lightly with cooking spray and sprinkle with 1/4 cup brown sugar. Bake at 425 degrees until apples are slightly soft, about 15 minutes; cool.

2. Combine remaining 1/2 cup brown sugar, flour, baking powder, baking soda, salt, and spices in large bowl. Mix in combined buttermilk, egg, oil, and lemon rind; mix in apples and raisins. Spoon batter into greased 10-inch springform pan; sprinkle with Brown Sugar-Granola Streusel.

3. Bake at 375 degrees until toothpick comes out clean, 45 to 50 minutes. Cool on wire rack 10 minutes; remove side of pan and cool.

JAM-GLAZED PEACH AND PLUM KUCHEN

Made on a pizza pan, this kuchen is perfect for serving a crowd. The kuchen can be made with all peaches too, and if out of season, they can be canned or frozen.

10 servings

2³/₄	cups all-purpose flour, divided
¹/₃	cup granulated sugar
1	package quick-rising dry yeast
¹/₂	teaspoon salt
¹/₂	cup hot water (115-120 degrees)
5	tablespoons margarine, melted
1	egg, beaten
1¹/₂	cups sliced, peeled, pitted peaches
1¹/₂	cups sliced, pitted plums
¹/₃	cup packed light brown sugar
¹/₄-¹/₃	cup peach spreadable fruit, warm
	Ground nutmeg, as garnish

Per Serving
Calories: 273
% Calories from fat: 21
Fat (gm): 6.5
Saturated fat (gm): 1.3
Cholesterol (mg): 21.2
Sodium (mg): 202
Protein (gm): 4.9
Carbohydrate (gm): 49.3
Exchanges
Milk: 0.0
Vegetable: 0.0
Fruit: 0.0
Bread: 3.0
Meat: 0.0
Fat: 1.0

1. Combine 2 cups flour, granulated sugar, yeast, and salt in large bowl; mix in hot water, margarine, and egg. Mix in enough remaining ³/₄ cup flour to make smooth dough. Knead on floured surface until smooth, 4 to 5 minutes. Return to bowl and grease top of dough. Let stand, covered, in warm place until double in size, 30 to 45 minutes. Punch dough down.

2. Pat dough onto greased 12-inch pizza pan. Arrange fruit attractively on dough, pressing lightly into dough; sprinkle with brown sugar.

3. Bake at 400 degrees until dough is puffed and browned, 20 to 30 minutes, covering edge of dough with aluminum foil if becoming too brown. Cool on wire rack. Brush with spreadable fruit and sprinkle very lightly with nutmeg.

PEACH-ALMOND STREUSEL KUCHEN

If peaches are difficult to peel, dip them in boiling water for 30 seconds, then rinse in cold water.

12 servings

- 1 cup all-purpose flour
- 1/3 cup wheat and barley cereal (Grape-Nuts)
- 1/2 cup packed light brown sugar
- 3/4 cup baking powder
- 1/4 teaspoon baking soda
- 1/2 teaspoon ground ginger
- 1/4 teaspoon salt
- 1/2 cup fat-free sour cream
- 1/4 cup fat-free milk
- 3 tablespoons margarine, melted
- 1 egg
- 1 teaspoon vanilla
- 1/2 teaspoon almond extract
  Brown Sugar-Granola Streusel (see p. 480)
- 3-4 tablespoons sliced almonds
- 3 cups thickly sliced, peeled, pitted peaches

Per Serving
Calories: 246
% Calories from fat: 30
Fat (gm): 8
Saturated fat (gm): 1.4
Cholesterol (mg): 17.8
Sodium (mg): 238
Protein (gm): 4.4
Carbohydrate (gm): 37.3
Exchanges
Milk: 0.0
Vegetable: 0.0
Fruit: 0.5
Bread: 2.0
Meat: 0.0
Fat: 1.5

1. Combine flour, cereal, brown sugar, baking powder, baking soda, ginger, and salt in large bowl. Mix in combined sour cream, milk, margarine, egg, vanilla, and almond extract. Spoon batter into greased 13 x 9-inch baking pan.

2. Make Brown Sugar-Granola Streusel, substituting almonds for the granola. Sprinkle half the streusel over the batter; arrange peaches on top and sprinkle with remaining streusel.

3. Bake at 375 degrees until toothpick inserted in center comes out clean, about 50 minutes. Cool on wire rack.

DRIED BERRY STREUSEL KUCHEN

Dried blueberries and cranberries are a flavorful combo in this sweet brunch treat; any dried fruit can be substituted.

10 servings

1²/₃ cups all-purpose flour

¹/₂ cup sugar

1¹/₂ teaspoons baking powder

¹/₂ teaspoon baking soda

¹/₄ teaspoon salt

²/₃ cup fat-free sour cream

2 eggs

¹/₄ cup orange juice

3 tablespoons vegetable oil

1 tablespoon grated orange rind

¹/₂ cup dried cranberries

¹/₂ cup dried blueberries

Crisp Streusel (see p. 46)

Vanilla Glaze (see p. 350)

Per Serving
Calories: 355
% Calories from fat: 19
Fat (gm): 7.7
Saturated fat (gm): 1.3
Cholesterol (mg): 42.4
Sodium (mg): 253
Protein (gm): 5.3
Carbohydrate (gm): 66.4
Exchanges
Milk: 0.0
Vegetable: 0.0
Fruit: 1.0
Bread: 3.0
Meat: 0.0
Fat: 1.5

1. Combine flour, sugar, baking powder, baking soda, and salt in large bowl. Mix in combined sour cream, eggs, orange juice, oil, and orange rind. Mix in cranberries and blueberries. Spoon batter into greased 9-inch round cake pan; sprinkle with Crisp Streusel.

2. Bake at 375 degrees until toothpick inserted in center comes out clean, about 30 minutes. Cool on wire rack; drizzle with Vanilla Glaze.

PEAR-PECAN KUCHEN

Substitute dried peaches, apricots, or apples for flavorful variations, or try a combination of dried fruit.

12 servings

₃/4 cup coarsely chopped dried pears
₁/2 cup boiling water
2 cups all-purpose flour
₃/4 cup packed light brown sugar
₁/4 cup finely ground pecans
1 teaspoon baking powder
₃/4 teaspoon baking soda
₁/4 teaspoon salt
1 cup buttermilk
2 eggs
4 tablespoons margarine, melted
2 teaspoons butter extract
2-3 tablespoons chopped pecans
3 tablespoons granulated sugar
Cream Cheese Glaze (see p. 498)

Per Serving
Calories: 293
% Calories from fat: 23
Fat (gm): 7.6
Saturated fat (gm): 1.4
Cholesterol (mg): 36.4
Sodium (mg): 276
Protein (gm): 5.2
Carbohydrate (gm): 52.3
Exchanges
Milk: 0.0
Vegetable: 0.0
Fruit: 1.0
Bread: 2.5
Meat: 0.0
Fat: 1.5

1. Combine pears and boiling water; let stand until pears are softened, 10 to 15 minutes. Drain.

2. Combine flour, brown sugar, ground pecans, baking powder, baking soda, and salt in large bowl. Mix in combined buttermilk, eggs, margarine, and butter extract; mix in softened pears. Spoon batter into greased 10-inch springform pan; sprinkle with chopped pecans and granulated sugar.

3. Bake at 375 degrees until toothpick inserted in center comes out clean, 30 to 40 minutes. Cool on wire rack 10 minutes; remove side of pan and cool. Drizzle with Cream Cheese Glaze.

GLAZED FRUIT FOCACCIA

This versatile Italian bread makes a delicious dessert! The baked focaccia can be frozen, which is an extra bonus.

2 focaccia (8 servings each)

5^1/$_2$ cups bread flour, divided
1 package (^{1}/$_4$ ounce) fast-rising yeast
2 tablespoons sugar
1 teaspoon salt
1^3/$_4$ cups hot water (125-130 degrees)
1 cup dried cranberries *or* cherries
1 cup dried fruit bits
2 cups boiling water
2 tablespoons melted margarine
^{2}/$_3$ cup packed light brown sugar
Butter-flavored vegetable cooking spray
Vanilla Glaze (see p. 350)

Per Serving
Calories: 304
% Calories from fat: 7
Fat (gm): 2.3
Saturated fat (gm): 0.4
Cholesterol (mg): 0
Sodium (mg): 168
Protein (gm): 6.1
Carbohydrate (gm): 65.2
Exchanges
Milk: 0.0
Vegetable: 0.0
Fruit: 1.0
Bread: 3.0
Meat: 0.0
Fat: 0.5

1. Combine 4 cups flour, yeast, sugar, and salt in large mixing bowl. Add 1^3/$_4$ cups hot water, mixing until smooth. Mix in enough remaining 1^1/$_2$ cups flour to make soft dough.

2. Knead dough on floured surface until dough is smooth and elastic, about 5 minutes. Place dough in greased bowl; turn greased side up and let rise, covered, in warm place until double in size, about 1 hour. Punch dough down.

3. Divide dough into halves. Spread dough into 2 greased 11 x 7-inch baking pans. Let dough rise until double in size, about 30 minutes.

4. Combine dried fruits and boiling water in bowl and let stand until softened, 10 to 15 minutes. Drain well.

5. Make ^{1}/$_4$-inch indentations with fingers to "dimple" dough. Spread 1 tablespoon margarine over dough in each pan; sprinkle with fruit and brown sugar. Spray with cooking spray.

6. Bake at 425 degrees until browned, 20 to 25 minutes. Cool 10 to 15 minutes on wire racks. Drizzle with Vanilla Glaze and serve warm.

TEN

Fruit Desserts

SWEET CHERRY SOUP WITH YOGURT SWIRL

A Merlot wine is an excellent choice for this sweet dessert soup. Serve in well-chilled bowls.

6 servings (about ¹/₂ cup each)

2 cups frozen, slightly thawed, sweet pitted cherries

1¹/₂ cups low-fat vanilla yogurt, divided

¹/₄ cup dry red wine *or* cranberry juice

2 tablespoons lemon juice

Per Serving
Calories: 138
% Calories from fat: 5
Fat (gm): 0.9
Saturated fat (gm): 0.5
Cholesterol (mg): 3.7
Sodium (mg): 41
Protein (gm): 3.5
Carbohydrate (gm): 28.9
Exchanges
Milk: 0.0
Vegetable: 0.0
Fruit: 2.0
Bread: 0.0
Meat: 0.0
Fat: 0.0

1. Process cherries in food processor or blender until finely chopped. Add 1 cup of yogurt, wine, and lemon juice; process until smooth (mixture will be frosty). Pour into chilled soup bowls. Dollop generous tablespoons of remaining ¹/₂ cup yogurt onto soup; swirl with a skewer or spoon.

TROPICAL FRUIT SOUP

If ripe mangoes are not available, the soup is quite delicious made with cantaloupe or muskmelon.

8 servings (about ¹/₂ cup each)

2¹/₂ cups sliced mangoes

1 can (11 ounces) Mandarin oranges, drained

1¹/₂ cups low-fat vanilla frozen yogurt

2 tablespoons lime juice

8 lime slices

Per Serving
Calories: 105
% Calories from fat: 7
Fat (gm): 1
Saturated fat (gm): 0.4
Cholesterol (mg): 3.8
Sodium (mg): 32
Protein (gm): 2.1
Carbohydrate (gm): 24.2
Exchanges
Milk: 0.0
Vegetable: 0.0
Fruit: 1.5
Bread: 0.0
Meat: 0.0
Fat: 0.0

1. Process mangoes and oranges in food processor or blender until smooth. Add frozen yogurt and lime juice; process until smooth. Serve in chilled soup bowls; garnish with lime slices.

SPICED ORANGE SLICES

A perfect dessert for winter, when many fresh fruits are not available. Serve with cookies—Cardamom Crisps (see p. 350) would be fabulous.

8 servings

- 1/3 cup orange juice
- 3 tablespoons packed light brown sugar
- 2-3 tablespoons orange-flavored liqueur
- 4 whole allspice
- 1 cinnamon stick
- 5 oranges, peeled, sliced
  Mint springs, as garnish

Per Serving
Calories: 72
% Calories from fat: 1
Fat (gm): 0.1
Saturated fat (gm): 0
Cholesterol (mg): 0
Sodium (mg): 2
Protein (gm): 0.8
Carbohydrate (gm): 16.8
Exchanges
Milk: 0.0
Vegetable: 0.0
Fruit: 1.0
Bread: 0.0
Meat: 0.0
Fat: 0.0

1. Heat orange juice, brown sugar, orange liqueur, allspice, and cinnamon stick to boiling in small saucepan; pour over orange slices in glass serving bowl. Refrigerate, covered, 8 hours or overnight for flavors to blend. Garnish with mint.

BLUEBERRY-PEAR COMPOTE

Serve this elegant fruit with Almond Tuiles or Sugared Lemon Squares (see pp. 347, 366).

6 servings

- 6 medium pears, peeled, cored
- 1 cup packed light brown sugar
- 2/3 cup water
- 2 tablespoons lemon juice
- 1 teaspoon grated lemon rind
- 2 tablespoons margarine
- 3 cups fresh, *or* frozen, blueberries
  Cinnamon Sour Cream (recipe follows)

Per Serving
Calories: 344
% Calories from fat: 11
Fat (gm): 4.7
Saturated fat (gm): 0.8
Cholesterol (mg): 0
Sodium (mg): 81
Protein (gm): 2.5
Carbohydrate (gm): 77.9
Exchanges
Milk: 0.0
Vegetable: 0.0
Fruit: 5.0
Bread: 0.0
Meat: 0.0
Fat: 1.0

1. Stand pears in baking pan. Heat brown sugar, water, lemon juice and rind, and margarine in small saucepan to boiling; pour over pears.

2. Bake pears at 350 degrees, covered, until tender, basting occasionally, 45 to 60 minutes. Remove pears to serving dish. Boil basting mixture in medium saucepan until reduced to about 2/3 cup; add blueberries and heat to boiling. Spoon warm blueberry mixture around pears. Serve with Cinnamon Sour Cream.

Cinnamon Sour Cream

- 1/2 cup fat-free sour cream
- 1 tablespoon light brown sugar
- 1/4 teaspoon ground cinnamon

1. Mix all ingredients.

FRESH BERRY RHUBARB

Frozen rhubarb can also be used so you can enjoy this light dessert all year.

6 servings (about ³/₄ cup each)

4 cups sliced rhubarb (about 1 pound)
¹/₂ cup sugar
¹/₂ cup water
¹/₄ teaspoon ground cinnamon
1 cup sliced strawberries
1 cup blueberries

Per Serving
Calories: 103
% Calories from fat: 3
Fat (gm): 0.3
Saturated fat (gm): 0.1
Cholesterol (mg): 0
Sodium (mg): 5.3
Protein (gm): 1
Carbohydrate (gm): 25.6
Exchanges
Milk: 0.0
Vegetable: 0.0
Fruit: 1.5
Bread: 0.0
Meat: 0.0
Fat: 0.0

1. Heat rhubarb, sugar, and water to boiling in small saucepan; reduce heat and simmer, uncovered, 10 minutes or until rhubarb is tender, stirring occasionally. Stir in cinnamon and cool; stir in strawberries and blueberries.

BAKED RHUBARB COMPOTE

Rhubarb is sweetened and baked with fruit for a simple dessert compote.

6 servings

3 cups sliced (1 inch pieces) fresh, *or* frozen, rhubarb
1 large tart apple, peeled, sliced
1 orange, peeled, cut into 8 wedges
²/₃ cup sugar
¹/₄ cup honey
3 tablespoons flour
Cinnamon Streusel (see p. 494)

Per Serving
Calories: 297
% Calories from fat: 12
Fat (gm): 4.2
Saturated fat (gm): 0.8
Cholesterol (mg): 0
Sodium (mg): 55
Protein (gm): 1.8
Carbohydrate (gm): 66.3
Exchanges
Milk: 0.0
Vegetable: 0.0
Fruit: 3.0
Bread: 1.5
Meat: 0.0
Fat: 0.5

1. Mix all ingredients, except Cinnamon Streusel, in 1¹/₂-quart casserole; sprinkle with Cinnamon Streusel. Bake at 350 degrees until fruit is bubbly, about 45 minutes.

GINGERED RHUBARB

One of spring's most awaited treasures, rhubarb is simmered to tender goodness with crystallized ginger and orange.

6 servings

1½ pounds fresh, *or* frozen, rhubarb, cut into 1-inch pieces
¼ cup fresh orange juice
1 tablespoon grated orange rind
⅔ cup sugar
¼ cup chopped crystallized ginger, divided
Ground nutmeg, as garnish

Per Serving
Calories: 144
% Calories from fat: 2
Fat (gm): 0.3
Saturated fat (gm): 0
Cholesterol (mg): 0.1
Sodium (mg): 7
Protein (gm): 1.1
Carbohydrate (gm): 36.5
Exchanges
Milk: 0.0
Vegetable: 0.0
Fruit: 2.5
Bread: 0.0
Meat: 0.0
Fat: 0.0

1. Heat rhubarb, orange juice and rind, sugar, and 3 tablespoons crystallized ginger to boiling in medium saucepan. Reduce heat and simmer, covered, stirring often, until rhubarb is thick, 10 to 15 minutes. Cool; refrigerate, covered, until cold.

2. Serve rhubarb in bowls; sprinkle with remaining 1 tablespoon crystallized ginger and nutmeg.

PEACHES AND BLACKBERRIES WITH BLACKBERRY COULIS

Blackberries have a limited season; fortunately they can be purchased frozen for year-round enjoyment.

4 servings

4 ripe medium peaches, peeled, halved
2 tablespoons brown sugar
Blackberry Coulis (recipe follows)
1 cup fresh, *or* frozen, thawed, blackberries
Fat-free sour cream, as garnish
Honey, as garnish

Per Serving
Calories: 144
% Calories from fat: 2
Fat (gm): 0.5
Saturated fat (gm): 0
Cholesterol (mg): 0
Sodium (mg): 3
Protein (gm): 1.4
Carbohydrate (gm): 36.5
Exchanges
Milk: 0.0
Vegetable: 0.0
Fruit: 2.5
Bread: 0.0
Meat: 0.0
Fat: 0.0

1. Toss peaches with sugar and arrange in shallow serving bowls. Spoon Blackberry Coulis around peaches and sprinkle with blackberries; garnish with dollops of sour cream and drizzle lightly with honey.

Blackberry Coulis

   2 cups fresh, *or* frozen, thawed, black-
     berries, divided
  1/2 cup water
  2-3 tablespoons sugar
  1-2 teaspoons lemon juice

1. Heat 1 cup blackberries and water to simmering in saucepan. Simmer, covered, until soft, about 5 minutes. Process mixture in food processor or blender until smooth; strain and discard seeds. Season to taste with sugar and lemon juice. Stir in remaining 1 cup blackberries.

STRAWBERRIES WITH BROWN SUGAR AND BALSAMIC VINEGAR

Balsamic vinegar and black pepper are sophisticated flavor accents in this fresh berry dish.

6 servings

   4 cups halved or quartered strawberries
  2-3 teaspoons balsamic vinegar
  1/4 cup packed light brown sugar
  1/8 teaspoon freshly ground black pepper
  3/4 cup fat-free sour cream
  1-2 tablespoons granulated sugar
   2 teaspoons grated lemon rind

Per Serving
Calories: 110
% Calories from fat: 3
Fat (gm): 0.4
Saturated fat (gm): 0
Cholesterol (mg): 0
Sodium (mg): 30
Protein (gm): 2.6
Carbohydrate (gm): 24.6
Exchanges
Milk: 0.0
Vegetable: 0.0
Fruit: 2.0
Bread: 0.0
Meat: 0.0
Fat: 0.0

1. Sprinkle strawberries with balsamic vinegar, brown sugar, and pepper and toss; let stand 15 to 20 minutes.

2. Mix sour cream, granulated sugar, and lemon rind; serve with strawberries.

STRAWBERRIES WITH PEPPERCORNS

An unusual combination of flavors creates a superb berry dessert.

6 servings

1 quart strawberries
2 tablespoons raspberry, *or* balsamic, vinegar
1/2 teaspoon lime juice
2 teaspoons sugar
1-2 tablespoons green peppercorns, drained

Per Serving
Calories: 39
% Calories from fat: 8
Fat (gm): 0.4
Saturated fat (gm): 0
Cholesterol (mg): 0
Sodium (mg): 1.5
Protein (gm): 0.7
Carbohydrate (gm): 9.4
Exchanges
Milk: 0.0
Vegetable: 0.0
Fruit: 0.5
Bread: 0.0
Meat: 0.0
Fat: 0.0

1. Cut strawberries into halves or quarters; spoon into serving bowl. Sprinkle combined remaining ingredients over strawberries and toss. Refrigerate 1 hour for flavors to blend.

STRAWBERRIES OLÉ

Touched with tequila and pepper, these strawberries are definitely South-of-the-Border.

4 servings

4 cups halved strawberries
1/3 cup orange juice
2-3 tablespoons tequila
2-3 teaspoons lime juice
Freshly ground pepper, as garnish

Per Serving
Calories: 71
% Calories from fat: 6
Fat (gm): 0.6
Saturated fat (gm): 0
Cholesterol (mg): 0
Sodium (mg): 2
Protein (gm): 1.1
Carbohydrate (gm): 12.9
Exchanges
Milk: 0.0
Vegetable: 0.0
Fruit: 1.0
Bread: 0.0
Meat: 0.0
Fat: 0.0

1. Toss strawberries, orange juice, tequila, and lime juice in bowl; refrigerate 1 to 2 hours, stirring occasionally.

2. Spoon strawberry mixture into bowls; sprinkle lightly with pepper.

Variation: **Berry Buñuelos**—Spray 4 flour tortillas lightly on both sides with butter-flavored vegetable cooking spray; sprinkle tops lightly with sugar and cinnamon. Bake on cookie sheet at 375 degrees until browned and crisp, 5 to 8 minutes. Make recipe as above, omitting orange juice and pepper; do not refrigerate. Spoon strawberry mixture on tortillas; top with dollops of fat-free sour cream and sprinkle with sliced almonds.

PEACHES AND BLUEBERRIES WITH LIME CREAM SAUCE

The creamy lime sauce has a texture similar to heavy cream, with virtually no fat!

6 servings

4 medium peaches, sliced
1 cup blueberries
   Lime Cream Sauce (recipe follows)
   Mint sprigs, as garnish

Per Serving
Calories: 119
% Calories from fat: 5
Fat (gm): 0.7
Saturated fat (gm): 0.4
Cholesterol (mg): 3
Sodium (mg): 208
Protein (gm): 6
Carbohydrate (gm): 23.6
Exchanges
Milk: 0.0
Vegetable: 0.0
Fruit: 2.0
Bread: 0.0
Meat: 0.0
Fat: 0.0

1. Arrange peaches and blueberries in bowls; spoon Lime Cream Sauce over and garnish with mint.

Lime Cream Sauce

makes about 1¹/₄ cups

1 package (8 ounces) fat-free cream cheese, softened
¹/₃ cup sugar
2-3 tablespoons lime juice

1. Beat cream cheese until smooth; beat in sugar and lime juice.

HONEY-LIME MELON WEDGES

A recipe that's so simple, but so very good.

4 servings

3-4 tablespoons honey

1 small cantaloupe *or* honeydew melon, cut into wedges

4 lime wedges

Ground nutmeg, as garnish

Per Serving
Calories: 112
% Calories from fat: **3**
Fat (gm): 0.5
Saturated fat (gm): **0**
Cholesterol (mg): **0**
Sodium (mg): 15
Protein (gm): 1.5
Carbohydrate (gm): 28.1
Exchanges
Milk: 0.0
Vegetable: 0.0
Fruit: 2.0
Bread: 0.0
Meat: 0.0
Fat: 0.0

1. Drizzle honey over melon; squeeze juice from lime wedges over and sprinkle lightly with nutmeg.

TROPICAL AMBROSIA

Enjoy tropical fruits served in pineapple shells with a creamy citrus topping.

6 servings

1 large ripe pineapple

2 kiwis, peeled, sliced

1 cup cubed mango *or* papaya

1 cup cubed cantaloupe *or* honeydew melon

1 carton (6 ounces) custard-style low-fat lemon, *or* orange, yogurt

3/4 cup light whipped topping

2 tablespoons orange marmalade

Toasted coconut, as garnish

Macadamia nuts *or* slivered almonds, as garnish

Mint sprigs, as garnish

Per Serving
Calories: 246
% Calories from fat: **7**
Fat (gm): 2
Saturated fat (gm): 1.3
Cholesterol (mg): 1.9
Sodium (mg): 36
Protein (gm): 3.1
Carbohydrate (gm): 54.7
Exchanges
Milk: 0.0
Vegetable: 0.0
Fruit: 4.0
Bread: 0.0
Meat: 0.0
Fat: 0.0

1. Cut pineapple in half; remove fruit with grapefruit knife, keeping shells intact. Cut pineapple into cubes, discarding core. Mix pineapple and remaining fruit and spoon into pineapple halves.

2. Mix yogurt, light whipped topping, and marmalade. Spoon dollops of topping over fruit; pass remaining topping. Garnish with toasted coconut and macadamia nuts and mint.

CARAMEL APPLE SLICES

Serve these fragrant apple slices over low-fat frozen vanilla yogurt for a sumptuous sundae, or serve over pancakes, waffles, or crepes.

4 servings

2 large sweet, *or* tart, apples, unpeeled, cored
$^1/_2$ cup apple cider
$^1/_4$ cup packed light brown sugar
Ground cinnamon, as garnish
Ground nutmeg, as garnish

Per Serving
Calories: 104
% Calories from fat: 2
Fat (gm): 0.3
Saturated fat (gm): 0
Cholesterol (mg): 0
Sodium (mg): 5
Protein (gm): 0.1
Carbohydrate (gm): 24.1
Exchanges
Milk: 0.0
Vegetable: 0.0
Fruit: 1.5
Bread: 0.0
Meat: 0.0
Fat: 0.0

1. Cut apples into fourths; cut into scant $^1/_4$-inch slices. Heat apples, cider, and brown sugar to boiling in medium skillet; reduce heat and simmer, uncovered, until apples are crisp-tender, 3 to 4 minutes. Remove apples to serving dish with slotted spoon.

2. Heat cider mixture to boiling; boil until mixture is reduced to a syrup consistency. Pour syrup over apples, and sprinkle very lightly with cinnamon and nutmeg.

BAKED STUFFED APPLES WITH CRÈME ANGLAISE

Apples are perfectly baked with fragrant fruit and elegantly served with Crème Anglaise.

4 servings

4 large baking apples (Rome Beauty, McIntosh, Jonathan, *or* Granny Smith)

$^{1}/_{2}$ cup chopped mixed dried fruit

2-4 tablespoons chopped toasted pecans

3 tablespoons sugar

$^{1}/_{2}$ teaspoon ground cinnamon

$^{1}/_{8}$ teaspoon ground nutmeg

2-3 tablespoons cold margarine, cut into pieces

Crème Anglaise (see p. 640)

Per Serving
Calories: 295
% Calories from fat: 29
Fat (gm): 10.2
Saturated fat (gm): 1.9
Cholesterol (mg): 54.4
Sodium (mg): 101
Protein (gm): 4
Carbohydrate (gm): 51.3
Exchanges
Milk: 0.0
Vegetable: 0.0
Fruit: 2.0
Bread: 1.5
Meat: 0.0
Fat: 1.5

1. Core apples, cutting to, but not through, bottoms; peel 1 inch skin from tops. Stand apples in baking pan.

2. Combine dried fruit, pecans, sugar, spices, and margarine; fill apples with mixture. Bake at 350 degrees, loosely covered with aluminum foil, until apples are tender, about 45 minutes. Cool to room temperature.

3. Spoon Crème Anglaise around apples in shallow bowls.

Variation: **Meringue-Glazed Baked Apples**—Make recipe as above, omitting Crème Anglaise; bake 30 minutes. Beat 1 egg white to stiff peaks, gradually adding $^{1}/_{4}$ cup sugar. Swirl meringue on top of apples; bake until apples are tender and meringue browned, about 20 minutes longer.

MIXED FRUIT KABOBS WITH RASPBERRY SAUCE

Bittersweet Chocolate Sauce (see p. 641) is another excellent sauce choice for the kabobs.

8 servings (2 kabobs per serving)

2 bananas
2 kiwi, peeled
2 peaches, unpeeled
2 pears, unpeeled
2 tablespoons margarine, melted
Raspberry Sauce (see p. 658)

Per Serving
Calories: 140
% Calories from fat: 21
Fat (gm): 3.5
Saturated fat (gm): 0.6
Cholesterol (mg): 0
Sodium (mg): 34
Protein (gm): 1.2
Carbohydrate (gm): 28.5
Exchanges
Milk: 0.0
Vegetable: 0.0
Fruit: 2.0
Bread: 0.0
Meat: 0.0
Fat: 0.5

1. Cut each piece of fruit into 8 equal pieces. Alternately thread fruit onto sixteen 6-inch wooden or metal skewers.

2. Broil, 6 inches from heat source, 5 to 8 minutes or until bananas are golden, rotating kabobs occasionally and basting with margarine. Serve with Raspberry Sauce.

HONEY-BROILED PINEAPPLE SLICES

This dessert beckons a selection of cookie accompaniments. Choose between Fruit Newtons and Hazelnut Macaroons (see pp. 341, 354).

4 servings

1 medium pineapple, peeled, cored, and cut into eight 1/2-inch slices
3 tablespoons honey
2 tablespoons frozen orange juice concentrate
2 tablespoons minced fresh cilantro *or* mint

Per Serving
Calories: 143
% Calories from fat: 4
Fat (gm): 0.7
Saturated fat (gm): 0
Cholesterol (mg): 0
Sodium (mg): 3
Protein (gm): 0.8
Carbohydrate (gm): 36.5
Exchanges
Milk: 0.0
Vegetable: 0.0
Fruit: 2.5
Bread: 0.0
Meat: 0.0
Fat: 0.0

1. Arrange pineapple on broiler pan; brush with combined honey and orange juice concentrate. Broil 6 inches from heat source 3 minutes; turn and baste with honey mixture. Broil 2 to 3 minutes more or until golden. Sprinkle with cilantro.

BANANAS FOSTER

Celebrate a taste of New Orleans!

4 servings

1/4 cup packed light brown sugar
11/2 teaspoons cornstarch
1/2 cup water
1 tablespoon light rum *or* 1/2 teaspoon rum extract
1 teaspoon vanilla
2 medium bananas, peeled, sliced
1/4 cup toasted pecan halves
11/3 cups low-fat vanilla frozen yogurt

Per Serving
Calories: 236
% Calories from fat: 20
Fat (gm): 5.5
Saturated fat (gm): 0.5
Cholesterol (mg): 0
Sodium (mg): 5
Protein (gm): 3.4
Carbohydrate (gm): 43
Exchanges
Milk: 0.0
Vegetable: 0.0
Fruit: 2.0
Bread: 1.0
Meat: 0.0
Fat: 1.0

1. Whisk brown sugar, cornstarch, and water in small saucepan; whisk over medium heat until mixture boils and thickens, 2 to 3 minutes. Reduce heat to low; stir in rum and vanilla.

2. Gently stir in bananas and simmer 1 to 2 minutes or until bananas are warm; stir in pecans. Serve warm over frozen yogurt.

SUGAR AND RUM PLANTAINS

Enjoy one of my favorite desserts from Mexico. Bananas can be substituted for the plantains—use bananas that are ripe but still very firm.

4 servings

1 tablespoon margarine

2 large ripe plantains, peeled, diagonally cut into ¹/₄-inch slices

¹/₂ cup dark rum *or* ¹/₂ cup water and 1 teaspoon rum extract

¹/₃ cup sugar

4 tablespoons fat-free sour cream

Ground cinnamon, as garnish

1 tablespoon pine nuts, toasted

Per Serving
Calories: 295
% Calories from fat: 13
Fat (gm): 4.4
Saturated fat (gm): 0.9
Cholesterol (mg): 0
Sodium (mg): 50
Protein (gm): 2.8
Carbohydrate (gm): 48.6
Exchanges
Milk: 0.0
Vegetable: 0.0
Fruit: 3.0
Bread: 0.0
Meat: 0.0
Fat: 2.5

1. Melt margarine in large skillet; arrange plantains in skillet in single layer. Cook over medium to medium-high heat until plantains are browned, 2 to 3 minutes on each side. Arrange on serving plates.

2. Add rum and sugar to skillet; heat to boiling. Reduce heat and simmer, stirring constantly, until mixture is reduced to a thick syrup consistency. Drizzle syrup over plantains; top each serving with a dollop of sour cream. Sprinkle with cinnamon and pine nuts.

FRESH FRUIT WITH ROQUEFORT SHERBET

Fruit and cheese pair beautifully for dessert. Enjoy a unique variation-fruit served with a frosty cheese sherbet.

8 servings

- 8 ounces fat-free cream cheese, softened
- 1-2 ounces Roquefort *or* other blue-veined cheese
- 1/4 cup sugar
- 1/2 cup 2% reduced-fat milk
- 1/4 cup lemon juice
- 2 pears, unpeeled, sliced
- 2 apples, unpeeled, sliced
- 1 pint strawberries
- 8 small bunches seedless grapes

Per Serving
Calories: 159
% Calories from fat: 12
Fat (gm): 2.4
Saturated fat (gm): 1.2
Cholesterol (mg): 6.6
Sodium (mg): 228
Protein (gm): 6.1
Carbohydrate (gm): 31.4
Exchanges
Milk: 0.0
Vegetable: 0.0
Fruit: 2.0
Bread: 0.0
Meat: 0.0
Fat: 0.5

1. Beat cream cheese and Roquefort cheese in small bowl until smooth; beat in sugar, milk, and lemon juice. Freeze in ice cream maker according to manufacturer's directions. Or, pour mixture into 6 x 3-inch loaf pan and freeze until slushy, about 1 hour; spoon into bowl and beat until fluffy. Return to pan and freeze until firm, 6 hours or overnight.

2. To serve, scoop sherbet onto 8 plates; arrange fruit around sherbet.

POACHED PEARS WITH BERRIES IN ROSEMARY SYRUP

Perfectly poached pears combine with fresh fruit in a fragrant herbed sugar syrup.

4 servings

   2 large pears, peeled, halved, cored
     Rosemary Syrup (recipe follows)
   1 cup raspberries
   1 cup fresh, *or* frozen, thawed, blueberries
   1 large orange, peeled, cut into segments
     Mint sprigs, as garnish

Per Serving
Calories: 313
% Calories from fat: 3
Fat (gm): 1.1
Saturated fat (gm): 0.1
Cholesterol (mg): 0
Sodium (mg): 6
Protein (gm): 1.6
Carbohydrate (gm): 73.1
Exchanges
Milk: 0.0
Vegetable: 0.0
Fruit: 5.0
Bread: 0.0
Meat: 0.0
Fat: 0.5

1. Add pears to Rosemary Syrup in medium skillet; simmer, covered, until tender, about 10 minutes. Remove pears to shallow bowl; strain syrup over pears and cool. Refrigerate until chilled, 1 to 2 hours.

2. Arrange pears and remaining fruit in shallow serving bowls; spoon Rosemary Syrup over fruit. Garnish with mint.

Rosemary Syrup

makes about 1 cup

   2/3 cup sugar
   2/3 cup dry white wine
   1 tablespoon balsamic vinegar
   1 tablespoon dried rosemary leaves
   1 bay leaf
   1 teaspoon grated orange, *or* lemon, rind

1. Heat all ingredients to boiling in medium saucepan.

PEARS BELLE HÉLÈNE

Tuck a Cocoa-Glazed Cookie Crisp (see p. 351) beside each dish to complete this elegant offering.

6 servings

4 cups water
1/4 cup sugar
6 small pears, peeled with stems intact
1 1/2 cups low-fat frozen vanilla yogurt
Bittersweet Chocolate Sauce (see p. 641)

Per Serving
Calories: 183
% Calories from fat: 5
Fat (gm): 1.1
Saturated fat (gm): 0
Cholesterol (mg): 0
Sodium (mg): 0
Protein (gm): 2.3
Carbohydrate (gm): 43.9
Exchanges
Milk: 0.0
Vegetable: 0.0
Fruit: 2.0
Bread: 1.0
Meat: 0.0
Fat: 0.0

1. Combine water and sugar in small saucepan; heat to boiling. Add pears; reduce heat to low and gently simmer, covered, 10 to 15 minutes or until pears are tender.

2. Cool pears in syrup; refrigerate until chilled, 1 to 2 hours. Drain.

3. To serve, flatten a scoop of yogurt in each of 6 dessert dishes. Place a pear on top and drizzle with Bittersweet Chocolate Sauce.

Variation: **Pears Melba in Meringue Shells**—Make recipe as above, substituting packed brown sugar for the granulated sugar, using 4 pears, omitting frozen yogurt, and substituting Raspberry Sauce (see p. 658) for the Bittersweet Chocolate Sauce. Use Meringue Shells (see p. 306), making shells with a diameter slightly larger than the base of the pears. Place poached pears upright in baked Meringue Shells; spoon Raspberry Sauce over.

SPICED PEACHES IN CHAMPAGNE

Enjoy this celebration dessert—champagne bubbles and all!

4 servings

4 cups champagne *or* sparkling white
   wine, divided
1/4 cup sugar
1 cinnamon stick
8 whole cloves
4 whole allspice
1 star anise *or* 1/2 teaspoon anise seed
4 small peaches, peeled, halved
2 envelopes unflavored gelatin
   Light whipped topping, as garnish
   Cinnamon sticks, as garnish

Per Serving
Calories: 258
% Calories from fat: 0
Fat (gm): 0.1
Saturated fat (gm): 0
Cholesterol (mg): 0
Sodium (mg): 9
Protein (gm): 1.3
Carbohydrate (gm): 31
Exchanges
Milk: 0.0
Vegetable: 0.0
Fruit: 2.0
Bread: 0.0
Meat: 0.0
Fat: 3.0

1. Heat 1 1/2 cups champagne, sugar, and spices to boiling in large skillet. Place peaches, cut sides down, in skillet and simmer, covered, until peaches are tender, about 5 minutes. Remove peaches; strain champagne mixture and discard spices.

2. Sprinkle gelatin over 1/2 cup champagne in small saucepan; let stand 3 to 4 minutes to soften. Cook over low heat, stirring, until dissolved. Add gelatin mixture to champagne mixture in bowl; add remaining 2 cups champagne. Refrigerate until mixture is the consistency of unbeaten egg whites, about 45 minutes, stirring occasionally.

3. Press gelatin mixture through strainer, using rubber spatula, to create "champagne bubbles." Spoon 1/2 the mixture into 4 large champagne glasses; refrigerate until firm, but not set, about 30 minutes. Place peach halves in glasses and spoon remaining gelatin mixture over. Refrigerate until set, 2 to 3 hours. Garnish with dollops of light whipped topping and cinnamon sticks.

WINE-POACHED PLUMS

White port wine is unique in this recipe, but red port can be used if necessary.

4 servings

2 cups white port wine *or* dry sherry *or* water
$^1/_3$-$^1/_2$ cup sugar
1 cinnamon stick
1 whole nutmeg
12 medium plums

Per Serving
Calories: 247
% Calories from fat: 4
Fat (gm): 1.2
Saturated fat (gm): 0.1
Cholesterol (mg): 0
Sodium (mg): 5
Protein (gm): 1.8
Carbohydrate (gm): 57.6
Exchanges
Milk: 0.0
Vegetable: 0.0
Fruit: 4.0
Bread: 0.0
Meat: 0.0
Fat: 0.0

1. Combine wine, sugar, cinnamon, and nutmeg in medium saucepan. Heat to boiling, add plums, and reduce heat to low. Gently simmer plums, covered, 10 to 15 minutes or until tender. Remove plums to serving dish.

2. Heat poaching liquid to boiling; boil gently 12 to 15 minutes or until slightly thickened. Serve over plums.

Variations: **Pears in Cider Syrup**—Make recipe as above, substituting 1 cup apple cider for the white port wine and 4 peeled, halved small pears for the plums. Stir 1 to 2 tablespoons rum *or* $^1/_2$ to 1 teaspoon rum extract into thickened poaching liquid; spoon around pears in serving dishes. Garnish pears with dollops of light whipped topping; sprinkle lightly with ground nutmeg and pomegranate seeds.

Ginger Poached Peaches with Mascarpone—Make recipe as above, substituting 1 cup peach nectar for the white port wine and 4 peeled, halved medium peaches for the plums; add 4 slices gingerroot to the peach nectar and omit sugar. Omit Step 2. Make $^2/_3$ cup ($^1/_2$ recipe) Mock Mascarpone (see p. 161); beat with 2 tablespoons sugar until fluffy and fold in $^2/_3$ cup light whipped topping. Spoon nectar mixture and peaches into serving dishes. Spoon mascarpone mixture into centers of peach halves and sprinkle with gingersnap crumbs.

BERRY BEST SHORTCAKE

A recipe from my Grandmother Spitler that I remember fondly. Glaze this tender-textured cake with Orange or Banana Glaze (see pp. 47, 64) for a special touch.

8 servings

- ¹/₃ cup vegetable shortening
- 1 cup sugar
- 1 egg
- 1 teaspoon vanilla
- 2 cups all-purpose flour
- 2 teaspoons baking powder
- ¹/₄ teaspoon salt
- ³/₄ cup fat-free milk
- 3 cups mixed berries *or* fruit
  Light whipped topping, as garnish

Per Serving
Calories: 320
% Calories from fat: 26
Fat (gm): 9.1
Saturated fat (gm): 2.3
Cholesterol (mg): 26.9
Sodium (mg): 216
Protein (gm): 5.2
Carbohydrate (gm): 54.4
Exchanges
Milk: 0.0
Vegetable: 0.0
Fruit: 1.0
Bread: 3.0
Meat: 0.0
Fat: 1.0

1. Beat shortening, sugar, egg, and vanilla in bowl until well blended. Mix in combined flour, baking powder, and salt alternately with milk, beginning and ending with dry ingredients.

2. Spread batter in greased 11 x 7-inch baking dish; bake at 350 degrees until browned, about 25 minutes. Cool on wire rack 10 to 15 minutes.

3. Serve warm cake squares with berries and garnish with whipped topping.

STRAWBERRY-KIWI SHORTCAKE

This moist, nutritious whole-wheat shortcake is made to order for a duo of fresh fruits.

8 servings

1 cup all-purpose flour
1 cup whole wheat flour
1/3 cup sugar
1 1/2 teaspoons baking powder
1/2 teaspoon baking soda
1/4 teaspoon salt
2/3 cup buttermilk
4 tablespoons margarine, melted
1 egg
2 egg whites
1 1/2 teaspoons vanilla
3 cups sliced strawberries
1 cup peeled, sliced, kiwi fruit

Per Serving
Calories: 39.1
% Calories from fat: 25
Fat (gm): 7.3
Saturated fat (gm): 1.5
Cholesterol (mg): 27.4
Sodium (mg): 319
Protein (gm): 6.5
Carbohydrate (gm): 39.1
Exchanges
Milk: 0.0
Vegetable: 0.0
Fruit: 1.0
Bread: 2.0
Meat: 0.0
Fat: 1.0

1. Combine flours, sugar, baking powder, baking soda, and salt in medium-size bowl. Mix buttermilk, margarine, egg, egg whites, and vanilla in small bowl until smooth; stir into flour mixture, mixing only until dry ingredients are moistened.

2. With floured hands, lightly pat dough into lightly greased 8-inch round or square baking pan. Bake at 400 degrees 12 to 15 minutes or until toothpick inserted near center comes out clean. Cool on wire rack 10 minutes.

3. Slice cake into wedges or squares and top with strawberries and kiwi fruit.

Variation: **Raspberries with Pecan Shortcakes**—Make Steps 1 and 2 as above, substituting all-purpose flour for the whole wheat flour and adding 1/3 cup chopped pecans. Beat 2/3 package (8-ounce size) reduced-fat cream cheese with 1/4 cup sugar and 1 teaspoon vanilla until fluffy; mix in 2 cups light whipped topping. Cut warm cake in half horizontally; spread 1/2 the cream cheese mixture on bottom layer. Replace top layer, and spread with remaining cream cheese mixture; cut into wedges. Substitute 4 cups fresh raspberries for the strawberries and kiwi; spoon over shortcake wedges.

FRUIT BAKED IN PARCHMENT PACKETS

An impressive presentation for an elegant dessert.

8 servings

2 cups peeled, sliced apples
1¹/₂ cups peeled, sliced pears
1 cup raspberries
3 tablespoons brown sugar
1 teaspoon ground cinnamon
¹/₄ teaspoon ground nutmeg
3 teaspoons flour
3 tablespoons margarine, melted

Per Serving
Calories: 119
% Calories from fat: 33
Fat (gm): 4.7
Saturated fat (gm): 0.9
Cholesterol (mg): 0
Sodium (mg): 52
Protein (gm): 0.6
Carbohydrate (gm): 20.4
Exchanges
Milk: 0.0
Vegetable: 0.0
Fruit: 1.5
Bread: 0.0
Meat: 0.0
Fat: 0.5

1. Combine all ingredients, except margarine, in large bowl; gently toss.

2. Cut eight 12-inch squares of parchment paper; fold each in half diagonally, making triangles. Open triangles and place on baking sheets; brush with margarine. Divide fruit mixture on papers and fold in half; fold edges inward twice to seal. Bake at 375 degrees 10 minutes.

3. Place packets on plates. To open, cut a 2-inch "X" in top of each packet with sharp knife.

FRUIT BAKED WITH MERINGUE PUFFS

Spoonfuls of golden baked meringue add a creative touch to warm, baked fruits.

4 servings

2 cups peeled, sliced peaches

1 pint raspberries

1/4 cup plus 3 tablespoons sugar, divided

3 egg whites

1/2 teaspoon vanilla

1/4 teaspoon ground nutmeg

2 tablespoons sliced almonds

Per Serving
Calories: 181
% Calories from fat: 11
Fat (gm): 2.3
Saturated fat (gm): 0.2
Cholesterol (mg): 0
Sodium (mg): 42
Protein (gm): 4.5
Carbohydrate (gm): 38.7
Exchanges
Milk: 0.0
Vegetable: 0.0
Fruit: 2.0
Bread: 0.0
Meat: 1.0
Fat: 0.0

1. Toss peaches and raspberries with 1/4 cup sugar; spoon into 4 custard cups and place in baking pan. Bake at 375 degrees 10 to 15 minutes or until hot through.

2. Beat egg whites to soft peaks in small bowl; beat to stiff peaks, adding remaining 3 tablespoons sugar gradually. Beat in vanilla and nutmeg. Spoon meringue over warm fruit mixture; sprinkle with almonds.

3. Bake until meringue is lightly browned, about 10 minutes. Serve immediately.

HONEYED BERRIES NESTLED IN FILLO

A medley of fresh berries, sweetened with honey, is served in an attractive "nest" of crisp fillo.

4 servings

    4 sheets frozen, thawed, fillo pastry
      Butter-flavored vegetable cooking spray
    1 tablespoon sugar
  1/4 teaspoon ground cinnamon
    3 tablespoons honey
    1 tablespoon lemon juice
    1 cup small strawberries
    1 cup blueberries
    1 cup raspberries
      Ground nutmeg, as garnish
      Light whipped topping, as garnish

Per Serving
Calories: 165
% Calories from fat: 8
Fat (gm): 1.6
Saturated fat (gm): 0.2
Cholesterol (mg): 0
Sodium (mg): 95
Protein (gm): 2.2
Carbohydrate (gm): 37.8
Exchanges
Milk: 0.0
Vegetable: 0.0
Fruit: 1.5
Bread: 1.0
Meat: 0.0
Fat: 0.0

1. Stack fillo and fold lengthwise into quarters; cut into 1/2-inch strips with sharp knife or scissors. Unwind fillo strips and toss together in a greased 8-inch pie plate, shaping to form a large "nest." Spray fillo generously with cooking spray and sprinkle with combined sugar and cinnamon.

2. Bake at 400 degrees until golden, 10 to 12 minutes. Cool on wire rack; carefully remove to serving plate.

3. Heat honey and lemon juice until warm. Fill fillo "nest" with combined berries and drizzle with honey mixture; sprinkle lightly with nutmeg. Garnish with light whipped topping.

APRICOT AND PEACH FILLO NESTS

A beautiful dessert that is quite easy to prepare; serve with Raspberry Sauce (see p. 658).

6 servings

12 sheets frozen, thawed, fillo pastry
Butter-flavored vegetable cooking spray
1¹/₂ pounds apricots, peeled, sliced
³/₄ pound peaches, peeled, sliced
3 tablespoons packed light brown sugar
¹/₂ teaspoon ground cinnamon
¹/₄ teaspoon ground nutmeg
Mint sprigs, as garnish

Per Serving
Calories: 219
% Calories from fat: 11
Fat (gm): 2.8
Saturated fat (gm): 0.4
Cholesterol (mg): 0
Sodium (mg): 188
Protein (gm): 4.7
Carbohydrate (gm): 45.8
Exchanges
Milk: 0.0
Vegetable: 0.0
Fruit: 2.0
Bread: 1.0
Meat: 0.0
Fat: 0.5

1. Cut fillo into twenty-four 8-inch squares. Spray 4 squares of fillo lightly with cooking spray; layer squares, turning each slightly so that corners are staggered. Carefully fit fillo into 8-ounce custard cup, shaping edges to form "nest." Repeat with remaining fillo squares lining a total of 6 custard cups. Arrange fruit in bottom of each "nest." Sprinkle combined brown sugar and spices evenly over fruit.

2. Place custard cups on cookie sheet and bake at 375 degrees until fillo is golden and fruit tender, about 15 minutes. Cool on wire rack; carefully remove "nests" from custard cups. Serve warm or room temperature garnished with mint.

Variation: **Blackberry Strudel Cups**—Make recipe as above, substituting 1 pint blackberries or raspberries for the peaches, granulated sugar for the brown sugar, and omitting spices. Bake fillo "nests" without filling with fruit. Mix 1 cup light whipped topping and 1 carton (6 ounces) custard-style low-fat yogurt; mix in fruit and fill fillo "nests."

FRESH FRUIT WITH CHOCOLATE YOGURT CHEESE

You won't believe that the richly textured cheese is actually low in fat!

4 servings

2 cups fat-free vanilla yogurt
2 tablespoons brown sugar
2 teaspoons unsweetened cocoa
2 pears, unpeeled, sliced
1/2 pint strawberries

Per Serving
Calories: 192
% Calories from fat: 2
Fat (gm): 0.5
Saturated fat (gm): 0
Cholesterol (mg): 0
Sodium (mg): 75
Protein (gm): 6.1
Carbohydrate (gm): 42.6
Exchanges
Milk: 0.5
Vegetable: 0.0
Fruit: 2.5
Bread: 0.0
Meat: 0.0
Fat: 0.0

1. Line a strainer with cheesecloth or a coffee filter and place over bowl; spoon yogurt into lined strainer and cover with plastic wrap. Refrigerate 12 hours or until yogurt is reduced to 1 cup in volume and is the consistency of softened cream cheese; discard liquid.

2. Transfer yogurt cheese to small bowl; mix in brown sugar and cocoa. Refrigerate 1 to 2 hours for flavors to blend. Serve with fruit.

BLUEBERRIES WITH MINTED GOAT CHEESE

Banon or Montrachet goat cheese would be an excellent choice for this recipe. If preferred, low-fat or fat-free cream cheese can be substituted for the goat cheese.

4 servings

4 ounces mild goat cheese

1 tablespoon finely chopped mint leaves

1 cup fresh, *or* frozen, thawed, blue-berries, divided

4 pieces luncheon-size lavosh (5-inch) *or* Gingersnappers *or* Tuscan Cornmeal Cookies (see pp. 330, 334)

Per Serving
Calories: 145
% Calories from fat: 28
Fat (gm): 4.6
Saturated fat (gm): 3
Cholesterol (mg): 13
Sodium (mg): 147
Protein (gm): 6.8
Carbohydrate (gm): 11.3
Exchanges
Milk: 0.0
Vegetable: 0.0
Fruit: 1.0
Bread: 0.0
Meat: 1.5
Fat: 0.0

1. Mix cheese and mint in small bowl until smooth; refrigerate 3 to 4 hours for flavors to blend. Shape cheese into flattened round on small, oven-proof serving plate.

2. Bake cheese at 350 degrees until warm and slightly softened, 5 to 10 minutes.

3. Process $1/2$ cup blueberries in food processor or blender until smooth. Spoon puree around cheese; sprinkle remaining $1/2$ cup blueberries over and around cheese. Serve with lavosh.

ELEVEN

Quick Desserts: Cakes, Cookies **AND** More

FOOD PROCESSOR CAKE

Or, make this cake in a blender. Either way, this is the quickest "scratch" cake we know!

8 to 9 servings

Rind of 1 small orange, cut into 1-inch pieces
1 egg
1/4 cup vegetable shortening
3/4 cup fat-free milk
1 teaspoon vanilla
1 1/4 cups all-purpose flour
1 cup packed light brown sugar
1 1/2 teaspoons baking powder
1/2 teaspoon salt
1/2 cup raisins
Cream Cheese Glaze (see pg. 498)
1/4 cup chopped hazelnuts *or* almonds

Per Serving
Calories: 374
% Calories from fat: 23
Fat (gm): 10
Saturated fat (gm): 2.1
Cholesterol (mg): 27.5
Sodium (mg): 308
Protein (gm): 5.4
Carbohydrate (gm): 67.2
Exchanges
Milk: 0.0
Vegetable: 0.0
Fruit: 0.0
Bread: 4.0
Meat: 0.0
Fat: 2.0

1. Process orange rind in food processor until finely chopped. Add remaining ingredients, except Cream Cheese Glaze and hazelnuts, to food processor; process just until ingredients are mixed, using pulse technique, and scraping bowl occasionally.

2. Pour batter into greased 8- or 9-inch square baking pan. Bake at 350 degrees until toothpick inserted in center comes out clean, 25 to 30 minutes. Cool in pan on wire rack. Spread with Cream Cheese Glaze and sprinkle with hazelnuts.

HONEY-ORANGE GLAZED YELLOW CAKE

So easy and so good—use your favorite kind of honey and enjoy!

12 servings

1 package (18.25 ounces) reduced-fat yellow cake mix
1¹/₃ cups orange juice
2 tablespoons vegetable oil
3 eggs
1 tablespoon finely grated orange rind
Honey-Orange Glaze (see pg. 106)
Orange slices, as garnish

Per Serving
Calories: 307
% Calories from fat: 20
Fat (gm): 6.9
Saturated fat (gm): 1.9
Cholesterol (mg): 53
Sodium (mg): 324
Protein (gm): 3.6
Carbohydrate (gm): 58.4
Exchanges
Milk: 0.0
Vegetable: 0.0
Fruit: 0.0
Bread: 3.5
Meat: 0.0
Fat: 1.0

1. Mix all ingredients, except Honey-Orange Glaze and orange slices, on low speed in large bowl until blended; mix on medium speed 2 minutes.

2. Pour batter into greased and floured 12-cup fluted cake pan. Bake at 350 degrees until toothpick inserted in center comes out clean, about 45 minutes. Cool cake in pan on wire rack 10 minutes; remove from pan.

3. Place warm cake on serving plate; pierce top of cake with long-tined fork and drizzle with Honey-Orange Glaze. Garnish with orange slices.

Variation: **Blueberry-Orange Cake**—Make cake as above, folding 1¹/₄ cups fresh, *or* frozen, blueberries into the batter. Pour batter into 2 greased and floured 9-inch cake pans; bake at 350 degrees until toothpick inserted in center comes out clean, 20 to 25 minutes. Cool on wire rack 10 minutes; remove from pans and cool. Omit Honey-Orange Glaze; frost with **Citrus Frosting:** Beat ¹/₂ package (4-ounce size) reduced-fat cream cheese and 2 tablespoons margarine until fluffy; beat in 3 cups powdered sugar. Mix in 1 cup light whipped topping.

RASPBERRY-ORANGE SWIRL CAKE

A swirl of raspberry puree enhances flavor and appearance in this delectable cake.

14 servings

2 cups fresh, *or* frozen, thawed raspberries
1 package (18.25 ounces) reduced-fat white cake mix
1¹/₄ cups water
2 tablespoons vegetable oil
3 eggs
1 teaspoon orange extract, divided
2 teaspoons grated orange rind
2 cups powdered sugar
3-4 tablespoons fat-free milk

Per Serving
Calories: 267
% Calories from fat: 20
Fat (gm): 6
Saturated fat (gm): 1.7
Cholesterol (mg): 45.5
Sodium (mg): 278
Protein (gm): 3
Carbohydrate (gm): 50.1
Exchanges
Milk: 0.0
Vegetable: 0.0
Fruit: 0.0
Bread: 3.0
Meat: 0.0
Fat: 1.0

1. Process raspberries in food processor or blender until smooth; strain and discard seeds.

2. Mix cake mix, water, oil, eggs, and ¹/₂ teaspoon orange extract on low speed in large bowl until blended. Mix on medium speed 2 minutes; stir in orange rind.

3. Pour half the batter into greased and floured 12-cup fluted cake pan; spoon on raspberry puree and top with remaining batter. With a knife, cut through batter a few times to swirl.

4. Bake cake at 350 degrees 40 to 45 minutes or until toothpick inserted in center comes out clean. Cool in pan on wire rack 10 minutes; remove from pan and cool completely.

5. Mix powdered sugar, remaining ¹/₂ teaspoon orange extract, and enough milk to make glaze consistency. Spoon over cake.

APRICOT SOUR CREAM CAKE

Any favorite preserves can be substituted for the apricot preserves in the recipe.

12 servings

1 package (18.25 ounces) reduced-fat white cake mix

1 cup water

1/3 cup fat-free sour cream

2 tablespoons vegetable oil

3 eggs

1/2 cup apricot spreadable fruit
    Creamy Apricot Frosting
    (recipe follows)

Per Serving
Calories: 326
% Calories from fat: 25
Fat (gm): 8.9
Saturated fat (gm): 3.9
Cholesterol (mg): 53
Sodium (mg): 343
Protein (gm): 3.7
Carbohydrate (gm): 55.7
Exchanges
Milk: 0.0
Vegetable: 0.0
Fruit: 0.0
Bread: 3.5
Meat: 0.0
Fat: 1.5

1. Mix all ingredients, except spreadable fruit and Creamy Apricot Frosting, in large bowl on low speed until blended; mix on medium speed 2 minutes.

2. Pour batter into 2 greased and floured 9-inch round cake pans. Bake at 350 degrees until toothpick inserted in center comes out clean, about 25 minutes. Cool on wire rack 10 minutes; remove from pans and cool completely.

3. Place 1 cake layer on serving plate; spread with spreadable fruit. Top with second cake layer and frost with Creamy Apricot Frosting.

Creamy Apricot Frosting

3 cups light whipped topping

1/3 cup apricot spreadable fruit

1/2 cup powdered sugar

1. Mix all ingredients.

CHOCOLATE-COVERED CHERRY CAKE

Serve with scoops of reduced-fat frozen yogurt or ice cream and Bitter-sweet Chocolate Sauce (see p. 641).

12 servings

1 jar (8 ounces) maraschino cherries, drained, syrup reserved
1 package (18.25 ounces) reduced-fat yellow cake mix
4 egg whites
1/2 cup margarine, softened
4-6 drops red food color
Chocolate Glaze (see p. 76)

Per Serving
Calories: 345
% Calories from fat: 28
Fat (gm): 10.9
Saturated fat (gm): 2.7
Cholesterol (mg): 0.1
Sodium (mg): 416
Protein (gm): 3
Carbohydrate (gm): 59.9
Exchanges
Milk: 0.0
Vegetable: 0.0
Fruit: 0.0
Bread: 3.5
Meat: 0.0
Fat: 2.0

1. Add enough water to reserved cherry syrup to measure 3/4 cup. Cut cherries in half; drain on paper toweling.

2. Mix cake mix, cherry syrup, egg whites, and margarine in large bowl on low speed until blended. Add food color and beat on medium speed 2 minutes; stir in cherries.

3. Pour batter into greased and floured 12-cup fluted cake pan. Bake at 350 degrees until toothpick inserted in center comes out clean, about 40 minutes. Cool on wire rack 10 minutes; remove from pan and cool. Drizzle with Chocolate Glaze.

CARRY-ALONG APPLE CAKE

The sugary apple topping can be spread on the cake, or spooned over pieces.

12 servings

1 package (18.25 ounces) reduced-fat yellow cake mix
1 package (3.4 ounces) instant vanilla pudding and pie filling
1 cup water
1/3 cup vegetable oil
4 eggs
Apple Topping (recipe follows)
Light whipped topping, as garnish

Per Serving
Calories: 362
% Calories from fat: 28
Fat (gm): 11.3
Saturated fat (gm): 2.6
Cholesterol (mg): 70.7
Sodium (mg): 457
Protein (gm): 4
Carbohydrate (gm): 61.4
Exchanges
Milk: 0.0
Vegetable: 0.0
Fruit: 1.0
Bread: 3.0
Meat: 0.0
Fat: 2.0

1. Beat cake mix, pudding and pie filling, water, oil, and eggs on low speed in large bowl until blended; beat on medium speed 2 minutes.

2. Pour batter into greased 13 x 9-inch baking pan. Bake at 350 degrees until toothpick inserted in center comes out clean, 30 to 35 minutes. Cool on wire rack.

3. Spread Apple Topping over cake; serve with light whipped topping.

Apple Topping

makes about 1 1/2 cups

2/3 cup sugar
3/4 cup orange juice
2 tablespoons lemon juice
3 cups shredded unpeeled apples

1. Heat sugar, orange juice, and lemon juice to boiling in medium saucepan. Reduce heat and simmer, uncovered, 10 minutes. Stir in apples; simmer until liquid is almost gone, about 10 minutes. Cool; refrigerate until chilled.

SWEET BEAN CAKE WITH BUTTERCREAM

A two-layer sheet cake, perfect for parties or picnics! The beans give the cake a wonderful moistness as well as a nutritional boost; 1 cup of canned pumpkin or mashed sweet potatoes can be substituted for the beans, if you wish.

16 servings

- 1 package (18.25 ounces) yellow cake mix
- 1 teaspoon ground cinnamon
- 6 egg whites *or* 1 cup no-cholesterol real egg product
- 2 tablespoons vegetable oil
- 1 1/3 cups water
- 1 can (15 ounces) great Northern beans, rinsed, drained, pureed *or* mashed
- 1 cup drained crushed pineapple
- 1 teaspoon vanilla
  Buttercream Frosting (recipe follows)

Per Serving
Calories: 355
% Calories from fat: 13
Fat (gm): 5.2
Saturated fat (gm): 1.5
Cholesterol (mg): 0.1
Sodium (mg): 248
Protein (gm): 4.7
Carbohydrate (gm): 72.9
Exchanges
Milk: 0.0
Vegetable: 0.0
Fruit: 0.0
Bread: 4.5
Meat: 0.0
Fat: 1.0

1. Mix all ingredients except Buttercream Frosting on low speed in large bowl until blended. Mix on medium speed 2 minutes.

2. Pour batter into 2 greased and floured 13 x 9-inch baking pans. Bake at 350 degrees until toothpick inserted in center comes out clean, 20 to 25 minutes. Cool cakes in pans on wire rack 10 minutes; remove from pans and cool completely.

3. Place 1 cake layer on serving tray; spread with scant 3/4 cup Buttercream Frosting. Top with second layer and frost top and side of cake.

Buttercream Frosting

makes about 3 cups

- 5 cups powdered sugar
- 2 tablespoons margarine, softened
- 1 teaspoon vanilla
- 3-4 tablespoons fat-free milk

1. Mix powdered sugar, margarine, vanilla, and enough milk to make spreading consistency.

RASPBERRY CREAM CAKE

As the frosting is made with whipped topping, this cake needs to be refrigerated. Serve with fresh raspberries for a summer treat, or make the cake with strawberry jam and serve with fresh strawberries.

12 servings

1 package (18.25 ounces) reduced-fat yellow cake mix
1¹/₃ cups water
2 tablespoons vegetable oil
3 eggs
¹/₂ cup seedless raspberry preserves
Raspberry Cream Frosting (recipe follows)

Per Serving
Calories: 321
% Calories from fat: 25
Fat (gm): 8.6
Saturated fat (gm): 3.7
Cholesterol (mg): 53
Sodium (mg): 325
Protein (gm): 3.3
Carbohydrate (gm): 55.8
Exchanges
Milk: 0.0
Vegetable: 0.0
Fruit: 0.0
Bread: 3.5
Meat: 0.0
Fat: 1.5

1. Mix all ingredients, except preserves and Raspberry Cream Frosting, on low speed in large bowl until blended; mix on medium speed 2 minutes.

2. Pour batter into 2 greased and floured 8- or 9-inch round cake pans. Bake at 350 degrees until toothpick inserted in center comes out clean, 20 to 25 minutes. Cool cake in pans on wire rack 10 minutes; remove from pans and cool completely.

3. Place 1 cake layer on serving plate; spread with raspberry preserves. Top with second cake layer and frost with Raspberry Cream Frosting. Refrigerate.

Raspberry Cream Frosting

makes about 2²/₃ cups

2²/₃ cups light whipped topping
¹/₄ cup powdered sugar
¹/₄ cup seedless raspberry preserves

1. Mix all ingredients.

CANDIED APPLE GOLD CAKE

A delicious cake, filled with pudding and topped with candied apple slices. Slip the apples in the oven during the last 10 to 15 minutes of cake baking time.

12 servings

1 package (18.5 ounces) reduced-fat yellow cake mix
1¹/₃ cups apple juice
2 tablespoons vegetable oil
3 eggs
Apple Cream Filling (recipe follows)
Candied Apple Topping (recipe follows)
Light whipped topping, as garnish

Per Serving
Calories: 329
% Calories from fat: 23
Fat (gm): 8.3
Saturated fat (gm): 2.5
Cholesterol (mg): 53
Sodium (mg): 456
Protein (gm): 3.3
Carbohydrate (gm): 60.1
Exchanges
Milk: 0.0
Vegetable: 0.0
Fruit: 0.0
Bread: 4.0
Meat: 0.0
Fat: 1.0

1. Mix cake mix, apple juice, oil, and eggs on low speed in large bowl until blended; mix on medium speed 2 minutes.

2. Pour batter into 2 greased and floured 9-inch round cake pans. Bake at 350 degrees until toothpick inserted in center comes out clean, 20 to 25 minutes. Cool in pans on wire rack 10 minutes; remove from pans and cool.

3. Place 1 cake layer on serving plate; spread with Apple Cream Filling. Top with remaining cake layer; arrange Candied Apple Topping on cake. Serve with whipped topping.

Apple Cream Filling

makes about 2 cups

- 1 package (3 ounces) vanilla pudding and pie filling
- 1¹/₄ cups apple juice
- ¹/₂ cup light whipped topping

1. Make pudding and pie filling according to package directions, using apple juice in place of milk. Cool. Fold in whipped topping.

Candied Apple Topping

- 2 medium baking apples, peeled, sliced
- 3 tablespoons granulated sugar
- 3 tablespoons packed light brown sugar
- 1 teaspoon grated orange, *or* lemon, rind
  Generous pinch ground nutmeg
- 1-2 tablespoons margarine

1. Arrange apples in 9-inch square baking pan; sprinkle with combined sugars, orange rind, and nutmeg. Dot with margarine and bake at 350 degrees until tender, 10 to 15 minutes. Cool.

Variation: **Caramel Candied Apple Cake**—Make cake as above, omitting Apple Cream Filling. Bake cake in 9-inch springform pan until toothpick comes out clean, 35 to 40 minutes. Cool on wire rack 10 minutes; remove side of pan and cool. Spoon Candied Apple Topping on cake. Heat 1¹/₂ cups fat-free caramel ice cream topping; spoon over cake slices and sprinkle with chopped nuts.

MARBLED CHOCOLATE CHERRY CAKE

This cake can be ready almost as quickly as you can say "party."

16 servings

1 jar (8 ounces) maraschino cherries, undrained
1 package (18.25 ounces) reduced-fat white cake mix
4 egg whites
6 tablespoons margarine, softened
4-5 drops red food color
2/3 cup fat-free chocolate syrup
Cocoa Drizzle (see p. 351)

Per Serving
Calories: 233
% Calories from fat: 26
Fat (gm): 6.7
Saturated fat (gm): 1.8
Cholesterol (mg): 0
Sodium (mg): 304
Protein (gm): 2.8
Carbohydrate (gm): 40.9
Exchanges
Milk: 0.0
Vegetable: 0.0
Fruit: 0.0
Bread: 2.5
Meat: 0.0
Fat: 1.0

1. Drain cherry syrup into measuring cup; add enough water to make 3/4 cup. Reserve 6 to 8 whole cherries; cut remaining cherries into fourths.

2. Make cake mix according to package directions, using 3/4 cup cherry syrup, egg whites, and margarine. Mix in quartered cherries and food color.

3. Pour 2/3 of the batter into greased and floured 12-cup fluted cake pan; mix chocolate syrup into remaining batter. Pour chocolate batter over batter in pan and swirl gently with knife.

4. Bake at 350 degrees until toothpick inserted in center comes out clean, about 40 minutes. Cool in pan on wire rack 10 minutes; remove from pan and cool completely. Top with Cocoa Drizzle and decorate with reserved cherries.

PEARS HÉLÈNE UPSIDE-DOWN CAKE

The easiest ever, using cake mix and canned pears. Yellow or white cake mix can be substituted for the chocolate.

8 servings

1/4 cup margarine

1/3 cup granulated, *or* packed light brown, sugar

1 can (16 ounces) pears, drained, sliced

6 maraschino cherries, halved

1 package (9 ounces) reduced-fat devil's food cake mix

2/3 cup water

1 egg

Chocolate Sauce (see p. 642)

Per Serving
Calories: 334
% Calories from fat: 26
Fat (gm): 10
Saturated fat (gm): 2.6
Cholesterol (mg): 27.1
Sodium (mg): 348
Protein (gm): 3.2
Carbohydrate (gm): 59.6
Exchanges
Milk: 0.0
Vegetable: 0.0
Fruit: 2.0
Bread: 2.0
Meat: 0.0
Fat: 1.5

1. Heat margarine and sugar until bubbly in small saucepan; pour into 8- or 9-inch round cake pan. Arrange pears and cherries in pan. Make cake mix according to package directions, using water and egg.

2. Pour batter into prepared pan; bake at 350 degrees until toothpick inserted in center of cake comes out clean, about 25 minutes. Immediately invert onto serving plate and cool. Serve with Chocolate Sauce.

CHOCOLATE CAKE TART

A cake decoratively topped with fruit to resemble a tart.

12 servings

1 package (18.25 ounces) reduced-fat devil's food cake mix

1¹/₃ cups water

2 tablespoons vegetable oil

3 eggs

¹/₄ cup cherry liqueur, optional

1 can (21 ounces) cherry pie filling

1-1¹/₂ cups light whipped topping

Chocolate curls, as garnish

Per Serving
Calories: 283
% Calories from fat: 25
Fat (gm): 8
Saturated fat (gm): 2.6
Cholesterol (mg): 53
Sodium (mg): 360
Protein (gm): 3.5
Carbohydrate (gm): 50
Exchanges
Milk: 0.0
Vegetable: 0.0
Fruit: 0.0
Bread: 3.0
Meat: 0.0
Fat: 1.5

1. Mix cake mix, water, oil, and eggs on low speed in large bowl until blended; mix on medium speed 2 minutes.

2. Pour batter into greased and floured 10-inch springform pan. Bake at 350 degrees until cake springs back when touched, 40 to 50 minutes. Cool cake on wire rack 10 minutes. Loosen side of pan with sharp knife; remove side of pan and cool cake completely.

3. Pierce top of cake with long-tined fork; drizzle with cherry liqueur. Spread cherry pie filling on top of cake. Spoon whipped topping into pastry bag fitted with medium star tip; pipe border on top and bottom edges of cake. Garnish with chocolate curls.

CHOCOLATE-DATE CAKE

The flavor of dates blends particularly well with chocolate in this easy cake. For chocolate addicts, the cake can also be frosted with Chocolate Buttercream (see p. 74).

16 servings

1 package (18.25 ounces) reduced-fat devil's food cake mix

1 cup water

1/3 cup applesauce

1/3 cup chopped dates

6 egg whites *or* 3/4 cup no-cholesterol real egg product
Chocolate Buttercream (see p. 74)

Per Serving
Calories: 320
% Calories from fat: 11
Fat (gm): 4.1
Saturated fat (gm): 1.4
Cholesterol (mg): 0.2
Sodium (mg): 289
Protein (gm): 3
Carbohydrate (gm): 67.7
Exchanges
Milk: 0.0
Vegetable: 0.0
Fruit: 0.0
Bread: 4.5
Meat: 0.0
Fat: 0.0

1. Mix all ingredients, except Chocolate Buttercream Frosting, on low speed in large bowl until blended. Mix on medium speed 2 minutes.

2. Pour batter into 2 greased and floured 8- or 9-inch round cake pans. Bake at 350 degrees until cakes spring back when lightly touched, about 25 minutes. Cool in pans on wire rack 10 minutes; remove from pans and cool completely.

3. Place 1 cake layer on serving plate; frost with about 1/2 cup Chocolate Buttercream. Top with remaining cake layer; frost top and side of cake.

TRIPLE CHOCOLATE BUNDT CAKE

Pudding mix adds flavor and moistness to this dark chocolate cake.

16 servings

1 package (18.25 ounces) reduced-fat devil's food cake mix

1 cup fat-free sour cream

1/3 cup fat-free milk

1/4 cup margarine, room temperature

1 teaspoon vanilla

2 eggs

1 package (3.9 ounces) chocolate fudge pudding mix

1-2 ounces white baking chocolate, melted

Per Serving
Calories: 220
% Calories from fat: 28
Fat (gm): 6.9
Saturated fat (gm): 2.1
Cholesterol (mg): 26.9
Sodium (mg): 423
Protein (gm): 3.5
Carbohydrate (gm): 36.1
Exchanges
Milk: 0.0
Vegetable: 0.0
Fruit: 0.0
Bread: 2.5
Meat: 0.0
Fat: 1.0

1. Mix all ingredients, except white chocolate, in large bowl on low speed until blended. Mix on medium speed 2 minutes.

2. Pour batter into greased and floured 12-cup fluted cake or tube pan. Bake at 350 degrees until toothpick inserted in center comes out clean, about 45 minutes. Cool on wire rack 10 minutes; remove from pan and cool completely.

3. Using small spoon or pastry bag, drizzle chocolate over top of cake.

Variation: **Caramel Spice Bundt Cake**—Make cake as above using spice cake mix and butterscotch pudding mix; omit white chocolate. Spread cake with warm Caramel Glaze. To make **Caramel Glaze**, heat 1 1/2 teaspoons margarine and 1 tablespoon light brown sugar in small saucepan until margarine is melted. Remove from heat; stir in 1/2 cup powdered sugar and 2 teaspoons hot water. Cook over medium-low heat, stirring constantly, until smooth.

ZANY BROWNIE BARS

Anything goes with this zany mix of flavors and textures.

24 brownies (1 per serving)

1 package (15 ounces) reduced-fat fudge brownie mix
Water
1 package (14 ounces) chocolate, *or* regular, caramels (about 50 caramels)
2 tablespoons water
1/2 cup chocolate-covered raisins
1/3 cup walnut pieces
1/3 cup flaked coconut

Per Serving
Calories: 166
% Calories from fat: 20
Fat (gm): 3.8
Saturated fat (gm): 1.3
Cholesterol (mg): 0.1
Sodium (mg): 67
Protein (gm): 1.4
Carbohydrate (gm): 32.5

1. Mix brownie mix with water according to package directions. Spread batter in greased 13 x 9-inch square pan. Bake according to package directions.

2. Heat caramels and water in small saucepan over medium-low heat, or microwave in glass measure until melted, 2 1/2 to 3 minutes, stirring every minute. Pour caramel mixture over brownies; sprinkle with chocolate-covered raisins, walnuts, and coconut. Broil 6 inches from heat source until coconut is toasted, 1 to 2 minutes. Cool on wire rack; cut into squares.

OATMEAL BROWNIES

Quickly made with a mix, these brownies are baked on a healthful oats crust.

3 dozen (1 per serving)

Oats Crust (recipe follows)
1 package (22 ounces) reduced-fat brownie mix
Water

Per Serving
Calories: 153
% Calories from fat: 32
Fat (gm): 5.5
Saturated fat (gm): 1.1
Cholesterol (mg): 0
Sodium (mg): 140
Protein (gm): 2.3
Carbohydrate (gm): 24.3
Exchanges
Milk: 0.0
Vegetable: 0.0
Fruit: 0.0
Bread: 1.5
Meat: 0.0
Fat: 1.0

1. Pat Oats Crust evenly in bottom of greased 13 x 9-inch baking pan. Bake at 350 degrees until lightly browned, about 10 minutes; cool on wire rack.

2. Make brownies with water according to package directions. Pour batter over Oats Crust. Bake according to package directions. Cool on wire rack.

Oats Crust

12 tablespoons margarine, melted
2¹/₂ cups quick-cooking oats
³/₄ cup packed light brown sugar
³/₄ cup all-purpose flour
¹/₂ teaspoon baking soda
¹/₄ teaspoon salt

1. Combine all ingredients; mix well.

CARAMEL ROCKY ROAD BARS

Super-easy to make with purchased cookie dough!

3 dozen brownies (1 per serving)

1 package (20 ounces) refrigerated re-duced-fat chocolate chip cookie dough
1 package (14 ounces) caramels (about 50 caramels)
2 tablespoons water
1/2 cup dry-roasted peanuts
2 cups miniature marshmallows

Per Serving
Calories: 125
% Calories from fat: 21
Fat (gm): 3
Saturated fat (gm): 0.2
Cholesterol (mg): 0
Sodium (mg): 71
Protein (gm): 1.3
Carbohydrate (gm): 23.5
Exchanges
Milk: 0.0
Vegetable: 0.0
Fruit: 0.0
Bread: 1.5
Meat: 0.0
Fat: 0.5

1. Cut cookie dough into 1/2-inch slices and arrange in bottom of 13 x 9-inch baking pan; press cookies together to form even layer in bottom and 1 inch up side of pan. Bake at 350 degrees until lightly browned, 15 to 18 minutes.

2. Microwave caramels and water in glass measure until melted, 21/2 to 3 minutes, stirring every minute, or stir in saucepan on low heat until melted. Pour caramel mixture over crust; sprinkle with peanuts and marshmallows.

3. Broil 5 inches from heat source until marshmallows are browned, 1 to 2 minutes. Cool on wire rack; cut into squares.

CAMPUS BARS

You don't have to be a college student to love these easy-to-make bar cookies!

30 bars (1 per serving)

2 1/4 cups graham cracker crumbs
1 can (14 ounces) fat-free sweetened condensed milk
1/2 cup reduced-fat semisweet chocolate morsels
1/2 can (3 1/2-ounce size) flaked coconut
1/3 cup chopped walnuts
2 teaspoons vanilla
1/4 teaspoon salt

Per Serving
Calories: 125
% Calories from fat: 27
Fat (gm): 4
Saturated fat (gm): 1.8
Cholesterol (mg): 0
Sodium (mg): 74
Protein (gm): 2.5
Carbohydrate (gm): 20.9
Exchanges
Milk: 0.0
Vegetable: 0.0
Fruit: 0.0
Bread: 1.5
Meat: 0.0
Fat: 0.5

1. Mix all ingredients in bowl; press evenly in greased 11 x 7-inch baking pan. Bake at 350 degrees until set and browned, 20 to 30 minutes. Cool on wire rack.

EASY ICED MOLASSES COOKIES

Quick-to-mix cookies are iced with an easy frosting made from a mix. Bake the cookies you need, then freeze remaining dough for a later time.

6 dozen cookies (1 per serving)

- ¹/₂ cup vegetable shortening
- ³/₄ cup packed light brown sugar
- ¹/₂ cup light molasses
- 1 egg
- 2¹/₄ cups all-purpose flour
- ³/₄ teaspoon baking soda
- ¹/₂ teaspoon salt
- 1-2 teaspoons ground allspice
  Easy Icing (recipe follows)

Per Serving
Calories: 66
% Calories from fat: 19
Fat (gm): 1.4
Saturated fat (gm): 0.4
Cholesterol (mg): 2.9
Sodium (mg): 47
Protein (gm): 0.6
Carbohydrate (gm): 12.9
Exchanges
Milk: 0.0
Vegetable: 0.0
Fruit: 0.0
Bread: 1.0
Meat: 0.0
Fat: 0.0

1. Beat shortening, brown sugar, molasses, and egg in large bowl until blended; mix in remaining ingredients, except Easy Icing. Refrigerate dough 2 to 3 hours.

2. Roll dough on floured surface to scant ¹/₄ inch thickness; cut into decorative shapes with 2- to 3-inch cutters. Bake on greased cookie sheets until browned, 8 to 10 minutes. Cool on wire racks. Frost with Easy Icing.

Easy Icing

- 1 package (15.4 ounces) creamy white frosting mix
- ¹/₃ cup very hot water
- 2 tablespoons light corn syrup
  Food color, optional

1. Make frosting mix according to package directions, using hot water and corn syrup; mix in a few drops of food color, if desired.

BERRY CREAM CHEESE TARTS

Fast to make with purchased crusts—use any berry in season.

6 servings

2 packages (8 ounces each) fat-free cream cheese, softened

2/3 cup sugar

2 eggs

6 graham cracker tart shells

1 1/4 cups blueberries *or* raspberries

1/3 cup currant, *or* apple, jelly, melted

Per Serving
Calories: 361
% Calories from fat: 22
Fat (gm): 8.8
Saturated fat (gm): 2.2
Cholesterol (mg): 76.7
Sodium (mg): 591
Protein (gm): 14.2
Carbohydrate (gm): 56.7
Exchanges
Milk: 0.0
Vegetable: 0.0
Fruit: 0.0
Bread: 4.0
Meat: 1.0
Fat: 1.0

1. Beat cream cheese in large bowl until fluffy; beat in sugar and eggs.

2. Pour mixture into tart shells. Bake at 350 degrees just until set, about 15 minutes. Cool on wire racks. Refrigerate 8 hours or overnight.

3. Arrange berries on tarts and brush with jelly.

BLENDER CHEESE PIE

A purchased crust with a blender filling—what could be easier?

8 servings

2/3 cup 1% low-fat creamed cottage cheese

1 package (8 ounces) fat-free cream cheese, softened, cut into pieces

1/2 cup sugar

2 eggs

2 teaspoons vanilla

1 reduced-fat graham cracker crust

1 can (16 ounces) cherry, *or* blueberry, pie filling

Per Serving
Calories: 282
% Calories from fat: 23
Fat (gm): 7.2
Saturated fat (gm): 1.9
Cholesterol (mg): 56.1
Sodium (mg): 346
Protein (gm): 9
Carbohydrate (gm): 45.2
Exchanges
Milk: 0.0
Vegetable: 0.0
Fruit: 1.0
Bread: 2.0
Meat: 0.0
Fat: 1.5

1. Process cottage cheese in blender or food processor until smooth; add remaining ingredients, except graham cracker crust and cherry pie filling, and process until smooth.

2. Pour filling into crust. Bake at 350 degrees until just set in the center, 20 to 25 minutes.

3. Cool on wire rack; refrigerate 8 hours or overnight. Spoon cherry pie filling over top of cheesecake.

BANANA SPLIT CHEESECAKE

Couldn't be easier or tastier! Garnish with whipped topping and chopped nuts for an extra touch.

8 servings

1 package (21.4 ounces) no-bake straw-berry, *or* cherry, cheesecake
2 tablespoons sugar
3 tablespoons margarine
2-3 tablespoons honey
1½ cups 1% low-fat milk
¼-½ teaspoon banana extract
2 bananas, sliced, divided

Per Serving
Calories: 352
% Calories from fat: 22
Fat (gm): 8.9
Saturated fat (gm): 3.7
Cholesterol (mg): 1.8
Sodium (mg): 383
Protein (gm): 5.9
Carbohydrate (gm): 63.4
Exchanges
Milk: 0.0
Vegetable: 0.0
Fruit: 1.0
Bread: 3.0
Meat: 0.0
Fat: 1.5

1. Make crust according to package directions, mixing graham cracker crumbs from package, sugar, margarine, and honey; reserve 2 tablespoons crumb mixture. Press remaining mixture evenly on bottom and ½ inch up side of 9-inch pie pan.

2. Make cheesecake according to package directions, using 1% milk and adding banana extract and 1 sliced banana.

3. Spoon filling into crust; sprinkle with reserved crumbs. Refrigerate until cheesecake is set, about 1 hour. At serving time, arrange remaining banana on top and drizzle with fruit packet from package.

BUTTERSCOTCH CHEESECAKE

Truly quick and easy, using the microwave oven and food processor. A purchased low-fat crust may be used when you are really in a rush; nutritional information will change, however.

12 servings

Chocolate Cookie Crumb Crust (see p. 134)

1/2 package (12-ounce size) butterscotch chips

2 packages (8 ounces each) fat-free cream cheese, softened

1 can (14 ounces) fat-free sweetened condensed milk

2 eggs

Per Serving
Calories: 330
% Calories from fat: 30
Fat (gm): 10.7
Saturated fat (gm): 5.1
Cholesterol (mg): 38.4
Sodium (mg): 416
Protein (gm): 10
Carbohydrate (gm): 46.6
Exchanges
Milk: 0.0
Vegetable: 0.0
Fruit: 0.0
Bread: 3.0
Meat: 0.0
Fat: 2.5

1. Make Chocolate Cookie Crumb Crust, pressing mixture evenly on bottom and 1/2 inch up side of 9-inch springform pan.

2. Microwave butterscotch chips in 4-cup glass measure until melted, 2 to 3 minutes, stirring every 30 seconds; or melt over medium-low heat in saucepan, stirring frequently.

3. Beat cream cheese in large bowl until fluffy; beat in melted chips, sweetened condensed milk, and eggs.

4. Pour filling into crust. Bake at 300 degrees until center is just set, 50 to 60 minutes. Cool on wire rack. Refrigerate 8 hours or overnight.

STRAWBERRY CREAM CHEESE SQUARES

Strawberries and cream cheese on a pretzel crust! The saltiness of the pretzels accentuates the sweetness of the strawberries.

9 servings

1¹/₂ cups coarsely crushed pretzels

2-3 tablespoons margarine, melted

2-3 tablespoons light corn syrup

1 package (8 ounces) fat-free cream cheese, softened

¹/₂ cup sugar

2 cups light whipped topping

2 cups boiling water

2 packages (3 ounces each) strawberry-flavored gelatin

2 packages (10 ounces each) frozen sweetened strawberries, partially thawed

Per Serving
Calories: 301
% Calories from fat: 15
Fat (gm): 5.3
Saturated fat (gm): 2.6
Cholesterol (mg): 2
Sodium (mg): 465
Protein (gm): 6.5
Carbohydrate (gm): 57.7
Exchanges
Milk: 0.0
Vegetable: 0.0
Fruit: 1.0
Bread: 2.5
Meat: 0.0
Fat: 1.0

1. Combine pretzels, margarine, and corn syrup; press mixture into bottom of greased 13 x 9-inch baking pan. Bake at 350 degrees until set, about 10 minutes. Cool on wire rack.

2. Beat cream cheese and sugar until smooth; fold in whipped topping. Pour mixture onto cooled crust. Refrigerate while preparing strawberry topping.

3. Pour boiling water over gelatin in large bowl; stir until dissolved. Add strawberries, stirring until thawed. Spoon strawberry mixture over cream cheese mixture. Refrigerate until set, about 4 hours.

EASY PEACH CRISP

This fast-to-make dessert can bake while you're eating dinner.

8 servings

6 cups sliced frozen, *or* canned, drained, peaches

1/4 cup sugar

Easy Crisp Topping (recipe follows)

Per Serving
Calories: 362
% Calories from fat: 17
Fat (gm): 7.2
Saturated fat (gm): 1.4
Cholesterol (mg): 0
Sodium (mg): 254
Protein (gm): 3.2
Carbohydrate (gm): 74.2
Exchanges
Milk: 0.0
Vegetable: 0.0
Fruit: 3.0
Bread: 2.0
Meat: 0.0
Fat: 1.0

1. Spoon peaches into 2-quart casserole; toss with sugar. Sprinkle Easy Crisp Topping over peaches. Bake at 350 degrees until cobbler is browned and bubbly, 35 to 45 minutes.

Easy Crisp Topping

1 cup reduced-fat baking mix
1/2 cup quick-cooking oats
1/3 cup packed light brown sugar
1/2 teaspoon ground cinnamon
Generous pinch ground nutmeg
4 tablespoons cold margarine, cut into pieces

1. Combine all ingredients, except margarine, in medium bowl. Cut in margarine until mixture resembles coarse crumbs.

APPLE PEACHY CRISP

Canned apple pie filling makes easy work of this granola-topped fruit crisp. Serve warm with reduced-fat ice cream.

8 servings

1 can (21 ounces) apple pie filling
2 cups coarsely chopped peeled peaches
1/4 cup dried cranberries *or* raisins
1/4 cup packed light brown sugar
1/2 teaspoon ground cinnamon
1/8 teaspoon ground mace
2 tablespoons flour
Granola Topping (see p. 495)

Per Serving
Calories: 277
% Calories from fat: 16
Fat (gm): 5.3
Saturated fat (gm): 3
Cholesterol (mg): 12.3
Sodium (mg): 130
Protein (gm): 2.9
Carbohydrate (gm): 57.2
Exchanges
Milk: 0.0
Vegetable: 0.0
Fruit: 2.5
Bread: 1.0
Meat: 0.0
Fat: 1.0

1. Mix all ingredients, except Granola Topping, in 1 1/2-quart casserole; sprinkle with Granola Topping. Bake at 350 degrees until fruit is bubbly, about 45 minutes.

SPICED BLUEBERRY COBBLER

Baking mix makes easy work of this summer fruit cobbler.

6 servings

4 cups fresh, *or* frozen, blueberries
1/3 cup packed light brown sugar
1/4 cup water, divided
1 tablespoon cornstarch
Spiced Cobbler Topping
(recipe follows)

Per Serving
Calories: 234
% Calories from fat: 20
Fat (gm): 5.4
Saturated fat (gm): 1
Cholesterol (mg): 0.2
Sodium (mg): 290
Protein (gm): 2.6
Carbohydrate (gm): 45.6
Exchanges
Milk: 0.0
Vegetable: 0.0
Fruit: 2.0
Bread: 1.0
Meat: 0.0
Fat: 1.0

1. Heat blueberries, sugar, and 2 tablespoons water to boiling in medium saucepan; stir in combined cornstarch and remaining 2 tablespoons water, stirring until thickened. Pour mixture into 1 1/2-quart casserole or 11 x 7-inch baking dish.

2. Spoon Spiced Cobbler Topping into 6 mounds on top of hot mixture. Bake at 375 degrees until browned, 15 to 20 minutes.

Spiced Cobbler Topping

    1 cup reduced-fat all-purpose baking mix
  1/4 cup fat-free milk
    2 tablespoons melted margarine
    2 tablespoons sugar
  1/2 teaspoon ground cinnamon
  1/8 teaspoon ground nutmeg
     Generous pinch ground mace *or* cardamom

1. Mix all ingredients in bowl, forming a soft dough.

BLUEBERRY BREAD COBBLER

Layers of buttered bread and berries bake to sweet goodness. Use a firm day-old bread—honey wheat, multi-grain, or sourdough are our preferences.

6 servings

    4 cups fresh, *or* frozen, blueberries
  3/4 cup sugar
  1/8 teaspoon ground nutmeg
    8 slices firm day-old bread
 2-3 tablespoons margarine

Per Serving
Calories: 274
% Calories from fat: 17
Fat (gm): 5.4
Saturated fat (gm): 1.1
Cholesterol (mg): 0.3
Sodium (mg): 229
Protein (gm): 3.4
Carbohydrate (gm): 55.3
Exchanges
Milk: 0.0
Vegetable: 0.0
Fruit: 1.0
Bread: 2.5
Meat: 0.0
Fat: 1.0

1. Heat blueberries, sugar, and nutmeg to boiling in large saucepan; reduce heat and simmer 2 to 3 minutes.

2. Trim 4 bread slices to fit in bottom of 8-inch baking pan; spread both sides of bread slices with margarine and place in pan. Pour 1/2 of the blueberry mixture over bread. Repeat with remaining bread slices and blueberry mixture.

3. Bake at 350 degrees until bubbly, 25 to 30 minutes. Serve warm.

RUM TRIFLE

This easy trifle uses pudding mix and purchased angel food cake. Substitute homemade Basic Angel Food Cake (p. 112), if you like.

10 servings

1/2 cup light rum *or* 2 tablespoons rum extract and 1/3 cup orange juice

3/4 cup golden raisins

1/4 cup chopped almonds

1 package (3 ounces) vanilla pudding and pie filling

2 1/2 cups fat-free milk

2 cups light whipped topping, divided

1 angel food cake (10 ounces), cut into 1/2-inch cubes

Sliced almonds, as garnish

Per Serving
Calories: 326
% Calories from fat: 9
Fat (gm): 3.2
Saturated fat (gm): 1.8
Cholesterol (mg): 1.1
Sodium (mg): 536
Protein (gm): 6
Carbohydrate (gm): 59.7
Exchanges
Milk: 0.0
Vegetable: 0.0
Fruit: 0.0
Bread: 4.5
Meat: 0.0
Fat: 0.0

1. Combine rum, raisins, and almonds in small bowl; let stand 1 hour.

2. Prepare pudding according to package directions, using 2 1/2 cups milk; cool. Fold in 1 cup whipped topping.

3. Layer 1/3 of the cake cubes, 1/3 of the raisin mixture, and 1/3 of the pudding mixture in glass bowl; repeat twice, ending with pudding. Cover. Refrigerate several hours or overnight. Spread trifle with remaining 1 cup whipped topping and sprinkle with almonds.

EASY APPLE PUDDING

Rich in flavor and texture, yet low in calories and fat.

4 servings

- 1/3 cup packed light brown sugar
- 1 tablespoon cornstarch
- 1/4 cup fat-free milk
- 2-3 tablespoons margarine
- 1 tablespoon lemon juice
- 1 can (21 ounces) apple pie filling
- Chopped pecans, as garnish

Per Serving
Calories: 284
% Calories from fat: 18
Fat (gm): 5.8
Saturated fat (gm): 1.2
Cholesterol (mg): 0.3
Sodium (mg): 147
Protein (gm): 0.8
Carbohydrate (gm): 59.8
Exchanges
Milk: 0.0
Vegetable: 0.0
Fruit: 4.0
Bread: 0.0
Meat: 0.0
Fat: 1.0

1. Combine brown sugar, cornstarch, and milk in small saucepan; whisk over medium-high heat until boiling and thickened. Stir in margarine and lemon juice; mix in pie filling. Spoon into dishes and refrigerate until chilled. Sprinkle with chopped pecans.

BAKED ALMOND FRUIT PUDDING

Canned fruit and pie filling bake into a comforting warm pudding.

8 servings

- 1 can (21 ounces) apple pie filling
- 1 can (16 ounces) sliced peaches in juice, drained
- 1/4 cup dried cranberries *or* raisins
- 1/4 cup packed light brown sugar
- 2 tablespoons flour
- 1/2 teaspoon ground cinnamon
- 1/8 teaspoon ground nutmeg
- 1/2 teaspoon almond extract
- 1/4-1/3 cup sliced almonds

Per Serving
Calories: 176
% Calories from **fat: 9**
Fat (gm): 1.8
Saturated fat (gm): 0.2
Cholesterol (mg): 0
Sodium (mg): 38
Protein (gm): 1.3
Carbohydrate (gm): 38.2
Exchanges
Milk: 0.0
Vegetable: 0.0
Fruit: 2.5
Bread: 0.0
Meat: 0.0
Fat: 0.5

1. Mix all ingredients, except almonds. Pour into 1 1/2-quart casserole; sprinkle with almonds. Bake, uncovered, at 350 degrees until bubbly, about 30 minutes.

CHOCOLATE TAPIOCA PUDDING

This dessert couldn't be easier!

6 servings

  3   tablespoons quick-cooking tapioca
¹/₈ teaspoon salt
  1   egg, beaten
2³/₄ cups chocolate-flavored 2% reduced-fat milk
  1   teaspoon vanilla

Per Serving
Calories: 107
% Calories from fat: 19
Fat (gm): 2.3
Saturated fat (gm): 1.4
Cholesterol (mg): 7.8
Sodium (mg): 126
Protein (gm): 4.3
Carbohydrate (gm): 17.2
Exchanges
Milk: 0.0
Vegetable: 0.0
Fruit: 0.0
Bread: 1.0
Meat: 0.0
Fat: 0.5

1. Mix all ingredients, except vanilla, in medium saucepan. Let stand 5 minutes. Heat to boiling, stirring constantly. Remove from heat; stir in vanilla. Let stand 20 minutes; stir. Refrigerate until cold.

EASY CARAMEL PUDDING

This easy stove-top pudding is flavored with caramels. It's delicious spooned warm over pound cake or warm baked apples, or top bowls of chilled pudding with sliced peaches or bananas.

6 servings

  3   tablespoons cornstarch
  3   cups fat-free milk
¹/₂ package (14 ounces) caramels (about 25 caramels)
  2   eggs, lightly beaten
  1   tablespoon margarine
¹/₄ cup chopped toasted pecans

Per Serving
Calories: 251
% Calories from fat: 28
Fat (gm): 7.9
Saturated fat (gm): 1.5
Cholesterol (mg): 72.9
Sodium (mg): 115
Protein (gm): 7.4
Carbohydrate (gm): 39.4
Exchanges
Milk: 0.5
Vegetable: 0.0
Fruit: 0.0
Bread: 2.0
Meat: 0.0
Fat: 1.5

1. Combine cornstarch and milk in medium saucepan; add caramels. Cook over medium heat until caramels are melted, stirring frequently, about 10 minutes.

2. Whisk about ¹/₂ of the caramel mixture into eggs in small bowl; whisk egg mixture into saucepan. Whisk over medium-high heat just to boiling, about 1 minute. Remove from heat and stir in margarine.

3. Pour into bowl; cover top of pudding with plastic wrap and cool to room temperature. Refrigerate until chilled.

4. Spoon pudding into serving dishes; sprinkle with pecans.

CITRUS PUMPKIN PUDDING

Use of convenience foods makes this creamy pudding one of the fastest desserts ever.

8 servings

1 package (3.9 ounces) instant lemon, *or* orange, pudding and pie filling
1 cup reduced-fat lemon, *or* orange, yogurt
1 cup canned pumpkin
1 tablespoon grated lemon, *or* orange, rind
1 teaspoon pumpkin pie spice
1 cup light whipped topping
Light whipped topping, as garnish
Chopped pecans *or* walnuts, as garnish

Per Serving
Calories: 105
% Calories from fat: 14
Fat (gm): 1.6
Saturated fat (gm): 1.3
Cholesterol (mg): 1.9
Sodium (mg): 187
Protein (gm): 1.6
Carbohydrate (gm): 21
Exchanges
Milk: 0.0
Vegetable: 0.0
Fruit: 0.0
Bread: 1.5
Meat: 0.0
Fat: 0.0

1. Beat pudding and pie filling and lemon yogurt in medium bowl on low speed 1 minute. Beat in pumpkin, lemon rind, and pumpkin pie spice; fold in 1 cup light whipped topping. Spoon into serving bowl or dishes. At serving time, top with dollops of light whipped topping and sprinkle with pecans.

BANANA BOURBON CRÈME

Creamy banana pudding, easy to make and spiked with bourbon!

6 servings

1 envelope unflavored gelatin

$1/4$ cup cold water

1 package (3.4 ounces) instant banana cream pudding and pie filling

1 cup fat-free milk

2 tablespoons bourbon *or* $1/2$-1 teaspoon brandy extract

2 tablespoons packed light brown sugar

$2^1/2$ cups light whipped topping

1 medium banana, sliced

Chopped pecans *or* walnuts, as garnish

Per Serving
Calories: 191
% Calories from fat: 17
Fat (gm): 3.6
Saturated fat (gm): 3.4
Cholesterol (mg): 0.7
Sodium (mg): 273
Protein (gm): 1.7
Carbohydrate (gm): 33.9
Exchanges
Milk: 0.0
Vegetable: 0.0
Fruit: 0.0
Bread: 2.0
Meat: 0.0
Fat: 1.0

1. Sprinkle gelatin over water in small saucepan; let stand 2 to 3 minutes. Cook over low heat until dissolved.

2. Beat pudding and pie mix, milk, gelatin mixture, bourbon, and brown sugar in medium bowl 2 minutes. Fold in whipped topping and bananas. Spoon pudding into serving bowl or dishes; sprinkle with pecans. Refrigerate until set, 2 to 3 hours.

STRAWBERRY CLOUD PUDDING

Quick, light, and delicious! Substitute lemon or orange gelatin and yogurt for the strawberry, or experiment with other combinations.

4 servings

1 package (3 ounces) strawberry-flavored gelatin

1 cup boiling water

1 cup cold water

1 cup low-fat strawberry yogurt

Fresh strawberries, as garnish

Per Serving
Calories: 100
% Calories from fat: 6
Fat (gm): 0.7
Saturated fat (gm): 0.4
Cholesterol (mg): 3.7
Sodium (mg): 59
Protein (gm): 3.2
Carbohydrate (gm): 21
Exchanges
Milk: 0.0
Vegetable: 0.0
Fruit: 0.0
Bread: 1.5
Meat: 0.0
Fat: 0.0

1. Dissolve gelatin in boiling water. Add cold water and chill until mixture mounds on spoon. Place bowl in larger bowl filled with ice and water. Add yogurt and beat at high speed until fluffy. Spoon into serving bowl or dishes; refrigerate until set. Garnish with strawberries.

RASPBERRY RHUBARB MOUSSE

This delicious mousse is made with frozen berries, which help set the gelatin. Frozen rhubarb can be used also, giving the flavors of summer even in mid-winter.

8 servings

- 4 cups sliced rhubarb (about 1 pound)
- 1/4 cup water
- 1/3 cup sugar
- 1 package (3 ounces) raspberry-flavored gelatin
- 1 package (12 ounces) frozen unsweetened raspberries
- 3 cups light whipped topping

Per Serving
Calories: 142
% Calories from fat: 20
Fat (gm): 3.1
Saturated fat (gm): 3
Cholesterol (mg): 0
Sodium (mg): 15
Protein (gm): 1.2
Carbohydrate (gm): 25.7
Exchanges
Milk: 0.0
Vegetable: 0.0
Fruit: 2.0
Bread: 0.0
Meat: 0.0
Fat: 0.5

1. Cook rhubarb, water, and sugar in large saucepan until tender, about 10 minutes. Add gelatin and stir until dissolved. Stir in raspberries until well mixed. Fold in whipped topping. Pour into serving bowl. Chill until set, about 4 hours.

CRANBERRY MOUSSE

This dessert couldn't be easier!

6 servings

1 cup boiling water

1 package (3 ounces) cranberry-raspberry-flavored gelatin

1 can (16 ounces) whole-berry cranberry sauce

2 cups light whipped topping

1/4 cup chopped toasted pecans

Per Serving
Calories: 220
% Calories from fat: 25
Fat (gm): 6
Saturated fat (gm): 2.9
Cholesterol (mg): 0
Sodium (mg): 40
Protein (gm): 1.2
Carbohydrate (gm): 40.4
Exchanges
Milk: 0.0
Vegetable: 0.0
Fruit: 2.5
Bread: 0.0
Meat: 0.0
Fat: 1.5

1. Combine boiling water and gelatin, stirring until dissolved; stir in cranberry sauce. Refrigerate until mixture mounds when dropped from a spoon, about 30 minutes. Fold in whipped topping.

2. Spoon into serving dishes and sprinkle with pecans. Chill until set, 2 to 3 hours.

CALYPSO PARFAITS

Tropical fruits combine to make this refreshing parfait.

6 servings

2 envelopes unflavored gelatin

1/2 cup orange juice

1 small banana, sliced

1 small ripe mango, peeled, diced

1 teaspoon chopped crystallized ginger

1/4 cup sweetened flaked coconut

1 pint orange sherbet

Per Serving
Calories: 164
% Calories from fat: 13
Fat (gm): 2.5
Saturated fat (gm): 1.8
Cholesterol (mg): 4.7
Sodium (mg): 37
Protein (gm): 1.5
Carbohydrate (gm): 35.8
Exchanges
Milk: 0.0
Vegetable: 0.0
Fruit: 1.0
Bread: 1.5
Meat: 0.0
Fat: 0.0

1. Sprinkle gelatin over orange juice in small saucepan; let stand 2 to 3 minutes to soften. Heat over low heat until dissolved.

2. Process fruit, ginger, and coconut in food processor or blender until smooth; pour in gelatin mixture with motor running. Add sherbet and process until smooth. Pour into parfait glasses. Chill until set, 2 to 3 hours.

CARAMEL BANANAS FOSTER

A new twist on Bananas Foster, using caramel candies.

4 servings

- $^1/_2$ package (14-ounce size) caramels (about 25 caramels)
- $^1/_3$ cup fat-free milk
- 1 tablespoon margarine
- $^1/_2$ teaspoon rum extract
- 2 medium bananas, sliced
- 1 pint fat-free vanilla ice cream *or* frozen yogurt

Per Serving
Calories: 355
% Calories from fat: 10
Fat (gm): 4.4
Saturated fat (gm): 1
Cholesterol (mg): 0.4
Sodium (mg): 127
Protein (gm): 6.3
Carbohydrate (gm): 77.9
Exchanges
Milk: 0.0
Vegetable: 0.0
Fruit: 1.0
Bread: 3.5
Meat: 0.0
Fat: 1.0

1. Heat caramels and milk in small saucepan on medium-low heat until melted, 3 to 4 minutes, stirring frequently. Stir in margarine and rum extract.

2. Add bananas to caramel mixture; cook over low heat 1 to 2 minutes. Spoon mixture over ice cream in bowls.

TWELVE

Free
AND
Equal® Desserts

Recipes in this chapter were tested only with Equal® brand sweetener; if you use another brand of artificial sweetener and want to use these recipes, you may need to experiment.

These recipes were carefully developed with the same low-fat guidelines used throughout the cookbook. The percentage of calories from fat noted in the Nutritional Analysis for each of these recipes is skewed, however, appearing higher than if the recipes were made with sugar; sugar contains 770 calories per cup and thus effects the mathematical calculation for determining fat percentage. For example, Dark Flourless Chocolate Cake (see p. 573), if made with 1 cup sugar instead of $7^1/_4$ teaspoons Equal® for Recipes, would calculate to be 35 percent calories from fat, rather than 47 percent. Even with the skewed higher figures for fat percentage, two-thirds of the recipes in this chapter meet our criterion of 35 percent calories or less from fat.

GLAZED APPLESAUCE-RAISIN CAKE

Cream cheese glaze is a perfect topping for this moist cake—or serve plain with scoops of sugar-free, fat-free frozen yogurt.

12 to 16 servings

   1 cup unsweetened applesauce
  ²/₃ cup vegetable oil
   2 eggs
   1 teaspoon maple extract *or* vanilla
  ³/₄ cup raisins
  ¹/₂ cup coarsely chopped walnuts, optional
   2 cups all-purpose flour
 7¹/₄ teaspoons Equal® for Recipes *or* 24 packets Equal® sweetener
   1 teaspoon baking soda
  ¹/₄ teaspoon salt
 1¹/₂ teaspoons ground cinnamon
  ¹/₄ teaspoon ground nutmeg
  ¹/₈ teaspoon ground cloves
    Vanilla Cream Cheese Glaze (recipe follows)

Per Serving
Calories: 263
% Calories from fat: 50
Fat (gm): 14.7
Saturated fat (gm): 2.9
Cholesterol (mg): 39.7
Sodium (mg): 211
Protein (gm): 6.6
Carbohydrate (gm): 26.5
Exchanges
Milk: 0.0
Vegetable: 0.0
Fruit: 0.0
Bread: 2.0
Meat: 0.0
Fat: 2.5

1. Mix applesauce, oil, eggs, maple extract, raisins, and walnuts in large bowl. Add combined flour, Equal® for Recipes, baking soda, salt, and spices, mixing until blended.

2. Spoon batter into greased 13 x 9-inch baking pan. Bake at 350 degrees until cake is browned and toothpick inserted in center comes out clean, 18 to 20 minutes (do not overbake!). Cool on wire rack. Drizzle with Vanilla Cream Cheese Glaze.

Vanilla Cream Cheese Glaze

makes about ¹/₂ cup

  ¹/₂ package (8-ounce size) reduced-fat cream cheese, softened
  ¹/₂ teaspoon vanilla
   1 teaspoon Equal® for Recipes *or* 3 packets Equal® sweetener
    Fat-free milk

1. Beat cream cheese, vanilla, Equal® for Recipes, and enough milk to make desired consistency.

DARK FLOURLESS CHOCOLATE CAKE

A chocolate indulgence, incredibly fudgey and sumptuous.

6 to 8 servings

4 tablespoons margarine, softened
1/4 cup raspberry spreadable fruit
1 egg
7 1/4 teaspoons Equal® for Recipes *or* 24 packets Equal® sweetener
1/2 cup fat-free milk
3 tablespoons Dutch process cocoa
1 cup all-purpose flour
1 teaspoon baking powder
1/2 teaspoon baking soda
1/4 teaspoon salt
Chocolate Glaze (recipe follows)

Per Serving
Calories: 291
% Calories from fat: 47
Fat (gm): 16.2
Saturated fat (gm): 6.7
Cholesterol (mg): 36.7
Sodium (mg): 417
Protein (gm): 13.3
Carbohydrate (gm): 27.2
Exchanges
Milk: 0.0
Vegetable: 0.0
Fruit: 0.0
Bread: 2.0
Meat: 0.0
Fat: 3.0

1. Beat margarine, spreadable fruit, egg, and Equal® for Recipes in medium bowl until smooth. Mix milk and cocoa in glass measuring cup until smooth.

2. Mix combined flour, baking powder, baking soda, and salt into margarine mixture alternately with milk mixture, beginning and ending with dry ingredients.

3. Lightly grease bottom and side of 8-inch round cake pan; line bottom with parchment paper; pour batter into pan. Bake in preheated 350 degree oven until toothpick inserted in center of cake comes out clean, about 20 minutes. Cool in pan; refrigerate, covered, 8 hours or overnight.

4. Place cake on serving plate. Within 1 hour of serving, spread with Chocolate Glaze.

Chocolate Glaze

makes about 1/2 cup

1/3 cup 2% reduced-fat milk
3 ounces unsweetened baking chocolate,
cut into small pieces
5 1/2 teaspoons Equal® for Recipes *or* 18
packets Equal® sweetener

1. Heat milk in small saucepan until very hot (do not boil). Remove pan from heat; immediately add chocolate, stirring until melted. Stir in Equal® for Recipes; return saucepan to low heat, stirring constantly, until smooth.

2. Cool to room temperature; refrigerate glaze until thickened enough to spread, about 15 minutes.

Variation: **Chocolate Lace Cake**—Make cake as above, omitting Chocolate Glaze. Place cake on serving plate. Melt 2 ounces unsweetened baking chocolate over low heat in small saucepan, stirring frequently; drizzle over top of cake in "lace" pattern. Refrigerate until chocolate has hardened, about 10 minutes. Garnish cake with dollops or rosettes of light whipped topping, raspberries, and mint sprigs.

BLUEBERRY CRUMB CAKE

Best served warm with light whipped topping or sugar-free frozen yogurt!

9 to 12 servings

    4 tablespoons margarine
    1 egg
 5¹/2 teaspoons Equal® for Recipes *or* 18
      packets Equal® sweetener
    1 cup all-purpose flour
 1¹/2 teaspoons baking powder
  ¹/2 teaspoon baking soda
  ¹/4 teaspoon salt
    1 teaspoon ground cinnamon
  ¹/2 cup reduced-fat buttermilk
  ¹/2 teaspoon vanilla
      Blueberry Crumb Topping (recipe
      follows)

Per Serving
Calories: 196
% Calories from fat: 50
Fat (gm): 11
Saturated fat (gm): 2.3
Cholesterol (mg): 24
Sodium (mg): 358
Protein (gm): 6.5
Carbohydrate (gm): 18
Exchanges
Milk: 0.0
Vegetable: 0.0
Fruit: 0.0
Bread: 1.0
Meat: 0.0
Fat: 2.5

1. Beat margarine, egg, and Equal® for Recipes until smooth in medium bowl. Mix in combined flour, baking powder, baking soda, salt, and cinnamon alternately with combined buttermilk and vanilla, beginning and ending with dry ingredients.

2. Pour batter into greased and floured 8-inch square cake pan; sprinkle Blueberry Crumb Topping evenly over batter. Bake at 350 degrees until toothpick inserted in cake comes out clean, 35 to 40 minutes. Serve warm.

Blueberry Crumb Topping

  ¹/3 cup all-purpose flour
 3¹/2 teaspoons Equal® for Recipes *or* 12
      packets Equal® sweetener
    1 teaspoon ground cinnamon
  ¹/2 teaspoon maple extract
    4 tablespoons cold margarine, cut into
      pieces
    1 cup fresh, *or* frozen, blueberries

1. Combine flour, Equal® for Recipes, and cinnamon in small bowl; sprinkle with maple extract. Cut in margarine until mixture resembles coarse crumbs. Add blueberries and toss.

DATE CAKE SQUARES

Perfect for picnics or potluck meals, this carry-along cake is one you'll make often.

8 servings

1 cup chopped pitted dates
3/4 cup chopped pitted prunes
1/2 cup dark raisins
1 1/4 cups water
8 tablespoons margarine, cut into pieces
2 eggs
1 teaspoon vanilla
1 cup all-purpose flour
5 1/2 teaspoons Equal® for Recipes *or* 18 packets Equal® sweetener
1 teaspoon baking soda
1/4 teaspoon salt
1/2 teaspoon ground cinnamon
1/4 teaspoon ground nutmeg
1/4-1/2 cup chopped walnuts

Per Serving
Calories: 336
% Calories from fat: 39
Fat (gm): 15.2
Saturated fat (gm): 2.9
Cholesterol (mg): 53
Sodium (mg): 382
Protein (gm): 7.5
Carbohydrate (gm): 46
Exchanges
Milk: 0.0
Vegetable: 0.0
Fruit: 1.0
Bread: 2.0
Meat: 0.0
Fat: 3.0

1. Combine dates, prunes, raisins, and water in medium saucepan; heat to boiling. Reduce heat and simmer, uncovered, until fruit is tender and water is absorbed, about 10 minutes. Remove from heat and add margarine, stirring until melted; cool.

2. Mix eggs and vanilla into fruit mixture; mix in combined remaining ingredients, except walnuts. Spread batter evenly in greased 11 x 7-inch baking pan; sprinkle with walnuts.

3. Bake at 350 degrees until cake springs back when touched, 30 to 35 minutes. Cool on wire rack; cut into squares.

PEACH-ALMOND UPSIDE-DOWN CAKE

Best served slightly warm, topped with sugar-free, fat-free ice cream, of course!

8 servings

- 1 can (8¹/₄ ounces) peaches in juice, well drained
- ¹/₂ cup unsweetened applesauce
- 5¹/₂ teaspoons Equal® for Recipes *or* 18 packets Equal® sweetener
- 1 egg
- ¹/₂ teaspoon vanilla
- 1 cup cake flour
- 1 teaspoon baking powder
- ¹/₄ teaspoon baking soda
- ¹/₂ teaspoon ground cinnamon
- ¹/₈-¹/₄ teaspoon ground nutmeg
- ¹/₄ teaspoon salt
- ¹/₂ cup reduced-fat buttermilk
  Fruit Topping (recipe follows)
- ¹/₄ cup sliced almonds, toasted

Per Serving
Calories: 136
% Calories from fat: 18
Fat (gm): 2.6
Saturated fat (gm): 0.4
Cholesterol (mg): 27
Sodium (mg): 207
Protein (gm): 6.1
Carbohydrate (gm): 19.8
Exchanges
Milk: 0.0
Vegetable: 0.0
Fruit: 0.5
Bread: 1.0
Meat: 0.0
Fat: 0.5

1. Cut peach slices into thirds; arrange in bottom of lightly greased 8-inch round cake pan.

2. Mix applesauce, Equal® for Recipes, egg, and vanilla until smooth in medium bowl. Mix in combined flour, baking powder, baking soda, cinnamon, nutmeg, and salt alternately with buttermilk, beginning and ending with dry ingredients. Pour batter over peach slices in pan.

3. Bake at 350 degrees until cake is browned and toothpick inserted in center comes out clean, about 20 minutes. Invert cake immediately onto serving plate. Cool 10 to 15 minutes; spread Fruit Topping over cake and sprinkle with almonds.

Fruit Topping

    3 tablespoons apricot spreadable fruit
    1 teaspoon lemon juice
    1 teaspoon cornstarch
 1³/4 teaspoons Equal® for Recipes *or* 6 packets
      Equal® sweetener
  ¹/4 teaspoon maple extract

1. Mix spreadable fruit, lemon juice, and cornstarch in small saucepan; heat to boiling, stirring constantly. Remove from heat; stir in Equal® for Recipes and maple extract.

APPLESAUCE RAISIN CAKE SQUARES

Serve warm with sugar-free, fat-free frozen yogurt, or drizzle cooled cake with Vanilla Cream Cheese Glaze (see p. 572).

16 servings

   1¹/2 cups unsweetened applesauce
    ¹/3 cup vegetable oil
      2 eggs
      1 teaspoon maple extract *or* vanilla
    ³/4 cup raisins
    ¹/2 cup coarsely chopped walnuts, optional
      2 cups all-purpose flour
  10³/4 teaspoons Equal® for Recipes *or* 36
        packets Equal® sweetener
      1 teaspoon baking soda
    ¹/4 teaspoon salt
   1¹/2 teaspoons ground cinnamon
    ¹/4 teaspoon ground nutmeg
    ¹/8 teaspoon ground cloves

Per Serving
Calories: 147
% Calories from fat: 32
Fat (gm): 5.4
Saturated fat (gm): 0.8
Cholesterol (mg): 26.5
Sodium (mg): 125
Protein (gm): 4.8
Carbohydrate (gm): 20.2
Exchanges
Milk: 0.0
Vegetable: 0.0
Fruit: 0.5
Bread: 1.0
Meat: 0.0
Fat: 1.0

1. Mix applesauce, oil, eggs, maple extract, raisins, and walnuts in large bowl. Add combined flour, Equal® for Recipes, baking soda, salt, and spices, mixing just until blended.

2. Spoon batter into greased 13 x 9-inch baking pan. Bake at 350 degrees until lightly browned and toothpick inserted in center comes out clean, about 20 minutes (do not overbake!). Cool on wire rack.

HEAVENLY PEACH PIE

Enjoy this pie in winter too, using frozen, thawed peaches, or drained canned peaches in juice.

8 servings

Double Pie Crust (see p. 128)
8¹/₄ teaspoons Equal® for Recipes *or* 27 packets Equal® sweetener, divided
6 cups sliced, pitted, peeled peaches
2 tablespoons flour
¹/₂ teaspoon ground cinnamon
2-3 pinches ground nutmeg

Per Serving
Calories: 238
% Calories from fat: 28
Fat (gm): 7.4
Saturated fat (gm): 1.5
Cholesterol (mg): 0
Sodium (mg): 230
Protein (gm): 7.2
Carbohydrate (gm): 36.6
Exchanges
Milk: 0.0
Vegetable: 0.0
Fruit: 1.0
Bread: 1.5
Meat: 0.0
Fat: 1.5

1. Make Double Pie Crust, substituting 1 teaspoon Equal® for Recipes for the sugar. Roll ²/₃ of the pastry on lightly floured surface to form circle 1¹/₂ inches larger than inverted 9-inch pie pan. Ease pastry into pan.

2. Toss peaches with combined flour, remaining 7¹/₄ teaspoons Equal® for Recipes, cinnamon, and nutmeg. Arrange fruit in pastry.

3. Roll remaining pastry on lightly floured surface to ¹/₈ inch thickness; cut into ¹/₂-inch strips. Lay pastry strips across top of pie and weave into lattice design. Trim ends of strips; fold edge of lower crust over ends of strips and seal and flute edge.

4. Bake pie at 425 degrees until bubbly, 30 to 40 minutes, covering edge of crust with aluminum foil if necessary to prevent excessive browning. Cool on wire rack.

CINNAMON APPLE PIE

One of the juiciest apple pies you'll ever taste! Use a tart baking apple—
Granny Smith is our favorite.

8 servings

Double Pie Crust (see p. 128)
8¹/₄ teaspoons Equal® for Recipes *or* 27
packets Equal® sweetener, divided
¹/₂ teaspoon ground cinnamon
2-3 pinches ground nutmeg
6 cups sliced, peeled baking apples
(about 6 medium)
³/₄ cup unsweetened apple juice
1 tablespoon cornstarch
1 teaspoon grated lemon rind

Per Serving
Calories: 246
% Calories from fat: 28
Fat (gm): 7.8
Saturated fat (gm): 1.5
Cholesterol (mg): 0
Sodium (mg): 232
Protein (gm): 6.2
Carbohydrate (gm): 39.1
Exchanges
Milk: 0.0
Vegetable: 0.0
Fruit: 1.0
Bread: 1.5
Meat: 0.0
Fat: 1.5

1. Make Double Pie Crust, substituting 1 teaspoon Equal® for Recipes for the sugar. Roll ²/₃ of the pastry on lightly floured surface into circle 1¹/₂ inches larger than inverted 9-inch pie pan. Ease pastry into pan.

2. Combine 5¹/₂ teaspoons Equal® for Recipes, cinnamon, and nutmeg; sprinkle over apples in large bowl and toss.

3. Mix apple juice, remaining 1³/₄ teaspoons Equal® for Recipes, cornstarch, and lemon rind in small saucepan; heat to boiling, whisking constantly until thickened, about 1 minute. Pour mixture over apples and toss; arrange in pastry.

4. Roll remaining pastry on lightly floured surface to ¹/₈ inch thickness and place over apples. Trim edges of pastry to within ¹/₂ inch of pan; fold top pastry over bottom pastry and flute. Cut decorative slits in top of pastry.

5. Bake pie in preheated 425 degree oven until pastry is golden and apples are tender, 40 to 50 minutes; cover edge of pie with aluminum foil if browning too quickly. Cool on wire rack.

APPLE CRANBERRY STREUSEL PIE

This pie will be a delicious addition to your holiday dessert table.

8 servings

Basic Pie Crust (All-Purpose Flour) (see p. 126)

10 teaspoons Equal® for Recipes *or* 33 packets Equal® sweetener, divided

1 tablespoon cornstarch

1 cup apple cider *or* unsweetened apple juice

1¹/2 cups cranberries, coarsely chopped

³/4 teaspoon ground cinnamon

¹/4 teaspoon ground nutmeg

¹/4 teaspoon salt

5 cups sliced, cored, peeled tart baking apples (about 5 medium)

Cinnamon Streusel (recipe follows)

Per Serving
Calories: 334
% Calories from fat: 36
Fat (gm): 13.7
Saturated fat (gm): 2.7
Cholesterol (mg): 0
Sodium (mg): 372
Protein (gm): 9.4
Carbohydrate (gm): 45.2
Exchanges
Milk: 0.0
Vegetable: 0.0
Fruit: 1.0
Bread: 2.0
Meat: 0.0
Fat: 2.5

1. Make Basic Pie Crust, substituting 1 teaspoon Equal® for Recipes for the sugar. Roll pastry on floured surface into circle 1¹/2 inches larger than inverted 9-inch pie pan. Ease pastry into pan; trim and flute.

2. Combine cornstarch and remaining 9 teaspoons Equal® for Recipes in small saucepan; stir in apple cider and cranberries. Heat to boiling; reduce heat and simmer, stirring constantly, until thickened, about 1 minute. Stir in spices and salt. Toss cranberry mixture with apples; arrange in pastry and sprinkle evenly with Cinnamon Streusel.

3. Bake pie at 400 degrees until pastry is golden and apples are tender, 50 to 60 minutes, covering pie loosely with aluminum foil during last 20 to 30 minutes of baking time if needed to prevent excessive browning. Cool on wire rack; serve warm.

Cinnamon Streusel

makes about 1/2 cup

1/4 cup quick-cooking oats
3 tablespoons all-purpose flour
3 1/2 teaspoons Equal® for Recipes *or* 12 packets Equal® sweetener
1 teaspoon ground cinnamon
1/2 teaspoon ground nutmeg
4 tablespoons cold margarine, cut into pieces

1. Combine oats, flour, Equal® for Recipes, cinnamon, and nutmeg in small bowl; cut in margarine until mixture resembles coarse crumbs.

BLUEBERRY PATCH PIE

Pastry strips weave a lattice topping for this garden fresh pie.

8 servings

Double Pie Crust (see p. 128)
11 3/4 teaspoons Equal® for Recipes *or* 39 packets Equal® sweetener, divided
4 tablespoons plus 2 teaspoons cornstarch, divided
1/3 cup apple juice
2 tablespoons lemon juice
6 cups fresh blueberries *or* 2 packages (16 ounces each) frozen unsweetened blueberries, thawed

Per Serving
Calories: 266
% Calories from fat: 26
Fat (gm): 7.7
Saturated fat (gm): 1.5
Cholesterol (mg): 0
Sodium (mg): 238
Protein (gm): 8.3
Carbohydrate (gm): 42
Exchanges
Milk: 0.0
Vegetable: 0.0
Fruit: 1.0
Bread: 2.0
Meat: 0.0
Fat: 1.5

1. Make Double Pie Crust, substituting 1 teaspoon Equal® for Recipes for the sugar. Roll 2/3 of the pastry on lightly floured surface into circle 1 1/2 inches larger than inverted 9-inch pie pan. Ease pastry into pan.

2. Mix remaining 10 3/4 teaspoons Equal® for Recipes, 2 teaspoons cornstarch, apple juice, and lemon juice in small saucepan; heat to boiling, whisking until thickened, about 1 minute.

3. Sprinkle remaining 4 tablespoons cornstarch over blueberries and toss; stir apple juice mixture into blueberries. Spoon blueberry mixture into pastry.

4. Roll remaining pastry on lightly floured surface to $1/8$ inch thickness; cut into $1/2$-inch strips. Lay pastry strips across top of pie and weave into lattice design. Trim ends of strips; fold edge of lower pastry over ends of strips and seal and flute edge.

5. Bake at 425 degrees until pastry is golden and pie is bubbly, 30 to 40 minutes; cover edge of pastry with aluminum foil if necessary to prevent excessive browning. Cool on wire rack.

CHERRY LATTICE PIE

This pie will disappear so quickly that you'd better bake two!

8 servings

Double Pie Crust (see pg. 128)
18 teaspoons Equal® for Recipes *or* 60 packets Equal® sweetener, divided
3 packages (16 ounces each) frozen no-sugar-added pitted tart cherries, thawed
3 tablespoons cornstarch, divided
2 tablespoons flour, divided
$1/8$ teaspoon ground nutmeg
6-8 drops red food color, optional

Per Serving
Calories: 290
% Calories from fat: 24
Fat (gm): 8.1
Saturated fat (gm): 1.6
Cholesterol (mg): 0
Sodium (mg): 233
Protein (gm): 12.2
Carbohydrate (gm): 43.9
Exchanges
Milk: 0.0
Vegetable: 0.0
Fruit: 1.5
Bread: 2.0
Meat: 0.0
Fat: 1.5

1. Make Double Pie Crust, substituting 1 teaspoon Equal® for Recipes for the sugar. Roll $1/2$ of the pastry on lightly floured surface into circle $1 1/2$ inches larger than inverted 9-inch pie pan. Ease pastry into pan.

2. Drain cherries, reserving $3/4$ cup cherry juice. Mix remaining 17 teaspoons Equal® for Recipes, 1 tablespoon cornstarch, 1 tablespoon flour, reserved cherry juice, nutmeg, and food color in small saucepan; heat to boiling, whisking constantly. Boil, whisking constantly, until thickened, about 1 minute.

3. Sprinkle remaining 2 tablespoons cornstarch and 1 tablespoon flour over cherries and toss; stir cherry juice mixture into cherries. Spoon cherry mixture into pastry.

4. Roll remaining pastry on lightly floured surface to $1/8$ inch thickness; cut into $1/2$-inch strips. Lay pastry strips across top of pie and weave into lattice design. Trim ends of strips; fold edge of lower pastry over ends of strips and seal and flute edge.

5. Bake pie at 425 degrees until pastry is golden and pie is bubbly, 35 to 45 minutes; cover edge of pastry with aluminum foil if necessary to prevent excessive browning. Cool on wire rack.

OLD-FASHIONED CUSTARD PIE

One of the best custard pies we've tasted! For a richer custard, use 2% reduced-fat milk.

8 servings

Basic Pie Crust (All-Purpose Flour) (see p. 126)

6¹/₂ teaspoons Equal® for Recipes *or* 21 packets Equal® sweetener, divided

4 eggs

¹/₄ teaspoon salt

2¹/₂ cups fat-free milk

1¹/₂ teaspoons vanilla

¹/₄ teaspoon ground cinnamon

¹/₈ teaspoon ground nutmeg

Per Serving
Calories: 199
% Calories from fat: 39
Fat (gm): 8.5
Saturated fat (gm): 2
Cholesterol (mg): 107.4
Sodium (mg): 284
Protein (gm): 10.3
Carbohydrate (gm): 19.3
Exchanges
Milk: 0.0
Vegetable: 0.0
Fruit: 0.0
Bread: 1.5
Meat: 1.0
Fat: 1.0

1. Make Basic Pie Crust, substituting 1 teaspoon Equal® for Recipes for the sugar. Roll pastry on floured surface into circle 1¹/₂ inches larger than inverted 9-inch pie pan. Ease pastry into pan; trim and flute.

2. Beat eggs and salt until thick and lemon colored in large bowl, about 5 minutes. Mix in milk, remaining 5¹/₂ teaspoons Equal® for Recipes, and remaining ingredients; pour into pastry.

3. Bake at 425 degrees 15 minutes; reduce temperature to 350 degrees and bake until sharp knife inserted halfway between center and edge comes out clean, about 12 minutes. Cool on wire rack. Serve at room temperature, or refrigerate and serve chilled.

Variation: **Coconut Custard Pie**—Make recipe as above, reducing milk to 2 cups, adding ¹/₂ cup flaked coconut, and substituting 1 to 2 teaspoons coconut extract for the vanilla.

SPICED SWEET POTATO PIE

A real Southern-style favorite!

8 servings

Basic Pie Crust (All-Purpose Flour)
(see p. 126)

8¹/₄ teaspoons Equal® for Recipes *or* 27
packets Equal® sweetener, divided

2 cups mashed, cooked sweet potatoes

2 eggs, slightly beaten

1 tablespoon margarine, softened

1 tablespoon flour

1 can (12 ounces) evaporated fat-free
milk

1¹/₂ teaspoons vanilla

1¹/₂-2 teaspoons ground cinnamon

³/₄ teaspoon ground nutmeg

¹/₄ teaspoon ground mace, optional

¹/₂ teaspoon salt

Light whipped topping, as garnish

Per Serving
Calories: 298
% Calories from fat: 27
Fat (gm): 8.9
Saturated fat (gm): 2
Cholesterol (mg): 54.7
Sodium (mg): 384
Protein (gm): 12
Carbohydrate (gm): 41.9
Exchanges
Milk: 0.0
Vegetable: 0.0
Fruit: 0.0
Bread: 3.0
Meat: 0.5
Fat: 1.5

1. Make Basic Pie Crust, substituting 1 teaspoon Equal® for Recipes for the sugar. Roll pastry on floured surface into circle 1¹/₂ inches larger than inverted 9-inch pie pan. Ease pastry into pan; trim and flute.

2. Mix sweet potatoes, eggs, margarine, remaining 7¹/₄ teaspoons Equal® for Recipes, and flour until blended in large bowl; mix in remaining ingredients, except whipped topping. Pour mixture into pastry.

3. Bake at 425 degrees 20 minutes; reduce heat to 350 degrees and bake until filling is set and sharp knife inserted halfway between center and edge comes out clean, 30 to 35 minutes. Cool on wire rack. Serve with light whipped topping.

Variation: **Spiced Pumpkin Pie**—Make recipe as above, substituting canned pumpkin for the sweet potatoes and omitting eggs, margarine, flour, vanilla, and mace.

PUMPKIN CHIFFON PIE

The perfect addition to any holiday menu.

8 servings

Basic Pie Crust (All-Purpose Flour) (see p. 126)
3¹/₂ teaspoons Equal® for Recipes *or* 12 packets Equal® sweetener, divided
1 envelope unflavored gelatin
1 teaspoon cornstarch
¹/₂ cup fat-free milk
2 egg yolks
2 cups canned pumpkin
1 teaspoon pumpkin pie spice
1 teaspoon vanilla
¹/₈ teaspoon salt
1 cup light whipped topping
Light whipped topping, as garnish

Per Serving
Calories: 196
% Calories from fat: 39
Fat (gm): 8.3
Saturated fat (gm): 2.7
Cholesterol (mg): 53.5
Sodium (mg): 191
Protein (gm): 5.5
Carbohydrate (gm): 24.1
Exchanges
Milk: 0.0
Vegetable: 0.0
Fruit: 0.0
Bread: 2.0
Meat: 0.0
Fat: 1.5

1. Make Basic Pie Crust, substituting 1 teaspoon Equal® for Recipes for the sugar. Roll pastry on floured surface to circle 1¹/₂ inches larger than inverted 9-inch pie pan. Ease pastry into pan; trim and flute. Pierce bottom of pastry with tines of a fork. Bake at 425 degrees until browned, about 15 minutes. Cool on wire rack.

2. Whisk remaining 2¹/₂ teaspoons Equal® for Recipes, gelatin, cornstarch, and milk over medium heat in medium saucepan until mixture boils and thickens, 2 to 3 minutes. Stir about ¹/₂ of the milk mixture into the egg yolks; whisk egg mixture into saucepan. Whisk over low heat until thickened, 1 to 2 minutes. Remove from heat and stir in pumpkin, pumpkin pie spice, vanilla, and salt. Cool to room temperature; refrigerate until mixture mounds when dropped from a spoon, about 20 minutes.

3. Whisk mixture gently until smooth; fold in 1 cup whipped topping and spoon into pie crust, smoothing top. Refrigerate until set, 3 to 4 hours. Garnish slices with dollops of whipped topping.

STRAWBERRY CREAM PIE

Celebrate spring with this colorful fresh berry pie.

8 servings

1¼ cups reduced-fat graham cracker crumbs

4-5 tablespoons margarine, melted

6¼ teaspoons Equal® for Recipes *or* 19 packets Equal® sweetener, divided

1 package (8 ounces) fat-free cream cheese, softened

1 teaspoon vanilla

1 cup boiling water

1 package (.3 ounces) sugar-free strawberry gelatin

2 cups sliced strawberries
Light whipped topping, as garnish

Per Serving
Calories: 165
% Calories from fat: 38
Fat (gm): 6.9
Saturated fat (gm): 1.6
Cholesterol (mg): 2.3
Sodium (mg): 330
Protein (gm): 8.9
Carbohydrate (gm): 17.1
Exchanges
Milk: 0.0
Vegetable: 0.0
Fruit: 0.0
Bread: 1.0
Meat: 1.0
Fat: 1.0

1. Mix graham cracker crumbs, margarine, and 1 teaspoon Equal® for Recipes in 8-inch pie pan; pat evenly on bottom and side of pan. Bake at 350 degrees until lightly browned, 6 to 8 minutes. Cool.

2. Beat cream cheese, vanilla, and 1¾ teaspoons Equal® for Recipes in small bowl until fluffy; spread evenly in bottom of crust.

3. Pour boiling water over gelatin and remaining 3½ teaspoons Equal® for Recipes in bowl, whisking until gelatin is dissolved. Refrigerate until mixture is the consistency of unbeaten egg whites, 20 to 30 minutes.

4. Arrange half the strawberries over the cream cheese; spoon half the gelatin mixture over strawberries. Arrange remaining strawberries over pie and spoon remaining gelatin mixture over. Refrigerate until pie is set and chilled, 2 to 3 hours. Serve with light whipped topping.

Variations: **Double Berry Pie**—Make recipe as above, substituting 1 cup blueberries for 1 cup strawberries. Arrange 1 cup blueberries over cream cheese in pie crust; spoon half the gelatin mixture over berries; top with 1 cup sliced strawberries and spoon remaining gelatin mixture over.

Strawberry Banana Pie—Make recipe as above, substituting sugar-free strawberry-banana gelatin for the strawberry gelatin and 1 small sliced banana for 1 cup strawberries. Arrange banana over cream cheese; spoon half the gelatin mixture over; top with 1 cup sliced strawberries and spoon remaining gelatin mixture over.

LEMON CREAM PIE

For best flavor, use fresh lemon juice.

8 servings

    Basic Pie Crust (All-Purpose Flour) (see p. 126)
1 teaspoon Equal® for Recipes *or* 3 packets Equal® sweetener
    Lemon Cream (recipe follows)
    Light whipped topping, as garnish
    Lemon slices, halved, as garnish

Per Serving
Calories: 215
% Calories from fat: 39
Fat (gm): 9.3
Saturated fat (gm): 2.1
Cholesterol (mg): 81
Sodium (mg): 192
Protein (gm): 8
Carbohydrate (gm): 24.6
Exchanges
Milk: 0.0
Vegetable: 0.0
Fruit: 0.0
Bread: 2.0
Meat: 0.0
Fat: 2.0

1. Make Basic Pie Crust, substituting 1 teaspoon Equal® for Recipes for the sugar. Roll pastry on floured surface to circle 1¹/₂ inches larger than inverted 9-inch pie pan. Ease pastry into pan; trim and flute. Pierce bottom of pastry with tines of a fork. Bake at 425 degrees until browned, about 15 minutes. Cool on wire rack.

2. Spoon Lemon Cream into baked crust and refrigerate until chilled, 2 to 3 hours. Garnish pie with rosettes or dollops of light whipped topping and lemon slices.

Lemon Cream

makes about 3 cups

$^1/_4$ cup cornstarch

2 tablespoons flour

$5^1/_2$ teaspoons Equal® for Recipes *or* 18 packets Equal® sweetener

2 cups fat-free milk

$^1/_2$ cup lemon juice

1 teaspoon finely grated lemon rind

3 egg yolks

1-2 tablespoons margarine

$^1/_2$ teaspoon lemon extract

1. Whisk cornstarch, flour, Equal® for Recipes, milk, lemon juice, and rind in medium saucepan to boiling; whisk until thickened, about 1 minute. Whisk about 1 cup milk mixture into egg yolks; whisk yolk mixture into saucepan. Whisk over low heat until thickened, about 1 minute. Whisk in margarine and lemon extract. Cool 15 minutes, whisking occasionally.

MOM'S LEMON MERINGUE PIE

Sweet and tart with a cloud of meringue!

8 servings

Basic Pie Crust (All-Purpose Flour) (see p. 126)

$15^1/_4$ teaspoons Equal® for Recipes *or* 49 packets Equal® sweetener, divided

$2^1/_4$ cups water

$^1/_2$ cup lemon juice

1 teaspoon finely grated lemon rind

$^1/_2$ cup cornstarch

2 eggs

5 egg whites, divided

2 tablespoons margarine

1-2 drops yellow food color, optional

$^1/_4$ teaspoon cream of tartar

Per Serving
Calories: 234
% Calories from fat: 38
Fat (gm): 9.9
Saturated fat (gm): 2.1
Cholesterol (mg): 53
Sodium (mg): 226
Protein (gm): 11.8
Carbohydrate (gm): 24
Exchanges
Milk: 0.0
Vegetable: 0.0
Fruit: 0.0
Bread: 2.0
Meat: 0.0
Fat: 2.0

1. Make Basic Pie Crust, substituting 1 teaspoon Equal® for Recipes for the sugar. Roll pastry on floured surface to circle 1^1/$_2$ inches larger than inverted 9-inch pie pan. Ease pastry into pan; trim and flute. Pierce bottom of pastry with tines of a fork. Bake at 425 degrees until browned, about 15 minutes. Cool on wire rack.

2. Mix water, lemon juice, lemon rind, 10^3/$_4$ teaspoons Equal® for Recipes, and cornstarch in medium saucepan. Whisk over medium-high heat until boiling; boil, whisking constantly, 1 minute. Whisk about 1 cup mixture into combined eggs and 2 egg whites; whisk egg mixture into saucepan. Remove from heat; add margarine, stirring until melted. Stir in food color; pour mixture into baked pie crust.

3. Beat remaining 3 egg whites and cream of tartar in medium bowl to soft peaks; beat to stiff peaks, adding remaining 3^1/$_2$ teaspoons Equal® for Recipes gradually. Spread meringue over hot lemon filling, sealing to edge of crust to prevent shrinking or weeping.

4. Bake at 425 degrees until meringue is browned, about 5 minutes. Cool completely on wire rack.

KEY LIME PIE

A Southern dessert that is famous for its smooth creamy texture and unique cool lime taste.

8 servings

1 cup reduced-fat graham cracker crumbs

3-4 tablespoons melted margarine

4^1/$_2$ teaspoons Equal® for Recipes *or* 15 packets Equal® sweetener, divided

1 envelope unflavored gelatin

1^3/$_4$ cups fat-free milk, divided

1 package (8 ounces) fat-free cream cheese, softened

^{1}/$_2$ cup key lime, *or* Persian lime, juice

Light whipped topping, as garnish

Mint sprigs, as garnish

Per Serving
Calories: 147
% Calories from fat: 32
Fat (gm): 5.4
Saturated fat (gm): 1.4
Cholesterol (mg): 3.2
Sodium (mg): 320
Protein (gm): 8.7
Carbohydrate (gm): 16.6
Exchanges
Milk: 0.0
Vegetable: 0.0
Fruit: 0.0
Bread: 1.0
Meat: 1.0
Fat: 0.5

1. Combine graham cracker crumbs, margarine, and 1 teaspoon Equal® for Recipes in 7-inch springform pan; pat evenly on bottom and ^{1}/$_2$ inch up side of pan.

2. Sprinkle gelatin over ^{1}/$_2$ cup of the milk in small saucepan; let stand 2 to 3 minutes; heat just to simmering, stirring constantly; cool.

3. Beat cream cheese until fluffy in medium bowl; beat in remaining 1^1/$_4$ cups milk and the gelatin mixture. Mix in lime juice and remaining 3^1/$_2$ teaspoons Equal® for Recipes. Pour into pan; refrigerate until set, 3 to 4 hours.

4. Remove side of pan; place pie on serving plate. Garnish with light whipped topping and mint.

NECTARINE AND BERRY TART

Fresh apricots or fresh or frozen, thawed peaches can be substituted for the nectarines in this summer-fresh, country-style tart.

6 servings

Basic Pie Crust (All-Purpose Flour) (see p. 126)

8¹/4 teaspoons Equal® for Recipes *or* 27 packets Equal® sweetener, divided

5 cups sliced nectarines (about 5 medium)

1 cup raspberries *or* sliced strawberries

1 cup fresh, *or* frozen, partially thawed blueberries

2 teaspoons lemon juice

3 tablespoons cornstarch

1 teaspoon grated lemon rind

¹/4 teaspoon ground allspice

Per Serving
Calories: 275
% Calories from fat: 27
Fat (gm): 8.5
Saturated fat (gm): 1.6
Cholesterol (mg): 0
Sodium (mg): 189
Protein (gm): 8.5
Carbohydrate (gm): 42.9
Exchanges
Milk: 0.0
Vegetable: 0.0
Fruit: 1.0
Bread: 2.0
Meat: 0.0
Fat: 1.5

1. Make Basic Pie Crust, substituting 1 teaspoon Equal® for Recipes for the sugar. Roll pastry on floured surface into 12-inch circle; transfer to ungreased cookie sheet.

2. Toss fruit with lemon juice in large bowl; sprinkle with combined cornstarch, remaining 7¹/4 teaspoons Equal® for Recipes, lemon rind, and allspice and toss. Arrange fruit on pastry, leaving 2-inch border around edge of pastry. Fold edge of pastry over edge of fruit, overlapping as necessary.

3. Bake at 425 degrees until pastry is golden and fruit tender, 35 to 40 minutes. Cool on wire rack.

APPLE WALNUT STREUSEL TART

A drizzle of warm apricot spreadable fruit is the perfect finishing touch for this pastry shop-pretty tart.

8 servings

Basic Pie Crust (All-Purpose Flour) (see p. 126)

2³/4 teaspoons Equal® for Recipes *or* 9 packets Equal® sweetener, divided

3 medium baking apples, peeled, sliced ¹/4 inch thick

Walnut Streusel (recipe follows)

¹/3 cup apricot spreadable fruit, warm

Per Serving
Calories: 218
% Calories from fat: 40
Fat (gm): 10
Saturated fat (gm): 1.8
Cholesterol (mg): 0
Sodium (mg): 187
Protein (gm): 4.7
Carbohydrate (gm): 28
Exchanges
Milk: 0.0
Vegetable: 0.0
Fruit: 1.0
Bread: 1.0
Meat: 0.0
Fat: 2.0

1. Make Basic Pie Crust, substituting 1 teaspoon Equal® for Recipes for the sugar. Roll pastry on floured surface into circle 1¹/2 inches larger than inverted 9-inch tart pan with removable bottom. Ease pastry into pan and trim.

2. Arrange apples in circles on pastry; sprinkle with remaining 1³/4 teaspoons Equal® for Recipes; sprinkle with Walnut Streusel.

3. Bake at 400 degrees until pastry is golden and apples are tender, 25 to 30 minutes. Cool on wire rack. Drizzle or brush spreadable fruit over tart.

Walnut Streusel

makes about ¹/2 cup

2 tablespoons flour

1³/4 teaspoons Equal® for Recipes *or* 6 packets Equal® sweetener

¹/2 teaspoon ground cinnamon

2 tablespoons cold margarine, cut into pieces

2-4 tablespoons coarsely chopped walnuts

1. Combine flour, Equal® for Recipes, and cinnamon in small bowl; cut in margarine until mixture resembles coarse crumbs. Stir in walnuts.

PINEAPPLE CRUMB TART

The rich crumb mixture is used both as a crust and topping in this delectable French-style tart. Substitute other canned fruit for the pineapple, if desired.

10 to 12 servings

1¼ cups all-purpose flour
5½ teaspoons Equal® for Recipes *or* 18 packets Equal® sweetener
4 teaspoons cornstarch
¼ teaspoon salt
10 tablespoons cold margarine, cut into pieces
1½ teaspoons vanilla
2 cans (8 ounces each) sliced pineapple in juice, well drained
¼ cup apricot spreadable fruit, warm

Per Serving
Calories: 207
% Calories from fat: 50
Fat (gm): 11.5
Saturated fat (gm): 2.3
Cholesterol (mg): 0
Sodium (mg): 201
Protein (gm): 3.7
Carbohydrate (gm): 22.3
Exchanges
Milk: 0.0
Vegetable: 0.0
Fruit: 0.5
Bread: 1.0
Meat: 0.0
Fat: 2.0

1. Combine flour, Equal® for Recipes, cornstarch, and salt in medium bowl; cut in margarine until mixture resembles coarse crumbs. Sprinkle vanilla over mixture and stir with fork to combine.

2. Reserve ½ cup crumb mixture. Pat remaining mixture evenly on bottom only of ungreased 10-inch tart pan or quiche dish. Bake at 350 degrees until browned, about 15 minutes. Cool on wire rack.

3. Cut pineapple slices in half and arrange on crust; sprinkle with reserved ½ cup crumb mixture. Bake at 400 degrees until topping is browned, about 10 minutes. Cool on wire rack; drizzle with spreadable fruit.

SUMMER FRUIT TARTS

Select the fruits for these pretty tarts according to season and availability, mixing colors and textures.

6 servings

Basic Pie Crust (All-Purpose Flour) (see p. 126)

2¹/2 teaspoons Equal® for Recipes *or* 8 packets Equal® sweetener, divided

¹/4 cup plain fat-free yogurt

¹/4 cup fat-free sour cream

¹/4 teaspoon almond extract

4 cups assorted fruit (strawberries, raspberries, blueberries, cubed pineapple, sliced peaches, pears, or kiwi)

³/4 cup pineapple juice

1 tablespoon lemon juice

2 teaspoons cornstarch

Per Serving
Calories: 242
% Calories from fat: 30
Fat (gm): 8.2
Saturated fat (gm): 1.6
Cholesterol (mg): 0.2
Sodium (mg): 203
Protein (gm): 6.1
Carbohydrate (gm): 36.2
Exchanges
Milk: 0.0
Vegetable: 0.0
Fruit: 1.5
Bread: 1.5
Meat: 0.0
Fat: 1.5

1. Make Basic Pie Crust, substituting 1 teaspoon Equal® for Recipes for the sugar. Divide pastry into 6 equal pieces; roll each piece on floured surface into 5-inch circle. Ease pastry circles into six 4-inch tart pans with removable bottoms and trim. Pierce bottoms of pastry with tines of a fork. Bake at 450 degrees until golden, 5 to 6 minutes. Cool on wire rack.

2. Combine yogurt, sour cream, almond extract, and ¹/2 teaspoon Equal® for Recipes; spread in cooled crusts. Arrange fruits attractively in tarts.

3. Combine pineapple juice, lemon juice, and cornstarch in small saucepan. Heat to boiling, whisking constantly, until thickened; stir in remaining 1 teaspoon Equal® for Recipes. Cool; spoon over fruit and chill until serving time.

RASPBERRY CREAM TART

Any berries can be substituted for the raspberries, or use a variety of berries, arranging the largest ones in the center of the tart.

8 servings

Basic Pie Crust (All-Purpose Flour) (see p. 126)

3¹/₂ teaspoons Equal® for Recipes *or* 12 packets Equal® sweetener, divided

¹/₃ cup cornstarch

1¹/₂ cups fat-free milk

3 eggs, lightly beaten

2 teaspoons finely grated lemon, *or* orange, rind

¹/₄ teaspoon lemon extract, optional

1¹/₂-2 pints raspberries

¹/₄ cup seedless raspberry spreadable fruit, warm

Per Serving
Calories: 225
% Calories from fat: 32
Fat (gm): 8
Saturated fat (gm): 1.8
Cholesterol (mg): 80.3
Sodium (mg): 198
Protein (gm): 7.9
Carbohydrate (gm): 30.1
Exchanges
Milk: 0.0
Vegetable: 0.0
Fruit: 1.0
Bread: 1.5
Meat: 0.0
Fat: 1.5

1. Make Basic Pie Crust, substituting 1 teaspoon Equal® for Recipes for the sugar. Roll pastry on floured surface to circle 1¹/₂ inches larger than inverted 9-inch tart pan. Ease pastry into pan; trim edges and pierce bottom with tines of a fork. Bake at 425 degrees until crust is browned, about 10 minutes. Cool on wire rack.

2. Mix remaining 2¹/₂ teaspoons Equal® for Recipes and cornstarch in medium saucepan; whisk in milk and heat to boiling, whisking until thickened. Whisk about ¹/₂ of the milk mixture into the eggs; whisk egg mixture into saucepan. Whisk in lemon rind and extract; whisk over low heat until thickened, 1 to 2 minutes. Cool to room temperature, stirring occasionally. Spoon into pie crust.

3. Arrange raspberries, pointed ends up, on custard. Brush raspberries with spreadable fruit. Refrigerate until chilled, 1 to 2 hours.

Variation: **Banana Cream Tart**—Make recipe as above, substituting 3 medium bananas, sliced, for the raspberries and omitting the raspberry spreadable fruit. Cover bottom of baked crust with layer of sliced bananas; cover with custard and refrigerate until chilled, 2 to 3 hours. Before serving, garnish top of tart with remaining bananas and dollops of light whipped topping.

ALMOND CHEESECAKE SQUARES

Rich in flavor and texture, yet made with fat-free cream cheese!

24 servings

3 packages (8 ounces each) fat-free cream cheese, softened

5¹/2 teaspoons Equal® for Recipes *or* 18 packets Equal® sweetener

2 eggs

2 egg whites

2 tablespoons cornstarch

1 cup fat-free sour cream

¹/2 teaspoon vanilla

¹/4 teaspoon almond extract
   Chocolate Crumb Crust
   (recipe follows)

¹/4 cup sliced almonds

Per Serving
Calories: 112
% Calories from fat: 34
Fat (gm): 4.1
Saturated fat (gm): 1
Cholesterol (mg): 19.9
Sodium (mg): 244
Protein (gm): 7.5
Carbohydrate (gm): 10.2
Exchanges
Milk: 0.0
Vegetable: 0.0
Fruit: 0.0
Bread: 1.0
Meat: 0.0
Fat: 1.0

1. Beat cream cheese until smooth in large bowl; beat in remaining ingredients, except Chocolate Crumb Crust and almonds, until smooth. Pour filling into crust; sprinkle with almonds.

2. Bake cheesecake at 300 degrees until set, about 30 minutes. Cool on wire rack; refrigerate until chilled, 6 hours or overnight. Cut into squares to serve.

Chocolate Crumb Crust

1¹/2 cups ground reduced-fat graham crackers

¹/4 cup Dutch process cocoa

2¹/2 teaspoons Equal® for Recipes *or* 8 packets Equal® sweetener

5 tablespoons margarine, melted

¹/2-³/4 teaspoon chocolate extract

1. Mix graham cracker crumbs, cocoa, and Equal® for Recipes in bottom of 13 x 9-inch baking pan; mix in margarine and chocolate extract. Pat mixture evenly on bottom of pan.

PUMPKIN CHEESECAKE

A creamy smooth cheesecake, scented with holiday flavors of pumpkin and spices.

12 to 14 servings

3/4 cup ground reduced-fat graham crackers
3/4 cup ground gingersnap cookies
8 1/4 teaspoons Equal® for Recipes *or* 27 packets Equal® sweetener, divided
4-5 tablespoons margarine, melted
2 packages (8 ounces each) fat-free cream cheese, softened
1 package (8 ounces) reduced-fat cream cheese
1 cup canned pumpkin
2 eggs
2 egg whites
2 teaspoons ground cinnamon
1 teaspoon ground cloves
1 teaspoon ground ginger
2 tablespoons cornstarch
1 cup light whipped topping
Chopped toasted pecans, as garnish

Per Serving
Calories: 213
% Calories from fat: 42
Fat (gm): 9.8
Saturated fat (gm): 4.3
Cholesterol (mg): 47.2
Sodium (mg): 444
Protein (gm): 12.1
Carbohydrate (gm): 18.2
Exchanges
Milk: 0.0
Vegetable: 0.0
Fruit: 0.0
Bread: 1.0
Meat: 1.0
Fat: 2.0

1. Mix graham cracker and gingersnap crumbs, 1 teaspoon Equal® for Recipes, and melted margarine in bottom of 9-inch springform pan; reserve 2 tablespoons crumb mixture. Pat remaining mixture evenly on bottom and 1/2 inch up side of pan. Bake at 350 degrees until lightly browned, about 8 minutes. Cool on wire rack.

2. Beat cream cheese until smooth in large bowl; beat in pumpkin, eggs, and egg whites. Mix in remaining 7 1/4 teaspoons Equal® for Recipes, spices, and cornstarch. Pour mixture into springform pan.

3. Bake at 300 degrees just until set in the center, 45 to 60 minutes; sprinkle with reserved crumbs and return to oven. Turn oven off and let cheesecake cool in oven with door ajar for 3 hours. Refrigerate 8 hours or overnight.

4. Remove side of springform pan; place cheesecake on serving plate. Spread with light whipped topping and sprinkle with pecans.

CREAMY CHEESECAKE MELBA

Topped with sour cream and a raspberry sauce, this cheesecake is a sweet ending to any meal.

16 servings

1¼ cups vanilla wafer crumbs
4-5 tablespoons margarine, melted
6½ teaspoon Equal® for Recipes *or* 21 packets Equal® sweetener, divided
2 packages (8 ounces each) fat-free cream cheese, softened
1 package (8 ounces) reduced-fat cream cheese, softened
2 eggs
2 egg whites
2 tablespoons cornstarch
1½ cups fat-free sour cream, divided
1 teaspoon vanilla
Melba Sauce (see p. 622)

Per Serving
Calories: 183
% Calories from fat: 37
Fat (gm): 7.4
Saturated fat (gm): 2.8
Cholesterol (mg): 39.9
Sodium (mg): 313
Protein (gm): 10.7
Carbohydrate (gm): 17.5
Exchanges
Milk: 0.0
Vegetable: 0.0
Fruit: 0.0
Bread: 1.0
Meat: 1.0
Fat: 1.0

1. Mix vanilla wafer crumbs, margarine, and 1 teaspoon Equal® for Recipes in bottom of 9-inch springform pan. Pat mixture evenly on bottom and ½ inch up side of pan. Bake at 350 degrees until lightly browned, about 8 minutes. Cool on wire rack.

2. Beat cream cheese and remaining 5½ teaspoons Equal® for Recipes in large bowl until fluffy; beat in eggs, egg whites, and cornstarch. Mix in ¾ cup sour cream and vanilla. Pour mixture into crust.

3. Bake at 300 degrees until just set in the center, 45 to 60 minutes. Turn oven off; let cheesecake cool in oven with door ajar 3 hours. Refrigerate 8 hours or overnight.

4. Remove side of pan; place cheesecake on serving plate. Spread top of cheesecake with remaining ¾ cup sour cream and drizzle with 2 to 3 tablespoons Melba Sauce. Drizzle remaining Melba Sauce on serving plates and top with cheesecake slices.

RICH CHOCOLATE CHEESECAKE

A chocolate lover's delight! Serve with Chocolate Sauce (see pg. 642), if you dare!

16 servings

1¼ cups graham cracker crumbs

4-5 tablespoons margarine, melted

6½ teaspoons Equal® for Recipes *or* 21 packets Equal® sweetener, divided

2 packages (8 ounces each) fat-free cream cheese, softened

1 package (8 ounces) reduced-fat cream cheese, softened

2 eggs

2 egg whites

2 tablespoons cornstarch

1 cup fat-free sour cream

⅓ cup Dutch process cocoa

1 teaspoon vanilla

1 cup light whipped topping

Unsweetened chocolate shavings, as garnish

Per Serving
Calories: 182
% Calories from fat: 43
Fat (gm): 8.5
Cholesterol (mg): 3.6
Sodium (mg): 320
Protein (gm): 10
Carbohydrate (gm): 14.9
Exchanges
Milk: 0.0
Vegetable: 0.0
Fruit: 0.0
Bread: 1.0
Meat: 1.0
Fat: 1.0

1. Mix graham cracker crumbs, margarine, and 1 teaspoon Equal® for Recipes in 9-inch springform pan; pat evenly on bottom and ½ inch up side of pan.

2. Beat cream cheese and remaining 5½ teaspoons Equal® for Recipes until fluffy in large bowl; beat in eggs, egg whites, and cornstarch. Beat in sour cream, cocoa, and vanilla, blending well; pour into crust.

3. Bake cheesecake at 300 degrees just until set in the center, 45 to 50 minutes. Turn oven off and let cheesecake cool in oven with door ajar for 3 hours. Refrigerate 8 hours or overnight.

4. Remove side of pan; place cheesecake on serving plate. Spread light whipped topping over top and garnish with chocolate shavings.

BING CHERRY CHEESECAKE

Two cheeses are combined with luscious Bing cherries in this easy cheesecake.

12 servings

1^1/$_2$ cups reduced-fat graham cracker crumbs

4^1/$_2$ teaspoons Equal® for Recipes *or* 15 packets Equal® sweetener, divided

1^1/$_2$ teaspoons ground cinnamon

4-5 tablespoons margarine, melted

2 envelopes unflavored gelatin

^{1}/$_4$ cup orange juice *or* water

1 package (8 ounces) fat-free cream cheese, softened

1 cup low-fat ricotta cheese

2 cups coarsely chopped, pitted Bing cherries

^{1}/$_2$ teaspoon cherry extract *or* vanilla

3-4 cups light whipped topping

Per Serving
Calories: 191
% Calories from fat: 35
Fat (gm): 7.3
Saturated fat (gm): 3.5
Cholesterol (mg): 5.1
Sodium (mg): 267
Protein (gm): 8.2
Carbohydrate (gm): 22.4
Exchanges
Milk: 0.0
Vegetable: 0.0
Fruit: 0.0
Bread: 1.5
Meat: 0.0
Fat: 1.5

1. Mix graham cracker crumbs, 1 teaspoon Equal® for Recipes, cinnamon, and margarine in bottom of 9-inch springform pan; press mixture evenly on bottom and ^{1}/$_2$ inch up side of pan. Bake at 350 degrees until browned, about 8 minutes. Cool on wire rack.

2. Sprinkle gelatin over orange juice in small saucepan; let stand 3 to 4 minutes to soften. Cook over low heat, stirring frequently, until dissolved. Beat cream and ricotta cheeses and remaining 3^1/$_2$ teaspoons Equal® for Recipes in large bowl until blended. Beat in gelatin mixture. Mix in cherries and cherry extract; fold in whipped topping.

3. Spoon mixture into crust, spreading evenly. Refrigerate until set, 4 to 6 hours. Remove side of pan and place cheesecake on serving plate.

LIGHT LEMON SQUARES

One of America's favorite bar cookies, made with no sugar added!

1 dozen cookies (1 per serving)

2 eggs
5¹/₂ teaspoons Equal® for Recipes *or* 18 packets Equal® sweetener
¹/₄ cup plus 2 tablespoons lemon juice
4 tablespoons margarine, melted, cooled
1 tablespoon grated lemon rind
Rich Pastry (recipe follows)

Per Serving
Calories: 138
% Calories from fat: 67
Fat (gm): 10.4
Saturated fat (gm): 2.1
Cholesterol (mg): 35.3
Sodium (mg): 146
Protein (gm): 3.9
Carbohydrate (gm): 7.5
Exchanges
Milk: 0.0
Vegetable: 0.0
Fruit: 0.0
Bread: 0.5
Meat: 0.0
Fat: 2.0

1. Beat eggs and Equal® for Recipes; mix in lemon juice, margarine, and lemon rind. Pour mixture into baked Rich Pastry.

2. Bake at 350 degrees until filling is set, about 15 minutes. Cool on wire rack.

Rich Pastry

³/₄ cup all-purpose flour
2¹/₂ teaspoons Equal® for Recipes *or* 8 packets Equal® sweetener
2¹/₄ teaspoons cornstarch
¹/₈ teaspoon salt
6 tablespoons cold margarine, cut into pieces
³/₄ teaspoon vanilla
1 teaspoon lemon rind

1. Combine flour, Equal® for Recipes, cornstarch, and salt in medium bowl; cut in margarine until mixture resembles coarse crumbs. Sprinkle with vanilla and lemon rind; mix with hands to form dough.

2. Press dough evenly on bottom and ¹/₄ inch up side of 8-inch square baking pan. Bake at 350 degrees until lightly browned, about 10 minutes. Cool on wire rack.

FUDGEY BROWNIES

Easy to make whenever you get an urge for something chocolate!

1¹/₄ dozen brownies (1 per serving)

6 tablespoons margarine
4 ounces unsweetened chocolate
¹/₃ cup fat-free milk
¹/₃ cup apricot spreadable fruit
1 egg yolk
1 teaspoon vanilla
¹/₂ cup all-purpose flour
10³/₄ teaspoons Equal® for Recipes *or* 36 packets Equal® sweetener
¹/₂ teaspoon baking powder
¹/₈ teaspoon salt
3 egg whites
¹/₈ teaspoon cream of tartar
¹/₂ cup coarsely chopped walnuts *or* pecans, optional

Per Serving
Calories: 120
% Calories from fat: 61
Fat (gm): 8.7
Saturated fat (gm): 3.4
Cholesterol (mg): 14.3
Sodium (mg): 111
Protein (gm): 4.7
Carbohydrate (gm): 7.9
Exchanges
Milk: 0.0
Vegetable: 0.0
Fruit: 0.0
Bread: 0.5
Meat: 0.0
Fat: 1.5

1. Heat margarine, chocolate, milk, and spreadable fruit in small saucepan, stirring frequently, until chocolate is almost melted. Remove from heat; continue stirring until chocolate is melted. Stir in egg yolk and vanilla; mix in combined flour, Equal® for Recipes, baking powder, and salt.

2. Beat egg whites and cream of tartar to stiff peaks in medium bowl; fold chocolate mixture into egg whites. Fold in walnuts, if using. Pour batter into greased 8-inch square baking pan.

3. Bake at 350 degrees until brownies are firm to touch and toothpick comes out clean, 18 to 20 minutes (do not overbake). Cool on wire rack. Serve warm or at room temperature.

PUMPKIN SPICE COOKIES

Soft, moist, and best eaten warm from the oven.

4 dozen cookies (1 per serving)

¹/₂ cup margarine, softened
9 teaspoons Equal® for Recipes *or* 30 packets Equal® sweetener
1 cup canned pumpkin
1 teaspoon orange extract
2 cups all-purpose flour
1 teaspoon baking soda
¹/₄ teaspoon salt
1¹/₂ teaspoons ground cinnamon
1 teaspoon pumpkin pie spice
¹/₂ teaspoon ground cloves
¹/₂ cup reduced-fat sour cream
¹/₂ cup finely chopped raisins
2 teaspoons grated orange rind
¹/₄ cup chopped pecans

Per Serving
Calories: 53
% Calories from fat: 44
Fat (gm): 2.6
Saturated fat (gm): 0.6
Cholesterol (mg): 0.8
Sodium (mg): 63
Protein (gm): 1.5
Carbohydrate (gm): 6
Exchanges
Milk: 0.0
Vegetable: 0.0
Fruit: 0.0
Bread: 0.5
Meat: 0.0
Fat: 0.5

1. Beat margarine and Equal® for Recipes until fluffy in large bowl; beat in pumpkin and orange extract. Mix in combined flour, baking soda, salt, and spices alternately with sour cream. Mix in raisins, orange rind, and pecans.

2. Spoon batter by heaping teaspoons onto greased cookie sheets. Bake cookies at 375 degrees until browned, 10 to 12 minutes. Cool on wire racks.

GRANOLA BITES

A sweet cookie, filled with healthful ingredients, that's good for you too!

2 dozen cookies (1 per serving)

2 cups corn, *or* wheat, flake cereal

²/₃ cup quick-cooking oats

¹/₄ cup bran cereal

¹/₂ cup chopped pitted dates *or* raisins

¹/₃-¹/₂ cup reduced-fat crunchy peanut butter

4 egg whites *or* ¹/₂ cup no-cholesterol real egg product

5 teaspoons Equal® for Recipes *or* 16 packets Equal® sweetener

2 teaspoons vanilla *or* maple extract

Per Serving
Calories: 57
% Calories from fat: 23
Fat (gm): 1.5
Saturated fat (gm): 0.3
Cholesterol (mg): 0
Sodium (mg): 71
Protein (gm): 2.8
Carbohydrate (gm): 8.7
Exchanges
Milk: 0.0
Vegetable: 0.0
Fruit: 0.0
Bread: 0.5
Meat: 0.0
Fat: 0.5

1. Combine cereals and dates in large bowl. Mix peanut butter, egg whites, Equal® for Recipes, and vanilla; pour over cereal mixture and stir until all ingredients are coated.

2. Shape mixture into 1-inch mounds; bake on greased cookie sheets at 350 degrees until cookies are set and browned, 8 to 10 minutes. Cool on wire racks.

SHORTBREAD COOKIES

A crisp yet tender cookie, with a wonderful buttery flavor.

1 dozen cookies (1 per serving)

1 cup all-purpose flour

3$^1/_2$ teaspoons Equal® for Recipes *or* 12 packets Equal® sweetener

1 tablespoon cornstarch

$^1/_8$ teaspoon salt

8 tablespoons cold margarine, cut into pieces

$^1/_2$-1 teaspoon butter extract

$^1/_2$ teaspoon vanilla

Per Serving
Calories: 113
% Calories from fat: 61
Fat (gm): 7.6
Saturated fat (gm): 1.5
Cholesterol (mg): 0
Sodium (mg): 113
Protein (gm): 2.1
Carbohydrate (gm): 8.7
Exchanges
Milk: 0.0
Vegetable: 0.0
Fruit: 0.0
Bread: 0.5
Meat: 0.0
Fat: 1.5

1. Combine flour, Equal® for Recipes, cornstarch, and salt in medium bowl; cut in margarine until mixture resembles coarse crumbs. Sprinkle butter extract and vanilla over mixture and mix with hands briefly until dough begins to hold together.

2. Pat dough evenly in bottom of greased 8-inch round cake pan. Lightly cut dough into 12 wedges with sharp knife, cutting about halfway through dough. Pierce each wedge 3 to 4 times with tines of fork.

3. Bake at 325 degrees until lightly browned, 25 to 30 minutes. Cool on wire rack; cut into wedges while warm.

Variations: **Almond Shortbread**—Make recipe as above, substituting almond extract for the butter extract and omitting vanilla. Separate 6 whole blanched almonds into halves; press 1 half into each shortbread wedge before baking.

Chocolate Shortbread—Make recipe as above, adding $^1/_4$ cup Dutch process cocoa, increasing Equal® for Recipes to 5$^1/_2$ teaspoons or 18 packets, and substituting vanilla for butter extract.

RASPBERRY-ALMOND BARS

A pretty bar cookie with a rich-tasting shortbread pastry.

2 dozen cookies (1 per serving)

2 cups all-purpose flour
3¹/₂ teaspoons Equal® for Recipes *or* 12
packets Equal® sweetener
¹/₈ teaspoon salt
8 tablespoons cold margarine, cut into
pieces
1 large egg, beaten
1 tablespoon fat-free milk *or* water
²/₃ cup seedless raspberry spreadable fruit
1 teaspoon cornstarch
¹/₄-¹/₃ cup finely chopped almonds, walnuts,
or pecans, toasted

Per Serving
Calories: 96
% Calories from fat: 45
Fat (gm): 4.6
Saturated fat (gm): 0.9
Cholesterol (mg): 8.8
Sodium (mg): 69
Protein (gm): 2.1
Carbohydrate (gm): 10.5
Exchanges
Milk: 0.0
Vegetable: 0.0
Fruit: 0.0
Bread: 0.5
Meat: 0.0
Fat: 1.0

1. Combine flour, Equal® for Recipes, and salt in medium bowl; cut in margarine until mixture resembles coarse crumbs. Mix in egg and milk.

2. Press mixture evenly in bottom of greased 11 x 7-inch baking dish. Bake at 400 degrees until edges of crust are browned, about 15 minutes. Cool on wire rack.

3. Mix spreadable fruit and cornstarch in small saucepan; heat to boiling. Boil until thickened, stirring constantly, 1 minute; cool 5 minutes. Spread mixture evenly over cooled crust; sprinkle with almonds. Bake at 400 degrees until spreadable fruit is thick and bubbly, about 15 minutes. Cool on wire rack.

APPLE-APRICOT BARS

Filled with a sweet, moist fruit filling, these bar cookies are a true comfort food.

2¹/₂ dozen cookies (1 per serving)

  ³/₄ cup chopped dried apples
  ³/₄ cup chopped dried apricots
  5¹/₄ teaspoons Equal® for Recipes *or* 18 packets Equal® sweetener, divided
  1 cup water
  5 tablespoons margarine, softened
  1 egg
  2 egg whites
  1 teaspoon vanilla
  1³/₄ cups all-purpose flour
  ¹/₂ teaspoon baking soda
  ¹/₄ teaspoon salt
    Fat-free milk

Per Serving
Calories: 63
% Calories from fat: 30
Fat (gm): 2.1
Saturated fat (gm): 0.4
Cholesterol (mg): 7.1
Sodium (mg): 71
Protein (gm): 1.9
Carbohydrate (gm): 9.1
Exchanges
Milk: 0.0
Vegetable: 0.0
Fruit: 0.0
Bread: 0.5
Meat: 0.0
Fat: 0.5

1. Heat apples, apricots, 3¹/₂ teaspoons Equal® for Recipes, and water to boiling in small saucepan; reduce heat and simmer, uncovered, until fruit is tender and water is absorbed, about 10 minutes. Process mixture in food processor or blender until smooth; cool.

2. Beat margarine and remaining 1³/₄ teaspoons Equal® for Recipes in medium bowl until fluffy; beat in egg, egg whites, and vanilla. Mix in combined flour, baking soda, and salt. Divide dough into 4 equal parts; roll each into a log about 5 inches long. Refrigerate, covered, until firm, about 2 hours.

3. Roll 1 piece dough on floured surface into rectangle 12 x 4 inches. Spread ¹/₄ of the fruit filling along a 1¹/₂-inch strip in the center of dough. Fold sides of dough over filling, pressing edges to seal. Cut filled dough in half and place seam side down on greased cookie sheet. Repeat with remaining dough and fruit filling.

4. Brush top of dough lightly with milk; bake at 400 degrees until lightly browned, 10 to 12 minutes. Remove from pan and cool on wire racks; cut into 1¹/₂-inch bars. Store in airtight container.

PEAR AND ROSEMARY BISCOTTI

Rosemary, with its sweetness, is a wonderful herb for desserts. Enjoy these biscotti with coffee or tea.

2 dozen biscotti (1 per serving)

    4 tablespoons margarine, softened
    2 eggs
    2 egg whites
2¹/₄ cups all-purpose flour
7¹/₄ teaspoons Equal® for Recipes *or* 24
      packets Equal® sweetener
    1 teaspoon baking powder
 ¹/₂ teaspoon baking soda
 ¹/₄ teaspoon salt
 ¹/₂ cup finely chopped dried pears
    1 tablespoon finely grated lemon rind
    1 tablespoon finely grated orange rind
    1 teaspoon dried rosemary leaves,
      crushed

Per Serving
Calories: 81
% Calories from fat: 27
Fat (gm): 2.4
Saturated fat (gm): 0.5
Cholesterol (mg): 17.7
Sodium (mg): 104
Protein (gm): 3.1
Carbohydrate (gm): 11.8
Exchanges
Milk: 0.0
Vegetable: 0.0
Fruit: 0.0
Bread: 1.0
Meat: 0.0
Fat: 0.5

1. Beat margarine, eggs, and egg whites in large bowl until smooth. Mix in combined flour, Equal® for Recipes, baking powder, baking soda, and salt. Mix in pears, citrus rinds, and rosemary.

2. Divide dough in half, and shape on greased cookie sheet into 2 flattened logs, each about 3 inches in diameter and 8 inches long. Bake at 350 degrees until browned, about 20 minutes. Cool on wire rack until cool enough to handle.

3. Cut bars diagonally into ¹/₂-inch slices. Place biscotti, cut sides down, on ungreased cookie sheet; bake until browned on the bottoms, about 10 minutes. Turn and bake until biscotti are browned on the other side and feel almost dry, about 10 minutes. Cool on wire racks (biscotti will become crisper as they cool).

CHOCOLATE FONDUE

The fondue is also delicious served as a sauce over sugar-free, fat-free ice cream.

8 servings (about ¹/₄ cup each)

1 package (8 ounces) unsweetened baking chocolate, coarsely chopped

1 cup fat-free milk

14¹/₂ teaspoons Equal® for Recipes *or* 48 packets Equal® sweetener

1 teaspoon vanilla *or* ¹/₂ to ³/₄ teaspoon rum *or* mint extract

Dippers: apple or pear slices, banana or melon pieces, orange segments, strawberries, and unsalted pretzel rods (not included in nutritional data)

Per Serving
Calories: 177
% Calories from fat: 61
Fat (gm): 14.2
Saturated fat (gm): 9.1
Cholesterol (mg): 0.6
Sodium (mg): 18
Protein (gm): 9.8
Carbohydrate (gm): 10.8
Exchanges
Milk: 0.0
Vegetable: 0.0
Fruit: 0.0
Bread: 0.5
Meat: 0.0
Fat: 3.0

1. Heat chocolate and milk in medium saucepan over low heat until chocolate is melted and mixture is smooth, stirring frequently. Stir in Equal® for Recipes and vanilla.

2. Pour chocolate mixture into serving bowl; serve with a variety of fruits and pretzel rods for dipping. If chocolate mixture becomes too thick, stir in 1 to 2 tablespoons warm fat-free milk.

BLACK CHERRY DESSERT DIP

Any desired flavor of spreadable fruit can be substituted for the black cherry.

4 servings (about ¼ cup each)

1 package (8 ounces) fat-free cream cheese, softened
½ cup black cherry spreadable fruit
2-3 teaspoons lemon juice
1 teaspoon grated lemon rind
⅛ teaspoon ground nutmeg
1 teaspoon Equal® for Recipes *or* 3 packets Equal® sweetener
Dippers: apple or pear slices, banana or melon pieces, orange segments, strawberries, and unsalted pretzel rods (not included in nutritional data)

Per Serving
Calories: 99
% Calories from fat: 7
Fat (gm): 0.8
Saturated fat (gm): 0.5
Cholesterol (mg): 4.5
Sodium (mg): 350
Protein (gm): 8.9
Carbohydrate (gm): 13.6
Exchanges
Milk: 0.0
Vegetable: 0.0
Fruit: 1.0
Bread: 0.0
Meat: 1.0
Fat: 0.0

1. Mix cream cheese and spreadable fruit, lemon juice, lemon rind, nutmeg, and Equal® for Recipes until smooth. Spoon into bowl; serve with a variety of fruits for dipping.

CREAMY LEMON PUDDING

For best texture, serve pudding the same day that it is made. The pudding is also excellent served warm as a sauce over fruit or any of the cakes in this chapter.

4 servings (about 3/4 cup each)

3 tablespoons cornstarch
2 tablespoons flour
Pinch salt
3 cups fat-free milk
1 egg
1 egg white
3-4 tablespoons lemon juice
1/2-3/4 teaspoon lemon extract
3 1/2 teaspoons Equal® for Recipes *or* 12 packets Equal® sweetener

Per Serving
Calories: 140
% Calories from fat: 10
Fat (gm): 1.6
Saturated fat (gm): 0.6
Cholesterol (mg): 56.3
Sodium (mg): 126
Protein (gm): 12
Carbohydrate (gm): 18.8
Exchanges
Milk: 1.0
Vegetable: 0.0
Fruit: 0.0
Bread: 0.5
Meat: 0.5
Fat: 0.0

1. Mix cornstarch, flour, and salt in medium saucepan; stir in milk. Whisk over medium to medium-high heat until mixture boils and thickens. Whisk about 1/2 of the milk mixture into the egg and egg white; whisk egg mixture into saucepan. Whisk over low heat 1 to 2 minutes.

2. Strain pudding into a bowl; cool to room temperature. Stir in lemon juice and extract and Equal® for Recipes. Refrigerate 1 to 2 hours.

PEACH CUSTARD

Use fresh, canned, or frozen, thawed peaches for this lovely light-textured custard.

6 servings (²/₃ cup each)

3 tablespoons cornstarch
2¹/₂ teaspoons Equal® for Recipes *or* 8 packets Equal® sweetener
2 cups fat-free milk
¹/₂ cup peach nectar
2 egg yolks, lightly beaten
1-2 tablespoons margarine, softened
1¹/₂ cups diced peaches
Light whipped topping, as garnish
Ground nutmeg, as garnish

Per Serving
Calories: 115
% Calories from fat: 29
Fat (gm): 3.8
Saturated fat (gm): 1
Cholesterol (mg): 72.5
Sodium (mg): 69
Protein (gm): 5.4
Carbohydrate (gm): 15.4
Exchanges
Milk: 0.5
Vegetable: 0.0
Fruit: 1.0
Bread: 0.0
Meat: 0.0
Fat: 0.5

1. Mix cornstarch and Equal® for Recipes in medium saucepan; whisk in milk and peach nectar. Whisk over medium to medium-high heat until mixture boils and thickens. Whisk about 1 cup milk mixture into the egg yolks; whisk egg yolk mixture into saucepan. Whisk over low heat until thickened, 1 to 2 minutes. Stir in margarine and cool to room temperature. Refrigerate until chilled, about 2 hours.

2. Whisk chilled custard until fluffy; fold in peaches. Spoon into dishes; garnish with dollops of light whipped topping and sprinkle lightly with nutmeg.

BAKED CUSTARD WITH ORANGE SAUCE

The custard has a shimmery light texture and lovely flavor, complemented with a lovely orange sauce.

6 servings (about ²/₃ cup each)

1 quart fat-free milk

5 eggs

5 teaspoons Equal® for Recipes *or* 16 packets Equal® sweetener

2 teaspoons vanilla

Orange Sauce (recipe follows)

Mint sprigs, as garnish

Per Serving
Calories: 174
% Calories from fat: 24
Fat (gm): 4.6
Saturated fat (gm): 1.5
Cholesterol (mg): 179.6
Sodium (mg): 138
Protein (gm): 14.3
Carbohydrate (gm): 17.7
Exchanges
Milk: 1.0
Vegetable: 0.0
Fruit: 0.0
Bread: 0.5
Meat: 1.0
Fat: 0.0

1. Heat milk just to simmering in medium saucepan. Beat eggs until foamy in medium bowl; gradually whisk milk into eggs. Stir in Equal® for Recipes and vanilla. Pour mixture through strainer into ungreased 1-quart casserole or soufflé dish.

2. Cover casserole with lid or aluminum foil and place in roasting pan on middle rack of oven. Pour 2 inches hot water into roasting pan. Bake at 325 degrees until custard is set and sharp knife inserted halfway between center and edge of custard comes out clean, 1 to 1¹/₄ hours.

3. Remove casserole from roasting pan; cool to room temperature on wire rack. Refrigerate until chilled, 6 hours or overnight. Spoon custard into dishes; spoon Orange Sauce over and garnish with mint.

Orange Sauce

makes about 1³/₄ cups

³/₄ cup orange juice

1 tablespoon cornstarch

1 teaspoon Equal® for Recipes *or* 3 packets Equal® sweetener

1 cup orange segments

1. Mix orange juice and cornstarch in small saucepan; whisk until mixture boils and thickens, 2 to 3 minutes. Stir in Equal® for Recipes and orange segments. Cool to room temperature; refrigerate until chilled.

Variation: **Baked Chocolate Custard**—Make recipe as above, increasing Equal® for Recipes to $6^1/4$ teaspoons and adding $^1/3$ cup Dutch process cocoa to the milk mixture. Omit Orange Sauce and mint sprigs.

APRICOT BAVARIAN

This delicately flavored dessert is party perfect.

4 servings (about $^2/3$ cup each)

$2^1/2$ teaspoons Equal® for Recipes *or* 8 packets Equal® sweetener
1 tablespoon cornstarch
1 envelope unflavored gelatin
1 cup apricot nectar
2 egg yolks
2 teaspoons finely grated lemon rind
2 cups light whipped topping
Light whipped topping, as garnish

Per Serving
Calories: 168
% Calories from fat: 38
Fat (gm): 6.6
Saturated fat (gm): 4.8
Cholesterol (mg): 106.5
Sodium (mg): 11
Protein (gm): 3.9
Carbohydrate (gm): 20.7
Exchanges
Milk: 0.0
Vegetable: 0.0
Fruit: 1.5
Bread: 0.0
Meat: 0.0
Fat: 1.0

1. Mix Equal® for Recipes, cornstarch, and gelatin in small saucepan; whisk in apricot nectar and heat to boiling, whisking until thickened. Whisk about $^1/2$ of the apricot juice mixture into the egg yolks; whisk egg yolk mixture into saucepan. Whisk over low heat until thickened, 2 to 3 minutes. Whisk in lemon rind. Cool to room temperature.

2. Fold 2 cups whipped topping into apricot mixture and spoon into serving bowl or individual dishes. Refrigerate until set, 3 to 4 hours. Garnish with light whipped topping.

Variation: **Orange Bavarian**—Make recipe as above, substituting orange juice for the apricot nectar, 1 tablespoon finely grated orange rind for the lemon rind, and adding $^1/2$ teaspoon orange extract. Garnish with light whipped topping and orange slices.

MANDARIN ALMOND CREAM

This Oriental-inspired dessert can be prepared in small bowls or stemmed goblets.

6 servings

2 envelopes unflavored gelatin

1 quart 2% reduced-fat milk, divided

2¹/2 teaspoons Equal® for Recipes *or* 8 packets Equal® sweetener

¹/4-¹/2 teaspoon almond extract

1 can (20 ounces) Mandarin orange segments, drained

Per Serving
Calories: 135
% Calories from fat: 21
Fat (gm): 3.1
Saturated fat (gm): 1.9
Cholesterol (mg): 12.2
Sodium (mg): 88
Protein (gm): 7.4
Carbohydrate (gm): 19.1
Exchanges
Milk: 1.0
Vegetable: 0.0
Fruit: 0.5
Bread: 0.0
Meat: 0.0
Fat: 0.5

1. Sprinkle gelatin over 1 cup milk in medium saucepan; let stand 2 to 3 minutes. Whisk over medium heat until beginning to simmer. Remove from heat; stir in remaining 3 cups milk, Equal® for Recipes, and almond extract. Refrigerate until mixture is the consistency of unbeaten egg whites, about 20 minutes.

2. Stir in Mandarin oranges; refrigerate until mixture is set, 2 to 3 hours.

CINNAMON BREAD PUDDING

For best texture, use day-old firm bread, such as French, Italian, or Vienna. Or, try sourdough bread, which lends a robust flavor.

8 servings

   2 cups fat-free milk
   4 tablespoons margarine, cut into pieces
   1 egg
   2 egg whites
3½ teaspoons Equal® for Recipes *or* 12 packets Equal® sweetener
1½ teaspoons ground cinnamon
   ⅛ teaspoon ground cloves
   3 dashes ground nutmeg
   ¼ teaspoon salt
   6 cups cubed day-old French, *or* Italian, bread (¾-inch cubes)

Per Serving
Calories: 153
% Calories from fat: 43
Fat (gm): 7.2
Saturated fat (gm): 1.7
Cholesterol (mg): 27.6
Sodium (mg): 308
Protein (gm): 6.8
Carbohydrate (gm): 14.8
Exchanges
Milk: 0.0
Vegetable: 0.0
Fruit: 0.0
Bread: 1.0
Meat: 0.5
Fat: 1.0

1. Heat milk and margarine to simmering in medium saucepan; remove from heat and stir until margarine is melted. Cool 10 minutes.

2. Beat egg and egg whites in large bowl until foamy; mix in Equal® for Recipes, spices, and salt. Mix in milk mixture and bread.

3. Spoon mixture into ungreased 1½-quart casserole. Place casserole in roasting pan on middle oven rack; pour 1 inch hot water into pan. Bake, uncovered, at 350 degrees until pudding is set and sharp knife inserted halfway between center and edge comes out clean, 40 to 45 minutes.

RAISIN-RICE PUDDING

Made on range top, rather than baked, this rice pudding is the creamiest ever.

8 servings (about ²/₃ cup each)

2 cups water
1 cup long-grain rice
1 quart fat-free milk
7¹/₄ teaspoons Equal® for Recipes *or* 24 packets Equal® sweetener
¹/₄ teaspoon salt
1 egg
¹/₂ cup raisins
2 teaspoons vanilla
¹/₂ teaspoon ground cinnamon

Per Serving
Calories: 179
% Calories from fat: 5
Fat (gm): 1
Saturated fat (gm): 0.4
Cholesterol (mg): 28.7
Sodium (mg): 147
Protein (gm): 9.8
Carbohydrate (gm): 32.2
Exchanges
Milk: 0.5
Vegetable: 0.0
Fruit: 0.0
Bread: 2.0
Meat: 0.0
Fat: 0.0

1. Heat water to boiling in large heavy saucepan; stir in rice. Reduce heat and simmer, covered, until rice is tender and water absorbed, 20 to 25 minutes.

2. Add milk to rice; heat to boiling over medium-high heat, stirring frequently. Reduce heat and simmer, covered, until mixture begins to thicken, 15 to 20 minutes, stirring frequently (milk will not be absorbed and pudding will thicken when it cools). Remove from heat and stir in Equal® for Recipes and salt.

3. Beat egg in small bowl; stir about 1 cup rice mixture into egg. Stir egg mixture into rice mixture in saucepan. Stir in raisins, vanilla, and cinnamon. Cook over medium-low heat 1 to 2 minutes, stirring constantly. Serve warm or chilled.

SWEET POTATO PUDDING

Although well-drained canned sweet potatoes can be used, we prefer the flavor and texture of the pudding made with fresh sweet potatoes.

6 servings

2 cups mashed cooked sweet potatoes
2 tablespoons melted margarine
2 eggs
1 cup fat-free sour cream
5¹/₂ teaspoons Equal® for Recipes *or* 18 packets Equal® sweetener
¹/₂ teaspoon ground cinnamon
¹/₂ teaspoon ground cardamom
¹/₄ teaspoon ground nutmeg
¹/₄ teaspoon salt
2-4 tablespoons chopped walnuts
Light whipped topping, as garnish

Per Serving
Calories: 249
% Calories from fat: 27
Fat (gm): 7.3
Saturated fat (gm): 1.5
Cholesterol (mg): 70.7
Sodium (mg): 211
Protein (gm): 10.1
Carbohydrate (gm): 35.4
Exchanges
Milk: 0.0
Vegetable: 0.0
Fruit: 0.0
Bread: 2.0
Meat: 1.0
Fat: 1.0

1. Mix all ingredients, except walnuts and light whipped topping, until well blended; spoon into 6 greased 1-cup soufflé dishes, or 1¹/₂-quart soufflé dish, and sprinkle with walnuts.

2. Bake at 350 degrees until puddings are puffed and set, 25 to 30 minutes for the small puddings, about 45 minutes for the large pudding. Serve warm with dollops of light whipped topping.

LEMON PUDDING CAKE

This lemony dessert separates into 2 layers while baking, creating both a cake and a pudding.

4 servings

3 tablespoons flour

3¹/₂ teaspoons Equal® for Recipes *or* 12 packets Equal® sweetener

¹/₄ teaspoon salt

2 pinches ground nutmeg

1 cup fat-free milk

2 egg yolks

3 tablespoons lemon juice

2 egg whites, beaten to stiff peaks

Per Serving
Calories: 95
% Calories from fat: 26
Fat (gm): 2.7
Saturated fat (gm): 0.9
Cholesterol (mg): 107.6
Sodium (mg): 209
Protein (gm): 8.7
Carbohydrate (gm): 8.7
Exchanges
Milk: 0.0
Vegetable: 0.0
Fruit: 0.0
Bread: 0.5
Meat: 1.0
Fat: 0.0

1. Combine flour, Equal® for Recipes, salt, and nutmeg in medium bowl. Beat milk, egg yolks, and lemon juice in small bowl until well blended; add to dry ingredients, beating well. Fold in egg whites.

2. Pour mixture into lightly greased 1-quart soufflé dish or casserole. Place in small roasting pan on middle oven rack and pour 1 inch hot water into pan. Bake at 350 degrees until top is set and sharp knife inserted halfway between center and edge comes out clean, 50 to 60 minutes.

3. Remove soufflé dish from hot water; cool on wire rack. Serve warm.

Variation: **Chocolate Pudding Cake**—Make recipe as above omitting lemon juice, increasing milk to 1¹/₄ cups, Equal® for Recipes to 5¹/₂ teaspoons or 18 packets of Equal® sweetener, and adding 2 tablespoons Dutch process cocoa and ¹/₂ teaspoon ground cinnamon.

SKILLET COBBLER

No need to heat the oven with this easy stove-top cobbler!

6 servings

1¹/₂ tablespoons cornstarch
8 teaspoons Equal® for Recipes *or* 26 packets Equal® sweetener, divided
¹/₂ cup water
1 teaspoon lemon juice
2 teaspoons finely grated orange rind, divided
4 cups fresh, *or* frozen, blueberries
1 cup all-purpose flour
1¹/₂ teaspoons baking powder
¹/₂ teaspoon ground cinnamon
¹/₈ teaspoon ground nutmeg
¹/₂ teaspoon salt
3 tablespoons cold margarine, cut into pieces
¹/₂ cup fat-free milk

Per Serving
Calories: 214
% Calories from fat: 26
Fat (gm): 6.3
Saturated fat (gm): 1.2
Cholesterol (mg): 0.4
Sodium (mg): 401
Protein (gm): 7.7
Carbohydrate (gm): 33.1
Exchanges
Milk: 0.0
Vegetable: 0.0
Fruit: 0.5
Bread: 2.0
Meat: 0.0
Fat: 1.0

1. Mix cornstarch, 5¹/₂ teaspoons Equal® for Recipes, water, lemon juice, and 1 teaspoon grated orange rind in 8-inch skillet. Add blueberries and heat to boiling. Boil, stirring constantly, until mixture is thickened, 1 minute. Reduce heat and simmer, uncovered, 5 minutes.

2. Combine flour, baking powder, remaining 2¹/₂ teaspoons Equal® for Recipes, spices, and salt in medium bowl; cut in margarine until mixture resembles coarse crumbs. Stir in milk, forming soft dough; stir in remaining 1 teaspoon orange rind.

3. Spoon dough in 6 mounds on simmering blueberry mixture. Cook, covered, over low heat until dumplings are done, 12 to 14 minutes. Serve warm.

CREAMY FRUIT FREEZE MELBA

A medley of flavorful fruit, frozen with cream cheese and sour cream, and served with brilliant-hued raspberry sauce.

12 servings

Per Serving
Calories: 102
% Calories from fat: 5
Fat (gm): 0.7
Saturated fat (gm): 0.2
Cholesterol (mg): 1.5
Sodium (mg): 122
Protein (gm): 6.5
Carbohydrate (gm): 18.2
Exchanges
Milk: 0.0
Vegetable: 0.0
Fruit: 1.0
Bread: 0.0
Meat: 1.0
Fat: 0.0

1 package (8 ounces) fat-free cream cheese
1 cup fat-free sour cream
2¹/₂ teaspoons Equal® for Recipes *or* 8 packets Equal® sweetener
2-3 teaspoons lemon juice
1 cup coarsely chopped fresh, *or* canned, peaches
1 cup fresh, *or* frozen, blueberries
1 cup fresh, *or* unsweetened frozen, raspberries *or* halved *or* quartered strawberries
1 cup canned, drained pineapple wedges in juice
1 can (11 ounces) Mandarin orange segments, drained
Chopped pecans, as garnish
Melba Sauce (recipe follows)

1. Beat cream cheese, sour cream, Equal® for Recipes, and lemon juice in medium bowl until smooth; gently mix in fruit. Spoon mixture into 10 x 6-inch baking dish and sprinkle with pecans. Freeze until firm, 6 to 8 hours.

2. Let stand at room temperature until slightly softened, 10 to 15 minutes; cut into squares. Serve with Melba Sauce.

Melba Sauce

makes about 2 cups

4 cups fresh, *or* frozen, thawed unsweetened raspberries
3¹/₂-5 teaspoons Equal® for Recipes *or* 12 to 16 packets Equal® sweetener

1. Process raspberries in food processor or blender until smooth; strain and discard seeds. Stir in Equal® for Recipes.

FROZEN YOGURT FRUIT CUPS

The texture of this frozen dessert is luxuriously creamy.

6 to 8 servings

   1 can (9 ounces) pineapple tidbits in juice, drained

   2 medium bananas, cut into scant $1/2$-inch pieces

  $1/2$ cup quartered small strawberries

   2 cups fat-free plain yogurt

   2 tablespoons lemon juice

$5^1/2$ teaspoons Equal® for Recipes *or* 18 packets Equal® sweetener

  $1/3$ cup walnut pieces

  $1/4$ teaspoon salt

 6-8 walnut halves, as garnish

Per Serving
Calories: 161
% Calories from fat: 23
Fat (gm): 4.3
Saturated fat (gm): 0.4
Cholesterol (mg): 1.4
Sodium (mg): 157
Protein (gm): 9.5
Carbohydrate (gm): 23.5
Exchanges
Milk: 0.5
Vegetable: 0.0
Fruit: 1.5
Bread: 0.0
Meat: 0.0
Fat: 0.5

1. Mix pineapple tidbits, bananas, and strawberries into yogurt; mix in lemon juice, Equal® for Recipes, walnut pieces, and salt.

2. Spoon mixture into small custard cups and garnish with walnut halves; freeze until firm, 4 to 6 hours. Let stand at room temperature 5 to 10 minutes before serving.

POACHED PEARS WITH RED WINE SAUCE

An elegant dessert that's remarkably easy to prepare.

6 servings

Per Serving
Calories: 189
% Calories from fat: 3
Fat (gm): 0.7
Saturated fat (gm): 0
Cholesterol (mg): 0
Sodium (mg): 6
Protein (gm): 2.1
Carbohydrate (gm): 33.7
Exchanges
Milk: 0.0
Vegetable: 0.0
Fruit: 2.0
Bread: 0.0
Meat: 0.0
Fat: 1.5

    2 cups dry red wine
    1 cup unsweetened apple juice
    2 cinnamon sticks
    1 whole nutmeg
    6 ripe, firm pears, peeled, cored, cut into
       halves
    2 tablespoons cornstarch
  $1/4$ cup cold water
  $2^{1}/_{2}$ teaspoons Equal® for Recipes *or* 8
       packets Equal® sweetener
       Mint sprigs, as garnish

1. Heat wine, apple juice, and spices to boiling in large skillet; add pear halves, cut sides down. Simmer, covered, until pears are tender, 10 to 15 minutes. Remove pears with slotted spoon and place in serving dishes; discard spices.

2. Heat wine mixture to boiling; whisk in combined cornstarch and cold water. Boil, whisking constantly, until thickened, about 1 minute; whisk in Equal® for Recipes. Spoon sauce around pears; garnish with mint.

PEARS BELLE HÉLÈNE

Serve Almond Shortbread Cookies (see p. 606) with this lovely dessert. To make Pears Melba, substitute Melba Sauce (see p. 622) for the Bittersweet Chocolate Sauce.

6 servings

2 cups unsweetened apple juice

1³/4 teaspoons Equal® for Recipes *or* 6 packets Equal® sweetener, divided

3 large pears, peeled, cored, cut into halves

3 cups sugar-free, fat-free ice cream

Bittersweet Chocolate Sauce (recipe follows)

Mint sprigs, as garnish

Per Serving
Calories: 235
% Calories from fat: 11
Fat (gm): 3
Saturated fat (gm): 0.8
Cholesterol (mg): 0.4
Sodium (mg): 85
Protein (gm): 9.7
Carbohydrate (gm): 45.3
Exchanges
Milk: 0.0
Vegetable: 0.0
Fruit: 1.0
Bread: 2.0
Meat: 0.0
Fat: 0.5

1. Heat apple juice and Equal® for Recipes to simmering in large skillet; add pear halves, cut sides down. Simmer, covered, until pears are tender, 10 to 15 minutes. Remove pears with slotted spoon.

2. Spoon ice cream into 6 serving dishes; top with pear halves. Spoon Bittersweet Chocolate Sauce over; garnish with mint sprigs.

Bittersweet Chocolate Sauce

makes about 1 cup

1/2 cup fat-free milk

1/2 cup Dutch process cocoa

3¹/2 teaspoons Equal® for Recipes *or* 12 packets Equal® sweetener

1-2 tablespoons margarine

1¹/2 teaspoons vanilla

1. Whisk milk, cocoa, and Equal® for Recipes until blended in small saucepan; add margarine and vanilla and whisk over medium heat just until simmering. Serve warm, or refrigerate and serve chilled.

CRANBERRY POACHED PLUMS

Serve the sweet plums and sauce warm over sugar-free, fat-free frozen yogurt or ice cream.

4 servings

2 cups sugar-free cranberry juice
1 cinnamon stick
3 whole allspice
8 large purple plums, cut into halves, pitted
2¹/₂ teaspoons Equal® for Recipes *or* 8 packets Equal® sweetener
1 tablespoon cornstarch
3 tablespoons cold water
Light whipped topping, as garnish

Per Serving
Calories: 119
% Calories from fat: 6
Fat (gm): 0.8
Saturated fat (gm): 0.1
Cholesterol (mg): 0
Sodium (mg): 13
Protein (gm): 3.2
Carbohydrate (gm): 26
Exchanges
Milk: 0.0
Vegetable: 0.0
Fruit: 2.0
Bread: 0.0
Meat: 0.0
Fat: 0.0

1. Heat cranberry juice, cinnamon, and allspice to boiling in large skillet; add plums, cut sides down. Reduce heat and simmer, covered, until plums are tender, about 10 minutes. Remove plums and discard spices.

2. Heat juice mixture to boiling; whisk in Equal® for Recipes and combined cornstarch and cold water, whisking until thickened, about 1 minute. Pour sauce over plums in serving dishes; garnish with light whipped topping.

SWEET BANANAS FOSTER

Also delicious served over pancakes and waffles as a sweet brunch offering.

6 servings

1¹/₂ cups apple cider

2 tablespoons lemon juice

3 tablespoons cornstarch

1³/₄ teaspoons Equal® for Recipes *or* 6 packets Equal® sweetener

1-2 teaspoons margarine

¹/₂ teaspoon rum, *or* maple, extract

1 teaspoon vanilla

2 medium bananas, sliced

1¹/₂ pints vanilla sugar-free, fat-free ice cream

Per Serving
Calories: 176
% Calories from fat: 4
Fat (gm): 0.9
Saturated fat (gm): 0.2
Cholesterol (mg): 0
Sodium (mg): 55
Protein (gm): 5.4
Carbohydrate (gm): 39.9
Exchanges
Milk: 0.0
Vegetable: 0.0
Fruit: 1.0
Bread: 1.5
Meat: 0.0
Fat: 0.0

1. Whisk apple cider, lemon juice, and cornstarch in medium saucepan over medium-high heat until mixture boils and thickens, 2 to 3 minutes.

2. Whisk in Equal® for Recipes, margarine, rum extract, and vanilla. Stir in bananas; cook 1 to 2 minutes longer. Serve over ice cream.

BERRIES ROMANOFF

Use 1 or more kinds of fresh berries in this lemon-scented Romanoff.

6 servings (about ¾ cup each)

2	cups light whipped topping
1	container (8 ounces) reduced-fat, sugar-free, custard-style lemon yogurt
1-2	tablespoons lemon juice
1¾	teaspoons Equal® for Recipes *or* 6 packets Equal® sweetener
3	cups fresh berries (strawberries, blueberries, raspberries, blackberries, *or* currants)
	Ground nutmeg, as garnish
	Mint sprigs, as garnish

Per Serving
Calories: 115
% Calories from fat: 28
Fat (gm): 3.4
Saturated fat (gm): 3
Cholesterol (mg): 2.5
Sodium (mg): 28
Protein (gm): 3.1
Carbohydrate (gm): 16.8
Exchanges
Milk: 0.0
Vegetable: 0.0
Fruit: 0.5
Bread: 1.0
Meat: 0.0
Fat: 0.5

1. Mix whipped topping, yogurt, lemon juice, and Equal® for Recipes; fold in berries. Spoon into stemmed goblets; sprinkle lightly with nutmeg and garnish with mint.

STEWED RHUBARB AND BERRIES

A great team of flavors—serve with light whipped topping and a sprinkle of toasted chopped pecans.

6 servings (about ⅔ cup each)

1	pound fresh, *or* frozen, rhubarb, cut into 1-inch pieces
¼	cup water
2	cups sliced strawberries
2½	teaspoons Equal® for Recipes *or* 8 packets Equal® sweetener

Per Serving
Calories: 36
% Calories from fat: 7
Fat (gm): 0.3
Saturated fat (gm): 0.1
Cholesterol (mg): 0
Sodium (mg): 4
Protein (gm): 2.3
Carbohydrate (gm): 6.9
Exchanges
Milk: 0.0
Vegetable: 0.0
Fruit: 0.5
Bread: 0.0
Meat: 0.0
Fat: 0.0

1. Combine rhubarb and water in medium saucepan; cook, covered, over medium heat until soft, about 10 minutes. Stir in strawberries and Equal® for Recipes; cook until hot through, 1 to 2 minutes. Serve warm, or refrigerate and serve chilled.

BRANDIED ORANGE COMPOTE

Serve this low-calorie dessert with moist Fudgey Brownies or crisp Short-bread Cookies (see pp. 603, 606).

4 servings

2 teaspoons cornstarch

1³/4 teaspoons Equal® for Recipes *or* 6 packets Equal® sweetener

³/4 cup orange juice

1 cinnamon stick

6 whole cloves

1-2 tablespoons brandy *or* ¹/2 teaspoon brandy extract

4 small oranges, peeled, sliced

Mint sprigs, as garnish

Per Serving
Calories: 102
% Calories from fat: 2
Fat (gm): 0.3
Saturated fat (gm): 0
Cholesterol (mg): 0
Sodium (mg): 1
Protein (gm): 3
Carbohydrate (gm): 21.5
Exchanges
Milk: 0.0
Vegetable: 0.0
Fruit: 1.5
Bread: 0.0
Meat: 0.0
Fat: 0.0

1. Whisk cornstarch, Equal® for Recipes, orange juice, and spices in small saucepan over medium heat until mixture boils and thickens, 2 to 3 minutes. Whisk in brandy.

2. Pour orange juice mixture over orange slices in serving bowl; cool to room temperature. Refrigerate until chilled, 1 to 2 hours; discard spices. Serve in small bowls; garnish with mint.

LIME MELON COMPOTES

A medley of melon, served with subtle-flavored Minted Lime Sauce.

6 servings (about 1 cup each)

2 cups each: cubed honeydew, cantaloupe, and watermelon
1 teaspoon Equal® for Recipes *or* 3
   packets Equal® sweetener
   Minted Lime Sauce (recipe follows)
   Mint sprigs, as garnish

Per Serving
Calories: 86
% Calories from fat: 23
Fat (gm): 2.3
Saturated fat (gm): 0.5
Cholesterol (mg): 0
Sodium (mg): 34
Protein (gm): 2.6
Carbohydrate (gm): 15.5
Exchanges
Milk: 0.0
Vegetable: 0.0
Fruit: 1.0
Bread: 0.0
Meat: 0.0
Fat: 0.5

1. Combine melon in serving bowl; sprinkle with Equal® for Recipes and toss. Serve with Minted Lime Sauce and garnish with mint.

Minted Lime Sauce

makes 1 1/4 cups

1 tablespoon cornstarch
1 3/4 teaspoons Equal® for Recipes *or* 6 packets
   Equal® sweetener
1 cup water
3 tablespoons lime juice
1 teaspoon dried mint leaves
1 tablespoon margarine, softened

1. Whisk all ingredients, except margarine, in small saucepan over medium-high heat until mixture boils and thickens, 2 to 3 minutes. Stir in margarine.

OLD-FASHIONED APPLE CRISP

Juicy apples baked with a crisp sweet-spiced topping will warm hearts in any season.

6 servings

3¹/₂ teaspoons Equal® for Recipes *or* 12 packets Equal® sweetener

1 tablespoon cornstarch

³/₄ cup unsweetened apple juice

1 teaspoon finely grated lemon rind

4 cups sliced peeled apples

Crispy Spiced Topping (recipe follows)

Per Serving
Calories: 198
% Calories from fat: 41
Fat (gm): 9.3
Saturated fat (gm): 2.5
Cholesterol (mg): 0
Sodium (mg): 93
Protein (gm): 4.8
Carbohydrate (gm): 25.7
Exchanges
Milk: 0.0
Vegetable: 0.0
Fruit: 1.0
Bread: 1.5
Meat: 0.0
Fat: 2.0

1. Whisk Equal® for Recipes, cornstarch, apple juice, and lemon rind over medium heat in medium saucepan until mixture boils and thickens, 2 to 3 minutes; add apples and simmer, uncovered, until apples begin to lose their crispness, about 5 minutes. Transfer mixture to 8-inch square baking pan.

2. Sprinkle Crispy Spiced Topping over apples. Bake at 400 degrees until topping is browned and apples are tender, about 25 minutes. Serve warm.

Crispy Spiced Topping

makes about ³/₄ cup

1/4 cup all-purpose flour

2¹/₂ teaspoons Equal® for Recipes *or* 8 packets Equal® sweetener

1 teaspoon ground cinnamon

1/2 teaspoon ground nutmeg

3 dashes ground allspice

4 tablespoons cold margarine, cut into pieces

1/4 cup quick-cooking oats

1/4 cup flaked coconut

1. Combine flour, Equal® for Recipes, and spices in small bowl; cut in margarine until mixture resembles coarse crumbs. Stir in oats and coconut.

CHUNKY SPICED APPLESAUCE

Just like Mom used to make, only without the sugar. Use your favorite cooking apple and adjust the amount of sweetener if necessary.

8 servings (about ²/₃ cup each)

3¹/₂ pounds tart cooking apples, peeled, chopped

¹/₂ cup water

7¹/₄ teaspoons Equal® for Recipes *or* 24 packets Equal® sweetener

¹/₂ teaspoon ground cinnamon

¹/₄ teaspoon ground nutmeg

1-2 dashes salt

Per Serving
Calories: 147
% Calories from fat: 5
Fat (gm): 1
Saturated fat (gm): 0.2
Cholesterol (mg): 0
Sodium (mg): 3
Protein (gm): 3.5
Carbohydrate (gm): 34.8
Exchanges
Milk: 0.0
Vegetable: 0.0
Fruit: 2.5
Bread: 0.0
Meat: 0.0
Fat: 0.0

1. Heat apples and water to boiling in large saucepan; reduce heat and simmer, covered, until apples are soft, about 20 minutes. Mash apples coarsely with fork; stir in Equal® for Recipes, cinnamon, nutmeg, and salt. Serve warm, or refrigerate and serve chilled.

FRUIT BAKED APPLES

Raisins or dried berries can be substituted for the dried fruit.

8 servings

3¹/₂ teaspoons Equal® for Recipes *or* 12 packets Equal® sweetener
1 tablespoon cornstarch
Pinch ground cinnamon
Pinch ground nutmeg
2 cups apple cider *or* juice
1 package (6 ounces) mixed dried fruit, chopped
2 tablespoons margarine
8 baking apples

Per Serving
Calories: 203
% Calories from fat: 14
Fat (gm): 3.5
Saturated fat (gm): 0.7
Cholesterol (mg): 0
Sodium (mg): 37
Protein (gm): 2.4
Carbohydrate (gm): 45.4
Exchanges
Milk: 0.0
Vegetable: 0.0
Fruit: 3.0
Bread: 0.0
Meat: 0.0
Fat: 0.5

1. Whisk Equal® for Recipes, cornstarch, spices, apple cider, and dried fruit over high heat in medium saucepan until mixture boils and thickens, 2 to 3 minutes. Reduce heat and simmer, uncovered, until fruit is tender and cider mixture is reduced to about 1 cup, 10 to 15 minutes. Stir in margarine.

2. Remove cores from apples, cutting to, but not through bottoms. Peel 1 inch from around tops. Place apples in greased baking pan; fill centers with fruit mixture and spoon remaining cider mixture over apples.

3. Bake, uncovered, at 350 degrees until apples are fork-tender, about 45 minutes.

DUTCH APPLE DESSERT PUFF

A no-sugar-added maple-flavored sauce replaces the honey or caramel sauce that would be used in this recipe. Maple Sauce is also delicious served over sugar-free, fat-free ice cream, pancakes, or waffles. Vary the flavor by substituting another flavor extract, such as almond or rum, for the maple.

6 to 8 servings

4	eggs
3/4	cup fat-free milk
3/4	cup all-purpose flour
7	teaspoons Equal® for Recipes *or* 24 packets Equal® sweetener, divided
1/4	teaspoon salt
3	tablespoons margarine, divided
5	large cooking apples, peeled, sliced
1/4	teaspoon ground cinnamon
1	cup apple cider *or* apple juice, divided
1	tablespoon lemon juice
4	teaspoons cornstarch
	Ground nutmeg *or* cinnamon
	Maple Sauce (recipe follows)
	Light whipped topping, as garnish

Per Serving
Calories: 342
% Calories from fat: 30
Fat (gm): 11.6
Saturated fat (gm): 2.7
Cholesterol (mg): 141.9
Sodium (mg): 249
Protein (gm): 12
Carbohydrate (gm): 48.5
Exchanges
Milk: 0.0
Vegetable: 0.0
Fruit: 3.0
Bread: 0.0
Meat: 1.0
Fat: 2.0

1. Mix eggs, milk, flour, 1 1/2 teaspoons Equal® for Recipes, and salt in bowl (batter will be slightly lumpy). Heat 1 tablespoon margarine in 12-inch oven-proof skillet until bubbly. Pour batter into skillet and cook over medium heat 1 minute. Transfer skillet to oven and bake at 425 degrees 20 minutes. Reduce oven temperature to 350 degrees and bake until crisp and golden, 7 to 10 minutes (do not open oven door during baking). Transfer puff to serving plate.

2. While puff is baking, saute apples in remaining 2 table-spoons margarine in large skillet until apples begin to soften, about 5 minutes; sprinkle with remaining 5¹/₂ teaspoons Equal® for Recipes and cinnamon. Add ³/₄ cup cider and lemon juice and heat to boiling; stir in combined remaining ¹/₄ cup cider and cornstarch. Boil, stirring, until thickened.

3. Spoon apple mixture into puff and sprinkle lightly with nut-meg. Cut into wedges; serve with Maple Sauce and dollops of light whipped topping.

Maple Sauce

makes about 1¹/₂ cups

- 1¹/₂ cups unsweetened apple juice
- 4 teaspoons cornstarch
- 1-2 tablespoons margarine
- 2¹/₂ teaspoons Equal® for Recipes *or* 8 packets Equal® sweetener
- 1¹/₂ teaspoons maple extract
- 1 teaspoon vanilla

1. Whisk apple juice and cornstarch over medium-high heat in small saucepan until mixture boils and thickens, 2 to 3 minutes. Stir in remaining ingredients. Serve warm.

CUSTARD-FILLED CREAM PUFFS WITH BLUEBERRY SAUCE

Cream puffs can also be filled with sugar-free, fat-free ice cream and served with Bittersweet Chocolate Sauce (see p. 625).

8 servings

Cream Puffs (see p. 266)
1 teaspoon Equal® for Recipes *or* 3 packets Equal® sweetener
Vanilla Custard (recipe follows)
Blueberry Sauce (recipe follows)
Light whipped topping, as garnish

Per Serving
Calories: 325
% Calories from fat: 38
Fat (gm): 13.4
Saturated fat (gm): 4.7
Cholesterol (mg): 161.3
Sodium (mg): 328
Protein (gm): 12.6
Carbohydrate (gm): 36.5
Exchanges
Milk: 0.0
Vegetable: 0.0
Fruit: 0.5
Bread: 2.5
Meat: 1.0
Fat: 2.5

1. Make 8 Cream Puffs, substituting 1 teaspoon Equal® for Recipes for the sugar.

2. Fill puffs with Vanilla Custard; serve with Blueberry Sauce and garnish with dollops of light whipped topping.

Vanilla Custard

makes about 4 cups

1/4 cup cornstarch
2 tablespoons flour
2 1/2 cups fat-free milk
3 egg yolks, slightly beaten
2 tablespoons margarine, softened
1 teaspoon vanilla
3 1/2 teaspoons Equal® for Recipes *or* 12 packets Equal® sweetener
2 cups light whipped topping

1. Whisk cornstarch, flour, and milk over medium-high heat in medium saucepan until mixture boils and thickens, 2 to 3 minutes. Whisk about 1 cup milk mixture into egg yolks; whisk egg mixture into saucepan. Whisk over low heat until thickened, 1 to 2 minutes. Stir in margarine, vanilla, and Equal® for Recipes.

· **2.** Cool custard to room temperature, stirring occasionally. Cover top of custard with plastic wrap and refrigerate until chilled, about 2 hours. Whisk custard until fluffy; fold in light whipped topping.

Blueberry Sauce

makes about 2 cups

　　2 teaspoons cornstarch
1³/₄ teaspoons Equal® for Recipes *or* 6 packets
　　　Equal® sweetener
　¹/₂ teaspoon ground cinnamon
　　1 cup unsweetened apple juice
　　1 tablespoon lemon juice
　　2 cups fresh, *or* frozen, blueberries

1. Whisk cornstarch, Equal® for Recipes, cinnamon, apple juice, and lemon juice over medium heat in small saucepan until mixture boils and thickens, 2 to 3 minutes.

2. Stir in blueberries; cook over low heat until berries are tender, 2 to 3 minutes. Serve warm, or refrigerate and serve chilled.

AUTUMN PEAR CREPES

Select perfectly ripened pears for this elegant dessert offering.

4 servings (2 crepes each)

Crepes (see p. 274)

2³/4 teaspoons Equal® for Recipes *or* 9 packets Equal® sweetener, divided

2 teaspoons cornstarch

1 cup pear nectar *or* unsweetened apple juice

2 cups cubed peeled pears

2 pinches ground nutmeg

Light whipped topping, as garnish

Toasted chopped walnuts, as garnish

Per Serving
Calories: 241
% Calories from fat: 17
Fat (gm): 4.8
Saturated fat (gm): 1
Cholesterol (mg): 53.6
Sodium (mg): 241
Protein (gm): 8.7
Carbohydrate (gm): 42.7
Exchanges
Milk: 0.0
Vegetable: 0.0
Fruit: 1.0
Bread: 2.0
Meat: 0.0
Fat: 1.0

1. Make 8 crepes, substituting 1 teaspoon Equal® for Recipes for the sugar; keep warm.

2. Whisk remaining 1³/4 teaspoons Equal® for Recipes, cornstarch, and pear nectar over medium heat in medium saucepan until mixture boils and thickens 2 to 3 minutes. Stir in pears and nutmeg; cook over medium heat until pears are tender, 3 to 5 minutes.

3. Fill each crepe with about ¹/3 cup pear mixture and place, seam sides down, on serving plates. Garnish with dollops of light whipped topping and sprinkle with walnuts.

THIRTEEN

Dessert Sauces

CRÈME ANGLAISE

Delicious served over pound cake, fruit pies, and tarts.

8 servings (about 2 tablespoons each)

1 tablespoon cornstarch
2 teaspoons sugar
1 cup fat-free milk
1 egg yolk
1/2-3/4 teaspoon ground nutmeg

Per Serving
Calories: 26
% Calories from fat: 24
Fat (gm): 0.7
Saturated fat (gm): 0.2
Cholesterol (mg): 27.2
Sodium (mg): 17
Protein (gm): 1.4
Carbohydrate (gm): 3.5
Exchanges
Milk: 0.0
Vegetable: 0.0
Fruit: 0.0
Bread: 0.5
Meat: 0.0
Fat: 0.0

1. Mix cornstarch and sugar in small saucepan; stir in milk. Cook over medium heat until mixture boils and thickens, stirring constantly.

2. Stir about 1/2 cup milk mixture into egg yolk; stir egg yolk mixture into saucepan. Cook over low heat, stirring constantly, until thickened (mixture will coat back of spoon). Remove from heat; stir in nutmeg. Serve warm or cold.

BITTERSWEET CHOCOLATE SAUCE

Bittersweet and scrumptious—serve over low-fat frozen yogurt, Chocolate Baked Alaska Pie, or Frozen Peppermint Cake Rolls (see pp. 461, 465).

12 servings (about 2 tablespoons each)

³/4	cup unsweetened cocoa
¹/2	cup sugar
³/4	cup fat-free milk
2	tablespoons margarine
1	teaspoon vanilla
¹/4-¹/2	teaspoon ground cinnamon

Per Serving
Calories: 64
% Calories from fat: 27
Fat (gm): 1.9
Saturated fat (gm): 0.4
Cholesterol (mg): 0.5
Sodium (mg): 39
Protein (gm): 1.1
Carbohydrate (gm): 10.7
Exchanges
Milk: 0.0
Vegetable: 0.0
Fruit: 0.0
Bread: 1.0
Meat: 0.0
Fat: 0.0

1. Mix cocoa and sugar in small saucepan; stir in milk and add margarine. Heat over medium heat until boiling, stirring constantly. Reduce heat and simmer until sauce is smooth and slightly thickened, 3 to 4 minutes. Remove from heat; stir in vanilla and cinnamon. Serve warm or at room temperature.

CHOCOLATE SAUCE

Quick and easy to make for instant dessert gratification!

8 servings (about 2 tablespoons each)

$^1/_4$ cup unsweetened cocoa
2 tablespoons sugar
1 tablespoon cornstarch
$^1/_3$ cup dark corn syrup
$^1/_4$ cup 2% reduced-fat milk
1 teaspoon margarine
2 teaspoons vanilla

Per Serving
Calories: 71
% Calories from fat: 8
Fat (gm): 0.6
Saturated fat (gm): 0.2
Cholesterol (mg): 0.7
Sodium (mg): 23
Protein (gm): 0.5
Carbohydrate (gm): 15.8
Exchanges
Milk: 0.0
Vegetable: 0.0
Fruit: 0.0
Bread: 1.0
Meat: 0.0
Fat: 0.0

1. Combine cocoa, sugar, and cornstarch in small saucepan. Stir in corn syrup and milk until smooth. Cook over medium heat until mixture boils and thickens, stirring constantly. Remove from heat; stir in margarine and vanilla. Serve warm or at room temperature.

RICH CARAMEL SAUCE

Egg and a bit of flour replace heavy cream to give this sauce its rich texture and flavor.

12 servings (about 2 tablespoons each)

2 eggs, lightly beaten
1 cup packed light brown sugar
1 tablespoon flour
1/4 cup light corn syrup
1/4 cup 2% reduced-fat milk
1 teaspoon vanilla
4 tablespoons margarine, cut into pieces

Per Serving
Calories: 140
% Calories from fat: 29
Fat (gm): 4.7
Saturated fat (gm): 1.1
Cholesterol (mg): 35.7
Sodium (mg): 72.6
Protein (gm): 1.3
Carbohydrate (gm): 23.9
Exchanges
Milk: 0.0
Vegetable: 0.0
Fruit: 0.0
Bread: 1.5
Meat: 0.0
Fat: 1.0

1. Mix eggs, brown sugar, flour, corn syrup, milk, and vanilla until smooth in small saucepan. Add margarine and whisk over medium-low heat until brown sugar and margarine are melted; continue whisking over medium-high heat until mixture boils and thickens, 2 to 3 minutes. Serve warm or at room temperature.

Variations: **Honeyed Caramel Sauce**—Make recipe as above, substituting honey for the light corn syrup and adding a pinch of ground nutmeg.

Rum-Raisin Caramel Sauce—Make recipe as above, adding 1/2 cup raisins and 1 to 2 tablespoons rum *or* 1/2 to 1 teaspoon rum extract.

QUICK-AND-EASY CARAMEL SAUCE

Just unwrap caramels and you're practically finished with this recipe. The sauce is quickly made in the microwave also; just heat in a microwave-safe dish until melted, stirring frequently.

12 servings (about 2 tablespoons each)

1 package (14 ounces) caramels
6 tablespoons 2% reduced-fat milk

Per Serving
Calories: 123
% Calories from fat: 7
Fat (gm): 1
Saturated fat (gm): 0.3
Cholesterol (mg): 0.6
Sodium (mg): 12
Protein (gm): 0.9
Carbohydrate (gm): 29.3
Exchanges
Milk: 0.0
Vegetable: 0.0
Fruit: 2.0
Bread: 0.0
Meat: 0.0
Fat: 0.0

1.   Heat caramels and milk in medium saucepan, stirring over medium heat until melted.

RUM-RAISIN SAUCE

Delicious over warm Oatmeal Cake, Moist Gingerbread Cake, or French Vanilla Ice Cream (see pp. 35, 55, 442).

10 servings (about 2 tablespoons each)

  1 cup plus 2 tablespoons water, divided
1/2 cup granulated sugar
1/2 cup packed light brown sugar
2-3 tablespoons margarine
    Pinch ground cloves
1/2 cup dark raisins
  1 tablespoon cornstarch
  1 tablespoon rum *or* 1 teaspoon rum extract

Per Serving
Calories: 128
% Calories from fat: 15
Fat (gm): 2.3
Saturated fat (gm): 0.5
Cholesterol (mg): 0
Sodium (mg): 32
Protein (gm): 0.3
Carbohydrate (gm): 27.2
Exchanges
Milk: 0.0
Vegetable: 0.0
Fruit: 0.0
Bread: 1.0
Meat: 0.0
Fat: 1.0

1. Heat 1 cup water, sugars, margarine, and cloves in medium saucepan, stirring until sugar is dissolved; boil, uncovered, until reduced to 1 cup. Add raisins and simmer 3 to 4 minutes. Combine remaining 2 tablespoons water and cornstarch until smooth. Add to saucepan and boil 1 minute; stir in rum.

WHISKEY SAUCE

A natural with Bread Pudding Soufflé (see p. 412), and delicious on ice cream with peaches.

8 servings (about 2 tablespoons each)

1 cup plus 1 tablespoon water, divided
1 cup sugar
2-3 tablespoons margarine
 Pinch ground nutmeg
1/2 teaspoon cornstarch
1 tablespoon whiskey *or* 1/2-1 teaspoon whiskey extract

Per Serving
Calories: 127
% Calories from fat: 20
Fat (gm): 2.8
Saturated fat (gm): 0.6
Cholesterol (mg): 0
Sodium (mg): 34
Protein (gm): 0
Carbohydrate (gm): 25.2
Exchanges
Milk: 0.0
Vegetable: 0.0
Fruit: 0.0
Bread: 1.0
Meat: 0.0
Fat: 1.0

1. Heat 1 cup water, sugar, margarine, and nutmeg in medium saucepan, stirring until sugar is dissolved; boil, uncovered, until reduced to 1 cup. Combine remaining 1 tablespoon water and cornstarch until smooth. Add to saucepan and boil 1 minute; stir in whiskey.

WARM RUM SAUCE

Delicious spooned over Old-Fashioned Baked Rice Pudding or Pumpkin Ginger Cake (see pp. 394, 54)

8 servings (about 3 tablespoons each)

$^1/_4$ cup sugar

1 tablespoon cornstarch

$1^1/_4$ cups fat-free milk

2 tablespoons rum *or* 1 teaspoon rum extract

2 tablespoons margarine

$^1/_2$ teaspoon vanilla

$^1/_8$ teaspoon ground nutmeg

Per Serving
Calories: 76
% Calories from fat: 34
Fat (gm): 2.9
Saturated fat (gm): 0.6
Cholesterol (mg): 0.7
Sodium (mg): 53
Protein (gm): 1.3
Carbohydrate (gm): 9.2
Exchanges
Milk: 0.0
Vegetable: 0.0
Fruit: 0.0
Bread: 0.5
Meat: 0.0
Fat: 0.5

1. Mix sugar and cornstarch in small saucepan; stir in milk and rum. Cook over medium heat until mixture boils and thickens, stirring constantly. Remove from heat; stir in remaining ingredients. Serve warm.

HONEY SAUCE

Serve warm or room temperature over low-fat frozen vanilla yogurt, Pumpkin Ginger Cake (see p. 54), or fresh fruit.

8 servings (about 2 tablespoons each)

1/2 cup honey
1/2 cup apple juice
   1 tablespoon cornstarch
   2 tablespoons cold water
   1 tablespoon margarine
   2 teaspoons lemon juice
1/8 teaspoon ground mace

Per Serving
Calories: 88
% Calories from fat: 14
Fat (gm): 1.5
Saturated fat (gm): 0.3
Cholesterol (mg): 0
Sodium (mg): 18
Protein (gm): 0.1
Carbohydrate (gm): 20.2
Exchanges
Milk: 0.0
Vegetable: 0.0
Fruit: 1.5
Bread: 0.0
Meat: 0.0
Fat: 0.0

1. Heat honey and apple juice to boiling in small saucepan over medium heat. Mix cornstarch in cold water until smooth; stir into honey mixture. Boil, stirring constantly, until thickened. Stir in margarine, lemon juice, and mace. Serve warm or at room temperature.

FRESH GINGER SAUCE

Enjoy the intense sweet-hot flavor of fresh gingerroot—wonderful over low-fat frozen vanilla yogurt, fresh fruit, or toasted angel food cake slices.

8 servings (about 2 tablespoons each)

- 1 cup boiling water
- 2 tablespoons chopped fresh gingerroot
- 3 tablespoons honey
- 1-2 tablespoons margarine
- 2 teaspoons lemon juice

Per Serving
Calories: 38
% Calories from fat: 31
Fat (gm): 1.4
Saturated fat (gm): 0.3
Cholesterol (mg): 0
Sodium (mg): 17
Protein (gm): 0.1
Carbohydrate (gm): 6.8
Exchanges
Milk: 0.0
Vegetable: 0.0
Fruit: 0.0
Bread: 0.5
Meat: 0.0
Fat: 0.0

1. Pour boiling water over gingerroot and honey in small saucepan. Cover; let stand 30 minutes. Cook over medium heat until boiling; reduce heat and simmer 2 minutes. Strain; stir in margarine and lemon juice. Serve warm or cold.

TART LEMON SAUCE

Blueberry Bread Pudding and Gingered Pear Cake (see pp. 396, 57) are perfect choices for this nicely tart sauce.

12 servings (about 2 tablespoons each)

2   tablespoons margarine
²/₃-1 cup sugar
1   cup lemon juice
2   eggs, slightly beaten

Per Serving
Calories: 77
% Calories from fat: 30
Fat (gm): 2.7
Saturated fat (gm): 0.6
Cholesterol (mg): 35.3
Sodium (mg): 33
Protein (gm): 1.1
Carbohydrate (gm): 13
Exchanges
Milk: 0.0
Vegetable: 0.0
Fruit: 0.0
Bread: 1.0
Meat: 0.0
Fat: 0.5

1. Melt margarine over low heat in small saucepan; stir in sugar and lemon juice. Cook over medium heat until sugar is dissolved.

2. Whisk about ¹/₂ cup of hot lemon mixture into eggs. Whisk egg mixture into saucepan; whisk constantly over low heat until mixture coats the back of a spoon, 2 to 3 minutes (do not boil). Serve warm or at room temperature.

SWEET LEMON SAUCE

Sweet, with a gentle lemon flavor and nutmeg accent. Perfect with angel food or pound cake, or over fresh fruit.

8 servings (about 3 tablespoons each)

2/3 cup sugar
1 tablespoon cornstarch
1/8 teaspoon salt
1/8 teaspoon ground nutmeg
1 cup water
2-4 tablespoons lemon juice
2 teaspoons grated lemon rind
1-2 tablespoons margarine

Per Serving
Calories: 82
% Calories from fat: 15
Fat (gm): 1.4
Saturated fat (gm): 0.3
Cholesterol (mg): 0
Sodium (mg): 53
Protein (gm): 0
Carbohydrate (gm): 18
Exchanges
Milk: 0.0
Vegetable: 0.0
Fruit: 1.5
Bread: 0.0
Meat: 0.0
Fat: 0.0

1. Mix sugar, cornstarch, salt, and nutmeg in small saucepan; stir in water, lemon juice, and lemon rind. Heat to boiling; boil until thickened, 1 to 2 minutes, whisking constantly. Remove from heat; stir in margarine.

ORANGE SAUCE

This sweet citrus sauce would be lovely with Berry Best Shortcake or Tropical Sundaes (see pp. 527, 473).

12 servings (about 2 tablespoons each)

¹/2 cup sugar
2 tablespoons cornstarch
1 cup orange juice
3 tablespoons lemon juice
2 tablespoons grated orange rind
2 egg yolks, beaten

Per Serving
Calories: 58
% Calories from fat: 13
Fat (gm): 0.9
Saturated fat (gm): 0.3
Cholesterol (mg): 35.5
Sodium (mg): 2
Protein (gm): 0.6
Carbohydrate (gm): 12.3
Exchanges
Milk: 0.0
Vegetable: 0.0
Fruit: 1.0
Bread: 0.0
Meat: 0.0
Fat: 0.0

1. Combine sugar and cornstarch in small saucepan; whisk in orange and lemon juices and orange rind. Whisk over medium-high heat until boiling and thickened, 2 to 3 minutes.

2. Whisk about ¹/2 of the orange juice mixture into egg yolks; whisk yolk mixture into saucepan. Whisk over low heat 1 minute. Serve warm or at room temperature.

ORANGE MARMALADE SAUCE

This very easy sauce can accent many cakes and pastries.

12 servings (about 2 tablespoons each)

3/4 cup orange marmalade

2 teaspoons cornstarch

2/3 cup cold water

2 teaspoons orange juice

Per Serving
Calories: 53
% Calories from fat: 0
Fat (gm): 0
Saturated fat (gm): 0
Cholesterol (mg): 0
Sodium (mg): 3
Protein (gm): 0.1
Carbohydrate (gm): 14.5
Exchanges
Milk: 0.0
Vegetable: 0.0
Fruit: 1.0
Bread: 0.0
Meat: 0.0
Fat: 0.0

1. Heat marmalade to boiling in small saucepan over medium heat. Mix cornstarch and water until smooth; stir into marmalade. Cook, stirring constantly, until thickened; boil 1 minute, stirring constantly. Remove from heat and stir in orange juice. Serve warm or cold.

PINEAPPLE-RUM SAUCE

A perfect complement to New York-Style Cheesecake (see p. 206) or low-fat frozen yogurt.

12 servings (about 2 tablespoons each)

1¹/₂ cups unsweetened pineapple-orange juice
1 cup coarsely chopped pineapple, peeled, cored
¹/₄ cup sugar
1 tablespoon rum *or* ¹/₂ teaspoon rum extract
2 teaspoons cornstarch
¹/₈-¹/₄ teaspoon ground nutmeg

Per Serving
Calories: 43
% Calories from fat: 2
Fat (gm): 0.1
Saturated fat (gm): 0
Cholesterol (mg): 0
Sodium (mg): 1
Protein (gm): 0.5
Carbohydrate (gm): 9.9
Exchanges
Milk: 0.0
Vegetable: 0.0
Fruit: 0.5
Bread: 0.0
Meat: 0.0
Fat: 0.0

1. Mix juice, pineapple, sugar, rum, and cornstarch in small saucepan; heat to boiling. Cook, stirring constantly, until thickened; boil 1 minute, stirring constantly. Remove from heat and stir in nutmeg. Serve warm or cold.

BRANDIED CHERRY SAUCE

Accent Ricotta Cheesecake or Risotto Pudding (see pp. 208, 395) with this flavorful sauce.

8 servings (about 2 tablespoons each)

2 tablespoons sugar

1 teaspoon cornstarch

1/4 teaspoon ground allspice

1 cup fresh, *or* frozen, thawed, pitted dark sweet cherries

1/2 cup water

1 tablespoon brandy *or* 1/2 teaspoon brandy extract

1 tablespoon lemon juice

Per Serving
Calories: 32
% Calories from fat: 1
Fat (gm): 0
Saturated fat (gm): 0
Cholesterol (mg): 0
Sodium (mg): 0
Protein (gm): 0.2
Carbohydrate (gm): 7.3
Exchanges
Milk: 0.0
Vegetable: 0.0
Fruit: 0.5
Bread: 0.0
Meat: 0.0
Fat: 0.0

1. Mix sugar, cornstarch, and allspice in medium skillet or chafing dish. Stir in cherries, water, brandy, and lemon juice. Stir over medium heat until mixture boils and thickens; boil 1 minute, stirring constantly. Serve warm.

FESTIVE CRANBERRY SAUCE

Delicious with Ginger-Orange Ice Cream (see p. 444) and cookies.

12 servings (about 2 tablespoons each)

$^1/_2$ cup sugar

1 tablespoon cornstarch

$^1/_4$ teaspoon ground cinnamon

1 cup water

$^1/_2$ cup fresh, *or* frozen, thawed, cranberries

Per Serving
Calories: 37
% Calories from fat: 0
Fat (gm): 0
Saturated fat (gm): 0
Cholesterol (mg): 0
Sodium (mg): 0
Protein (gm): 0
Carbohydrate (gm): 9.6
Exchanges
Milk: 0.0
Vegetable: 0.0
Fruit: 0.5
Bread: 0.0
Meat: 0.0
Fat: 0.0

1. Combine sugar, cornstarch, and cinnamon in small saucepan. Stir in water and cranberries; heat to boiling. Cook, stirring constantly, until thickened. Serve warm or cold.

CRANBERRY COULIS

This mildly tart sauce is excellent served over sliced fresh fruit, Dundee Cake, or Almond Rice Pudding (see pp. 122, 393).

6 servings (about 3 tablespoons each)

1¹/2 cups fresh, *or* frozen, cranberries
1 cup orange juice
2-3 tablespoons sugar
1-2 tablespoons honey

Per Serving
Calories: 59
% Calories from fat: 2
Fat (gm): 0.1
Saturated fat (gm): 0
Cholesterol (mg): 0
Sodium (mg): 1
Protein (gm): 0.4
Carbohydrate (gm): 14.8
Exchanges
Milk: 0.0
Vegetable: 0.0
Fruit: 1.0
Bread: 0.0
Meat: 0.0
Fat: 0.0

1. Heat all ingredients to boiling in small saucepan; reduce heat and simmer, covered, until cranberries are tender, 5 to 8 minutes. Process mixture in food processor or blender until almost smooth.

RASPBERRY SAUCE

Entertain with flair, adding this fresh berry coulis to Apricot and Peach Fillo Nests or Kiwi Tart (see pp. 532, 177).

8 servings (about 2 tablespoons each)

> 1 pint fresh, *or* frozen, thawed, raspberries
> 1/4 cup sugar
> 1 teaspoon lemon juice

Per Serving
Calories: 39
% Calories from fat: 3
Fat (gm): 0.2
Saturated fat (gm): 0
Cholesterol (mg): 0
Sodium (mg): 0
Protein (gm): 0.3
Carbohydrate (gm): 9.9
Exchanges
Milk: 0.0
Vegetable: 0.0
Fruit: 0.5
Bread: 0.0
Meat: 0.0
Fat: 0.0

1. Process raspberries, sugar, and lemon juice in blender or food processor until smooth. Strain the puree; discard seeds.

MANGO COULIS

An easy and delicious sauce to serve with Lemon Soufflé Crepes (see p. 417), fresh fruit, or sherbet.

8 servings (about 2 tablespoons each)

3/4 cup diced ripe mango
1/4 cup sugar
1/4 cup orange juice
1 tablespoon lime juice
1/2 teaspoon rum extract

Per Serving
Calories: 42
% Calories from fat: 1
Fat (gm): 0.1
Saturated fat (gm): 0
Cholesterol (mg): 0
Sodium (mg): 1
Protein (gm): 0.2
Carbohydrate (gm): 10.6
Exchanges
Milk: 0.0
Vegetable: 0.0
Fruit: 1.0
Bread: 0.0
Meat: 0.0
Fat: 0.0

1. Process all ingredients in food processor or blender until smooth.

KIWI COULIS

A favorite tropical fruit, transformed into a honey-scented dessert sauce. Try it with Tropical Fruit Strudel or Classic Sponge Cake with fresh strawberries (see pp. 298, 100).

6 servings (about ¼ cup each)

- 4 large kiwi, peeled, cut into pieces
- 4-5 tablespoons honey
- 1-2 tablespoons lemon juice

Per Serving
Calories: 84
% Calories from fat: 4
Fat (gm): 0.4
Saturated fat (gm): 0
Cholesterol (mg): 0
Sodium (mg): 2
Protein (gm): 0.8
Carbohydrate (gm): 20.3
Exchanges
Milk: 0.0
Vegetable: 0.0
Fruit: 1.5
Bread: 0.0
Meat: 0.0
Fat: 0.0

1. Process all ingredients in food processor or blender until smooth.

BERRIES 'N CREAM SAUCE

First-prize honors will be awarded when this sauce is served with fresh fruit or Rich Lemon Pound Cake (see p. 89). Also try it with pancakes or waffles for brunch!

8 servings (about 2 tablespoons each)

1 cup fresh, *or* frozen, thawed, unsweetened raspberries
3 tablespoons sugar
3 tablespoons fat-free sour cream
2 tablespoons lemon juice

Per Serving
Calories: 33
% Calories from fat: 2
Fat (gm): 0.1
Saturated fat (gm): 0
Cholesterol (mg): 0
Sodium (mg): 5
Protein (gm): 0.5
Carbohydrate (gm): 7.9
Exchanges
Milk: 0.0
Vegetable: 0.0
Fruit: 0.5
Bread: 0.0
Meat: 0.0
Fat: 0.0

1. Process raspberries and sugar in food processor or blender until smooth. Strain and discard seeds. Stir in sour cream and lemon juice.

HERB-SCENTED CITRUS CREAM

Cilantro adds a fresh sparkle of flavor to this refreshing sauce; fresh mint would be a delicious variation. Serve over Basic Angel Food Cake (see p. 112), sliced fresh fruit, or Mixed Fruit Kabobs (see p. 519).

8 servings (about 2 tablespoons each)

- ¹/₂ cup fat-free sour cream
- ¹/₂ cup low-fat custard-style lemon yogurt
- 1 tablespoon sugar
- 2 tablespoons minced fresh cilantro
- 1 tablespoon grated orange rind

Per Serving
Calories: 39
% Calories from fat: 5
Fat (gm): 0.2
Saturated fat (gm): 0.1
Cholesterol (mg): 0.8
Sodium (mg): 22
Protein (gm): 1.7
Carbohydrate (gm): 7.4
Exchanges
Milk: 0.0
Vegetable: 0.0
Fruit: 0.0
Bread: 0.5
Meat: 0.0
Fat: 0.0

1. Combine sour cream, yogurt, and sugar in small bowl until smooth. Stir in cilantro and orange rind. Refrigerate 1 to 2 hours for flavors to blend.

INDEX